The Emptied Christ of Philippians

The Emptied Christ of Philippians
Mahāyāna Meditations

JOHN P. KEENAN

Foreword by Ruben L. F. Habito

WIPF & STOCK · Eugene, Oregon

THE EMPTIED CHRIST OF PHILIPPIANS
Mahāyāna Meditations

Copyright © 2015 John P. Keenan. All rights reserved. Except for brief quotations in critical publications or reviews, no part of this book may be reproduced in any manner without prior written permission from the publisher. Write: Permissions, Wipf and Stock Publishers, 199 W. 8th Ave., Suite 3, Eugene, OR 97401.

Wipf & Stock
An Imprint of Wipf and Stock Publishers
199 W. 8th Ave., Suite 3
Eugene, OR 97401

www.wipfandstock.com

ISBN 13: 978-1-4982-2131-3

Manufactured in the U.S.A.

For
my children
Dan and Teresa, Melanie and Life

and for my grandchildren
Ayla, Eliza, Thomas, and Zoe

Looking at his face, what do we see? Before all, the face of a God who is emptied, a God who has assumed the condition of servant, humble and obedient until death. The face of Jesus is similar to that of so many of our humiliated brothers, made slaves, emptied. God had assumed their face. And that face looks to us. If we do not lower ourselves we will not see his face. We will not see anything of his fullness if we do not accept that God has emptied God's self.

—Pope Francis[1]

---

1. Speaking in Florence, Italy, November 10, 2015. Quoted by Joshua J. McElwee in "Catholicism can and must change, Francis forcefully tells Italian church gathering." Published on National Catholic Reporter (http://ncronline.org), November 10, 2015.

Contents

Foreword by Ruben L. F. Habito | ix
Preface | xv
Acknowledgments | xvii
Abbreviations | xviii

1 Introduction | 1
   Christian Exegesis and Mahāyāna Hermeneutics in Paul's Letter to the Philippians | 1
   About the Text of Philippians | 9

2 Self-Sufficiency Letter A | 14
   Self-sufficiency in Any and All Circumstances (4:10–14) | 19
   Thanks Be to God (4:15–20) | 24

3 Emptiness Letter B, Part 1 | 31
   Greeting (1:1) | 31
   Grace and Peace (1:2) | 44
   Prayer and Relationships (1:3–11) | 46
   Paul's Imprisonment Strategy (1:12–14) | 71
   Partisan Preaching (1:15–18a) | 78
   Christ Enlarged (1:18b–20) | 90
   The Tensive Equality of Life and Death (1:21–24) | 98
   Conventional Confidence (1:25–26) | 116
   Conventional Citizenship (1:27–30) | 121
   Selfless Attending in Concrete Judgments (2:1–4) | 130

4 Emptiness Letter B, Part 2: The Central Meditation on the Emptied Christ (2:5–11) | 141
   "Attend to this . . ." (2:5) | 144
   ". . . although he was in the form of God . . ." (2:6) | 150
   ". . . he emptied himself . . ." (2:7) | 169
   ". . . he humiliated himself . . ." (2:8) | 183
   ". . . God did more than exalt him . . ." (2:9) | 193
   ". . . every knee shall bend . . ." (2:10–11) | 199

5 **Emptiness Letter B, Part 3** | 207
   The significance of the empty Christ for the Philippians (2:12–13) | 207
   Empty Murmuring (2:14–16) | 220
   Pouring out Life (2:17–18) | 230
   Travel Plans (2:19–30) | 236
   Finding Refuge (3:1) | 242
   Personal Affairs and Struggles (4:1–3) | 244
   Eschatological Joy (4:4–7) | 249
   Discernment (4:8–9) | 255
   Good Wishes and Grace (4:21–23) | 258

6 **Resurrection Letter C** | 261
   Canine Confidence (3:2–4a) | 261
   Paul's Identity (3:4b–6) | 268
   Self-reckoning (3:7–11) | 274
   Stretching Forth (3:12–14) | 294
   The Mind of Abiding without Clear Answers (3:15–16) | 306
   Patterned Imitation (3:17) | 313
   Hostility to the Cross (3:18–19) | 318
   Governing Councils and Cosmic Reconfigurations (3:20–21) | 323

7 **Postscript: On the Interfaith Reading of Paul** | 335

Selected Bibliography | 339

Foreword

Divine Self-Emptying:
A Buddhist Lens on Christian Scripture and Doctrine

The entire Christian tradition stands by the mind-boggling claim that God became human, taking on our flesh ("becoming incarnate") in the person of Jesus of Nazareth, called the Christ ("Anointed One"). The foundational doctrine of Christianity, proclaimed by the early church and confirmed by successive elders and leaders of the Christian faith community in their official councils, is the logic-defying affirmation that this Jesus—an itinerant Jewish preacher and teacher who walked and talked, wined and dined, rubbed elbows with and taught a small band of disciples about God's ways during a three-year period of public ministry in Galilee and environs, and who was eventually arrested by the authorities and ignominiously put to death on a cross—is as truly God as he is also truly human.

The devoted followers who came together to form a community after Jesus' death went about proclaiming that he rose again from the dead. They must have experienced something so powerful and life-changing throughout all this that it could not have been conveyed with due justice otherwise. In the words of the Roman centurion who witnessed Jesus' death: "Truly, this was the Son of God" (Matt 27:54). As the word quickly spread around the neighboring areas, believers increased by leaps and bounds over a relatively short period of time. This community of faithful stood firm in their proclamation from generation to generation on through the centuries: No, Jesus Christ was not a (mere) human being who was elevated to a quasi-divine status (Arius), nor was he God who merely took on a human appearance to show us the Way (the Docetists). This Jesus was, if anything, nothing less than fully human and at the same time one in being (*homoousios*, ὁμοούσιος) with God the Father, as declared in the creed that was formalized at the Council of Chalcedon (451 CE) and became a hallmark of the Christian faith.

Paul's Letter to the Philippians, written some two or three decades after the death of Jesus, is one of the earliest documents that can provide us with a window into the faith of the early Christian community. This letter contains excerpts of an early hymn they sang highlighting the mystery of the Incarnation, or God taking on human flesh:

> [6] who, though he was in the form of God, did not regard equality with God as something to be exploited, [7] but emptied himself, taking the form of a slave, being born in human likeness. And being found in human form, 8 he humbled himself and became obedient to the point of death—even death on a cross [9] Therefore God also highly exalted him and gave him the name that is above every name, [10] so that at the name of Jesus every knee should bend, in heaven and on earth and under the earth, [11] and every tongue should confess that Jesus Christ is Lord, to the glory of God the Father. (Phil 2:6–11)

This passage has provided impetus for theological reflection and speculation since the early church fathers through the medieval ages and up to our contemporary times. We find commentaries on this passage by an illustrious line of theologians—including Clement of Alexandria, Tertullian, Hippolytus, Cyprian, Origen, Athanasius, Cyril, Nestorius, Gregory of Nyssa,[1] Hilary of Poitiers, John Damascus, Ambrose, Augustine, Chrysostom, and others—all seeking to elucidate this doctrine of the Incarnation with their distinctive approaches to this Philippian hymn. There has been a resurgence of interest in the theological significance of kenosis, or God's self-emptying, since the nineteenth century and in more recent times.[2]

As has been frequently pointed out, the pivotal phrase of Phil 2:6–11, "emptied himself," strikes a resonant chord with a central theme in Mahāyāna Buddhism, the notion of *śūnyatā*, or "Emptiness." This theme of emptiness or kenosis has thus caught the attention of thinkers engaged in the ongoing Buddhist-Christian dialogue, where it is providing an impetus for fresh spiritual insights and renewed theological exploration.[3]

A unifying theme in the work of John P. Keenan, now spanning nearly three decades and including a number of hefty tomes as well as significant journal articles, can be described as applying a Buddhist lens in reading Christian scripture and for understanding Christian doctrine. It is welcomed and appreciated as a major contribution in the ongoing Buddhist-Christian conversation (see the bibliographical listing

---

1. See Sarah Coakley, "Does Kenosis Rest on a Mistake?" in C. Stephen Evans, ed., *Exploring Kenotic Christology: The Self-Emptying of God* (Oxford: Oxford University Press, 2009), 246–264), examining kenotic models in patristic exegesis and focusing on Cyril, Nestorius, and Gregory of Nyssa.

2. See Note 14 in the Introduction to this book for recent works on Kenotic Theology. See also Jennings B. Reid, *Jesus: God's Emptiness, God's Fullness* (Mahwah: Paulist, 1990); Onno Zijlstra, ed., *Letting Go: Rethinking Kenosis* (Bern, Switzerland: Peter Lang, 2002); David Brown, *Divine Humanity: Kenosis and the Construction of Christian Theology* (Waco, TX: Baylor University Press, 2011); Anna Marmodoro and Jonathan Hill, *The Metaphysics of the Incarnation* (Oxford: Oxford University Press, 2011).

3. See John B. Cobb, Jr., and Christopher Ives, editors, *The Emptying God: A Buddhist-Jewish-Christian Conversation* (Maryknoll, NY: Orbis, 1990); Donald Mitchell, *Spirituality and Emptiness* (Mahwah: Paulist, 1991); and John B. Lounibos, *Self-Emptying of Christ and the Christian: Three Essays on Kenosis* (Eugene, OR: Wipf and Stock, 2011), also mentioned in the notes of Keenan's Introduction.

at the end of this book). But more importantly, as hopefully may be more clearly recognized in due time by wider circles of readers, his work invites and challenges Christian theologians to consider taking on a fresh and radically new approach in their proper task of doing Christian theology, whether one takes this task in the traditional sense as "faith seeking understanding," or as "the fully reflective understanding of the Christian witness of faith as decisive for human existence,"[4] or as "critical and constructive reflection on Christian experience in the light of contemporary understanding, and critical and constructive reflection on contemporary understanding in the light of Christian experience."[5]

The Meaning of Christ: A Mahāyāna Theology, Keenan's first major tome in this vein, takes a passage from the Letter to the Ephesians as a starting point: "Wake up from your sleep, rise from the dead, and Christ will enlighten you" (Eph 5:14). Keenan invites the reader to an experience of awakening to what he calls "the Christ meaning," as he seeks "to present in clear language the meaning of being enlightened by Christ, the meaning of Christian awakening and rising from the dead."[6] In other words, his stated approach is "not to sketch the objective meaning of Jesus as a statement of Christian belief to which all must assent in order to retain their union cards as believers. Rather, the Christ meaning is considered and recommended from an understanding of the faith consciousness from which it is generated."[7]

Keenan derives inspiration from his many years of engagement as a scholar of Buddhism, an area where he has also made significant contributions—specifically in the elucidation of Mahāyāna Yogācāra teachings, elaborations on the central notion of *śūnyatā* grounded in Buddhist meditative practice. In a similar vein, Keenan's approach to reading Christian scripture and understanding Christian doctrine seeks to place these in the context of the spiritual experience out of which scriptural and doctrinal expressions emerge: "a mystic realm of meaning in which meaning is constituted not by thinking and judging, but by the immediacy of contact, of being touched. *Indeed, this base experience is the source from which all theologizing springs.*"[8]

A very important theme in all of Keenan's writing is his proposal for a different conceptual framework to convey this "mystic realm of meaning" that Christians are able to enter into through their experiential encounter with the mystery of Christ. Since early times, articulation of Christian understanding of the gospel message has

---

4. Schubert Ogden, *On Theology* (Dallas: Southern Methodist University Press, 1992), 1.

5. Adapted and expanded from the Editors' Introduction to John Makransky and Roger Jackson, eds., *Buddhist Theology: Critical Reflections by Contemporary Buddhist Scholars* (Routledge, 1999), 19, referring to their use of the term "Buddhist Theology."

6. Keenan, *Meaning of Christ*, 1.

7. Ibid.

8. Ibid. Italics mine. Keenan's *The Gospel of Mark: A Mahāyāna Reading* (Maryknoll: Orbis, 1995); *The Wisdom of James: Parallels with Mahāyāna Buddhism*, (Mahwah: Paulist, 2005); and *I Am / No Self: A Christian Commentary on the Heart Sūtra* (Leuven: Peeters, 2011) co-authored with Linda K. Keenan, draw the reader into this realm.

been characterized by a "substantialistic" frame of mind, i.e., one that takes the Aristotelian concept of "substance" as a primary building block for understanding reality. Arising within the context of the Greco-Roman, Medieval European, and Western cultural matrix in which Christian life and thought thrived and developed over these two millennia, this frame of mind finds its expression in notions like *ousia* (ουσια, "substance") a term that is the root for *homoousios* (όμοουσιος, "consubstantial"), used in conveying the understanding of Christ's oneness in being with God the Father, as well as the term *hypostasis* (ὑποστασις, "nature"), used for articulating the distinctive human and the divine natures of Christ, and so on.

These expressions, Keenan points out, are linked to "ontotheological interpretations" of the nature of reality, relying as they do on an understanding of self-enclosed ("substantial") being as the basic unit of all things that exist. Seen from a Buddhist perspective, this is a deluded view that prevents us from seeing the intimate interconnectedness of all things in the universe—a key insight into the nature of reality that stems from the awakening experience of the Buddha. Keenan turns to Mahāyāna Buddhist thought in seeking a different set of conceptual tools for articulating Christian doctrine that might more suitably convey the experiential meaning underlying its often convoluted expressions and that may resonate more with contemporary modes of thinking.[9]

The doctrine of the Incarnation that is the centerpiece of the Christian gospel message is intimately linked to another key Christian doctrine that blatantly goes beyond the normal parameters of logical discourse: the teaching that God is One and at the same time Three (God the Father, Jesus the Son, and the Holy Spirit). This seemingly logic-defying statement continues to be firmly affirmed through the centuries, with the double emphasis first that God's distinctly threefold mode of being (ὑποστασις hypostasis) is upheld in a way that is not tritheistic—that is, that divine Threeness does not compromise divine Oneness—and second, that neither is Threeness subsumed into Oneness. Much of trinitarian theology through the centuries, beginning with the early church fathers up to recent times, has also been characterized by what Keenan refers to as an ontotheological frame of mind, that is, based on a substantialistic view of reality that many of our contemporaries no longer find viable. How a Mahāyāna Buddhist view centered on the notion of Emptiness and the concomitant understanding of the interconnectedness of reality may shed new light on trinitarian theology is a task still waiting to be addressed with more thoroughness.[10]

---

9. See also Keenan's article entitled "A Mahāyāna Theology of the Real Presence of Christ in the Eucharist," *Buddhist-Christian Studies* 24 (2004) 89–100, for a superb example of how a Buddhist experiential perspective can shed new light on a longstanding theme that has caused division among Christians, which arises from different ways of taking the meaning of the term "transubstantiation" in the context of liturgical celebration, and could be avoided by approaching the doctrine of the Real Presence from the standpoint of Emptiness.

10. For a collection of essays that address this theme and invite further reflection and development, see Roger Corless and Paul F. Knitter, eds., *Buddhist Emptiness and Christian Trinity* (Mahwah:

FOREWORD

In this book, *The Emptied Christ of Philippians: Mahāyāna Meditations*, by building upon as well as critiquing previous attempts at comparing Christian kenotic theology with the Buddhist understanding of Emptiness, the author walks the reader through the entire Letter to the Philippians to unveil the rich world contained therein. This is one more gem in John P. Keenan's impressive array of works that teem with his thought-provoking comments and spiritually enriching insights on reading Christian scripture and understanding Christian doctrine.

Ruben L. F. Habito
Professor of World Religions and Spirituality
Director of Spiritual Formation
Perkins School of Theology, Southern Methodist University
Dallas, Texas

Paulist, 1990).

Preface

This endeavor, from beginning to end, is a Christian reading of the apostle Paul's message to the Philippians. At the same time, it is a work of interfaith theology, for it employs the philosophy of Mahāyāna Buddhism as its hermeneutic guide in lieu of the primarily Greek philosophies that shaped Christian understandings in the past and that lie silently behind the work of even Christian exegetes who express a distaste for philosophy. I believe that we have an urgent need today to think the gospel and to learn Christ in unfamiliar cultural mindsets, for vast and still-shifting cultural changes are occurring in our understanding of what it means to be human, what it means to speak of God, and what it means to confess Christ faith.

Those readers who are familiar with the dialogue between Buddhists and Christians over the past few decades will be aware that an important focus of that interfaith conversation has been the "emptiness hymn" of Phil 2:6–11. Perhaps the most prominent, indeed dominant, Buddhist voice in that discussion for many years was that of Japanese Zen practitioner and adherent of Kyoto School philosophy ABE Masao (1915–2006).[1] I have discussed Abe's somewhat problematic approach to Buddhist-Christian dialogue in an article entitled "Mahāyāna Emptiness or 'Absolute Nothingness'? The Ambiguity of ABE Masao's Role in Buddhist-Christian Understanding."[2] I would like to clarify at the outset that the present endeavor, which employs Mahāyāna philosophy as a way to overcome essentialist thinking about Christ, is quite distinct from Abe's Kyoto School interpretation of the Philippian emptiness hymn. Moreover, whereas most Buddhist-Christian discussions of the emptiness theme in Philippians tend to focus almost exclusively upon the hymn in 2:6–11, this work treats Paul's Philippian correspondence in its entirety.

My understanding of emptiness as presented in the Indian and Chinese texts of Mahāyāna Buddhism is as a spiritual practice—the practice of abandoning all forms of self, including particularly any viewpoint that pretends to capture religious doctrine

---

1. To avoid confusion, Japanese family names will be indicated in small caps when the full name is used. The Japanese practice is to give the family name first, but Japanese-Americans and some Japanese scholars who publish in English follow the American order.

2. In *Revue Théologiques* (Montréal); see bibliography. For more on Abe, see Angelo Rodante, *Sunyata buddhista e Kenosi christologica in Masao Abe* (Rome: Città Nuova Editrice, 1995), which includes a comprehensive presentation of Abe's understanding of "dynamic emptiness" and its critiques.

or truth in freeze-dried categories.³ In its early Indian and Chinese context, emptiness is an inculcated spiritual critique of our deluded notions about a self-enclosed being, of the philosophies that such notions engender, and of the dead-end to which they lead. We do not live in a world of fixed and identifiable layers of meaning, some merely natural and some supernatural. I am something of a theological Darwinist, holding that there are no fixed identities or species that can assure us of living in a well-ordered and hierarchical world; in my view, theology in its most vital enunciation would undermine the sovereign status of any fixed order that presents ready answers.⁴ An emptiness theology offers no well-defined political stance. Precisely by liberating us from all ideological stances, it directs attention to this world as it is and creates a space for common people to discern the dependently arisen common good, adopting whatever stance best furthers justice and peace at this time, in this place.

Two themes that are central to Mahāyāna philosophy run through my meditations on the apostle Paul's correspondence with the community in Philippi. Those themes are (1) the indivisible link between emptiness and dependent arising; and (2) the unbridgeable chasm between ultimate meaning and conventional, or contextual, meaning. My philosophic mentors in this are the classical Indian Mahāyāna thinkers Nāgārjuna and his disciple Āryadeva, as well as Asaṅga, Vasubandhu, and Bandhuprabha,⁵ proponents of the Yogācāra branch of that tradition. More immediately, my understanding of Mahāyāna Buddhism has been informed by Japanese Buddhist scholars Nagao Gadjin, Takasaki Jikidō, and Hakamaya Noriaki, as well as by Professor Minoru Kiyota, my mentor in Buddhist Studies at the University of Wisconsin–Madison. My theological guide is Paul's Philippian text itself, enriched by the commentarial literature, particularly the work of John Reumann, Jean-François Collange, Gordon D. Fee, and Peter T. O'Brien on Philippians, as well as works on identity issues in Paul's thought and theology by James D. G. Dunn and William S. Campbell.

English translations of Philippians used herein are generally based on the NRSV, as adjusted in light of my understanding of the many possible translations suggested in the commentaries. The Greek text of Philippians is from "ΑΩ The Online Greek Bible: Greek New Testament Resources," http://www.greekbible.com/index.php.

---

3. Jacques May, *Chandrakīrti: Prasannapadā Madhyamika-vṛitti. Douze chapitres traduits du Sanskrit et du Tibétain, accompagnés d'une édition critique de la version tibétaine* (Paris: Adrien-Maisonneuve, 1959) 15.

4. See Mitchell, *Church, Gospel, & Empire*, 3–59, on "Theological Dislocation."

5. The otherwise unknown author of *The Interpretation of the Buddha Land*. See Keenan, *Study of the Buddhabhūmyupadeśa*.

Acknowledgments

My deep appreciation goes to three colleagues and friends who took precious time from their schedules to read this manuscript and offer thoughtful suggestions for its improvement: Kristin Beise Kiblinger, Francis X. Richards, and Amos Yong.

Sincere gratitude to Ruben L. F. Habito for his generous contribution of the foreword to this book.

And to Wipf and Stock copyeditor par excellence Alex Fus, many, many thanks!

Abbreviations

BDF	F. Blass, A. Debrunner, Tr. R. W. Funk. *A Greek Grammar of The New Testament and Other Early Christian Literature.* Chicago: University of Chicago Press, 1961.
Chi.	Chinese
JB	Jerusalem Bible
Js.	Japanese
L.	Latin
NovT	*Novum Testamentum*
NRSV	New Revised Standard Version
NTS	*New Testament Studies*
Skt.	Sanskrit
TDNT	*Theological Dictionary of the New Testament*, ed. G. Kittel and G. Friedrich. Grand Rapids: Eerdmans, 1964–1976.

1

Introduction

Christian Exegesis and Mahāyāna Hermeneutics in Paul's Letter to the Philippians

Many fine exegetical commentaries elucidate the text of Paul's letter to the Philippians, both building upon and challenging one another in the process. The following meditation on Philippians takes careful account of that mainstream scholarship on this letter and its author, but this is a commentary of an altogether different ilk. This is a reading of Philippians from the philosophical perspective of Mahāyāna Buddhism and its understanding of the mind of emptiness. My hope is that a thoughtful rereading of Philippians in this less familiar key will allow the music of Paul's words and of the Philippian hymn to seep into our minds and suggest new understandings of this epistle.

The Letter to the Philippians is the apostle Paul's side of a correspondence he carried on with a Christian community in the Greco-Roman town of Philippi during the years 54–55 CE. In other words, we are reading someone else's mail here. And because we have only Paul's side of a back-and-forth correspondence, we are forced to conjecture from his words what the Philippians, in their turn, may have written to him. Extensive scholarly work on Paul's epistles has contributed much to our understanding of the background of this correspondence by sketching the broad social and cultural milieu of Paul's time and place, as can be ascertained from other sources. Careful studies on issues of authorship, composition, rhetoric, and implied audience have also helped to throw light on the meaning of Paul's letters to his various correspondents in furtherance of the gospel.

I refer to a broad array of these Christian commentarial works in my treatment of Philippians. At the same time, my reading of the epistle is informed by my long engagement with an entirely different set of scriptures possessing their own distinct set of philosophical commentaries—the scriptures of Mahāyāna Buddhism. Weary of the metaphysical certitudes of my own scholastic seminary training, and dubious of recent scholars' attempts to read Christian texts with "fresh" innocence by retrojecting themselves back over the centuries, I have chosen to look at Paul's correspondence with the Philippians through the lens of the Mahāyāna philosophy of emptiness. The Mahāyāna approach aims consistently to empty all things and every viewpoint of any presumed essence so that their dependently arisen being and truth may thereby emerge to shed new light and new understanding. The hope here is that a Mahāyāna approach to Philippians will enable this ancient Christian manuscript—possibly our earliest Christian text—to offer new insight to its readers.

Paul's epistle to the Philippians is distinctive among New Testament texts for the hymn in 2:6–11, which sings of a Christ who empties himself. In fact, this provides the recurring theme of the entire Philippian correspondence. Despite the importance of the theme of emptiness in this very early Christian text, however, theological thinking over the centuries has been so overwhelmingly dominated by ontological philosophies that Christian theologies of emptiness emerged only in relatively modern times. In the nineteenth and early twentieth centuries, a vigorous kenotic theology was developed in Germany by Gottfried Thomasius and in England by P. T. Forsyth. However, even these kenotic theologians, who attended carefully to the theme of the empty Christ, remained faithful to the Chalcedonian insistence upon Christ's essential being.[1] These theologians focused on how, given the commonly affirmed consensus on God as essential being, we might explain the assertion in Phil 2:7 that Christ emptied himself. Despite the hymn's unambiguous declaration that Christ himself did not consider divinity as anything to be grasped, they nevertheless adopted an interpretation that protects the ontotheological essence of Christ as God.

In contrast to this late-blooming and rather peripheral Christian kenotic theology, Mahāyāna—Buddhism's Great Vehicle of liberation—begins and ends with emptiness. Mahāyāna emptiness does not, as sometimes imagined by westerners, signify a spiritual philosophy of nihilism.[2] It is instead a robust discourse about the being of things as they emerge, with a strong insistence upon our abandonment of any confidence that we can ever capture the truth of things in the self-assured language of viewpoints. An emptiness theology is thus the polar reverse of the many Christian theologies that—with great conviction but a singular lack of success—endeavor to bolster our sense of Christian selfhood and assuage Christians' increasing fear of a loss of religious self-identity.

---

1. See Dawe, *Form of a Servant*, for a summary of western kenotic theology, especially its German and English proponents.

2. See Nagao, *Mādhyamika and Yogācāra*, esp. "Emptiness," 209–18, and "'What Remains' in Śūnyatā: A Yogācāra Interpretation of Emptiness," 51–60. For a full exposition, see Nagao, *Foundational Standpoint*.

INTRODUCTION

Identity issues will permeate this commentary, for although no particular or intrinsic Christian identity is anywhere to be found, Christian exegetes and interpreters all too often urge upon us just such an assured theology. In fact, appeals to "Christian identity" misdirect our attention, miss the point, and paint churches into a corner where they assume a defensive stance and fail to critically examine the cultural and social worlds around them. Ultimate meaning as offered by Christic faith—what Paul calls life in Christ—is that which we stretch towards without ever grasping a truth that we might claim as the prized possession of a Christian identity. We are not to cling to spiritual realities as though they are attainable goals, but neither are we to cling to this life of ours as though the horizons of the self constitute what is really real. When our minds are emptied of such self-assurance, we may be found in him, stretching forth to be conformed to his empty mind of wisdom. Such a radical conversion of consciousness can enable us to let go of imagined realities and essential identities, freeing us to engage our world with the offer of an eschatological Christian faith that looks to the future in hope.

To anyone who appreciates the Mahāyāna philosophy of emptiness, the Philippians hymn, with its enunciation of a Christ who empties himself (ἑαυτὸν ἐκένωσεν), reverberates with the very foundational insight of Mahāyāna Buddhism's wisdom scriptures: that all things and all persons are empty of any inner essence or core self that could possibly be the stable subject, or object, of a supernatural relationship. Traditional Christian theologians borrowed from Plato and Aristotle when they identified the core of human beings as an immortal soul infused into the human body by a creative God. That theological notion of "soul" then precipitated into our cultural consciousness so thoroughly that it came to be understood as the personal, core identity of who we are. Many in the twenty-first century take this view to the extent of assuming that, individually, we are exactly who we define ourselves to be—and we tend to understand God as well in the context of that definition of ourselves.

Mahāyāna regards any form of a "core" personal identity as something that we ourselves have constructed in the course of our living. As such, it can never be the starting point of a spiritual quest. A self-*less* person, by contrast, is capable of recognizing and acknowledging the very transience of our being here and so, freed from any *a priori* definition of identity, is able to engage in bodhisattva[3] practices of wisdom and compassion in this world. So it is that, to those like myself who are involved in the conversation between the Buddhist and Christian traditions, no other Christian text is more pregnant with the potential for interfaith contemplation and insight than Paul's letter to the Philippians, with its theme of the emptying Christ. This is precisely what has drawn me to engage in this Mahāyāna-driven *lectio divina* of the Philippian correspondence.

---

3. A bodhisattva is a compassionate wisdom-being who, instead of seeking cessation, remains within the world of suffering in order to teach, heal, and liberate sentient beings.

In Mahāyāna's teaching of emptiness, no viewpoint can capture the very being of beings, for all ideas and all viewpoints are recognized as having been constructed in the context of our conventional world and expressed in human language. Nothing that we humans understand through insight and judgment has its own self-enclosed essence. Indeed, we can never grasp the "essence" of things in clear and distinct ideas, for there is no essence there to be apprehended. In constructing theologies, we filter our insights—and the judgments we ground upon them—through what we ourselves have experienced and understood from that experience. All things and views are contextual and empty of essence, for all things and views come into being in dependence upon countless converging causes and conditions. Still, Mahāyāna emptiness is not a denial of the existence (Skt. *sat*) of beings (*sattva*); it is rather a denial of the existence of *essences* (*svabhāva*). At the same time, it is an affirmation—of the pervasively interdependent and transient existence of all things and all beings.

The Perfection of Wisdom sūtras, which mark the rise of Mahāyāna thought, were the first Buddhist scriptures to present the notion of emptiness. The classical explication of emptiness and its implications is found in Nāgārjuna's *Stanzas on the Middle*.[4] Especially important is the famous chapter 24 of that work, in which Nāgārjuna insists that the scope of emptiness encompasses not only the deluded world and its false viewpoints about the real, but also applies even to the true teachings of the Buddha. This was a remarkable turn in Buddhist thinking. Buddhist thinkers could not thereafter simply contrast the truth of their own tradition to the false views of their opponents. They were henceforth forced to turn the critique back upon their own affirmations of truth and to inquire into the status of those affirmations as judgments of truth.

Christians have long held that the devil is a good theologian, able to verbally spout correct doctrine without any inner conversion of understanding. The Mahāyāna philosophers of truth have taken to heart such an insight, making it the entryway into their doctrinal thinking. They acknowledge that even *correct* doctrinal viewpoints are empty, able to lay no claim to capturing the truth of awakened discourse. Indeed, truth may even be an obstacle to awakening, for we tend to cling with idolatrous tenacity to our enunciated truths. So Mahāyāna empties *all* viewpoints, not just those that we categorically reject as false, but even those that we cherish and follow. No absolute truth that pretends to represent a self-enclosed essence can capture the reality of things. Indeed, such a captured truth obfuscates and occludes the practice of the Middle Path, where truth emerges ever more fully as we hold in creative tension both the emptiness of all theology and the fullness of its long and varied traditions.

Emptiness does not lead us to some special realm of nothing-at-all. Rather, it serves to clear away all views so that we may enter into doctrine, realize its meaning, and enunciate it persuasively. To the extent that we achieve insight into the emptiness of doctrines and viewpoints, we are enabled to enunciate doctrinal truth skillfully, in

---

4. See Garfield, *The Fundamental Wisdom of the Middle Way*.

Introduction

as many tongues as there are in this world. But those tongues are always *our* tongues, even when inspired by the breath of the Spirit. Scriptural truth flows from the Spirit into words, but words remain always words—contextual and embedded in the shifting webs of our languaged horizons. They do not exist in the self-enclosed splendor of a manageable deposit dropped by a birdlike spirit from above. Nevertheless, our ancestors in the faith have handed down to us teachings that are indeed true expressions of their embodied, living practice within their worlds.

In the Middle Path philosophy developed by Nāgārjuna, emptiness and dependent arising comprise a "middle path" of empty and awakened wisdom. Later, the critical philosophers of the Yogācāra school sought a deeper understanding of the mind of empty wisdom. Their work sketches out the underlying structure and activity of human consciousness—which they find is not a stable platform for generating views, even when those views are correct. The Yogācāra thinkers find human consciousness itself to be a dependently arisen structure comprised of a combination of unconscious influences, together with the conscious activities of understanding that arise from insight into images and issue in skillful, contextual judgments.

In the critical philosophy of Yogācāra, emptiness is employed as a useful approach to understanding the meaning of our lives in this world. As such, it offers a hermeneutic principle for reading and understanding Christian scripture as well.[5] Yogācāra thinkers employ emptiness to analyze the deluded pattern of thinking that is characterized by imagined attachment. In that deluded pattern of thinking, a presumably stable self is the subject that apprehends presumably stable objects. But all objects must be emptied, even if they are the heart of one's tradition—the Buddha and his Dharma, or God and the Christ. As the Philippian hymn declares, Christ is to be emptied. This is the mind of Christ. But emptiness is not the ultimate meaning of anything;[6] it is but a *remedy* to purify our understanding. It is a reminder that we are—and function as—human beings who bring to speech, as skillfully as we are able, truths disclosed only darkly in the mirror of wisdom. Before proclaiming our truths, we are to pass through the dark night of theology.

The hermeneutics of emptiness point the reader of scripture toward an ultimate meaning that lies beyond any word or any image, beyond capture and apart from mediated meaning.[7] Grounded in meditative awakening, empty truth negates the calculus of self-power, which is so assured in its own theologies and which blocks our practice of risen life. When first I encountered Nāgārjuna's Mādhyamika philosophy of emptiness, enmeshed as I was in the scholastic ontotheologies of my Christian

---

5. See Asaṅga, *Summary of the Great Vehicle*, 54–55. At the end of chapter 3, section 32, the overall doctrine of the Mahāyāna is summarized as, first, the character of the dependent arising of consciousness through the permeations of language; then, second, the character of things that arise within the dependently arisen pattern of mind; so that, third, one interprets scriptures in the light of their dependent arising, and not as a literal grasp of stable essences. See also Keenan, "Intent and Structure."

6. *Pace* Abe, "Kenotic God and Dynamic Sunyata."

7. See Lonergan, *Method in Theology*, 29, 76–77, 106, 273.

tradition, I thought him a shortsighted humbug. In my view, he failed miserably even to acknowledge the most basic principles of logical thinking. It was only after I tired of being such a clearheaded thinker that I was able to appreciate Nāgārjuna's efforts to free my faith practice from the naively realistic pattern of an assured subject (me) reaching out to know an equally assured object (God). That pattern of thinking had created in my mind a theological bondage to sureties that failed to precipitate into engaged practice. Whenever one has a firm grasp on the ultimate, one may be certain to have constructed idols.

The doctrines that developed over time within our Christian tradition are not in fact to be found in so many words in our scriptures, for the questions that drove the development of those doctrines did not arise until some time after those scriptures were written. As questions arose—Who is Jesus? Who is God? Who are we?—the edifice of doctrine was erected piece by piece as Christian thinkers grappled in turn with Arius, Nestorius, Eunomius, and others. Brick by brick, the tower of Christian thought took on a metaphysical structure, borrowing from the cultural discourses that limned the contours of truth in their day. German theologian Adolf von Harnack famously rejected all such endeavors as a Hellenistic departure from the early scriptures and a domestication of the simple and pure gospel message.[8] Yet I think he failed to appreciate the organic place of metaphysics in Hellenistic times and throughout the Middle Ages into the modern world. Nurtured by and trained within that metaphysical discipline, I see it differently. Anyone who learns the contours of the development of the doctrines of incarnation and Trinity soon realizes that it is indeed an edifice leading, step by step, to a "high" christology, but that it was never meant to be one perspective among many. At each point, our Greek ancestors in the faith rejected one perspective after another, thereby "circumscribing" the mystery and "defining" it beyond all perspectives.[9]

The edifice of doctrinal argument moves through its terms to reach a point, not of completion, but of launching into the silence of prayer and liturgy. The structure and intent of that edifice is to move from idea to idea—not to reach a final definition of the mystery, but to provide a pathway to follow on our journey into the night of darkness, where prayer and liturgy spontaneously take over. Gregory of Nyssa and the church fathers the spoke of the two paths of theology: the apophatic way of abiding in the mystery of unknowing, and the kataphatic path, which attempts to enunciate that mystery in words and ideas. But these two paths are not to be seen as sequential, as if one mounts through words and ideas to a pinnacle, there to abide in the unknowability of God. Rather, at each step and every stage, the very enunciation of truth is

---

8. See Adolf von Harnack, *Lehrbuch der Dogmengeschichte* [History of Dogma] (Freiburg im Breisgau: Germany, 1885), which forms the background context for Jaroslav Pelikan's five-volume *Christian Tradition*.

9. Marinus de Jonge, *Christology in Context: The Earliest Christian Responses to Jesus* (Philadelphia: Westminster, 1988) 194–99.

confessed to be surrounded by unknowing and silence. The exercise of theology does not move from assured and solid ideas into a silence in which all words and symbols disappear in the dark night of unknowing. Rather, it begins and is at every point twinned with that silence from which we all emerge to bring into speech the teachings through which we may learn Christ.

Philosophy begins, Aristotle said, in wonder. The metaphysical elaboration of our earliest creeds drew upon that wonder, excluding at every turn some perspectival account of Christ: He is not a creature, as Arius thought; not adopted, as Nestorius claimed; and not an embodiment of the *known* essence of God, as Eunomius taught. He is not a "divine," godlike man—not an angel, not a prophet, not a sage, and so forth. It was at every stage an exercise in negation. Christ cannot be defined in his unique individuality, for always he is non-dual with Father and Spirit, and with us.

The creeds circumscribe the faith by refusing to collapse the mystery into ideas, insisting simply that Jesus is the wisdom of the Father, the Word made flesh, of one being with the Father. As the grammar of faith, the creeds shape how we may talk about being in Christ.[10] But if the gospel faith were solely a matter of ideas, it would have no salvific power to transform our identities and our minds, which move before and beyond the engendering of ideas. To carry out their doctrinal task of responding to all perspectival explanations of the mystery, our ancestors in the faith developed creeds employing the metaphysical ideas that were so richly persuasive in their Greek culture. They did not, however, set about to *explain* the mystery, realizing throughout that God is ineffable and known only in unknowing.

It is, alas, the sadness of our age that such a metaphysical edifice no longer serves as an effective launching place for mystical engagement. What once was the pinnacle of thought—ascending to heights that brought all intellectualization to naught in wonder and prayer—has become just one more verbal edifice among many other constructs. In a world with many perspectives, it has become but one perspective among perspectives. Incarnational confession remains the Christian viewpoint, but in many churches nowadays, staunchly defended stances on social and cultural issues have become almost more important, as though those are the defining marks of the faith. By contrast, traditional theologies have lost much of their persuasive energy and their ability to nurture insight; they appear rather forbidding alongside more easily understood and attractive alternatives.

Classical Christian ontotheologies attract few people today into any sustained engagement with either doctrine or prayer. Not even many Christian professionals bother much to learn traditional Christian doctrine in depth, satisfied to allude to doctrines such as Trinity and incarnation as "mysteries" beyond our understanding. They tend to eschew theology in favor of pastoral simplicity, passing on to more easily understood and urgent issues of Christian identity—stances on abortion, sexual

---

10. See Joseph S. O'Leary, *L'art du judgment en théologie* (Paris: Les Éditions du Cerf, 2011) 289–316, on "Le dogme à l'épreuve de la vacuité."

identity issues, and unfaltering commitment to the privileged status of a still actively cherished clerical ontology.[11] It is not impossible, however, to study and understand the development of Christian doctrine; plentiful textual and historical sources are available. Perhaps in the attempt to overcome the ancient metaphysics that no longer speaks to modern culture, we pass too quickly from the central doctrines of our incarnational history to reductive recommendations for dynamic community models of Trinity that swirl around Father, Son, and Spirit, or a social trinitarian model wherein the Father displays our mutual interdependence in sending Jesus and the Spirit to this world.[12]

The lazy versions of Christian doctrine about Christ often amount to nothing more than recommendations for community and engagement. For that, however, one hardly needs any doctrine at all; wholehearted affirmation of the United Nations Declaration of Human Rights would suffice. But when faith traditions become as culturally inaccessible as metaphysical theology, they hardly constitute a persuasive invitation to meditative engagement. Today any number of alternative doctrines, responsible perspectives, and philosophies of life are on offer, none of which require the study of ancient languages or philosophical systems as a prerequisite to understanding.

In the traditional metaphysical theologies of the Hellenistic Fathers, the descent/ascent imagery of the Philippian hymn was conceived as the interplay of two layers and three stages. The three stages were: from the time before, when Jesus was in the form of God; until his emptying of himself on the cross; and then his exaltation beyond death. All this was seen as a double-layered metaphysical drama that unfolded between the natural realm and a supernatural truth understood to be what is essentially real. Within that now archaic but then vibrant framework, one can hardly imagine a more skillful employment of cultural language. And for those able—through much study—to read themselves into those ancient idioms and to move within that world of discourse, it still retains its beauty and truth.[13]

In the present commentary, however, I attempt to read Paul's correspondence—and indeed the entire tradition—apart from these very balanced models. I do so not because I think of these models as intrusions or betrayals, but because for most of my contemporaries they have long ceased to occupy the place assigned to them in ancient

---

11. Archbishop of Philadelphia Cardinal Bevalaqua, in his testimony before the 2005 Philadelphia Grand Jury, testified that priests are "ontologically" different from laypersons, thereby supporting his claim that, in the case of an accused abuser priest who declared his innocence, the cardinal had no authority simply to remove the priest; he was required to refer the case to the Vatican courts, which might or might not find him guilty.

12. Inspired perhaps by Karl Rahner's work *The Trinity* (New York: Herder & Herder, 1970) and Rahner's identification of the "theological" discourse on the Trinity with the "economic" discourse, theologians such as Leonardo Boff have devoted their thinking to enunciating this most central of Christian doctrines in a more phenomenological key, drawing out its implications for personal and social praxis. See Leonardo Boff, *Trinity and Society* (Maryknoll: Orbis, 1985).

13. As in the seven volumes of Hans Urs von Balthasar's *The Glory of the Lord: A Theological Aesthetics* (San Francisco: Ignatius, 1967).

days. It is not that our incarnational understandings have become irrelevant, but that the metaphysics used to express them is no longer accessible. As a result, the churches seem sometimes to have assumed a strange role as adjudicator of philosophies rather than as witness to gospel faith, with the result that they neglect the task of enunciating the gospel in ever-new languages and philosophies with broader insight and appeal. But our scriptures and traditions themselves urge upon us the understanding that doctrine is not inextricably tied to any single perspective either ancient or modern. Scriptures invite us into the mystery that is our life in Christ, and that lies beyond the parameters of any perspective whatsoever.

For this reason, it seems to me that a Mahāyāna philosophy that grants central attention to emptiness and to the mind of wisdom can be of some help in enunciating the ancient mysteries of the Christian faith. There are newer kenotic theologies that do move in this direction[14]—albeit tentatively, for they have to bear in mind the immense weight of the ontological traditions. A classical Mahāyāna approach can assist these endeavors because it affords a vast philosophical account of the implications of emptiness and the mind of wisdom. Like all others, this Mahāyāna account is a conventional discourse undertaken in a particular context, but perhaps it can map avenues for deeper theological engagement.

About the Text of Philippians

Written just two decades after the death of Jesus, Paul's letter to the Philippians not only reveals a great deal about his understanding of the gospel, it also provides evidence for the existence of an emergent community of Christ followers in the Roman colony of Philippi.[15] For most of those two decades, Paul has preached the gospel of Christ. During his years at Ephesus, from which he writes to the community in Philippi, Paul also writes to communities in Galatia and Corinth, as well as to Philemon in the nearby Lycus Valley. His letter to the Romans lies further in the future.

Paul experiences some contention during this Ephesian period. In Galatia, he encounters opposition from Jewish Christians; in Corinth, he deals with a hotbed of

---

14. See John B. Lounibos, *Self-Emptying of Christ and the Christian: Three Essays on* Kenosis (Eugene, OR: Wipf & Stock, 2011) esp. "Self-Emptying in Christian and Buddhist Spirituality," 85–102. Also see Lucien Richard, *Christ the Self-Emptying God* (Mahwah, NJ: Paulist, 1997). See also the essays in John Polkinghorne, ed., *The Work of Love: Creation as Kenosis* (Grand Rapids: Eerdmans, 2001). Especially note Donald Mitchell, *Spirituality and Emptiness: The Dynamic of the Spiritual Life in Buddhism and Christianity* (Mahwah, NJ: Paulist, 1991). Mitchell is trained in Zen meditation, a practitioner in the Focolare movement, and a scholar of Buddhist studies. Like Lounibos, Mitchell is able to delve into Mahāyāna teachings and offer judicious insights into the meaning of self-emptying. Also see Louis Roy, *Mystical Consciousness: Western Perspectives and Dialogue with Japanese Thinkers* (Albany: State University of New York, 2003), which, from the perspective of Bernard Lonergan, treats an array of western thinkers as well as members of the Kyoto School, in particular Nishitani Keiji.

15. See Campbell, *Paul and the Creation*, 12–13, on the terminological fitness of using "Christ followers" rather than "Christians," for the latter was not yet a recognized social identity.

cliques and party spirit (1 Cor 1–4) and becomes the target of outside agitators (2 Cor 11). Moreover, we learn in Phil 1:15–17 that there are other preachers who do not see eye-to-eye with Paul, some of whom selfishly preach Christ in such a way as to increase Paul's suffering during his imprisonment. Paul works and writes as the *oikonomos*, the head of the church household—one who fills the steward's role in the Greek Council. This was an office usually held by a "slave," and thus Paul introduces himself here as a slave of Christ.[16] This role also implies that Paul shares responsibilities with others. Indeed, as becomes apparent in his correspondence with the Philippians, Paul accepts the emptiness hymn as a faith confession offered by the community in Philippi.

Although we have only Paul's side of his correspondence with the Philippians, the communication between them was clearly not a one-way street from God to Paul to his hearers.[17] No one has ever been able to identify with certainty the source of the emptiness hymn, but most scholars do regard it as a pre-Pauline liturgical hymn.[18] Perhaps it is best to see it, along with John Reumann, as a composition by the Philippians themselves, who send it to Paul after receiving his first letter with its protestations of self-sufficiency. It would appear that this faith confession from the Philippians challenges Paul's faith and leads him toward deeper insight into the mystery of Christ at a time when he is already close to fifty years of age and a Christ follower for over twenty years. Through it, Paul grows in his faith and understanding.

It is the analysis of Reumann,[19] among many others, that Paul's epistle to the Philippians actually contains three distinct letters. Very likely these were combined into the present canonical form near the end of the first century, to be shared with the wider church community. This conclusion in no way impugns the integrity of the epistle or its authority in the tradition. However, recognizing that the text contains portions of three different letters does help to account for some rather abrupt and discordant breaks in its flow. And the three-letter scenario can resolve some of the difficulty in a consistent rhetorical reading of Philippians as part of a back-and-forth correspondence. Reumann concludes that these are letters written by Paul "to Christian house churches at Philippi from Ephesus in 54–55" and that "the canonical four-chapter Philippians contains parts of three letters from Paul."[20]

According to Reumann, the first letter, Letter A, written in 54 CE, is comprised of Phil 4:10–20. This initial message expresses to the Philippians Paul's hesitant appreciation for their gift of money and for their concern about him. After writing that their relationship gladdens him, Paul briefly describes his situation, with no indication that

---

16. Reumann, "Oikonomia-Terms in Paul," 159. See also Reumann, *Philippians*, 78–79; 82.

17. Campbell, *Paul and the Creation*, 33–53.

18. Reumann, *Philippians*, 366–74. Because 2:6–11 only roughly fits the parameters of a hymn, he sees it as an "encomium," or a "speech of praise." Having heard many a clumsy hymn, I retain the more usual term, "hymn."

19. Ibid., 8–13.

20. Ibid., 3. See also ibid., 5–13.

INTRODUCTION

he is at that time in prison. It is a letter of friendship, but nevertheless Paul seems to want to distance himself from the perceived implications of a Greco-Roman friendship, with its attendant role expectancies. Thus, Paul asserts that in all circumstances he is "self-sufficient," not actually in need of their gifts, although he thinks it was a good thing that they did send a gift. Paul's less than gracious response here to the Philippians' help is often described as a "thankless thanks." Here, and nowhere else in his writing, Paul claims a "self-sufficiency" that is more akin to Stoic ideas than to the gospel. He seems to be concerned lest the acceptance of the Philippian gift make him the Philippians' client, bound by the duties of friendship to accept and carry out their preferred strategy for social and cultural acceptance as Christians in the Roman Empire. I will refer to Letter A as the "Self-Sufficiency Letter."

Paul's concern about remaining self-sufficient appears to have been assuaged by the time he writes Letter B. This second letter comprises 1:(1)2 to 3:1(2), and likely parts of 4:1–9 and 4:21–23, written in late 54 or early 55 CE while Paul is imprisoned in Ephesus. This letter expresses joy and appreciation at the Philippians' sharing with him in the gospel and praises the ministry of an otherwise unknown Philippian named Epaphroditus. Paul tells of his dire situation in prison but also rejoices in the more positive prospects for the progress of the gospel, urging the Philippians toward unity in the face of opposition. The central meditation of Letter B is the hymn of the empty Christ, which, as mentioned above, may well have been composed by the community in Philippi. It appears that they may have sent it to Paul in response to his earlier claim of self-sufficiency, to share with him their understanding of Christ. Paul agrees with their hymn of Christ-emptiness, draws out its implications in his reply, and never again in these letters or elsewhere claims to be self-sufficient. I identify Letter B as the "Emptiness Letter."

Letter C, comprised of 3:2–21 (with perhaps parts of 4:1–9), was written in the year 55 CE and contains no evidence that Paul is still imprisoned. This third letter contains a polemical warning against enemies, whom Paul calls "dogs," and expresses concerns about divisive doctrines, ethics, and unity. The same understanding of Christ as that expressed in the hymn of the empty Christ in Letter B is here repeated in terms of knowing Christ through the power of his resurrection and our participation in his sufferings. Paul now describes his own path as an emptying of all the identity markers that characterized his former life. I refer to this letter as the "Resurrection Letter."

These three letters were combined sometime between 90 and 100 CE, probably in Philippi, no doubt with the purpose of preserving the words Paul wrote to his favorite congregation.[21] Apparently the letters that the Philippians themselves wrote to Paul, which Epaphroditus carried to him, were not preserved. The best that we can do is to deduce the content of Paul's correspondents' letters from the clear shifts in what Paul wrote—from his initial claim of self-sufficiency, to his own confession of the empty Christ, to the path of sharing in Christ's sufferings and risen life.

21. Ibid., 3, 8–15. Also see Collange, *Epistle of Saint Paul*, 3–8.

There is persuasive evidence for this three-letter schema.[22] As we read the unified text in the New Testament, 3:2 introduces an abrupt shift in mood and content from the text that precedes it. The heavy-duty polemics that ensue do not seem to flow from the first and second chapters of the given text. Moreover, if this were a single letter, it seems highly unlikely that Paul would have withheld his thanks to the Philippians for their support until almost the end of the letter (beginning in 4:10). It is more likely that he would have sent his "thanks," such as they are, promptly upon receipt of their gift. It may be that the three letters were combined into a single text by a local congregation, or perhaps by some individual like Onesimus, later bishop of Ephesus, or by a Pauline school. In any case, partition theories about this letter go back to the nineteenth century, and the issue has been much debated. German scholarship has advocated for partition, while many in the Anglo-Saxon world defend the unity of the canonical text. To my mind, the three-letter schema does make the letter easier to read and understand.[23] Thus, this commentarial meditation will treat the three letters in the order described above in an attempt to recapture the sequence of Paul's thinking from the flow of his correspondence with the Philippians.

As to style, Paul tends to introduce and revisit themes in his letters in a rather cyclic, random fashion as occasion suggests, returning again and again to tease out meanings from his experience of the risen Christ—meanings that he may not have been able to express satisfactorily in an earlier sentence or discourse. He writes repeatedly of Christ faith, of being saved by Christ faith, of righteousness and gift, of the risen Christ, and of our participation in and oneness with Christ. It seems as though each time Paul attempts to share with the Philippians his experience of Christ, he articulates it differently. He does not, however, write as though he has experienced Christ while they have not, for he and they are joined in the same empty Christ the Philippians celebrate. Their shared experience of Christ flows into the many gospel insights and commitments that permeate the correspondence between them—although

---

22. Some still hold that it is a single letter. See Markus Bockmuehl, *A Commentary on the Epistle to the Philippians* (Peabody: Hendrickson, 1998) 20–25.

23. Reumann, *Philippians*, 675–76. "Philippians 4:10–20 [is] only loosely connected to 3:2–4:9. Paul delays clear appreciation of the Philippians' gift till here in Philippians and then puts it oddly. Why? . . . In the 1950s, proposals for *three* letters gained ground, 4:10–20 (or –23) the first of three. Garland [Garland, "Composition and Unity," 141] heard a 'crescendo of voices' against the unity of Philippians. Among German critics, partition theories dominated; unity theories continued in the Anglo-Saxon world . . . There has been a trend away from historical reconstruction, to take documents 'as received.' Rhetorical criticism and emphasis on friendship have been used to support unity, but each can also fit partitioning. Any verdict is unproven. 4:10–20 is best read as the body of Letter A but must also be treated as part of a four-chapter letter" (ibid.). See ibid., 676 n. 1 for a partial list of partition advocates. Reumann adds, "Lack of direct thanks is eased by prompt acknowledgment in Letter A of the safe arrival of the gift. Possibly Paul wrestled with whether he should accept this financial support, especially if he was not yet imprisoned. He asserts his independence (4:11 *autarkēs*) and his dependence on the Lord (4:13), not on the Philippians . . . The phrase "*danklose Dank*" arose prior to consideration of 4:10–20 as the body of a separate letter" (ibid., 677). As Reumann states, "Our conclusion: 4:10–20 = the body of Letter A" (ibid., 678).

INTRODUCTION

of the Philippian side of this exchange we have only the emptiness hymn that Paul cites from their liturgical practice. It is sometimes quite difficult to pin down what Paul means to say in his letters precisely because we do not have his correspondents' letters, nor do we know much about them.

Broadly, what we see in these three letters to the Philippian community is Paul groping his way toward friendship with this most stable of the early churches—first in his hesitating thanks in Self-Sufficiency Letter A; his appreciative reception of the Philippians' Christ understanding in Emptiness Letter B; and then, in Resurrection Letter C—after a harsh warning against any who would mar their friendship by imposing additional identity markers on the body of the organic Christ—in his emptying of his own identity in the knowledge of the empty power of the risen Christ.

2

Self-Sufficiency Letter A

According to John Reumann, Paul's earliest extant letter to Philippi was written from Ephesus in the year 54 CE. This Letter A, which I term the Self-Sufficiency Letter, is comprised of verses 4:10–20 of the canonical epistle, and it acknowledges a monetary gift to Paul from the Philippians. Reumann notes that the message would originally have had "a salutation (1:1–2 or similar) and a prayer report (1:3–11 or some form of it), followed by brief greetings and a benediction (cf. 4:21–23)."[1] It is a personal letter, paralleling Paul's friendly, persuasive letter to Philemon.[2]

We do not see in this letter any mention of the empty Christ of Emptiness Letter B or the risen Christ of Resurrection Letter C, for this first letter was not occasioned by those doctrines. Nor does it speak of self-interested Christ preachers or of "dog" preachers who insist on circumcision,[3] both of whom Paul mentions elsewhere in this correspondence. Verses 4:10–20 are limited to an expression of Paul's gratitude for the Philippians' concern about him and for their gift of money, as well as his joy in the friendly relationship between them. There is no hint that Paul is in prison at the time he is writing this message.[4] It is but "a brief note of thanks addressed to the Philippians by the apostle when he received the aid they had sent him through Epaphroditus (verse 18)."[5]

---

1. Ibid., 699.

2. Ibid., 688. In 4:10–20, "'I, me' language occurs in virtually every verse except 20, the 'I'-style of personal confession in 12–13; 'you' (pl.) in verses 10, 14–19" (ibid.).

3. Ibid., 718. "But 4:10–20 is not Christo-emphatic; it speaks of God (4:13, 19, 20) far more than Christ. The false teachers, so vivid in 3:2, 18–19, are not apparent in 4:10–20" (ibid.).

4. Ibid., 3.

5. Collange, *Epistle of Saint Paul*, 148. He continues: "The independent nature of the pericope, its curious position as a 'thank you' passage at the end of a letter which used to be thought a unity, and the necessarily long period of time which passed between the receipt of the gift and the writing of the first chapters of the epistle, all point to the independent composition of these verses, even prior to the rest of the epistle" (ibid.).

As it transpires, however, friendship has its complications. Although Paul writes here in the recognizable style of friendship letters of his time and culture,[6] he is nevertheless troubled by the perceived implications of this friendship with the Philippians, and he "seems to wish to extricate himself from aspects of its culture."[7] Friendships come with mutual expectations, and in his world this entailed the back-and-forth giving of gifts.[8] Seneca describes the reciprocal relationship between friends as establishing demands on both parties, for friendships flourish on reciprocity.[9] Cicero speaks of cultivating friends in less transactional terms: "For we do not put favors out at interest, but are by nature given to acts of kindness—so we believe that friendship is desirable, not because we are influenced by hope of gain, but because its entire profit is the love itself."[10] Nevertheless, like everything human, friendships often do entail benefits beyond mutual pleasure and joy; they are socially useful in business and politics and often express themselves culturally in terms of patron-and-client role expectations.[11]

Thus, Epaphroditus' arrival with a gift of money puts Paul in something of a quandary, torn between cherishing his friendship with the Philippian community and yet wishing to avoid any sense that he has become a client by accepting their gift.[12] Thus his apparent hesitancy to offer wholehearted thanks to the Philippians, writing merely that "they have done well," and that they can expect a reciprocal reward from God.[13] Paul's "almost churlish" gratitude startles.[14] Many Christian interpreters are

---

6. Reumann, *Philippians*, 678: "Since the mid-1980s, Philippians has often been called a 'letter of friendship,' with a friendly relationship between writer and recipient(s)." Reumann cites Luke Timothy Johnson's *Writings of the New Testament* and others to the effect that "In Philippians, the greatest concentration of friendship terms occurs in 4:10–20," so "[w]e shall conclude that elements in the friendship *topos* appear, but not all is explained by *philia*" (ibid., 679).

7. Ibid.

8. See Peter Marshall, *Enmity in Corinth: Social Conventions in Paul's Relations with the Corinthians*, WDNT 2:23 (Tübingen, Germany: Mohr Siebeck, 1987) 1–34.

9. Reumann, *Philippians*, 682.

10. Cicero, *De amicitia*, 9.30–31.

11. Reumann, *Philippians*, 683. The pattern repeats in many societies where one is beholden to a benefactor.

12. Ibid., 683: "But in 4:10–20 bonds of friendship have 'become strained either by Paul's or Epaphroditus's situation'; a house-church patron, perhaps Euodia or Syntyche, 'decided no longer to support Paul.'" Reumann goes on, "Sociologically, Paul desired to avoid status implications of patronal friendship" (ibid., 684).

13. Ibid., 685: "In 4:10–20 Paul acknowledges gifts from Philippi but never in Philippians expresses thanks with a verb like *eucharistein* (1:3, 'I thank my God . . . ?')."

14. Ibid., 690: "4:11–13 strikes a jarring note for Paul's 'favorite church,' singular among his *peristasis* [one's situation] catalogues in so fully accepting Hellenistic views. The almost churlish intrusion, 'I am content, I know, I can do all things,' without you, redefines the problem of friendship." Reumann adds, "4:11–13 with its '*autarkia* catalogue' is 'almost discourteous' in a letter of thanks . . . Paul thereby dampens the Philippians' zeal for their kind of *philia* . . . Paul presents the Philippians' gift to the real recipient, God" (ibid., 692). Friendship and fellowship shift to sacrifice and sharing: "Paul changes the paradigm from Greco-Roman friendship to the real partner in *koinōnia*, God, who will

clearly embarrassed that this earliest of Christian thinkers sounds so ungracious; others seem to read into his words their own awkward experiences of diffidence in asking for or receiving money.[15] Paul's writings rarely reveal reticence, however, and he is not reticent in expressing himself here. His words in verses 11–13 seem to be intended almost to "distance him from what the Philippians imply with their gift and their ideas of 'friendship' . . . [which] meant acknowledging a gift promptly (as Paul does) but then a (bigger) gift in response."[16]

So Paul avoids "getting caught up in such a reciprocal relationship, even with Philippi. It would prove endless, blunt his apostolic authority and freedom, and eventually color the concept of God and the Christian faith with *do ut des*, 'I give this in order that you will give that.'"[17] Surprisingly, however, Paul makes his point by emphasizing his own self-sufficiency, expressed in a philosophic term then current in Stoic writings. Paul asserts in 4:11 that he has learned in all circumstances to be self-sufficient (ἐγὼ γὰρ ἔμαθον ἐν οἷς εἰμι αὐτάρκης εἶναι), adding in 4:13 that he "can do everything (πάντα ἰσχύω)."[18] Reumann understands that here Paul is reshaping Greco-Roman patterns of friendship "toward Christian *koinōnia* by insistence on God who reverses *do-ut-des* concepts."[19] This explains much about this early letter, for Greco-Roman friendship patterns did not support innocent and disinterested intercourse between friends, but rather the mutual self-interest that pervaded aristocratic

---

take Paul's place, the One who alone can fulfill *every* need . . . (4:19)" (ibid.).

15. Silva, *Philippians*, 201: "Every minister has probably learned from experience how difficult it is to accept gifts graciously. How does one, without appearing ungrateful, discourage parishioners from spending their substance? Conversely, how does one give full, enthusiastic, and sincere thanks without suggesting that more is expected?" Caird writes, "He knows that they cannot really afford the money, but he cannot tell them so openly without seeming ungracious" (Caird, *Paul's Letters from Prison*, 152). One wonders how he knows that. Bruce adds, "Paul greatly appreciated the Philippians' kind thought, but he assures them that he had not been *in need* of support of this kind. His language may suggest the embarrassment felt by his independent and sensitive spirit at saying 'Thank you' for a spontaneous gift even from such well-loved and loving friends as the Christians in Philippi" (Bruce, *Philippians*, 149). Martin states, "That these verses do betray a certain tenseness on the apostle's part is undisputed, but this may be explained by his reserve, akin to embarrassment, over money matters in general, which has been detected in 1 Corinthians 9:15–18. The sense of uneasiness results from a conflict between his desire to express sincere appreciation of the help given and a concern to show himself superior to questions of money. In the writer's opinion this natural idiosyncrasy in regard to money, which other servants of God have shared, satisfactorily disposes of the difficulties which Michael raises [about a prior resentment caused by something Paul had previously said]" (Martin, *Philippians*, 176).

16. Reumann, *Philippians*, 704.

17. Ibid.

18. Ibid., 703: "Paul and the Philippian Christians knew the term *autarkeia*, if not all the philosophical views." But, in 4:13, "Adding . . . 'able to do all things,' makes Paul sound like a superman, Stoic self-sufficiency plus braggadocio as in W. E. Henley's 'Invictus,' 'I am the captain of my own soul'" (ibid.).

19. Ibid., 722.

society.[20] In asserting self-sufficiency, then, Paul is distancing himself from such networks of mutually beneficial friendships.

Underlying this reading of the passage, which takes Paul's tepid thanks for the Philippians' monetary gift as an implied refusal of that kind of friendship, unanswered questions remain about Paul's sources of financial support. While he thanks the Philippians for supplying him more than once with the wherewithal to carry on his missionary endeavors, we know very little about how Paul managed to sustain his adventuresome life in service of the gospel over the long term. Possibly he derived funds from business arrangements, such as one dealing with a woman named Lydia in Philippi.[21] Paul, however, never mentions such things in his letters. Or he may have had other sources—perhaps a wealthy wife, as Eusebius of Caesarea thought, or a supportive family back in Tarsus. And Paul himself did have a craft as a tentmaker. Indeed, in modern-day theological discourse about ministry, Paul is frequently taken as the example of someone who preaches the gospel without receiving a salary from those he preaches to. We speak today of "tentmakers" as those preachers of the gospel who also engage in a trade or profession through which they are able to earn their own living.

As a crafter of tents, Paul likely traveled the trade routes, where tents were a necessity. According to Bruce Chilton, Paul traveled those routes from Damascus down into Arabia in his early days. Later, he followed the trade routes from Jerusalem up through greater Greece into Philippi and Thessalonica, down into the cities of Athens and Corinth, and further yet to the city of Rome, where he ended his days with the unfulfilled expectation that he would journey on into Spain to preach the gospel of

---

20. See Marchal, *Hierarchy, Unity, and Imitation*, 34–50. On gift-giving, see James D. G. Dunn, *Beginning from Jerusalem*, vol. 2 of *Christianity in the Making* (Grand Rapids: Eerdmans, 2009) 1017. Also see G. W. Peterman, *Paul's Gift from Philippi: Conventions of Gift Exchange and Christian Giving* (Cambridge: Cambridge University Press, 2005) 53–68; he maintains that "in each point of his response the apostle corrects a possible Greco-Roman understanding of the significance of the gift with the Jewish understanding of it" (ibid., 158–59).

21. As described by J. Fleury, "Une société de fait dans l'Église apostolique (Phil 4:10 a 22)," in *Historie du droit*, vol. 2 of Mélanges Meylan (Lausanne: Université de Lausanne, 1963) 41–59. Fleury suggests that Paul had begun a business enterprise with Lydia, a dealer in purple cloth in Philippi (Acts 16:14–15). They formed a legal *societas* for an agreed purpose with a common treasury and records of expenditures and income. In Phil 4:18, Fleury suggests, Paul is issuing a receipt dissolving the society; he has been paid enough. That fits the present Letter; he did not need gifts from Philippi, but drew on earnings with Lydia. Perhaps that partnership expanded into a "consensual *societas* between Paul and the Philippians church," as envisioned by J. P. Sampley in "Societas Christi: Roman Law and Paul's Conception of Christian Community," in *God's Christ and His People*, edited by J. Jervell, and W. A. Meeks (Oslo: Universitetsforlaget, 1977) 158–74. Lydia, who is named in Acts but not in this Letter, may then have been the "partner" or "yoke fellow" (*syzyge*, Phil 4:3) whom Paul asks, as a community leader, to work for peace between Euodia and Syntyche—two community members who were in disagreement, possibly over supporting Paul's citizenship strategy of challenging Roman power. The arrangement described above is speculative (Reumann, *Philippians*, 693–94), but in the absence of clear information, we are left with speculation.

The Emptied Christ of Philippians

Jesus.[22] One can easily imagine tents such as those made by Paul being used in caravan communities along the trade routes he traveled. Perhaps some Christian communities also gathered in tents in remembrance that, in Christ, God has come to tent among us.[23] In constant use, such impermanent dwellings would also require repairs that, as a tentmaker, Paul could provide.

As a craftsman and a merchant, Paul would certainly have been conversant with the financial terms that appear in Letter A. Yet we have no way to ascertain how well he was able to support himself and his mission, especially when he became involved in defending the gospel before political judges. It seems that Paul must not have had a steady source of income otherwise, for he writes in 1 Thess 2:9 that when he left Philippi and began to preach in Thessalonica, the capital of Macedonia and its largest city, "we worked night and day" to support the mission and not burden the congregation. So it is likely that the gifts from Philippi were needed, even if they came with friendship-strings attached and created some tensions within the community. Perhaps Epaphroditus himself provided some of the funds, not only carrying the gift but drawing upon his own resources to supplement it.[24]

Paul's claim to self-sufficiency in his response to the gift he received must have been jarring to the ears of the Philippian community, whose emptiness hymn celebrates the Christ who, in emptying himself, clearly relinquishes any guise of self-sufficiency. As we will see in Letter B, Paul cites that hymn not as his own composition, but as an already-existing confession of faith in the empty and exalted Christ. That hymn served then as a corrective to all claims of self-sufficiency and all claims of self-status. Such claims subsequently disappear from Paul's writings altogether. Apparently he came to accept that the people in Philippi were not attempting to reduce him to client status or seeking to use their mutual friendship to persuade him to accept their approach in carving out space for Christ fellowship in the Greco-Roman world. Paul does argue the reasons for his own gospel strategy at the beginning of Letter B, but he leaves room for other approaches, pleading always for unity and harmony within the community of Christ followers.

---

22. Chilton, *Rabbi Paul*, 64–67. Paul offers precious few tidbits of information about himself in his letters, which often leaves us wishing to fill in our picture of him. The concise portrait offered by Chilton in *Rabbi Paul* relies upon a close reading of Paul's texts and is apparently consonant with such facts as we do have. He insists that "[i]t takes more to encounter Paul than reading an ancient text or two . . . We need to parse his words to access the person speaking, and we have to appreciate the settings and milieus that he addressed . . . Paul is inexplicable apart from the environment of apocalyptic zeal, intense mysticism, and incipient violence that characterized first-century Judaism and Christianity" (ibid., xiv–xv). We are probably best served by curbing our imaginations about Paul's biography and remaining minimalist in that regard. We just do not know enough, and the blank spaces in the story are wide enough to drive almost any exegetical bus through. Paul himself offers very brief autobiographical summaries in Gal 1:11—2:14 and in Letter C of this Philippian correspondence (3:5–6).

23. Keenan, *I Am / No Self*, 97–98.

24. Reumann, *Philippians*, 708.

SELF-SUFFICIENCY LETTER A
Self-sufficiency in Any and All Circumstances (4:10-14)

4:10 I am very much gladdened in the Lord that once again your constant care for me has blossomed, now that the opportunity presents itself. ¹¹ I do not speak from lack; for I have learned to be self-sufficient in any circumstances. ¹² I know what it is to be down and out, and I know what it is to be flush. In any and all circumstances, I have learned the secret of being [content] in good times and in bad, in abundance and in poverty. ¹³ I can do all things through him who strengthens me. ¹⁴ Still, you do well to share my distress.

4:10 Ἐχάρην δὲ ἐν κυρίῳ μεγάλως ὅτι ἤδη ποτὲ ἀνεθάλετε τὸ ὑπὲρ ἐμοῦ φρονεῖν, ἐφ' ᾧ καὶ ἐφρονεῖτε ἠκαιρεῖσθε δέ. ¹¹οὐχ ὅτι καθ' ὑστέρησιν λέγω, ἐγὼ γὰρ ἔμαθον ἐν οἷς εἰμι αὐτάρκης εἶναι. ¹²οἶδα καὶ ταπεινοῦσθαι, οἶδα καὶ περισσεύειν· ἐν παντὶ καὶ ἐν πᾶσιν μεμύημαι καὶ χορτάζεσθαι καὶ πεινᾶν, καὶ περισσεύειν καὶ ὑστερεῖσθαι. ¹³πάντα ἰσχύω ἐν τῷ ἐνδυναμοῦντί με. ¹⁴πλὴν καλῶς ἐποιήσατε συγκοινωνήσαντές μου τῇ θλίψει.

Paul is "very much glad" (Ἐχάρην δὲ . . . μεγάλως)[25] that the Philippians have sent him a gift. He is happy because "once again" (ὅτι ἤδη ποτὲ) the care, or "concern," (φρονεῖν) of the Philippians "has blossomed" (ἀνεθάλετε),[26] and been "focused on his situation" (τὸ ὑπὲρ ἐμοῦ φρονεῖν),[27] "as indeed it had long been, but without opportunity" (ἐφ' ᾧ καὶ ἐφρονεῖτε, ἠκαιρεῖσθε δέ) for concrete expression. The Philippians have sent Paul funds to continue his work, and he assures them that he appreciates their generosity, suggesting that they offered that gift because of their experienced oneness with him in Christ. That phrase "in the Lord" (ἐν κυρίῳ, *en kyriō*) is not a throwaway line. Again and again Paul asserts that all his efforts for the furtherance of the gospel are moved not by self-benefit or self-profit, but by his being one in the Lord with others.

Nevertheless, commentators suggest that Paul expresses his gratitude somewhat tepidly in this passage because he suspects that the Philippians may attempt to use this financially unequal friendship to influence Paul's missionary conduct vis-à-vis the Roman Empire. As we learn in Acts 16, Paul has publicly claimed his Roman citizenship, and this accommodation to the Roman system may have had disturbing implications for other Christians. He may have become wary that the Philippians expect him to reciprocate by agreeing with their own strategy for furthering the gospel within Roman

---

25. Ibid., 647, on "I rejoiced" reads, "A true past tense, I *rejoiced* when you again showed concern for me."

26. Ibid., 647-48, on ἀνεθάλετε. *Thallō* means "to grow" or "to flourish," and, with the prepositional prefix, *ana*, has a causative sense. "Nowhere else in the New Testament" (ibid.).

27. Ibid., 720, on τὸ ὑπὲρ ἐμοῦ φρονεῖν reads, "The verb [φρονεῖν] occurs throughout Philippians (10x), the heaviest concentration of occurrences in the New Testament." It is so often used because of the consistent stress on attentiveness and mental focus. Again, Reumann adds that this verb "echoes through the correspondence, 2:2 bis, 16, 19, 4:2, and 4:10 bis" (ibid., 148). *Phronein* is found in the introductory verse to the meditation on the empty Christ (2:5).

culture. So he responds to the gift rather coolly, presenting himself as something of a Stoic philosopher who knows how to be satisfied with whatever his merchant craft affords him. Paul has "learned to be content" (ἐγὼ γὰρ ἔμαθον ἐν οἷς εἰμι αὐτάρκης εἶναι 4:12), and he does "not speak from a sense of lack" (οὐχ ὅτι καθ'ὑστέρησιν λέγω 4:11). He is a merchant. When he makes a sale, he's "flush" (οἶδα καὶ περισσεύειν), and when he doesn't, he's "broke" (οἶδα καὶ ταπεινοῦσθαι). Even during an earlier period when the Philippians contributed to Paul's endeavors, he likely depended primarily on his own trade to make a living.

It is not that Paul "is clearly sensitive about money matters in general."[28] It is not that he feels he must defend himself, as he does in other letters, against charges of sponging off assemblies he preaches to.[29] Paul, in his financial life, differs not at all from the rest of us humans, but he does not go begging. He has been "initiated into the secret" (μεμύημαι) so that "in all circumstances" (ἐν παντὶ καὶ ἐν πᾶσιν), "in good times and in bad" (καὶ χορτάζεσθαι καὶ πεινᾶν),[30] "in abundance and in poverty" (καὶ περισσεύειν καὶ ὑστερεῖσθαι), he is content and sufficient unto himself. The verb in the phrase "I have learned the secret" (μεμύημαι) is derived, it would seem, from Greek mystery religions into whose secrets one is initiated by ritual acts.[31] Paul has been initiated into the secret of material contentment. But what secret is that? And how has he been initiated? Has he learned a supernatural method to rise above the physical circumstances of his life? Is he aloof and somehow beyond it all? It does not seem so: When he is poor, he is hungry. When he has no money, he gets by as best he can, like poor people all over the world both in his day and in ours.

When Paul says in 4:12 that he is "content" (αὐτάρκης εἶναι), he means it quite literally. But this "contentment" is a culturally packed term, flowing directly from Stoic and Cynic philosophies that recommend such contentment in all circumstances. The adjective "self-sufficient" (αὐτάρκης, *autarkēs*) in 4:11 is another "important term in Stoic, Cynic, and other philosophies"; used "only here in the New Testament."[32] It comes from *autos*, meaning "self," plus *arkeō*, "suffice, be enough," and was "a central concept in ethical discussions from the time of Socrates."[33] The noun form, αὐτάρκεια, does occur in 2 Cor 9:8, but there it refers to the sufficiency of good things that God will provide to cheerful givers. First Timothy 6:6 later uses the noun

---

28. *Pace* O'Brien, *Epistle to the Philippians*, 514.

29. Johnson, *Apostle Paul*, 23, on the Corinthians, who "think that Paul is unreliable and possibly even fraudulent in his dealings with money (11:7–11; 12:16–18). (Paul had emphasized that he preached for free, but he did not tell the Corinthians that the Philippian church was financing him on the side. The Corinthians then suspected that his collection [for the poor in Jerusalem] might be fraudulent)."

30. Reumann, *Philippians*, 655, on χορτάζεσθαι reads, "to get my fill . . . From *chortos*, feeding place, fodder for animals, + *azō* as verbal suffix."

31. Ibid., 655.

32. Ibid., 651.

33. Ibid.

form "self-sufficiency" (αὐτάρκεια) to mean simply contentment; in that instance, it is twinned with godliness and accompanied by a reminder that since we brought nothing into the world, we can take nothing out of it. After this first letter of the Philippian correspondence, Paul never again uses the adjective "self-sufficient" in referring to himself.[34] But whatever nuance he intended by its use in this passage, his claim startles like a "meteor fallen from the Stoic sky."[35] The assertion is so personal and its impact so jarring that "Philippians 4:10–20 has had no great impact on doctrinal or ethical themes in Christianity, even 'stewardship.'"[36]

Apparently the secret that Paul has learned is self-sufficiency in all circumstances. But how did he learn that secret? Did Jesus teach it? In the Gospel of Matthew, Jesus tells us—however impractical the advice—not to worry about anything. We are to be like the lilies of the valley, unconcerned about our passing beauty. We are to be like the birds of the air, unconcerned about our next meal. But Paul is not appealing here to that advice from Jesus. In any case, there is no indication that Jesus ever preached self-sufficiency or self-contentment. The point of the self-sufficiency that Paul declares here is Stoic philosophy's well-known reversal of the human instinct to grasp and protect. In this correspondence with his Philippian benefactors, he applies that Stoic attitude to the practical affairs of his life. Certainly, Stoic contentment is not in any way a supernatural or a specifically Christian virtue, although people in many faith traditions do practice contentment with their circumstances,[37] and such a practice is not unworthy of Christ followers. But Paul's assertion of self-sufficiency in this letter is discordant to Philippian ears. And, as we will see in the Emptiness Letter that follows, once the Philippians share with Paul their christology of emptiness and exaltation, he drops any further reference to self-sufficiency. For Christ, the emptiness hymn declares, emptied his own self entirely.

34. Pace Fee, *Paul's Letter to the Philippians*, 431 n.37: "The usage in 2 Cor 9:8 is certain evidence that the word is part of Paul's regular vocabulary and that it can come close to 'sufficiency,' without the sense of 'self-sufficiency.'" It is not then surprising that commentators play down the sentence, insisting, as Martin does, that what Paul really means is "that in every conceivable circumstance, 'in any and every situation,' he finds the strength which vital union with Christ supplies to be adequate for maintaining his apostolic work and for the fulfillment of his desire to accelerate the process of the gospel. This statement, then, does not make Paul a wonder-worker, a spiritual 'super-man,' who towers so far above the rest of us that his life is no encouragement to lesser mortals" (Martin, *Philippians*, 180).

35. Fee, *Paul's Letter to the Philippians*, 431.

36. Reumann, *Philippians*, 724.

37. The Buddha is said to have once preached a Sermon to the Birds about not becoming attached to anything. See Edward Conze, *The Buddha's Law among the Birds* (Delhi: Motilal Banarsidass, 2002) for this medieval Tibetan folktale about the Buddha, who took the compassionate form of a cuckoo to teach the Dharma of liberation to the birds. See also "Sufficiency and Satisfaction in Zen Buddhism: Recovering an Ancient Symbolon" in James W. Heisig, *Dialogues at One Inch above the Ground: Reclamations of Belief in an Interreligious Age* (New York: Crossroad, 2003), a meditation on the properly understood ascetic attitude as written on a stone in the garden of Ryōanji Temple in Kyoto: "All I know is how much is enough" (or, "I just know what suffices"). See also "The Message of Bapu's Hut," in Illich, *Mirror of the Past*, 65–70, on Gandhi's simplicity and the poverty he embraced in a world of so many poor.

Some Buddhist thinkers describe the realization of a true and authentic self once a person attains enlightenment and abides in absolute nothingness. Philosophers of the Kyoto School, especially Nishitani Keiji, teach that we all flow from an "absolute nothingness" (Js. *zettai-mu* 絶対無), which we cannot comprehend and cannot control. This absolute nothingness is not, however, the opposite of being—which they define as a "nihility," or the relative nothingness of the empty forced into a putative relationship with being.[38] In classical Mahāyāna treatises, such a relative, anti-being nothingness is described as the "inept apprehension of emptiness" (惡取空), for it negates all images and ideas in a nihilistic drive toward simply nothing; it is more of a death wish, wherein one attends only to human mortality and welcomes being no more. One can—and indeed philosophers and thinkers often do—grow weary of this world and simply desire to stop and get off or, like philosopher Gilles Deleuze, jump out of the window of life to end its chronic pain. There are sometimes urges within us to blot out our very existence, for it is not assured or stable, and we can become weary of being existentially condemned to meaningless freedom.

However, while Buddhists do teach that all is empty, they maintain that one may not settle down there and wallow. For Buddhists, emptiness (空) functions in service of practice, which issues in a broad and deep awareness of the reality of all things as they come into being in dependence (Js. *engi* 縁起) upon uncountable causes and conditions, as the life and being of that which is empty. This notion is crucial in Mahāyāna: Emptiness is *not* to lead us into despair but rather into the celebration of a life that in actual experience is full.[39]

In this passage, Paul is adopting a Stoic attitude of contentment and self-sufficiency in that he too is able to be at ease, whether in circumstances of abundance or of lack. Indeed, circumstances of lack afford him opportunities to depend upon others and for them to support him, which Paul finds acceptable so long as no strings are attached. But in the context of the Christ who empties self, this cannot mean wallowing in lack and penury, for that is useless. Truly poor people seldom wallow in their own poverty; they do not have time to wallow. They work to scratch out a living and get by, and in so doing they depend upon one another in ways that rich people, isolated in their wealth, often do not. Rich or poor, however, none of us—even the steely Stoics—possess or control our own lives. Although we may, like captains of our own ships, stand at the helm and attempt to steer the course of our journey, we do not control the sea and can go only where wind and waves allow. But, whatever befalls, we are not to throw ourselves into the blank depths of the deep, dark sea. In

---

38. See Nishitani Keiji, *Religion and Nothingness*, trans. Jan van Bragt (Berkeley: University of California Press, 1982) 46–76, on "The Personal and the Impersonal in Religion," and 77–118, on "Nihility and Śūnyatā."

39. See David R. Loy, *Lack and Transcendence* (Amherst, NY: Humanity Books, 2000) and ibid., *A Buddhist History of the West* (Albany: State University of New York Press, 2002). Loy draws upon psychotherapy, existentialism, and Buddhism in discussing the non-duality of life and death and in examining the deluded human desire for permanence of self.

Kyoto School philosophy, acknowledgment of absolute nothingness does not signify an end-time despair; it is imagined, rather, as a "locus" wherein all affirmation and negation cease—much as some exegetes see being "in Christ" as the sphere or location of risen life.

There is, however, neither any special enlightened place nor any way for us to assert a permanent value of the self. We do not control the conditions that make our life possible. If we stop a moment to contemplate, it is readily apparent how precarious is our passage through this world. And faith begins with this acknowledgment of our bare humanity, the truth that there is nothing upon which we can depend to support our special and cherished individual selves. (Darwin was spot-on: The world is rife with contingency and happenstance.) Nevertheless, in this first letter to the Philippians Paul appears to have adopted—which means he read and understood—the Stoic notion of self-sufficiency. And though this Stoic virtue seems so discordant with the confession of the Christ who abandons his own self, Paul seems here to be following the advice that he gives the Philippians later in Letter B (4:8)—to take account of whatever they find to be honorable, praiseworthy, and good.

Indeed, in Greek and more specifically Stoic philosophical ethics, the virtue of self-sufficiency (αὐτάρκεια) "was regarded as the essence of all virtues. It described the cultivated attitude of the wise person who had become independent of all things and all people, relying on himself, because of his innate resources, or on the lot given to him by the gods."[40] The Stoic doctrine was "that man should be sufficient unto himself for all things, and able, by the power of his own will, to resist the force of circumstances."[41] And this Stoic path does embody a brave and worthy ideal: to make the best of life as you find it by being courageous enough to live and die well. It is an ideal much cherished in western cultures to this day. I envisage the resolute attitude of Marcus Aurelius, Emperor of Rome, who in his meditations determines to enjoy and appreciate life to the fullest by recognizing its clear and defined limits. It also calls to mind existentialist philosophers like Albert Camus who, realizing the certainty of life-unto-death, yet engendered the courage to face life and death boldly and without pretense.

Paul, however, was brought up within the Hebrew faith and endeavored in every way possible to live that tradition zealously and intensely. It must have been obvious to him that the Stoic notion of an independently sufficient self is inimical to Torah, wherein we are servants of God and are commanded to love both God and neighbor. To be authentically human is to acknowledge that in fact we are *not* in control, for we are creatures and not the authors of our own lives. The Stoic philosophy of Paul's time, by contrast, emphasized the unreliability of other people and the consequent need for the individual to cultivate inner strength; each and every person must rely upon the

---

40. O'Brien, *Epistle to the Philippians*, 521.
41. Vincent, *Critical and Exegetical Commentary*, 143.

self alone. So although Paul here professes the very Stoic virtue of contentment, he must somehow adapt that to his still very Hebrew faith in Christ.

Later in the correspondence, Paul will assure the Philippians that he has abandoned all self-markers. Even here, his assertion that "I can do all things" is followed by the words *"through him who strengthens me"* (πάντα ἰσχύω ἐν τῷ ἐνδυναμοῦντί με 4:13), a confession of dependence that no Stoic would ever utter.[42] Throughout the remainder of the Philippian correspondence, we will see that Paul no longer professes to draw his strength from an inner core as a Stoic would, but rather from the erasure of all self-boundaries to be one with Christ. This is how he is empowered and enabled to do all things, for he has learned Christ and, as we would say, reconfigured his neural pathways to live in Christ. In this first letter, however, Paul's assertion of self-sufficiency, along with his halfhearted expression of gratitude for the Philippians' gift, does hold a ring of arrogant boasting, whatever he may say elsewhere.

Despite Paul's apparent ambivalence toward the Philippians' gift in this passage, he does suggest that he understands they have not sent him money simply because of his need. His lackluster expression of thanks conveys that there is something more to it when he writes, "Still, you do well to share my distress" (πλὴν καλῶς ἐποιήσατε συγκοινωνήσαντές μου τῇ θλίψει 4:14). No matter what their motivations, they still (πλὴν) did well[43] to share his "distress,"[44] for that sharing (συγκοινωνήσαντές)—a term used only here and in Eph 5:11[45]—denotes their interconnectedness.

Thanks Be to God (4:15–20)

> 4:15 *You Philippians well know that in the early days of the Gospel, when I left Macedonia, no church had partnered with me in the matter of giving and receiving, except you alone.* [16]*For even when I was in Thessalonica, you sent me help for my needs more than once.* [17]*Not that I crave the gift. Rather, I crave the profit that accumulates to your account.* [18]*I have been paid in full and have more than enough; I am fully satisfied, now that I have received from Epaphroditus the gifts you sent, a fragrant offering, a sacrifice acceptable and pleasing to God.* [19]*And*

---

42. Reumann, *Philippians*, 722, thinks the sentence was added by a later scribe to soften its bluntness.

43. Ibid., 705. On *plēn*, "Anyway," Reumann cites Hawthorne in noting that *plēn* "expresses goodwill, *captatio benevolentiae*, commendation, the way friends speak. It 'comes as close to saying "Thank you" as Paul ever does in Philippians'" (ibid.).

44. Ibid., 702. Reumann writes on *peristasis*, a catalog of circumstances recounting "[v]icissitudes of the wanderer or (suffering) sage, how he perseveres, credentials, place in the divine scheme of things, a path 'to the stars, through perseverance'" (ibid.). Martin takes *thlipsis* (θλίψις) in verse 14 not to mean "merely 'my difficulties' or 'my personal need,'" for *thlipsis* "is a technical term for the affliction or tribulation to come on the earth at the end of the age" (Martin, *Philippians*, 180). And so Martin sees Paul's eschatological struggles here indicated.

45. Reumann, *Philippians*, 658.

Self-Sufficiency Letter A

my God will fully satisfy every need of yours according to his riches in glory in Christ Jesus. ²⁰To our God and Father be glory forever and ever. Amen.

4:15 Οἴδατε δὲ καὶ ὑμεῖς, Φιλιππήσιοι, ὅτι ἐν ἀρχῇ τοῦ εὐαγγελίου, ὅτε ἐξῆλθον ἀπὸ Μακεδονίας, οὐδεμία μοι ἐκκλησία ἐκοινώνησεν εἰς λόγον δόσεως καὶ λήμψεως εἰ μὴ ὑμεῖς μόνοι· ¹⁶ὅτι καὶ ἐν Θεσσαλονίκῃ καὶ ἅπαξ καὶ δὶς εἰς τὴν χρείαν μοι ἐπέμψατε. ¹⁷οὐχ ὅτι ἐπιζητῶ τὸ δόμα, ἀλλὰ ἐπιζητῶ τὸν καρπὸν τὸν πλεονάζοντα εἰς λόγον ὑμῶν. ¹⁸ἀπέχω δὲ πάντα καὶ περισσεύω· πεπλήρωμαι δεξάμενος παρὰ Ἐπαφροδίτου τὰ παρ' ὑμῶν, ὀσμὴν εὐωδίας, θυσίαν δεκτήν, εὐάρεστον τῷ θεῷ. ¹⁹ὁ δὲ θεός μου πληρώσει πᾶσαν χρείαν ὑμῶν κατὰ τὸ πλοῦτος αὐτοῦ ἐν δόξῃ ἐν Χριστῷ Ἰησοῦ. ²⁰τῷ δὲ θεῷ καὶ πατρὶ ἡμῶν ἡ δόξα εἰς τοὺς αἰῶνας τῶν αἰώνων· ἀμήν.

Paul traveled from city to city across the Greco-Roman world. But he was not a solitary pilgrim, nor would he have traveled with just a companion or two. It is likely that for sake of security he traveled with the caravans, where he could also find customers for his trade and a source of income. Indeed, financial matters were of considerable concern to Paul. Money is our ability to live in this world and to support our families. As Karl Marx well knew, economics is the most basic of all human sciences, for it has an immediate, experienced impact.

Paul's letters to the Thessalonians and the Corinthians demonstrate his concern about financial issues, and he acknowledges that money is a point of some contention within both of those early Christian communities. Indeed, it appears that in those letters Paul is responding to money-related criticisms that had been leveled against him: allegations that even though he had no proper credentials, he nevertheless made money from his preaching. But Paul makes the point more than once in the correspondence with the Thessalonians and Corinthians that although a preacher of the gospel is entitled to support from the communities he visits, he himself has not made use of that entitlement (1 Thess 2:9; 2 Thess 3:7–10; 1 Cor 9:3–18; 2 Cor 12:12–18). Monetary support for preachers does seem to have been a common practice; itinerant preachers of any gospel who lacked a gainful trade certainly would have found it difficult to carry on. Paul maintains that just as a soldier expects to be supported by his army, so ministers of the gospel should not have to take time out from their gospel endeavors to earn their sustenance. Nonetheless, he does not demand such support from the communities he visits.

Having declared at the beginning of this first letter to the Philippians (4:11) that he has learned the Stoic virtue of self-sufficiency in all circumstances, Paul stresses in 4:17: "It is not that I seek after the gift" (οὐκ ὅτι ἐπιζητῶ τὸ δόμα). Yet, with Paul as with us, the calculus of money is never straightforward and simple. He has been sent to preach the gospel by a risen Christ who does not pay salaries. Nor does that Lord provide Paul with a letter of recommendation. Indeed, Paul does not represent the church in Jerusalem. He has not been sent by any of the Lord's apostles gathered in

Jerusalem, in Galilee, or anywhere else. Rather, as Paul boldly avows, he has been sent by the risen Lord. Thus, has no proper ecclesial identity. His only worldly credential for preaching the gospel is that he has no credentials to proffer at all. Nothing. Just that he is "under orders"—"I *have been appointed* for a gospel defense" (1:16)—and is sent by the Lord. It is not, then, very surprising that some within the early Christian communities might take issue with him, pointing out his lack of direct linkage to Jesus and the earliest disciples. No one ever ordained Paul. No one sent him out from a mother church. He is not a cleric paid a salary by the church. He is not a bishop, although he does mention overseers. He is not a servant deacon, although he writes about deacons. Paul really does function without any properly credentialed identity.

All of which highlights Paul's stark singularity, for it is this same Paul who is so central to our understanding of Jesus of Nazareth. It is Paul who gives us our paradigmatic enlightenment account of risen life in Christ, and yet never does he provide an unambiguous description of his Damascus Road encounter with Jesus. Nowhere does Paul clearly communicate that personal experience of awakening, although he does from time to time describe its implications for his life, explaining that because of it he has lost everything—even, one supposes, his self-sufficiency. In fact, Paul spends his life unfolding, not systematically but in diverse and rhetorically powerful ways, what that experience of radical transformation meant to him. The content of Paul's enlightenment is visible in his every effort to further the gospel and to live in oneness with Christ. Rather than dwelling upon the initial bare experience itself, he lives out its meaning from day to day.

Some Buddhist practitioners present the awakening of the Buddha simply as an experience that is beyond all discrimination and all words. They do not bother to spell out its lived implications, which they assume flow naturally and without effort. This is particularly true of the "import Zen" that Alan Watts and D. T. Suzuki introduced into the United States in the mid-twentieth century, wherein the core experience of enlightenment (Js. 悟り, *satori*) is assumed to be at the heart of all religious traditions, although it is never accessible in words. The Buddha Śākyamuni and his silent enlightenment under the Bodhi tree do indeed provide the paradigm of awakening for later Buddhist practitioners. However, far from ending in that silence, accounts of the Buddha's mystic and ineffable awakening proliferated over time into a vast literature that propounds the teachings of the Dharma—the Four Noble Truths and the Twelvefold Chain of Causality. Later Mahāyāna philosophers make a clear differentiation between the silent ultimate meaning of awakening and the tensive enunciation of that experience in doctrine and practice.

Paul similarly embodies his ineffable Christ enlightenment within the concrete struggles of his life, which never transcend human pain or brokenness. Just as he strives to further the gospel that enunciates our oneness with Christ, Paul identifies his own pain with the sufferings of Christ—and it is clear that his tangible struggles include matters of money. So in responding here to the monetary gift sent by the

Philippians, Paul addresses financial matters directly. He reminds the Philippians of what they already know,[46] that from "the early days of the Gospel, when I left Macedonia, no church had partnered with me in the matter of giving and receiving, except you alone. For even when I was in Thessalonica, you sent me help for my needs more than once" (4:15–16). So we see that the Philippians not only share a friendship with Paul, they also have a history of funding his endeavors. Although Paul indicates at the beginning of the letter (4:10–11) that he does not need support, having learned the virtue of self-sufficiency, the Philippians have in fact partnered with him before. And so he speaks here of his finances.

The phrase he uses in 4:15, "in the matter of giving and receiving" (εἰς λόγον δόσεως καὶ λήμψεως), is a commonly used business term.[47] Paul also speaks of "the account ledger" (λόγον) "of credits and debits" (δόσεως καὶ λήμψεως) and refers directly to the monies he has taken in and the expenses he has incurred. In financial matters, "you Philippians well know" (Οἴδατε δὲ καὶ ὑμεῖς, Φιλιππήσιοι) that "you alone" (οὐδεμία . . . εἰ μὴ ὑμεῖς μόνοι) of all the churches "have partnered with me" (μοι ἐκκλησία ἐκοινώνησεν).[48] Indeed, they are the only church to have done so "from the beginning" when Paul "first began to preach the Gospel" (ὅτι ἐν ἀρχῇ τοῦ εὐαγγελίου), when he "left Macedonia" (ὅτε ἐξῆλθον ἀπὸ Μακεδονίας) to travel on throughout Greece and beyond. And they have sent monies "for my use" (εἰς τὴν χρείαν μοι ἐπέμψατε) not "only once but twice," that is, "again and again" (ὅτι . . . καὶ ἅπαξ καὶ δὶς).

In fact, when Paul wrote later to the Thessalonians and the Corinthians that he had preached the gospel to them without charging them for it, he had at that time been able to rely to some degree on support from these Philippians. It was not that they had once sent him a gift, perhaps as a going-away present; they supported his "foreign mission"—for Paul's vision was to preach to all lands and cultures. He seems always to have bitten off more than he could actually chew. Furthermore, those other congregations—particularly the Thessalonians, who lived only about a hundred miles from Philippi—must have known that he was supported by this one Philippian church, for Paul's letters soon became public, circulated and read openly in the Christian gatherings. Indeed, contention about Paul's financial situation may have been triggered precisely because his critics were aware that the church in Philippi was supporting

---

46. Ibid., 659–60. On "you know," Reumann writes, "a question on what the Philippians now need to recall" (ibid.).

47. Ibid., 662, on giving and receiving accounts. See John Dominic Crossan, *The Historical Jesus: The Life of a Mediteranean Jewish Peasant* (New York: Harper, 1991) 20–29, on the story of an apprentice and his father, vividly reconstructed. The phrase about a settlement of mutual accounts, literally giving and receiving of debt and credit, is "long known from classical sources." Reumann explains, "Thus *logos doseōs kai lēmpseōs* was a 'constitutive principal' of society in Philippi. Paul appeals to Christians, with their *politeuma* in heaven, not to invest in fountains or festivals but Paul and mission" (Reumann, *Philippians*, 663).

48. Ibid., 661, on church: "The Philippian house churches are an *ekklēsia* (term not used in 1:1b but to be understood there). Philippians 3:6 gives *ekklēsia* a broader sense. 4:15 = the total Christian community in Philippi and environs."

his efforts. Thus Paul thanks the Philippians for their generosity "even when I was in Thessalonica" (καὶ ἐν Θεσσαλονίκῃ), perhaps at the very time he was encountering unfounded complaints that he was a financial drain on the communities he served.

Still, in 4:17, Paul "does not crave" (ἐπιζητῶ) their money, but rather he craves that "they may make money" (ἀλλὰ ἐπιζητῶ τὸν καρπὸν τὸν πλεονάζοντα)—in that great bank account in the sky! These Philippians "have an account ledger" (εἰς λόγον ὑμῶν) in which their credits and debits are reckoned. Just as their names are written in "the book of life" (4:3), so their bank accounts are in a heavenly depository, and Paul rejoices to see "the growth" (τὸν πλεονάζοντα) "of their profit" (τὸν καρπὸν). All these terms are financial. The increase in their account book here deals with metaphorical finances and "fruit" (τὸν καρπὸν); their assets are stored up far offshore. Preachers sometimes highlight the frequent use of financial terms in the New Testament. Often these terms are employed metaphorically, but sometimes real money is a necessity. And Paul, driven as he is by his experience of the risen Christ, occasionally requires financial assistance from partners like the Philippians in order to press forward in furthering the gospel. There is another reckoning, indeed, but it is not one that appears on anybody's bank statement.

Paul writes in fact that he has been "paid in full" (ἀπέχω δὲ πάντα 4:18).[49] This phrase is another "technical term for receiving a sum of money in full and giving a receipt for it."[50] The Stoics use the same term where "to be paid in full" (ἀπέχω δὲ πάντα) is "a near equivalent of αὐτάρκεια [contentment],"[51] the virtue of self-sufficiency that Paul practices. "Paul then has more than enough" (καὶ περισσεύω) and "he is fully satisfied" (πεπλήρωμαι), for not only has he "received from Epaphroditus the gifts that were sent" (δεξάμενος παρὰ Ἐπαφροδίτου τὰ παρ'ὑμῶν) by the Philippians, but more basically he has learned this Stoic "self-sufficiency" and thus abandoned the craving that drives a deluded quest for security. Paul has learned all this not from the radical Damascus Road reorientation of his consciousness that drove him to the task of furthering the gospel, but from his meditation on Stoic philosophy. He could read.

In this first letter, Paul does not mention prison, nor is he expecting an imminent trial. Probably because he is not now in jail, he tends to be optimistic. Still, he writes so frequently elsewhere about his many tribulations that apparently he is not an altogether carefree fellow. Later, in Letter B when he is indeed a prisoner, he writes that if he could have his preference, he would rather die to be with Christ, yet he waits so that he may serve to benefit others, for their life is the same Christ-life that beats in his own heart. Paul uses many rather transcendent images—about the book of life, heavenly bank accounts, the crown of victory for those who run the race—but none seem to be

---

49. Ibid., 711, on being paid in full: This "assures the Philippians they have discharged all the obligations attached to *philia*. If a principle is present from Galatians 6:6 (paying the teacher materially for spiritual goods), Paul is crossing that off too, they have amply taken care of him. 'Account closed.'"

50. O'Brien, *Epistle to the Philippians*, 540.

51. See Fee, *Paul's Letter to the Philippians*, 450 n. 7.

adequate. What happened to Paul on the Damascus Road is not a once-and-for-all-experience; it provides him with a constant inner drive to strive toward what lies ahead. He looks forward to his own death, employing constantly shifting images to express a hope that cannot be articulated by or captured in any image that might delineate an expectation. Paul is a multifaceted and sometimes ambiguous writer. But whatever his various concerns, he does not dismiss gifts received. He neither rejects nor fixes his particular attention upon the effort of the Philippians to see to his financial needs. He does, however, seem to rather belittle their generosity.

After talking straightforwardly of money, Paul now shifts the metaphor to speak in 4:18 of the gift sent to him as "a fragrant offering" (ὀσμὴν εὐωδίας), "a sacrifice acceptable and pleasing to God" (θυσίαν δεκτήν, εὐάρεσρον τῷ θεῷ).[52] The first phrase literally means "an odor of a sweet smell" and is frequently used of sacrificial offerings in Torah.[53] God takes pleasure in the aroma of sacrifices that mark the commitment of his people Israel to his gracious covenant. If the aroma marks an acceptable sacrifice that is pleasing to God, it is because it is offered with a contrite heart, for that is the "new covenant" announced by Jeremiah (31:31–34). It is not that one actually gains interest in some heavenly bank account, and Paul knows well enough that one does not profit so much from good works. But Paul is not finished talking about needs and wants. He practices self-sufficiency and in 4:19 recommends that the Philippians do the same, knowing that their experience of "*my* God" (ὁ δὲ θεός μου) "will fully satisfy every need of *yours*" (πληρώσει πᾶσαν χρείαν ὑμῶν). He recommends in fact that his readers abandon themselves and in their hearts render glory to—that is, "light up" (ἡ δόξα)—"this Father God" (τῷ δὲ θεῷ καὶ πατρὶ ὑμῶν),[54] who "indeed" (ἀμήν) "abides forever and ever" (εἰς τοὺς αἰῶνας τῶν αἰώνων, ἀμήν 4:20).[55]

This last passage, 4:19–20, clearly counters any suggestion of a client status foisted upon Paul by the friendly gift from Philippi. He seems to be saying here, "God shall supply all your need and do so with coruscating radiance and splendor[56] (so don't look to me to provide any reciprocal gifts to you)." Indeed, "The Philippians have paid Paul fully what they owe him; now his God will supply their needs. Is such a *do-ut-des* concept ('I'll do this so that you'll do that for me') unworthy of Paul's theology?"[57]

---

52. Reumann, *Philippians*, 712 n. 84: "Banking and animal sacrifice were related in antiquity in that temples served as repositories for money and savings accounts." So the shift in metaphors is not as stark as it appears to us.

53. Ibid., 667. On sacrifice, Reumann says that the three phrases—"a fragrance with aroma, a sacrifice acceptable, and well pleasing to God"—are "from cultic sacrifice, also found in the Greco-Roman world . . . [I]n Genesis 8:21, 'the Lord God smelled the pleasing odor' of Noah's sacrifice" (ibid.).

54. Ibid., 674: "The article can be taken with *theō [i]* only; then *kai patri hēmōn* is epexegetical: 'To God, that is, to our Father.'"

55. Ibid., 674–75, notes that "forever and ever" comes "from Hellenistic philosophy and Zoroastrian concepts, 'periods in world history,' *aiōnes* ruled by more-than-human 'powers' (cf. Philippians 2:10c; 1 Corinthians 2:6–8, rulers of this age, 15:24, and Romans 8:38)."

56. Ibid., 672. "Glory" (ἡ δόξα) means "brightness," "splendor," or "radiance."

57. Ibid., 670.

Commentators often try to soften the impact and to see it merely as an optative wish on the part of Paul: May God take care of you. But the whole issue is awash in paradox tending to conundrum: The model Christ who is revealed in the Philippians' hymn invites us to both the dying and the risen life that comprise the central themes of the next two letters. And these divine riches are "[s]een paradoxically in the impoverished figure of Jesus Christ: 'though rich, for your sakes he became poor, so that by his poverty you might become rich' (2 Cor 8:9; cf. Phil 2:5–11)."[58] Paul knows all too well that God does not literally shower riches upon the needy. Furthermore, in Letter B he expresses the hope that this forever-father-God will save him from suffering and death.

At this point, however, Paul is in no imminent legal danger, and perhaps he sees his concrete needs as supplied by the variously constituted communities. He does not envisage the sharing of all one's possessions as described in Acts 2–5, but he may envision some sharing in common, as taught among visionary Greek philosophers such as Pythagoras in his commune.[59] Certainly, although Paul tells us that God will satisfy our needs "according to his riches in glory in Christ Jesus" (κατὰ τὸ πλοῦτος αὐτοῦ ἐν δόξῃ ἐν Χριστῷ Ἰησοῦ 4:19), this meting out of riches is not very promising for our organic life; poor Christ followers no doubt starved as often as anyone else. In fact, this Jesus Christ himself had no money or treasure and died a hungry criminal. And his death did not somehow trigger a reverse victory whereby peace sprang up across the earth and all suffering was banished. Although Paul has been enabled by this rich and ever-helpful-yet-absent Christ to practice Stoic self-sufficiency, he knows full well that being human entails inevitable suffering and death. No utopian dreams for Paul, only entrustment in Christ and an eschatological hope that the gospel may transform people—and that Stoic virtue of self-sufficiency.

How would Paul's protestations of self-sufficiency have been received back in Philippi, where the people had gathered and sent money to him through Epaphroditus? They may well have felt that Paul was boasting, not in Christ, but in his own autonomy. They would have understood his desire not to be a client to their patronage, but they may also have felt that he was belittling their partnership. So the Philippians send another message that relocates their friendship within the empty Christ, thereby assuaging his concerns. This message elicits a reply in the form of Letter B—an enthusiastic response from Paul to their hymn of the empty Christ and his assurance of his love for them and their shared commitment to the gospel.

---

58. Ibid., 672.
59. Ibid., 662.

3

Emptiness Letter B, Part 1

Letter B runs from the introductory greeting in 1:1 to 3:1, then skips ahead to 4:1–9 and 4:21–23. This second letter is Paul's meditation on having the mind of Christ. Whatever friendship difficulties may have arisen earlier between Paul and the people in Philippi, he turns here to matters of life and death. He is now in prison and has received a letter carried to him by Epaphroditus from Philippi, a letter that scholars conclude must have contained the emptiness hymn the Philippians were using in their liturgies. Paul repeats the words of that hymn in his reply, unfolding its implications for himself and other Christ followers. All reference to self-sufficiency has now disappeared from his correspondence.

Greeting (1:1)

1:1 *Paul and Timothy, slaves of Christ Jesus, to all the saints in Christ Jesus who are in Philippi, including the overseers and servants.*

1:1 Παῦλος καὶ Τιμόθεος δοῦλοι Χριστοῦ Ἰησοῦ πᾶσιν τοῖς ἁγίοις ἐν Χριστῷ Ἰησοῦ τοῖς οὖσιν ἐν Φιλίπποις σὺν ἐπισκόποις καὶ διακόνοις.

"Paul and Timothy" (Παῦλος καὶ Τιμόθεος) are here described as "slaves"—often translated more gently as "servants"—"of Christ Jesus" (δοῦλοι Χριστοῦ Ἰησοῦ). Both are proper translations of the Greek word *doulos*, signifying one who has no ability to direct his own personal life. But that word holds for us a somewhat troubling tone, for we know that Paul and Timothy lived in a slave society, and using the term appears to acquiesce in that oppressive social structure.[1]

---

1. See Marchal, *Hierarchy, Unity, and Imitation*, in which Marchal—borrowing from Schüssler Fiorenza's term "kyriarchy" as the rule of the powerful "lords"—describes the kyriarchal structure of the Greco-Roman world in which Paul lives and participates. In *Church, Gospel, and Empire*, Mitchell

Paul proclaims in his letter to the Galatians (3:28), that in Christ there is no longer slave or free. However, household codes in the Deutero-Pauline epistles of Colossians, Ephesians, Titus, and 1 Peter evidence clear acquiescence in the institution of slavery, with Eph 6:7 even recommending that slaves be cheerful in their service. The household codes in those later letters were not of course written by Paul himself, but slavery was a given in his world; it was integral to the stable order that supported the economic health of the entire Roman Empire. We would like our scriptures to exemplify throughout the values of a kingdom wherein indeed there is no longer male or female, slave or free, but the gospel message is directed to people who remain entangled in the broad, seemingly ineradicable, injustices of their social and cultural times.[2] Very likely Paul was unable even to envision a social order without slavery.

Commentators often spiritualize the meaning of "slave" in this passage and tend to move on without any discussion of the institution of slavery. After all, neither Paul nor Timothy were actual slaves. As used here, the word is taken to denote someone under the control and guidance of another—much as a Muslim (literally, "slave" or "servant") embraces "submission" (Islam) to the guidance of Allah. Paul is identifying himself here not by affirming his own self-definition as a free man or even as an apostle, but in terms of common slavery. While to Rome he is a citizen with all the rights of citizenship, he is a slave to his Lord, Jesus.

Jean-François Collange believes that "the word [*doulos*, slave] has pejorative force here. Linked with Jesus Christ, it cannot but evoke echoes of the 'slavery' applied in 2:7 [of this Emptiness Letter] to the condition of the incarnate Christ."[3] Later in Resurrection Letter C, Paul will list the elements of his self-definition and negate each one of them, just as in the Emptiness hymn (2:6–11) Christ empties himself of anything that might identify him as equal to God. As a slave, Paul would have no right to an identity. It seems that, having read the Philippians' emptiness hymn, he now sees himself and Timothy as slaves with no claim whatsoever to self-sufficiency. Nor does Paul substitute a new Christian identity in place of his former status as a highly regarded Pharisee and a zealous Jew. There is no record of Paul undergoing some type of sociological conversion from this to that. Instead, he has had disclosure experiences

---

points out that power-hungry society is countered by the vision of "kenarchy" found in the empty Christ of these Philippian letters.

2. Reumann, *Philippians*, 55, explains: "The Christian movement included slave-owners (Philemon) and slaves (Onesimus), though not the 'lowest menials,' working in mines near Philippi (C. F. D. Moule, *The Birth of the New Testament* [San Francisco: Harper & Row, 1982] 209). Perhaps a third of the people in Corinth were slaves, another third ex-slaves (J. Murphy-O'Connor, 1 *Corinthians*, New Testament Message 10 [Wilmington, Glazier, 1979] xi) . . . Roman law sometimes ameliorated conditions. Stoics promoted egalitarianism. Only the Essenes launched 'a programmatic denunciation of institutional slavery' (Philo, Prob. 79 = LCL Philo 9:56–57; IDBSsupp 831). But by and large slavery 'was never really questioned in antiquity . . . Almost no one, slaves included, thought to organize society in any other way'; slaves sometimes had slaves (D. B. Martin, *Slavery as Salvation: The Metaphor of Slavery in Pauline Christianity* [New Haven: Yale, 1990] 42, cf. 7 and 32)."

3. Collange, *Epistle of Saint Paul*, 36.

that deepen his humanity and erase all reified identity markers. This is why he is a slave. This is why Timothy is also a slave. They exercise no autonomy over their own lives; they are not captains of their own souls. It is in this frame of mind that Paul, with his silent partner Timothy,[4] now writes "to all of the saints in Philippi" (πᾶσιν τοῖς ἁγίοις . . . τοῖς οὖσιν ἐν Φιλίπποις).

Philippi was a colonial city in Macedonia.[5] It was on the trade routes from Rome towards Asia Minor and all points to the east. It had been granted status as a colony of the Roman Empire and was an important trade center. Paul went to the city to preach the gospel and, according to The Acts of the Apostles (16:11–15), there he met Lydia, a woman who would come to the riverside to pray with her friends. Most commentators on Philippians construct the scene differently from the account in Acts. Paul's correspondence here assumes a more established community with overseers and agents—leaders like Syntyche, Euodia, Epaphroditus, and Clement, who were able to gather funds and send them to Paul. The Philippian community was comprised of a number of local church communities that gathered in the private homes of those members who could accommodate them: "Paul writes to Christian house churches at Philippi from Ephesus in 54–55."[6]

In other locales, Paul—who always regarded himself as an authentic Jew—would go to the synagogue, which for Jews in the Diaspora was the meeting place for prayer as well as for other community activities. But not in Philippi; there is no evidence for the existence of a synagogue there, nor even any community of Jews.[7] Perhaps the earliest Christ group in Philippi did meet by the river as described in Acts, but the

---

4. Reumann, *Philippians*, 80. "In Philippians, Timothy looms large. Paul hopes to send him to the congregation until he himself can come; see on 2:19–24. Lohmeyer (*Die Briefe an die Philipper, an die Kolosser und an Philemon*. [Götingen: Vandenhoeck & Ruprecht, 1974] 119–20) inferred that Timothy was 'the chosen successor of the apostle,' as Paul contemplated death. Timothy could be the 'true yokefellow' of 4:3" (ibid.).

5. Ibid., 699: "[C]onverts in this 'little Rome' had shared the gospel at home and supported Paul and his team through financial gifts, several times in Thessalonica (4:16), possibly Beroea and Athens, certainly Corinth, where other Macedonian churches helped also (2 Cor 11:7–9; cf. Acts 18:5). For this work the Philippians developed a structure of *episkopoi* and *diakonoi* within and among the house churches (1:1). There were congregational *apostoloi*, like Epaphroditus (4:18; cf. 2:25–30), commissioned for specific tasks" (ibid.).

6. Ibid., 3. Also, "The Christian community in Philippi, as elsewhere, consisted of several house churches . . . Till mid-2nd century, most Christians met in private houses, with little or no building-renovation for religious needs . . . But each house church likely carried out every type of ecclesial activity. They 'networked,' perhaps through periodic meetings of patrons, *episkopoi*, or a counsel of leaders. Assemblies in homes permitted worship and fellowship apart from temples (in Jerusalem, or pagan ones in Philippi) or synagogues and emphasized the family unit and with it the *paterfamilias* and patron-client structures of the day, so that the early church was not entirely 'a poor man's organization' . . . Epaphroditus, Euodia, Syntyche, Clement, and perhaps the 'loyal companion' in Phil 4:2–3 may have each headed local churches. Size of each? Guesses range from 10 to 50" (ibid., 84–85).

7. Ibid., 3–4. "The approach in this commentary will not be understood unless it is grasped that Philippi was almost unique among cities Paul addressed in his letters: it differed from other places he evangelized because of its 'Roman-ness' and lack of a Jewish community . . . Acts 16 and archeology report no synagogue (at best a 'place of prayer' for a few women like Lydia, a convert)" (ibid.).

community Paul writes to is more stable and organized. It may be that Euodia and Syntyche were *episcopoi* in local church gatherings. They may at times have met in "guild halls," meeting places for merchants, for later in Resurrection Letter C Paul speaks of civic gatherings (*politeuma*). Perhaps both Paul and the Lydia in Acts, a trader in purple dyes, were merchants who traveled with the caravans.

Even after so much scholarly endeavor, we still do not know much about the specific makeup of the people in Philippi who received Paul's missives, although they appear to have been Greek Christians more familiar with Greco-Roman culture and society than with the Hebrew scriptures, which Paul never cites in this letter.[8] Immense gains have been made in recent scholarship in understanding the Greco-Roman culture and society in which these people lived. We learn some particulars about the Christian community in Philippi from Paul's epistle itself: There were overseers and agents among them, they were dear to Paul, and they sent him money. Syntyche and Euodia were gospel partners there, probably leaders and perhaps themselves overseers or agents, and they disagreed. The group could have met wherever they found a pleasing location, but it is hard to imagine such a bucolic setting as a riverside glade for the public reading of Paul's letters. All that we actually know is that wherever they met, they were an assembly gathered to hear the word, learn the gospel, and enter into the mysteries.[9]

This is why Paul calls them "saints" (ἀγίοις, *hagiois*). They are people "set aside" who live "in Christ Jesus." To be "in Christ" becomes their shared identity, expressing itself in the varied ethnic and cultural forms identity took within a broadly Greco-Roman city, in a community attentive to the life and death of a particular risen Jew. By the very fact of gathering together, these people have set themselves aside from their fellow Philippians. They not only share their saintly life with each other, they are "saints in Christ Jesus" (πᾶσιν τοῖς ἁγίοις ἐν Χριστῷ Ἰησοῦ). That is what makes them saints, setting themselves apart from their pagan neighbors by reformulating their very identity even as they retain their native Philippian identities and their Greco-Roman heritage.[10] They are set apart as holy by maintaining a Jesus path-practice, following a high moral code, and participating in meditative prayer and a welcoming liturgy—all for the sake of transforming their minds and hearts in an awakened practice of shared life in Christ.

---

8. Johnson, *Writings of the New Testament*, 340.

9. See Reumann, *Philippians*, 16–18, for the chronology on Paul and Philippi. The founding of the mission at Philippi is in 48–49 CE. In 53–54, Paul settles in Ephesus, eventually locating his ministry in the hall of Tyrannus for two years, perhaps 27 months (Acts 19:10). During the same period from 53–54, Paul writes Letter A to Philippi (4:10–20), a note of thanks. He may not as yet be imprisoned. In 54–55, Paul writes Letter B to Philippi (1:1 or 1:3–2:30 or 3:1, plus perhaps parts of the present 4:1–9 and 21–23). Then in 55, Paul writes Letter C to Philippi expressing the polemic against a group that sounds much like the opponents encountered in Galatia. In the year 60 CE, Paul arrives in Rome, after which he disappears from the pages of history.

10. See Campbell, *Paul and the Creation*, 156, in which Campbell argues that the new identity of believers is not "fused with the identity of the Christ in such a way that their particularity is lost."

Any group that adopts a set practice and pursues a clear goal does set itself apart by that very fact, from basketball players dedicated to their team practice to New Testament exegetes as they practice their exegesis. If Christ followers imitate Christ, they aim to share ever more deeply in the community of his dying and rising life. If basketball players imitate Michael Jordan, they strive to perfect their jump shot and learn the dynamics of team play. In both instances, they become set apart, as stars in the firmament (Phil 2:15). Paul would say that the latter strive for a perishable goal, and the former for an imperishable goal (1 Cor 9:25)—to be holy as God is holy by sharing in the suffering and rising of Christ.

It is fairly easy to understand the identity of an athlete, for she is defined by her skills. But it is difficult to know what it means today to share in the dying of Jesus, who died on his cross some two thousand years ago, and even more difficult to know what it means to share in his resurrection. We might admire the prowess of legendary sports figures, but we hardly share in their lives and, as time goes on, old role models are forgotten and new ones take their place. Paul, though, never upholds Jesus as a role model. But he does recommend that his Philippian hearers imitate Jesus in sharing his sufferings and participating in the power of his resurrection (3:10–17). Models are most effective when immediately present, but Jesus' life was not immediately present to the Philippians. Even the first gospel narrative of Jesus' life and teaching was not composed until some twenty years after Paul wrote to the Philippians in 54–55 CE.[11] Such Jesus narratives as would have been available to the Philippians may have been but meager pre-Synoptic versions. In any event, Paul does not offer the Philippians a character sketch of Jesus. For Paul, Jesus' meaning is summed up in his shared dying and rising, and that is what holds Paul's world together.

Paul must have known something of the Jesus traditions that lie behind our canonical gospel accounts, but he does not employ them to model Jesus for his hearers, who live in a very different culture and society.[12] So we are to live "in Christ," who died on the cross and rose again, not model ourselves on him as one might imitate an admired teacher. Perhaps Paul did not know very much about the character and life of Jesus of Nazareth. He apparently never met him in life, but only when he encountered the luminous Christ on the Damascus Road in a blinding disclosure was it revealed to him that the historical Jesus had been crucified in abject humiliation and yet lived. Paul was already a Pharisee who believed in a bodily resurrection, but his faith now

---

11. Reumann, *Philippians*, 7.

12. Ibid., 3. Philippi "was twice founded as a Roman *colonia* (Acts 16:12), first by Gaius Octavian (later Augustus Caesar) and Mark Antony after a double battle there in 42 B.C. when they defeated Cassius and Brutus and ended the Roman Republic; and then, after the defeat of Anthony and Cleopatra in 31 b.c., as *Colonia Iulia Augusta Philippensis*. This 'little Rome' had legal status as if in Italy, with some 10,000 inhabitants, many of them citizens, in a walled city of 167 acres plus over 700 square miles around it. Philippi reflected Thracian underpinnings, Hellenistic culture, but dominant *Romanitas*. Its religions included classic Greco-Roman gods and goddesses, Thracian deities, and Oriental cults (Isis). The dominant new factor was Imperial religion and the Emperor cult, the faith of some 50 million people, more or less, with rituals and celebrations that touched most of life" (ibid.).

became grounded in his own actual experience of the living presence of the same Jesus who, ascending beyond the clouds, had absented himself to abide as the eschatological Lord of the communities Paul was then persecuting.

After that Christ experience, Paul abandoned his prior zeal as a persecutor of Christians and went on to learn Christ from others, including the church community in Damascus, and spend years in Arabia meditating on the meaning of life in Christ. Perhaps the knowledge he gained of Christ, as Paul reports in 3:7–11, came from divergently remembered traditions such that he never saw Jesus' life in any Synoptic overview. Indeed, he was writing a generation before there was any recorded Synoptic account. He was seeing through a glass darkly—which is why he spends so much time talking about Jesus and yet still his language of resurrection faith remains so opaque and inchoate. He is striving to bring to speech an experience of life that swirls beyond the tongue-tied enclosure of our lives. To be "saints" in Philippi means to be set aside from the endless cycles that lead to death and nothingness to live instead a life beyond the confines of any affirmed self-identity. That was the starting point, then to be lived out in the context of the actual Greco-Roman world that limned Philippian living.

More is meant here than merely that the Philippians have joined up with the Christ cause or accepted a new social and personal identity.[13] That would not entail one person living "in" another person, and then Paul could hardly say that Christ lives in him. He might say that he is a Christ follower. Yet, if following Christ means merely taking on a different personal and social identity within a given culture, we are left with a pale sketch of living in Christ as following a fearless leader in a community with a common cause. Such a meager life in Christ would leave its participants secure in newly minted and even more tenaciously affirmed assurances that bolster a common sense of a precious, set-apart selfhood. A new group identity could perhaps offer surcease from the oppressive definitions of familiar social structures, but one could gain the same thing simply by moving into a new culture or learning a new language. To be "in Christ" refers to the Jesus who died in Palestine a generation before Paul's mission journeys. So the Philippians' lives are tied up with the actual Jesus of Nazareth, the person we now call the historical Jesus. But how are these Macedonians to live "in Christ Jesus," to live in another person whom they have never met in their historical life?

So in this very first sentence, Paul is writing to his friends in rich and highly ambiguous gospel speech that, as the correspondence progresses, will undermine all notions of what it means to live a human life and what it means to be an individual

---

13. Crossan and Reed contend that "faith does not mean intellectual consent to a proposition, but vital commitment to a program" (Crossan and Reed, *In Search of Paul*, 385). By contrast, I would contend that faith is neither proposition nor program, but the transformation of consciousness that enables one to adopt whatever program best furthers human peace and justice in one's own present circumstance. Christian thinkers who would mirror Jesus in terms of their own ideological commitments—depicting an image of the historical Jesus that is compatible with those ideologies—come to grief in Paul, who never bothers to offer any portrait of Jesus that one might see as a model.

person. To be set aside in Christ is not to claim a cause or a new identity, but "to take on the form of a slave" (μορφὴν δούλου λαβών 2:7). Yet not as a servile person who meekly submits to authority. Paul never bows to any Roman official, always confronting and negotiating with them. He seeks and receives approval for his Gentile mission from the pillars of the Christian movement in Jerusalem, but he hardly kisses anyone's ring. In this letter, to be a slave is—as becomes apparent in the hymn of the empty Christ—to abandon self-identity in the eschatological experience and hope of risen life. There is no particular ideological or theological stance that might bring that about. We are not saved by our ideas or by our self-definitions, but rather by living the very life of the risen Christ as we share in his sufferings in our own bodies and minds. Claims of denominational identity are not salvific; they tend rather to express our slavish attachment to our own treasured and reassuring self-identities, even identities that are deemed to be Christian.

Still, whether then or now, one person cannot live inside another. We might identify with a historical person, but we can hardly get inside and live their life as this verse suggests. We are bounded by our skins, our bodies, our neighborhoods; ethnic identities and patriotic loyalties proliferate. Encased as we are in our varied identities—corporeal, historical, religious, national—our common human life is ruled by a geopolitics that is rooted in the organic instinct to assure our own survival against all others, which issues in the competitive struggle for power. Humanistic philosophies like the Stoicism of Paul's day recommend that we relate to one another altruistically and rationally for the common good, but these function well only in times of reasonable peace and security. For the most part, visions of common peace and shared justice for all lie beyond the scope of possibility and thus beyond our practical vision. We regret oppression in Syria under Bashar al-Assad and bemoan starvation in Somalia, but we are largely unable to do much about either. So we contract our vision, contribute some money to a nonprofit engaged in the region, and go on about our lives as best we can. How can it be, then, that we live in Christ together with Chaldean Christians? Or together with the sufferings of Palestinian Christians or Muslims?

The highest of humanistic ideals never suggests that we live "in" one another. Their base reality is the individual person who can espy the rational structures of the cosmos and, by following reason, verbally affirm all individuals' right to wellbeing: All people are created equal and endowed by their creator with certain inalienable rights to life, liberty, and the pursuit of happiness. However, such a declaration cannot but ignore the blunt fact that all our endeavors toward happiness are erased as we each grow old, fall sick, and die. It is unlikely that we can expect any more than that from a humanistic philosophy or from a political strategy. Progressive politics are founded on at least aspiring to protect the individual rights of all so that as we live our daily lives, fall in love, and live together, we may prosper on this earth. But never do we submerge our individual personhood in that of another! Some individuals do immerse their sense of self in political parties, but Yellow Dog Democrats think little of the fragile transience of life, and Red State Republicans ignore death and put their faith in the magic of the free market. All too often, these political self-definitions mean submitting slavishly to the will of another.

Even "Christian identity" is often understood in this way—that the authentic practitioner will submit unquestioningly to Jesus as represented by sovereign church dignitaries. But in this letter from Paul, Christ is not a ruling sovereign; he is an emptied Lord who is more than exalted by God and yet cannot exercise any effective control over us at all. Ecclesial insistence on the proper form of Christian identity only reduces the gospel to party affiliation and engenders the very secularism it so vocally abhors.[14]

Such a quest for a stable identity is perhaps reflected in the Paul who claims self-sufficiency in Letter A. However, that stance drops away as he endeavors to live "in Christ," and it hardly characterized the early followers of the Jesus path. Indeed, for them the singular meaning of Christ is that he emptied his self-identity. This introductory verse suggests that the ongoing task of the Christian is to reconfigure our very sense of self, not to be slavishly codependent but to be re-formed. Abandoning the deluded sense of independent and standalone selfhood, we are to be freed in the risen life of Christ, wherein we may find refuge from our bounded self-identities. When the boundaries dividing life from death, male from female, slave from free, and Jew from Greek cease to exist, we are freed to embrace in all its rich diversity the very bodily life that we lead here. That is the only way in which we might all, whether overseers or servants or slaves, live in Christ—by practicing a love and faith that decenters selfhood in the Christ who erases his own self-boundaries.

Exegetes and interpreters are properly concerned with the grammatical and semantic relationships of Paul's words, but all too often they push grammatical relationships beyond their semantic scope, suggesting a gospel that is all about relationship between persons. The gospel then becomes a grammatical handbook of transpersonal psychology. Relationships between human and divine persons become the default setting for scriptural interpretation, and flesh-and-blood gospel experience and insight are supernaturalized to accommodate such stable relationships. We are indeed to relate to one another in love and stand in and against this world as children of our Father. But the language of relationship cannot even begin to make clear what it means to live "in Christ."

I would hold that we should be more circumspect when we speak "relating" to Jesus. Neither Paul nor any of the four Gospels recommend that we enter into a relationship with him. To be in Christ is not to nurture an imagined relationship with the man Jesus, but rather to abide in the wisdom-mind of Christ. That is what reconfigures the notion of friendship pervading Letter A. Paul never recommends to the Philippians

---

14. Mitchell, *Church, Gospel, and Empire*, 136–40, speaks of the commodification of transcendence into sovereign rule. Also see Mitchell's blog, http://rogerhaydonmitchell.wordpress.com, especially under the topic of "kenarchy."

that we become friends with Jesus. With Paul, we share in the body of Christ within our very bodies. Moreover, the Jesus of John's Gospel invites us into a loving friendship that redefines friendship: "On that day you will know that I am in my Father, and you in me, and I in you" (John 14: 20). Neither text is speaking of bridging the space between two standalone individuals.

To live in Christ Jesus somehow signals a reconfiguration of our personal being. It means a conversion from self—from our genetic and biological attachment to me and mine—to living the path taught in the gospels by Jesus of Nazareth. At least that. But once we enter into this practice of no-self, we learn Christ to fill up what is lacking in Jesus' sufferings (Col 1:24), through our lived commitment to resurrection faith within our particular cultural worlds and biological identities. It is more than simply following Jesus' teachings;[15] there were many teachers in those days, and there were many excellent teachings. Today as we read and study our gospels and other ancient texts, we can see that the teachings of Jesus do not differ greatly from the teachings of progressive rabbis like the great Hillel, who lived a generation or two before him. So to live in Christ is more than adopting the moral precepts of the Gospels. The agent of continuity from this life to the afterlife of resurrection is not the self-defined self but rather the "new creation" of the "inner nature" spoken of in 2 Cor 5:17 and 4:16.[16] The totality of the Torah is love of God and neighbor, but there is more to being in Christ than practicing good relationships. The gospel calls for a fundamental conversion and transformation of the basis of all relationships away from the fleshy attachment to selfhood—a reorientation, a *metanoia*, that re-centers our lives within the organically living body of Christ.

We used to think that we might find our true self in the immortal soul infused within us by a provident God who creatively loves each and every person. But Aristotle's philosophic notion—and Aquinas' theological idea—of soul have disappeared from our cultural awareness. "Soul" has mutated into a self-affirmed identity that differentiates us from all other humans as the carrier of self-awareness. Rather than attempting to wrestle back the medieval notion of soul from its now-pervasive meaning of an inner self, we would do better to heed Paul's counsel to conform our minds and our bodies to the mind of the risen Christ by sharing in his sufferings. In any case, the New Testament contains no mention of soul as the principle of immortal life.

As is abundantly clear from the earliest days of our Hebrew ancestors and evidenced in the words of the prophet Amos, we are to be dedicated to the practice of justice. We know that the Lord God, although he does not bring it about, nevertheless insists upon justice. When Jesus speaks in the gospels of the great commandment to love God and neighbor, he draws directly from Leviticus and Deuteronomy. And these teachings reverberate in all four of our gospels. Certainly Paul, Pharisee that he

---

15. As in Thomas Jefferson's *The Life and Morals of Jesus of Nazareth*, which selects progressive ideas from the New Testament.

16. See Thrall, "Paul's Understanding."

was, was steeped in that tradition from his study of Torah. It may be assumed that when he spoke to the Philippians before the gospels were written, he was familiar with the Jesus traditions yet to be recorded. But Paul grounds justice and love in Jesus as Christ—not as a political or social messiah who might deliver Israel from its Roman occupation, but as the Christ who delivers the Philippians from their self-enclosed and dead-end lives.

Only once (Phil 3:20) does Paul describe Jesus as "savior" (*sotēr*), a term that does suggest a hoped-for shift in political fortunes that most often leaves self-delusion firmly in place. But Paul was not living or preaching in Palestine, and presumably the Philippians were not looking for a "messiah" to save them from Rome. The Empire set the social horizon within which human life was lived, and most of the early Christian communities did not see themselves as outliers or Essene-like separatists who railed against society precisely because they were not a part of that society. The Philippians were members of a Roman colony, quietly accepting the violence that was all too commonly entailed in maintaining the Pax Romana.

Among canonical Christian texts, only the book of Revelation embraced a full-blown rejectionist stance against the "whore of Babylon," that is, the Roman Empire. The stance of Paul and the Philippians vis-à-vis the Roman Empire was much more nuanced in its effort to negotiate the best possible public path for the early Christian communities. Despite the fact that the gospel path of risen life is at stark variance with Roman power and privilege, our ancestors could not and did not carve out a social place for themselves that was in direct opposition to the regnant culture. Then, as now, communities of Christ followers had to discover how best to live and thrive within their own circumstances.

So for Paul, the title of "Christ" does not signify a messiah deliverer. "Christ" simply became Jesus' surname, identifying him as a savior who, by delivering us from death, delivers us to live transformed lives in the midst of our crooked and perverse times.[17] Paul's interpreters raise social and cultural issues again and again, for his strategy tends toward assimilation, and he does often repeat—and thus re-inscribe—social norms and values then prevalent in his world.[18] Indeed, if we follow the trajectory of the letters of the authentic Paul and then on to the Deutero-Pauline letters and the Pastorals, the salient feature is an increasing willingness to carve out a space within Roman society so as to endure in a world of structural violence.[19]

---

17. Reumann, *Philippians*, 132, writes, "Biggest difference from the Greco-Roman concept of *dikaiosynē* [justification]: God's righteousness as deliverance, working vindication for the oppressed (Psalm 103:6), far beyond notions of distributive justice ('to each his or her own')." In parallel, Christ as savior brings a deliverance from the cyclic degeneration of distributive justice into the dog-eat-dog world that is our biological inheritance.

18. Ibid., 67. "Early Christians sometimes adapted to Caesar's rule (Luke–Acts, 1 Clement), sometimes resisted (the book of Revelation). Paul's stance is complex" (ibid.).

19. Ruden, *Paul Among the People*, 173–76.

Paul was no less limited in his social horizons than he was in his geographic purview—with Spain at the outer limits of his known world—or in his archaic geocentric cosmic picture. Neither did he live in our pluralistic world of multiple faith traditions, each with its own ancient scriptural and commentarial tradition. Paul does seem to have been familiar with Greek cultural philosophies, Stoic and Platonic, and must have been aware of the mystery religions that flourished in cities like Philippi,[20] but never does he directly discuss any philosophic ideas. Paul was well aware of the goddesses Artemis and Bendis, whose place seems to have been taken over by the Roman goddess Diana—all of whom were associated with the lower regions because of their connection to childbirth and death.[21] Other contemporary deities were linked to worldly affairs, and some dwelt in the sky. All of these, in the hymn of the empty Christ, are subjected to his absent Lordship.[22] By contrast, Paul and his coworkers knew nothing of the Indian Vedas or Upanishads, which predated them by more than a millennium. Likewise, nothing was known of the Chinese philosophers Lao Tzu or Chuang Tzu and their quest for immortality. Nor was Paul familiar with the Buddhist Pāli Canon, scriptures that record the teachings of the Buddha Śākyamuni, who lived about five hundred years before Jesus. And for Paul, the stars in the sky were moved by angels who just might be demonic gods.

All of which is to say that Paul preached the gospel message within his own cultural world, and just as no one would urge us to adopt Paul's geocentric picture of the cosmos, so we today are under no obligation to affirm his social or cultural values.[23] Indeed, Paul instructs his readers to test the times and discern in actual situations what is the best course of action (Phil 1:10; 4:8–9). He was a man of his times, not of ours. We need to acknowledge Paul's intellectual and cultural horizons in order to understand his writings, but we do not need to act as though we live in the same archaic world of cosmic and geographic narrowness or of colonial oppression. Our geography encircles a globe that Paul never knew existed. Our faith traditions today are in tension not with a set of mystery religions or Hellenistic cults, but rather with traditions of wisdom and salvation with their own long histories, some of which flourished long before Paul's known world. And our knowledge of the cosmos has expanded so much

---

20. See Portefaix, *Sisters Rejoice*, 33–58, on "Religion and Female Existence," and ibid., 75–128, on "Deities of Importance to Women in Philippi."

21. Ibid., 76–77.

22. Marchal, in *Hierarchy, Unity, and Imitation*, argues convincingly that Paul repeats and thus reinscribes the kyriarchal power structures of his oppressive society. The term "kyriarchal" is coined by Elisabeth Schüssler Fiorenza to signify a more broadly oppressive practice than patriarchy. Still, I prefer to talk about patriarchy, for the empty Jesus is granted the name of Kyrios only when exalted above any empirical exaltation.

23. See Dunn, *Theology of Paul the Apostle*, 670–712, on "Ethics in Practice." Dunn adds, "Paul's timetable did not envisage an ethical or social programme extending across several generations," and "The policy Paul advocated was one of political realism or, alternatively expressed, political quietism," and "It was hardly even thinkable for Paul, then, that his Roman readers could or should try to change political or social structures" (ibid., 673, 579, 680).

as to mock any claim that our Jesus has been exalted over far distant galaxies and nebulae.[24]

Nevertheless, even now—millennia after Paul, with his archaic horizons—to live "in Christ Jesus" in some sense means to be incorporated, to be one-bodied with, the crucified and risen Christ.[25] We do well to follow Paul—as he does in the remainder of this epistle and all his epistles—in always stretching forth to enunciate the ramifications of what it means to live in Christ. Paul's frequent use of that expression, to be "in Christ," has long attracted the attention of exegetes, who sometimes describe it as his "mystical" use of grammar. And indeed it is difficult to interpret.[26] Christ is the location in which we live, some say. But Christ is the location of no location, a place of no place at all. Rather, some say, Christ is the sphere in which we live. But our human imaginations are no longer restricted to this earthly sphere—we have walked on the moon. The phrase "in Christ," it seems to me, has much more to do with how we think

---

24. Our Milky Way galaxy is but one of billions of other such galaxies within an expanding multiverse without fixed limits. Paul's setting of the exalted Christ over his archaic world draws its impact from the beings—divine, human, demonic—who populated that world, but this can be translated into our present cosmology only with a studied absence of attentiveness.

25. See Reumann, *Philippians*, 58–61, in which Reumann explains that the phrase "in Christ Jesus . . . 'utterly defies definite interpretation' (BDF #219[4])." Some of the principal options Reumann lists include: A. Deissmann in *Die Neutestamentlichte Formel "in Christo Jesu"* (Marburg, Germany: Elwert, 1892), who sees the phrase "in Christ" as "a technical formula" perhaps coined by Paul himself and without parallels (such as "in Socrates," or "in Moses"), which leaves us to discern what Paul himself meant when he used the term. That seems to be a good starting point, curbing the exegetical quest for parallel sources that might lie behind Paul's usage. Some see "a local sense: Christ is the redeemed person's habitat, dwelling place, sphere, or atmosphere the air the person breathes . . . a mystical relationship, a Christ mysticism" (Reumann, *Philippians*, 59). Schweitzer, in *Mysticism of Paul*, holds that to be in Christ signifies an eschatological mysticism and means to partake of God's reign. For E. Lohmeyer, the phrase has a metaphysical interpretation, contrasting with "under the law." It is "not mystical but derives from an eschatological revelation of God in Christ in time and history, a Christusmetaphysik" (E. Lohmeyer, *Grundlagen paulinischen Theologie*, BHT 1 [Tübingen, Germany: Mohr Siebeck, 1929] 139–46). For Bultmann, the eschatological body of Christ is interchangeable with "in the spirit." For Buschel, it is a dynamic conception that means we are "en route," not at the goal (F. Buschel, "'In Chrisus' bei Paulus," *ZNW* 42:141–58). Others think of Christ's as a corporate and all-inclusive universal personality, a representative figure. Reumann himself writes that "Societal barriers are transcended (Gal 3:26–28; Rom 12:4–5; I Cor 1:30; Gal 5:6); everyday thinking, feeling, and actions become part of a world wherein one lives 'in Christ,'" then citing from an entry on "Ritual" by E. M. Zeusse, in *The Encyclopedia of Religion* 12:406, that persons "transcend the individual self" and "are linked together into enduring and true forms of community." I would argue that to be in Christ involves not mystery—up in the sky where some kind of overarching universal personality includes us all—but first and primarily the realization of no-self (Skt. *anātman*), and then the taking on of the particular patterns of dependently arisen identity, as described in the gospel. Reumann notes that "None of the 10 proposals for interpreting *en Christō(i)* fit every passage" (Reumann, *Philippians*, 84). By contrast, I think that primary self-emptying, as expressed in the hymn of the empty Christ, does fit all cases, whereas the filling out of the essence-free development of gospel persons often starkly differs over space and time, in accord with historical circumstances.

26. See Schweitzer, *Mysticism of Paul*, 1–25, on "the distinctive character of Paul's mysticism" as a Christ-mysticism, not a God-mysticism as found in the Gospel of John.

of ourselves, or how we allow ourselves to be changed, than with any imagined shift of location or sphere.

Paul includes the overseers (ἐπισκόποις, *episcopois*) and servants (διακόνοις, *diakonois*) in his greeting to the Philippian community. Acts describes "servants" as those who assist the community and take care of the weak, the poor, and the needy. (It also describes the deacon Stephen as preaching the gospel and witnessing to its power, but that description of *diakonoi* is not found in Philippians.) In Paul's Greco-Roman context, these "servants" are perhaps better understood as agents, go-betweens who are assigned tasks in civil affairs.[27] The word "overseer" in Greek is *episcopos* (ἐπίσκοπος), the word we translate today as "bishop." In the Greco-Roman world, it referred to "the ubiquitous overseer/supervisor in government, guilds or associations."[28] The role of these overseers was unlike today's bishops, who combine oversight of the faith and practice of the church with administrative concern for the care and feeding of clergy. There is no evidence that these Philippian "overseers," plural in number, had any administrative duties at all[29] or that the Christian assembly in Philippi was so well-ordered as to need many administrative skills. In any case, there were then no clergy to oversee. We do not know the job description of either the *episcopois* or the *diakonois* in such a community, and yet the fact that they are mentioned witnesses to some development among the Christ followers in Philippi.[30] Perhaps the "overseers" were assigned various temporary duties to carry out on behalf of the Philippian community, such as Epaphroditus' mission to carry letters and financial contributions to Paul.

Grace and Peace (1:2)

1:2 *Grace to you and peace from God our Father and the Lord Jesus Christ.*

---

27. Reumann, *Philippians*, 63.

28. Ibid., 62–63.

29. Martin, *Philippians*, 59: "In the church at Philippi there were a number of such *episcopoi* drawn from the rank and file of the church, and although these persons are specially mentioned in the opening salutation, they are not given any prominence in the body of the letter, nor are they referred to at 4:10–20 where Paul expresses his thanks for the Philippians' gifts. The apostle writes to a whole church and there is no suggestion of a small group which held ecclesiastical office as in 1 Clement 42."

30. See Reumann, *Philippians*, 86: "The titles [*episkopoi* and *diakonoi*] were widespread in the Greco-Roman world for persons with responsibilities in government, social, or religious groups." Again, Reumann writes, "Such references as exist in Paul's letters to local leaders showed *no uniformity* but instead an *ad hoc* development . . . [Paul] cared little more for congregational organization than he did for baptizing (cf.1 Cor 1:17)" (ibid., 87). Reumann adds, "In summary, the overseers and agents were leaders developed by the Philippian congregation (invented by them, see John Reumann, 'Contributions of the Philippian Community to Paul and to Earliest Christianity,' *NTS* 39 [1993] 438–57, here 449–50) . . . Terms come from their world of government, society and (to a minor extent) religion" (ibid., 89). See also the excursus in Collange, *Epistle of Saint Paul*, 37–41.

1:2 χάρις ὑμῖν καὶ εἰρήνη ἀπὸ θεοῦ πατρὸς ἡμῶν καὶ κυρίου Ἰησοῦ Χριστοῦ.

Paul wishes "grace and peace" (χάρις . . . καὶ εἰρήνη) to his readers ("you," ὑμῖν). The phrase "grace and peace," perhaps coined by Paul, means that this peace comes not from the Pax Romana maintained by the emperor, but from God's favor, the source of all rejoicing and delight that pervades the cosmos.[31] Grace and peace come "from God our Father" (ἀπὸ θεοῦ πατρὸς ἡμῶν), a common notion in the Hebrew scriptures as well as in the mystery religions.[32]

So the reality underlying Paul's understanding of the cosmos has a benevolent countenance, that of a father toward his children. But this leaves our reading of Paul with an immense problem, for it is not so apparent that this cosmos is unremittingly kind and fatherly. Surely Paul is perfectly aware of the violence that surrounds and at times tortures him. Still, he holds to the notion of a fatherly presence, focused though he is on the emptying of Christ even to death on a cross. This cosmic father is not the sweetly benevolent presence of a set-apart great Self, but rather a benign absence that is realized in the emptying that is to die and then to rise in Christ.

Paul's naming of God as Father appeals less to cosmic benevolence than to the single most recognized image of a well-ordered society.[33] A fatherly God assures Paul's readers of belonging to a family wherein all share the same familial benefits. This image, so embedded in Paul's culture and society, causes us some discomfort, for cultural understandings have changed since Greco-Roman times. But if we read Paul in his time and place, we can see that he is carving out a cultural space for Christians—not in a world that acknowledges universal principles of equality and liberty, but rather in a world where power, violence, and exploitation reign unchallenged.[34] The immense distance between Paul's time and our own sometimes leads us to anachronistic readings, so that we hear his words as if from a conservative father figure standing in for a yet more powerful Father who demands subservience from all others.[35]

---

31. John Dominic Crossan, *The Birth of Christianity: Discovering What Happened in the Years Immediately After the Death of Jesus* (San Francisco: HarperSanFrancisco, 1989) 411.

32. Reumann, *Philippians*, 70: "Mystery cults used 'father language' . . . In Cybele cult, cries of 'Atte pappa,' 'Attis, father!'" are found.

33. Ruden, *Paul Among the People*, 162: "On this topic, I can let 'er rip. If you want one word to define social organization, religion, and the values in general for the Greeks and Romans, you can't do better than 'fatherhood.'"

34. See ibid. Ruden is a classical scholar, uniquely able to read Paul against the background of Greco–Roman literature and to contrast his teachings on sexual and familial issues not with modern norms, but with the ancient norms then firmly in place.

35. The case is not difficult to make. Castelli writes, "He (i.e., Foucault) teaches us by implication that the emerging institutions of early Christianity—*ekklesia*, modeled on family, bound up with the language of sameness and identity—need to be interrogated for what they say about early Christian understandings of the circulation of power" (Castelli, *Imitating Paul*, 48). Castelli adds, "Early Christianity may be thought of as an emerging regime of truth" (ibid., 49). One can hardly deny that church behavior has most often functioned just so, as a regime of truth that regards difference as deviance, and yet the "church" of Paul's day had hardly developed the mechanisms to enforce any common

Nevertheless, grace and peace here are tied to a fatherly God and enunciated in the dying and rising of Jesus Christ, the Lord of death and life. Christ becomes more than the Lord of life, embodying the care and concern of a paterfamilias father for the worldly prosperity of his children. He is also the Lord of death, acknowledging its sway over all and accepting dying as part and parcel of living. Such an emptying unto death is more than a dramatic price to be paid to appease a sovereign god; that would hardly make sense in view of the clear indifference of the cosmos to ongoing human need and suffering. Only if we also can share in Christ's empty dying, and thus in the power of his resurrection, can we somehow espy the benevolent face of a father in the solar storms that impact our planet and will someday cease as the sun itself singes the earth into nothingness. From this Father-God come both grace and peace—a statement that if read by Roman power-holders would be sure to evince strong censure, for it supplants Caesar as the savior who brings peace.[36]

The source of this grace and peace is not just an unconcerned Father-God who watched Jesus die, but is doubly "from God our Father *and the Lord Jesus Christ*" (ἀπὸ θεοῦ πατρὸς ἡμῶν καὶ κυρίου Ἰησοῦ Χριστοῦ), for the base Christ insight is incarnational: the cosmic Father-God is made real only in the Christ who dies and yet lives. Always God and Christ transcend the margins of discriminative categories, neither up there nor down here but incarnationally emptying the definitions of imminence and transcendence and erasing the margins between living and dying. Here there is a non-duality between God, our Father, and the Lord Jesus Christ (καὶ κυρίου Ἰησοῦ Χριστοῦ) such that no Christian discourse on God can proceed apart from the emptying Christ. He is confessed as Lord not only to counter Lord Caesar, but also to identify the empty Christ with the "over-exalted" Lord in the hymn in the second chapter of Philippians, where Christ is named with the name of the most august God, however counterintuitive that may be.

This is the salient confession of Christian faith: that Christ is Lord not alongside God, but within God and non-dual with God, for Christ faith makes God actually real in the mud of the earth and the detritus of human lives. Many commentators interpret the phrase to denote the divine nature of Christ or his preexistence, as expressed in later theology. But that Patristic interpretation, although early, is anachronistic. Paul nowhere teaches Christ's preexistence; he does, however, confess Christ to be the wisdom hidden in God from the beginning and disclosed to enlightened minds.[37]

It is perhaps better and more skillful to understand the phrase here as expressing the non-duality of Christ with the Father. That is why he is confessed as Lord—the Lord of that wisdom that awakens us to the risen life we share with him. The person of Jesus is not a second entity alongside God, but "not-two" with God, for the

---

regime. Better the gospel notion of kenarchy—rule through emptying power—as it is expressed in the emptiness hymn at the heart of this correspondence.

36. Thurston, "Philippians," 46–47.

37. Dunn, *Theology of Paul the Apostle*, 266–93.

ultimate meaning of God is not numerical. It is as in John's Prologue: Christ is the fleshy Word with the Father in the beginning, with God and divine.[38] Jesus naturalizes God, identifying God as the powerless "watcher" whose care for Jesus remained ineffective against Roman authority. The Word became flesh not only in the body of the historical Jesus, but in a flesh-and-blood embodiment to be shared organically by all flesh, for therein humans can find their primal and boundless life. What grounds the fatherly presence of a distantly benign God is to be found in the monstrously benign death of Christ,[39] which we as followers are to share. Jesus does not make God more caressingly fatherly, but drags that image into the dirt and blood of Golgotha. God the Father in his blissful heaven is forced to watch Christ die. This Father does not intervene in any of the passion narratives.

It is a hard grace and a difficult peace, this peace and grace that Paul wishes upon his readers.

Prayer and Relationships (1:3–11)

> 1:3 *I thank my God every time I remember you, ⁴constantly praying with gladness in every one of my prayers for all of you, ⁵because of your sharing in the Gospel from the first day until now. ⁶I am confident of this, that the one who began a good work among you will bring it to final fullness at the day of Jesus Christ. ⁷Indeed, it is right that I focus my attention on all of you, because you all have me in your hearts, for you share grace together with me, both in my chains and in the defense and confirmation of the Gospel. ⁸For God is my witness, how I long for all of you with the compassion of Christ Jesus. ⁹And this is my prayer, so that more and more your love may overflow with wisdom and full insight, ¹⁰that you may examine the alternatives, so that you may be transparent and inoffensive for the day of Christ, ¹¹filled with the fruit of righteousness that comes through Jesus Christ for the glory and praise of God.*

> 1:3 Εὐχαριστῶ τῷ θεῷ μου ἐπὶ πάσῃ τῇ μνείᾳ ὑμῶν, ⁴πάντοτε ἐν πάσῃ δεήσει μου ὑπὲρ πάντων ὑμῶν μετὰ χαρᾶς τὴν δέησιν ποιούμενος, ⁵ἐπὶ τῇ κοινωνίᾳ ὑμῶν εἰς

---

38. See Keenan, *I Am / No Self*, 100–103.

39. See Žižek and Milbank, *Monstrosity of Christ*, 74, where Žižek stresses the visceral and bodily Christ and cross: the "monstrosity" of his self-emptying on the cross. Christ again becomes the prime symbol that empties God from being God: "What dies on the cross is not only the earthly-finite representative of God, but God himself, the very transcendent God of beyond" (ibid., 60). The cross I can identify with my own body, as it ages and grows weaker by the day, but here Jesus is the point where both he and God are evacuated from faith experience. Žižek is well read in Hegel, whose trinitarian theology had swept through the Danish churches—it was this "established" church theology that so nauseated Søren Kierkegaard. My conclusion is that we do not need to empty God or Jesus, but to empty ourselves of our fantasies about God and Jesus, in whatever skillful ontological or deontological language best serves. A theology of the empty Christ issues not only in a deontologizing of our notions, but in a deontological insistence on ethics and praxis.

τὸ εὐαγγέλιον ἀπὸ τῆς πρώτης ἡμέρας ἄχρι τοῦ νῦν, ⁶πεποιθὼς αὐτὸ τοῦτο, ὅτι ὁ ἐναρξάμενος ἐν ὑμῖν ἔργον ἀγαθὸν ἐπιτελέσει ἄχρι ἡμέρας Χριστοῦ Ἰησοῦ. ⁷καθώς ἐστιν δίκαιον ἐμοὶ τοῦτο φρονεῖν ὑπὲρ πάντων ὑμῶν, διὰ τὸ ἔχειν με ἐν τῇ καρδίᾳ ὑμᾶς, ἔν τε τοῖς δεσμοῖς μου καὶ ἐν τῇ ἀπολογίᾳ καὶ βεβαιώσει τοῦ εὐαγγελίου συγκοινωνούς μου τῆς χάριτος πάντας ὑμᾶς ὄντας. ⁸μάρτυς γάρ μου ὁ θεός, ὡς ἐπιποθῶ πάντας ὑμᾶς ἐν σπλάγχνοις Χριστοῦ Ἰησοῦ. ⁹καὶ τοῦτο προσεύχομαι, ἵνα ἡ ἀγάπη ὑμῶν ἔτι μᾶλλον καὶ μᾶλλον περισσεύῃ ἐν ἐπιγνώσει καὶ πάσῃ αἰσθήσει, ¹⁰εἰς τὸ δοκιμάζειν ὑμᾶς τὰ διαφέροντα, ἵνα ἦτε εἰλικρινεῖς καὶ ἀπρόσκοποι εἰς ἡμέραν Χριστοῦ, ¹¹πεπληρωμένοι καρπὸν δικαιοσύνης τὸν διὰ Ἰησοῦ Χριστοῦ εἰς δόξαν καὶ ἔπαινον θεοῦ.

Paul gives thanks to his God (Εὐχαριστῶ τῷ θεῷ μου) "every time I remember you" (ἐπὶ πάσῃ τῇ μνείᾳ ὑμῶν) and "in every one of my prayers for all of you" (πάντοτε ἐν πάσῃ δεήσει μου ὑπὲρ πάντων ὑμῶν), for he does "make his prayers" (τὴν δέησιν ποιούμενος). He does not just remember them in passing but "makes" his prayers deliberately.

In Mark's Gospel, we see Jesus go apart to pray: in the desert after his baptism (1:12–13); in a deserted place in the darkness of early morning after many healings at Peter's house (1:35); and in the garden of Gethsemane before his passion (14: 32–41). In Matt 6:9–13, Jesus teaches the disciples to pray the Lord's Prayer. But it is in Paul that we have the earliest witness of Jesus' disciples praying. Paul is not only an apostle-theologian, unfurling the meaning of risen life, but an engaged practitioner who "makes," "composes," or "constructs" (ποιούμενος) his prayers (τὴν δέησιν 1:4). The word *deēsis* (δέησις) comes from a verb meaning to lack, and then to request or beseech, so it may be rendered as "entreaty."[40] But prayer is not a matter of our entreaties, or Paul's, causing God to answer and act in gracious response. In prayer we are consciously acknowledging our human inability to get a purchase on life itself, and by this acknowledgment we are transformed and refocused—beyond the boundary between living and dying, beyond the evolutionary impulse to survive at all costs.[41] We engage in prayer to change and transform our minds, come face-to-face with the experienced reality of our lives. Here, the result of Paul's prayer is that he is "confident of this" (πεποιθὼς αὐτὸ τοῦτο): that "he who has begun a good work in you will bring it to completion" (ὅτι ὁ ἐναρξάμενος ἐν ὑμῖν ἔργον ἀγαθὸν ἐπιτελέσει 1:6).

Religious prayer often does begin with appeals for desired outcomes, as when I prayed for my basketball team to win. As Jonathan Haidt writes, "Religion is . . .

---

40. Reumann, *Philippians*, 104.

41. See Gazzaniga, *Who's In Charge?*, 30: "Modern neuroanatomists are quick to point out that as you climb the primate scale to humans, it is not that additional skills are simply being added on as once was hypothesized, but the whole brain is getting rearranged throughout." Gazzaniga adds, "So here we are, born with this wildly developing brain under tremendous genetic control, with refinements being made by epigenetic factors (nongenetic factors that cause the organism's genes to behave differently) and activity-dependent learning" (ibid., 40). The gospel learning is an epigenetic metamorphosis of our organic consciousness, overcoming the "selfish" genes to live in communities of eschatological hope.

well suited to be the handmaiden of groupishness, tribalism, and nationalism."[42] But prayers, like religions themselves, are known by their fruits, so Paul here reports that his praying has led not to a specific outcome, but rather to his confidence in the continuation of the good work already begun among the Philippians. This prayer goes beyond group or kinship altruism to shared organic life in Christ.[43]

Paul prays "with gladness" (μετὰ χαρᾶς 1:3) in the joy and wonder that arises from the bare awareness that we are here, alive, and promised life beyond life and death. And so he gives thanks (Εὐχαριστῶ, *eucharistō*). This is perhaps the primal emotion of a human being who comes into this world completely bereft of any self-power: gratitude for life as a pure gift. No more talk here of Paul's self-sufficiency. All his prickly concern about that, so startling in Letter A, has now disappeared.

Paul likely composed his prayers as his ancestors had, in set form and at set times. Not merely expressing a fleeting emotion toward an unknown god, but directed to a strangely personal God. I give thanks "to my God" (τῷ θεῷ μου), he says as he looks back at the course of his gospel engagement with the Philippians (ἐπὶ πάσῃ τῇ μνείᾳ ὑμῶν), for the awareness of the dependently arisen course of our lived lives is a construct of our memory. So he prays "for all of you" (ὑπὲρ πάντων ὑμῶν), because they have been intertwined in his own gospel life. No matter what, he is confident "in the Gospel meaning" (εἰς τὸ εὐαγγέλιον) that "you share" (ἐπὶ τῇ κοινωνίᾳ ὑμῶν) will be brought to final fulfillment (ἐπιτελέσει) because gospel life erases the boundaries between life and death, enabling the formation of the community of the people in Philippi.[44] If the gospel is just about how to live a good life, as Thomas Jefferson thought, then it is a failure. But it is not just about living a good life. Rather, it is about living and dying, about how we can live attentively and kindly when surely we will die and lose everything that constitutes the good life.[45]

---

42. Haidt, *Righteous Mind*, 268.

43. *Pace* ibid., 265: "Whatever Christ said about the good Samaritan who helped an injured Jew, if religion is a group-level adaptation, then it should produce *parochial* altruism." Haidt adds, "The only thing that was reliably and powerfully associated with the moral benefits of religion was *how enmeshed people were in relationships with their co-religionists*. It's the friendships and group activities, carried out within a moral matrix that emphasizes selflessness. That's what brings out the best in people" (ibid., 267).

44. See Reumann, *Philippians*, 107, on community (*koinonia*): "Pythagoras taught a communal order (derived from the order of the *kosmos*), all held in common. Plato's ideal Republic had communal, not private, property. Behind visions of an ideal society lurked the notion of 'a golden age' (Hesiod, *Opera*, 109ff.) and tales about ideal communities. Cynic teachers aimed at no property, just an itinerant's sack; Stoics, a consortium of gods and humans, a brotherhood with equality; also Neo-Pythagoreans like Apollonius of Tyana . . . Luke's account of the Jerusalem church in Acts 2–5 suggests 'the ideal which the Greeks sought with longing was achieved in the life of the primitive community' (G. Kittle, *Thological Dictionary of the New Testament* [Grand Rapids: Eerdmans, 1964–1976] 3:796)."

45. Compare Haidt, *Righteous Mind*, 296: "I love the movie *Avatar*, but it contained the most foolish evolutionary thinking I've ever seen. I found it easier to believe that islands could float in the sky than to believe that all creatures could live in harmony, willingly lying down to let others eat them." Such evolutionarily "impossible" eschatological harmony and self-sacrifice is the message of many faith traditions. See Keenan, *I Am / No Self*, 138–45, for a discussion of John 6, in which Jesus insists

The Philippians have shared in this "good endeavor" (ἔργον ἀγαθὸν) "from the very first day until now" (ἀπὸ τῆς πρώτης ἡμέρας ἄχρι τοῦ νῦν 1:5). The very first day is when they embraced that gospel in Philippi, continuing until their common "now" (νῦν), a concrete point in the flow of time that for them is grounded on a primal time. The Philippians have supported Paul's endeavors in the past, and now, whether or not money is involved, they will continue. Paul is speaking concretely about their shared life in Christ, not about any cosmic beginning. Mircea Eliade, in his book *The Sacred and the Profane*,[46] speaks of the time "at the beginning" as the original time of the people, our seers, and our prophets. It is the primal time described in myth to which we all, in our various traditions, look back to in wonder, focused upon the dream time—or eschatological time—to which we hope to return.[47] But that primal time for Paul is grounded in the shared immediacy of these early Christians' common life, both in his primal faith disclosure of Christ along that Damascus Road (Gal 1:11–12)[48] and in the time when the Philippians first heard the gospel and entered into its shared faith.

In many Buddhist teachings, especially from Zen masters like Bankei,[49] we are reminded to live in the present moment. The past is gone and is no longer ours. The future does not yet exist and thus cannot yet be ours. We only have the present moment, and so we are to attend to our lives as we actually live them, moment by moment. This is also a theme of Christian spiritual theology: we are to practice the sacrament of the present moment and not be concerned over the past or worry about the future. So Paul here recognizes that the Philippians have not only furthered the gospel in the past, from the very first days of its planting in Macedonia, but also that they further it in the present moment when he writes, when they hear, and when they

---

that his followers are to eat him.

46. Mircea Eliade, *The Sacred and the Profane: The Nature of Religion* (New York: Harcourt, 1959).

47. But see Everett, *Don't Sleep*, 133: "This principle [of immediacy as the epigenetic cultural filter for truth] also explains the absence of history, creation, and folklore in Pirahã. Anthropologists often assume that all cultures have stories about where they and the rest of the world come from, known as creation myths. I thus believed that the Pirahãs would have stories about who created the trees, the Pirahãs, the water, other living creatures, and so on." But they didn't have such mythic accounts, nor were they interested in other peoples' primal myths.

48. Paul himself never describes his experience on the Damacus road. That account comes from Acts, which repeats it three times. I accept the conclusion of Robert M. Price that it is a paradigmatic narrative, much like the account of the Buddha's Awakening, except that accounts of the Buddha contain little of Price's reconstruction of the real, factual redaction history of that narrative (Robert M. Price, "The Legend of Paul's Conversion," 2009, http://www.robertmprice.mindvendor.com, art_legend_paul_conv.htm). Asian Buddhists have never been interested in unearthing the historical facts of the Buddha Śākyamuni's life, for they regard it as a narrative construction of the meaning of awakening. By contrast, empiricist western interpreters try to get at bare facts, bereft of their meaning—something like like throwing out Tolstoy's *War and Peace* to get at the actual history of Napolean's invasion of aristocratic Russia.

49. See Peter Haskel, *Bankei Zen: Translations from the Record of Bankei* (New York: Grove, 1984) for Bankei's teachings on the immediacy of the pure mind.

all live and move and have their being in Christ. In Paul's memory, their shared past is his present.[50] And as we read, Paul's past becomes our present as we await a future called eschatological, for it is a time of grace and peace that we can only imagine in contrast to all our presents.[51]

Still, for Paul, as indeed for all Christians since, the furtherance of the gospel does not take place in an eternal "now." The immediacy of the present moment includes a beginning in remembered time and is completed in some future "end of time," for Christ, ever present, is the conventional voice of the Father from silence. But the last moment of conventional time is not the last tick of the cosmic clock as our sun runs out of its energy. Rather, "the good endeavor [God] started in you" will be "brought to its final fullness at the day of Christ Jesus." That is what Paul says. It will be completed at the day of Christ Jesus (ἄχρι ἡμέρας Χριστοῦ Ἰησοῦ 1:6). This day of Christ is more than the particular historical moment retrievable by studies of the historical Jesuses and more than an imagined future victory moment projected on our calendars.[52]

The day of Christ Jesus is the consummation and completion of the entire cosmos, but it is not "a definite point of time when Christ will appear."[53] Rather, this end time, in all its otherness from linear time, is the present eschatological structure of a hope-imbued future beyond the bonds of our captivity to self-referential time. Christians do not, in point of fact, control cosmic time, and we cannot project any future day when our Christ will end time. Our Jesus is not going to appear and show

---

50. Compare the popular Eckhart Tolle, *The Power of Now: A Guide to Spiritual Enlightenment* (Vancouver, BC: Namaste, 1997) 106: "Never personalize Christ. Don't make Christ into a form identity. Avatars, divine mothers, enlightened masters, the very few that are real, are not special as persons. Without a false self to uphold, defend, and feed, they are more simple, more ordinary than the ordinary man or woman. Anyone with a strong ego would regard them as insignificant or, more likely, not see them at all." For Paul, however, although he too will repeat the hymn that sings of Christ emptying his "form identity," the expression "being in Christ" is identified with the actual Jesus of Nazareth, experienced personally by Paul on the Damascus Road. The symbols of faith scripted on the experience of the risen Christ are not interchangeable, for they are sacramental symbols, even if merely the words of scripture. Tolle seeks the essential core of all religions in an experience of no-self, for he has meditated on Buddhist scriptures and taken the name of Meister Eckhart, the German Christian mystic much beloved of interfaith thinkers. From a Mahāyāna perspective, however, emptiness and no-self do not float free as some universal, common experience. They are grounded in our dependently arisen lives—for Paul and his readers, in the concrete presence of Christ; for Buddhists, in Śākyamuni.

51. See Everett, *Don't Sleep*, 129, on the Pirahã word *xibipíío*: "Eventually, I realized that this word referred to what I call experiential liminality, the act of just entering or leaving perception, that is, a being on the boundaries of experience. A flickering flame is a flame that repeatedly comes and goes out of experience or perception." The transience of immediate experience is employed in the many metaphors for emptiness, which stress what is available to experience. Everett concluded that the Pirahãs were not amenable to biblical narratives, which led him to question his missionary endeavors. Paul, however, would agree with the Pirahãs, for the gospel message is shared risen life experienced here, as yet not fully here. That is the eschatological structure of the transformed mind of wisdom.

52. As in Robert Hugh Benson's 1907 apocalyptic novel *Lord of the World* (London: Pitman, 1907).

53. O'Brien, *Epistle to the Philippians*, 65.

up all the other religious traditions and their revered founders. There will be no great judgment between the Christ and the Buddha. Christians will not get to lord it over Mohammed or any of his followers. No Christian Jesus will appear to Jews to validate our theological biases and religious hatreds. All of our histories are and remain human and, as any physicist knows, we do not know the nature of time or how it will unfold. We know only that time moves with us, marking our passage from birth to death, stretching forward and straining in Christ wisdom toward an eschatological point beyond picturing, imagined only negatively as the collapse of all conventional margins and mergers. Apocalyptic scenarios are the stuff of disappointed Christian visionaries and Hollywood film producers.[54] Eschatological time is the pattern of awakened minds freed from evolutionary determinism.[55]

"The day of Christ Jesus" (ἡμέρας Χριστοῦ Ἰησοῦ 1:6), here Paul's day of Christ Jesus, is the summation of his life and of our tradition, projected in this present moment upon the transience of our day-after-day living and dying onto an envisaged future sketched by our past memory—when first the good work of the gospel was begun, again and again. It is not a moment in linear time, for it is both near but always future, not here, and it is past—the day of Jesus Lord, who died and rose again. We are to envision in opaque hope the summation of our lives in the cosmos as the fulfillment of our constant desire for love and peace, realized through justice and embodied in the hearts and minds of Christ men and Christ women everywhere. Concretely, we see our eschatological consummation in the faces of men and women who live the risen life of resurrection faith now, even as they suffer and grow tired. Paul's end-time consciousness is here expressed not by any telling of the future or any biblical calculation, but by his "confidence," for he is sure "about all this" (πεποιθὼς αὐτὸ τοῦτο): Awaiting the day of the Lord describes an always-present mind that is grounded in the past death and resurrection of Jesus but that is never satisfied with the past, always stretching forward for the furtherance of this gospel of the ever-present moment.[56]

---

54. See Stephen D. Moore, *Empire and Apocalypse: Postcolonialism and the New Testament* (Sheffield: Sheffield Phoenix, 2006), in which Moore argues that the book of Revelation is an anti-assimilationist argument to replace Rome, the "Whore of Babylon," with the reign of God and his co-regent Christ. It makes its case through rhetorical mimicry and parody of the imperial cults practiced in Hellenistic cities such as Philippi.

55. Gazzaniga, *Who's In Charge?*, 21, on the death knell for strict behaviorism: "Thus, while the overall connectivity pattern is under genetic control, outside stimuli from the environment and training also affect neuronal growth and connectivity. The current view of the brain is that its large-scale plan is genetic, but specific connections at the local level are activity-dependent and a function of epigenetic factors and experience: Both nature and nurture are important, as any observant parent or pet owner can report." Gospel learning is an epigenetic knowledge that effects a neural transformation in the organizational structure of genetic consciousness.

56. Reumann, *Philippians*, 150: "Paul does not begin here with Christ or the cross, God's plan, or Israel's history, but the Philippians and their Christian experience. There is also a third decisive moment to come (verse 6)—who knows when?—Christ's parousia, final judgment and completion of God's work. Thus: gospel heard and believed —> now —> the Day of Christ. This 'existential salvation history' is marked by *sharing in the Gospel*, receiving and passing it on."

Paul thanks the Philippians for sharing in the gospel (ἐπὶ τῇ κοινωνίᾳ ὑμῶν εἰς τὸ εὐαγγέλιον 1:5) not because they have supported him financially, but because they too are engaged in enunciating gospel meaning in their lives. After all Paul's talk of his not needing the money, he does thank them for their engagement. They are not just supporting his gospel endeavors; they themselves share in the gospel, nurturing their own communities, and apparently they themselves have composed the hymn of the empty Christ for use in their liturgies. The gospel is always a common endeavor, never a one-way transmission from special individuals to their clients.

Paul has high regard for his Philippian friends. He pays "attention to all of you" (φρονεῖν ὑπὲρ πάντων ὑμῶν 1:7) and turns his mind to them with esteem and affection. The verb here is *phroneo* (φρονέω), used frequently in this letter to indicate a turning of one's mind and attention, or an intent focusing of practical consciousness.[57] "It is right and proper for me to mentally attend to all of you" (καθώς ἐστιν δίκαιον ἐμοὶ τοῦτο φρονεῖν ὑπὲρ πάντων ὑμῶν), "for you too hold me in your hearts" (διὰ τὸ ἔχειν με ἐν τῇ καρδίᾳ ὑμᾶς 1:7). They steadfastly attend to one another.

In Mahāyāna philosophy there is no stable and standalone self, no sovereign mental attention that could constitute for us a valid self-consciousness that waits neutrally for the appearance of something to think about—an "in here" in attentive attendance on an "out there." There is no *tabula rasa*, as if our minds were bland and inorganic. We make our minds to be as they are by the latent force of habits and patterns of thinking[58] ingrained in our sociobiological genetics and formed over the centuries through the evolutionary course of our biological living.[59] And so we grow into and attend to many human relationships. But like all things human, those relationships change over time, sometimes maturing, sometimes lapsing; they are not permanent features of an unchanging self. Still, we often regard our inner self as a sort of ready container, able to create relationships just as they come. For the Mahayanist, this is merely the habitual, deluded impulse that pulls us with primal force this way and that in the vain attempt to survive being so very human. It is the mind, intent on its various activities of seeking the wanted and warding off the unwanted, sinking into delusion.

---

57. Ibid., 116: "The stem *phrēn* (verb from Homer on) meant 'mind, understanding, consciousness.' With Plato and Aristotle *phronēsis* came to mean 'practical wisdom,' reckoned with virtues like wisdom (*sophia*), justice, and courage; a gift of God, moral insight."

58. The first verse of the *Dharmapāda*, from the earliest layer of Buddhist scriptures, includes: "All that we are is the result of what we have thought. It is founded on our thoughts. It is made up of our thoughts. If a man speaks or acts with an evil thought, pain follows him, as the wheel follows the foot of the ox that draws the wagon" (Irving Babbitt, *The Dhammapada* [New York: Oxford University Press, 1936] 1).

59. The neural functions are described by Gazzaniga: "As a person is walking, the sensory inputs from the visual and auditory systems go to the thalamus, a type of relay station. Then the impulses are sent to the processing areas in the cortex and then relayed to the frontal cortex. There they are integrated with other higher mental processes and perhaps the information makes it into the stream of consciousness, which is when a person becomes consciously aware of the information" (Gazzaniga, *Who's In Charge?*, 76).

However, when awakened to the cessation of false ideas and lustful anger, the mind can be converted and focused upon active and compassionate wisdom.

In furtherance of such an awakening, Buddhist meditation begins by a focusing (φρονεῖν; Skt. *samādhi*) of the mind, often on one point, so as to tame the monkey mind that jumps from this to that in an associative nervousness that worries about everything.[60] With a mind focused on one point—the flame of a candle or, for Buddhists, an image of the Buddha sitting in concentrated wisdom—one turns attention away from imagined states of greed and anger to try to become aware of the rhythmic breathing in and out of one's very own body. This is a common practice, I think, among both Buddhists and Christians. It is known in Christian history as "centering prayer," or as the practice of "meditative reading" (*lectio divina*), which begins with repeated recitation and measured breathing as in the Jesus prayer, wherein one attends to breathing in and out with a mantra-like enunciation of Jesus' name, all to calm the mind for meditation and learning Christ. But in this passage, Paul is not practicing the quietude of meditation. He directs his attention to his fellow Christians in Philippi, expressing his affection for his friends there and rejoicing in "your shared participation with me in grace" (συγκοινωνούς μου τῆς χάριτος πάντας ὑμᾶς ὄντας 1:7).

Such attending to others means that "the way one thinks is intimately related to the way one behaves."[61] Life in Christ overflows the prayer of silence into a common and shared speech. Paul here anticipates the great emptiness hymn of this letter, where the Lord Christ empties himself of all self-interest and all self-attention to focus not on his own self-as-so-great-a-godly-personage, but on humanly being human. Paul here likewise turns his attention away from self-concern and toward others. Paul's attentive life is expressed later in the phrase that for him "to live is Christ," as he demonstrates in his endeavors for the furtherance of the gospel. Paul carries his friends in his heart, in the center of his attentive mind. And together they work "towards the defense and validation of the Gospel" (καὶ ἐν τῇ ἀπολογίᾳ καὶ βεβαιώσει τοῦ εὐαγγελίου 1:7). It

---

60. Buddhists have never had arguments over determinism versus free will, because they have assumed some space for free choice within the conscious patterns of delusion. Gazzaniga writes that some scientists "suggest that a belief in free will may be crucial for motivating people to control their automatic impulses to act selfishly, and a significant amount of self-control and mental energy is required to override selfish impulses and to restrain aggressive impulses" (ibid., 115). Most faith traditions assume that the mind can be tamed, as indeed do all scientists, no matter what their views, to which again see Gazzaniga, "The human interpreter has set us up for a fall. It has created the illusion of self and, with it, the sense we humans have agency and 'freely' make decisions about our actions. In many ways it is a terrific and positive capacity for humans to possess . . . The illusion is so powerful that there is no amount of analysis that will change our sensation that we are all acting willfully and with purpose. The simple truth is that even the most strident determinists and fatalists at the personal psychological level do not actually believe they are pawns in the brain's chess game. Puncturing this illusionary bubble of a single willing self is difficult to say the least" (ibid., 105). Mahāyāna's central teaching of no-self does, however, recognize the continuity of personal consciousness and the validity of selfless personhood.

61. O'Brien, *Epistle to the Philippians*, 67.

is a changing, dynamic relationship that challenges Paul's discordant self-sufficiency claims in Letter A and focuses all their minds on their mutual gospel endeavor.

"Defense" (ἀπολογία, *apologia*) of the gospel means that Paul and the Philippians, from the beginning of their gospel experience, felt a need to present a clear and public apologetic validation (βεβαιώσει) for the path of the Jesus gospel. Such a defensive corroboration of the gospel is not the province of Paul alone, or of any professional class of Christ followers—all of the Philippians, whether they be overseers or servants or slaves like Paul and Timothy or anyone else, share in the fellowship of grace that floods into our hearts from the Christ who defended himself by completely emptying himself. That is a strange kind of defense, for it is not expressed as one ideology contending with another, nor does it provide any justification for self-righteousness.[62] It is nevertheless a defense—of what it means to be human on this Jesus path, a defense without any corresponding offense whatsoever. One walks a path but is hard pressed to map either its origin or its terminus.

This is what Paul feels, and he calls "God to be witness" (μάρτυς γάρ μου ὁ θεὸς 1:8) "to how much I cherish you" (ὡς ἐπιποθῶ πάντας ὑμᾶς) "in the very depths of the innards of Jesus Christ" (ἐν σπλάγχνοις Χριστοῦ Ἰησοῦ). He would not have needed to stress how he cherishes the people in Philippi had there not been the estrangement over issues of friendship and status that is discernable in Letter A. The word "cherish" means to feel sympathy or to be moved deeply, and it signifies that Paul loves these Philippians profoundly. The term "innards" indicates the visceral feeling at the bottom of one's stomach (σπλάγχνον) or bowels when one is moved emotionally by love for someone else. But, strangely, it is not Paul's innards that are moved but Christ's, for Christ is neither an external source of the love that embraces and lays visceral claim to the apostle's whole personality, nor the object of Paul's cherishing, his Philippian friends. Paul not only lives in a spiritual Christ but shares in the organic life of Christ; his own life and Christ are indivisible. Their innards are intertwined such that Christ loves the Philippians in and through Paul, and Paul in and through the Philippians. "It is not Paul who lives within Paul but Jesus Christ, which is why Paul is not moved by the bowels of Paul but by the bowels of Jesus Christ."[63] This can get confusing, for we are not moving here within a world of discrete selves reaching out to relate to other discrete selves.[64] Rather than read the phrase as though Paul himself is extending his

---

62. Haidt, *Righteous Mind*, xiii: "I want to show you that an obsession with righteousness (leading inevitably to self-righteousness) is the normal human condition. It is a feature of our evolutionary design, not a bug or error that crept into minds that would otherwise be objective and rational." In Christian theology, that obsession is referred to as original sin, while in Mahāyāna, it is called imagined delusion. In all cases, it constitutes an obsession from which one is to be liberated.

63. Johann Albrecht Bengel, *New Testament Word Studies* (Grand Rapids: Eerdmans, 1971) 2:426.

64. "The Western conception of the person as a bounded, unique, more or less integrated motivational and cognitive universe, a dynamic center of awareness, emotion, judgment, and action organized into a distinctive whole and set contrastively both against other such wholes and against its social and natural background, is, however incorrigible it may seem to us, a rather peculiar idea within the context of the world's cultures" (Haidt, *Righteous Mind*, 14). Haidt quotes Clifford Geertz, "From

relationship with Jesus to the Philippians, we should understand that there is no final relational validity to the dichotomy between Paul and Christ or Paul and the Philippians, for they all recognize that they share the same organic life of Christ. They are two but they are not two; their entrails are entangled one amidst the other so that Paul's pulse actually "beats with the pulse of Christ."[65]

The life pulsing in our bodies is not a thing apart from life itself, apart from the risen life of Christ that Paul experiences. Whether then or now, it does stand in need of an apologetic, for it counters the most obvious value of the standalone individual, each with his or her own bowels and heart, ready to reach out in survivalist cunning to establish beneficial relationships, even with God as the counterpoint to this absolute self. In the consumer market of religions, a gospel like this finds no purchase. How can anyone in this day and age promote a religion that deprives one of the suzerainty of selfhood?[66]

Paul "prays" (καὶ τοῦτο προσεύχομαι 1:9), and here he identifies the content and purpose (τοῦτο) of his prayer. But who is this Paul who prays? Later on in this letter Paul abandons and empties all his conventional self-definitions so that he is not even the center of his own praying. Yet, even empty of self-definitions, Paul personally is Jewish, and Jews have been taught to pray from ancient times. They talk to God, as did Abraham and Moses. So Paul talks to God. But, unlike Abraham and Moses in the Torah, Paul in the New Testament receives no reply from God—at least Paul never reports that he does. (Although in Acts, Luke does describe the risen Christ as speaking to Paul as he lies in the roadway.) Neither Paul nor his readers, then or now, really expect God to respond, for we know that those ancient conversations between humans and God are not conversationally true. Paul knew that too. Still, he prays. One would suppose that such praying is more than just wish-making. Indeed, Paul could have said, "I wish to God that . . ." but he didn't. He says that he prays, embracing a one-way speech that acknowledges the silence of the God that encompasses all. And through this silence-inviting prayer, Paul is enabled to hear the speaking of the Philippians and heed their words about the self-emptying Christ.

---

the Native's Point of View: On the Nature of Anthropological Understanding," in *Culture Theory*, ed. R. Shweder and R. LeVine, 123–36 (Cambridge: Cambridge University Press, 1984) 126. In Mahāyāna, however, no matter how culturally constructed, self-attachment remains the experienced delusion, engendering the entire realm of *saṃsāra*. Self-clinging permeates eastern cultures as well as western, even if social harmony of the group is prized over the standalone person.

65. J. B. Lightfoot, cited in Martin, *Philippians*, 66.

66. Gazzaniga, *Who's In Charge?*, 70: "Yet we are still confronted with the question of why do we feel so unified and in control? We don't feel like there is a pack of snarling dogs in our brains. And why, for those who suffer from schizophrenia, does it feel as if someone else is in control of their actions or thoughts? Your friends at the cocktail party with no knowledge of psychology or neuroscience are fascinated or disbelieving if told about these nonconscious processes, only because they aren't apparent to the individual's personal experience. It's all very counterintuitive to us humans, with our strong sense of being unified into one self and feeling in control of our actions."

The Emptied Christ of Philippians

As will become increasingly clear in this letter, prayer calls for a radical reorientation not just of one's activity, but also of one's very self. So when Paul prays, he seeks to enter into the mind of Christ and to share the prayer of Christ, even if he himself never learned the "Our Father" from Jesus. To enter into the mind of Christ means not only to move out of the mediated conventions of grammatically controlled worldly discourse, but also to move back into our cultural worlds as they are constructed by our languages. The words of prayer, sometimes silent, sometimes enunciated, go beyond argument, discourse, and grammar.⁶⁷ They are the numbing words of broken speech going beyond its own borders into glossolalia (1 Cor 14:1–28).⁶⁸ The Pentecostal churches are surely on the mark here, for at its deepest, prayer is not an individual's recitation of someone else's words. One enters for a time into an identity beyond constructed identity—that of the Christ whose name is above naming. In such an unnamed Christ identity, Paul's prayer is more than a wish: it is a remembrance of a new and primal, all-inclusive identity summons to transform delusion into Christ consciousness.

Paul prays "so that more and more your love may grow and overflow" (ἵνα ἡ ἀγάπη ὑμῶν ἔτι μᾶλλον καὶ μᾶλλον περισσεύῃ 1:9), richer and richer, into the wisdom and insight that flows from that Christ mind. The phrase translated as "overflow more and more" announces a theme that will appear a number of times in the letter: that our life is not the static, self-enclosed, and very personal story of our autobiographical imaginations,⁶⁹ but rather an ever increasing, ever deepening, ever more other-centered groping and squirming into a love for others, which tumbles from silence to enunciate wisdom. It is an outflow that does not stop,⁷⁰ but that can be blocked by the vast array of evolutionary forces impelling us toward delusion, hatred, and craving. Yet even dirty death does not bring it to a halt, for its source lies in an identity beyond our personal identification—a life beyond death, welling up from the cosmic beginnings that increasingly engender self-awareness and selflessness throughout the

---

67. In arguing for the absence of recursion in Pirahã language, against the universal grammar as postulated by Noam Chomsky, Everett argues that "Pirahã imposes and enforces a cultural value on its grammar. It is not . . . simply that Pirahã accidentally lacks recursion. It doesn't want it; it doesn't allow it because of a cultural principle" (Everett, *Don't Sleep*, 237).

68. See Bauer, *Greek-English Lexicon*, 162.

69. Gazzaniga, *Who's In Charge?*, 41: "You will still feel that someone, you, is in their making the decisions and pulling the levers. This is the homuncular problem we can't seem to shake: The idea that a person, a little man, a spirit, *someone* is in charge." One wonders why neuroscientists so often speak, as does Gazzaniga here, of the homunculus, which hearkens back to medieval alchemy, rather than contrasting and comparing their findings on the brain with notions of the human person, either in Christian thinkers like Bernard Lonergan or in Buddhist thinkers who speak of the selfless person of the bodhisattva. I suspect once again that academic specialization disallows the time and effort needed to enter into unfamiliar areas of discourse.

70. Asaṅga, in discussing treating the four pure states of perfected awakening, teaches that "the truly enunciated doctrine of the Great Vehicle" is "an outflow (*niṣyanda*) from the pure reality realm (*viśuddha-dhrmadhātu*)" (Asaṅga, *Summary of the Great Vehicle*, 2:26, 50). See Hakamaya, "Realm of Enlightenment."

biosphere (Skt. *anātman*). Prayer engenders and witnesses to a oneness with the mind of Christ, a non-dual consciousness that bubbles up in silent wisdom and engaged discernment.

But this is not just any growth or outflow, for always there are mutations, some of which make us better able to survive as individuals rather than as members of an embodied Christ.[71] In this passage, however, focused prayer is intentional, for it is an outflow of "love" (ἡ ἀγάπη).[72] Better said, our love grows ever more, for it is a dimension—underlying all of the personal constructs that define our relational lives—that overcomes our primal evolutionary heritage of greed and hatred to grow into wisdom and insight.[73] Paul speaks of love directed to fellow human beings not as a characteristic of our struggle for survival, but as a conscious and constructed space apart from survival struggles. That "Paul speaks only rarely of love for God"[74] brings to mind the words of 1 John 4:20: "those who do not love a brother or sister whom they have seen, cannot love God whom they have not seen."

Paul's mind is not defined by a direct and oh-so-very-personal intercourse with God, not even when he gives thanks "to my God" (τῷ θεῷ μου 1:3). Nor does he frame his participation in the risen life of Christ through the imagined relational terms of a secure self.[75] Paul calls into question not only his "I" but also the object of a God "out there" whom he might love.[76] It is not that *he directs* his mind toward Christ, but that *Christ has directed* Paul's life. He once lived a strong faith, and his mindset as a young man was pledged avidly to the spread of its truth. Now he is dedicated to the Christ who empties all enclosed truth claims, all identity characteristics, all self-esteem.[77] If

---

71. Haidt, *Righteous Mind*, 136: "Evolutionary theorists often speak of genes as being 'selfish,' meaning that they can only influence an animal to do things that will spread copies of that gene. But one of the most important insights into the origins of morality is that 'selfish' genes can give rise to generous creatures, as long as those creatures are selective in their generosity. Altruism toward kin is not a puzzle at all. Altruism toward non-kin, on the other hand, has presented one of the longest-running puzzles in the history of evolutionary thinking."

72. Ruden, *Paul Among the People*, 38: "As many Bible readers will already know, this 'love' is *agapē* (a word not often used before the New Testament). It is selfless love, as opposed to the common Classical Greek words *philia*, which meant the exclusive love of one's own circle, and *erōs*, which meant erotic love."

73. In treating the emergent mind, Gazzaniga writes, "In his wonderful book *A Different Universe*, Robert Laughlin, who won the Nobel Prize in Physics in 1998, said about the dawning of the understanding of emergence, 'What we are seeing is a transformation of worldview in which the objective of understanding nature by breaking it down into ever smaller parts is supplanted by the objective of understanding how nature organizes itself'" (Gazzaniga, *Who's In Charge?*, 135). The gospel communities represent a radically new organization of our natural, evolutionary heritage.

74. *TDNT* 1:50.

75. Schweitzer, in his *Mysticism of Paul the Apostle*, speaks of Paul's "Christ mysticism," perhaps because being "in Christ" is being here, selflessly (Schweitzer, *Mysticism of Paul the Apostle*, 5–6).

76. See Dunn, *Theology of Paul the Apostle*, 472–77, on "The Divided 'I.'"

77. *Pace* Haidt, *Righteous Mind*, 77: "For a hundred years, psychologists have written about the need to think well of oneself. But Mark Leary, a leading researcher on self-consciousness, thought that it made no evolutionary sense for there to be a deep need for *self*-esteem (*The Curse of the Self*:

Jesus empties himself of being equal to God, we can equally empty ourselves of being self-enclosed Christians, encamped within our sacred societies.[78] Paul is saved not by directing his mind and life toward a new Christ as object, but by abandoning the very power of grasping after objects in the delusion of a subjective foolishness.

This growth of love is not described in ever more intense relational categories, but as entering "into wisdom and insight" (ἐν ἐπιγνώσει καὶ πάσῃ αἰσθήσει 1:9) as the natural outflow of the love of which Paul speaks. Such love does not issue in imagined intimacies but flows ever more into the wisdom that abides quietly in a Christ-emptiness that enables multiple engagements.[79] Rudolf Bultmann explains this wisdom recognition (ἐν ἐπιγνώσει) as "almost a technical term for the decisive knowledge of God which is implied in conversion to the Christian faith."[80] It is perhaps better said that such wisdom recognition, as entailed in conversion, is a radical reorientation of consciousness—but not toward enclosure within a particular faith tradition, which would merely redefine a secure place for self-delusion.[81] Paul himself never converted from being a Jew and a Pharisee to being a Christian.[82] There were no so-named

---

Self-Awareness, Egotism, and the Quality of Human Life [Oxford: Oxford University Press, 2004]). For millions of years, our ancestors' survival depended upon their ability to get small groups to include them and trust them, so if there is any innate drive here, it should be a drive to get *others* to think well of us. Based on his review of the research, Leary suggested that self-esteem is more like an internal gauge, a 'sociometer' that continuously measures your value as a relationship partner. Whenever the sociometer needle drops, it triggers an alarm and changes our behavior." By contrast, *agapē* admits no relational limitations and hardly increases one's self-esteem, for Christ did not esteem his being in the form of God as anything precious.

78. Haidt, *Righteous Mind*, 139: "The male mind appears to be innately tribal—that is, structured in advance of experience so that boys and men *enjoy* doing the sorts of things that lead to group cohesion and success in conflicts between groups (including warfare)." Thus, "if you think, as I do, that one of the greatest unsolved mysteries is how people ever came together to form large cooperative societies, then you might take a special interest in the psychology of sacredness. Why do people so readily treat objects (flags, crosses), places (Mecca, a battlefield related to the birth of your nation), people (saints, heroes), and principles (liberty, fraternity, equality) as though they were of infinite value? Whatever its origins, the psychology of sacredness helps bind individuals into moral communities" (ibid., 149). Such tribal grouping, under whatever flag or god is taken to be sacred, may well describe the cultural adhesion of religion, but it fails to reflect the communities Paul and the Philippians envisaged: no Jew or Greek, male or female, slave or free.

79. See Reumann, *Philippians*, 124–25, where *epignosis* is world transcendent wisdom—almost a technical term for the decisive knowledge of God—while *aisthēsis*, only here in the New Testament, is the ability to distinguish between good and evil. If transcendent wisdom is apophatic, then *epignosis* is kataphatic, engaged in insightful discerning in the concrete situations of our lives.

80. Cited in O'Brien, *Epistle to the Philippians*, 76.

81. Haidt, *Righteous Mind*, 273: "We humans have an extraordinary ability to care about things beyond ourselves, to circle around those things with other people, and in the process to bind ourselves into teams that can pursue larger projects. That's what religion is all about." That may be an apt description of the common phenomenon of religion as group bias, but it hardly acknowledges faith as the emptying of all boundary markers.

82. *Pace* Segal, *Paul the Convert*, 117–49. Segal sees Paul's conversion as a radical reorientation and commitment, but also as an ideological or theological shift in perspective and affiliation—as indeed do most Christian theologians. But see Campbell, *Paul and the Creation*, 46–50, on "A Non-Sectarian

Christians in his day, just the gospel path of freedom learned by sharing in Christ's dying and rising life. In the letter to the Romans, Paul remains a skilled Pharisee, able to develop extended midrash on Torah.[83]

Paul's wisdom is suggestive of Gnostic ideas about wisdom; indeed, the term *epignosis* (ἐπίγνωσις) is used to express the main idea of Gnostic *gnosis*. Paul will take up the theme again in 3:7–11 of Letter C, where he speaks of the "all-surpassingness of knowing Christ." Gnostic though this may sound, it has been adapted here. Whereas Gnostic wisdom is attained only by a very spiritual person and removes one further and further from engagement in this sorry world, Paul's wisdom moves from love to wisdom that goes beyond God-awareness to "the varied insights" (πάσῃ αἰσθήσει 1:9) that enable one to act tactfully in this world. That insight is employed in engagements in the concrete, actual, messy situations that furtherance of the gospel always entails. It is an insight and a "sensitivity" (αἰσθήσει) that covers situations as they arise. This kind of insight is not a special, once-and-for-all insight into something particular, for the text has "all insight" (καὶ πάσῃ αἰσθήσει), suggesting a breadth of insight that may be directed to many and various situations. It may be translated as "tact," or a sensitivity to an actual situation at a particular time.[84]

All this recalls the Mahāyāna discourse on awakening as inclusive of both *non-discriminative wisdom*—the wisdom that, apart from all image and idea, experiences the depths of emptiness—and *subsequently-attained wisdom*—which in this dependently arisen world of many cultural and social conventions displays itself in all the skillful approaches and teachings that lead beings towards wisdom and awakening. On the Mahāyāna path, the bodhisattva is the ideal, for the bodhisattva aspires not only to transcendent awakening, but also to compassionate engagement in the world. Paul's discourse here works much to the same effect: The mind of Christ is not directed simply and entirely toward the silently benign Father, but also toward humans, so that he is fully embodied in his presence among us as the powerful absence of anything that might direct our attention away from the furtherance of gospel life.

The purpose of this wisdom and insight is that we might "examine the alternatives" (εἰς τὸ δοκιμάζειν ὑμᾶς τὰ διαφέροντα 1:10).[85] We do not only enter into prayer and converse with a silent God to experience a primal belonging. It is also equally an

---

Reading of Paul." I doubt that conversion to risen life in Christ is to be equated bluntly with conversion to Christianity.

83. Segal, *Paul the Convert*, 122–23.

84. Martin, *Philippians*, 66–67. See Nagao for an analogous notion of wisdom as both transcendent and conventional in the Mādhyamika understanding of being: "Thus, while conventional being-to-its-limit [Skt. *yāvad-bhāvikatā*] denotes the broad expanse (*udāra*) of wisdom and insight, ultimately meaningful being-as-such [*yathāva-bhāvikatā*] points to their depths. Worldly convention is described in the Buddhist texts as blunt (*audārika*), while ultimate meaning is spoken of as sharp and incisive (*sūkṣma*)" (Nagao, *Foundational Standpoint*, 34).

85. See Caird, *Paul's Letters from Prison*, 108: "The verb δοκιμάζειν can mean *approve*, but the sense required here is rather 'to learn by experience.' Ethical judgment becomes mature only by constant exercise."

entirely worldly choice that depends upon our examination (τὸ δοκιμάζειν ὑμᾶς) of different life options (τὰ διαφέροντα) so as to choose what is best (τὰ διαφέροντα) for skillfully advancing the gospel in our own context. This wisdom flows from abiding in silent wisdom, then increases in love through conventional insight, enabling us to choose what is best among the myriad options available to us.[86] Often the phrase is translated "to approve what is best," as if that is perfectly clear to Paul and his readers and requires no deliberative effort. But it is more than a slogan about striving for some pre-determined, known form of excellence. We are to "probe" and "test" what is best; it is not a given "God-the-Father-knows-best" as if all the varied dynamics of our personal and communal lives are laid out for us and we need only follow.

The myriad religious and cultural issues that have arisen from recent advances in medical knowledge and technology raise issues that Paul never faced: Is there ever a case for ending the life of an unborn fetus? Or allowing a person in constant, intractible pain to choose an end to that suffering? Are we morally obliged to continue artificial life support for an individual who has no reasonable prognosis of ever regaining consciousness? And who has the right to determine such cultural and social policies?

Paul, cranky fellow that he sometimes was, never removed himself from the struggles that characterized his own life. And he does not prescribe what, upon examination, might be "the most excellent alternative" for others; he is not the master of the lives of the Philippians. Nor can Paul's stance vis-à-vis his own culture determine the stance we should take in our present circumstances. Life in Christ, as the central offer of salvific freedom, overflows into all human situations, so Paul prays that the Philippians may sort out the concrete implications for themselves with insight and tact by weighing their resurrection faith along with what is of value in their own lives—political, social, and cultural.[87] Paul witnesses to the gospel; he makes no attempt to manage anyone else's life. Sensitive to being managed himself, he does not adopt a patron role vis-à-vis the Philippians, for they would not tolerate that. If we have interpreted Letter A correctly, the Philippians were more inclined to assume the patron role in regards to Paul. Furthermore, his polemic against "the dogs" in Letter C is so intense precisely

---

86. Vincent, *Critical and Exegetical Commentary*, 13. Reumann notes that the term *ta diapheronta* means either "things that excel" or "things that differ" and further observes that in 1:10 we are not dealing with a "once and for all times" morality, for new ethical situations keep arising (Reumann, *Philippians*, 157). I take the verse to be recommending that we follow the advice in 4:8–9 and strive for whatever is virtuous and best by testing each situation in the light of transcendent wisdom to discern and gain insight in the concrete course of our practice of prudent and skillful judgment and action.

87. I agree with Haidt that we are best served by following what is most excellent. See his *Righteous Mind*: "I don't know what the best normative ethical theory is for individuals in their private lives. But when we talk about making laws and implementing public policies in western democracies that contain some degree of ethnic and moral diversity, then I think there is no compelling alternative to utilitarianism. I think Jeremy Bentham was right that laws and public policies should aim, as a first approximation, to produce the greatest total good. I just want Bentham to read Durkheim and recognize that we are *Homo duplex* before he tells any of us, or our legislatures, how to go about maximizing the total good" (Haidt, *Righteous Mind*, 272). Yet that utilitarian approach is not to be aimed at self-benefit, but to serve the common good by embracing an ethic of *agapē*.

because Paul cannot simply order them to obey but must instead persuade them. By contrast, our varied cleric-ridden churches today often feel the need to usurp these choices, establishing political stances and determining what Jesus would do, as though we are excused from probing the courses of our own lives.[88]

Beyond insisting on mutual love in the face of these crooked and perverse times, Paul seldom took it upon himself to adjudicate and provide answers to the particular questions confronting others. When he was perceived to do so, as in Galatia, he encountered strong resistance. His task is to announce the unfailing truth of the gospel of resurrection faith that, by overcoming the evolutionary heritage that pushes us always to look out for Number One, will enable path-followers to weigh their affairs fearlessly. When Paul does enunciate the implications of the gospel path for his own time and place, he violates regnant expectations: He rejects the then-current culture of pederasty[89] and offers possibilities of reformed marriage relationships, instigating a change in the status of women.[90] Still, the advice Paul gave was embedded within his culture and society and so cannot be applied to our diverse cultures without an examination of the present alternatives.

In the next link of Paul's multi-membered prayer, he says that the wisdom and insight leading to engaged judgments, and then to action, are intended "to render us transparent and inoffensive in the day of the Lord" (ἵνα ἦτε εἰλικρινεῖς καὶ ἀπρόσκοποι εἰς ἡμέραν Χριστοῦ 1:10). Often these terms are translated as "pure" and "blameless," and that would accord with reading the preceding phrase as "approve what is best." But this reading seems to me desultory and not in harmony with the intensity of the letter, which soon turns to questions of deliberative wisdom and factional strife (1:15–18). The word for "transparent" (εἰλικρινεῖς) comes from εἴλη, which describes the sun's warmth (noun ἥλιος, "the sun") and means to be lit up by sunshine, just as we now speak of sunshine laws needed to make political dealings transparent. "Without giving offense" (ἀπρόσκοποι) means not to cause others to stumble.[91] This does not

---

88. See ibid., 85, esp. the section entitled "We can believe almost anything that supports our team."

89. Ruden, *Paul Among the People*, 58: "The bridegroom Catullus celebrates has the 'proper' attitude: use the kid and throw him aside when convenient. Once you have polluted him, you can catch the same pollution by getting close emotionally. This is how twisted and doubled back the ethics of homosexuality were among the Greeks and Romans. This was what Paul and his readers were seeing."

90. Ibid., 117–18: "Paul did make a huge change in the status of women and in marriage, but not the one we ascribe to him. By bringing the question of happiness into it, he let loose not only that hope and possibility, but with it all of the complexity that ancient customs had tamped down. People now had to figure out relationships between the sexes: whether to have relationships at all, whether they bring too much pain and trouble, whether something else would be more fulfilling, how to balance relationships with the spiritual life, and how to love each other selflessly rather than take each other for granted as providers and breeders."

91. Reumann, *Philippians*, 128, cf. 157: "'transparent' in character." For ἀπρόσκοποι, see Vincent, *Critical and Exegetical Commentary*, 13: "not causing others to stumble." Silva observes that "the only other occurrence of this adjective in Paul's letters has the active sense, 'not causing to stumble,' as in 1 Cor 10:32, 'Give no offense [*aproskopoi ginesthe*] to Jews or to Greeks or to the church of God'" (Silva,

mean simply that the people of Philippi are to be of good moral character, but that in strategies for advancing the gospel—whether Paul's willed imprisonment or perhaps other strategies as to the degree of resistance to Roman power—they should be transparent in their motives and their stances. They should not deliberately offend the larger communities in Philippi or in Ephesus, where Paul is in prison, or more broadly the Roman authorities who hold power, or even, as in Romans, the broader church of God (1 Cor 10:32).

To be inoffensively transparent means to abide in a consciousness purified of all self-attachment, whether in image or in idea, including even one's own constructed situation in the world. The grace of risen life enables us to take responsibility by expanding the horizons in which we experience and think about our personal, cultural, and political lives with a transparently pure focus on the path-practice of prayer and a critical openness to all possible cultural horizons. Only in such a mind of hopefulness and waiting are we enabled to prepare "for that day of Christ" (εἰς ἡμέραν Χριστοῦ), for that eschatological day lies beyond all horizons, in recognition of our human transience. As soon as one defends the Christian position, one has lost Christian faith. In ecclesiastical politics of whatever variety, strategy sessions are most effective not when they engender counterpositions in culture wars, but when they urge their theology in terms of basic gospel insight into the rule of emptiness (i.e., kenarchy).

Paul may have read Plato's dialogues and Aristotle's *Nicomachean Ethics*, but he does not bolster his teachings by appeal to the regnant role of any universal natural reason. Human reason is swayed by the passionate insistence on being right, and rightness is circumscribed within team spirit against an opponent. If no opponent exists, the claim of having the only "rational" position will surely create one, and the gospel is then mutated from being the good news of risen life to one option among the plethora of options offered by a multicultural world.

Indeed, there will be a final end to all days within time, when the time of our world comes to an end and our earth-home is swallowed in a searing supernova. But linear end time lies beyond scriptural discourse and draws on the conclusions of astrophysics witnessing the birth and destruction of galaxies in numbers too great to reckon. That cosmic finality is not the "day of the Lord," for the day of the Lord is a day of fullness—the completion or fullness of all our efforts. But it is not "our day." We are the makers of our contextual worlds, caught as we are between deluded, death-destined sin and the overflowing grace of an ever-risen life. But we do not control our own days or our own lives. Even though we construct our life course and cultivate our varied identities, we are never the heroes of our own lives and do not direct human affairs by the pure light of reason.[92] That is a boy's imaginings in Charles Dickens'

Philippians, 51).

92. Haidt, *Righteous Mind*, 73: "Plato (who had been a student of Socrates) had a coherent set of beliefs about human nature, and at the core of these beliefs was his faith in the perfectibility of reason. Reason is our original nature, he thought; it was given to us by the gods and installed in our

David Copperfield, but it is a novelistic conceit. We are not called to be heroes, but to be transparent in character and inoffensive in gospel behavior. Secrecy poisons human relationships, because it takes its valence from competitive interests, masking our evolutionary delusions of either escaping a feared attack or pouncing upon our enemies. In both instances, it sidesteps the gospel call to practice transparency—even if it kills us.

"To be transparent and inoffensive for the day of the Lord" emerges from the love that displays itself as wisdom and insight so as to engage us in the lives of all of our brothers and sisters. That occurs when we live here and now in Christ-mindedness: to share in the mind that empties itself from all self-justifying meanderings. That is the fullness that Paul talks about. This resonates with the "plenitudes" in the Mahāyāna scriptures, where all the talk about emptiness is paired with a kind of fullness that is not self-referential. Those plenitudes or fullnesses describe the various aspects of wisdom as it unfolds into engagement, in awareness that we live in the emptiness of cosmic space (Skt. *dharmadhātu*) and do not have the script for the future of time, even though time does seem always to be moving, arrow-like, straight ahead.[93] The earth, nested in its Milky Way, moves through deep space, but we are not at the controls of this enterprise. Such empty wisdom awakens onto a fullness that is realized by emptying the self and all of its tricky deceits and allowing the life that bubbles up to fill our bodies and our minds beyond bodily boundaries of self or other.

So Paul prays that the Philippians may experience "the fullness of the fruit of righteousness" (πεπληρωμένοι καρπὸν δικαιοσύνης 1:11). To be empty of self is to be filled with a fruitful life abiding in justice and compassion. "Righteousness" is the constant cry of the prophets, enunciating the passion of the gracious God for "the right and the fair" among all peoples in a cry that echoes throughout the entire Tanach. When later in Resurrection Letter C Paul lists his spiritual credentials, he describes himself as zealous to practice the righteousness of the Lord God. Here he sees that the fruits of the righteousness he practices are not his; they come from the other-power (Js. *tariki*)[94] of Jesus Christ. No one can bring themselves into a right relation with God, for God is not a self-referential object of the mind. That is quite a blow—that even after a whole lifetime of blamelessness and dedicated practice, still no one gets to

---

spherical heads. Passions often corrupt reason, but if we can learn to control those passions, our God-given rationality will shine forth and guide us to do the right thing, not the popular thing." So, Haidt concludes, "In this chapter I'll show that reason is not fit to rule; it was designed to seek justification, not truth" (ibid., 74). By contrast, Yogācāra thinkers maintain that all our attempts at overarching and all-determining reasoning operate within the imagined (Skt. *parikalpita*) pattern of self-delusion.

93. See Bandhuprabha, *Interpretation of the Buddha Land*, 97–121, on the ten similes for the "pure realm of the real" (Skt. *dharmadhātu*). Compare Sean Carroll, *From Eternity to Here: The Quest for the Ultimate Theory of Time* (New York: Dutton, 2010), for a parallel meditation on time and space from a theoretical physicist.

94. A key concept in Pure Land Buddhism. For a clear and insightful introduction to Pure Land thought in Japan, see Taitetsu Unno's *Tannisho*. Also see Alfred Bloom, *Shinran's Gospel of Pure Grace* (Tuscon: University of Arizona, 1965).

be the hero, no one gets to be the saint.[95] One doesn't even get to abide, self-satisfied, in an all-confident mind.

As followers of Christ, we reclaim being just human, just as we are. For Paul, as for us, that awareness dawns only with the eclipse of all self-powered efforts. It is not that somehow Paul discovers a new source of inspiration within a cherished new identity. Instead, he experiences the collapse of all traditions in the immediacy of an enlightening Christ who moves him to loosen the identity boundaries that define. Only in the collapse of the powers of the standalone person does the power of the resurrection flow through these bodies of our living and dying. Otherwise, we keep thinking that we possess our own bodies and have a stable individual existence apart from the richly interdependent and interpersonal cosmos in which we have our being—that we are stable selves who might have a stable relationship with a self-conscious god. But all life is ever changing, and a stable god would be a lifeless idol.

So these fruits are not our own fruits, and they do not arise naturally from our biological or karmic heritage, for that is the human heritage that Augustine calls original sin. Hindus and Buddhists speak much of karmic theory—sometimes in a popular fashion and sometimes in a highly nuanced and thoughtful way. Karmic maturation (Skt. *vipāka*) means simply that actions we perform (*karma*) mature into their congruent results. One reaps what one sows. Such karmic complexes cause the world to be as we experience it: a realm of suffering delusion that engenders anger and rewards greed. In its traditional Indian presentation, the Buddhist theory of karma accounts for the very existence of our world as it is.[96] The accumulated karmic actions of living beings from time before time have led us to be who and how we are. So, in Indian thought, the actions of sentient beings—including animals and whatever other nonhuman sentient beings one may imagine either in the upper realms of life or in the lower hells reaching back to the entirety of our evolutionary prehistory—are seen as the cause of the present world's suffering.[97] So consistent did the notion of karmic

---

95. See Zen teacher Steward Lachs' critique of the hagiographic presentation of Chan/Zen masters in his "When the Saints Come Marching In: Modern Day Hagiography," March 9, 2011, http://www.thezensite.com/ZenEssays/CriticalZen/When_the_Saints_Go_Marching_Marching_In.pdf.

96. See Vasubandhu's *Viṃśatikā-kārikā* in Stefan Anacker, *Seven Works of Vasubandhu: The Buddhist Physchological Doctor* (Delhi: Motilal Banarsidass, 1984) 159–79. This is a Yogācāra text often incorrectly understood as teaching idealism. The issue throughout Yogācāra is not to invalidate sense perception, but to question the karmic formation of images and insight as they arise from defiled thinking (*kliṣṭa-manas*), under the permeations of the karmically conditioned *ālaya* consciousness. Yogācāra is not a form of idealism, but a critical examination of how our minds become defiled by passionate attachments that block understanding and occlude awakening.

97. Julian Paul Keenan, *Face in the Mirror*, 241: "Similar complications arise with the self-based emotion of pride. It is possible that a person experiencing a sense of accomplishment, that 'I did this,' might enjoy this sensation and try to feel this emotion again. Imagine that some early prehuman managed to make a device capable of trapping animals and experienced a reinforcing sense of pride (not to mention a good meal) in the accomplishment. Pride must have been a great motivator in the development of ideas, tools, and strategies, and we imagine that early leaders might have maintained their rule with a hefty measure of pride."

determinism become that escape into some nirvanic state was seen as the only remedy. This conception of the world may well have contributed to the oft-noted Indian disregard for recording history.

By contrast, the ancient Chinese were enthralled with the history of human endeavor. Confucius looked back to a golden age of sage emperors and treasured such early historical accounts as the *Shu Ching* (Book of History) and the *Tso Chuan* (Chronicles of Tso), which cover events from the hoary past, providing human models for present living. The *Shu Ching*, in its commitment to model history, attends to actual events; it records an eclipse that scientists date as most likely to have occurred October 22, 2134 BCE, long before the 763 BCE eclipse recorded in Amos 8:9. Within their humanistic Confucian context, the Chinese have been firmly grounded in their history. In fact, the Buddhists' initial introduction of a nonhistorical wheel of karmic transmigration was so startling to the Chinese that the *Hou Han Chi* (Record of the Later Han) relates that the "princes and nobles, once they considered the limits of death, rebirth, and retribution, in every case each succumbed to panic."[98]

So in East Asia there has long been a tendency to reinterpret the Indian version of transmigration. Are we, or are we not, the agents of our own lives? Does the inexorable law of karmic retribution negate the significance of any human action in the world? If that is so, what are the sources for "the good works that have been begun" in the Philippians? The Chinese themselves have always insisted on human ethics and choice as the only way to construct human culture and civilization. It is perhaps noteworthy that the practical effect of Chinese thought is in large part responsible for the longest continuous social and cultural entity in human experience. But in ancient Indian thinking (and in large part, all traditions within the Indian subcontinent), history was regarded as a web of lies and foolishness that we wish were erased from all human activity. Karma (or human action) is seen as the motive force that impels living beings from one life into the next on the constant and beginningless wheel of suffering—a Dharma teaching that is akin to Darwinian insights from evolutionary science.[99]

However, the more nuanced and profound doctrinal elaborations of karmic theory in Buddhist texts and commentaries strive to make it clear that what transmigrates is not a personal self (Skt. *pudgala; ātman*), for there is no personal self and

---

98. *Hou Han Chi*, 10, cited in TSUKAMOTO Zenryū, *A History of Early Chinese Buddhism: From Its Introduction to the Death of Hui-yüan*, trans. Leon Hurvitz (Tokyo: Kodansha, 1979) 475–76.

99. See William S. Waldron, "Common Ground, Common Cause: Buddhism and Science on the Afflictions of Identity," in *Buddhism and Science: Breaking New Ground*, ed. B. Alan Wallace (New York: Columbia University Press, 2003) 145–91. The issue was troubling even to Darwin himself. Haidt notes, "Darwin was fascinated by morality because any example of cooperation among living creatures had to be squared with his general emphasis on competition and the 'survival of the fittest.' Darwin offered several explanations for how morality could have evolved, and many of them pointed to emotions such as sympathy, which he thought was the 'foundation-stone' of the social instincts" (Haidt, *Righteous Mind*, 30–31). He was forced to conclude that "natural selection gave us minds that were preloaded with moral emotions" (ibid.).

thus no standalone agent who might turn the wheel of karmic retribution. What does transmigrate is the bare consciousness that links one lifetime to another but is bereft of memory. In modern parlance, karmic conditioning from the past is inscribed in the genetic structure of our evolutionary consciousness so that forgetfulness, greed, and anger drive us forward into ever-repeating experiences of suffering. The path-practice of the Buddha thus focuses attention on the karma-laden minds of sentient beings so that we might bring our latent forgetfulness (*avidyā*) into the light of understanding, tame greed and anger, and thereby trigger a reorientation of our minds and bodies. The promise is that if we can identify the causes of suffering, we can transform our consciousness, attain awakening, and liberate all sentient beings. As Darwin knew so well, sentient beings are born with the neural ability to fight for bodily survival. In Indian Buddhist doctrinal history, freedom from these karmic networks is called *nirvāṇa*, literally the "blowing out" of the fires of greed and hatred that emerge from the deluded self-clinging of our struggle for survival. Darwin describes the phenomenology of what occurs; the Buddha Dharma offers an alternative: a life of wisdom and compassion.

The cherished goal of cessation from the wheel of suffering issued first in the ideal of the arhat—the saintly being who has stopped the transmigratory wheel from turning and abides alone, hermit-like, in full and complete nirvanic cessation. Having put an end to karmic impulses, such an arhat remains on this earth only so long as the spinning of a potter's wheel might continue moving after the potter removes her foot. As soon as that karmic motion is exhausted, the saintly hermit figure disappears, never to be seen again. Mahāyāna practitioners revised that ideal, for if self is an empty category as Mahāyāna teaches, then self-attainment is meaningless. Thus, they empty even the goal of a final state of nirvarnic cessation, sketching the life of practice as a path toward awakening to the emptiness of all and then re-engagement in the suffering world as a compassionate bodhisattva.

Although not of course a Mahāyāna practitioner, Paul—in his engagement with the Philippians and with all the communities he founded and served, and indeed with the entire world in which he lived—never aimed to remove people from their lived lives. His aim was the compassionate furthering of the gospel that restructures all human relationships by reorienting our minds—and our bodies—to conform to Christ in suffering and dying and sharing in risen life. Even after adopting the Jesus path, Paul remained a Jew, and that means he was tied to this earthy world in which we live, for there was among the Jews no flight of Platonic fancy into ethereal realms.[100] Paul's teachings in his varied correspondences exhibit no withdrawal from the messiness of

---

100. Except perhaps for Philo of Alexandria (10 BCE–ca. 50 CE), a fully Hellenized Jew who was widely read in Greek philosophy and therefore more popular among Christian scholars than Jewish. Roman armies put down the Diaspora Jewish revolt of 115–17 CE, devastating Alexandria and the Hellenistic Judaism that had flourished under thinkers such as Philo, while leaving a vacuum that was filled by rabbinic Judaism rooted firmly in Palestine. See Joseph Mélèze Modrzejewski, *The Jews of Egypt: From Ramses II to Emperor Hadrian* (Princeton: Princeton University Press, 1997).

this organic earth. The Philippians are not to recoil, as Plato did, from this barbarously muddy world. Although our earliest monastics did flee into the Egyptian desert, western monastic orders became the civilizing centers of their medieval worlds, even opening the first schools and hospitals.

No one escapes from being human, not even celibates, who have not only to tame, but also suppress the hormonal impulses we all share. Rather than escape, Paul urges the practice of transparent righteousness that flows from Christ's self-emptying. Indeed, that is why Paul recommends that we test and probe what is best, for otherwise we cannot effectively strive for those goals. The first step is that we dedicate ourselves to emptying ourselves of pretense and self-interest. Still, we hope not for empty nothingness in our lives, but rather for fullness of life (πεπληρωμένοι) through our identity with Christ-life and righteousness (δικαιοσύνης) so that we may strive and be filled with "the fruits" (καρπὸν . . . τὸν), such as "come through Jesus Christ" (διὰ Ἰησοῦ Χριστοῦ). All this in the hope that on the eschatological day of the Lord we may be filled with life that comes "from Christ for the glory and praise of God" (τὸν διὰ Ἰησοῦ Χριστοῦ εἰς δόξαν καὶ ἔπαινον θεοῦ 1:11)—a packed sentence, indeed. The fruits of the Philippians' righteousness will flow not from their self-sufficient human agency, but from Christ, and result in the glory of God.

In the New Testament, glory is regularly attributed to God, not to Jesus Christ, for it carries the connotation of power and ability. Glory is the renown attributed to God, but here Paul's didactic prayer concludes with that transcendent glory functioning through Jesus Christ, perhaps foreshadowing the "more than superlative exaltation" (2:9) of the emptied Christ who fills the center of our personal consciousness. In so doing, Paul makes God's glory indivisible with the gory death of Jesus on the cross. The transcendent glory we imagine to surround the unnamable God, here "the glory of God" (καὶ ἔπαινον θεοῦ), is grounded in the empty Christ, who is engulfed in pain and suffering. The image of glory is of a primal and beautiful world flowing from a creative source, worthy of recognition and praise, of a stark and savage goodness in a world so transient that its fleeting beauty draws our minds forth in glimpses of wonder simply at our being-here, wherever we are. In the New Testament, it becomes an eschatological beauty, glimpsed in transfigured hope and dreams within horizons of meaning that counter both the evolutionary violence that flows from our selfish genes[101] and the institutionalized violence of power that impoverishes and starves people to death in their millions.

---

101. Haidt, *Righteous Mind*, 197: "Richard Dawkins . . . in his 1976 best seller *The Selfish Gene*, grant[s] that group selection is possible but then debunk[s] apparent cases of group adaptation. By the late 1970s there was a strong consensus that anyone who said that a behavior occurred 'for the good of the group' was a fool who could be safely ignored . . . Theories in a wide variety of disciplines rest on the assumption that 'man is selfish.'" By contrast, see Mark 9:2–8, where the vision of the transfigured Jesus is followed by Peter's desire to cling to that vision by setting up "shelters" there, to abide in that mountain (Keenan, *Gospel of Mark*, 208–16).

Emptiness means that we need not envisage a comforting creator who looks out for the care and nurture of individuals. Rather, the Spirit breathes order into the chaos of nothingness and bellows the cosmos into being, filling and inflating world realms as savage as they are beautiful. Which is why images of creator gods tend to be threatening and mercurial—the world is so designed. When we see that same creative aspiration in the uttering of the Word that is Christ, we do not see a separate second-god but rather the same savage beauty suffocating the life from Jesus' lungs so that we all may live in the spirit of Christ, sharing his sufferings and participating in his resurrection.

Paul and the Christian tradition that followed him affirm the re-orientation of identity (*metanoia*) that is engendered through sharing the mind of Christ, shifting away from a fixation on otherworldly glory and toward the Christ wisdom that abides in the indivisibility of that sought-after bliss with this present life of striving and karmic struggle. Eschatological wonder becomes the re-inscribed pattern of present life, and the supernatural becomes indivisible with the natural, for they are but ideas about otherworldly reality and truth that we employ to localize our eschatological longings. Sometimes, perhaps often, we use supernatural categories to domesticate our longing and imagine a special realm to which an imagined self has assured access. But there is no supernatural or ecclesiastical realm that will take us out of this world, for worldly actions always have their results: karma does function in its pedestrian linkages.[102]

Still, the gospel urges that human endeavor be directed toward a hoped-for consummation in justice and peace, envisaged as the day of the Lord when, negating the karmically confined horizons of the world, justice may flow from the heavens and peace will pervade all relationships—a dream of consummation that structures our every moment of practice in our refusal to accept the rightness of oppression or greed. End-time living is a way of living the now time, always engaged in hope for the wellbeing of all peoples while eschewing the self-affirmation of jingoistic boasting in one's own national or religious identity. Eschatology is not an exercise in future-telling. We are urged to reject any suzerainty of power that sees itself as the guarantor of peace and order, acquiescing in the joy of the few while allowing the suffering of the many. Heeding the eschatological prophets from Daniel to Jesus to Paul, we are to await the day of Christ and work to accomplish it.[103]

It is an old saw that characterizes Buddhism as world denying, and Christian leaders often critique Buddhism in just such terms.[104] True, some Buddhists have

---

102. J. F. Powers, in his novel *Morte D'Urban* (New York: Doubleday, 1962), portrays a Father Urban of the Clementine Order who, despite his effort to modernize the gospel and reinvigorate his order, falls into the accustomed mediocrity of clerical life.

103. Reumann, *Philippians*, 124. Reumann argues that fullness in the New Testament is "'an eschatological catchword' for a 'fulness present and proclaimed in the age of salvation as compared with the old aeon' (*TDNT* 6:59)" (ibid.).

104. The representations of Buddhism in Pope John Paul II, *Crossing the Threshold of Faith* (New York: Knopf, 1994) 85–90, and in Cardinal Joseph Ratzinger, *Truth and Tolerance: Christian Belief and World Religions* (San Francisco: Ignatius, 2003) 175–76, 227, fail even to attempt engagement with

shown that tendency, historically and doctrinally, but stereotypes are based on snapshots—frozen images that refuse revision even with new insight. Christians might want to take care of their own glass houses: Thomas à Kempis' classic *Imitation of Christ* is as world denying as any Buddhist text ever was. Moreover, many Buddhist thinkers today insist upon social justice and engagement. Indeed, social engagement is the hallmark of modern Buddhist living and thinking; awakening is seen not as withdrawal, but as waking up to what is truly real and authentic in human living.[105]

There are parallels here between Christians who teach selfless living as the implied meaning of the gospel and Mahayanists who teach such living as the very decentered meaning of the Dharma. And yet there are differences, for while Christian exegetes often move from the theological portions of Paul's writings to his paraenetic advice, Mahayanists make no such distinction. That is because in Mahāyāna, there is no central theological viewpoint that must first be in place before one may practice. In Nāgārjuna's *Stanzas*, the Buddha taught emptiness to eliminate all views whatsoever, including even the central teachings of the tradition. The point of such a blanket negation of holding views is that practitioners can easily get stuck in their viewpoints, focusing on their own righteousness or attainment and neglecting the very path-practices meant to liberate from suffering and meaninglessness. Views filter experience and imprison people in their cherished ideas.[106] So, in Buddhist tradition, the first doctrinal truth appeals to an easily recognized truth: that once given life, we suffer, age, and die. That recognition, as obvious as it is, is difficult to accept, for the controller-self imagines itself to be godlike and immortal.

It is difficult to accept life as a human—mixture that it is of selfish desires centered on survival, together with desires to experience an end-time love of this life that goes on beyond us, cherishing every life from generation to generation until the linear end, across the world, and always with the hope that apart from the cosmic ending there will be an eschatological Pure Land of Bliss for all. Nevertheless, at death we have no need to surrender our lives, for they have not been ours from the beginning. Our self-power has always been an illusion. What happens in the course of an awakened life is brought about not by individual effort and self-power, but by the other-power of the eschatological Lord Jesus Christ.

---

actual Buddhist scholarship, remaining content to repeat stereotypes long since rejected by scholars and by Buddhists themselves. For a response from a Theravada Buddhist monk, see Bhikkhu Bodhi, "Toward a Threshold of Understanding" (Kandy, Sri Lanka: Buddhist Publication Society, 1995).

105. See Christopher S. Queen and Sally B. King, eds., *Engaged Buddhism: Buddhist Liberation Movements in Asia* (Albany: State University of New York Press, 1996).

106. Everett, *Don't Sleep*, 218: "Sapir even goes so far as to claim that our view of the world is constructed by our languages, and that there is no 'real world' that we can actually perceive without the filter of language telling us what we are seeing and what it means. If Sapir and Whorf are correct, the implications for philosophy, linguistics, anthropology, and psychology, among other fields of study, are vast." The fifth-century Yogācāra philosophers similarly taught that the world we experience is only a construct (Skt. *vijñapti-mātra*) of consciousness, imbued by the permeations of language.

There is here in 1:11 a significant textual variant about glory that reads εἰς δόξαν καὶ ἔπαινον μοι in place of εἰς δόξαν καὶ ἔπαινον θεοῦ. That is, rather than "for the glory and praise *of God*," the alternative reads "for *my* glory and praise." If that reading were to be accepted as authentic, it would appear that Paul is here pushing himself to the fore.[107] Perhaps in the formation of our present text, that just seemed too egoistical and was therefore changed; perhaps it sounded too similar to Paul's claims of self-sufficiency in Letter A. But the alternative is the more difficult reading, and thus has a better claim to represent the original text.

Later in this Letter B, Paul does boast—that the people in Philippi are his joy and crown (4:1). And in the present context of eschatological wonder "at the day of Christ," perhaps this variant and embarrassing reading can be taken to mean: "for the glory [of God] and praise to me," mirroring 2:15–16, where Paul looks forward to the day when the Philippians will shine like stars in the sky and he can boast of not having run in vain.[108] If indeed Paul's identity is tangled up with Christ, who empties himself and is more than exalted in glory (2:9), he can well envisage end-time praise for his efforts—efforts that were sometimes questioned by fellow Christ followers in his day. But Paul's glory comes not from self-sufficiency, but from God in Christ, who empties selfhood. Such a reading further brings to ground the transcendent glory of God, not in the praise of a now-absent Christ, but his presence in Paul himself. The reconfiguration of Paul's mind in the empty Christ does not mean that he is swallowed up in a cosmic soup wherein all of Christ's followers disappear into a monistic sameness.[109] That is not the eschatological structure of the mind of the empty Christ. Paul's relationship with the Philippians now moves away from self-referential categories to a shared glory that they all find in the empty Christ.

---

107. See Ruden on Paul's boasting: "he is always boasting; he even makes fun of himself boasting (as in 2 Corinthians 11)" (Ruden, *Paul Among the People*, 178).

108. See Reumann, *Philippians*, 135, 159: "1:11c, *for God's glory and praise*, is usually taken to show Paul's theocentricity or theoultimacy . . . 1:11c is not human praise of God (doxology) but praise and glory given to human beings by God at the End, commendation of believers. [Since "God's glory" can be a subjective genitive], the reading in a few MSS, including P46, can be understood as accurate interpretation, 'for the glory (of God) and praise *to me*.'" That would harmonize with Phil 4:1, where Paul talks about his joy and his crown.

109. See the Foucaultian reading by Castelli: "Out of this survey of the ancient discourses on mimesis will come a series of generalizations about the notion of imitation which Paul inherited from the Greco-Roman Culture: (1) Mimesis is always articulated as a hierarchical relationship, whereby the 'copy' is but a derivation of the 'model' and cannot aspire to the privileged status of the 'model.' (2) Mimesis presupposes a valorization of sameness over against difference. Certain conceptual equations accompanied this move: unity and harmony are associated with sameness while difference is attributed characteristic of diffusion, disorder, and discord. (3) The notion of the authority of the model plays a fundamental role in the mimetic relationship" (Castelli, *Imitating Paul*, 16). She argues, "Furthermore the expectation to imitation underwrites the apostles' demand for the erasure of difference, and links that erasure to the very possibility of salvation" (ibid., 17). But if imitation functions only in relationship to those we love, none of this erasure need occur.

If this alternate textual reading be preferred and Paul's didactic prayer in 1:3–11 ends with a hope for his own end-time praise, it simply twins the personal tone of verse 3, where he gives thanks "to my God" (τῷ θεῷ μου) with a hope for his own share in the life of that personal "my God." And, in so doing, it affirms the emptiness of self that Paul celebrates in Christ in 2:6–11 and in 3:4–11 of Letter C. In no way does embracing emptiness negate his personal consciousness. Affirming the emptiness of self as normative entails as well the affirmation of a conventional self that is able to hear and spread the gospel—a self that, having been dethroned from its stable perch as the center of attention, is freed to launch into the adventure of gospel life.[110]

Paul's Imprisonment Strategy (1:12–14)

Here in Letter B there is no question that Paul has been arrested and is in a prison somewhere. The immediate issue reflected in the correspondence with the Philippians is why that is so and whether his strategy for furthering the gospel by appearing and pleading before a Roman court is an intelligent move. The main social and cultural issue for these early Christ communities was how to carve out a space for their communal practice, for in diverging from their Jewish tradition, which Rome recognized as legal, they had become an illegal religious sect:[111]

> 1:12 *I want you to know, brothers and sisters, that what has happened to me has served to advance the gospel rather than otherwise,* [13]*to the extent that it has become known throughout the whole imperial guard and to all the rest that I am bound over in Christ;* [14]*and the majority of the brothers and sisters, having been made confident in the Lord by my chains, grow bolder all the time in speaking the word without fear.*

> 1:12Γινώσκειν δὲ ὑμᾶς βούλομαι, ἀδελφοί, ὅτι τὰ κατ' ἐμὲ μᾶλλον εἰς προκοπὴν τοῦ εὐαγγελίου ἐλήλυθεν, [13]ὥστε τοὺς δεσμούς μου φανεροὺς ἐν Χριστῷ γενέσθαι ἐν ὅλῳ τῷ πραιτωρίῳ καὶ τοῖς λοιποῖς πᾶσιν, [14]καὶ τοὺς πλείονας τῶν ἀδελφῶν ἐν κυρίῳ πεποιθότας τοῖς δεσμοῖς μου περισσοτέρως τολμᾶν ἀφόβως τὸν λόγον λαλεῖν.

---

110. Ruden, *Paul Among the People*, 182: "What could be less coherent and satisfying than Paul's earthly life? He disappeared for long periods after his conversion, three years in Arabia and a number of years back home in Tarsus. He may have worked in his family business, argued with his parents, married and argued with his wife. He then helped with the new movement in Antioch, and later in a long series of other cities. He pitched and vomited on boats. He was shipwrecked three times, and once floated a whole day and night on wreckage. Time after time, he lay awake hungry and cold in long grass by the road, perhaps listening terrified as bandits passed."

111. Ibid., 127. Ruden comments on how Paul negotiates state authority with the Roman community: "How on earth was Paul going to talk to his Romans about authority? He did need to talk to them, or they would never form orderly communities, let alone work out a conscientious relationship with the state, let alone conceive of a God who, in asking for obedience, wanted nothing but their good."

After praying for the Philippians, Paul continues his letter with a "disclosure statement," wherein he informs his "brothers and sisters" (ἀδελφοί, *adelphoi*) how he himself regards his present situation.[112] He says, "I want you to know" (Γινώσκειν δὲ ὑμᾶς βούλομαι), clarifying his present situation and its implications for the gospel. Apparently there have been rumors and some disagreement. Philippi, with its colonial status, its Roman citizens, and its ability to raise significant funds for Paul's endeavors, was perhaps the polar opposite of the community that expressed itself in the rejectionist book of Revelation. Philippi was Roman; the book of Revelation ("The Apocalypse") was anti-Roman. In any case, the appropriate social options and cultural strategies were not always clear, just as such things often puzzle Christ followers today.

The Book of Acts (25–26) reports that Paul refused release from prison in Ephesus; instead, he made public his Roman citizenship and so was remanded into custody to be sent to trial in Rome. That was a gutsy move, for it forced the issue. Once before, when he was arrested and beaten in Philippi (Acts 16), Paul refused at first to disappear quietly, claiming his Roman citizenship and demanding an apology from the local magistrates. But when they came and did apologize, Paul left the city.[113] Yet in Ephesus, before the governor Festus (Acts 25) and King Agrippa, Paul appeals directly to Caesar, and his claim of citizenship leaves no room for a quiet departure. King Agrippa concludes that "this man could have been set free, if he had not appealed to Caesar" (Acts 26:32). And so Paul was taken by stages to Rome as a prisoner, lodged in prisons all along the route.

Paul does not in this Philippian correspondence retell the dramatic narrative of Acts; he is not recounting his experiences but rather writing letters to people who already know his situation. It does seem reasonable then to understand Paul's defense of his imprisonment in terms of the challenge he presented to the Roman officials by his claim to citizenship.

This leaves the exegetes to speculate on the question of how Paul's status as citizen prisoner was received by other Christians. He is writing a letter, so he could presuppose that his readers know, as we cannot, the course of particular events they have shared in common. It is clear from what he does write, however, that Paul is distancing himself from their criticism. The criticism may have been that by claiming his citizenship and seeking a Roman trial, Paul is acquiescing in the legitimacy of the Empire and so acting in a manner unworthy of the gospel. Perhaps detractors argued that he ought to take a more militant stance against Rome, as did The Apocalypse. Or perhaps the criticism was just the opposite: that by his claim of citizenship and forthcoming trial, Paul brings undue Roman attention to nascent Christ communities

---

112. Reumann, *Philippians*, 191.

113. Acts 16:37: "And Paul said to them [i.e., the magistrates in Philippi], 'They have beaten us publicly, men who are Roman citizens, and have thrown us in prison, and do they now cast us out secretly? Let them come themselves and take us out.'" So they apologized to them and sent them on their way.

seeking to ground their faith and practice less confrontationally within the regnant Greco-Roman society. Perhaps such critics thought Paul ought to be less belligerent and more accommodating to the powers that in fact control the world, for Philippi holds special status as a Roman colony. Both suppositions imply that to other Christians, Paul's enthusiastic welcome of his present imprisonment is troublesome.[114]

Whatever the criticisms, Paul sees his situation, whether arisen from his claim of citizenship as in Acts or perhaps somehow through another conflict, as the natural outcome of the shared life of the gospel and as an opportunity to continue sharing that gospel "to the extent that" (ὥστε) his bonds (τοὺς δεσμούς μου) are seen to be "in Christ" (ἐν Χριστῷ 1:13).[115] Already at the start of Letter A, Paul identifies himself, together with Timothy, as a slave of Christ (1:1 δοῦλοι Χριστοῦ Ἰησοῦ), and so here he remains enslaved to Christ. Now Letter B affirms that "my situation" (ὅτι τὰ κατ' ἐμὲ),[116] "has turned out" (ἐλήλυθεν), "for the Gospel's advance" (εἰς προκοπὴν τοῦ εὐαγγελίου) and not otherwise (μᾶλλον 1:12). That this is the outcome may be surprising to many, for imprisonment would seem to be a setback, hardly promising any advance for the gospel.[117]

This term "advance" (προκοπή)—borrowed from Stoicism, where it denotes moral progress in virtue—here indicates the social and cultural progress of the gospel. In Stoicism, it meant an advance "essentially connected with the acquisition of individual virtues to be gained or developed from man's own natural disposition,"[118] underlying the attainment of the virtue of self-sufficiency. That notion may be in play in Letter A,

---

114. Reumann cites Collange on Paul's "determination to secure release for himself, a change of mind that may have angered and alienated his radical followers" (Reumann, *Philippians*, 192). They apparently saw in his conduct "an attitude of infidelity to the Cross," and indeed of "cowardice" ibid.). Collange notes the sharp contrast between the opponents' "radical, doctrinaire commitment" and Paul's "realistic," opportunistic commitment" (Collange, *Epistle of Saint Paul*, 51–52). Reumann explains, "Early Christian attitudes toward the Roman Empire varied from the positive view in Romans 13:1–7 (reflecting the OT; cf. Jer. 29) to the negative assessment in apocalyptic writings like Rev 13" (Reumann, *Philippians*, 194). Reumann and Collange see Paul's critics as these ideologically pure advocates of a Cross stance that would reject any entanglement with the Roman authorities. According to Martin, some are "deliberately courting the hostility of the civil authorities . . . stirring up agitation by a message aimed at subverting Roman rule" (Martin, *Philippians*, 74–75). Indeed, his critics could have been partisan Christians trying to urge a Christian identity, rejecting his citizenship strategy as a cowardly assimilation to worldly power. Or perhaps they feared that strategy would bring the gospel communities into unwanted public prominence and hinder the task of grounding the progress of the gospel within a Roman society that was accustomed to many religions. Caird suggests that members of the church "might have taken his imprisonment as a warning to do nothing that would attract the attention of the authorities" (Caird, *Paul's Letters from Prison*, 109). Indeed, in 1:10 above, Paul advises the Philippians to give no offense.

115. Collange, *Epistle of Saint Paul*, 54 n. 1, interprets "*hōste*" in verse 14 to mean, not "so that," but "that is to say" or even "to the extent that."

116. Ibid., 53. According to Collange *ta kat'eme* (v. 12) is his Roman citizenship.

117. O'Brien, *Epistle to the Philippians*, 90: "Here the adverb μᾶλλον does not mean 'more, to a greater degree,' but 'rather' in the sense of 'instead.'"

118. Ibid.

where Paul insists on his personal self-sufficiency. But here in Emptiness Letter B, it is used to indicate communal progress in furthering the gospel. In 1:25, Paul uses the term again to close the paragraph where he speaks about the Philippians' progress (εἰς τὴν ὑμῶω προκοπὴν), thereby framing the focus of his attention on progress in a gospel understanding. Such progress does not here refer to the acquisition of new virtues that contribute to a stable selfhood; rather, it signifies the reorientation of the entirety of any individually constructed life.

If we compare these first two letters, we can recognize clear differences in Paul's self-awareness. Perhaps because of response he has received from Philippi, Paul has learned more of the mind of Christ. And this understanding has deepened still further when in Letter C he writes of the surpassing knowledge of Christ and abandons all his self-identity markers so as to know Christ in his dying and rising. It should be no surprise if, in a back-and-forth correspondence on such central questions of following Christ, new understanding should occur on both sides. Here, to be bound in Christ, in actual imprisonment, effects a decentering of Paul's very self so that he may share in the risen life of Christ. The term "progress" comes from a verb *prolopeō* which means to "go forward" and suggests clearing the gospel path, removing obstacles—something like "pioneers *cutting* a way *before* an army, and so *furthering* its march"[119]—at the very time that Paul's own path is blocked.

In speaking of the furtherance or progress of the gospel, Paul seems addicted to sports metaphors about striving and stretching, about running races and passing the finish line. He speaks of accomplishing much and bearing fruit. His gospel is not a static "something" contained in any book or outlined in any canon—there was no canon in Paul's day, not even a written set of gospels. The gospel message that is being passed along from one person to another in Paul's time is an onrushing assault that opens self-enclosed minds and draws communal attention to the significance here and now of the coming day of the Lord. It has clear implications for social and political living, and that was its attraction to many who suffered under the regime of Roman power. It was not, however, a program for change that would leave minds content in their self-attachment. Paul's gospel is not about private experiences that uplift and carry the enlightened mind toward detached, mystical heights. Moreover, Paul's letters are not one-way presentations of truth to people who are unaware of this path. Consequently, he is able to learn from others who engage in this same gospel path.

When Paul waxes eloquent about his oneness "in Christ" (ἐν Χριστῷ, *en Christō*), at a minimum he means that one is not just to live the gospel of Christ personally but to strive to enunciate and preach that life to others. Just as Paul was a tentmaker accustomed to plying his trade within the merchant caravans that passed continually along the Roman roads,[120] so now he plies his rhetorical skills to weave the words of his letters so that they may elicit shared insight and commitment. The Philippians, in

---

119. Vincent, *Critical and Exegetical Commentary*, 16.
120. See Chilton, *Rabbi Paul*, "On the Road," 48–71.

the midst of their own daily endeavors, have been journeying forth as well. They are focused on a work that goes beyond any mystic experience of ultimate meaning, looking instead to the wisdom and insight that enables one to witness to and enunciate Christ in everyday living.

Still, the gospel is neither a program in need of implementation by the courageous, nor a collection of comforting beliefs for the timorous. Neither of those alternatives would have elicited the spirited back-and-forth that marks Paul's letters. When preached with a transparent purity, this gospel path gives no offense to the brave or to the timid, but at times it does trigger conversions that embolden people beyond their fear of death. In 1:13, Paul asserts that "it has become apparent" (φανεροὺς . . . γενέσθαι)[121] "to everybody, to the Praetorian Guard," which enforces Roman power, "and to everybody else" (ἐν ὅλῳ τῷ πραιτωρίῳ καὶ τοῖς λοιποῖς πᾶσιν) that he is "in chains" (ὥστε τοὺς δεσμούς μου) because of, or "in Christ" (ἐν Χριστῷ). It is clear to all that still Paul lives "in Christ."

Unlike his critics, those in prison with Paul have no doubt about the reason he is there; it is certainly not because he is cowardly or because he seeks to make a public display of himself. They know his motives because they are in direct contact with him. Like the centurion who stood face-to-face with the dying Jesus in Mark 15:39 (parallel in Matt 27:54 and Luke 23:47), they see that Paul also is truly (ἀληθῶς) God's son.[122] Just as in the Synoptics the first witnesses to Jesus' innocence were Roman soldiers, so here Roman soldiers witness to Paul's innocence; they know why he has been put in those chains. He is concretely a slave of and because of Christ, and he has learned the emptiness of the suffering Christ. The phrase "in Christ" is mystical grammar, and the expression is understandably "unusual if not awkward."[123] But here, "it has become apparent or become visible" that what was hidden in Paul's own mind is now clear to everyone because of his actions in preaching the gospel. What then was hidden and has now become plain?

The passage that follows (1:15–18), in which Paul refers to his fellow preachers of Christ, suggests that the criticism they level at him lies in the commonly understood fact that to be in a Roman prison is nothing but disaster for most people. Even in many places today, those perceived to have troubled the powers-that-be disappear into prisons, never again to emerge. In fact, it is not clear whether Paul ever did get his trial. We have no court records. Although Paul had envisaged his anticipated trial as a stellar opportunity to witness to the gospel, that event is nowhere reported. His

---

121. See Reumann, *Philippians*, 170, which translates *phaneros* as "come to light."

122. See C. S. Mann, *Mark: A New Translation with Introduction and Commentary*, Anchor Bible (New York: Doubleday, 1986) 654: "Mark uses the word *kenturiōn*, a Latinism found in the papyri, whereas Matthew and Luke use the equally late *hekatontarchos*, a word whose meaning is essentially the same—the commander of what we woud call a company of soldiers." Furthermore, Matthew reports not only the witness of the centurion, but mentions that person "and those who were with him" (Ὁ δὲ ἑκατόνταρχος καὶ οἱ μετ' αὐτοῦ), which echoes Paul's "and to all the rest" (καὶ τοῖς λοιποῖς πᾶσιν).

123. O'Brien, *Epistle to the Philippians*, 91.

impressive address to King Agrippa described in Acts 26 apparently was not repeated before another Roman judge. The brute fact is that even if Paul did eventually regain his freedom, he soon disappeared from our common history.

Nevertheless, Paul insists here that, although not apparent to his Philippian critics, it is clear to him that all has turned out quite well for the furtherance of the gospel. His eschatological attending upon the Christ whose heart beats through his own organic life—and that is the significance of our doctrine of incarnation—has been made manifest to all. Even in prison, Paul rejoices in this end-time Christ. He will not be dislodged from the world of his own understanding and engagement. He will continue as a preacher of the gospel busy dreaming of and announcing the coming day of the Lord, when a new path to life will counter the human calculus of power, greed, and anger. Here, the end-time sign of Paul chained in Christ is apparent to all who see, even "the entire Roman Praetorian Guard" (ἐν ὅλῳ τῷ πραιτωρίῳ 1:13) who hold him in prison.[124]

Therefore, says Paul in 1:14, "the majority of the brothers and sisters" (καὶ τοὺς πλείονας τῶν ἀδελφῶν),[125] "because of my chains" (τοῖς δεσμοῖς μου), have been persuaded "to be more and more confident in the Lord" (ἐν κυρίῳ πεποιθόντας) so that "even more" (περισσοτέρως) "they dare" (τολμᾶν) "to speak the word" (τὸν λόγον λαλεῖν) "without fear" (ἀφόβως), even if they themselves are arrested and imprisoned. His brothers and sisters in Philippi and throughout the world are moved "to enunciate the word" (τὸν λόγον λαλεῖν) of the gospel more fearlessly all the time.

In John's Prologue, the Word from the beginning is made flesh and dwells among us, after which all words are meant to be spoken. By becoming flesh, the eternally abiding Word becomes decentered and is spread through the speaking of many. Here, Paul and his coworkers try to enunciate the Christ meaning of those deep and broad experiences through which Paul shares his being with Christ and with his readers—an experience of being saved from the confines of selfhood by this Word of life. That is why he is so driven to enunciate (λαλεῖν) the meaning (τὸν λόγον) of that experience—that is his gospel.[126] The ground from which Paul speaks here is the ground from which all gospel coworkers also speak "in the Lord" (ἐν κυρίῳ, *en kyriō*), for those transformative experiences are open and present to all gospel practitioners who

---

124. Martin, *Philippians*, 70. The term *praitōrion* "denotes the residence of the governor of a province in the other New Testemant references (Pilate's residence, as Roman procurator, in Jerusalem; Herod's palace in Caesarea)" (ibid.).

125. Collange, *Epistle of Saint Paul*, 55, translates *hoi pleiones* as "majority," not "more."

126. *Pace* Hubert Ritt, "λόγος," *Exegetical Dictionary of the New Testament*, ed. H. Batz, G. Schneider (Grand Rapids: Eerdmans 1990–1993) 2:358. "For Paul the creative '*word* of God' (ὁ λόγος τοῦ θεοῦ), which was originally directed to Israel, 'has not failed' (Rom 9:6); this would not be at all possible, for God himself is the source of this *word* (1 Cor 14:36; 2 Cor 4:2), the gospel, which is clearly distinguishable from any 'human *word*' (λόγος ἀνθρώπων), 1 Thess 2:13; 1:5; 2:5)" (ibid., cited in Heil, *Philippians: Let Us Rejoice*, 51 n. 4). That makes the word of God an imagined divine speaking and not the sometimes contentious discourse we find in Paul. In Mahāyāna philosophy, the word of God is not the word of God. That is why it is the word of God.

are thus urged and driven to enunciate that word fearlessly. To be "fearless" (ἀφόβως) is also a characteristic of all buddhas and bodhisattvas, for they are grounded in that emptiness in which there is nothing whatsoever to lose.[127] For Paul, it has a very concrete meaning: he is preaching the crucified Christ as the counter to all Roman pretensions and comforting theistic conceits. Negating the many gods who each embody a far-away power, he is the atheist in their midst, celebrating a god who embodies weakness and emptiness.

Although imprisoned, Paul does not represent himself as a victim of justice long denied. His attitude is not ideologically or theologically driven, but rather a practical concern about how best to clear a cultural space for the gospel communities.[128] It was Paul himself who caused his troubles, refusing to back away from the gospel and challenging the Romans to hear its message. The gospel demands justice but is about more than justice, for if we had to await the establishment of justice in linear time, few would ever find deliverance. Paul continues to understand his life in self-effacing slavery to Christ. He is not the central symbol of the gospel; Christ is that symbol.

Paul's imprisonment for Christ leads most of his friends "to grow confident in the Lord" (ἐν κυρίῳ πεποιθότας) regardless of the course of their individual lives. It is not merely a matter of their being cheered or encouraged; it is confident entrustment in the empty Christ, whereby one empties oneself of all expectations and is thereby freed to work skillfully with wisdom and insight in speaking the word. Paul's brothers and sisters are not persuaded by any judicial or theological argument. They become bold, even bolder, because they are not speaking their own words at all. And yet it is they who do speak the words that bring to speech the primal Word from the beginning. The Chinese philosopher Chuang Tzu once queried, "Where may I find a man of few words, that I might have a word with him?"[129]

Partisan Preaching (1:15–18a)

> 1:15 *Some indeed preach Christ out of jealous contention, but others out of goodwill.* [16]*The latter [live] out of love, knowing that I have been appointed for a gospel defense;* [17]*the former proclaim Christ out of selfish partisanship, not sincerely, for they imagine that they will stir up trouble in that I am in my chains.* [18]*What*

---

127. See Asaṅga, *Realm of Awakening*, 218.

128. Collange, *Epistle of Saint Paul*, 51: Paul's "attitude could only be an initiative which the imprisoned apostle has taken in order to be set free, doubtless by revealing his Roman citizenship. Having himself perhaps entertained the idea of 'glorifying Christ' (v. 19) by martyrdom, Paul realized as time went by that the occasion had not yet arrived and that for the present the Gospel demanded his life rather than his death. It is easy to see that this sudden turn about could have opened him to the charge of cowardice, especially in the light of the Cross itself." Collange adds, "Paul offers no theological justification for his choice—it is merely *anangkaioteron* (v. 24), more profitable or more necessary; and this is no more than to state a subjective principle of opportunism" (ibid., 52).

129. Chuang Tzu, *Complete Works*, 302.

does it matter? Just this: that Christ is preached in every way, whether in pretense or in truth, for in that I rejoice.

1:15 Τινὲς μὲν καὶ διὰ φθόνον καὶ ἔριν, τινὲς δὲ καὶ δι' εὐδοκίαν τὸν Χριστὸν κηρύσσουσιν: ¹⁶οἱ μὲν ἐξ ἀγάπης, εἰδότες ὅτι εἰς ἀπολογίαν τοῦ εὐαγγελίου κεῖμαι, ¹⁷οἱ δὲ ἐξ ἐριθείας τὸν Χριστὸν καταγγέλλουσιν, οὐχ ἁγνῶς, οἰόμενοι θλῖψιν ἐγείρειν τοῖς δεσμοῖς μου. ¹⁸τί γάρ; πλὴν ὅτι παντὶ τρόπῳ, εἴτε προφάσει εἴτε ἀληθείᾳ, Χριστὸς καταγγέλλεται, καὶ ἐν τούτῳ χαίρω.

Who are the ones who preach Christ "out of jealous contention" (διὰ φθόνον καὶ ἔριν), as Paul says? Who are those who are intent on selfish partisanship (ἐξ ἐριθείας) and preach Christ "without sincerity" (οὐχ ἁγνῶς)? It seems unlikely that Paul would rejoice even in insincere preaching, for how would that help the faith to flourish and thrive?¹³⁰ Perhaps it is not that these preachers are insincere in their gospel preaching itself but that their insincerity lies elsewhere—in alloying the gospel with their own partisan concerns. Paul further describes these preachers as intent on a factional godly "ambition" (ἐριθεία) that engenders contention and strife (ἔρις). Disputation may have been an admired exercise in Paul's time,¹³¹ but it would hardly have served to further the gospel.¹³² One exegete notes that the cognate form for "one who is ambitious" (ἔριθος) refers to "a mercenary" who is ambitious for his own gain.¹³³

But Paul is not saying that these preachers are seeking personal gain or to satisfy personal self-interest. He says that they do "preach the Christ" (τὸν Χριστὸν κηρύσσουσιν) and that he "rejoices in that" (καὶ ἐν τούτῳ χαίρω), for they do not, like some other opponents, preach a different gospel. Nor do these preachers appear to be the "Judaizers" (so called by the exegetes), who demand circumcision and observance of dietary rules among Christ followers. Rather, these are fellow preachers and coworkers with Paul, perhaps both in Ephesus and in Philippi. Thus, exegetes puzzle over exactly who these preachers who preach Christ from contention and partisanship might have been.

These are not opponents of Paul whom we might recognize from his other letters. Commentators on Paul's letter to the Romans identify his opponents there from the

---

130. Vincent, *Critical and Exegetical Commentary*, 22: "Christianity thrives even through insincere preaching."

131. See Reumann, *Philippians*, 178, on strife (*eris*): "Greeks divinized Dispute or Emulation, which they considered the energizing spirit of the world and one of the primordial forces (C. Spicq, *Theological Lexicon of the New Testament* [Peabody: Hendrickson, 1994] 2:71)." Again, Reumann, writes, "In the NT, 'Paul virtually holds the copyright' on its [*eris*, strife] use (Schütz, 161) for church divisions and controversies" (ibid., 200).

132. I read Paul here, as in the factional disputes in 1 Cor, not as adopting any position in factional disputes, but rather as adopting a strategy to focus on what is most profitable in clearing a space for the advance of the gospel within his culture and times.

133. Max Zerwick, *Analysis philologica Novi Testamenti graeci* (Rome: Pontificii Instituti Biblici, 1953) 439. Also consider "one for hire" (Vincent, *Critical and Exegetical Commentary*, 21).

way they are reflected in the rhetoric of that letter.[134] Paul argues there against someone identified only as "The Judge" or "The Teacher"; he appears to be a self-righteous Christian teacher, not the Christian trope of a "stereotypical Jew"[135] but a Christian preacher who insists that the gospel does entail Torah observance—including circumcision, dietary regulations, and religious festivals.[136] Perhaps such teachers insisted on that observance in order to keep their communities identifiably Jewish and thus legal under Roman law.

In Resurrection Letter C of this Philippian correspondence, Paul dismisses in no uncertain terms those who insist that all Christians be circumcised as a necessary mark of their faith; he even calls them "dogs." Paul's ire is stirred whenever the gospel of free and risen life in Christ is circumscribed within divisive identity walls by any preacher, even one who lives and preaches within the Christ communities. For example, in Corinth Paul caricatures opponents who are clearly Christians as self-satisfied individuals: "already realized, already fulfilled, already entered into the kingdom" (1 Cor 4:8). By contrast, when Paul was blithely dismissed by the Athenian philosophers on the Areopagus, he did not launch into a diatribe but simply noted that this gospel of resurrection faith appears as foolishness to them. He saves his harsh rhetoric for Christian factions or preachers who would reserve the free offer of risen life to their communities. In this passage his words are milder, however, and he acknowledges that these are coworkers who preach the same Christ in whose risen life Paul rejoices. It is just that, although preaching the very same Christ, they do so from a position of contention and party spirit, and they seem to hope to gain some partisan advantage from the fact of Paul's imprisonment.

Perhaps the immediate issue is one of strategy—whether Christians ought to confront Rome, as Paul is doing by asserting his citizenship status, or should instead avoid such confrontation—and these Christian preachers reject Paul's strategic submission to imprisonment. But the text here does not clarify what their position is. They all preach the same content, which is Christ and his resurrection, so the issue is not correct doctrine or understanding of the gospel message. Perhaps they are simply unconvinced that Paul's orders (κεῖμαι, keimai) indeed come from Christ, or that Christ has appointed him to defend the gospel. After all, Paul received no prior approval from the Jerusalem apostles. But he contends that these preachers "know that I have been appointed for a Gospel defense" (εἰδότες ὅτι εἰς ἀπολογίαν τοῦ εὐαγγελίου κεῖμαι 1:16) and nevertheless indulge in partisan preaching.

---

134. See Stowers, *Rereading of Romans*, for a reading of that epistle within its historical and rhetorical contexts of meaning. On "The Teacher," see ibid., 143–58.

135. See "Stereotyping Judaism" in Amy-Jill Levine, *The Misunderstood Jew: The Church and the Scandal of the Jewish Jesus* (New York: HarperOne, 2007) 119–66.

136. See Stowers, *Rereading of Romans*, and also Campbell, *Deliverance of God*, 765–832, on Romans.

If these preachers did think Paul an upstart apostle, they might well have seen his imprisonment as an opportunity to further their own gospel strategy by throwing him to the Roman lions and casting him as an example of a rejectionist stance like that championed in the book of Revelation. But, as critical scholars have convincingly shown, Paul is hardly a radical reformer opposing the cultural norms of his time.[137] He is, rather, an apostle of an ambiguous freedom to all hearers—even the entire Praetorian Guard (ἐν ὅλῳ τῷ πραιτωρίῳ 1:13) holding him in prison. Although Paul is energized to preach a gospel of liberation from any identity markers that other Christ preachers might impose upon communities, he is hardly a partisan of social freedom from Roman society or culture. Opposed as he is to any norms that would define the follower of Christ, he nevertheless certainly does see his Christian critics in partisan terms: "they see my imprisonment as as a chance to stir up trouble" (οἰόμενοι θλῖψιν ἐγείρειν τοῖς δεσμοῖς μου 1:17).

Paul today is seen as a singular and foundational figure in the history of Christian mission, and so it is difficult for us to imagine him as not fully accepted by his gospel coworkers. But his letters clearly reveal that Paul had his opponents, although it is a challenge to discern the identity of those he criticizes or the context of their disagreements. Whoever the "insincere" preachers in this passage may be, we only learn something about their character traits—that they are contentious and fractious. Perhaps the point that Paul intends to make here, in any case, is that even if someone preaches the gospel within a factional or party context, still it is an announcement of the life, death, and resurrection of the Lord, and in that he rejoices. Some embarrassed commentators perform exegetical gymnastics to reach the conclusion that these "selfish" preachers are hostile not to Paul, but to the authorities who imprisoned him.[138] Or possibly they were itinerant preachers who held a different notion of Christ. Then again, they may have been preachers who simply felt a personal rivalry with Paul. But the text supports none of these interpretations; it expresses only Paul's understanding of these preachers' motivations, which is that they wish to stir up trouble about his imprisonment. The rest is speculative, no matter how necessary for interpreting our text.

Perhaps it is best to see these preachers simply as factional—good team players who are attempting to protect the gospel message from all other parties. If they did regard Paul as an upstart apostle, they very well may have "seen my imprisonment as a chance to stir up trouble" (οἰόμενοι θλῖψιν ἐγείρειν τοῖς δεσμοῖς μου 1:17). Their "lack of sincerity" (οὐχ ἁγνῶς 1:17) in that case is not global or motivated by petty personal jealousy, but would rather reflect party postures and positions. If they were

---

137. See Ruden, *Paul Among the People*, 148, in which Ruden critiques the contention in Crossan and Reed's *In Search of Paul* that Paul rejected slavery. Her criticism is grounded on comprehensive attentiveness to the Greco-Roman literature, as it sets the social parameters within which the early communities lived.

138. T. Hawthorn, "Philippians i.12–19: With Special Reference to vv. 15.16.17," *Expository Times* 62 (1950–1951) 316–17; and F. C. Synge, *Philippians and Colossians* (London: SCM, 1951) 24–25, cited in O'Brien, *Epistle to the Philippians*, 103.

theological rejectionists, as in the book of Revelation, Paul certainly would not have agreed with them, for he was no advocate of opposing the social and cultural norms of his time. Paul is an apostle of freedom to all, including the Praetorian Guard (ἐν ὅλῳ τῷ πραιτωρίῳ 1:13) holding him in prison; surely that alone would gall anyone whose gospel strategy was to reject the Empire and its values. Only by the exercise of great exegetical sleight of hand could Paul be construed as a radical partisan for freedom *from* Roman society or culture.[139] If, on the other hand, his opponents' social stance was accommodationist toward the surrounding culture, they certainly would not have welcomed Paul's imprisonment, resulting as it did from his own appeal to Roman citizenship. In sum, Paul does not see the gospel from the same viewpoint as his critics, whatever their stance may be, and "they see Paul's imprisonment as a chance to stir up trouble." Clearly, Paul's adversaries in his own time did not regard him with the same awe and reverence we have learned over the past two millennia.[140]

There remains much space in which to exercise one's exegetical imagination regarding these contentious preachers. For my part, I see them as insisting on their cultural and social evaluation of how the church communities are to prosper and how Paul's situation hinders that prosperity, whether from purists who demand a confrontational stance against the Empire or from assimilationists who would rather soft-pedal the issue until some later day. In either case, they are caught in their "imaginings" (οἰόμενοι) and are thus attached to their staunch positions. Paul, meanwhile, is weighing the most skillful alternatives in a delicate situation where communities whose faith undermines Roman ideology must still of necessity live within a world defined by Roman power. Paul never was a team player, but his critics insist on team spirit.

For his part, Paul is content "that I have been appointed" (ὅτι . . . κεῖμαι) "for a gospel defense" (εἰς ἀπολογίαν τοῦ εὐαγγλίου 1:16).[141] He never claims he has been arrested in the night like Jesus in the garden, and the textual evidence of this Philippian

---

139. Pace Horsley, who holds that "Paul reflects a 'counter imperial mission' and 'alternate society'" (R. A. Horsley, "Paul and Slavery: A Critical Alternative to Recent Readings," in Callahan et al., *Semeia* 83–84, 176).

140. It is very difficult to question the privileged status of Paul within the tradition. See Castelli, *Imitating Paul*, 35–36: "My focus on Paul is a matter of necessity, because this text is the earliest coherent expression of what one might call an early Christian position. In contrast to some other interpreters I do not attempt to privilege Paul's viewpoint or position. I do, however, claim that Paul himself does just that and the later tradition reinscribes this privilege." Castelli's reliance on Foucault, however, grants that postmodern philosopher a highly privileged status in analyzing the power relationships in Paul's discourse. Ruden, situating Paul in his time and place, does a better job of avoiding either claims for Paul as radical social reformer or as reinscribing power in *Paul Among the People*.

141. Collange, *Epistle of Saint Paul*, 47: "'[A]pologia' often in the New Testament means the defence made by an accused person before a tribunal (Acts 19:33; 22:1; 25:16, etc.). So Paul is alluding to his imminent appearance in court at Ephesus brought about by the revealing of his true citizenship." Collange adds, "The application of the word [*apologia*] to the Gospel, which occurs only here and at 1:7, therefore denotes that by making his own personal defence the apostle proposes to offer a defence of the Gospel also (cf. v. 13)" (ibid., 57).

letter does suggest that in some way Paul welcomes his situation. His words here lend credence to the Acts account of Paul in Ephesus—that he refused freedom by making an appeal to his citizenship, forcing the Roman officials to send him in chains to Rome, all for the sake of the gospel. He wants to bring the issue to a head and solve it once and for all.

It is not difficult to see how other Christian preachers would think Paul's action ill advised, perhaps unnecessarily putting him and thus the entire Christian movement in legal jeopardy. The verb he uses in explaining that he has "been appointed" was originally a military term and is often interpreted theologically as a "divine passive." In other words, Paul was divinely appointed for this defense of the gospel: he has been commissioned (κεῖμαι) and has received his marching orders. Perhaps, more concretely, the word refers to his prospective trial and the defense of the faith he will make there. As Acts 23:11 reports: "That night the Lord stood near him and said, 'Keep up your courage! For just as you have testified for me in Jerusalem, so you must bear witness also in Rome.'" In chains, Paul is not actually the master of his own life, and neither does the Lord set his trial date. But it does seem likely that he has been given a court date when he is to appear before some magistrate or other. This is another obvious meaning for the passive voice in Paul's statement that "I have been appointed for a Gospel defense"—not that God has ordered him, but that the Roman judge has. He is under indictment[142] and required to make a defense—an opportunity Paul welcomes just as "those who preach out of love recognize" (οἱ μὲν ἐξ ἀγάπης εἰδότες 1:16). They cherish Paul; they know and love him.[143]

The irony is that Paul has been ordered by Roman law to appear in a Roman court, and he has also been ordered by God to defend the gospel. These two points, although not identified in the minds of the insincere Christ preachers, are indeed identified in the mind of Paul, who sees in the empty Christ a more-than-empirical vindication. So, even in chains, Paul prepares himself to be "transparent and not contentious" (εἰλικρινεῖς καὶ ἀπρόσκοποι 1:10) on his day in court, which he has identified as his "day of Christ" (εἰς ἡμέραν Χριστοῦ 1:10), or his own moment of eschatological witness. Paul will make his defense in love and gentleness in neither ecclesiastical nor civil contention. Such love goes beyond the tribal altruism of party spirit. Faith is a communal engagement, not a team sport.

"Others however" (Τινὲς μὲν καὶ . . . οἱ δὲ) apparently neither cherish Paul nor recognize his commission, and so they stir up trouble because Paul welcomes the opportunity to witness from prison. Paul was not the recognized head of the early communities, and his life has not yet become the cause célèbre it became in later times.

---

142. O'Brien, *Epistle to the Philippians*, 101. But Collange adds, "The verb '*keimai*' could simply mean 'I am here, in this situation, so that . . . ;' unless it is taken with the sharper meaning of 'I am appointed, put here (by God) so that . . . '" (Collange, *Epistle of Saint Paul*, 57).

143. Collange, *Epistle of Saint Paul*, 49. This love (*agapē*) is "not so much as of absolute value (as in Barth, Beare, Gnilka, Lohmeyer) but as the love which the Philippians have just shown to Paul (Bonnard)" (ibid.).

Despite Paul's assertion in 1:30 that his ordeal is the same (τὸν αὐτὸν ἀγῶνα) that they all experience as Christ followers in a legally delicate situation, the other preachers are motivated "by jealous contention" (Τινὲς μὲν καὶ διὰ φθόνον καὶ ἔριν 1:15) and preach Christ from selfish partisanship or party spirit (οἱ δὲ ἐξ ἐριθείας τὸν Χριστὸν καταγγέλλουσιν 1:17). Those preachers, moved by the gospel and saved by Christ faith, see *themselves* as the champions of a gospel party, and so they are sealed within a factionalism that encloses them in their preacherly status. Although brothers and sisters in the faith, Paul describes them as acting from a spirit of jealous contention (φθόνος καὶ ἔρις), not an uncommon phenomenon among marginalized social factions.

It is not at all difficult to imagine these early communities smarting from feelings of being marginalized. It is a difficult thing to be elected out of the world and yet to avoid factionalism. Consequently, some function from a spiritual factionalism (ἐριθεία) in taking the gospel as yet another religious viewpoint or social option among many others—the best option, to be sure, but still in competition with lesser alternatives. Competition may indeed drive our evolutionary history, and it certainly has a clear impact on economic growth, but it finds scant justification in the gospel. In our day, some insist on a liberal gospel program, some on a conservative one. Yet, whenever we reduce the gospel to a viewpoint or a program, we encourage factionalism and construct dividing walls.

Paul shows himself to be intent on breaking down such factional divides by launching his harshest critiques against those who draw boundaries beyond which the risen life of Christ does not extend. But Paul is neither a revolutionary social figure nor a conservative protector of cultural values. He is a wily gospel strategist. When Paul mentions the Praetorian Guard, he does so without a whiff of revolutionary resentment or ideological anger. At the end of this Letter B, he sends greetings from those "in Caesar's household," for they are among the people in his circle of friends. The gospel Paul preaches is a gospel of the dying and rising Christ with whom we may be one and in whom we are enabled to die and rise. That gospel is hardly the affirmation of anybody's political stance or traditional life values.

Paul does offer culturally sensitive negotiations on a host of current issues, without either accommodating cultural values and social institutions or wasting lives in bootless resistance to them. His central concern, which is to announce the gospel teaching, would hardly hold up in any court that values empirical evidence. Still, even with all its eschatological hope, this Philippian letter recommends sensible political choices, so long as they are honorable and praiseworthy. The gospel is not a recommendation to substitute one set of cultural goals for another or to adopt one social program as more effective than another; all goals and programs can merely sketch envisioned linear futures. The gospel is imaginable only in end-time terms—which is to say that it is not imaginable at all. It is the undermining of all programmed goals and philosophic options in favor of awakened participation in life identified as risen with Christ.

Paul often writes polemically, but he is no Spartacus who rebels against institutionalized slavery, as both Onesimus and Philemon learned. He frequently does find himself in conflict with other people—people within the church assemblies as well as people in the broader social and political world. But he is not himself a sectarian thinker.[144] Rather, Paul finds that "in Christ" all self-protective distinctions and all ideological differences are swallowed up and rendered naught.[145] No Greek and no Jew. No male and no female. No rich and no poor (Gal 3:28). This is a revolutionary teaching indeed, but it offers no strategic revolutionary program to bring it about. Paul does not speak much about the kingdom of God, the Synoptic Gospel teaching cherished by later social reformers and liberationists. His letters do not reflect the Synoptic Gospels' end-time hopes for the almost-here arrival of the just and peaceful kingdom. The Philippians did not expect a Messiah, for in their Greco-Roman world a savior signified the kind of political deliverance that is embodied in emperors and kings. There was no need to wean the people of Philippi from Palestinian expectations of a political messiah; they were not looking for one. But Paul does look toward the coming of Jesus Christ.

In the words of Luke Timothy Johnson, when Paul meets party conflict as he did in Corinth, he opts not for one side or the other but to stand squarely for righteousness beyond any ideological position—not being right but being righteous.[146] This is why he fights so insistently against reducing the gospel to an ideological program or a one-and-only strategy. The gospel cannot be posted on the bulletin boards of our deluded minds or argued in the courts; it has to be realized internally. It is not an ideologically defensible position among other sorts of positions; rather it is existentially grounded in the courses along which our lives flow, leading and leaving people judiciously to make their own social and political decisions. This becomes apparent in 2:3–4 and 4:8–9, both passages included in Letter B. We are to be our own politicians; God is not a partisan God. The gospel path abides in the middle, between extremes, but it is not a middle that hovers equidistantly between two contrasting poles. It is a middle that embraces the practice of both living in Christ and dying with Christ.

Although Paul was attracted by some Stoic ideas, he adopted none of the available philosophies of his day, which is why the church fathers were later free to employ an adapted version of Greek metaphysics. Paul, like Plato, wants us to practice dying, but not as abandonment of the world for a higher truth. We are instead to transform the world, for that is what risen life in Christ means: We practice dying and rising not as frightful events to be sealed off into a "rather-not-think-about-that" future, but as

---

144. See Campbell, *Paul and the Creation*, 46–50.

145. Castelli, *Imitating Paul*, 41, notes: "That Foucault focuses so much of his analysis on the construction of the 'deviant' is no accident. For Foucault, the identification of the 'other' is what enables the production of identity and the privileging of the 'same.'" According to the work of neuroscientists I have read, that encounter with the other is indeed crucial for the development of self-awareness. Yet, the horizons of *agapē* broaden self-awareness to include all sentient beings.

146. See "Lecture 6: Life in the World—First Corinthians" in Johnson, *Apostle Paul*.

practices to be embraced in their indivisibility with here-and-now life. Living and dying are everyday events of our gospel faith. Certainly church people attend a great number of funerals.

And so here Paul has been called to offer a gospel defense of the course of his life and his actions in some political court, whether in Rome or Caesarea or Ephesus. Yet his defense is a no-defense, for this gospel is not a defensible ideology. He does not plead simply his own innocence but defends this sometimes-troubling gospel. This fact is recognized by some of Paul's coworkers "who preach Christ out of good will, out of love" (τινὲς δὲ καὶ δι' εὐδοκίαν τὸν Χριστὸν κηρύσσουσιν . . . οἱ μὲν ἐξ ἀγάπης 1:15–16), for that is the only visible mark of gospel living. They know and acknowledge (εἰδόντες) the call that has been given to Paul for his day in court, and they expect him to follow his own advice in his gospel defense—that it will be transparently pure and without offense, embodying the love of Christ throughout.

Paul's "Gospel defense" (εἰς ἀπολογίαν τοῦ εὐαγγελίου) is often understood as "a defense of the Gospel." After all, it is reasonable to think that his task is to defend the gospel he preaches, for this is why he is in chains. So the phrase is often taken to be an objective genitive–with the second term, "the Gospel," as the object of the action of the first term, "defending." However, it may be better to see it as a subjective genitive: a defense that is informed by this gospel that has grasped Paul. He is to offer not a defense of the objective truth of the gospel, but a gospel-informed defense of Christian communities in the Greco-Roman world. He merely wants to testify once and for all that the communities of faith pose no imminent, revolutionary threat to the common order and should be left alone to spread their more-than-revolutionary message of freedom. These are early days in our common history when the communities had yet to make very much impact on the broader world, so Paul does not want anyone to discredit the Christian communities and prevent their growth. He wants to give a defense that is informed by the gospel and inspired by the good news of the risen Christ so as to articulate a gospel-infused defense for all the Christ followers in their varied gatherings.

Since the text lacks specificity about those other, questionably-motivated preachers, we would do best to listen to Paul, who says merely that some preachers, in their factional insistence, do not act "sincerely" (οὐχ ἁγνῶς). They do not act sincerely precisely because they are caught in factional images. Paul's irenic attitude toward them befuddles easy commentary, for one might expect Paul to criticize people who act from self-serving motives. But he recognizes that they are well intentioned in their preaching for the furtherance of the gospel. Perhaps such people envisage a legal circus wherein Paul will either vanquish his accusers and vindicate the gospel, or—as they fear—the gospel will be criminalized by his failure. In either case, these are fellow Christ followers who are motivated by party sectarianism. They are presenting the gospel as an ideology over against the prevailing culture, and they "stir up trouble" (θλῖψιν ἐγείρειν) because of Paul's chains (τοῖς δεσμοῖς μου). Perhaps they are preachers who, unlike Paul, continue to insist upon their own self-sufficiency.

In Christian history, there have been more than a few such junctures when different factions rallied around particular figures or points of view. Paul, however, clearly does not regard Jesus as a visionary figure around whom we are to rally. Perhaps that is why he neglects to give us any picture of the historical Jesus as a hero. In 1 Corinthians, the "Jesus party" is one of the factions that Paul rejects; for social and political stances—even when informed by gospel freedom—remain social and political stances. In this letter, Paul instructs the Philippians to be skillfully attuned to the times and attentive to the conditions of their lives. If they are, they will see his situation in a favorable light as the conventional endeavor it is. He is doing the same thing here as he did with the Corinthian community when he distanced himself from the various factions of Apollo, of Paul, and of Christ. Paul does not regard himself as the champion of one party over another; that is the whole point of his stance against factionalism among the Corinthians, and the same is true here.[147] Some of Paul's coworkers want him to serve as such a symbol because they "imagine" (οἰόμενοι) that thereby they will be able to stir up trouble and win the day. Much like the disciples in the Synoptic Gospels, they wish their Christ to win the day and not to suffer but instead to emerge fresh with victory and to be recognized as innocent. Yet Paul does not entrust himself to their imaginations.

While his coworkers are caught up in their imaginations and want to make trouble, Paul is intent on preaching this crucified and defenseless Christ whose resurrection constitutes no empirical victory at all. His coworkers thrive on their imagination (οἰόμενοι), motivated by their self-referential interest in what is right and true. The term "imagining" (Skt. *parikalpa*) reverberates in Mahāyāna discourse. In the Yogācāra philosophy, there is an extended discourse on the three different patterns of mental attentiveness. The perfected (*pariniṣpanna*) pattern of one who is awakened entails insight into the emptiness of things and their dependently-arising occurrences. The second, synergistic or other-dependent (*paratantra*) pattern of mind is freed from clinging to imagined truths, enabled to gain critical insight into the structure and activity of our thinking, and understands that things arise from a host of causes and conditions; it does not therefore freeze things in fixed images.[148] The third pattern of

---

147. "Excursus: The 'Parties'" in Hans Conzelmann, *1 Corinthians: A Commentary on the First Epistle to the Corinthians* (Philadelphia: Fortress, 1975) 33–38, esp. 38: "The transformation of the understanding of faith into the support of a standpoint leads automatically to a multiplicity of standpoints, and hence to division. Over against this, Paul defines his position first of all in negative terms, as a nonstandpoint."

148. Compare Gazzaniga, *Who's In Charge?*, 102: "The view in neuroscience today is that consciousness does not constitute a single, generalized process. It is becoming increasingly clear that consciousness involves a multitude of widely distributed specialized systems and disunited processes, the products of which are integrated in a dynamic manner by the interpreter module." The "interpreter" here refers to the self-awareness that unifies all the disparate sensations, insight, and judgments into coherent wholes. For Gazzaniga, the concern is to understand and defend self-awareness

mind is that of fantasy—"clinging to what is imagined" (*parikalpita*), wherein—like Paul's misled coworkers—one attends only to images without ever gaining insight into their meaning. This image-driven attentiveness concentrates, laser-like, on one's own ideas or party ambition.

That third, imagined pattern of thinking, even when it enunciates true doctrine, leads to pain and suffering, rejection and misunderstanding, and—what is here to the point—to a diminished capacity to work for the position-free gospel. Frozen at imagined images and lacking insight, such persons become idealists, both by mistaking their images as real and by reducing the gospel to a program of ideas. They preach Christ in pretense as a "smokescreen" (εἴτε προφάσει 1:18) for their own religious self-interest. They incorporate a true belief into their own expanded self-power, fusing that self with a partisan Christ belief without ever allowing the knowledge and wisdom of Christ to enter deeply into their minds and uproot their selfish assurances. Yet whether they act "in pretense or in truth" (εἴτε προφάσει εἴτε ἀληθείᾳ), still they preach the very same risen Christ.

So Paul asks in 1:18, "What is one to make of this situation?" (τί γάρ)—a situation in which his coworkers, who share in Christ, apparently wish him to represent their own party stance, pushing him forward as a symbol around which others might coalesce in a broader cultural movement to the benefit of this gospel. If they are belligerent young Christ followers, they may well be saying: "Let's you and them fight." Or, if more timorous elders: "Let's you and them *not* fight." For Paul in prison, there's not much to say, for events are already in motion, so he concludes with "only this" (πλὴν): "that in all ways" (ὅτι παντὶ τρόπῳ) of attending to our shared reality in the risen Christ, he himself truly and unreservedly "rejoices in this one singular fact" (καὶ ἐν τούτῳ χαίρω) "that Christ is indeed made known" (Χριστὸς καταγγέλλεται).

Even partisan preachers preach the same Christ, despite their failure to understand the wisdom that is awakening in Christ. Whether one preaches with a mind grounded in awakened truth (εἴτε ἀληθείᾳ),[149] or with a mind caught "in mere appearances" (εἴτε προφάσει), it is the enunciation of the Christ gospel that matters. Whether one preaches with a mind awakened to the dependently arisen complexity of actual conditions, or with a mind affixed to imagined realities, it is the enunciation of gospel truth that matters. The phrase "in every way" (παντὶ τρόπῳ) is more than a meaningless modifier; it displays Paul's awareness that mindset or "character" (τρόπος)

---

against scientific determinism. For Yogācāra, the concern is to free our consciousness from taking its constructs as conduits of assured truth and reality.

149. Reumann, *Philippians*, 184, notes that "Bultmann (*TDNT*, 1:232–51), and others made much of the etymology (*alpha* privative [BDF 117.1] + lanthanō, lēthō, a vb. that means 'hide'; therefore, 'not hidden,' 'what is seen, expressed, or disclosed')." That etymology reflects Heidegger's understanding of truth, or ἀλήθεια, as the uncovering of what is forgotten and hidden, as in William J. Richardson, *Heidegger: Through Phenomenology to Thought* (The Hague: Msrtinus Nijhoff, 1963) 484–89. It also parallels the Yogācāra notion of conventional truth as revelatory (*saṃvṛti-udbhāvana*), for what is hidden (*saṃvṛta*) by that very fact marks a truth covered by langauge.

differs from preacher to preacher, much as do the "patterns" (Skt. *lakṣaṇa*; *svabhāva*) of consciousness that figure so centrally in the Yogācāra critical understanding of our own understanding.

Because the patterns of human activity become ingrained in us over the course of our genetic and biological living, we spontaneously react to images that trigger survival responses.[150] However, this common pattern in our deluded struggle for the survival of self may be countered through engaged meditative practice, which can induce a reversal of the habit of clinging to our cherished images so that we come to recognize the world as it is—radically transient, lacking in any enduring support for selfhood, and extending far beyond the stable confines of any self-definition.

Of all the traditions within Mahāyāna, it is the Yogācāra thinkers who focus exceptional attention upon the consciousness that underlies our living—both the commonly deluded state of our consciousness and the potential to reverse that delusion by awakening to wisdom and compassion.[151] The religious traditions do not rest easily with the determinism of some neuroscience; however, their teachings demonstrate a clear awareness of the human drive toward repetitive karmic entanglement in the delusion, greed, and anger that characterize our evolutionary heritage and inscribe themselves on our neural structures. Paul is likewise aware—both of the distortions in some of the gospel preaching against which he reacts so strongly, and also of the distortions in the minds of those partisan preachers he criticizes as contentious trouble seekers.

Seldom in our human experience do we encounter a person whose witness is unalloyed; more often we see there a mixture of wisdom and foolishness. "Trouble-seeking" preachers are often frozen in the mere appearance of gospel teaching, as if the images and ideas they entertain actually represent the reality of the world around us. Still, they can and do preach Christ from within their constricted horizon. Despite his protestations to the contrary, even Paul is not immune to selfish desires, which is why he is so circumspect in explaining his present course of action and why he so enthusiastically embraces the empty Christ as the path to liberation.

Better not to cling to images and to move instead in a mind of truth which, awakened to the essence-free emptiness of things, is able to function skillfully in garnering insight into the images that flow through our minds and uprooting habit-engendered seeds that would otherwise proliferate into a jungle of delusion and factional violence. One cannot beat Rome by being factionally anti-Roman, for the realpolitik that rules nations for their own political interest—and churches for their own ecclesiastical

---

150. See James Atlas, "The Amygdala Made Me Do It," *New York Times Sunday Review*, May 12, 2012, which discusses the work of Jonah Lehrer, Charles Duhigg, Daniel Kahneman, and Leonard Mlodinow on the neurobiology of our organic brains.

151. The closest parallel among western theologians is found in the philosophic works of Bernard Lonergan on critical understanding, but he was never able to translate his philosophic insight into the theologies of the church, encrusted as they were in a naïve medieval ontology.

benefit—easily slips into a deluded game of fools who are all too ready to impose their discordant realities on others through war, mayhem, or quiet exclusion.

Paul never reveals himself to have reached any final personal or social stance, much to the regret of both progressive and conservative Christians who would like to claim him for their side. Nor does he offer a philosophical explication of the patterns of human consciousness as did the Yogācāra philosophers. He is not a philosophical thinker. Even in his gospel commitments, he never claims to have reached any goal at all; in his concluding letter to the Philippians on resurrection faith and Christ knowledge, he describes himself only and always to be "stretching forth" or "pressing on" toward the goal (3:12–16). Of one thing alone he is sure: He has been called to offer a gospel-inspired defense, and this is the reason he critiques those who wish to engage in imagined factional struggles, even if they are his coworkers.

Paul does rejoice that Christ is being preached, despite the factional attitude of some of the other preachers. But he criticizes those who, in one way or another, imagine a scenario of symbolic victory. He would not have been pleased to learn of the legend of some three centuries later that Constantine the Great was vouchsafed a vision of the cross of Christ as a sign of victory ("*In hoc signo vinces*," the vision informed him).[152] Such victory-seekers are unable to "recognize" (εἰδότες) that—although Paul has been "given his marching orders" (κεῖμαι) "to mount a gospel defense" (εἰς ἀπολογίαν τοῦ εὐαγγελίου)—he does not share their ideological stance. Nor could they understand his apparent unconcern about the outcome of his own imprisonment.

Unfortunately, we do not know the outcome of Paul's endeavors, for after he wrote the letters that have come down to us, he passed into the great silence of those who have been rendered mute. In the historical event, Paul's death went unreported, and he passed quietly from the scene. Possibly his strategy for a skillfully nuanced defense of the gospel did succeed in court, but he himself was then swallowed up in Nero's persecution. We have no way of knowing. In any case, some three centuries later, the Roman Empire itself would become Christian under Emperor Constantine. And then Christianity did begin to erect walls between insiders and outsiders in earnest, building a vastly powerful alliance with Roman power and constricting the gospel into the ontological enclosures of our shared and sorry history.

---

152. Nor would Paul have been pleased with Eusebius. On Eusebius, see Mitchell, *Church, Gospel, and Empire*, 28–59, in which he concludes: "As a result of the continued masking of the human kenotic Jesus consequent on the assumption of the imperial nature of divine sovereignty, the originally counterpolitical impact of the Gospel was gradually displaced from the developing Christendom." Mitchell goes on to examine the "continuing impulses of this ontologically configured sovereignty" through selected "conduits" or representative chapters in the history of the tradition (ibid., 59).

Christ Enlarged (1:18b–20)

> 1:18b *Yes, and I will continue to rejoice,* ¹⁹*for I know that through your entreaties and Jesus Christ whom the Spirit supplies this will turn out for my deliverance,* ²⁰*[all] in accord with my eager longing and hope: that in no way will I be put to shame, but that with full openness, in my body Christ will be enlarged now as always, whether by life or by death.*

> 1:18b ἀλλὰ καὶ χαρήσομαι. ¹⁹οἶδα γὰρ ὅτι τοῦτό μοι ἀποβήσεται εἰς σωτηρίαν διὰ τῆς ὑμῶν δεήσεως καὶ ἐπιχορηγίας τοῦ πνεύματος Ἰησοῦ Χριστοῦ, ²⁰κατὰ τὴν ἀποκαραδοκίαν καὶ ἐλπίδα μου ὅτι ἐν οὐδενὶ αἰσχυνθήσομαι, ἀλλ' ἐν πάσῃ παρρησίᾳ ὡς πάντοτε καὶ νῦν μεγαλυνθήσεται Χριστὸς ἐν τῷ σώματί μου, εἴτε διὰ ζωῆς εἴτε διὰ θανάτου.

Paul "continues to rejoice" (ἀλλὰ καὶ χαρήσομαι 1:18b), because he feels confident that he will be acquitted. His refuge and support lies in "the entreaties" of the Philippians (διὰ τῆς ὑμῶν δεήσεως) and "Jesus Christ whom the Spirit supplies" (καὶ ἐπιχορηγίας τοῦ πνεύματος Ἰησοῦ Χριστοῦ).[153] "For I know" (οἶδα γάρ), he says, that all "this will turn out for my salvation" (ὅτι τοῦτό μοι ἀποβήσεται εἰς σωτηρίαν 1:19). Paul is sure that this imprisonment he embraces will result in acquittal, that he will be released from his chains, and that his gospel defense will be accepted. In historical hindsight, perhaps those who feared his imprisonment would not result in the furtherance of the gospel were correct, and Paul's insistence on his chosen strategy was simply mistaken. Maybe things did not turn out as he expected. The extant textual and historical witnesses do not provide enough evidence for any certainty. Perhaps factional preachers, driven as they were by gospel jealousy, would have been better served to welcome martyrdom.[154] Maybe Paul was wrong, and those who opted for a conciliatory strategy were not moved by selfish motives at all. No scriptural authority guarantees the accuracy of Paul's personal evaluation of others.

Paul's strategy never really was a sure thing, and in 1:20 he does entertain the possibility of failure: he might lose his life, or his gospel defense might fall on deaf ears. Gospel strategies are not disclosed to us through gospel faith. These are fully worldly, contextual decisions, depending upon our prudential insight into common experiences, and issuing in carefully weighed judgments rightly called "knowledge" (οἶδα). Yet human judgments may miss the mark; one can hardly take every factor

---

153. Following Reumann, *Philippians*, 209–12, who interprets the phrase epexegetically, with "Spirit" in apposition to "supply," for "Spirit of Christ" is rare in Paul, but often he speaks of the spirit as "a life-giving spirit" (1 Cor 15:45), the unitive linkage between Christ and the believer (1 Cor 6:17). Christ, the empty mirror of the Father, is accessible, not in imagined relationship, but through the spirit who discloses him.

154. The quest for martyrdom is the overarching theme of J. B. Lightfoot, *Saint Paul's Epistle to the Philippians*, The Epistles of Paul 3.1 (London: Macmillan, 1868). He maintains that Paul writes this letter to encourage all to seek such martyrdom.

into account. In light of his own judgment, Paul hopes for acquittal and release based on a persuasive defense "in accord with my eager longing and hope" (κατὰ τὴν ἀποκαραδοκίαν καὶ ἐλπίδα μου) that "in no way (ὅτι ἐν οὐδενὶ) will I be put to shame" (αἰσχυνθήσομαι), whatever occurs.[155] His knowledge here is more personal and modest than any expectation of a grand finale. He is confident, not certain, of the outcome—although, if Letter C is taken into account, he seems to have been freed from prison.

Grounded in the Hebrew scriptures that nurtured and formed him from the time he was a child, Paul—now arrested and in chains—pleads his case to his readers in the manner of Job. The book of Job is a perceptive and troubling scripture, dealing as it does with the universally experienced unfairness of human life and suffering.[156] Quoting a passage from Job here, Paul says that he is sure that (οἶδα γὰρ ὅτι) whether his present circumstances "will turn out for my deliverance" from suffering. That phrase (τοῦτό μοι ἀποβήσεται εἰς σωτηρίαν) exactly reproduces the Septuagint Greek translation of Job 13:16,[157] showing that Paul sees himself as experiencing the same kind of predicament as Job. He does not think he is in chains justly, but "in Christ." But just as Job maintains his faith in God despite his sufferings, so will Paul remain faithful to his Christ faith. Just as Job experiences redemption and salvation, so here also Paul knows that he will share in that ultimate vindication, whether "he receives a favorable or an unfavorable verdict before Caesar's tribunal."[158] Just as Job has to contend with argumentative friends who are confident of their theological understanding of his sufferings, so Paul contends with other Christ preachers who have their own decided slant on the place of gospel faith in the Greco-Roman world. Paul envisages deliverance from the Roman courts, and yet this is more than merely the hope of a favorable judicial ruling that will release him from his chains. Like Job's final vindication, Paul's vindication will be before God as his witness.

Paul lives in an unjust society where random official cruelty could hardly have been unknown to him, so one wonders how he could expect all to turn out aright. Nevertheless, Paul is confident: "indeed I know" (οἶδα γὰρ), he writes, that things will turn out well. Such confident awareness comes not from reliable connections (perhaps with Christ followers in the imperial household), but because of the "entreaties" that the Philippians offer on his behalf (διὰ τῆς ὑμῶν δεήσεως). In scriptural writings, the

---

155. According to Caird, *Paul's Letters from Prison*, 112, "ashamed" means "be daunted, intimidated, or put out of countenance."

156. Collange, *Epistle of Saint Paul*, 59: "It is not suffering in a general sense which has led the apostle to ponder on the Book of Job, but more particularly the dispute even with his friends about his attitude towards it." According to Job 13:16, "This moreover shall be (*'apobēsetai eis*) my salvation."

157. Caird, *Paul's Letters from Prison*, 112, on verse 19: "'[T]his will turn out for my deliverance' should be printed as a quotation. Paul is quoting Job 13:16 in the Septuagint version, and his words are liable to misinterpretation unless we recognize their source." But according to Reumann, "All Old Testament wordings in Philippians are 'embedded,' not cited," for "it is speculative to assume familiarity among the Philippians with the words as Scripture" (Reumann, *Philippians*, 232–33).

158. F. F. Bruce, cited in O'Brien, *Epistle to the Philippians*, 110.

word "entreaty" (δέησις) most often means prayer to God, and so most commentators take it to mean just that here—that the Philippians make prayers to God on Paul's behalf. Yet the verb "to entreat" (δέομαι) does have a broader sense that could include an appeal to worldly authorities. Both kinds of entreaty may be envisaged here—prayers to God on Paul's behalf and entreaties to the Roman legal authorities from Roman citizens in Philippi. Certainly the powerless power of prayer, employed when humans can do little else, would be strengthened by entreaties to Roman judges on behalf of a fellow Roman citizen.

Paul clearly thinks that these entreaties from his friends do help. But prayer evokes the power of not having power, the solidarity of standing with the weak, weakly. It is not as though one person or group of people addresses a prayer request upward to the Great God who then downwardly assists the person prayed for. Prayer is not divine triangulation from one human to God and back to another human. In the poetic body of the book of Job (disregarding the added prose passages—the cosmic preface and the comforting conclusion), Job learns the folly of prayerful triangulation when, in the whirlwind, he encounters a God who has better cosmic things to do. In point of fact, prayers did not deliver Paul, nor did the Father save Jesus from the cross. The scandal of Jesus' weakness has often led Christian thinkers—in their reluctance to embrace such powerlessness[159]—to imagine some all encompassing and victorious salvific design wherein an all-powerful and effective God could in turn make us powerful and effective and able to evade the humiliation of the cross. Jesus' crucifixion in that scheme represents a one-off event that appeases a sovereign God who will never again need to be appeased. But this is theological balderdash; it understands the cross not as the mark of our being in Christ, but as an external event intended to benefit all Christ followers to come.

For Paul, with all his end-time hopes, such entreaties from his friends are perhaps meant to influence his hope of acquittal. He does not know how his case will be adjudicated, but he is assured of their solidarity with his efforts, and perhaps some had influence among the powerful. Still, entreaties are hardly restricted to the worldly powerful. If we share in a communal life that flows like a river rushing onward without ceasing—a life that is given to us before we are conscious and goes on beyond our death—then such entreaties deliver us whatever occurs: Christ will be enlarged in his body.

Entreaties by his Philippian friends are for Paul conjoined with "Jesus Christ whom the Spirit supplies" (καὶ ἐπιχορηγίας τοῦ πνεύματος Ἰησοῦ Χριστοῦ). He does not put all his eggs in one basket. The term "supply" or "help" (ἐπιχορηγία) is one of the words—the many words—that seem specific to Paul. Jesus does not come directly to Paul and establish a personal relationship; the Spirit is the supplier of Jesus Christ.

---

159. The gospel understanding embraced by John D. Caputo in *The Weakness of God: A Theology of the Event* (Bloomington: Indiana University Press, 2006). The "event" is the cross, which exposes the presence of God as a "weak force" drawing us away from the strong forces of self-clinging.

Here we have one of the central doctrines of Paul's gospel: the Spirit experienced within the context of worldly communities is the ongoing presence of the absent Christ in the church, and thus in Paul. No Spirit, no Christ—Christ is "supplied" to his followers as his face (πρόσωπον) is reconfigured within the community in the faces (πρόσωποι) of his brothers and sisters. This Spirit is the conventional presence in the world of the risen and exalted Christ, who is now absent from that suffering world. In Rom 8:26 the Spirit "groans" wordlessly, and in Eph 4:30 the Spirit can be grieved by human sin.

However, in our tradition the Spirit never takes on the personal characteristics we attribute to the Father, nor is the Spirit ever depicted in the way we describe the man Jesus. The face of the Spirit is visible only in human lives within the communities. Here the Spirit supplies the Christ presence that flows through Paul and the community, beyond any calculated attempt by one standalone self to reach out in deluded imagining to a standalone Jesus to establish a personal relationship with him. This Spirit support (ἐπιχορηγία) erases the restrictive boundaries of the kind of stand-apart friendship (*philia*) with reciprocal benefits that worried Paul in Letter A. It reconfigures Paul and the Philippians in the one body that is Christ.[160]

It is then no wonder that in Resurrection Letter C Paul tells us that we not only share in his risen body, we are to participate in his body of suffering as well, for our skin no longer defines the margins of our organic life. The Spirit is the embodiment of the risen Christ, here and now, in the lives of actual people who follow this *agapē* path. Jesus Christ does not actually reign over the hectoring church from deep within its devout recesses, nor does he manage the world from somewhere far above the planet Earth. Neither does the phrase "Jesus Christ whom the Spirit supplies" express a Spirit-mediated relationship, but rather a single truth: The world-present Spirit, who supplies the risen Christ, flows into the same empty presence of that which, filling the cosmos, encompasses Paul in self-emptying embrace.

Nothing in Paul is defined in neat boxes or kept in separate categories. There is nothing supernatural here either that would merely support the bloated status of an overblown church. But Paul is confident that Christ-help comes to him through his unity with his Philippian coworkers in the Christ spirit of resurrection power. This is an eschatological help realized here and now through transformative enlightenment in Christ, as he says later in this letter. Together with the entreaties of his friends, such will help direct his life, no matter what legal verdict may be handed down. There is, moreover, nothing natural here either: All neural drives toward self-survival have been transformed to intermingle through the communities to benefit and gladden all. Grace permeates the cosmos.

---

160. Gazzaniga, *Who's In Charge?*, 133, discusses the emergent evolution of group cohesiveness: "I think that we scientists are looking at these [neural] capacities from the wrong organizational level. We are looking at them from the individual brain level, but they are emergent properties found in the group interactions of many brains." Gazzaniga treats only the emergence of consciousness as interdependent group formation. By contrast, Paul's neural networking erases group boundaries to constitute one organic body enlivened by the Spirit-supplied Christ.

This is why Paul feels assured, for such life "accords with my eager longing and hope" (κατὰ τὴν ἀποκαραδοκίαν καὶ ἐλπίδα μου 1:20). This "eager longing" surely includes the conventional hope that Paul's trial will turn out in his personal favor, but it is also a hope that in no way will he suffer disgrace, whatever may happen. This is the same as Job's hope that he would not be disgraced because of the sufferings he has experienced. It is a hope that people everywhere feel—that we not be boxed in to the calculus of sin because of the sad events that overtake us.

The content of Paul's hope is clear—not only for a legal victory, but that he "in no wise be disgraced" (ὅτι ἐν οὐδενὶ αἰσχυνθήσομαι). Disgrace is the sense of total weakness experienced by those who suffer and are sick, or who stand accused before whatever court has power over them. Paul, himself abused by his chains, does experience weakness; however, it becomes clear as we read on that he boasts in the weakness of the cross. Disgrace we sometimes earn by our deeds; we are sinners focused by our evolutionary biology on self-preservation through greed and anger. But sometimes disgrace comes unjustly, apart from any good or bad action of our own, and then Paul embraces it as Christ-weakness.

For Paul, the threat of disgrace has come by his own volition as the result of claiming his Roman citizenship and thus setting into motion this journey toward a Roman trial. Yet because of the entreaties of his friends and the help of the Spirit presence of Jesus Christ, Paul may be confident that even though bound over to trial, in the final reckoning he will suffer no lasting disgrace. Paul, a reformed abuser of others, will have sufficient courage and openness so that Christ might be exalted even in his broken human body. The term *parrēsia* (παρρησία 1:20), translated often as "courage," may also be rendered as "openness." Paul faces his legal disgrace "with openness in all things" (ἀλλ' ἐν πάσῃ παρρησίᾳ), for Paul knows and is confident that he will have the courage, whether he lives or dies, to welcome the exalted Christ into his empty body, whether whole or broken to pieces, because "in all aspects" (ἐν πάσῃ) he is open to Christ being glorified through him—whatever the outcome.

"Whether by life or by death" (εἴτε διὰ ζωῆς εἴτε διὰ θανάτου), still Paul says, "in my body Christ will be enlarged" (μεγαλυνθήσεται Χριστὸς ἐν τῷ σώματί μου)—by the transparent openness to the Spirit presence of the risen Christ in his very body. He has skin in the game—his own skin. Commentators note that Paul's attitude here "might appear to be sublime indifference."[161] But it is not disengagement. Rather, it is that in Paul's bodily being (as opposed to his "self"[162]), Christ will be expanded and exalted. That is a very Mahāyāna notion, for a bodhisattva is one who abides beyond both living and dying.[163] The awakened bodhisattva—by emptying all the boundary

---

161. R. P. Martin, *Philippians*, New Century Bible, 76, cited in O'Brien, *Epistle to the Philippians*, 116.

162. *Pace* Reumann, *Philippians*, 215.

163. See Kazuaki TANAHASHI, ed., *Moon in a Dewdrop: Writings of Zen Master Dōgen* (San Francisco: North Point, 1985) 74: "'Because a buddha is in both birth and death, there is no birth and

markers and by deep insight into the equality between the suffering of samsaric life and the peaceful cessation of nirvana—abides in non-abiding cessation, engaging totally in the conventional world in order to bring benefit and gladness to all sentient beings. The Diamond Sūtra teaches that a bodhisattva is authentic insofar as he does not entertain the thought of a self (Skt. *ātman*), a person (*pudgala*), a being (*sattva*), or a life force (*jīva*), for there is no stable reality behind these notions.[164]

Still, once emptied, all these bodhisattvas do live within this multiply-interdependent world of ours, and so this Mahāyāna scripture can say that noble persons (Skt. *ārya-pudgala*) are "exalted" (*prabhāvita*) by the "unconditioned" (*asaṃskṛta*) in their abandonment of all self-attachment. Edward Conze, the principal English interpreter of the Prajñāpāramitā scriptures, glosses the term *prabhāvita* (exalted) as "glorified," for these bodhisattva persons have "arisen" from the unconditioned, having been brought forth by it.[165] For his part, Paul sees this unconditioned and uncompounded life in the risen life of Christ supplied by the Spirit. It is not a spirit-linkage between two realms—the conditioned world of suffering (Skt. *saṃsāra*) and the unconditioned world (*nirvāṇa*). Indeed, in the Mahāyāna practice, both are emptied of any stable being. These realms need not be linked, for they already interpenetrate, and we are encompassed in the one world, although it is perceived differently by the wise and the foolish.

The Chinese Buddhist Huayan tradition has a worked-out schema for the shifting world awareness of practitioners of the path. Initially, we are aware of the appearances or the phenomena (事) that we encounter in the world—sun and stars, family and foreigners, and all the concrete factors among which we strive to live and prosper. Only by hearing the Dharma Teaching and becoming aware of true reality (理) can we transcend this sorry life of struggle and become aware of the true realm. But to cling to that true realm is an escapist goal, for transcendent insights clash with day-to-day living. So by attending to Mahāyāna teaching, one realizes the interpenetration of worldly appearances and true reality (理事無礙). Transcendent reality and worldly appearances neither stand against nor obstruct (無礙) one another. This sounds very much like Paul here meditating on the erasure of the boundaries between life and

---

death.' It is also said, 'Because a buddha is not in birth and death, a buddha is not deluded by both birth and death.'" See also "The Problem of Death in Dōgen and Shinran, Part I," in Masao ABE, *A Study of Dōgen: His Philosophy and Religion* (Albany: SUNY Press, 1992) 145–67, and "The Unborn and Rebirth, Part II" in ibid., 169–220. DŌGEN Kigen (1200–1253) is the Japanese founder of Sōtō Zen tradition and a master of meditative rhetoric, weaving common themes back upon themselves to collapse doctrine into practice, as in his essay, "Actualizing the Fundamental Point," in *Moon in a Dewdrop*, 69–74. He seems to me most like Paul, who brings all his teachings to ground in life "in Christ."

164. Mu Soeng, *Diamond Sutra*, 80, section 3. Mu Soeng comments, that contrary to popular belief, the Buddha "did not teach a nihilistic doctrine of 'no soul,' which would have rendered the issues of ethics and wholesome conduct completely irrelevant" (ibid., 85). What he did teach is that we delve into what the notions of "soul" and "no soul" might mean in actual living, whether they encumber practice or liberate one from attachment.

165. See Conze, *Buddhist Wisdom Books*, 38–39. See Mu Soeng, *Diamond Sutra*, 94, section 7.

death within an expanded and enlarged Christ who, in rising, collapses the boundaries between life and death, between secular and sacred.

In the Huayan schema, there is yet a deeper awareness that is described as the interpenetration or the non-obstruction of one phenomenon by another phenomenon (事事無礙); a bodhisattva functions in life with an awakened awareness that obliterates all dichotomies whatsoever.[166] Perhaps that is what Paul means by this enlarged body of Christ—that his life and the lives of the Philippians are encompassed in the enlarged body of Christ. To be so encompassed is to resituate our very identity and being. This is not about a conventional relationship—even a supernatural relationship—between on the one hand Christ followers secure in their self-awareness and, on the other, an imagined Christ restored to selfhood in the heavens.

Paul writes similarly in 1:23–24 when he says that although he longs to die and be with Christ, his skillful and conventional task is to live, focused on this world alone. This enables him to engage in his present course with confidence in its outcome, regardless of whether he lives or dies. Whenever Paul speaks of living in Christ, he sketches the structure of awakening and arising from the dead. However, the goal for him is not his individual wellbeing, but rather that Christ be exalted and enlarged in Paul's physical body—not just on the day of judgment, but "always and at every present moment" (ὡς πάντοτε καὶ νῦν 1:20) in the shared body of the believers. Paul speaks of his actual physical body, which suffers pain, which can be chained, which can be broken, and which—at least according to later tradition—was executed by beheading. It is "his living body" that experiences pain and suffering.[167] Paul does not withdraw from the rough-and-tumble Hellenistic world in which he works for the furtherance of the gospel such that Christ may be exalted and enlarged beyond the confines of any mapped selfhood.

What does it mean that "Christ be enlarged and exalted" (μεγαλυνθήσεται Χριστὸς 1:20)? Perhaps that Christ is magnified by the forthright openness of Paul in prison and proleptically before Paul's judges, whether by his life or his death. Christ's Spirit presence is widened by the envisioned impact of Paul's witness. This means more than that Paul celebrates Christ and makes much of him. The word *megalunthēsetai* (μεγαλυνθήσεται), so often rendered as "magnified," literally means "to be enlarged"[168] or to be made great and expand beyond current boundaries. Here, as soon as Paul speaks of life in Christ, he says that the risen Christ-life has been enlarged from its narrative margins in the Jesus traditions to become the risen life that pervades Paul's own body, defines his life, and is Spirit-shared throughout the wide world of all beings,

---

166. See LAI Pan-chiu, *Trinitarische Perichorese und Hua-yen Buddhismus* [In den letzten Jahren rückte die Trinitätslehre in den Mittelpunkt des christlichbuddhistischen] 45–61 (4.1 Einleitung).

167. Reumann, *Philippians*, 215. Also see ibid., n. 16: "Paul does not use *psyche* ('soul') at any point in Phil 1:20–23)." Participation in the risen life of Christ is bodily, sharing in organic life beyond the margins of these individual bodies.

168. Vincent, *Critical and Exegetical Commentary*, 25.

even when the Spirit who presences Christ does not whisper his Palestinian name. The Spirit blows where it will and is not confined within the languaged borders of any faith tradition. Just as the Father sent the Spirit to breathe order into the chaos of nothingness, so ever-anew the Spirit breathes Christ wisdom into risen life. There lurks within Christian piety the danger of a supernatural individualism wherein Christ remains bounded within his individually risen body and acts somehow behind the scenes to glorify some people who are similarly confined within their own selfhood. But this is to shrink Christ and fail to understand that this enlarged Christ resides in our very bodies. Christ is more than his Palestinian history, because risen life has been magnified and enlarged to the limits of the real.

The hymn that follows in 2:6–11 in this letter about Christ's emptying himself speaks of Christ's exaltation beyond his Galilean career to become the life-source of all who entrust themselves in faith. But this much should be clear: to be executed means to be killed, and to be crucified means to die of suffocation, losing the strength to raise oneself up to gulp down a breath of life-giving oxygen, and then to collapse in death, bowels loosened, fetid odors emanating. The gospels recount that women came to take the body of Jesus, wash it, and spread ointment on its wounds. We do not know how Paul himself died or whether anyone treated his broken body with care and respect. Yet he envisions that he will not be disgraced, imagining that he will, in his body, enlarge the life of Christ.

Japanese Shingon Master Kūkai (774–835 CE) wrote about "the meaning of realizing awakening in this very body" (Js. 即身成佛義, *sokushin-jōbutsu-gi*), explaining that awakening is an organic realization that encompasses the cosmos in the very body of the practitioner. This teaching is perhaps why practitioners of Shingon Buddhism, when venerating Kūkai's *stupa* on Mount Kōya, do not think of him as dead, although he died in the year 835 CE. They confess that he abides in the *samādhi* of not abiding in either life or death. Here too in Philippians, the very life of Christ expands beyond the historical Jesus to become the life of Paul and of the communities of faith. The lives we live are not separate and apart from one another. That is what being "in Christ" means—supplied not magically, but organically by the Spirit that breathes unbounded life in all sentient beings.

The Tensive Equality of Life and Death (1:21–24)

1:21 *For to me, to live is Christ and to die is gain.* ^{22}*If I am to live in the flesh, that means fruitful labor for me; but I do not know which I prefer.* ^{23}*I live in tension between the two: I long to depart and be with Christ, for that is far better;* ^{24}*but to remain in the flesh is more necessary for you.*

1:21 ἐμοὶ γὰρ τὸ ζῆν Χριστὸς καὶ τὸ ἀποθανεῖν κέρδος. ^{22}εἰ δὲ τὸ ζῆν ἐν σαρκί, τοῦτό μοι καρπὸς ἔργου· καὶ τί αἱρήσομαι οὐ γνωρίζω. ^{23}συνέχομαι δὲ ἐκ τῶν δύο, τὴν ἐπιθυμίαν ἔχων εἰς τὸ ἀναλῦσαι καὶ σὺν Χριστῷ εἶναι, πολλῷ [γὰρ] μᾶλλον κρεῖσσον: ²⁴τὸ δὲ ἐπιμένειν [ἐν] τῇ σαρκὶ ἀναγκαιότερον δι' ὑμᾶς.

"For me to live is Christ and to die is gain" (ἐμοὶ γὰρ τὸ ζῆν Χριστὸς καὶ τὸ ἀποθανεῖν κέρδος). Stark words, these, but central to the letter. Reumann maintains that "Philippians 1:21–23 is one of the three most influential passages in the epistle, along with 2:5–11 and 3:20–21."[169] The hymn of the empty Christ who is exalted beyond exaltation (2:5–11) is one of our earliest christological confessions, while chapter 3, here treated separately as Resurrection Letter C, addresses the energizing power of risen life in Christ knowledge. Here, in 1:21–24, Paul speaks of the difference between life and death. His words do not reflect the way in which we commonly cherish our lives and fear our deaths,[170] but rather his experience of being identified with—rather than related to—Christ.

Some commentators see a rhetorical comparison (*synkrisis*) here between two possible alternatives.[171] On the one hand, humans expect life to afford opportunities for progress and gain, whereas death means the end of those opportunities: "Work for the night is coming," as the old hymn tells us. Not so with Paul. Here we have an autobiographical account of Paul's state of mind, and it counters that commonsense preference for life over death. Some scholars see in this passage an enthymeme, an incomplete statement that the reader has to tangle with, or an enigmatic proposition with strong similarities to Chan (Zen) kōans.[172]

Autobiographical though the passage is, the subject of the first clause is not Paul himself but the infinitive of the verb "to live" (τὸ ζῆν), the predicate of which is "Christ" (Χριστὸς, Christos). That is, to live is indivisible (Js. 即 *soku*) with Christ.[173]

---

169. Reumann, *Philippians*, 259. He notes that Veronica Koperski, in her *The Knowledge of Jesus Christ my Lord: The High Christology of Philippians 3:7–11* (Kampen, the Netherlands: Pharos, 1996), makes a cogent case that these verses are just as central to the correspondence as the emptiness hymn.

170. Gazzaniga, *Who's In Charge?*, 69: "What we always must keep in mind is that our brains, hence all these processes, have been sculpted by evolution to enable us to make decisions that increase our reproductive success." It is strange that the Roman Church insists on supernatural realities, and yet in its sexual ethics reinforces the evolutionary exigency of reproductive success. Paul's strategy before the Roman tribunal envisions not reproductive success, but the enlargement of the common body of risen life. We are liberated from the constraints of our evolutionary heritage.

171. See Reumann, *Philippians*, 235–37.

172. See Aitken, *Gateless Barrier*, 7, for Wu-men's comments on Chao-chou's dog. A monk, knowing the orthodox teaching that all sentient beings have Buddha nature, still asked Chao-chou (b. 778) whether a dog has Buddha nature. Chao-chou's reply is the famous dismissal: "Not!" (無), seemingly negating the common teaching and thereby causing confusion in the minds of well-taught disciples. But Wu-men's (1181–1260) comments, recorded in the *Wu-men Kuan* (Gateless Barrier) do not make things easier, insisting on the "Not!," for that "Not!" is the gateless barrier through which one passes unimpeded: "You will walk hand in hand with all the Ancestral Teachers in the successive generations of our lineage—the hair of your eyebrows entangled with theirs, seeing with the same eyes, hearing with the same ears" (ibid.). More is meant here than simply receiving teaching from the ancestors; one is to share in one's own body their bodily experience of seeing and awakening.

173. The character 即 (Chi. *qi*) is pervasive in Mahāyāna scriptures and commentaries, indicating

Paul and Christ are not two standalone persons; they share one indivisible life, for Christ's personal life has been enlarged in his resurrection. This is the reality of risen life. Risen life means life reconfigured from its evolutionary, bounded forms to an awakened life shared by all. Paul enters the picture only indirectly, expressed in a dative of reference: "for me" (ἐμοὶ γὰρ). This life—indivisible with Christ—collapses an individual's life and death into the broader, "enlarged" Christ. Paul is not the anxious disciple "who wallows in indecision,"[174] somehow hoping for a blessed afterlife, none too sure, and therefore all too assured. Nor is Christ the metaphysical "out-there" core of a separate Christ-life. Paul identifies flesh-and-blood life—just as he lives it—as itself Christ. Just that and nothing more. It is not that Christ, here the predicate, adds anything special to life over and above life itself. Paul does not say that for him life has *become* Christ but that life *is* Christ. For Paul, simply to live is Christ, recognizing that in resurrection faith the dichotomy between life and death no longer holds. That is why this Christ has to be supplied by the Spirit, for only a freshly creative breathing can bring about such an indivisibility of this-my-life and the life of the Christ. But the breathing of life into inert bodies remains as strange and even as savage as the initial creation—all being made personal in the face of Christ, wherein we face one another.

Ignatius of Antioch, in his *Letter to the Ephesians*, similarly speaks of our inseparable life (τὸ ἀδιάκριτον ὑμῶν ζῶν) with Christ, for risen life is not distinguished individually.[175] Christ performs no magical function for Paul, nor does he provide added meaning to Paul's already by then well-understood life. What reconfigures Paul is this Spirit-wisdom awareness of who he is. His life as formerly understood has been redefined, and he now recognizes life to be identified as Christ, just as it is, in all its humanness. Christ becomes the suchness (Skt. *tathatā*) of life, breaking down the boundaries of Paul's historical personality and opening him to a life that is first emptied of its individual margins by apophatic negation of the reality of those margins and then reformulated by his learning Christ—word-by-word learning of what it actually means to live in Christ.

The initial emptying of the empirical self is, I think, shared broadly among traditions, each in their fashion. And each tradition, in accord with its teachings, then sketches a reconstituted life: a shared risen life in Christ here, as in this very early Christian scripture; an awakening to compassion, as with Buddhists; moving from sin to actualizing Torah, as with Jews; and becoming truly a "slave" in service to Allah, as with Muslims. We might have thought Christ would provide an added level to already well-ordered lives. Not so here. Paul realizes what was always so—that to live is Christ

---

an identity where none is apparent. For example, *saṃsāra* is identical with (即) *nirvāṇa*. In Chih-i's T'ien-t'ai thought, this term expresses the indivisibility between emptiness, everyday life, and the middle path, which form the three-in-one (三而有一) and one-in-three (一而有三) truth of the teaching. See my forthcoming work on T'ien-t'ai thought and Ephesian theology.

174. Reumann, *Philippians*, 236.

175. Vincent, *Critical and Exegetical Commentary*, 26, citing Ignatius's *Letter to the Ephesians*, iii., IX.

just as living occurs. He never was a secure, standalone individual who owned his life. Paul's indivisible identity with Christ takes place by living "in Christ" without the delusion-engendered self-attachment that gives rise to fear for the loss of our organic boundaries, as if losing those boundaries would mean the erasure of our life. We are to erase *self*, not life, to inscribe Christ into our sinews and skeleton, so that our very bones may participate in that Ezekiel scenario of skeletal reconstruction. Paul shares Ezekiel's eschatological vision of the enfleshment of the dry bones scattered in the valley of death, accomplished by that windy Spirit who breathes renewed life into the dead (Ezek 37:1–14). So here Christ is "supplied" by the Spirit, whose visage is the renewed Christ-life that shines in our faces. The age of the Spirit comes whenever the renewed life of the gospel takes on communal form, enlivening people to reach beyond their neural impulses.

We are invited to entangle ourselves in these verses and—in one way or another—to unpack their meaning for our lived lives. Paul's words are not expressed in clear propositional form. He employs a kōan-like rhetoric: a comparative rhetorical form (*synkrisis*) that presents the reader with a task that goes beyond merely absorbing theology as revealed information. Some scholars see enthymemes—syllogisms yet to be worked out—scattered throughout Paul's writings. Perhaps the entire gospel is such an enthymeme, and we can appropriate its meanings only by wrestling with our own lives.[176] Paul's inchoate discourse guards precisely against theological reduction so that we might viscerally clear away and abandon distinct ideas in favor of direct engagement in the practice of living beyond life-and-death.[177] The meaning of Paul's words has to be wrestled with in personal reflection over the course of a lifetime, as one sometimes longs to be with Christ in the "full perfection in his resurrection"[178] and sometimes realizes the presence of the absent and risen Christ in one's own body, here and now.

---

176. See P. A. Holloway, "The Enthymeme as an Element of Style in Paul," *Journal of Biblical Literature* 120 (2001) 329–39; also see M. J. Debanné, "An Enthymematic Reading of Philippians: Towards a Typology of Pauline Arguments," in *Rhetorical Criticism and the Bible*, S. E. Porter and D. L. Stamps, eds. (Bloomsbury: T. & T. Clark, 2002) 481–503. Reumann, in an excursus entitled "Enthymemes?," finds the discussion on enthymemes both "promising" and "problematic" (Reumann, *Philippians*, 143). See also the critical comments of David E. Aune in "The Use and Abuse of Enthymeme in New Testament Scholarship," *NTS* 49 (2003) 299–320; and also in "Enthymeme" in *The Westminster Dictionary of New Testament and Early Christian Literature and Rhetoric* (Louisville: Westminster John Knox, 2003) 150–57. Aune presents in brief summary the protean uses of classical enthymemes, arguing that this rhetorical form, from Aristotle's *Ars Rhetorica*, was not available to Paul because the *Ars Rhetorica* was not. Nevertheless, a broader use of similar rhetoric—wherein the consent of the hearer depends not on the formal logic of the argument, however truncated, but relies on the conscious contribution of the hearer from within personal experience—is hardly absent from any scriptural writing.

177. On inchoate discourse, see my foreword to Habito, *Living Zen, Loving God*, xiii.

178. See Reumann, *Philippians*, 250, in which death can be "gain," because of risen life through Christ (Rom 5:21; 6:22, 23). Reumnann cites M. Bockmuehl, "A Commentator's Approach to the 'Effective History' of Philippians," *Journal for the Study of the New Testament* 60 (1995) 88, that dying with Christ means "full perfection in his resurrection."

In a different context, in early Buddhism full perfection was the goal of the model of the saintly arhat—one who seeks an individual awakening (Skt. *pratyeka-buddha*) that will lead him to escape into a *parinirvāṇa*, or a full (*pari*) cessation (*nirvāṇa*). Such a practitioner is described as fleeing into the forest to engage in assiduous practices until all karmic baggage is eliminated. Then this rhinoceros-like saint, alone in the forest thickets, simply disappears from this samsaric world. But the scriptures of the later Mahāyāna movement redefine the "full perfection of awakened wisdom" (*prajñāpāramitā*) to mean wisdom's insight into the emptiness of that arhat goal. They equate cessation with samsaric life in this very world, and thus recommend, in place of the arhat paradigm, the bodhisattva model of "non-abiding" cessation: continuing compassionate engagement in the midst of this life in the world. These Mahāyāna scriptures engage the same life-or-death issue as the earlier Abhidharma. However, the arhat's goal is the full cessation of *parinirvāṇa* at actual personal death, once the karmic influences that keep a person in *samsara* are exhausted. In Mahāyāna, by contrast, the bodhisattva's final death (*parinirvāṇa*) occurs only after the tasks of compassionate engagement to benefit and gladden the sentient beings of this world are completed; then the energy needed for engagement is exhausted, and the bodhisattva passes by dying. Mahāyāna wisdom abides neither there in nirvana nor here in samsara.

In the Mahāyāna doctrine of emptiness, the awakened one (buddha or bodhisattva) gains deep insight and wisdom into the equality (Skt. *samatā-jñāna*) between life and death.[179] Such enlightenment does not discriminate between life and death, giving preference neither to life over death nor to death over life. Both living and dying are empty of any final definitive status. The underlying Mahāyāna notion is that the self, which we always assume to be the stable subject of our delimited organic life, is in fact a construct. It does have a personal, conventional reality as the humans we are, but it has no ultimate status in truth.[180] When we search our consciousness for a stable self-identity—who we are and what we have become—we find no bedrock self, but rather a cluster of causes and conditions that have led us to be whoever it is that we regard our-

---

179. Keenan, *Study of the* Buddhabhūmyupadeśa, pt. III, ch. 10, 424–25.

180. Gazzaniga, *Who's In Charge?*, 75: "The lingering conviction that we humans have a 'self' making all the decisions about our actions is not dampened. It is a powerful and overwhelming illusion that is almost impossible to shake. In fact, there is little or no reason to shake it, for it has served us well. There is, however, a reason to try to understand how it all comes about. Once we understand why we feel in charge, even though we know we live with a slight tape delay on what our brains are doing, we will understand why and how we make errors of thought and perception." Buddhist tradition sees much reason to shake that self-assurance, for even though it serves our evolutionary survival, its attachment to self leads to endless suffering and pain. In agreement with Gazzaniga, "There is no ghost in the machine, no secret stuff that is you" (ibid., 108). Since neuroscientists find no neural location for self, they envision their task as developing broader frameworks in which to understand our common experience of self-consciousness. Mahāyāna explicates the genesis of self-consciousness as delusional, recognizing the myriad false narratives of self-awareness that humans weave, and so negating any stable stuff that might constitute a perduring self. Yet, once awakened, personal consciousness as dependently arisen is heartily affirmed as the everyday living of a bodhisattva practitioner.

selves to be. That is, what we have become by our own efforts, what our families have provided, how our genealogical prehistory set our familial and ethnic heritage, and how our long evolutionary inheritance is rooted in an all-but-unimaginable past.[181] We are left wondering how this upsurge of our living ever came about, grateful to our ancestors for our existence, often critical of our ethnic heritage and personal families and their mixed imprint on our habits and patterns, and more or less confident in our own efforts to become the individuals we are or mean to be.

But never in these conscious excavations do we empirically discover some stable core that might have remained constant and unchanged throughout the entire course of the causes and conditions that have led us to be here. Names are verbal handles that we employ in daily living, but they uncover nothing finally real. Life goes beyond personal individuality and reaches that far shore from which one sees that our imagined notions of a permanent self merely enable us to grasp tenaciously onto our fleeting being. Upon awakening, one enters a pure reality (Skt. *pariśuddhi-dharmadhātu*), depicted mythically as a luxuriant grove of abundant life or the vast ocean into which all enter.[182] Life overflows the margins of selfhood and cannot be contained in any single corporeal vessel. Buddhist teachings about no-self are meant to serve as rafts to carry us beyond the raging torrents of saṃsāra to abide in a nirvana of no abiding, wherein life, just as it is (Skt. *tathatā*), is lustily affirmed in end-time joy.

No verbal elaboration can inform people of the truth and reality of awakened life. The Tathāgata Buddha in the Diamond Sūtra teaches his disciples to recognize that his teaching is a non-teaching that serves only as a raft—effective for the journey across the waters, but to be abandoned upon reaching that far shore of awakened wisdom. So even the teaching (Dharma) is to be cast aside, for there is no stable reality (*dharma*) underlying any teaching. Nor is there any non-teaching to be affirmed as the Buddha teaching, for emptiness itself is not a real thing, as if mere negation could capture what is really not.[183] The teaching of emptiness is a broom to sweep away the accumulated detritus of the years, and once its cleansing is done we can put it away in some corner or other until it is needed again. We received life, and what remains after the sweeping that empties is the house of being here.

---

181. Ibid., 102: "Consciousness is an emergent property ... We do not experience a thousand chattering voices, but a unified experience. Consciousness flows easily and naturally from one moment to the next with a single, unified, and coherent narrative. The psychological unity we experience emerges out of the specialized system called 'the interpreter' that generates explanations about our perceptions, memories, and actions and the relationships among them. This leads to a personal narrative, the story that ties together all the disparate aspects of our conscious experience into a coherent whole: order from chaos. The interpreter module appears to be uniquely human and specialized to the left hemisphere. Its drive to generate hypotheses is the trigger for human beliefs, which, in turn, constrain our brain." Mahāyāna philosophers similarly affirm a continuity of consciousness, but teach that it is basic error and ignorance to identify that "interpreter" as a stable and essential self.

182. Keenan, *Study of the* Buddhabhūmyupadeśa, pt. III, ch. 13, 469–72.

183. Mu Soeng, *Diamond Sutra*, 92; Conze, *Buddhist Wisdom Books*, 34.

Paul's household of the faithful, in all its vital beauty and disheartening sadness, is the arena for bodhisattva action. We are given life, but from the beginning it is not ours at all. We all become who we are by slow, karmic maturation over months and years of neural development and our psychological mirroring of others.[184] So it is that the life we live we do not own. Everything is a gift. We cannot lose our life because we do not own our life. Since it is not ours at the beginning, we can't lose it at the end. If to live is Christ, then it is not true that "you have only one life to live." We don't "have" any life. Life is not about having or succeeding but about taking on the mind of Christ so that all may succeed in living in wisdom and kindness.

Paul says in 1:21 that to live is Christ, by which Christ is not one's own individual possession. Whenever Paul encounters Christ and realizes his oneness with Christ-life, whether on the Damascus Road or elsewhere, he describes Christ as the center of his decentered mind—as life going beyond the grave, liberated from its confinement within his imprisoned dilemma. It is not just an undefined and ineffable truth that Paul encounters, as if all concrete situations disappear in clouds of misty emptiness. Rather, it is the conventional truth of the risen presence of the absent Jesus, witnessed within Paul as the risen Christ, who by emptying his consciousness, transformed it. That is why in Resurrection Letter C Paul speaks of the power of the resurrection: our lives, hidden in Christ, rise even now in Christ in all their dependently arisen beauty and transparent transience. Risen life is not peaceful cessation from the blood-pumping and wind-breathing life we each individually and personally name. The same life is pumped through every living heart and into every living mind since the very beginningless beginning, even after hearts stop beating and lungs no longer draw in air. Perhaps earthly life is a unique phenomenon in the vastness of cosmic space, but if so, then this one exception disproves the rule that the cosmos is cold and lifeless.[185]

Such life is not a Christ-principle. It is not our innate "Christness," as if that were a new and stable self-identity. Religious attempts to define Christian identity, or Buddhist or Muslim identity, fail because they start and end with assuring people of an illusion: that we can define our identity as somehow in itself salvific. Although here Christ is indivisible with Paul, Christ is not any Christian's possession. Paul, in Acts 9, comes to recognize the concretely lived life he shares with the Damascus community of Ananias as indivisible with his own breath-and-blood living. Just as Saul, as the persecutor of Christians, had earlier failed to recognize that shared life, so attachment to any bounded religious truth prevents us from recognizing this same life shared around the globe. When religious traditions get ensnared within their theological

---

184. Gazzaniga, *Who's In Charge?*, 161, writes that mirror neurons "were the first concrete evidence that there is a neural link between observation and imitation of an action, a cortical substrate for understanding and appreciating the actions of others . . . The mirror neurons are implicated not only in the imitating of actions, but also in understanding the intention of actions." In the writings of Paul, who speaks of seeing enigmatically in a mirror, one is to mirror the mind of Christ as embodied in practitioners.

185. Ibid., 121: "As Richard Feynman once pointed out, exceptions prove the rule . . . wrong."

ideas and forget their primary practice, they withdraw into more and more impregnable enclaves and, neglecting to be of service to the world, begin to regard the world in all its rich panoply as the enemy.

If at some future time we have to write of the failure of Vatican II to open the church to the wealth and wisdom of our many worlds, no doubt we will then understand why institutional power so often fails to engender life visions: institutions grow by ever more protectively circumscribing their corporate selfhood. Only when Paul got his wits about him—abandoning his claims to self-sufficiency and gaining insight into the risen Christ already known to the community of Christ followers in Damascus and Philippi—did Paul realize that his conventional identity as a Pharisee no longer had any enduring validity. That does not mean, however, that while alive in his body Paul lost all sense of his own constructed personhood. Paul is always Paul, with no blurred contours or fuzzy boundaries. He remains a well-taught if irascible Pharisee, driven to go beyond the comfort levels of first the Jerusalem authorities who agreed on his mission to persecute Christians, then later the Jerusalem apostles who agreed to his mission to preach Christ to the Gentiles, and after that, even some of his fellow Christ preachers in Philippi.

Faith entrustment to the risen Christ relativizes the absolute status of Paul's character constructs, realigning them with the conventional realities of his life as it unfolded before him—the very life Paul refers to when he says, "If I am to live in the flesh" (εἰ δὲ τὸ ζῆν ἐν σαρκί 1:22). This flesh-and-blood life is the lived samsaric course from birth to death that we all experience as our bodily being, whether lived in awakened wisdom or clung to in deluded sin. Paul did both: He first ignorantly clung to his former identity, and then he was freed from such clinging. But that freedom still does not exempt one from living within the dependently arisen horizons of a particular life. So when Paul talks about living in the "flesh" (σαρξ, sarx), he means his earthly, samsaric life, and the term "flesh" retains its common meaning of life enmeshed in the world of sin and delusion. But Paul living "in Christ" entails a wisdom that recognizes the indivisibility between samsara and nirvana, seeing both as empty of any core essence: "For me to live is Christ and to die is gain" (1:21). These words startle, and as readers we find ourselves again entangled in a rhetorically constructed kōan-like conundrum that challenges common judgment. Everyone knows that to die is loss, not gain.[186] But for the Mahāyāna and for Paul, chastened by the Philippians, there is

---

186. See Ernest Becker, *The Denial of Death* (New York: Free Press, 1973) 16, 285, in which Becker sees the vitalistic refusal of humans to acknowledge their own mortality and concludes that "fear of death is a biological and evolutionary problem," leading him to call for a "new heroism" whereby "the orientation of men has to be always beyond their bodies, has to be grounded in a healthy repression, and toward explicitly immortality-ideologies, myths of heroic transcendence." He would agree that humans live in a constant forgetfulness of their very humanity, yet his stress on heroic human projects still seems to reflect eighteenth-century Enlightenment approaches, despite the fact that in his mature years he rejected the Enlightenment confidence in the basic goodness of human nature. He identified the human "problem" as our evolutionary heritage to fight against death itself and was open to faith traditions, but he contextualized them within self-generated "immortality" projects, as if we might

an equality between living and dying. Indeed, if one has to choose, perhaps dying is preferable, for with it comes a cessation of suffering.

In 1:23, Paul "longs or desires" (τὴν ἐπιθυμίαν ἔχων) "to depart and be with Christ" (εἰς τὸ ἀναλῦσαι καὶ σὺν Χριστῷ εἶναι). The term used here for this "longing" (ἐπιθυμία) is surprising and does not denote a "good desire," but almost always is used of an "evil desire."[187] Thus the translation of τὴν ἐπιθυμίαν ἔχων ("I have a longing") is "I long for." An old Latin translation of Philippians has it that "I lust after being dissolved and being with Christ" (*cupio dissolvi et esse cum Christo*). This, I think, does catch the sense of the phrase, for Paul is tied and shackled, dragged from place to place along the route to his trial, and he feels ready to rest for good—to "strike camp" (τὸ ἀναλῦσαι) one last time and have done with it. He has an arhat desire to disappear from his contentious life into eschatological peace, but that is not the bodhisattva course. The term here translated as "depart" (τὸ ἀναλῦσαι) is rendered in the Latin of the Vulgate as *dissolvi*, "to be dissolved," and thus mingled with the ongoing flow of Christ-life. But it is used also for striking a military camp or loosing a ship from its moorings so that it may sail away to the deep ocean.[188] The term becomes a metaphor for death, for death frees us from not only sin and suffering, but also from the sometimes ambiguous engagements and struggles we experience in the furtherance of truth and compassion. Perhaps its more concrete military connotation "striking camp" was at the front of Paul's mind.

In any case, we ought not to imagine Paul as sitting in some windowed jail with his friends in attendance upon him; he is a prisoner in chains, moved along from place to place on the journey from Jerusalem to Rome. He had hoped to go as far as Spain one day but wound up just "with Christ."[189] He rests at night with his companion Timothy (1:1, 2:19–24), to whom perhaps he dictates a few paragraphs as he is able. Images of a forced journey permeate Paul's language: here, "striking camp" and later "stretching forth" toward the final goal as well as the "marching orders" suggested in 1:16, where he says that "I have *been appointed* for a Gospel defense." Paul is a tired apostle; he is in his fifties, a venerable age in his time and place. He bears on his body

---

overcome death by ourselves becoming heroes. Also see Jay Robert Lifton, *Revolutionary Immortality: Mao Tse-tung and the Chinese Cultural Revolution* (New York: Norton, 1976) 149–63, on "Beyond the Last Stand."

187. Martin, *Philippians*, 81. Also Collange, *Epistle of Saint Paul*, 64: "Paul always uses '*epithumia*' ('desire') with a bad sense (except for 1 Thess. 2:17) and in this sense it must also be understood here."

188. O'Brien, *Epistle to the Philippians*, 130. The Buddha Land Sūtra (*Buddhabhūmi-sūtra*) offers two similes of non-discriminative wisdom and its realization of the ultimate reality. The first is a garden image of the "luxuriant grove of unified experience," wherein all notions of "me-and-mine" have vanished in the common experience of wisdom, and the second likens that reality realm (Skt. *dharmadhātu*) to a great ocean wherein all rivers intermingle their waters. Bodhisattvas who have entered that ocean "experience the phenomenal wisdom of one unified taste." See Bandhuprabha, *Interpretation of the Buddha Land*, 196–97.

189. Crossan and Reed, *In Search of Paul*, 400–403. Crossan and Reed speculate that Paul was acquitted and did not die as the result of his imprisonment, but, together with Peter, was martyred in Nero's persecution in 64 ce, unnoticed among the crowds of Christians slaughtered at that time.

the marks of Jesus Christ (ἐγὼ γὰρ τὰ στίγματα τοῦ Ἰησοῦ ἐν τῷ σώματί μου βαστάζω, Gal 6:17). He has heard the accounts of Christ's passion, and he too has been shackled, beaten, and forced to march under the cross.

Nevertheless, both living and dying are Christ. If Paul dies, he will be with Christ. But Paul does not imagine he will live with the historical Jesus or that they might sit down together and have friendly chats by a tranquil and stormless sea at the center of the cosmos. Paul seldom lets his imagination run free, and he does not describe risen life in any recognizable form.[190] He knows the accounts of the early Jesus traditions and recognizes that he is "born out of time" (1 Cor 15:8), never having known Jesus here in the flesh (τὸ ζῆν ἐν σαρκί). Neither does he think Christ is the metaphysical One Beyond Being. Christ is not Christians' ontological or cosmic milieu, into which one might "be dissolved" (τὸ ἀναλῦσαι; L. *dissolvi*). Thus, I do not favor translating the phrase in 1:23 as "I want to be dissolved and be with Christ." Much as the boundaries of selfhood are to be emptied, they are dependently arisen realities that indeed do describe our actual life situation. Even after we die, those boundaries remain for some time in the memories of our progeny. For example, Confucians are to cherish the ancestors back to the seventh generation. Nevertheless, Paul's Christ-life is inextricably one with the same Jesus who died and rose in Palestine. That unmixed life is not a newfound milieu, but a sharing of this organic life in the risen-to-life Christ. It is, simply put, our life lived in the knowledge and wisdom of the empty Christ. "Depart" is more to the point, for Paul was so weary that he did long to leave those endeavors to share a life with the risen Christ. And still, perhaps the military metaphor "to break camp" and be on one's way is more apropos as Paul stretches forth to Rome and beyond.

We find in Paul's letters a paradigm of the tensive identity between life lived here *in* Christ and life beyond *with* Christ. He is constrained to live here humanly, Christ-awakened to boundless life while yet enmeshed in the concrete limitations of his situation, which has been brought about by his own upayic (skillful) strategy to further the gospel by claiming his Roman citizenship. Most narratives about bodhisattvas in the Buddhist teachings are idealized, and even the existentially powerful Zen stories have become paradigmatic over the ages. We possess no personal letters from anyone named "Bodhisattva."[191] But perhaps in Paul's letters we may glimpse something of a bodhisattva-like person who, while yet alive, has cleared away preconceived notions and abandoned the parameters of his individual selfhood. Perhaps that is why these epistles—these postcard-like snippets that express such a mixture of the personal and faith concerns of our early ancestors in the faith—were accepted as Christian scrip-

---

190. Collange, *Epistle of Saint Paul*, 68: "Yet although Paul expresses a belief in communion with Christ *at the time of* and *after* death he never speculates about it and a less embellished affirmation of it than his could hardly be imagined."

191. See Heinrick Dumoulin, "The Person in Buddhism: Religious and Artistic Aspects," *Japanese Journal of Religious Studies* 11 (1984) 143–67.

ture. They have been preserved not as incomplete historical records of early Christian events that tease the skills of exegetes, but rather as mirror images, or paradigms, for all later readers—so that, whatever the circumstances, we too might learn Christ in our own all-too-human lives. The details of Paul's personal circumstances, however crucial for interpretive clarity, are not the important part. Paul's mirroring of Christ is.[192]

Simply to live and simply to die is Christ, and therefore for Paul to die is gain, because at that point one no longer need carry the burdens of a conventionally personal course of life that demands we strive in concrete situations for the furtherance of gospel wisdom. We are not in Paul's situation, are not informed on the specifics of the issues, and cannot model our lives on his historical world. Neither can we mimic his life in an imagined imitation of Christ, for that would leave us entrapped within proliferating images of imagined selves, attempting to recreate his life "in Christ."[193] We cannot pretend to live within the ancient histories of Ephesus, Philippi, or Palestine without refusing to live our own histories. However, by the simple fact that Paul's correspondence with the Philippians has been preserved and received as canonical in the ongoing Christian tradition, the image of Paul as "betwixt and between" life and death that we find here can serve as a mirror that reflects each beholder in a myriad of different life situations, collapsing our selfhood so that living and dying may be reconstituted beyond individual identity markers.

From what we have gained in understanding about Paul's time, we know that some Greeks did see death as gain for those who experienced life as a burden, considering it a release from pain and suffering.[194] When Paul says that to die for him is profitable, he might strike us once more as the self-sufficient Stoic, but he makes no claim here to self-sufficiency. No doubt he too craves surcease from pain and suffering. And the loss of pain *is* a gain.[195] Just as Paul longs (L. *cupio*) to be freed from his shackles

---

192. See Keenan, *Study of the* Buddhabhūmyupadeśa, pt. III, ch. 9, 391–416, on mirror wisdom as the nondiscriminative experience of the real just as it is, transcending the pattern of subject-object apprehension.

193. See Jaroslav Pelikan, *Jesus through the Centuries: His Place in the History of Culture* (New Haven: Yale, 1985). Pelikan offers a corrective to the many different portraits of the historical Jesus—each of which presents a particular Jesus as the real Jesus—by reminding readers of the many "real Jesuses" we have seen over the ages. A similarly shifting cultural portrayal of Paul could run the gamut from the ambiguous Paul of 2 Pet, to the saintly missionary of the Fathers, to the deep theologian of the Reformation, to the adventuresome apostle who suffered many trials, to the martyr of the faith, the woman hater of feminist commentators, and the cantankerous narrow-minded authority-enforcer of postmodern critiques. All of these divergent images are constructed by thinkers attempting as best they can to place Paul in his proper context.

194. O'Brien, *Epistle to the Philippians*, 122–23.

195. Everett, *Don't Sleep*, 165, recounts the scene of Alfredo's dying: "'No, Daniel,' he replied. 'One knows when one is dying. But there is no reason to be sad. I am happy to end this pain in death. And I can tell you that I am not afraid of death. I know that I am going to be with Jesus. And I am grateful that I had a long life and a very good life. I am surrounded by my children and my grandchildren. They all love me. They are all here for me. I am so thankful for my life and my family.'"

The Emptied Christ of Philippians

and escape into being with Christ (τὴν ἐπιθυμίαν ἔχων εἰς τὸ ἀναλῦσαι καὶ σὺν Χριστῷ εἶναι), so—often—do we. But the take-away point is this: Christ is identified with life, and life is identified with Christ. And life for Christ followers is the emptiness of the empty Christ, and the empty Christ is our everyday life. Thus, although Paul does indeed earnestly wish to sink into the being of Christ, yet he does not. Although some opine that Paul had a suicidal desire,[196] an option not yet deemed unacceptable among early Christians, he resists the urge to resolve the tension between his eschatological life with Christ and his not-yet-final passing.

Christ is not the ontologically set-apart realm of metaphysical being.[197] The being of the risen Christ is beyond imagining and beyond metaphysics altogether. That tension empties any imaged ideas that would bifurcate life into different realms. Paul "doesn't know which alternative is best" (καὶ τί αἱρήσομαι οὐ γνωρίζω 1:22)—whether to live or whether to die. He "is on tenterhooks between two alternatives" (συνέχομαι δὲ ἐκ τῶν δύο 1:23); indeed, to be freed from suffering and be with Christ is "far better" (πολλῷ [γὰρ] μᾶλλον κρεῖσσον),[198] "yet to remain in the flesh" and continue his life endeavors (τὸ δὲ ἐπιμένειν [ἐν] τῇ σαρκὶ 1:24) for others is "more necessary for" them (ἀναγκαιότερον δι' ὑμᾶς). Here is the heart of Paul's dilemma in the context of the conventional life he strives to live to the benefit of others.[199] If he goes on living in the body, in the flesh-and-blood world of his samsaric history, then he can continue to be engaged "in fruitful work" (τοῦτό μοι καρπὸς ἔργου). Death would be "gain" (κέδρος), for that is "far better" (πολλῷ [γὰρ] μᾶλλον κρεῖσσον),[200] but a "fruitful" (καρπὸς) life

---

196. See "Did Paul Contemplate Suicide?" in Reumann, *Philippians*, 237–39, for a critical discussion of A. J. Droge's claims in "Mori Lucrum: Paul and Ancient Theories of Suicide," *NovT* 30 (1988) 278–85.

197. A similar critique against "realm-ism" (the supernatural) was raised by Japanese Buddhologist and Zen priest HAKAMAYA Noriaki, in his book *Hihan Bukkyō* [Critical Buddhism] (Tokyo: Daizō Shuppan, 1990) 249–75. In that work, he reiterated the Mahāyāna critique against doctrinal notions of an innate "Buddha nature" (Skt. *garbha*), taking the rejection of "realm-ism" (*dhātuvāda*) beyond the academic study of doctrinal development and applying it to the center of Japanese Buddhist life and practice. His argument that such doctrinal views unconsciously but actually enshrine social discrimination and bias (ibid., 275–303) caused such controversy that he eventually lost his professorial position at the Sōtō Zen university where he taught. Furthermore, he was constrained by the intensity of the ensuing arguments to abandon his status as a Zen priest and become "laicized" in a lengthy ritual that mirrored the ordination ceremony step-by-step. Metaphysical tenets have their effects in this real world.

198. O'Brien, *Epistle to the Philippians*, 130: literally "much rather better."

199. Collange, *Epistle of Saint Paul*, 65: Paul "now sets a single adjective—'*anangkaioteron*,' 'it is more necessary.' In 1 Cor 9:16 proclaiming the Gospel is also presented as the result of necessity, though this idea has no real theological significance in Paul; most frequently it states mere fact, an inevitable result." Perhaps it is better to see this "necessity" as a dependently arisen "need" to preach the quite conventional gospel in Philippi rather than to depart into the silence of ultimate meaning.

200. Ibid. "The expression is a pleonasm and over-emphatic and for this reason can only be ironical . . . By such forced praise Paul in fact condemns what he has himself stamped as a self-centred desire ('*epithumia*')" (ibid.).

of gospel engagement has drawn Paul into his present situation as a compassionate preacher of Christ wisdom (i.e., a bodhisattva).

When Paul comes to treat the ultimate meaning of death and resurrection, of dying and being with Christ, he resorts to "goblet words"[201]—words that overflow the grammatical and semantic limits of his language—for he sees in a mirror, darkly.[202] Here he longs to die, because to be with Christ is, as he says, piling up comparative words, "much more better." It is not simply "better" (κρεῖσσον), for Paul adds the comparative "much" (μᾶλλον) to heighten the meaning, then appends "more" (πολλῷ) and adds, in the best texts, the superfluous "for" (γὰρ) to an already overpacked pleonasm. All this heaping up of words beyond grammatical common sense emphasizes how preferable Paul sees being *there* with Christ to be. "The truth is ungraspable and inexpressible," teaches the Diamond Sūtra. "It neither is nor is not, for all noble persons are exalted by the unconditioned."[203] Incapable of describing in words what it means to be with Christ beyond death, Paul multiplies the words as if the more, the better. He resorts to this rhetorical pattern wherever he speaks of things he cannot express, for the transformative experience of encountering the risen Christ is not the reinstatement of a known pattern of human relationship, but the falling away of all relational categories in an unconditioned exaltation whereby Christ is exalted and enlarged in one's own body. Imagination is curbed, and Paul's grammar becomes overloaded.[204]

If being with Christ, which is what Paul longs for, were simply a separate transcendent state, it would be easy to describe it as a limit category: the unconditioned, the ultimate reality, or the really real. That is the description in the Diamond Sūtra. It would be the final horizon that draws us beyond all conventional horizons, sparking the undying desire of men and women to reach beyond whatever life horizon they have attained. But here in Philippians, it is a "being with" (σὺν εἶναι) that is simultaneously a loosening of all relationships (τὸ ἀναλῦσαι). The phrase "being with Christ" (σὺν Χριστῷ εἶναι) signifies a relationship between the terms "Paul" and "Christ." But the being beyond that is implied in departure warns against any insistence on a stable

---

201. See Chuang Tzu, *Complete Works*, 373: "Chuang Chou heard of their views and delighted in them. He expounded them in odd and outlandish terms, abandoning himself to the times without partisanship, not looking at things from one angle only. He believed that the world was drowned in turbidness and that it was impossible to address it in sober language. So he used 'goblet words' to pour out endless changes."

202. Ruden, *Paul Among the People*, 186: "The NRSV has it that we now see only 'in a mirror, dimly'; literally, this is 'through, by means of a mirror, in a riddle.' The correction from the old translation 'glass' (old-fashioned English for 'mirror'), which is confusing to the modern ear, is good: I used to picture a dirty pane of window glass myself. Ancient mirrors were made not of glass but of bronze, which does not reflect terribly well; people don't, on their own, in their immaturity, see even themselves clearly. But if they practice love, they will someday look into a mirror and see not only themselves but God. They will have the answer to the riddle and understand."

203. Mu Soeng, *Diamond Sutra*, 94; Conze, *Buddhist Wisdom Books*, 36.

204. Paul reminds one of Wittgenstein's adage that we should be silent about things we do not know. But instead of keeping silent, Paul continues to try to express meanings that clank against the constrictive, grammatical structures of his Greek idiom.

base to such a relationship, making it impossible to clearly express what "being with Christ (σὺν Χριστῷ εἶναι) entails.[205]

205. See Caird, *Paul's Letters from Prison*, 113: "This verse [23] seems to present the ... view that those who die 'in the Lord' go directly into his presence." Silva, in discussing this verse, mentions the notion of soul-sleep: "Proponents of soul-sleep argue that death in fact does away with time as far as the consciousness of believers is concerned: when they awaken at the resurrection, no time has passed for them" (Silva, *Philippians*, 74). The issue concerns the continuity between the being "in Christ" while alive and "'with Christ' after death," how to understand that "interim state" between dying here and now and the final resurrection. Reumann sees Paul here in 1:23 as "asserting a continuity of the individual's relationship with Christ ... He expects the relationship to continue at death. His phrase for the immortality of the Christ-relationship is *to be with Christ* ... No details, certainly not golden streets or heavenly banquet feasts" (Reumann, *Philippians*, 252). Mahayanists, for their part, also see a continuity perduring after dying, which they call the "interim state" (Skt. *antara-bhāva*), but they restrict its import to the karmic continuity (*saṃtāna*) of consciousness from one life to another within the frame of samsara. In accord with the inexorable force of karmic actions accumulated over the ages, at death any particular life is "reborn" in full retributive continuity with the past, in the various "destinies" (*gāti*), from the deepest of the hells to the ethereal realms of gods and angels. Yet, even the realms of divine beings, as well as hell denizens, is not final determination, for one cycles through life until the attainment of *parinirvāṇa*, or the cessation of the entire karmic wheel of suffering. In common practice, this is often taken to entail a personal rebirth, such that one might be an animal in one destiny and a human in the next. But the notion is more nuanced than that, for the carrier of such life-to-life continuity is not the personal self—which does not exist in any of the destinies—but mere consciousness bereft of all memory and thus all identity. Identity remains a construct and has no reality that might support any relationship beyond the constructed environment of a particular place and time. The "interim state" is deemed to consist in that time before consciousness again embodies itself. The Yogācāra thinkers, trying to offer an explanation for such continuity within a theological framework of no-self, taught that there is a "storehouse consciousness" (*ālaya-vijñāna*), or an unconscious substratum of mind that is impregnated with all the karmic seeds from the past and propels life onward along its karmic trajectory. However, for an awakened buddha, the karmic stream has been exhausted once awakening occurs, and the birth-appearance of buddhas and bodhisattvas is driven, not by past karma, but by compassionate engagement. Risen life, once experienced, continues in the reemergence of compassionate engagement in the tasks to be done, much as Paul came to regard his continued presence among the Philippians as the more necessary outcome. But it all hinges on experiences of awakening to abundant life beyond attachment to delusion and the greed and hatred thus engendered. The final state of a buddha, however, remains indescribable as an afterdeath continuity or not, for in the final state of a buddha, nothing can be said. The theo-cosmological framework for such Buddhist meditations is a regard for this world as merely the "container world" (*bhājana-loka*), the scene of the working out of the salvation of all sentient beings. When all the karma of all beings has been exhausted, this world would logically disappear completely. But that is not a conclusion welcomed by any Buddhist. For the most part, it constitutes a limit question, signaling a boundary beyond which questions cannot be answered and should not be asked. The only text that treats the issue squarely, *The Interpretation of the Buddha Land*, shies away from that complete collapse of the entire karmically-driven universe to say that for one reason or another, it will never happen. There will always be deluded beings needing bodhisattva compassion to lead them toward awakening. By contrast, in Paul, the cosmos itself is redeemed and shares in the redemption of individuals. This all makes for interesting speculation, but the point here is that there is no reason to superimpose on Paul a theory of perduring relationships, for all the relationships we know are worldly and conditioned by our here-being, even our learned relation with the figure of the risen Christ. In a locative theology that envisages a place there, in contrast to our placement here, one might indeed imagine a continuity of relationship. But Paul never teaches the existence of a self, nor does he speak of any relationships. That relational theology grows from the grammatical analysis of verbal relationships within his semantic world, which promotes grammar to theology and results in a locative theology that contrasts "here"

Perhaps the earliest of Christian heresies is Docetism, a mistake that has no identified intra-Christian proponent. Celsus—the non-Christian philosopher Origen addressed in his *Against Celsus*—first used it to describe Christians. He maintained that if Christian claims about Jesus being both divine and human are true, this implies that Jesus only *seemed* (*dokeō*) to be human. Since the early councils, Christian thinkers have rejected that notion, yet the temptation to sacralize Jesus as more than human is found throughout the tradition. The letter to the Hebrews enjoining its readers not to regard Christ as an angel (1:5–14) suggests that some did just that. The doctrine of the incarnation as taught in the first five centuries insisted that Jesus is fully human and fully divine, without any admixture of his two natures. And yet the divine nature of Christ still pushes people to regard Jesus as more than (and thus not really) human. Philosophy, as now practiced, has for the most part abandoned the ontotheologies that the Greek Fathers of the church employed, so that their balanced doctrinal teaching has become all but unintelligible today. Simple repetition of the Chalcedonian theology on the indivisibility of the two natures of Christ, both divine and human, is ineffectual today because—apart from professional scholars—no one now thinks in the terms originally used to enunciate that theology.

Orthodox though the Chalcedonian endeavor is, it rests uneasily with the gospel narrative and is even less compatible with Paul's inchoate theology. If we regard Jesus in terms of a divine self, then there is no way to avoid thinking of him as a sacral self as opposed to the earthly selves of his disciples. This, however, is to reify Jesus and to imagine that we stand *here* in relationship to him *there*. Better to focus upon the kenotic hymn—with its tensively irreducible discourse on the empty and more-than-exalted Christ, as well as its intimations of the indivisibility between the ultimate meaning we seek in being "with Christ" beyond our death and the worldly context in which we (and Paul) actually find ourselves "in Christ" here and now. All our notions of being God and being human are thereby reaffirmed as the contextual and human discourse they have always been.

The function of emptiness is to clear away all essentialist notions in favor of a silently divine stillness, which itself is one with this dependently arisen world of becoming and constant change. Mahāyāna Buddhists prefer to empty the mind-screen of ideas and theologies by erasing their underlying reality (Skt. *svabhāva*), then stepping back and attending to what lies transparently before the windows of our eyes. Having cleansed the screen, one realizes that all along it has been an open window through which we can now gaze with clear vision into the everyday life that surrounds us in all its sundry comings and goings. Grace is everywhere, both in our emergent past and in our end-time future, for it is ever present right here and now. To be "in Christ" is not to be in a relationship with some sacral image of Jesus in his heaven, but rather to recognize that the same life that pulses in our physical bodies, and all bodies, is joined to the historical body of Christ through our sharing in his risen and awakened life.

---

and "there" in bipolar fashion.

In the Mahāyāna, karmic action comes in its varieties: Bad karmic actions sow seeds of delusion and suffering. Good karmic actions lead one to enter upon the path, which even when brought to completion does not bring about awakening or enlightenment. Awakening does not come from human action (*karma*) at all but instead emerges spontaneously in the second when one's eyelids are opened, without effort, by grace—not as the culminating achievement of a path of practice. What is achieved by self-mastery are good karmic results, or good fruits that spread among all sentient beings to counter our evolutionary instincts toward greed and anger and "tame" our natural heritage. Good actions do not, however, engender awakening to the risen Christ.

In this vein, Paul says that for him, to live is to continue working for the gospel to benefit and gladden human beings in Philippi. Yet he cannot dispel the always-present tension between what is best for Paul and what is necessary for others. He is pinioned on the horns of a constant and irresolvable dilemma not merely because of his claim of Roman citizenship, but also because of the very structure of his adventuresome faith. Really, as he writes, he has no need to decide for one side or the other, for the choice is no longer in his control. So he rehearses the considerations that led him to be where he is, for "I do not know," and he does not need to know, "what is the best choice" (καὶ τί αἱρήσομαι οὐ γνωρίζω 1:22). The verb here, "to choose" (αἱρέω), "frequent in the Septuagint and secular Greek, meant . . . 'to take into one's hands, seize' in a very realistic way."[206] It means here that the choice is his. Still, confident as Paul is of his strategy, he cannot choose between two such alternatives. Paul's life, like all life, is dependently arisen, given as a mission-inspiring task, and exhausted when the force of human energies wane, diminish, and finally end.[207]

Paul is facing a trial for his life. He does long to be released from all the very concrete tasks that characterize his life as a gospel worker and by which he engages in a constant drive for the preaching of Christ. Paul is always at a disadvantage with his opponents, for he is forever having to counter a theology that is clearly outlined with a protean life "in Christ" that involves more than he can properly articulate. His opponents see the issues clearly, but Paul is looking through a mirror, wondering what it all means. He does not look at the mirror as though its surface holds the truth, but rather he glimpses in its reflections the shape of a truth embodied in the lives of the Philippians. Letters are for him mirrors, affording him an indirect vision of people who are far away. But for Paul, the tensive ambiguity remains, for the actual life-and-death

---

206. O'Brien, *Epistle to the Philippians*, 126.

207. Collange, *Epistle of Saint Paul*, 62, sees Paul as rhetorically posing the alternatives "presented to him at the time when he took the decision to reveal his Roman citizenship, alternatives underlying the debate reflected in verses 15ff." Also, Collange points out that the use of the verb *haireō*, meaning "to choose" or "to take into one's own hands," could hardly reflect the actual sitiation of an imprisoned person (ibid., 63).

decision comes, "not by some kind of special enlightenment, but just by the simple fact that for the time being he is still there. To that fact he bows."[208]

Paul is being very human and thus it is, I think, a mistake to supernaturalize him as though he lived on some sacred or higher plane that is unavailable to the rest of us. Having encountered numerous people in a variety of sacral vestments and having donned those same vestments myself, I can attest that there are no sacred individuals. Indeed, the image of Paul from his correspondence is hardly holy, for he sweats blood and tears, and one can still almost smell them on the pages of his letters. Many a reader would like to sit down and argue with him, as his interpreters so often do. No one bothers to argue with Caesar. Few argue with the Buddha. But everybody wants a go at Paul, whether to support him in his conflicts by depicting his enemies in stark contours, to defend those he disparages as "dogs," or to convince him that he should have acted differently in light of more progressive ideas.

I too like to contend with Paul as I unpack his elegantly turgid theology, if not to reevaluate his cultural choices. I can make my own cultural choices and feel no need to confine my options to those of his archaic world. But in this passage Paul is describing the context of his life in light of his Christ awakening, and this is what I find fascinating, for his is not such an unusual dilemma. We too have glimmers of awakening experiences and can witness to the light we glimpse from time to time in our own lives. Those brief glances of light put us in conflict with the ubiquitous structures that employ power, sometimes violently, to keep people in the dark today. We too live with the dichotomy that is forced upon us by the very transience of our lives, and we likewise lack any true ability to choose.

When I held a position in the church, I could to some degree influence ecclesial affairs. When I held a position in the academy, I could exert a little influence on academic affairs. Now in retirement, like Paul tucked safely away in his prison cell, my power to influence has been reduced to scribbling words on paper. But steely submission to transient fate is not enough. We who read Paul's letters over the shoulders of the past are to live like Paul—in that same tension—recognizing that our dying is organic to our living. In no way are we to pretend that we will never actually die, for that pretense disenables us from living in gospel engagement. The answer lies in refusing to resolve the dilemma while yet living in its creative interstices, shouldering our task to further the gospel for the benefit and gladdening of all beings and rejecting the endless summer that would delude us into thinking sickness, old age, and death will never touch *us* in any imaginable future.

In his present imprisoned situation, it may not be up to Paul whether he lives or dies, but he *can* decide whether to live in the delusion of self-affirmation or to live in the risen awareness that embraces both ultimate Christ-life and conventional Christ-life—life with Christ there and life in the body of Christ here. Paul is not contemplating spiritual euthanasia; that would end his continual striving for the gospel. He chooses

---

208. Barth, *Epistle to the Philippians*, 41.

to live within the dynamic tension between life and death, "hemmed in on both sides by the two" (συνέχομαι δε ἐκ τῶν δύο 1:23). The basic sense of the verb συνέχομαι in that phrase is "to hold together," to be constrained.[209] It does not mean to be neatly balanced between two contrasting alternatives. Neither is it a one-dimensional either/or dilemma needing a resolution, but always a wise struggle embodied in a tensive coinherence that urges Paul to work in love throughout his worldly and conventional life. By being in Christ, we are pushed toward that objective that is a life inscribed in Christ, that which we are ever striving towards both in our worldly and conventional furtherance of the gospel and in our prayerfully-induced calm and courageous acceptance of the equality between living and dying.

The Mahāyāna doctrine of the two truths (Skt. *satya-dvaya*) complements the doctrine that emptiness and dependent arising are one and the same thing. It affirms the creative and tensive otherness between the ultimate (*paramārtha*) truth—which is beyond language and ineffable as something we may move toward but never capture—and the worldly, contextual (*saṃvṛti*) truth, which is expressed in language and only sketches our path toward the ultimate.[210] Neither is to be collapsed into the other, for ultimate truth is always beyond any controlling grasp, while contextual truth functions only conventionally, never invading the silence of ultimate truth.

The fractured and fractious history of Christianity demonstrates full well just how viscerally unconvincing are ecclesiastical claims to channel the ultimate truth. The ultimate truth is the truth of the final objective, an ever-alluring goal (Skt. *artha*) that draws us forth toward an unattainable (because it is ever-deepening and expanding) ultimate (*parama*) meaning (*artha*) that recognizes and stretches the creedal design of our lives as practitioners and as human beings to an end-time fulfillment.[211] The Mahāyāna path is to walk in the tensive awareness of an ineffable ultimate that is only more or less skillfully embodied in conventional terms. There are no other terms. To be a buddha or bodhisattva means to be enlightened to the here-and-now presence of the unattainable ultimate that drives us to engage in worldly, conventional practice and enunciate the truth of the teaching. It is like setting out on a space journey to a distant galaxy, enlivened by the quest but knowing full well that there are no discernible margins to an ever-expanding universe. I suspect we never will find those wormholes or time-travel gateways of science fiction that promise to whisk us off faster than the speed of light to places so far distant that their now-perceived light marks where they were millions of eons ago. What we are given is this world and our near solar system. We are hemmed in by unattainable horizons, with the nearest Andromeda galaxy perhaps as much as 2.5 million light-years away. We are hemmed

---

209. Collange, *Epistle of Saint Paul*, 64. Collange notes that Paul uses the term *sunechō* ("hold together," or "hem in") in only one other instance: 2 Cor 5:14.

210. See Nagao, *Foundational Standpoint*, 21–32, on "The Two Truths."

211. Reumann, *Philippians*, 556, on skopos: "A goal or target at which one aims."

in precisely because of our understanding that we never can explore or conquer such immensely distant realms.

What then becomes important is our shared human endeavor and our shared life, which we seek perhaps to share more expansively. Astrophysicists have taken over the old Aristotelian task of engendering wonder. We can send probes and spacecraft on journeys that will far outlast our lifetimes, so exploration into the depths of space becomes a multigenerational endeavor, drawing us beyond any imagined profit into selfless wonder of a sort Aristotle never imagined. In the meantime, wisdom awakened to the expanding divine presence throughout the multiverse finds its complement in engaged compassion right here on earth. This is why we are drawn to Paul: to see and to question the ways in which he expressed his Christ-life in concretely personal terms. We may imagine the earth as our mother, but no one envisions the multiverse as either motherly or fatherly. In face of its vastness, those terms of family life lose their purchase in our minds. Paul is held in tension between the life that is Christ and the dying that is Christ—in the bosom not of a comforting mother, but of an absentee Father. Gregory of Nyssa read Paul's Philippian letter about stretching forth as indicating that life, here and hereafter, is a constant stretching forth and forward to ever-new experiences, insights, and depths, from glory to glory.[212] In this letter, Paul witnesses to the dynamism that pushes him forward to be fruitful in the tasks of the gospel and outward to be organically dissolved and embodied with Christ. And in order to stretch forth, Paul wishes to be "loosened" (ἀναλῦσαι) even from his body.

The expression "to be with Christ" (σὺν Χριστῷ εἶναι) is apparently truly distinctive to Paul. There is no corresponding phrase in rabbinic literature, but there are parallels, particularly in the psalms, that speak of fellowship with God. Psalm LXX 138(139):18, for example, "appears to mean, 'I will be awakened to fellowship with God.'"[213] Such fellowship with God conquers death and probably does indeed figure in Paul's statements. Yet it is but a metaphor drawn from images of relationships of allegiance between just and mighty kings and their obedient subjects. Paul has reconfigured this covenant theology, and for him, to be with Christ includes both the oneness with Christ he looks forward to after the death of the body as well as the here-and-now experiences of Christ's always-eschatological, not-yet presence. It is as if, gazing into the immensity of the cosmos, we catch a present glimpse of the refracted light from a distant star and, in awareness of the warmth on our skin from our nearby star, we conclude with Isaac Newton that that light flows through and permeates our bodies too. The darkness is everywhere graced with light, and thus life.

Paul, in his endeavors and in his end-time faith, holds in creative tension two culturally distinct traditions: first, the end-time thought he reads in the prophets; and second, a oneness with the soon-to-come Christ, which reflects notions of Greek mystery religions surrounding initiation and participation in the mysteries. But what

212. See Keenan, *Meaning of Christ*, 93–103.
213. O'Brien, *Epistle to the Philippians*, 133.

is basic to Paul is that his end-time theology is rooted in the events of the cross and resurrection—events he has been awakened to in this here and now, stretching from his Damascus Road experience to this moment when, held in chains, he writes to the Philippians. Paul frequently expresses the meaning of Christ in cosmic terms, but his cosmos was so much smaller than ours. It is our task, then, to reimagine eschatological events in our own context, and that cannot be done using the archaic worldview of Greco-Roman times.

Note that Paul speaks of being *in* Christ, not being in fellowship or relationship with Christ. It is not that a self-enclosed and standalone individual called Paul somehow establishes a mystic fellowship with a standalone and self-enclosed Christ who, once crucified but now in his risen realm, is available to Christians who pray. "It is Christ who lives in me (ζῇ δὲ ἐν ἐμοὶ Χριστὸς)," Paul writes in Gal 2:20. The Jewish Paul does not think in terms of body and soul, as if upon dying his real self-soul migrates above to be with Christ.[214] Indeed, "Paul does not distinguish between body and soul, but speaks simply of himself as being with Christ. Life with Christ at death is no problem for the apostle; it flows like a pure spring from the victory of Easter."[215] As usual, it is always easier to say what things are not than what they are. And that Easter victory itself is an eschatological experience without empirical validation.

Conventional Confidence (1:25–26)

1:25 I am quite sure that I will remain and continue with all of you for your progress and joy in faith, ²⁶so that your boasting in Christ Jesus might abound through me because of my return to you.

1:25 καὶ τοῦτο πεποιθὼς οἶδα ὅτι μενῶ καὶ παραμενῶ πᾶσιν ὑμῖν εἰς τὴν ὑμῶν προκοπὴν καὶ χαρὰν τῆς πίστεως, ²⁶ἵνα τὸ καύχημα ὑμῶν περισσεύῃ ἐν Χριστῷ Ἰησοῦ ἐν ἐμοὶ διὰ τῆς ἐμῆς παρουσίας πάλιν πρὸς ὑμᾶς.

In asserting that he "confidently knows" (καὶ τοῦτο πεποιθὼς οἶδα) that he "will remain and continue with all of you for your progress and joy in faith" (ὅτι μενῶ καὶ παραμενῶ πᾶσιν ὑμῖν εἰς τὴν προκοπὴν καὶ χαρὰν τῆς πίστεως), Paul apparently expresses assurance about the outcome of his trial.[216] He has said in 1:24 that his continued presence

---

214. See Thrall, "Paul's Understanding."

215. O'Brien, *Epistle to the Philippians*, 137. O'Brien alludes to Collange in noting, "The apostle is . . . not so much interested in giving details of what life after death can be like as in the present conditions which will permit participation in it. 'To die' and 'to be with Christ' are therefore in large measure synonymous" (ibid.). See also Collange, *Epistle of Saint Paul*, 69.

216. Collange, *Epistle of Saint Paul*, 59. Collange interprets concretely the "this" (τοῦτο) about which Paul "confidently knows" (καὶ τοῦτο πεποιθὼς οἶδα) as the "that" (ὅτι) clause—the outcome of his Roman trial, "the sequence of events which he has just set in motion" (ibid.).

among the Philippians is necessary for them.[217] So here Paul is confident that surely he will be found innocent, thus postponing his departure to be with Christ—and yet in 1:27 Paul does acknowledge that his fate is not in his own shackled hands. We do not have Paul's legal records, so we do not know the outcome of his trial. However, because there is no suggestion in Resurrection Letter C that Paul was in prison when writing that letter, he was most likely acquitted, or at least freed from prison. As usual, historical information is so scant that we have to fall back on mirror speculations to catch a glimpse of what may have happened.

Paul talks so confidently about his success before the court and his continued presence (μενῶ καὶ παραμενῶ) among them (πᾶσιν ὑμῖν) for their progress and joy in the faith (εἰς τὴν ὑμῶν προκοπὴν καὶ χαρὰν τῆς πίστεως), because he is sure of the outcome and that "through my return among you," (διὰ τῆς ἐμῆς παρουσίας πάλιν πρὸς ὑμᾶς) "your boasting in Christ Jesus" (τὸ καύχημα ὑμῶν ... ἐν Χριστῷ Ἰησοῦ) "might increase" (ἵνα ... περισσεύῃ).

Paul's end goal is the progress of the faith, and the means to accomplish that goal are available before the court—a strategy in which he is confidently assured. If the central dispute between Paul and the Philippians is indeed about Paul's self-sufficiency and his assertion of citizenship, he now assures them that he "actually knows" (πεποιθὼς οἶδα 1:25) he is on the right track. Paul envisages his legal acquittal followed by his return to Philippi and his dear friends there, for his life remains tensively balanced between a much-desired departure to be with Christ and the need for compassionate engagement in the preaching of the gospel. Within the horizons of his conventional knowing, he is as sure as he can be. We have no sure evidence whether, in the historical event, he was correct. Scripture is infallible in the meaning of its teachings, but the hopes and expectations expressed therein are not themselves infallibly realized. Nevertheless, Paul was at ease walking the middle path between an awareness of the power of Christ beyond dying and the driving force of Christ in living his life, to the point that even his very mundane decisions take on something of his faith-inspired confidence (πεποιθώς). He wants to encourage the faith of the Philippians, for in Christ he has overcome the dichotomy between God-way-out-there and Paul-way-down-here. He lives even now in Christ and, if he has not yet passed beyond his life to be with Christ, he will remain with the Philippians for their progress in their joy in the faith. If he should die, Epaphroditus will still deliver his letter.

Disputes over how to live Christ in the Greco-Roman world would continue in any case, as indeed they did. Regardless of whether Paul himself was acquitted or taken to his death in Rome, we do not know how effective his strategy of gospel defense proved to be. Only after Constantine made the Empire Christian was Christianity

---

217. Reumann, *Philippians*, 254: "Paul's presentation of aims begins with wordplay in Greek, brought out as *stay on* (v 24 *epimenein*), *stay* (25, using *menein*), and *stay on in service* (25, *paramenein*)." I interpret this as Paul's bodhisattva vow to remain within his world to carry out the deeds necessary for others, rather than to seek the arhat goal of final cessation with Christ.

accepted, but then not as a leaven within the broader Greco-Hellenistic society but as a sovereign power alongside the Empire.[218] The history is as it is, but once it became socially normative to be Christian, gospel challenges to the larger society ceased, only to be replaced by endless power negotiations between church and state.

Unlike negotiations between entities like church and state, Paul's embrace here of both life and death does not involve competing interests. He lives, fully alive, in a tensive end-time awaiting. In his Christ faith, each moment is both fully here-and-now present and at the same time pregnant with a beyond-death future that beggars theological imagination. Paul's eschatology is this balancing between, on the one hand, his final cessation and dissolution when he will be with Christ and, on the other, his present being in Christ in the world with all his strength devoted to striving for the sake of others. Paul is confident that in Christ he is ambidextrous: With his right hand he will teach the gospel message of an all-encompassing and transcendent life with Christ, while with his left he will see to the everyday health of the body of Christ in Philippi as well as in Ephesus, Corinth, Rome, and elsewhere.

But what does Paul mean when he talks about "the faith" of the Philippians, about which they "can both make progress and experience joy" (εἰς τὴν ὑμῶν προκοπὴν καὶ χαρὰν τῆς πίστεως)? Joy seems clear enough, for a Christic faith allows the erasure of boundaries between people and between people and God, bringing the joy of convivial living and peace beyond the realpolitik of competing powers.[219] But how can one speak of the "progress of faith" (προκοπὴν . . . τῆς πίστεως)? How does faith progress? Does it mean one simply believes more intensely, with greater fervor? I do not think so, since that would hardly be progress, just more self-assertion: "I really, really believe!" Does it mean drawing more and more people into the church? This is what people often understand the progress of faith to mean. But Paul is focused upon the teaching of faith doctrine, not on grasping after the power to make Christ belief normative by force, nor on some popular self-actualization nonsense.

What Paul writes of life in Christ and of Christ's death is not an invitation to embark upon spiritual journeys into our inner selves. He invites his readers instead to abandon self-definition altogether and to live in freedom, even while his own embodied self is shackled and awaiting trial. Christ too was in chains, and it is to his unfettered risen life that Paul witnesses and that he boldly and bodily offers to others. He proffers a taught faith, not some amorphously open mind that lusts after every idea that strikes its fancy. Quite specifically, he teaches the learned gospel as it empowers resurrection.

---

218. See Mitchell, *Church, Gospel, and Empire*. Also see Mitchell's blog, http://rogerhaydonmitchell.wordpress.com, especially under the topic of "kenarchy."

219. See Ivan Illich, *Tools for Conviviality* (London: Boyers, 2001) and David Cayley, *The Rivers North of the Future: The New Testament of Ivan Illich* (Toronto: Anasi, 2005). Also see Barbara Ehrenreich, *Dancing in the Streets: A History of Collective Joy* (New York: Metropolitan, 2007).

Paul could not have imagined a gospel that is enforced upon others, for his experience of being in Christ is not an ideological viewpoint that could be affirmed so fervently as to banish all other positions. It is all about dying and rising with Christ, not about increasing power but about increasing faith. The gospel teaching is clear enough: To save one's life is to lose one's life. Most assuredly Paul, and indeed all Christian preachers in those early days, were offering an alternative to the state religion of the Roman Empire. But that alternative was not one on a spectrum of mappable options; it was and still is Christ faith in life resurrection.

Paul must have known the Jesus traditions that, after he wrote these letters, were eventually brought together to form the four Gospel narratives. Even so, he does not say much at all in his letters about the historical Jesus or his teachings. Even as a zealous Pharisee, he would probably have found nothing particularly surprising or objectionable in the Synoptic narratives. Like the original disciples in Palestine, Paul focuses single-mindedly upon the living Christ he encountered. But having met the risen Christ, his aim is to enlarge the risen life of Christ through his own bodily witness for the larger body of Christ followers.

One can hardly imagine that Jesus' teachings as recorded in the Synoptic Gospels would have triggered much prosecutorial zeal to eradicate the early communities of his followers. One can well imagine, however, that claims in those same Synoptic Gospels that somehow Jesus embodied God would indeed have been a point of contention.[220] Paul does not repeat Jesus' social gospel teachings, nor does he bother to describe the social and economic conditions of the Greco-Roman world at the time, for his correspondents were certainly familiar with them. Surely, Paul was committed to the justice demanded by the prophets. But what he teaches and attempts to foster in his audience is the resurrection faith, so that they may grow in understanding and appreciation of the truth of the gospel that Christ is the primal wisdom of God beyond death. That growth in gospel learning is the mark of their progress in faith—that they too may live fearlessly in confidence of life beyond organic and political limitations. And this involves human learning and participation in the prayers and common liturgies of the communities, all of which comes to ground in gospel learning. It is communal progress furthered by the common activities of the communities. It is not a party platform.

It is not only a matter of learning the faith-nurturing doctrine, but also of progress in cleansing the mind from all barriers that hinder faith so that one may experience "joy in faith" (καὶ χαρὰν τῆς πίστεως). By this, Paul clearly implies the erasure of final status distinctions between rich and poor, male and female, free and slave, Jew

---

220. See Alan Segal, *Two Powers in Heaven: Early Rabbinic Reports about Christianity and Gnosticism* (Leiden: Brill, 2002), which describes the rabbinic rejection of any theology that would place another "power" in heaven, whether the Merkabah mystical traditions with their emphasis on Enoch, or the Christian focus on Jesus as being with God from the beginning. Compare Dunn, *Theology of Paul the Apostle*, 266–93, on "The Preexistent One." Paul sees Jesus as embodying the wisdom of God from the beginning, but he lacks the Johannine teaching on the Logos.

and Gentile. So it is indeed about overturning any society that clings to such distinctions, as of course all known societies do. We are all to be one in Christ. This is not a Pauline afterthought; it is the center of his gospel experience and preaching. Progress in faith is, first if not last, the ongoing erasure of boundaries, which allows us actually to live in Christ, to be one-bodied with Christ, and one-bodied even with those whose bodies we find unacceptable. This demands, subsequently and necessarily, an arduous effort of prayer and meditation; it does not drop down from heaven in a package, nor can we make it come about by our own effort. Grace is everywhere and always a gift—and it always demands effort from us.

The result of all this is that Paul's hearers may no longer boast about their own status or accomplishments. But they may, more and more, boast in Christ Jesus because of Paul. In Paul's writings, "boasting" (καύχημα 1:26) is usually an act of self-sufficiency and self-attachment. It is the quintessential affirmation of pride and delusion, as when Paul speaks of boasting according to the flesh (2 Cor 11:18), or boasting in human ability (1 Cor 3:21), or boasting in appearances (2 Cor 5:12). By contrast to such self-boasting, to boast "through me in Christ" (ἐν Χριστῷ Ἰησοῦ ἐν ἐμοὶ) is to move beyond self-attachment to glory in the same life force that beat in the heart of Christ and that beats in our hearts. It is to abandon all images of self, for indeed there is not one of us who is not tempted to boast of self—our achievements, our stellar lives, our inestimable value, our spiritual or financial portfolios. This is the constant temptation, and to Paul it is the basic delusion.

And so it is startling when Paul says that the Philippians may boast "in me" (ἐν ἐμοὶ). One would expect that one is to boast only in Christ and not in (ἐν) Paul. Is this not yet another form of Paul's pushing himself forward? It surely is so, but only inasmuch as Paul entrusts himself to the incarnate Jesus, for all his efforts flow from "him who strengthens me," as he will confess in 4:13. By being one with Christ and boasting in Paul, the Philippians are to regard him not in patronage terms as a favorite son or their dear leader, but as an apostle of Christ in a shared risen life. It is also an invitation: The Philippians too, in virtue of their participation in risen life, may boast in their communal assembly and their selfless careers in the town of Philippi. But this Christ with whom we are to be one is not some mythical and imagined Christ who hovers above and calls us all to live in pretended relationship and cozy fellowship. This is a concrete oneness that pervades our lives and flows from one person to another in the here and now, drawing us all to be one not only with God through Christ—and not only with Christ in God, but also with all of our brothers and sisters everywhere, renouncing our evolutionary impulse to serve "me and mine" (Skt. *ātma-ātmīya*).

Such is the spirit call of this gospel—as it is of the Buddha Dharma—that we are to begin by abandoning self and its preoccupations. The same life that beats in the hearts of our enemies is the life that beats in our hearts. In one way or another, we are all Samaritans to somebody. But there is no real life difference. And all our boasting should celebrate life together beyond ethnic, nationalistic, religious, and personal boundaries. That is what it means for us Christians to be in Christ, and this understanding is so globally countercultural that it can hardly be reduced to any political program or power rearrangement. That same life circulates in the bodies and minds of people of different traditions, whether they call it Christ-life or Buddha awakening. Wherever we find life, we identify it as Christ-life, for there is no other life envisaged in our scriptures and traditions. Others identify it differently—as the awakening of the Buddha, as submission to Allah, as being one with Brahman, as living the Mosaic covenant and following God's commandments. No matter. It is all a gift and none of it is under our control. We all begin with life as we experience living, and the first step, throughout all these traditions, is to abandon the self-centered life that imprisons experience.

The Philippians may so glory in Christ and boast in Paul because he indeed expects to come to them. Not yet being dead, he plans for his future, knowing that he lives in a tensive awaiting of the outcome of his case before the authorities. Paul's awakening is an advancing awakening. It is not a stay-at-home waiting, Godot-like, for an end time. It is an awakening that is on the move and engaged for the sake of the gospel. Even if Paul dies, still the teaching of resurrection faith will be delivered to the Philippians. Paul was a work in progress.

Another reading of this passage might see Paul's confidence that he will visit the Philippians as somewhat like the spiritual insight vouchsafed in a vision to the fourteenth-century English mystic Julian of Norwich: "All shall be well, and all shall be well, and all manner of thing shall be well."[221] No matter what the difficulty, if one loves Christ and lives in faith, nothing can cause harm and nothing can separate us from the love of Christ. This insight is not of course a guarantee of a successful outcome in worldly terms, but rather a widening of the spectrum in which all outcomes are seen.

Conventional Citizenship (1:27–30)

1:27 Only, exercise your citizenship in a manner worthy of the gospel of Christ, so that, whether I come and see you or am absent and hear about you, I will know that you stand firm in one spirit, striving together with one life for the gospel faith, 28and do not be at all frightened by anything that comes from opponents: this is a sign of their dissolution, but of your salvation. [All] this comes from God: 29for he has graciously granted to you not only to believe in Christ, but also to suffer for him—30since you experience the same struggle that you saw in me and now hear about me.

1:27 Μόνον ἀξίως τοῦ εὐαγγελίου τοῦ Χριστοῦ πολιτεύεσθε, ἵνα εἴτε ἐλθὼν καὶ ἰδὼν ὑμᾶς εἴτε ἀπὼν ἀκούω τὰ περὶ ὑμῶν, ὅτι στήκετε ἐν ἑνὶ πνεύματι, μιᾷ ψυχῇ

---

221. Julian of Norwich, *Showings*, trans. Edmund Colledge and James Walsh (New York: Paulist, 1978) 225.

συναθλοῦντες τῇ πίστει τοῦ εὐαγγελίου, ²⁸καὶ μὴ πτυρόμενοι ἐν μηδενὶ ὑπὸ τῶν ἀντικειμένων, ἥτις ἐστὶν αὐτοῖς ἔνδειξις ἀπωλείας, ὑμῶν δὲ σωτηρίας, καὶ τοῦτο ἀπὸ θεοῦ· ²⁹ὅτι ὑμῖν ἐχαρίσθη τὸ ὑπὲρ Χριστοῦ, οὐ μόνον τὸ εἰς αὐτὸν πιστεύειν ἀλλὰ καὶ τὸ ὑπὲρ αὐτοῦ πάσχειν, ³⁰τὸν αὐτὸν ἀγῶνα ἔχοντες οἷον εἴδετε ἐν ἐμοὶ καὶ νῦν ἀκούετε ἐν ἐμοί.

The issue that is front and center in these Philippian letters is how to engage in this everyday world while at the same time realizing the gospel equality between life and death. For Paul, "to live is Christ and to die is gain," for he has overcome the dichotomy of either clinging to life or rushing toward death. He accepts the condition in which he finds himself—although in chains, he is still alive and expects to visit the Philippians again. Here, Paul urges them to engage in their lives just as they are, as citizens of a Christ assembly located in the Romanized colony of Philippi.[222] Philippians are citizens of the Empire and not likely to revolt against it.

Certainly, there are many passages in Paul, as elsewhere in the New Testament, that insist upon justice and that contrast the gospel, the good news that comes from Christ, with the "good news" that comes from Caesar. But Paul was most likely innocent of reformist politics,[223] and there is little evidence of political turmoil in Philippi, considering its location on a rich trade route and the status it enjoyed as an important city in Macedonia. Paul does not recommend that Christ followers comport themselves in an otherworldly fashion; to the contrary, he urges their civil engagement in the world. Fulfill your civic obligations and be good citizens (πολιτεύεσθε), he tells them. They are to act as citizens of a Roman colony should act and to participate in the good governance of Philippi.

Paul himself is exercising his citizenship in his appeal to Caesar, and he wants his readers likewise to practice their civic duty. That is the first and obvious meaning of the term, "to exercise your citizenship" (πολιτεύεσθε 1:27). It refers to social and political matters "in the public place (*politeia*),"[224] that is, to matters of the city (πόλις, *polis*). The overall point is engagement in conventional life, for the main verb "exercise your citizenship" "spreads its aura over" all that follows in the rest of the passage, enjoining continued involvement in public life.[225] This also reflects Paul's legal struggle

---

222. Reumann, *Philippians*, 275: "1:27–30 form a discrete unit, a single Greek sentence, with one main verb *politeuesthe* in 27a."

223. Ruden, *Paul Among the People*, 122, on Paul's Tarsus: "While he grew up, Tarsus was thriving as a peaceful provincial capital. If anyone persecuted Jews there, we don't know about it. He lived his entire life, in fact, in an era of relative order and safety following the Roman civil wars: crime was not allowed to grow chaotic enough to embarrass Rome; there were no local potentates doing whatever they wanted; and no wars were being fought except on the edges of the empire."

224. Reumann, *Philippians*, 280. Also see where Reumann notes "relations in the 'public space' of the Roman *colonia* and Roman adversaries. Social 'givens' included courts, civic officials, economic livelihood, social relations, trade guilds, neighbors of various religions, and a formal state cult (not yet as in the last years of Nero or Domitian's time, but emphasized more than in any city where Paul previously ministered)" (ibid., 281–82).

225. Ibid., 285, 295. Many commentators who hold for one unified letter interpret "to exercise

to carve out a space for Christ followers within the Empire under the umbrella of his citizenship defense. If perhaps those ill-motivated Christ preachers he refers to above are actually trying to cause turmoil by making Paul into an anti-government symbol, then it would make sense for Paul to tell his friends to stay responsibly engaged in their civic life because of their gospel practice.

Similar wording occurs in Resurrection Letter C, where Paul writes that "our political engagement is in heaven" (ὑμῶν γάρ τὸ πολίτευμα ἐν οὐρανοῖς ὑπάρχει 3:20), leading unwary commentators to think that "heavenly citizenship" is otherworldly. But that cannot be the meaning in 1:27, for it makes no sense. Here, Paul is calling Christ followers to exercise their citizen duties in a manner worthy of the gospel, with a reconfigured social and cultural consciousness. But this is not supernatural politics, an agenda flowing from the heavens. There simply is no such agenda and no such politics. All politics are local. Although the demand for justice flows from God's prophets, politics and policy remain contextual—matters for intelligent human insight and decision.

There is no authentic faith politics, although the boundaries of our political actions must be congruent with the gospel call for compassion in just practices. But the how to do it is always a matter of informed human intelligence and committed action that must emerge in the lived interstices between ultimate life and the always-conventional context of political affairs. Religious pedigrees and sectarian ideology founded on the conviction that one's own ideas are the absolute truth are inappropriate and unreliable guides in the arena of secular policy-making.[226] Religious thinkers the world over tend to urge their ideas as if validated by some divine suzerainty. But Paul lives in the interstices between conventional life and life in Christ, and he does not reduce the gospel to a political program. He does recommend striving to enlarge Christ faith by constructing a strategy for furthering the cultural and social scope of that faith.

Paul enjoins the Christians in Philippi to act intelligently in the social and political world, "always in a manner worthy of the gospel of Christ" (Μόνον ἀξίως τοῦ εὐαγγελίου τοῦ Χριστοῦ 1:27), whatever the specific content of their stance in the world. His is a utilitarian approach that is grounded in this Christ gospel and witnesses to

---

your citizenship" (πολιτεύεσθε) in light of the "heavenly commonwealth" in 3:20 (τὸ πολίτευμα ἐν οὐρανοῖς ὑπάρχει), weakening the stress here on actual public engagement. For example, Silva approvingly cites Diognetus' description of Christians "who pass their time upon the earth, but . . . have their citizenship in heaven (ἐν οὐρανῷ πολιτεύονται)" (Silva, *Philippians*, 88). The gospel is not a political cause, yet neither is it a supernatural escape from living among the welter of worldly conditions. There is no Christian party, nor ought there to be any Christian lobby, for political deliberations are hardly advanced by entertaining the often absolutist claims of religious leaders and clerics. Which is perhaps why Paul here recommends that the Philippians themselves, not their ecclesial leaders, determine what might be of value to them.

226. See Haidt, *Righteous Mind*, 107: "Each [moral] matrix provides a complete, unified, and emotionally compelling worldview, easily justified by observable evidence and nearly impregnable to attack by arguments from outsiders."

our shared human condition. "Whether I come and see you" (εἴτε ἐλθὼν καὶ ἰδὼν ὑμᾶς 1:27) "or am absent and hear about you" (εἴτε ἀπὼν ἀκούω τὰ περὶ ὑμῶν), the Philippians are to stand firm and strive together for the gospel faith. But Paul gives them no platform for political action; he does not direct them as to what to think about their social and political life together.

Meanwhile, Paul confidently defends his own strategy before Roman law and power, making it clear that this is why he is in prison awaiting trial. Nevertheless, he insists that the context in which politics and policy are to be considered is our shared life in Christ, which erases boundaries between rich and poor and impels us toward social and active engagement. All are encompassed in gospel grace, and Paul's oppressors—who do indeed oppress—have the same lifeblood flowing through their own hearts and the same energies active in their minds. Yet, enthralled by power and status, their minds move within the ever ancient and ever new geopolitics of self-preservation. Paul rejects the factionalism of self, so he elegantly and viciously excoriates any faction that would seek to draw new boundaries for competing selves. He insists that the Philippians "stand firm in one spirit" (ἵνα ... ὅτι στήκετε ἐν ἑνὶ πνεύματι 1:27) and act in a manner consonant with their gospel faith. That Spirit is the same Spirit that supplies Christ and emboldens Paul's endeavors.

Here Paul teaches that gospel faith—which critiques ideology by dethroning selfhood and factionalism—should set the parameters within which Christians carefully consider all ideologies and political movements.[227] But to strive "within the gospel faith" (τῇ πίστει τοῦ εὐαγγελίου) does not mean faith in the gospel as an objective set of assured truths. The genitive term τοῦ εὐαγγελίου (of the gospel) functions as an appositional genitive to πίστις (faith); thus, it is not faith that takes the gospel as its object, but rather faith that is informed by the gospel[228] and supplied by the Spirit.

This is a hard lesson to learn. I have met many influential people who embody their factional positions as truth. As a young Roman Catholic curate enamored with the liberal theology of Vatican II, I was dismayed one evening in 1966 to hear a bishop of the church boast over a rectory dinner table that he had no need for theology; he already knew the truth. Indeed, he went on rather proudly to explain that he had not

---

227. Ivan Illich (1926–2002), in *Celebration of Awareness*, argues that the gospel is not an ideology to be implemented but rather a path of faith and practice. I attended seminars with Illich at his Intercultural Documentation Center in Cuernavaca, Mexico, in the late 1960s. Illich (a philosopher, secularized Roman Catholic priest, and social critic who is perhaps best remembered for his 1971 book *Deschooling Society*) followed Christ with a simple and critical practice. He urged upon the many progressive Christians who came to his center that the gospel is not an ideology and that it cannot be identified with any political option, even the liberation theology then current in Latin America. In light of this non-ideological gospel, Illich critiqued left-leaning as well as centrist and right-leaning options, refusing to acknowledge the Christian status of the "Christian Democratic" parties then spreading throughout Europe and into Latin America. His counter-advice was that people everywhere appropriate their own native ability to govern themselves, apart from any supervening theology from any quarter whatsoever.

228. Reumann, *Philippians*, 268.

read a book since his ordination some thirty years earlier. Unfortunately, such studied ignorance has flourished over the last four or five decades and effectively cancelled out the ecumenical and interfaith openness of that Vatican Council. When recourse is made to religiously held ideologies, every reformation calls forth a counterreformation and factionalism that snuffs out the Spirit on both sides, leaving them behind ramparts designed to repel one another. Denominationalism is the social formation of deluded selfhood.

Paul can easily be misread and misused as an ideological and factional partisan of the gospel truth. Whether or not he was in the end able to visit the Philippians, he instructs them here "to stand in one spirit" (ὅτι στήκετε ἐν ἑνὶ πνεύματι) and "to struggle and to contend" (συναθλοῦντες) in common accord and a common "single life" (μιᾷ ψυχῇ) "for the gospel faith" (τῇ πίστει τοῦ εὐαγγελίου). It is as if they are engaged in an athletic contest, for the term "struggle" comes from the gladiatorial arena. There is nothing more factional than gladiators. Ever fond of military and athletic imagery, Paul pictures "the Philippian Christians as wrestlers or gladiators in the arena of faith."[229] Were he writing today, Paul might well opt for football metaphors. Certainly, he recommends struggle, not ease or comfort in some assured truth. Moreover, it is *concerted* action that he urges—that we "stand in the one spirit-informed mind" (ὅτι στήκετε ἐν ἑνὶ πνεύματι), be of the "one life," and act with common purpose.

But although he employs this imagery of struggle, Paul decries factionalism and party spirit. He does not say we are to march side by side like comrades-in-arms as Christian soldiers on the march. He would never have imagined a "Christian" army or a "Legion of Mary." Paul's fondness for military imagery is merely a fondness for commonly available images. Sarah Ruden writes, "Since the army was the part of government that could really work, protecting and enriching the people, many polytheistic authors show that in civic life, people should behave like good soldiers. 'Staying where you are posted'—that is, in the assigned position in the line—was an apt metaphor for public responsibility."[230] While tax officials and judicial courts exhibited the kinds of corruption that plague empires, the army demanded a discipline of purpose that was widely admired throughout Greco-Roman society. It offered one of the only avenues for males to prosper in life,[231] precisely because it inculcated mutual trust and enforced discipline. Then, as now, military imagery was powerful because armies embody the sense of a larger corporate self for the sake of which soldiers the world over are willing to die.

---

229. O'Brien, *Epistle to the Philippians*, 150.

230. Ruden, *Paul Among the People*, 138, on Paul and military imagery.

231. Ibid., 128–29: "More important for most of Paul's male followers, joining the Roman army was the best deal in the empire, a way for fit, tough, and disciplined provincials to get what they were not born to: Roman citizenship (often just through joining up), careers and status (through promotion), and wealth (through plunder)."

Paul nevertheless rejects the calculus of self-survival. He does not see each and every Christian as a standalone individual who ought to join in a common endeavor to protect one party against another; his was not an era of independent nation-states. The only march Paul actually joins is his forced march as a shackled prisoner, and even there he finds kindred souls in the ranks of the Praetorian Guard. But the martial metaphors stand out: We are to stand together, in one spirit, advancing fearlessly. My conclusion is that Paul simply liked military language.

The term "life" (ψυχῇ, *psychē*) here is the same term used in the gospel when Jesus says that in order to save our lives, we must lose them (Mark 8:35). So "one life" in this passage means more than "with one accord." Paul has just spoken about the one life that is Christ, gained both by living and by dying. We should not then understand Paul to be saying that Christ followers are differentiated from all other living beings because of their Christian identity, or that they should strive to make others assume that cultural identity.[232] That would mean there are at least two lives: Christian life and the life of others. But this is a shallow, us-against-them reading. When in 1:28 Paul says that "we should let nothing frighten us" (καὶ μὴ πτυρόμενοι ἐν μηδενὶ) "that might come from our opponents" (ὑπὸ τῶν ἀντικειμένων), he does not speak of Christ-life versus the life of others with whom Christ followers are locked in worldly competition for power and influence. The opponents are not "the other side" but rather any who would divide and destroy the shared life we all live, unconverted by faith in any gospel and intent solely upon the struggle for self-survival.

In 1:16, Paul asserts that he has been appointed—that is, he is under orders (κεῖμαι, *keimai*)—to defend the gospel. And in 3:16, in Letter C, he tells the Philippians "to march in formation" as soldiers would (τῷ αὐτῷ στοιχεῖν). But this "soldiering on" is in witness to shared life "in Christ," who led no army. In John 18:36, before Pilate, Jesus claims an otherworldly kingdom, saying that if his kingdom were "from this world," then his followers would indeed fight for him. But it wasn't and they didn't. Even Jesus' claim in Matt 26:53—that he could call upon more than twelve legions of angels to save him from arrest—was not realized, for Jesus' point in saying that is to rebuke Peter's swordplay in his defense. "Those who march in opposition" (ὑπὸ τῶν ἀντικειμένων) and of whom we are "not to be frightened" are those who, opposing Paul in their self-delusion, stand over against and frustrate efforts to further the gospel by dragging him in chains along toward his appointed trial.

The adversaries and opponents mentioned by Paul are seldom identified in terms of their teaching or their viewpoints. He simply pictures them as factional people who work out on others their imagined need to protect and nourish their own sense of self, demanding that a privileged "we" be set in opposition to some detested "they."

---

232. Jaroslav Pelikan's masterful five-volume *Christian Tradition* follows the development of Christian culture from Patristic times to the present age, demonstrating that resurrection faith is not a separate culture among other cultures; it remains always countercultural, emptying cultural forms and bringing into question the exercise of power wherever it be found.

In this passage, they seem to be those who have arrested Paul and are forcing him to march—in other words, the Roman authorities.[233] But again and again Paul tells us that we are to march selflessly. The opponents need not be identified other than as those who march to the tune of a fractious and factional drummer. In Paul's world, we are to recognize that we live the very same life (μιᾷ ψυχῇ) as our opponents, the same life Paul lives in Christ and urges upon us all. And we are not to fear deluded opponents who can indeed kill—but only the body.

The struggle for one life, identified with Christ beyond life and death, negates any effort to gain evolutionary advantage over the lives of others, and so serves as a sign for the saving of our common lives—that is, "for our salvation" (ἥτις ἐστὶν . . . ὑμῶν δὲ σωτηρίας), precisely because we are organically grounded in "life from God" (καὶ τοῦτο ἀπὸ θεοῦ), which we live as shared with all other living beings. Salvation here means risen life in these very bodies of ours. Salvation means taking refuge in an eschatological vision of life expanding beyond the limits of death, not a transfer ticket to another realm where the rightness of our self-defense will be forever vindicated. That kind of self-serving struggle characterizes instead those who would differentiate life—*my life is good and beautiful, and your life can be negated and eliminated*. Their labors will come to a sad end—"it is a sign for their destruction" (ἥτις ἐστιν αὐτοῖς ἔνδειξις ἀπωλείας). Such people's efforts will be squandered and wasted in the delusion of a concocted need to define their unique identity in competition with others, even as they cling to a narrowly restricted life in the false hope of assuring its continuance.

The term "dissolution" (ἀπωλεία) in 1:28 contrasts with Paul's earnest wish in 1:23 that he be dissolved (εἰς τὸ ἀναλῦσαι) to be with Christ. The opponents he speaks of fall away from life through entrenched self-interest and barricaded spheres of self. It is not a matter of their death or their eternal damnation, nor does it mean that Christ followers should welcome such an outcome. *Schadenfreude* is not a gospel value. The killing of every Islamist terrorist lessens the life of every Christian. John Donne knew this better than Ernest Hemingway ever imagined; Donne used the phrase "for whom the bell tolls" to evoke the corporate unity of being human.[234] In 3:19, Paul asserts that the final end of enemies of the cross is likewise "destruction" (ἀπώλεια), for when they die, they simply cease to be, disappearing altogether without sharing the common risen life in which all are invited to participate.

Such situations of struggle and contention come, Paul says, "from God" (καὶ τοῦτο ἀπὸ θεοῦ), because for Paul everything comes from God, the ultimate presence that in harsh benevolence transcends all worldly categories of gain and loss. This does not mean that God sows contention or prizes human suffering and struggle. Rather, the life-source God drives us toward ever-receding horizons, which does entail a common struggle and generally results in resistance from those who demand stable horizons.

---

233. Reumann, *Philippians*, 278: "Roman officials and the populace."

234. Meditation XVII of John Donne's *Devotions upon Emergent Occasions*. Hemingway borrowed Donne's words for the title of his novel about the Spanish civil war.

The Emptied Christ of Philippians

At the same time, Paul demands that we act selflessly in all our conflicts. And so Paul can say it has been "graciously granted to us not only to believe in Christ" (ὅτι ὑμῖν ἐχαρίσθη τὸ ὑπὲρ Χριστοῦ, οὐ μόνον τὸ εἰς αὐτὸν πιστεύειν 1:29), "but also to suffer for him" so that we may find meaning for our lives, meditate in quiet peace, and at the end be gathered to our fathers and mothers in the eschaton-life of Christ. This struggle is directed inward, countering our evolutionary survival instincts so that we may respond and share in Christ's struggle. Christ is the paradigm not only for transcendent wisdom, but for the struggle we humans encounter. The narrative of his passion and death portrays a human ordeal. We are likewise to enter into the fray—with all the suffering that may entail—for the furtherance of the gospel. Rather than taking up arms to protect, we are to suffer with Christ, for only such humanness can assure that this gospel actually serves to gladden and benefit all beings.

It is not an altogether happy fact that "we are granted then to suffer on his account" (ἀλλὰ καὶ τὸ ὑπὲρ αὐτοῦ πάσχειν). Job knew all about suffering and pain, about the sense of desolation and isolation. Paul too, in his chains, has known hardships, beset as he was on every side—by Roman soldiers on the one hand, and on the other, by factions in the Corinthian community, challengers in Galatia, contending preachers in Ephesus, and culturally obtuse apostles in Jerusalem. Does God will people to suffer? Job knew such was not the case. He retained his commitment to Torah despite the sufferings he endured and despite his inability to understand or explain why he suffered. The austere poetry sections that constitute the original book of Job, however, proved too stark and discomforting for many, so another hand added a prose introduction and conclusion. These sections recast the entire painful ordeal by painting the more reassuring scenario of divine testing and divine reward.[235] Job himself was more down to earth.

Like Job, Paul is not saying that God, out of some sense of divine super-knowledge, sends sufferings because in his divine omniscience it's a good idea. Anyone who identifies with the one life that Christians experience to be Christ—indeed anyone encouraged to work for the benefit of all—can expect conflict and suffering, for this gospel transgresses norms and threatens entrenched self-interests. Even apart from the boundary transgression of the empty Christ, ordinary living entails human-created suffering whenever we differentiate mine from yours and cling to personal identities defined as "me and mine" (Skt. *ātma-ātmīya*) as over against "you and yours." All of this inevitably triggers suffering. Beyond such human-created pain and distress, our very organic life entails suffering, for our bodies are wonderfully fragile. Attachment to delusions and imagined projections may bolster our (false) sense of a well-defended self-identity, but that identity in the end is always threatened by the suffering that precedes death.

---

235. Bernhard W. Anderson, *Understanding the Old Testament* (Englewood Cliffs: Prentice Hall, 1986) 590: "It is generally agreed that the author of the poetic sections did not compose the story that appears in the prologue and epilogue."

Paul himself experienced both gospel conflict and bodily pain, and yet he says insight into the one life flowing through all beings everywhere drives us to work toward the recognition by all that this life is a shared life—whether Jew or Greek, male or female, straight or gay, right or left, Christian or Muslim, and on and on. Although we all suffer, the only identifiable reason for much of the suffering in our many worlds lies in discrimination and attachment to self, not in some perverted will of God. Thus, wise people do endure their suffering with patience and do die peacefully in the hope of risen life.

The Philippians also "experience the same conflict" (τὸν αὐτὸν ἀγῶνα ἔχοντες), "that you saw in me and now hear about me" (οἷον εἴδετε ἐν ἐμοὶ καὶ νῦν ἀκούετε ἐν ἐμοί 1:30). In no known universe are we eternally sheltered from strife and free from pain. We are human. We experience not only the transience of life and all the frailty and suffering this entails, but also the conflict that arises from necessarily incomplete viewpoints to which we cling as though they are absolute truths. But once we awaken to the one life that is Christ, we can attend to and meditate upon the vanity of self-interest and proceed joyously like sightless Paul along the Damascus Road.

Upon reading this letter, knowing the same human struggles as Paul, the Philippians recognize that even he has not realized a composed state of sweet and easy wisdom. He, too, is still striving toward the goal, stretching forth in his efforts. He does not pronounce that suffering for Christ is some arbitrary directive from an all-knowing Father who demands pain from his children for their own good. In fact, suffering in this world is often simply the result of actions taken by people in their primal ignorance (Skt. *avidyā*), usually actions that deny our common humanity and result in the dissolution of shared life that comes when we insist we shall live a life others may not share. Yet shared life is all there is.

Human suffering is the first truth of the Buddhist path. It remains true even when times are good and bodies are healthy, for the brute fact remains that no one escapes from the transience and impermanence of being alive. That plain fact is perhaps what leads to all our bootless attempts to endure and prosper in the evolutionary struggle for the survival of the fittest. But awakening to the potential of a shared risen life can counter the passions of that strife and alleviate that primal ignorance by erasing the very boundary between living and dying. That is why all discussion of Christ in Paul is centered on his dying and rising, offered in an uncontentious spirit to all.

Selfless Attending in Concrete Judgments (2:1–4)

> 2:1 *If then there is any encouragement in Christ, any consolation from love, any communion in the Spirit, any mercy and compassion,* ²*make my joy complete by meditatively attending to the same: having the same love, sharing the same life, and attending to unity:* ³*Nothing from selfish ambition or empty self-glorification,*

but in humiliation regard others as better than yourselves, ⁴each of you having an eye not to your own interests, but to the interests of others.

2:1 Εἴ τις οὖν παράκλησις ἐν Χριστῷ, εἴ τι παραμύθιον ἀγάπης, εἴ τις κοινωνία πνεύματος, εἴ τις σπλάγχνα καὶ οἰκτιρμοί, ²πληρώσατέ μου τὴν χαρὰν ἵνα τὸ αὐτὸ φρονῆτε, τὴν αὐτὴν ἀγάπην ἔχοντες, σύμψυχοι, τὸ ἓν φρονοῦντες, ³μηδὲν κατ' ἐριθείαν μηδὲ κατὰ κενοδοξίαν, ἀλλὰ τῇ ταπεινοφροσύνῃ ἀλλήλους ἡγούμενοι ὑπερέχοντας ἑαυτῶν, ⁴μὴ τὰ ἑαυτῶν ἕκαστος σκοποῦντες, ἀλλὰ [καὶ] τὰ ἑτέρων ἕκαστοι.

Paul has just written about how constrained he is by the tension between longing to die to be with Christ and remaining alive to benefit the Philippians and others through his strategy to defend and promote the gospel. Far from collapsing that dilemma, he embraces it as an act of eschatological hope. And now, turning to moral and ethical advice, Paul relies on a similarly tensive creativity to be practiced attentively by his readers in Philippi. They themselves are to identify just what constitutes the actual manifestation of the following: consolation, love, communion in the Spirit, and merciful compassion. Paul sets the larger frame within which this is to be practiced—love, life, and unity, all beyond our constant urge to live and act selfishly. Were he to die, to be with Christ would bring rest and surcease for him. But this approach would still work for the furtherance of the gospel. He builds on that single eschatological tension, recommending what it means to live in Christ, identifying the contours of that which is contrary to the Christ mind, and—having set that gospel framework—confidently leaving to the Philippians any actual decisions about their civic life in Philippi. All the while, Paul defends his own approach, about which he is confidently knowledgeable.

To make decisions "in Christ" refers not to a locative realm whereto one might retire for decision-making, but rather to the eschatologically transformed consciousness of the Philippians that will set the pattern for their deciding. This entire passage teases out the configuration of consciousness with which the Philippians are to attend to and understand the emptiness hymn that follows, then lays out the concrete effects Paul has experienced in his encounters with the empty Christ, and finally recommends the context for all skillful approaches to daily and civic life.

Paul is writing a letter to the assembly in Philippi, but it is not like a letter or email message we might send today. Paul's letters are more than friendly communications and more than letters of encouragement to groups he has founded or supported. They are crafted discourses on the theme of what it means to follow Christ—what it means to take on Christ identity as selfless disciples. They are well thought out and rhetorically crafted; the discourse is paratactically coherent, while all the parts relate to and flow back and forth from one another in rhetorically organic circles, expanding the breadth of his gospel to the far horizons and narrowing its focus to one's own mind. Its themes and words echo back and forth from start to finish. If Paul had adopted a Greek philosophy, the parataxis likely would have been clarified by sharply delineated overviews, making his letters easier to read and alleviating the need for 2 Pet 3:15–16 to apologize for their difficulty.

But here the difficulty is ours, not in interpreting an opaque Paul, but in deciding exactly how to embody love, compassion, and mercy. In the previous passage Paul wrote of fulfilling civic duties as citizens of the colony of Philippi while insisting that his hearers always be attentive to acting in a manner worthy of the gospel. Christian communities are called not to withdraw, but rather to engage in public affairs for the furtherance of the gospel faith. That may be a struggle, and indeed it did cause trouble and distress for Paul and for the Philippians. So here Paul is offering words of encouragement.

The passage that follows this contains the famous hymn of the emptying Christ, which constitutes the very heart of Letter B. That hymn probably had its origins in a time before Paul came to Philippi or undertook any of his mission journeys. As noted above, Paul introduces it here as an already recognized summation of the mind of Christ, leading us to conclude that it has come to him in a letter from the Philippians, for it occurs nowhere else. In any event, it is a gem that distills early Christian understanding of the empty Christ. By way of preview, these opening verses of chapter 2 contain "a number of linguistic correspondences with the following hymn (2:5–11)" and "prepare the way for the hymnic paragraph that follows."[236] I understand these preparatory verses, along with those that follow the hymn, as Christian meditations on self-emptying and world engagement. Paul begins here with a series of conditions about life in Christ. He says "if there be any encouragement," "comfort," or "urgent exhortation" (εἴ τις οὖν παράκλησις) to be found "in Christ" (ἐν Χριστῷ), then his hearers should prepare their minds to meditate upon that in Christ. It should drive them forward to engage in the urgent tasks of furthering the gospel—an urgency that Paul has expressed above and that should be recognized as springing from Spirit-supplied life and embodied in an enlarged Christ.

Commentators consider all possible meanings for the above term *paraklēsis* (παράκλησις)—including "encouragement," "exhortation," "appeal," "request," "comfort," and "consolation." Then, after analyzing the phrase in its semantic history and its contextual significance, they usually opt for one or another of the possible meanings. Perhaps it is better, however, to make no choice. Since this term does embrace all that it can signify, none of those meanings are excluded by the semantic context. Paul's language is particularly rich in its semantic range, and we are not wise to restrict that range. It is not that a word can mean anything a particular person might want it to mean. However, words do derive their significance from common webs of semantic usage that are often quite broad, so any one dictionary definition cannot be excluded

---

236. O'Brien, *Epistle to the Philippians*, 166. Collange notes the number of terms in this passage that also occur in the hymn of the empty Christ—*phroneō* ("to focus"), *pneuma* ("spirit"), *psychē* ("life"), and *agapē* ("love")—and concludes that 2:1–5 "is a sort of 'overture' to [the hymn], and hence there are a number of identical words and the 'in Christ' occurs twice, in verses 1 and 5" (Collange, *Epistle of Saint Paul*, 77).

entirely just because one chooses an alternative definition. We create dictionary entries by drawing upon common usages.

The term *paraklesis* (παράκλησις) is of particular interest because it is the same term used by the Gospel of John to refer to "the advocate, the comforter," or the Paraclete (παράκλητος John 14:16), who comes as the Spirit of the risen Christ, reminding one of the above phrase in 1:19 explaining that Paul is helped by the Philippian entreaties and by the Spirit who supplies Christ. I believe Paul's usage here lies within the broad context of the meanings available to John to express an ongoing resurrected life in Christ—the Spirit Comforter sent from the Father. Indeed, it has here something of the Johannine sense, in that Paul sees life in Christ as springing from the spirit of Christ working in the hearts and minds of his followers. The Spirit, then, is the ongoing and urgent presence that both Paul and the Philippians experience as risen life "in Christ." The phrase has much greater significance than simply a word of encouragement; it speaks of that transformed life in Christ with which Paul begins and ends his writings.

"If there is any consolation of love" (εἴ τι παραμύθιον ἀγάπης) that comes from living in Christ and having gained insight into the equality between living and dying, that too should become an object of one's meditative attention. "If there is any participation in the Spirit" (εἴ τις κοινωνία πνεύματος), in a shared fellowship with the spirit of the risen and living Christ present in the community, that also becomes an object of Paul's meditation. Such spirit-participation is not just a mental attitude. It transcends both objective and subjective poles of consciousness and allows believers to experience the very roots of their being. Participation in the Spirit is the source of the fellowship and community (κοινωνία) that constitutes the ecclesial gatherings. Thus, I hesitate to capitalize the word "spirit" consistently, lest we reify that pervasive breath of God that flows from the silent stillness of the Father to permeate our minds and bodies with the circulating oxygenation that graces our minds with the same spirit comforter Paraclete that flows within and emanates from the body of Jesus. This spirit participation is a reorientation of the mind—away from selfishness to the mind of an engaged Christ-wisdom. Participation in the Spirit evokes the same spirit as Jesus washing the feet of his followers in John's Gospel. It is the same message in the Synoptics when Jesus speaks of loving our neighbor. It is the same message as Torah when it teaches love of God and of neighbor.

These first three comforting phrases seem to echo Paul's final prayer for his Corinthian community. Second Corinthians concludes with: "The grace of the Lord Jesus Christ and the love of God and the communion of the Holy Spirit be with you all" (Ἡ χάρις τοῦ κυρίου Ἰησοῦ Χριστοῦ καὶ ἡ ἀγάπη τοῦ θεοῦ καὶ ἡ κοινωνία τοῦ πνεύματος μετὰ πάντων ὑμῶμ 2 Cor 13:13). Pierre Benoit sees here in Philippians a parallel but veiled allusion to trinitarian themes.[237] Christ and the Spirit are explicitly mentioned while, as in 2 Corinthians, "love" characterizes the Father. Indeed, such inchoate trinitarian

---

237. Benoit, *Les épîtres*, 25e.

awareness permeates Paul, for he speaks constantly of our union with Christ in the Spirit, by which we are adopted by the Father, thereby reconfiguring our understanding of the one God to include not only an active outpouring of God-grace into our hearts and minds, but also our indwelling within the heart and bosom of that Father. Perhaps, again, it might be best not to capitalize "father," lest that be taken to signify an all-controlling figure who reigns supremely over the entire world, for this father clearly does no such thing, simply representing the harshly benevolent transcendence that is immediately experienced before discriminative knowledge arises, and thus exercising no control, no power. In this reading, we are swept up into the interflowing life of God, and thus feel—and are led by the Spirit in meditation to have—compassion for one another everywhere.

"If there are any feelings of visceral mercy or compassion" (εἰ τις σπλάγχνα καὶ οἰκτιρμοί), that too is an outflow from participation in the Spirit—from the consolation of love between all beings and engagement in the urgency of living in Christ and preaching the gospel however best serves to alleviate suffering and bring justice and peace. Mahāyāna theology teaches a wisdom that becomes real only when embodied in compassion (Skt. *karuṇā*). Here the mind of Christ is not just the peace and quiet beyond death; it is with equal force the engagement displayed in loving one another in life and living in the Spirit. We are to direct our empty lives by taking charge of our orientations and commitments. Recognizing the emptiness of self does not lead to withdrawal; it opens up broad horizons for engagement and bodhisattva commitment.

And so Paul asks his readers to "fulfill my joy" (πληρώσατέ μου τὴν χαρὰν) by attentively "focusing your minds on the same" (ἵνα τὸ αὐτὸ φρονῆτε) themes as objects of meditative attention. The main verb of this long paragraph/sentence is "fulfill" (πληρώσατέ), which is explained by the next phrase, where Paul uses a favorite verb, "to attend to, to focus, to bear in mind" (φρονέω). He is not merely writing a theological tractate, he is offering practical advice on how Christ followers are to meditate and how they are to attend to their experience. They are to take on the mind of Christ, but not in the way that one might adopt an attitude or outlook in the pattern of discriminative delusion, or even in the way that one might consider an idea or a doctrine. Rather, in prayerful meditation—very likely in the context of a liturgy that sings the hymn to the empty Christ—one's whole focus of attention shifts away from worldly delusion and attachment and toward the wisdom of life in Christ engagement. The struggle to abandon a mindset that imagines and clings to idols requires us to chip away at all the layers of protective self-covering and carve out the innards of our self-referential minds, leaving them empty, ready, and alert to the interests of others.

So Paul's joy will be fulfilled and complete when the Philippians meditatively attend not to his words or to his social stratagems, but to the reality of life in Christ in their own minds. There are urgent struggles with a gospel that directs us toward the deep needs of others, and there is spirit comfort in the fellowship of love and compassion. These are the things that characterize the mind of Christ, and this is what Paul means by living in Christ. He wants his hearers to practice this: to bend their knees in prayer. Whether we kneel or bend our knees by sitting cross-legged hardly matters; the important thing is to focus the mind, for consciousness is configured by what it focuses upon, by that which it places at the forefront of life and love.

In Yogācāra theology, the conversion (of the basis, Skt. *āśraya-parivṛtti*) that awakens our consciousness may occur when one so focuses the mind on the truths of the doctrine that those truths seep in, reconfigure our attention, and make us ready for that moment of reorientation. This is what Paul wants the Philippians to do: to focus on the mind of Christ in these proposed meditative themes. Not on Jesus' ideas, or on what we imagine Jesus would do, but on his dying and rising. The outcome of such meditative prayer is that we should all "have the same love" (τὴν αὐτὴν ἀγάπην ἔχοντες) and "share the same life" (σύμψυχοι). This latter expression, "same life," appears only this once in the New Testament. Indeed, many terms that Paul uses in this letter are rare, and some only he uses in the New Testament.[238] This phrase is often translated as being "like-minded" or "of one accord." But I believe those renderings are too weak. Paul is not a spiritual coach urging his players to show some team spirit.[239] He is writing from the heart of deep experience. This is not simply something he experienced once in the past, a once-and-for-all event, but an ongoing experience shared by the Philippians and countless practitioners after them. When Paul says we are to "share life," he means precisely that: We are to participate in the life of Christ, which flows from the beginning, for to live is Christ and Christ means to live. We do not own our life, ever. We experience it as we are born, grow into adulthood, commit ourselves to a life course, and enter into the tasks of the gospel. We are to live as life is given, within our bodies and within our cultures. As we pass through old age and die, we bring that life to its cessation, and that again is the one life in Christ.

Paul spells it out: We are "to focus upon that oneness" (τὸ ἕν φροωοῦντες). The shared life of the community is furthered in our common attentiveness to the one—the one God of Torah, the one of whom the Shema proclaims: "The Lord your God is one" (Deut 6:4). In Paul, that one life is identified also with the life we share with and through Christ, in the common unity of being human. This is the second affirmation of our Christian tradition from the beginning: The first is the Shema, and the second is the identity of Christ with God.[240] But how is one to attend to this "one unity" (τὸ ἕν)? Surely by attending to the one life beyond living and dying that is Christ. But who is this God who is one—with Christ one, with us one? To answer that, it is best to say again and again what God is *not*, lest images and ideas rush in to trivialize both practice and teaching. When that happens, either we make those images and ideas into

---

238. O'Brien, *Epistle to the Philippians*, 178.

239. Haidt, *Righteous Mind*, 198. Haidt sees human beings as "the giraffes of altruism. We're one-of-a-kind freaks of nature who occasionally—even if only rarely—can be as selfless and team-spirited as bees" (ibid.).

240. Pelikan, *Credo*, 330–35, on "The Paradigm: *Shema* and *Homoousios*."

idols we cling to in our tireless quest for religious self-identity, or—eventually—we come to reject them, along with the practice and the teaching, in favor of the attractions of life in this world.

This much one can say: God is one, not as a center of self-consciousness, as if God were a "Great Self" (Skt. *mahātman*) to be differentiated from other, lesser consciousnesses. The Buddhist rejection of theism aims at just such a notion of a mind-centered power that reigns over life from a distance. But self-consciousness arises from a dichotomy of subject and object, and if we take creation *ex nihilo* as true, then there is nothing anywhere for a "creator" God as subject to apprehend as creatable object. Rather, Paul's life "in Christ"—a life that is reconfigured in emptying self—means that God is everywhere encompassed in a transcendent emptiness that is beyond discriminative awareness, and is thus apart from any divine perspective whatsoever. God has no perspective, and as Mahāyāna teaches, such perspective-free consciousness is best characterized as wisdom that does not differentiate this from that and that cannot be expressed in languaged discrimination. Such empty God consciousness is consciousness of no-self, for it is not mirrored in yet another, much bigger, self. Even the three persons of the Trinity are not to be characterized as separate selves or separate consciousnesses, but rather as identical in the one that is God. Trinity as a hall of mutually reflecting mirrors is a carnival sideshow.

Consciousness of no-self entails a no-self wisdom. Not enthralled with self within, one may direct attention toward others, even to the point of bringing them from blank nothingness into the being we live. This is why Christ is the primal wisdom of God, present from the beginning with God. Still, the person of God is beyond perspectival enunciation. We characterize God as person because non-discriminative wisdom flows forth compassionately and embraces the entirety of the multiverse in all its sentient being and all its personal character. At depth, then, a person is not a set-apart and standalone individual but an embodiment of an ever-silent wisdom that speaks compassionately into the actual world we inhabit.[241]

---

241. The American Roman Catholic Bishops criticized Elizabeth A. Johnson's book *Quest for the Living God* for its "failures" to appreciate the philosophy of analogical knowledge (*analogia entis*), insisting that although our knowledge is inadequate, we nevertheless do know very well what we do know—analogically. In a Mahāyāna theology of the two truths, the emptiness of all knowing is intertwined with dependently arisen understanding and language, much as apophatic truth and kataphatic truth were intertwined in the Christian mystical tradition, neither of which have need of a mediating "analogy" to assure the theologian that at least there is a little light in our darkness. Thus, the teachings, being dependently arisen, already constitute the enlightened path we practice. It is a liberative theological meditation to move—as does Johnson, and before her, Sallie MaFague—within an engaged practice of the faith wherein none of our ideas capture God (Johnson, *Quest for the Living God*, 200–210). Yet, insight into the symbolic power of our language is best preserved in interfaith endeavors, I think, by acknowledging the "indivisibility" of our symbols, dependently arisen as they are, from the path understandings they engender. In the same way, Chinese T'ien-t'ai Buddhist theologian Chih-i insists on the indivisibility between emptiness and our conventional languages within the practice of the Middle Path. See my forthcoming work on T'ien-t'ai thought and Ephesian theology.

Commentators often take the phrase "attending to unity" (τὸ ἕν φροωοῦντες 2:2) as meaning to be of one accord, of one purpose, and thus expressing here Paul's "intent" for the Philippians to live in unity and harmony. The significance of the phrase is then explicated in terms of the entire passage on unity within the Philippian community, which is often seen to be disunited because of differences among its members. This interpretation portrays Paul as exercising apostolic authority in relationship to the community, and it denigrates the Philippians. But this phrase about attending to unity echoes—is in chiastic relation with—the phrase "attending to the same" (ἵνα τὸ αὐτὸ φρονῆτε) earlier in the same verse. So one can surmise from the context that Paul in this passage is actually urging the Philippians to be single-mindedly "Gospel oriented" toward a shared risen life in the empty Christ.[242]

Disputes are real and a natural part of communal living, but truth seldom lies solely on one side or the other. Moreover, the disunity of the Philippian church tends to be overstated; both Clement and Epaphroditus are Philippians, but neither is ever described as contentious or fractious. As Christians over the centuries have meditated on these scriptures, we have not found the experience of these ancient Christian communities to be so very strange, despite the sketchy state of our knowledge about them, for we do assume a commonality of life with the ancients—with Peter and Paul, Mary and Lydia. And Paul here does not leave us in the dark; he takes pains to present in these points of meditation what he considers to be the mind of Christ: it is the one life that we lead, characterized by compassion and love, marked by an urgency to work in fellowship and love, and focused upon the one beyond duality. More than social cohesion and harmony, this one life is our end-time present. Such a unitary focus on end-time life is far more than a change of attitude or an agreed-upon set of opinions. It is the collapse of any secure sense of being a standalone self and the conscious construction of being "in Christ."[243]

The oneness of our life with Christ leads to the oneness of God, who is one beyond a second. In like manner, Mahāyāna thinking consistently critiques discrimination and duality, teaching that we and Buddha, life and death, delusion and enlightenment are all non-dual (Skt. *advaya*) and that the wisdom (*bodhi*) that is awakening (*buddhatva*) is non-discriminative wisdom (*nirvikalpa-jñāna*). Similarly, when the Patristic writers speak of the oneness of God, it is not an assertion that our God is real, while yours is not; it is a oneness beyond serial enumeration, an unrestricted horizon

---

242. O'Brien, *Epistle to the Philippians*, 179.

243. For example, Thurston translates "having the same opinions, the same love," and comments that "'Having opinions' (*phronēte*) suggests a mental attitude" (Thurston, "Philippians," 72–73). Silva likewise renders the phrase, "Adopt this frame of mind" (Silva, *Philippians*, 94). These translations and comments seem to me to water down the strength of τὸ αὐτὸ φρονῆτε, making it merely a change of attitude or opinion rather than the radical conversion of consciousness the text entails. Caird rightly notes that "Paul is not asking for doctrinal orthodoxy or uniformity of opinion, nor is he here referring to the process, well attested in the early church, by which the Spirit brought members of an assembly to a common mind (Acts 15:28)" (Caird, *Paul's Letters from Prison*, 117).

within which all horizons come into view. It is the gravitational pull that impels us ever deeper into the cloud of unknowing beyond God as this or that. Indeed, such an awareness, described in the mountaintop scenes of Exodus, leads directly to the apophatic emphasis that is to accompany all our enunciations of any teaching about God.

The experience of shared comfort and consolation—focused on the shared life among us and thus upon the one God that lies within each and beyond each—is signaled by relinquishing any sense of "party spirit" (κατ'ἐριθείαν), whether ethnic, national, or ecclesiastical. Factionalism has no part in the tasks of the gospel, and the unending need to "take a stance" leads us away from the mind of Christ. To embrace the gospel is not to embrace an ideology. It is not a political or a religious platform. It is not a factional viewpoint.[244] And so we must avoid such party spirit and self-ambition and refrain from engaging "in vain and empty self-glorification" (μηδὲ κατᾶ κενοδοξίαν 2:3). This last term is constructed from the adjective "empty" (κενός) and the noun "glory" (δόξα). In 2:6–11, Paul will offer the hymn that speaks of Christ emptying himself of any putative identifying characteristics we might use to pin him down, for he is more than exalted into the glory of God the Father. But in 2:3, Paul rejects empty vainglory precisely because it does not empty self; it is mere bootless boasting about how right my viewpoint is, my religion is, indeed even how special "my Jesus" is. No matter what the content, if a spirit of selfish ambition and vain boasting motivates our preaching, we do not preach the mind of Christ.

"Rather" (ἀλλά), "regard others as better than yourselves" (ἀλλήλους ἡγούμενοι ὑπερέχοντας ἑαυτῶν 2:3), Paul writes. Even if our relationships result "in humiliation" (τῇ ταπεινοφροσύνῃ),[245] we are to regard others as better. But Paul is not, I think, recommending blind obedience and servile humility. He does not speak of humility but of humiliation, and when that occurs, it is a social fact, not an inner attitude. In the social reality of the Greco-Roman world, the majority of people suffered some measure of humiliation in their social status, which would indeed lead to resentment, psychological envy, and to the factional strife that often occurs among oppressed people. But Paul instructs the members of the community in Philippi that no matter what their status, whether citizen or not, even when humiliated, they are to regard others

---

244. As I learned from Ivan Illich. See his *Celebration of Awareness*.

245. See Reumann, *Philippians*, 309–15. Here is apparently the first use of the word ταπεινοφροσύνη in Greek literature. It is most often taken in Old Testament terms as a favorable virtue, but in the Greek world of Philippi, "*tapeinophrosynē* was no virtue but a servile characteristic of inferior classes" (ibid., 309). It suggests groveling and abject status, a point brought to present-day attention by feminist critiques of patriarchy and kyriarchy. The unfavorable "Greek view was exacerbated in Roman society . . . In the social pyramid, the underling was 'my nothingness' or 'most worthless slave.' This late-classical social order was the foil for Christian teaching on *tapeinophrosynē*" (ibid., 310). In contrast to the positive regard for "humility" elsewhere in the scriptures, Reumann writes, "*tapeinophrosynē* = the social-world humiliation that Philippian Christians experienced in daily life from their 'betters' in Roman social structures" (ibid., 315) and, Reumann adds, "If *tapeinophrosynē* appears here for the first time in Gk. literature, it is Paul's creation in light of . . .Phil 2:8 ['he humiliated himself'] . . . There is no prior history of *tapeinophrynosynē* to which one can appeal" (ibid., 319 n. 5).

as better than themselves. Status is not the register of worth. The corrosive influence of self-clinging, empty boasting (κενοδοξία), and selfish ambition (ἐριθεία) is in stark contrast to the model of Christ, who although regarded as so far above us all, still emptied himself to become the most despised of men—a criminal under sentence of crucifixion,[246] the worst of imagined humiliations.[247]

The Buddha taught that we are to empty ourselves—not because of any particular illusion we may entertain of our superiority over other individuals, but because we truly *are* empty and there is nothing real to be clung to. There is no self beyond the constructs that our brains, our bodies, and our minds develop over time under the tutelage of teachers and the nurture of parents. Indeed, humans are not born with self-awareness; it is some eighteen months before young children develop the capacity to distinguish themselves from others.[248] Selflessness is likewise a learned awareness, involving prayerful meditation and a recognition of the fact that the idea of self is something we have learned over the course of our evolutionary development.[249] Delusion arises when that self-construct, which is truly necessary in day-to-day living,

---

246. See Ruden, *Paul Among the People*, 42: "For maximum humiliation, and maximum edification of others, crucifixion was public."

247. Reumann takes *tapeinophrosynē* as "humiliation," writing that his "translation breaks with 'humility,' a virtually unanimous rendering since patristic times, but to be avoided here" (Reumann, *Philippians*, 327). Philippians 2:3 "may be the first occurrence of *tapeinophrosynē* in Gk" (ibid.). Its "meaning was not yet fixed, certainly not 'humility' in a good sense" (ibid.). It indicates a negative humiliation of self or group, and it would be recognized as such by the Philippians. The point is that each member of the community, no matter what their status in the Roman public sphere, "is to regard every other Christian as superior, rejecting selfish quests for personal or class glory" (ibid., 328). Within the communities, whatever social status obtained, such self-boundaries are to be emptied, not by declaring an ideal equality, but by countering any measured reckoning of self-status. "The problem in Philippi was not the legitimacy of government (Romans 13:1–7), but how the worst practices in the civic-social system could affect Christians in the church . . . People were proud of positions obtained" (ibid., 330). This led Paul to recommend attending concretely to the gospel of equality, and that is why each is to regard others as better, no matter what status is involved. Despite the fact that "*tapeinophrosynē* came to be read in light of the virtue of 'Christian *humility*,' rather than as the *humiliation* of 'inferiors' by 'superiors' in the social system of Paul's day," recent theologies of liberation altered our critical awareness of the culturally specific advice Paul offers, seeing it as his caving in to oppressive social structures (ibid., 331). Just as Paul's life within that ancient world provides no set model for modern Christians, likewise his advice to fellow Christians within their culture at the time offers itself only for a broad, contextually nuanced consideration, which we are then tasked to render into actual practice. If we need a revolution, our gospel task is to revolt. If we need to overturn social mores, we need to overturn them—but not by appealing to Paul's time-bound advice to people in Philippi, or to the household codes in the Deutero-Pauline letters to the Colossians or Ephesians, but rather by attending to our own life here and now, in these evil days. As he did in those evil days.

248. Julian Paul Keenan, *Face in the Mirror*, 67: "Other researchers have sought to establish the precise relation of self-recognition and self-awareness in children. Michael Lewis, who is the foremost expert on children and self, has extensively studied self-awareness and self-recognition in children. Like Amsterdam, Lewis has found the magic period of self-recognition to occur in the latter half of the second year."

249. Ibid., 148: "Further, these studies provide a sensitive measure of self. No longer is the self-face all or none; we now have gradations of self we can measure."

is misconstrued as constituting the central value of our lives or as an ultimately real reality in a world that is itself entirely contextual.

Nevertheless, now and again one does meet selfless people who truly help and truly teach. They help others to stand out while disregarding their own part in the matter. It is the compassionate deeds of the bodhisattva that signal the presence of transcendent wisdom. It is the engaged saint who presences God as immanent in human gatherings. It is the engagement and love for the sake of others that marks the presence of a Christ mind. The goal of such a mind is to abandon one's own interest, not "looking out for" (σκοποῦντες, "scope out" 2:4) those things that redound to our own benefit. Rather, we "should look out for other people's benefit" (ἀλλὰ [καὶ] τὰ ἑτέρων ἕκαστοι), which here, most particularly, is the meaning and joy the gospel can bring to gladden and benefit unfocused and scattered lives that run off in distraction and end in dissolution. Such "a negation and forgetfulness of self" (μὴ τὰ ἑαυτῶν ἕκαστος σκοποῦντες 2:4) does not just signify a prohibition of "any interest in one's own affairs."[250] That is too soft a reading, coming just after Paul has recommended that we conform our lives to the pattern of Christ's consciousness. To forget the self is more troubling than any teaching to love others as one loves oneself, for that instruction tends to invite the spurious conclusion that the self is indeed to be prized, nurtured, and loved.[251] Our sense of personhood is, as the Mahayanists say, a dependently arisen construct, which is indeed to be nurtured as the life we have been given in this world and with which we may create a wise and compassionate course of living, but never is it to become the focus of our attention or our striving. We are to strive for the furtherance of the gospel so that—forgetting self—we may look to the interests of others.[252]

---

250. Pace O'Brien, *Epistle to the Philippians*, 185. Better is Moule's "persuasive defense of the view that Paul is urging his readers to manifest the same self-denying mind as Christ manifested" (C. F. D. Moule, "Further Reflexions on Philippians 2:5–11," in *Apostolic History and the Gospel*, edited by W. W. Gasque and R. P. Martin [Exeter: Paternoster, 1970] 264–76). Citing Moule, Bruce continues, "[Moule] suggests the amplification *touto to phronēma phroneite en hymin ho kai en Christō Iēsou*, which he translates, 'Adopt towards one another, in your mutual relations, the same attitude which was found in Christ Jesus' (265)" (Bruce, *Philippians*, 67). Similarly, "Barth reminds one that she or he 'climbs down' from the throne of self in order to mind 'that which is minded *in Christ Jesus*'" (Thurston, "Philippians," 76). Collange comments that the selfless behavior of a disciple "shifts a man's centre of concern from himself turning him to Christ, to other people, and to the future (verse 28)" (Collange, *Epistle of Saint Paul*, 73). There is broad agreement on the self-effacement entailed in all these passages. The Mahāyāna critique of selfhood is in harmony with all that, but goes further by emptying the ontological basis of any stable notion of selfhood as the carrier of attitudes, relationships, or opinions.

251. Haidt, *Righteous Mind*, 225: "Durkheim argued ... that *Homo sapiens* was really *Homo duplex*, a creature who exists at two levels: as an individual and as part of the larger society." In Mahāyāna terms, Durkheim's *homo duplex* is oriented both to conventional living and to an ultimate transcendence. For Paul, these two orientations are included in *agapē*, which accepts no limitations on the conventional love that binds all people together in one life.

252. Caird, *Paul's Letters from Prison*, 117. Caird notes that the Greek is vague here, merely talking about "his own things" (τὰ ἑαυτῶν) and "the things of others" (τὰ ἑτέρων). "It could refer to possessions, gifts, rights, or points of view. Perhaps Paul deliberately used a vague expression to include them

Still, this passage is framed as conditional: "if there is something" (Εἴ τις 2:1). Even if Paul has no doubt that there is encouragement, consolation, and love,[253] he nevertheless leaves the actual identification of those marks of life in Christ to the discernment of his readers. Rather than spelling out his own view, Paul contents himself with upholding their gospel endeavors by enunciating a framework for the selfless common life in Christ, leaving the details—what is actually important in people's lives—to the people themselves.

---

all" (ibid.). Mahāyāna would sum them all up as "me and mine," laying stress on "points of view" (Skt. *dṛṣṭi*), all of which occlude insight into the no-self of our conventional selfhood.

253. Sumney, *Philippians*, 40.

4

Emptiness Letter B, Part 2
The Central Meditation on the Emptied Christ (2:5–11)

Philippians 2:6–11 contains an ancient Christian meditation upon the meaning of life in Christ, which later comes to be called the incarnation. Indeed, this passage provides the leitmotif of Paul's understanding of Christ, which he expands upon in this second letter to the community in Philippi. After his introductory exhortation that we should attend to our Christ-life, Paul quotes this "emptiness hymn."[1] Even though its content seems to undermine the assured ontological assumptions of later theology, this hymn has attracted the attention of well-known and perceptive scripture scholars, many of whom attempt to fit its message into the Chalcedonian doctrine of the two natures of Christ. In so doing, most argue that Christ, being unique, cannot be our paradigm and that we cannot actually take on his mind. Nevertheless, Paul himself introduces the hymn with the explicit call for us to take on the mind of Christ, implying more than mere imitation.

A hymn that extols Jesus' emptying of himself does not sit comfortably within the ontological framework of Greek theology. Indeed, a Christ who empties his own essence to become fully human transgresses any fixed boundary delineating human and

---

1. Reumann, *Philippians*, 361–64. Reumann identifies 2:6–11 rhetorically, not as a hymn because it "fits neither OT, Jewish nor Greco-Roman hymnody," but as an *encomium*, an ancient "speech of praise." So Reumann interprets that "Paul employs in verses 6–11 an encomium the Philippians had worked out to use in mission proclamation about Christ and God in their Greco-Roman world" (ibid., 333). I hesitate to disagree, yet if indeed the Philippians themselves composed the passage, there is no guarantee that they knew the proper rhetorical format. More likely, when they came together in worship, "each one having a hymn, a lesson, a revelation, a tongue, or an interpretation" (1 Cor 14:26), they drew on their experienced life in Christ poetically to enunciate the meaning of Christ. As Thurston asserts, they drew upon Wisdom literature and Psalms so that "by the late 40s, Christians were singing 'Jesus Wisdom hymns' in their worship, and those hymns served the dual purpose of worship and catechesis" (Thurston, "Philippians," 77). Even if "encomium" is the correct identification of the hymn's rhetorical structure, it fails to call attention to the poetic flow of the rhetoric, with all its challenging allusions and seldom-used words.

divine essences. And yet, when Greek theology affirms a paradoxical identity between two essences that are defined in opposition to one another, that does harmonize with the movement of the Philippian Christ who, being in the form of God, empties himself so as to be more than exalted and draw all toward risen life. The argument of the present commentary is that Mahāyāna philosophy can perhaps offer a better vehicle for meditating upon the emptiness hymn than that which is provided by Christian ontological thinkers, but not that it need replace their theology.

Most commentators conclude that the hymn in 2:6–11 is a pre-Pauline composition, since Paul presents it here as an already known and recognized confession of the significance of Christ.[2] Ernst Lohmeyer concludes that it is the product of a Jewish Christian community who sang the hymn in their Eucharistic liturgies.[3] Embedded as it is within this particular correspondence between Paul and the Philippians, it seems most likely that the latter composed the hymn and that Paul then cites it as an expression of their common faith: "Paul's dialogue with the Philippians is not a monologue. They wrote to him and made contributions to his work."[4] The immediate context would have been Paul's affirmation of his self-sufficiency in Letter A. In response to that, the Philippians (in a letter that no longer exists) assure Paul that they are not attempting by their gift to become his patrons, then present him with this hymn as their Christ understanding of the gospel. Dropping any further reference to self-sufficiency, Paul here cites the Philippians' hymnic confession and then draws from it further implications for their common life. Still later in the correspondence, in Letter C—while refuting those who would insist on the necessity of identity markers such as circumcision for Christ followers—Paul unpacks the emptying of all his own identity claims and reaffirms the significance of the hymn in more familiar resurrection terminology.[5]

Many aspects of this hymn are quite striking and alluring. Its rhetoric is not paralleled anywhere else in Paul's letters. Its vocabulary is unusual; many terms appear

---

2. *Pace* N. T. Wright, "ἁρπαγμός and the Meaning of Philippians 2:5–11," *Journal of Theological Studies* 37 (1986) 321–52. Wright notes that the hymn "was originally written by Paul himself precisely in order to give christological and above all theological underpinning to the rest of Philippians, especially chapters 2 and 3. I for one find it hard to produce convincing counter arguments" (ibid., 352).

3. E. Lohmeyer, *Kyrios Jesus: Eine Untersuchung zu Phil 2, 5–11*, Sitzungsberichte der Heidelberger Akademie der Wissenschaften, Philosophisch-Historische Klasse, Jahrg (Heidelburg, 1928) 7. Also see R. P. Martin, *Carmen Christi: Philippians 2:5–11 in Recent Interpretation and in the Setting of Early Christian Worship* (London: Cambridge University Press, 1967) 27, reprinted as *A Hymn of Christ* and cited in O'Brien, *Epistle to the Philippians*, 189–90.

4. Reumann, "Resurrection in Philippi," 408.

5. Ibid., 418. Reumann contends that in 3:10–11, Paul corrects the Philippians' hymn for what it lacked: "the cross and suffering of Christ, the resurrection, and final judgment" (ibid.). Yet, the hymn explicitly does speak of death on a cross, which surely entails suffering. Reumann, however, thinks that the phrase is not part of the original hymn but was added to 2:8 by Paul himself. Although no images of the final judgment appear, the hymn ends with a cosmic image of the universal acknowledgement of the empty Christ as the more than exalted Christ.

here and nowhere else, neither in Paul nor elsewhere in the New Testament. This is a principal reason that the hymn is thought to predate Paul. If indeed this is the case and the hymn is not Paul's composition, that would place it in Philippi just twenty years or so after the death and resurrection of Jesus, providing us with a window into early Christian experiences and attitudes toward the central teachings of faith. So although this emptiness hymn fits uneasily with later Christian theology, the many scholars who have studied it constitute something of a "who's who" of biblical scholarship, and their commentaries offer a plethora of analyses of the hymn's rhetorical structure and a myriad of interpretations.[6]

Numerous studies have attempted to ascertain the background of the hymn. Ernst Käsemann sees Gnosticism in its background, for it speaks of the descent and ascent of a Gnostic-like savior. Lucien Cerfaux sees its ideas as emerging from the theme of the servant of the Lord in Isa 53. Eduard Schweizer espies in the hymn the image of a righteous sufferer as found in post-biblical Judaism, particularly such Jewish martyrs as the Maccabees. Dieter Georgi takes the background theme to be from the Wisdom of Solomon. Jean Héring, Oscar Cullmann, and James D. G. Dunn, in varied ways, see the hymn's background in terms of a contrast between the first Adam of Genesis and the second Adam, Christ. There are also many modern kenotic theologies that focus on the self-emptying (kenosis) of God. These do not focus on exegesis of Philippians, but rather on developing new patterns of understanding a God who "withdraws" from his creation to create space for the ever-unfolding evolution of the cosmos.[7]

Elucidations of this passage are many, and mostly plausible, but in the judgment of Peter O'Brien,[8] none seem to perfectly explain its background or its rhetorical structure. Perhaps the difficulty in identifying the hymn's background lies in its strikingly new character. Along with O'Brien, I would follow more theological interpretations such as those proposed by L. W. Hurtado and G. F. Hawthorne. These exegetes view the hymn not against the template of any particular background or rhetorical form, but simply as an early, prayerful meditation formed from new insights and couched in new vocabulary. If, as John Reumann argues, it was composed by the Philippians themselves and sent by letter to Paul, then it flows not from previous ideas or a particular genre or even from Paul's own experience of Christ,[9] but rather from the experience of risen life that is shared by all participants in the Philippian community.

---

6. Among the broad array, many notable scholars focus on its rhetoric: Joachim Jeremias (who stressed the rhetorical parallelism within the hymn), Ralph P. Martin (who had a different analysis of that structure), Jean-François Collange (who opted for yet another rhetorical arrangement), C. H. Talbert (who sees there an adoptionist christology), Ernst Käsemann (who sees in it the story of salvation history), and Morna Hooker (who emphasizes its theological interpretation rather than its structural rhetoric).

7. See the works of Arthur Peacocke, John Polkinghorne, Ilia Delio, and Pierre Teilhard de Chardin.

8. O'Brien, *Epistle to the Philippians*, 197.

9. *Pace* Alain Badiou, *St. Paul: The Foundation of Universalism* (Stanford: Stanford University

I would not want to narrow the focus of this meditation to any one event as does G. F. Hawthorne, who asserts that no matter who actually composed it, the hymn may have been rooted in "one particular event from the life of Christ, namely Jesus' washing his disciples' feet (John 13:3–17)."[10] This seems perhaps too specific, and in any case the hymn makes no mention of foot washing. But that suggestion does certainly catch the theological import of the hymn as an early and profound meditation on the meaning of encountering Christ in liturgy, where disciples pray, sing hymns, and sometimes do wash one another's feet. Indeed, Paul says as much in his introductory verse (2:5), which directs us to focus our meditative attention on the content of the hymn. It is not to be a once-sung-and-then-forgotten piece of Christian hymnody, but an oft-repeated and deeply inculcated liturgical form embodying the basic message of the gospel—the emptying of Christ.

Thus, I follow John Reumann in regarding the hymn as having been composed by the Philippians, who sent it to Paul after receiving his hesitant thanks, with its attendant claim of Stoic self-sufficiency, to share with him their understanding of the mind of the Christ who claimed no such self-sufficiency. Thus assured that their gift did not signify a patron-client relationship, Paul concurs in his reply with their liturgical expression of what it means to be "in Christ."

Lohmeyer and most other commentators agree that this hymn was used in the context of the Eucharistic liturgy. We do not, however, know the form of first-century Eucharistic liturgies. It could be a prayer chant used in meditation gatherings, for the body of the hymn is introduced by an admonition to attend and focus on the mind of Christ. Or, it may come from the first portion of a communal liturgy that begins with readings from the Greek scriptures (Septuagint), then flows into the cadenced confession of the hymn, and follows with the simple Eucharistic words that Paul enunciates in 1 Cor 11:23–26. Paul's own letters were probably read before or after the common liturgy, but since they were not at the time considered to have canonical value, they would not have been a part of the liturgy itself.

"Attend to this . . ." (2:5)

2:5 *Attend to this among you, which also in Christ Jesus:*

2:5 τοῦτο φρονεῖτε ἐν ὑμῖν ὃ καὶ ἐν Χριστῷ Ἰησοῦ,

One can hardly imagine a more ambiguously paratactic sentence. Its semantic ambiguity draws interpreters to develop a variety of exegetical and theological elaborations

---

Press, 2003) 19–22, 40–54.

10. Cited in O'Brien, *Epistle to the Philippians*, 197. See L. W. Hurtado, "Jesus as Lordly Example in Philippians 2:5–11," in *From Jesus to Paul: Studies in Honor of Francis Wright Beare* edited by P. Richardson and J. Hurd (Waterloo: Laurier, 1984) 113–26.

Emptiness Letter B, Part 2

for Paul's reticent wording here. Literally, the sentence says: "Attend to" (φρονεῖτε) "this" (τοῦτο) "among yourselves" (ἐν ὑμῖν) "which also" (ὃ καὶ) "in Christ Jesus" (ἐν Χριστῷ Ἰησοῦ). There is no mention of Christ's *mind* at all, but "this" (τοῦτο) is interpreted as "this mind," for the hymn does describe the wisdom of Christ's mind. Hence, the NRSV has: "Let the same mind be in you that was in Christ Jesus."

I understand this initial phrase to be an injunction to the community "gathered together," that is, "among you" (ἐν ὑμῖν), to meditate on the meaning of "being in Christ."[11] That gathering should not be seen as restricted to believers, unless one supposes all hearers of the letter to be baptized into membership in that community; Paul does not specify that, and there is no reason to assume his intended audience excluded anyone within hearing distance. The main verb, "attend" (φρονεῖτε, *phroneite*), used immediately above in 2:4 in the sense of "attending to the same" (τὸ αὐτὸ φρονῆτε), here expands to signify "set one's mind on, have this mental configuration."[12] Many render it interpretively as "have this mind in you," for the sentence surely relates to the conscious state of mind of the hearers, soon to be encircled by the consciousness of Christ in his dying and rising. This is where the translation of "mind" comes from, unfolding the sense of the verb "attend to" (φρονεῖτε).

This is not about adopting a mindset or attitude, but rather about actively focusing one's mind upon a Christ consciousness that goes beyond one's own mind, as qualified by the next phrase, "which also in Christ Jesus." But how can one attend to another's mind? If we are each sealed off in our individual, private minds, we can do no more than guess what might be in another's mind. But Paul suggests a sharing of minds freed from the margins of selfhood. He uses a kōan-like structure to leave the reader without clear directions, even in something of a quandary,[13] for one is left questioning one's own questioning and one's own private inner space. I understand it as a directive to engage in focused meditation on being "in Christ Jesus": Set your mind on this. Focus meditatively upon this. Make this the center of your attention.

What, then, is "this" (τοῦτο), this object for meditative attention? As is so often true, there are numerous interpretations, but I would urge that we see "this" as referring both backward to what has just been said and forward to the hymn itself, for Paul has said twice in 2:2 that we are to "attend to the one" (τὸ ἓν φρονοῦντες) and "to attend to unity" (τὸ αὐτὸ φρονῆτε), which here comes to signify the mind of being here "in

---

11. Reumann, *Philippians*, 341. Reumann notes that the Philippians "*do* think this way about Christ, for they wrote verses 6–11" (ibid.). Reumann opines that Philippian converts composed the hymn as "an assertion for the Greco-Roman world about Christ and God, used in witnessing to neighbors" who had no felt need for a messiah or a savior (ibid., 362).

12. Fabricatore, *Form of God*, 142: "Paul is referring back to the attitude or mindset that he just described in 2:1–4."

13. Morna D. Hooker, "Philippians 2:6–11," in *Jesus und Paulus: Festchrift für Werner Georg Kümmel zur 70. Geburstag*, edited by E. E. Ellis and E. Grasner (Gottingen: Vandenkoeck & Ruprecht, 1975) 157. On the polysemous meaning of the hymn, Hooker writes: "I have myself produced six or seven analyses—and found each of them convincing at the time" (ibid.).

Christ" and, after dying, there "with Christ" (1:23). Paul is suggesting that we share in this one mind of Christ, in unity with one another, by means of attentive, meditative practice. "This" (τοῦτο) signifies the topic of meditation: the one conscious life beyond duality, which is described in the verses that follow as the mind of Christ.[14] We are to attend closely to the emptying of self in the humiliation of the cross and to the over-exaltation of the risen Christ. For if we empty ourselves of duality and take on the mind of Christ, we do more than imitate the mind of Christ: we participate in Christ by reconfiguring our minds through grace and faith.

The second part of the sentence is highly elliptical, literally meaning "which also in Christ Jesus" (ὅ καὶ ἐν Χριστῷ Ἰησοῦ), such that the reader is left to supply a verb. And the commentators do not hesitate to supply verbs here, often using the verb "was" (ἦν) not only to refer back to Jesus' own mind but even beyond, to that "time" when he was "in the form of God." One might instead supply the present tense of the verb "is" (ἐστί), referring not to the mind that was—past tense—in Christ Jesus on earth or beyond earth, but to the mind that is, signifying the mind of the living Christ that is present to those who engage in prayer and meditation.[15] That is the mind we are to enter, for it is the enlightened mind that once and again engulfed Paul and in which he invites all to participate. One then translates: "attend to this which [is] in Christ Jesus." This I would take to mean: attend to this mind, which is what it means to live right now in Christ Jesus, beyond any duality posed between present and future, beyond any duality between our minds and Christ consciousness, and indeed beyond any duality between Christ and God. Such a mind is apart from any defined limits of selfhood, beyond any of our definitions of God. What that mind is forms the subject of the meditation that follows. Nonetheless, the text does not supply either past or present tense for the verb "to be" (ἐστιν), so perhaps it is best to leave it grammatically ambiguous, as Paul leaves it to the minds of his readers to understand. Refusing to supply any verb, we can take the latter phrase "which also in Jesus Christ," to be in apposition to the former (τοῦτο φρονεῖτε): "Attend to this, which also in Christ Jesus" (ὅ καὶ ἐν Χριστῷ Ἰησοῦ).[16]

The literature on this hymn is immense, for it is one of our earliest confessions of Christ, and it is so tantalizingly vague at many key points. My interpretation tends to favor the group of mystical readings offered by such commentators as C. H. Dodd and A. Deissmann, but I would insist that a "veiled" reading not float freely into ethereal realms. Many other commentators see in 2:5 advice from Paul to imitate the mind

14. See L. A. Loise, "A Note on the Interpretation of Phil. 2:5," *Expository Times* 90 (1978) 52–53.

15. As does Thurston, "Philippians," 80.

16. Caird, *Paul's Letters from Prison*, 118–19. Caird argues against supplying a verb because that gives an unusual sense to the phrase "in Christ Jesus," which Paul uses to signify the common life of the Philippians. Such difficulties, however, disappear "if we take the Greek exactly as it stands, without supplying a verb ('which also in Christ Jesus'), and then treat the words 'which also' (ὅ καί) as the Greek equivalent of the Latin *id est*: 'this is the disposition which must govern your common life, i.e., your life in Christ Jesus, because he . . . .'" (ibid.).

that was in Christ Jesus—that is, the mind that was in Jesus as an individual person as manifested in his teachings, and in his living and dying. These include C. F. D. Moule and G. F. Hawthorne, who supply the verb "was" (ἦν) to the latter half of the verse to indicate that it is the individual Christ of whom Paul speaks. But Paul never met the individual Christ and, although he surely was familiar with the Jesus traditions, he writes very little about what Jesus of Nazareth may have thought or felt.[17]

Nor does Paul speak of Christ as a paradigm or example for us to imitate; he never bothers to provide us with a characterization of what Jesus was like in his daily life. What is important to Paul is to live "in Christ Jesus," the risen Christ who was disclosed to him in his Damascus Road encounter. Paul evinces no interest in drawing a character sketch of Christ's personality or subjectivity. Rather, he directs our attention to a Christ who empties himself of everything, even the character of being Christ, or of being God. This is the entry into the Christ mind that Paul celebrates. Not Jesus as Messiah (Christ), for Paul never speaks of Jesus' messiahship at all, and no one in Philippi was waiting for a messiah or a savior to deliver them from anything. "Christ" in these letters has become simply Jesus' surname.[18]

Other thinkers, notably Ernst Käsemann, offer a kerygmatic interpretation, seeing Paul here as urging the Philippians to take as the object of their attention the kerygma, the proclamation that has led them to be in Christ.[19] As Peter O'Brien ex-

---

17. See Dunn, *Theology of Paul the Apostle*, 182–206, on "How Much Did Paul Know or Care about the Life of Jesus." Historical Jesus studies return the favor and hardly mention Paul or this earliest of confessions in their understanding of Jesus of Nazareth. See Crossan, *Cross That Spoke*, which appeals only to sources that can be seen to lie behind the Passion accounts but makes no reference to these early accounts of "being in Christ" throughout Paul, as they have no ascertainable historical warranty.

18. See Collange's work on Christ becoming Jesus' last name (Collange, *Epistle of Saint Paul*, 92).

19. Ernst Käsemann understands the phrase "in Christ" (ἐν Χριστῷ) as meaning "in the realm of Christ" (Robert Morgan, "Incarnation, Myth, and Theology: Ernst Käsemann's Interpretation of Philippians 2:5–11," in *Where Christology Began: Essays on Philippians 2*, edited by Ralph P. Martin [Louisville: Westminster John Knox, 1998] 56). Although that is a common interpretation in some Christian theology, it can engender immense problems, for we have no realm other than the life we live, graced as it is by being "in Christ" here and "with Christ" when we depart. We have no notion of any realm beyond Christ-life, only the resurrection faith that prefigures an eschatological being in Christ here and now with our end-time hopes for being with Christ at the end. Any double-decker theological notion of another "realm" superimposes on our life an imagined fabrication that signifyies nothing real. In the 1980s, two Japanese Zen scholars, HAKAMAYA Noriaki and MATSUMOTO Shirō, launched a spirited attack on Buddhist notions of a separate realm, which they called *dhātuvāda*, the theory of realms. They saw this notion as underlying facile Buddhist ideas about Buddha Nature, the inherent existence of an already pure inner mind that is covered over by adventitious defilements. That notion, they saw, was responsible for much disengaged practice and social forgetfulness, for already we all are enlightened. The Christian version of *dhātuvāda* is supernaturalism—the theory that above and beyond this world there is another, higher realm, to which we have ready access (if only we would) by prayer and ecclesial participation. In fact, above this natural world there is simply space, the metagalactic expanse of an ever-expanding multiverse. In harmony with these Mahāyāna scholars—Hakamaya and Matsumoto—and their spirited attack on Buddhist notions, I would argue that the supernatural realm reflects nothing beyond the institutional ease of an ecclesial establishment that is all too ready to assume its own supernatural status and serve as the purveyor of grace from

plains, these thinkers take the phrase "in Christ Jesus" to signify not the thoughts or attitude of Christ but the union of believers with Christ as members of his body. This seems close to a mystical reading in that it moves beyond the confining margins between self and others; still, such a being in Christ is a separate realm and a different reality to be sought beyond this day-to-day life in our world. The people in Philippi did not have to reclaim the kerygma, for they were already attuned to life in Christ. In his teaching, Paul rarely points either to the subjective life of Jesus or to the objective kerygma of his teachings. And the center of gravity in this hymn is Christ's lordship over the universe—which itself constitutes an empty center beyond exaltation.[20] Better perhaps is the understanding of Ralph P. Martin, who thinks that this "imitation" of Christ is more than following a model and rather constitutes a transformation of our being to "become what we already are"—that is, risen with Christ to life[21] beyond the boxed-in confines of our inner selves.

There are many ecclesiastical interpretations of the passage as well. These would equate the mind of Christ with church teachings that attempt to establish a "Christian identity" to which the faithful are to conform their minds.[22] Yet this reading hardly attends to or accords with a Christ who emptied himself of identity. All claims in favor of salvific identity end up drawing boundaries between the faithful and all others, assuring us of salvation by self-definition and condemning them to exclusion. Strangely, the most pervasive secularization of the gospel today occurs when churches (whether liberal or conservative) ignore the self-emptying of Christ and embrace modern western notions of standalone Christian individualism by engaging in the vainglory and self-boasting of identity theology. Such identity issues are grounded not in Christian scripture or tradition, but rather in the United Nations Declaration of Human Rights.[23] That Declaration serves well to further justice and respect for all individuals,

---

another realm. Yet grace is here and now, everywhere, available free of charge.

20. See Reumann, *Philippians*, 361: "From the earlier confessions, 'Jesus is the Christ' and 'Jesus is Lord,' 'Christ' developed as 'Jesus' last name,' not a title; *kyrios* became the decisive affirmation, a fundamental, known to the Philippian Christians in, among other places, the salutation of all Paul's letters (1:2) . . . 'Jesus is Lord' was connected with the resurrection (Romans 10:9), but for the Philippians more with an 'apotheosis' to lordship." As described in the present hymn, where Jesus' self-emptying issues in his super-exaltation as risen lord.

21. R. P. Martin, *Philippians*, New Century Bible, 93, cited in O'Brien, *Epistle to the Philippians*, 257.

22. W. S. Campbell's *Paul and the Creation of Christian Identity* is an account of the construction of Christian identity vis-à-vis its Jewish root context, stressing the contextual milieu of that construction and arguing that it does not constitute a "universal" account of what it means to be Christian but instead would be understood within the ever-shifting cultures wherein Christians live and have their being.

23. Pelikan, *Credo*, 304–305, on "A Modern Secular Parallel." Pelikan treats the Universal Declaration of Human Rights as a creedal statement that in its prospective universality mimics the traditional creeds of Christendom, finding broad acceptance of its celebration of human rights and its demand that these rights be acknowledged and practiced.

but its underlying philosophy derives from western Enlightenment thinkers and is hardly relevant to gospel insistence upon reconfiguring our very self-consciousness.

I much prefer a more hesitant, mystical understanding of Phil 2:5, for the very minimal interpretation is to admit that we do not know and can never adequately enunciate exactly what it means to be "in Christ" as one beyond duality. "Mystical" here means apophatic—experienced but not imagined as known in clear ideas. Apophasis is not a higher kind of knowing; it is simply the wise realization that we do not know. Apophatic understandings come to ground only in lived encounters with our empty selves and with the fullness of risen life, in all the myriad forms that has taken in Christ-lives over the centuries. But such "mystical" discourse is not a special species of knowing something. It abides, rather, in a clear and consistent *refusal* to take human knowing beyond its language and cultural context, remaining at ease at the stillpoint where we encounter the small, still voice of silence before reentering mediated realms of language and human endeavor toward gospel progress among men and women. It is mystical because it is apophatic, without any claim to supernatural knowledge.

We really do not know the answers to the deepest questions: Where do we come from? Who are we? Who is God? Why does the multiverse exist at all? Over-bloated confessions that pretend to surpass the limited scope of human knowing, as often as not, invite skepticism from the many who distrust absolutist claims. By contrast, a hesitant and apophatic mysticism neither boxes us in to a positivist or empiricist philosophy nor requires a supernatural affirmation of inherent personhood or stable individuality. A mystical understanding of this meditation invites us to deeper experiences and insights, the content of which may become clear through contemplation of the revealed scriptures with an ever deeper focus upon the Christ who emptied himself of being everything, even of being Christ.

The gospel is not one consumer option for a questing mind that seeks religious answers to the felt needs of an inner self. It is, rather, a witness and an invitation—to the practice of focused attending to life *beyond* the quest for self-realization or self-definition. It is not that the answers of our catechesis are not true, but that the truth surpasses their enunciation and leaves the questioner in ever more pervasive wonder.[24] The "mind" recommended in 2:5 opens upon a new experience and entices with a strikingly participatory invitation into what Jesus is (and is not) and what God is (and is not). It is not meant simply to provide a set, well-defined exemplar for us to follow, as one might admire and emulate an impressive hero or follow a charismatic political leader. By becoming one with the mind of Christ, in accord with the words of the hymn, perhaps we may also empty ourselves of everything and be more-than-exalted with Christ in the glory of the glory-less Father beyond imagined glory. It is more than imitating Christ. It is to be one with Christ.

The commentaries that have been written on this hymn in Phil 2:6–11 frequently go beyond the context of Paul's letter and reflect later doctrinal teachings of the church,

---

24. Maximus Confessor, *Patrologia Graeca* (Paris: Monge, 1857–1866) 44:8731–b.

for this is one of the very earliest incarnational confessions in our scriptures. And if this hymn is not congruent with later Greek theologies, then it would seem we have divergent christologies from our very beginnings. Certainly this hymn is a very early witness, coming as it does from the Philippian congregation and appearing here in Paul's letter, and yet it is also one of the most overlooked passages of Christian scripture. Christian incarnational doctrine did not spring directly from Paul and his letters, certainly not from this Philippian confession of the empty Christ. Incarnational theology flows, rather, from the traditions of John and from Hebrews, with the notion of Christ as the character of God and as the Word with God from the beginning.[25] So it is not surprising that the many Pauline commentators, themselves committed Christians, tend to reflect the later doctrines of the early church as expressed in creed and councils.

Nevertheless, Paul's letters are an organic part of our faith tradition, and even though they do not move in the traditions of John and Hebrews, their wisdom christology is not in disharmony with later doctrinal development. Indeed, inchoate confessions of trinitarian awareness permeate Paul's writings. But if we look back at this hymn of the empty Christ from the well-defined perspective of our ontotheologies, we do run the risk of taking as our parameters for understanding Christ wisdom those time-frozen notions of God as an omniscient, almighty, unmitigated being vis-à-vis limited and transient human beings. This is the framework our early Greek ancestors drew from Plato and their own Greek traditions of philosophy, which set the course for our doctrinal history of objectifying God and defining humanness. But to confine ourselves to that orthodox trajectory constrains any interpretation of Christ as self-emptying or as cosmically over-exalted. In this hymn we have not an alternate ontological version of Chalcedon, but rather a confession of Christ wisdom that is innocent of any ontology. The Philippians produced no known philosophers.

" . . . although he was in the form of God . . ." (2:6)

> 2:6 *Who, although he was in the form of God, did not regard being equal to God as anything advantageous.*

> 2:6 ὃς ἐν μορφῇ θεοῦ ὑπάρχων οὐχ ἁρπαγμὸν ἡγήσατο τὸ εἶναι ἴσα θεῷ,

This is yet another difficult verse, each of whose terms are much discussed. The affirmation of divine being as Christ's form (ἐν μορφῇ θεοῦ)—whether seen as his essence, his divine image in contrast to Adam, his salvific mode of being, his status, or his share in glory—sets up a massive paradox, for in any case it is Jesus of Nazareth who died on the cross to whom that divine form is attributed.

---

25. Dunn, *Theology of Paul the Apostle*, 266–93.

The active participle *uparchōn* (ὑπάρχων) means, in the most common interpretation, simply to exist, to be present. Thus, Christ existed in that divine form. In Paul's Hellenistic diction, ὑπάρχω was commonly substituted for εἶναι, "to be," and most interpret it here to mean simply that he "was"—taking its past tense from the main verb "he regarded" (ἡγήσατο) in the aorist—or perhaps that he "is," since the participle itself is in present tense. The force of the participle is concessive: "Although in the form of God," setting up a contrast with what follows.[26] This "was" has often been taken to refer to Christ's preexistence—in harmony with the ontotheology of Chalcedon—or at least to his prior, if not eternal, existence before he emptied himself.[27] Lightfoot argues that it refers to prior existence without necessarily denoting eternal existence, but Lightfoot does see it to exactly reflect the opening sentence of John's Gospel: "In the beginning was the Word and the Word was with God" (ἐν ἀρχῇ ἦν ὁ λόγος καὶ ὁ λόγος ἦν πρὸς τὸν θεόν).[28] This sounds much like Arius, for whom the Word in John referred to wisdom as first among creatures, the pre-cosmic word of God. But Arius comes later, and his ideas led to the Nicene Confession's clarification that the Word incarnate is God, not merely the incarnation of the primal Word as the first among creatures. Possibly the present verse did play a part in the Arian controversy, but that would seem to be reading issues of the fourth century back into the middle of the first century.

We might tease another interpretation from the text. Even though ὑπάρχω was commonly used for εἶναι, "to be," and meant simply "was" or "is," still here the verb is composed of the preclitic ὑπ- and ἄρχω. This suggests a primal beginning, as if the idea were "from" (ἀπο) "the beginning" (ἀρχῇ). Even though it is pushing things to read John's primal Logos here,[29] the hymn does use a term that suggests the primal form of

---

26. Daniel B. Wallace, *Greek Grammar Beyond the Basics* (Grand Rapids: Zondervan, 1996) 634, cited in Fabricatore, *Form of God*, 144.

27. Fabricatore, *Form of God*, 143. Fabricatore sees Christ's prior existence in the appearances of the Lord in the Tanach (ibid., 204–209); in the theophanies in the Tanach to Moses; and in John 1:14, which says, "we all have witnessed his glory." Caird is circumspect: "Indeed, the term pre-existence is somewhat glibly used in theological discussion without any clear definition of its significance. When Jewish theology spoke of persons or things as existing before the Creation, this was always to be understood in one of two ways. The pre-existent Wisdom, for example, was the personification of an attribute of God, and her apparently independent personal existence could readily be recognized as a figure of speech (Prov. 8:22 ff; Ecclus. 24; Wisd. 7:22 ff) . . . Other persons or things said to pre-exist did so in the mind or predestining purpose of God" (Caird, *Paul's Letters from Prison*, 119).

28. Joseph B. Lightfoot, *Saint Paul's Epistle to the Philippians* (London: Macmillan, 1913) 110. Bruce is more confidently insistent: "It seems fruitless to argue that these words do not assume the pre-existence of Christ" (Bruce, *Philippians*, 68).

29. Pace James H. Moulton and George Milligan, *The Vocabulary of the Greek New Testament: Illustrated from the Papyri and other Non-Literary Sources* (London: Holder & Stoughton, 1914–1929) 651. Moulton and Milligan conclude from their materials that here ὑπάρχων cannot be pressed to mean "being originally" (cited in Fabricatore, *Form of God*, 183 n. 70). Reumann also translates "form" as "sphere" and comments: "Verse 6a seems to express state of being, a continuing state at that. The participle, virtually an equivalent of ōn, 'being,' is the only one in 2:6–11 in the present tense. But neither philosophical concepts of ontology nor notions about 'being *from the beginning*' are to be

Christ as that occurs in the Deutero-Pauline letters to the Colossians and Ephesians. In 3:20 Paul uses the same verb in stating that "our civic association from the beginning is from the heavens" (ὑμῶν γὰρ τὸ πολίτευμα ἐν οὐρανοῖς ὑπάρχει), connoting more than merely it "is" in heaven, but that all along it has been our primal home.[30] Here in 2:6, the hymn speaks not of a deeper dimension of Christ's ontological being, but rather describes the primal being of Christ from the very beginning. A cognate phrase from the same root, τὰ ὑπάρχοντα, denotes "existing circumstances, present advantages,"[31] or the things that one has and owns from the start. This resonates with the following phrase about Christ not deeming his godly form to be to his advantage. We could perhaps render the translation to say not that Christ "*was* in the form of God," but rather that Christ "*abided* in the form of God," hinting at the primal enfoldment of Christ within the divine presence. Since this "form" of God can be understood philosophically as God's essence, it may surely be read in harmony with the Chalcedonian declaration. But that formulation of course represents a different trajectory of theological issues that go well beyond its more common meaning here—the visible and perceptible form or shape of God.

The phrase "in the form of God" (ἐν μορφῇ θεοῦ) in 2:6 is much debated. The traditional understanding since Augustine has been in terms of later ontotheology—that Christ is the essence of God.[32] Nineteenth-century theologians, however, differentiated the inner attributes of the essence of divine being from outer and discernible attributes like omniscience and omnipotence, which are not manifest in the life of Christ. Pierre Benoit explains the phrase to mean "the essential attributes that manifest the nature [of something],"[33] leaving room for those kenotic theologies to understand that Christ has emptied himself of the outer attributes but not of his inner essence, for in that case he would negate his very being. This allows that Christ actually emptied something, if not his essence. He could not empty his essence under

---

read in, though many have seen an ongoing implication, that *morphē theou* continues, even as this person takes on *morphē doulou*" (Reumann, *Philippians*, 367). Yet Reumann sees form as implying a "movement from the sphere of deity to the sphere of servitude" (ibid.). By contrast, I hold that there are no distinct realms or spheres, but there are indeed distinct patterns of deluded living in bondage to selfhood, as well as awakened living in the risen Christ.

30. Martin, *Philippians*, 100. Martin comments anachronistically, "Being in very nature God looks back to our Lord's pre-temporal existence as the second person of the trinity. The verbal form translated *being, hyparchōn*, need not necessarily mean this, but it seems clear that this sense is the only satisfactory one in the context. RV margin translates 'being originally,' and this must refer to the pre-incarnate state to which Paul elsewhere makes reference" (ibid.).

31. Liddell and Scott, *An Intermediate Greek-English Lexicon* (Oxford: Clarendon, 1990) 831.

32. Vincent, *Critical and Exegetical Commentary*, 57–58: "Μορφὴ here means that expression of being which is identified with the essential nature and character of God, and which reveals it. This expression of God cannot be conceived by us, though it may be conceived and apprehended by pure spiritual intelligences." Such pure spiritual intelligences recall Platonic notions of the *nous* as the higher organ of mystic intelligence.

33. Benoit, *Les épîtres de saint Paul aux Philippiens*, 26c.

this interpretation because "if God did this [emptied himself of his divinity], then he would cease, *ipso facto*, to be God."[34]

Still, the overwhelming tendency of interpreters is to insist that, in one way or another, "the form of God" is to be aligned with later metaphysical notions of essence and nature, which then forces the hymn into the parameters of later christology and misconstrues Christ's emptying in the following verse as nothing more than a metaphor for already explicated notions of God's graciousness. But the notion that *morphē* (form) means "essence" comes to grief in the very next sentence, which speaks of the "form of a slave" (*morphē doulos*). In anybody's ontology, an essence is the unchanging core identity of something or someone, but slaves can be manumitted, in which case they are indeed changed—no longer slave but free.[35] If slave essences can be changed, then why not divine essences? Maybe God can abandon his essence and still be God? Or perhaps if God abandons his essence, he is no longer God. The latter is the reading adopted by Buddhist thinker ABE Masao in his dialogues with Christian theologians,[36] but those theologians, aware of the history of New Testament exegesis, by and large were not persuaded. What, they wondered, would be an essence-less God?

In any case, commentators generally agree that the term "form" must have the same meaning in verse 6 and verse 7. It seems best to heed Fabricatore's opinion that "form" in this hymn signifies the visible manifestation or appearance of God's glory,[37] rather than the core being envisioned by later ontotheology. Fabricatore examines the lexical definitions of "form" as it shifts meaning over time, from early Greek philosophers through thinkers of the Greco-Roman world and on to the Patristic theologians. Fabricatore concludes that when Philippians was written, the term did not mean the ontological essence of Aristotle and Plato or of the later councils, but rather the visible manifestation of God's glory as seen in Christ. In this early Christian period, terms are used more innocently, so the phrase "form of God" is more flexible than it would later become, indicating simply the visible appearance of God.[38] In the narratives of the Tanach, God often appears in glorious theophanies, as for example to Moses on

---

34. John Harvey, "A New Look at the Christ Hymn in Phillippians 2:6–11," *Expository Times* 76 (1964–1965) 338, cited by Fabricatore, *Form of God*, 161.

35. Collange, *Epistle of Saint Paul*, 97–98. Collange avoids essentializing the "form of God" when he writes, "Why, then, '*morphē*'? Because the word indicates a most profound and genuine identity, as early exegesis rightly divined, yet one which was *hidden*, not manifest" (ibid.). This recalls the Yogācāra notion that the conventional truth, which is a covering over of ultimate truth (Skt. *paramārtha-satya*), marks the presence of that ultimate *precisely by being so covered and hidden* (*saṃvṛta*). See Nagao, *Foundational Standpoint*, 51–59.

36. See Abe, "Kenotic God and Dynamic Sunyata."

37. Fabricatore, *Form of God*, 152–56. Both Paul D. Feinburg ("The Kenosis and Christology: An Exegetical-Theological Analysis of Phil 2:6–11," *Trinity Journal* 1 [1980] 21–46) and Robert B. Stimple ("Philippians 2:6–11 in Recent Studies: Some Exegetical Conclusions," *Westminster Theological Journal* 41 [1979] 247–68) also interpret μορφή as referring to God's glory.

38. Fabricatore, *Form of God*, 153–56.

the Exodus mountaintop and to the prophets.[39] In the gospels, Jesus shines in translucent light at his transfiguration before his disciples, and many witness his luminous form in the resurrection appearances. The glory of this visible divine form contrasts starkly with the form of a humiliated slave that we encounter in the next verse of this Philippian hymn.

But the weight of the ontological tradition presses heavily on exegetes and theologians working to bring this early christological confession into line with later Chalcedonian doctrine. So—rather than to recognize a historical trajectory whereby, over time, an early understanding of Christ as self-emptying and more-than-exalted became overshadowed by the ontological categories of later theologians—modern commentators have felt constrained to force the meaning of the emptiness hymn into that more orthodox and ontological Procrustean bedframe. Consequently, when they do discuss this hymn, they say very little that veers from the ontological understanding of Christ's two essences or natures. A Mahāyāna understanding, by contrast, would see the hymn as a distinct and complementary pattern for understanding the mind of Christ—who he is, and thus who we are.

Many commentators collapse the emptiness themes of this hymn by having it both ways: Since the divine form implies glory (δόξα)—the seen, perceived, visible glory of God—this is the manifestation of Christ's underlying essence. Nineteenth-century German commentator H. A. W. Meyer finds the glory of God to be the form of manifest being corresponding to the divine essence, whereby glory exhibits that essence.[40] If we link form (μορφή, morphē) as essence with glory (δόξα, doxa), we arrive upon the metaphysical heights, where we find a dualistic philosophy of inner and outer. But there is none of this in the Philippian hymn; the hymn does not indulge in metaphysical speculation about essence and attributes or about essence and its manifestation.

Other commentators avoid the language of essences, equating "form" (μορφή, morphē) with "image" (εἰκών, eikōn). They read here, in light of Gen 1:26–27, a contrast between Adam, who was created in the image of God, and the Christ, who is the image (εἰκών) of God—the new Adam (Col 1:15). This explanation, proposed by Jean Héring among others,[41] draws upon the book of Genesis in the Greek Bible and contrasts that to Christ as the new configuration of human being that Paul speaks of elsewhere. Ralph Martin argues that "form" (μορφή) is synonymous with "image" (εἰκών),[42] but most commentators disagree, holding that the two terms are not

---

39. Ibid., 205–10.

40. H. A. W. Meyer, *Critical and Exegetical Handbook to the Epistles to the Philippians and Colossians*, translation of 4th edition by J. C. Moore and W. P. Dickson (New York, 1875) 80, cited by O'Brien, *Epistle to the Philippians*, 208.

41. See O'Brien, *Epistle to the Philippians*, 196–97.

42. See Martin, *Hymn of Christ*, 108: "It may be shown that εἰκών and μορφή are used as interchangeable terms in the Greek Bible, and are regarded as synonyms in other places." Archibald M. Hunter also sees the εἰκών of Adam as equivalent to the μορφή of Christ, for the meaning of εἰκων "fits

equivalent. However, even if the hymn could not have made such an equation, there is a clear contrast between the selfish Adam who sought equality with God and the Christ who did not bother.

Yet another ontological suggestion, this one offered by Ernst Käsemann, is that form (μορφή) signifies "mode of being (*Daseinsweise*) or 'a way of being under particular circumstances.'" This would mean that *morphē* refers not to an individual entity but to "'a mode of being in a specific direction, such as, for example, being in divine substance and power.'"[43] Others criticize that interpretation because, in order to develop these notions, Käsemann draws upon later Hellenistic and Gnostic redeemer myths of a cosmic savior figure who descends to earth to save the elect and then returns to higher realms—a theme that is unavailable and unacceptable to Paul and the Philippians. (Such a mythic descent/ascent model for understanding Christ is not altogether unknown to us, however. Not infrequently, one encounters such docetic accounts of the heavenly Christ descending to save us and take us to heaven. The Gnostics have no monopoly on mythmaking.)

All these notions of essence, glory, mode of being, or image seem to be have a common background metaphysics of the divine, and in modern philosophical discourse they cannot but appear to suggest that the interpreter actually knows about divine nature and its modes of being. And so they are received today as pretentious attempts to see things from God's perspective. That is of course impossible, for God has no perspective.

Another interpretation is that of E. Schweizer and Ralph Martin: that *morphē* here means a condition or status and refers to Christ's original position vis-à-vis God. Martin maintains that, on balance, this view has the most in its favor, in part because of the close tie between "the righteous one" and the personalized figure of wisdom in Jewish sapiential literature.[44] Others reject this view, seeing nothing about status in this hymn. Yet if we interpret Christ's "humiliation" in verse 8 not as a virtuous act of self-effacing humility, but rather—following Reumann, as I do—as social degradation, the hymn is indeed addressing issues of status and identity. But how can any of us know what Christ's original position vis-à-vis God might mean? We can recognize what it means to be humiliated, and we know what social humiliation and low status are, but what does God's status mean, especially considering that here Christ does not regard his equality with God as a particularly advantageous status? What is God's status, when God has no status at all? I do not know what God is, and thus I hesitate to concur with those who read "form" as signifying what is really real about God and

---

our passage perfectly" (Archibald M. Hunter, *Paul and his Predecessors* [London: SCM, 1961] 43). For a critique, see Dave Steenburg, "The Case Against the Synonymity of Morphē and Eikōn," *Journal for the Study of the New Testament* 34 (1988) 77–86. Steenburg argues convincingly that there is no tie between *morphē* here and the use of *eikōn* in Gen 1:26-27.

43. Käsemann, "A Critical Analysis of Philippians 2:5-11," *Journal for Theology and the Church* 5 (1968) 60, cited in O'Brien, *Epistle to the Philippians*, 209. See Fabricatore, *Form of God*, 148–50.

44. O'Brien, *Epistle to the Philippians*, 210.

then go on to promote that insight into a philosophical metalanguage we can only pretend to understand.

Paul did live and write in a Hellenistic culture where the terms "form" and "being" were in general use, much as we in our culture employ the word "real" without necessarily consulting either Heidegger or Aquinas to determine those thinkers' precise definition of the word. The "form of God," as it appears here, is then the commonly understood nature of God, "that which truly characterizes a given reality."[45] In much the same way, we speak of human "nature" to describe the ways we observe human beings acting. Form, then, is the shape of something that is perceived by the senses, or the concrete presentation and character of what is. Exegetical and theological problems arise here because, as these terms are used in the Philippians hymn, they do not have the precise metaphysical definitions found in Plato and Aristotle.

The interpretations of many scholars, including J. B. Lightfoot and Pierre Benoit, nevertheless do look to the Hellenistic culture of ancient Greece to assume that this hymn is relying upon Greek philosophical ideas, particularly Aristotelian notions of form. Lightfoot writes: "Though μορφή [form] is not the same as φύσις [nature] or οὐσία [essence], yet the possession of the μορφή [form] involves participation in the οὐσία [essence] also: for μορφή [form] implies not the external accidents but the essential attributes."[46] This notion of form, taken straight from Greek metaphysics, defines and delimits beings each according to its form. To be "in the form of God" is then to be essentially distinct from all other forms, such as "to be in human form" or "to be in plant form." If one takes Paul rather than the Philippians to be the author of this hymn—as I would not—he then becomes our first metaphysician. The difficulty with this, even if one does believe that Paul himself composed the hymn, is that nowhere else in Paul's writing do we see any affinity for such metaphysics; he appears content throughout his writings to use terms that are familiar in common discourse. And if, as I am persuaded, the hymn is indeed the product of the Philippian community, it seems even less likely that the word "form" is used here to mean anything beyond what we would commonly intend today when speaking of the "form" or outward appearance of someone or something—that is, their visible characteristics, innocent of ontological entanglements.[47]

A few hundred years after Paul's exchange of letters with the Philippians, the pressing needs of classical Christian theology would not be satisfied by such an undeveloped notion of what is real, and theologians then did come to rely upon metaphysical interpretations. Some teachers at the time were proffering perspectives on Christ and God that seemed discordant with the gospels, and so, feeling a need to develop a clear philosophical understanding of life in Christ, Greek Christian thinkers turned to

---

45. Fee, *Paul's Letter to the Philippians*, 204.

46. J. B. Lightfoot, *St. Paul's Epistle to the Philippians* (London, 1881) 110, cited in O'Brien, *Epistle to the Philippians*, 207.

47. See Fabricatore, *Form of God*, 263.

their own classical culture, which they accepted and adapted to their own purposes.[48] Greek metaphysics, which stressed the delimited and individual being of what is real, was a useful tool, and they employed its philosophical notions in crafting each and every Christian creed and confession. They consistently refused, however, to collapse the mystery of Christ into any perspective, always firmly insisting on the paradox of the incarnation. The famed *homoousios* (ὁμοούσιος)—"of one being with," or "consubstantial with," the Father in our creedal confessions—guards the mystery by rejecting less paradoxical explanations. The efforts of these early Greek Christian ancestors who Hellenized the gospel in their theologies served the tradition well, for they held as central our participation in the incarnate life of Jesus Christ. That is, we are who we are not by our natural "ontological" heritage, nor as standalone individuals, but because human nature itself is reconfigured in Christ. This formulation was so satisfactory that for centuries—indeed, until the Renaissance and Reformation—Greek ontotheology permeated classical Christian culture and replaced the ancient philosophers.[49]

In any case, the Christian adoption of the Hellenistic complex of ideas came about only in the fourth century, long after the composition of this Philippian hymn about participating in Christ Jesus. We know nothing of the thinking of the Philippians with whom Paul corresponded, but these hymnic words would have held resonance for them only if they found therein a reflection of their own enlightened and reconfigured awareness of risen life—a life they experienced themselves and heard about in the Jesus narratives. Those narratives, which circulated among the Christian communities, were not mere reports of interesting events in the past; they sketched out an offer of immediate and experienced life in Christ.[50]

Even with an everyday understanding of the "form" of God, this hymn stacks the rhetorical deck by setting up a dexterous and fungible notion—the "form of God," which then is to be left behind. It leaves us wondering just what it might mean that Jesus, who is truly God's formal reality, empties himself and evinces no concern about being divine. One can read back into these words a "high christology" of Christ being both truly divine and really human, but in the hymn itself, everything remains

---

48. Aloys Grillmeier, *From the Apostolic Age to Chalcedon*, vol. 1 of *Christ in Christian Tradition* (Atlanta: John Knox, 1965) 107. Grillmeier describes the process as "two steps forward and one step back" (ibid.). On the adoption of Greek patterns of thought and their role in setting the framework for the christological and trinitarian discussions of the patristic churches, see Keenan, *Meaning of Christ*, 46–50.

49. See Pelikan, *Christian Tradition*, 1:44: "The victory of orthodox Christian doctrine over classical thought was to some extent a Pyrrhic victory. For the theology that triumphed has continued to be shaped ever since by the language and thought of Greek metaphysics." See Charles Taylor, *A Secular Age* (Cambridge: Belknap, 2007).

50. Everett speaks of the immediacy of experience that is structured in the language of the Pirahã people of the Amazon: "Declarative Pirahã utterances contain only assertions related directly to the moment of speech, either experienced by the speaker or witnessed by someone alive during the lifetime of the speaker" (Everett, *Don't Sleep*, 132). Although not so inscribed in other languages, this kind of immediacy is pervasive in the theology of Paul; it is all about sharing in risen life.

inchoate. Its fruit is envisaged not as maturing in the realm of philosophical discourse, but rather in the lives of faith-imbued practitioners. Its truth is disclosed not on pages of discursive reasoning, but only to a mind that conforms to the empty Christ in prayer and practice.

This sense of inchoate participation expressed here and in many other passages by Paul offers a trinitarian structure to our experience of life and meaning. Similarly, in the transfiguration account in Mark 9:2–8, Jesus' very form is trans-*formed* (μεταμορφώθη) before Peter, James, and John; but, having been advised by Jesus not to spread it about, all they are left with is "just Jesus" in his simple humanness.[51] Despite the lack of any mention of the Spirit in the Philippian hymn, trinitarian teachings remain just below the surface of its text, urging its hearers to transform and reconfigure their minds. This is a constant theme of Paul, and it parallels Jesus' call for conversion (*metanoia*) at the beginning of Mark's Gospel. Trinitarian themes are not mistakes foisted upon us by the Greek councils and the Latin theologies. Yet scripture is foundational precisely because it speaks in an inchoate register, inviting us to practice and experience, and only then to study and develop old and new christologies.[52]

The old christologies are encoded in creeds that we still recite in our liturgies. They retain their force by circumscribing the mystery, disallowing all our varied attempts to rationalize the being of Christ. Our creeds are called "Symbols of Faith" (L. *symbola fidei*) not because they are "mythic" signposts for something else, but because they delineate the teaching of Christ by a common "throwing" (*bolē*) "together" (*sym*) of the faith of the diverse parties attendant at each of the ecumenical councils. No one, I imagine, went home from those councils fully satisfied—not Athanasius, not Cyprian, and certainly neither Arius nor Eunomius—for the conciliar statements "throw together" the common faith in a verbal balancing act that glories in paradox and mystery. The councils refused time and time again to collapse the common faith down to any single perspective.

Although our creeds are called "symbols" of faith, we do entrust ourselves in commitment to a tradition, and so it is not appropriate for us to simply make the words of those creeds mean anything at all we might wish. That is a common liberal Christian move: first to identify orthodox insights as symbolic, and then to leave them quite behind to sketch a more modernly compatible view of the matter. Yet the conciliar creeds are not the *only* way in which we may understand the meaning of Christ. Indeed, with the passing of metaphysical surety, they become less useful and more befuddling to people who are not trained in Greek philosophical thought. The

---

51. On Mark 9:2–8, "The Epiphany of Just Jesus," see Keenan, *Gospel of Mark*, 208–12.

52. Habito writes that the Zen injunction to kill the Buddha if one sees him "is the command to do away with one's mental images of the Buddha," and that a "parallel injunction to the Christian about 'crucifying Christ' may have a different ring, but its purport is the same—to clear away all our pious images of Christ and thus 'put him in his place,' which is on the cross, where he is one with all beings in their suffering, where he is reduced to nothing in total emptying (*kenosis*)" (Habito, *Living Zen, Loving God*, 37).

Philippians emptiness hymn, on the other hand, offers a skillful approach to enunciating the same Christ faith in perhaps a more accessible key, though it is nevertheless very much rooted in scripture.

The second part of verse 2:6 makes clear that Jesus' being in the "form of God (μορφή θεοῦ)" means his being "equal to God" (τὸ εἶναι ἴσα θεῷ). The grammar of this verse is pretty straightforward, but the interpretive problem for commentators is theological: What does it mean to say that Jesus is equal to God? God has no equal, no second. Who and what is God? Could God, the "one God" of the Shema, have an "equal"? Is it any wonder that Jews and Muslims find Christian ontotheologies to be idolatrous? However we might read this verse today, "being in the form of God" apparently caused no disagreement among the Philippians; they must simply have accepted that Christ is our linkage to the primal God. This much is reflected in the concessive form of the sentence: "although he was in the form of God . . ."

Bishop Nestorius thought the incarnate Christ was adopted as God's son and became equal only at his baptism in the Jordan, when the heavens opened and the voice of God proclaimed, "You are my son." But this view was deemed heretical, and Nestorius and his followers had to flee the wrath of the orthodox by journeying as far as China, where "Nestorian Christians" left records in Chinese of their "adoptionist" faith.[53] Indians, by contrast, recognizing a variety of incarnations, were ready to welcome Jesus as yet another. But this is not the teaching of the gospel or of the churches. Jesus is not confessed as the best in a series, for there is no serial elaboration of God or any equal to God. From the earliest days, Paul and his comrades confessed Jesus to somehow share in the glory of God, but this Philippian hymn makes us hesitate to confess what Christ himself did not confess: that he was God's equal. In fact, this represents yet another heresy: that there are two gods, whether equal or not. The Chalcedonian trajectory confesses a Christ who is not divine *alongside* God, but rather is of one being with God, indivisible with the Father, leaving all this non-duality for later generations to figure out.

Often we have erred by insisting that Jesus Christ is the best of all incarnations. But again and again the creeds refuse to collapse faith into explanatory viewpoints, going so far as to invent newfangled words like *homoousios* to guard the most central of Christian kōans.[54] In fact, the creeds hardly explain anything, simply repeating

---

53. See Martin Palmer, *Jesus Sutras: Recovering the Lost Scrolls of Taoist Christianity* (New York: Ballentine, 2001). The "Jesus Sutra" is a collective term for a number of texts written by Christian communities in T'ang China and discovered over the last hundred years. Their interpretation and translation is disputed, but they do exist, reflecting a Christian community legally established in the cosmopolitan T'ang dynasty. Nestorian Christian presence has long been recognized in China, and some see that lineage in these texts. But the texts themselves contain no sectarian Christian argument, contenting themselves with expressing the meaning of Christ in terms borrowed, as Palmer says, from Taoist traditions.

54. See Rowan Williams, *Arius: Heresy and Tradition*, rev. ed. (Grand Rapids: Eerdmans, 2007) 82–99 and 175–78. The conclusions to the first two sections show that Arius himself was "a committed theological conservative," rejecting the new enunciations of faith in terms of Hellenistic philosophy as

over and over the same formulas. Thus, to recite the Nicene Creed is not to state the Christian perspective, but to remember the stark mystery that challenges all assurance of our standalone being. Christ does not stand alone as the best, but rather stands as one with all who welcome risen life. So if Christ does not consider himself God's equal, we do best to interrogate our own assumed knowledge of who we humans are and who God is, with all defined boundaries fading into insignificance.

The passage, however, does not merely state that Jesus is God's form; it implies that actually he "is God's equal" (τὸ εἶναι ἴσα θεῷ), even though Jesus is not attached to that divine equality. *In his own mind*, the hymn declares, Jesus did not think his own divine equality anything particularly to be grasped after, anything particular to be exploited, or anything that might be an advantage to him. He seems to have a cavalier attitude toward his own divine status. I have heard so many Christian preachers declare that bedrock Christian faith is that Christ is God, but Christ here does not care about being God.[55] He takes being equal to the deathless God, and he makes little of it. The sentence says: "He did not regard being equal to God *as anything very special*" (ἁρπαγμὸν, *harpagmon*). There are many interpretations of the term *harpagmon*, for it occurs only here in the Greek Bible and only rarely in other Greek texts. Its meaning is widely discussed and disputed.[56] Jesus, the Philippian hymn sings, "didn't think that being equal to God" (οὐχ ἡγήσατο τὸ εἶναι ἴσα θεῷ) "was *harpagmon*."

The noun *harpagmon* (ἁρπαγμὸν)—derived from the verb (ἁρπάξω) for "to snatch or seize"—means a "snatching" or "seizing," or perhaps "that which is seized or snatched" or that which is stolen as prey or booty, a prize, or a gain. So then, his core being is not regarded as "something to take advantage of, or something to use for his own advantage."[57] J. B. Lightfoot understood the term as meaning "a prize" or "treasure."[58] Jesus did not think his divine equality was something to be particularly treasured. Ralph P. Martin interprets the term as "something to be retained as booty," something that Jesus regarded as a personal gain. In the same vein, Morna Hooker emphasizes that unlike Adam in the garden, Christ did not snatch at equality with God.

Indeed, the only garden in the gospels is Gethsemane; Jesus was not born into a garden of Eden like Adam or into the gardens of Lumbini like the Buddha Śākyamuni,

---

found in the Nicene creed (ibid., 175).

55. *Pace* Caird, *Paul's Letters from Prison*, 124. In discussing verse 11 on Jesus as Lord, Caird writes, "It is not surprising therefore that at an early date it [i.e., naming Jesus as Lord] became the most popular designation for Jesus, or that its ambiguity provided a setting in which Christian devotion to Jesus could expand. But Paul at least never took the step of calling Jesus God" (ibid.).

56. Collange, *Epistle of Saint Paul*, 98. In 1979, Collange wrote: "Everything relevant has been said about the meaning of '*harpagmos*'" (ibid.). The contours of the issue have become clearer, but no noticeable stoppage in the upsurge of commentarial interpretation has ensued.

57. See R. W. Hoover, "The *Harpagmos* Enigma: A Philological Solution," *Harvard Theological Review* 64 (1971) 95–119.

58. O'Brien, *Epistle to the Philippians*, 212.

but rather into a world filled with threat and danger. Nevertheless, this early Christian hymn tells us, he did not crave after being like God, knowing good and evil. Although in the form of God and thus equal with God, he cared little for the unmitigated being of God. As it will work out, we too have no need to repeat Adam's sorry quest to seize on "God's being"—to become immortal, beyond suffering and death—because taking on the mind of Christ entails the abandonment of grasping after anything at all. In their Greek world, Christians were identified as "atheists" (ἄθεοι) because they did not recognize the divinities that populated that world. Perhaps, rather than mounting defenses of theism, we would do better to meditate upon Christ's abandoning the very notion of divinity as applied to himself, for this is the reason we confess him to be "fully human" and yet "of one being" with the Father. Christ is God because he does not regard that as particularly important.

Can we be clearer? What might *harpagmos* mean here? It does appear to denote "robbery" where it appears (rarely) in Greek literature. But that is "a meaning that can hardly obtain here," writes Gordon Fee,[59] and so some scholars have concluded that the only choice is to emend the text. But textual emendation in the absence of clear textual indications seems like an interpreter's dodge—an extreme move to solve a theological conundrum that arises because we feel sure we know what it means to be God, and that clearly has nothing to do with robbery! By contrast, C. F. D. Moule, unwilling to emend the text, takes the word *harpagmos* in the active sense of snatching something. Jesus, Moule argues, did not think of equality with God as a trophy to be taken at the end of some spiritual journey,[60] but rather as an emptiness—not as a snatching at something but "as an openhanded spending, even to death."[61] Moule elaborates: "precisely *because* he was in the form of God he reckoned equality with God not a matter of getting but giving."[62]

This theme is taken up by Karl Barth and many kenotic theologians who suggest that Christ's emptying was a free act of giving, befitting the gracious being of God.[63]

59. See the discussion in Fee, *Paul's Letter to the Philippians*, 205–206.

60. And thus not Joseph Campbell's archetypical *Hero With a Thousand Faces*, who passes through trials and sufferings to emerge in Vedāntic oneness with the heart of the real (Campbell, *Hero With a Thousand Faces*, 377–78). There is no culture-free and universal faith that might subsume all religions within the overarching apprehension of any single truth, for faith is always local and embedded in the actual lives of practitioners.

61. C. F. D. Moule, "Further Reflexions on Philippians 2:5–11," in *Apostolic History and the Gospel*, edited by W. W. Gasque and R. P. Martin (Exeter: Paternoster, 1970) 272, cited by O'Brien, *Epistle to the Philippians*, 213.

62. C. F. D. Moule, "The Manhood of Jesus in the New Testament," in *Christ, Faith, and History*, edited by S. W. Sykes and J. P. Clayton (Cambridge: Cambridge University Press, 1972) 97.

63. On the German kenotic understanding of emptiness, Collange writes that "for Barth kenosis could only mean this: 'As God, therefore, (without ceasing to be God) he could be known only to himself, and unknown as such in the world and for the world. His divine majesty could be in this alien form. It could be a hidden majesty . . . He had the freedom for this condescension, for this concealment of his Godhead. He had it and he made use of it in the power and not with any loss, not with any diminution or alteration of his Godhead' (*Church Dogmatics* IV Pt. 1, ET 1956, 180)" (Collange,

Yet this interpretation suffers, in my estimation, from too high a divine perspective—"being God, he did not have to try to be God"—for this is a perspective that is unavailable to any human commentator at all. Moreover, it says nothing more than does the assertion that an immeasurably rich man does not have to crave wealth—a trivial observation.[64] Similarly, when Roy W. Hoover places the issue in a full christological context and claims that Christ "did not regard being equal with God as something to take advantage of,"[65] this again assumes that we have a stable notion of what God means and so ends up meaning that "being God, he did not have to act like God." How can anyone know what it might mean to be, but not act, God?

Gordon Fee offers two possible understandings, both of which seem insightful and both of which lead us, I think, in the right direction. He posits that *harpagmos* is first and foremost verbal in force, signifying the act of "grasping"; secondly, it is a synonym for its cognate noun, *harpagma*, meaning "booty or prey." The term thus indicates a grasping after something we wish to clutch to ourselves. Reading this in the context of the Mahāyāna discourse about mind, it would be a grasping that bespeaks persistent delusion or "unreal imagining" (Skt. *abhūta-parikalpa*).[66] Such delusion perceives, or grasps, only imagined things and yet treats them as though they are real. In this hymn, God is not a stable entity that may be grasped and clung to as the most precious of deathless objects. And that very negation opens up new trajectories for christological thinking that are distinct from ontotheologies that express themselves in terms of a knower reaching out to know what is really so. People do in fact live within images—of race, ethnicity, religion, role, job, and all the myriad ways we have of self-clinging. This imaginative consciousness, according to the Buddhist texts, is "unreal" (*abhūta*), for none of these images actually represent anything that is truly real or that abides firmly in its definition.

Epistle of Saint Paul, 102).

64. Caird, *Paul's Letters from Prison*, 121: "There is no justification here for what in modern times has come to be known as Kenotic Christology, the idea that Christ could not have become man without divesting himself of the attributes of deity, particularly those of omnipotence, omniscience, and omnipresence. Paul is not talking about these matters, but about Christ's renunciation of rank, privilege, and rights." One can see the renunciation of rank and privilege, but where in Paul is there any discourse on Christ's rights?

65. R. W. Hoover, "The *Harpagmos* Enigma: A Philological Solution," *Harvard Theological Review* 64 (1971) 118, cited by O'Brien, *Epistle to the Philippians*, 215.

66. Nagao, *Foundational Standpoint*, 91. Nagao interprets a passage on unreal imagining from *The Analysis of the Middle Path and Extremes* (Madhyāntavibhāga), which states: "Unreal imagining exists, but in it the two do not exist. However, herein emptiness exists, and in that [unreal imagining] exists." Nagao explains, "The phrase 'unreal imagining' refers to the appearance of dependently arisen things in consciousness. There 'the two'—namely, subject and object—have no final status as existent beings. Rather, as expressed in the third phrase, 'emptiness exists' in unreal imagining, because no subjective or objective essence can lay claim to being. It is in the context of the emptiness of subject and object that the dependently arisen state of 'unreal imagining' exists" (ibid.). Emptiness denies essential being to both the apprehending subject and the apprehended object, thereby reclaiming the purified pattern of other-dependent consciousness as a conventional subject apprehending conventional objects, for therein lies the truth of conventional language and doctrine.

With this in mind, we may then read the Chalcedonian confession not as a christological definition, but as a kōan-like refusal to rationalize the ineffable indivisibility that we affirm of Christ with the Father and of Christ with us—our being "in Christ." To be attached to any confessional expression is to fail to imitate the mind of Christ; no matter how orthodox, it amounts to the same "unreality" that Qoheleth describes as vanity and mist. In fact, there is nothing to hold onto: neither ordinary things like wealth and status, nor lofty things like philosophy and theology. Everything vanishes in the misty passing of any object grasped to the self, and self-referential consciousness, so assured in its hold on what is objectively real, ceases to be the measure of what is real.

For Yogācāra thinkers, unreal consciousness is the assumption that an object apprehended (Skt. *grāhya*) stands in front of an abiding subject who apprehends (*grāhaka*). This pattern of an apprehended something that defines the apprehender is the subject/object dichotomy that fractures consciousness, lures us toward mirages, and supports our deluded mind in its varied functionings. The Mahāyāna cure for this delusion is a "dose of emptiness," which through meditative concentration can free the mind from its attachments and transcend the entire framework of subject-object apprehension and the grasping that engenders delusion.[67] This, in turn, calls attention to the entire field of human experiences that come before and remain after the discriminating mind at last recognizes and acknowledges the contextual pattern of its bifurcating operations.

Once a practitioner of meditation has awakened to emptiness, however, that person, because they are human, cannot simply abide in liberation from clinging to what is unreal. Rather, the practitioner but must reappropriate ordinary patterns of understanding whatever images and sensations present themselves as objects to subjective experience and insight.[68] Scripture and philosophy, whether inchoate or articulated, are then once again affirmed, but not with the unreal imagining that an objective truth is perceived by an objectively real subject. Rather, our putatively stable

---

67. For the meaning and the use of emptiness, see José Ignacio Cabezón, *A Dose of Emptiness: An Annotated Translation of the Stong Thun Chen Mo of Mkhas Grub Dge Legs Dpal Bzang* (Albany: State University of New York Press, 1992). On the Mādhyamika teaching of emptiness, see also C. W. Huntington, *The Emptiness of Emptiness: An Introduction to Early Indian Mādhyamika* (Honolulu: University of Hawaii Press, 1989). For the broader scope of Mahāyāna thought, including Yogācāra, see Nagao, *Foundational Standpoint*, and also Jay L. Garfield, *Buddhist Philosophy and Cross-Cultural Interpretation* (Oxford: Oxford University Press, 2002).

68. The patterns of human understanding are treated by Bernard J. F. Lonergan in his *Insight: A Study of Human Understanding* (Toronto: University of Toronto, 1992) and worked out in his schema of theological endeavor in his *Method in Theology* (Toronto: University of Toronto, 1990). Lonergan's insights have been so fruitful that Lonergan studies have evolved into their own full-blown scholasticism over the last half-century. Lonergan's theological schema, sketched in *Method in Theology*, has not gained universal support, but I do follow his basic understanding of human consciousness as enfolding experience, insight, and judgment, explicated in *Insight: A Study of Human Understanding*. The "unreal imagining" of the Mahāyāna parallels Lonergan's "already-out-there-now-real" as the deluded mode of naïve realism.

minds are "reclaimed" as being themselves contextual—dependently arisen in all their discourses about what flows through and beyond discrimination, ever striving to disclose the visceral presence of our bodily oneness with Christ. And that is what the early ecumenical councils in effect did: they set within the dependently arisen philosophies then available to them a framework for enunciating the non-duality of Christ with the Father.

Some commentators on Phil 2:6 understand Christ's "non-grasping" in terms of his refusal to enter rapture by embarking on a spiritual quest to mount above this weary world into realms of the divine. *The Greek–English Lexicon of the New Testament* gives one meaning for *harpagmos* as a mystical rapture but notes that this is an ancient mistake. Still, if this is a grasping after special experiences, then the hymn means that for Christ "to be like God was no rapture" (cf. 2 Cor 12:2; 1 Thess 4:17; Rev 12:5).[69] Jesus rejected "being caught up" into heaven to escape suffering. Paul himself is familiar with rapturous experiences, as he recounts in 2 Corinthians and 1 Thessalonians. However, in the Christ wisdom discourse of 1 Corinthians he distances himself from the authoritative status of such special experiences,[70] in favor of enunciating the always hidden wisdom of God: "We speak God's hidden wisdom in mystery" (λαλοῦμεν θεοῦ σοφίαν ἐν μυστηρίῳ τὴν ἀποκεκρυμμένην 1 Cor 2:7). And this is an everyday, lived wisdom that enlivens ordinary people in resurrection faith. P. Trudinger "takes it [*harpagmos*] as meaning that Christ refused to ascend to God by way of mystical raptures."[71] Christ's disregard for being equal to God is his abandonment of the arhat's goal of attaining a blissful and final cessation apart from this world. God has chosen the things that are not, in order to bring to nothing the things that are (ἐξελέξατο ὁ θεός τὰ μὴ ὄντα, ἵνα τὰ ὄντα καταργήσῃ 1 Cor 1:28). Christ has emptied himself of his divine equality.[72] Christ wisdom does not mean that we are already filled or that we have already become rich (1 Cor 4:8); it is not a matter of any ontological thing to be grasped or any ontological subject who grasps.

---

69. Bauer, *Greek-English Lexicon*, 108 n. 3. For a critique, see Reumann, who concludes that this interpretation "has found little support" (Reumann, *Philippians*, 345). Nevertheless, Bauer does provide an extensive list of supporters.

70. See Keenan, *Meaning of Christ*, 40–43.

71. P. Trudinger, "'Harpagmos' and the Christological Significance of the Ascension," *Expository Times* 79 (1967–1968) 279, cited in Collange, *Epistle of Saint Paul*, 99.

72. Alain Badiou, *Saint Paul: The Foundation of Universalism* (Stanford: Stanford University Press, 2003) 47. Badiou writes on 1 Cor 1:17–29 that "One must, in Paul's logic, go so far as to say that *the Christ-event testifies that God is not the god of Being, is not Being*. Paul prescribes an anticipatory critique of what Heidegger calls onto-theology, wherein God is thought of as supreme being, and hence as measure for what being as such is capable of. The most radical statement in the text we are commenting on is in effect the following: 'God has chosen the things that are not (*ta mē onta*) in order to bring to nought the things that are (*ta onta*).' That the Christ event causes nonbeings rather than beings to arise as attesting to God; that it consists in the abolition of what all previous discourses held as existing, or being, gives a measure of the ontological subversion to which Paul's antiphilosophy invites the declarant or militant" (ibid.).

Emptiness turns practitioners back toward the world to affirm their human existence—in all its dependently arisen beauty as well as in its unstable truth—as the arena for compassionate action. We are freed from unreal imagining to recover the dependently arisen pattern (Skt. *paratantra*) of our very conventional selves, in all our organic, genetic, neural, and conscious functionings. By attending to that which is in Christ's non-grasping mind, we reaffirm our day-to-day human consciousness of being "in Christ" not by a display of objects perceived by a discerning subject, but now in an awakened pattern of recognizing ourselves as human subjects within a particular culture and society, without any pretension of having captured the being of God, and without boasting of any special relationship with God. The Christ path here recommended is a path of non-attachment and simplicity that boasts in having nothing to boast about at all. That is why we confess the creeds of the church—not to *capture* truth, but to bask in its radiant glory. The less we boast of Christ's divinity, the more the divine light of Christ illumines our worlds.

When we come, then, to consider God, as well as what it means for Christ to be equal to God, we would do well to harness our imaginations and, welcoming in the insights of less familiar philosophies, to suspend the classical, ontological pattern of grasping after meanings we clutch to our bosoms. The Philippian emptiness hymn affirms that Jesus' "theological" focus was not to apprehend being equal to God as something to be grasped—not anything that might be snatched as a prize, nor anything that might indicate victory for a deluded prize-seeker. Being equal to God is not something to steal—nothing to be had there, nothing precious or prized, for being God means precisely emptying oneself from being God, so that by entering the cloud of unknowing we may know God. Here, we are to adopt the mind of Christ, wherein no God is found but only the very transient and empty Christ. This does not mean that the human Jesus is humanly promoted or exalted above other humans, but that the entire framework encompassing all promotions and demotions is undermined, and God is no longer safe in his heavenly haven from putatively existential complaints from humans who have a firm hold on their Job-like lives.

If the Philippian christology here is indeed the highest in the New Testament—or if, as Gordon Fee puts it, verses 6 and 7 contain "the strongest expressions of Christ's deity in the New Testament"[73]—it remains by design an inchoate christology. Thus it ought not immediately morph into the later Greek ontotheologies, even though those may comprise the cherished confessions of our immensely true and elegant tradition. In the historical event, the doctrinal history of the later Hellenistic theologies and the early ecumenical councils did not attend to this hymn of the empty Christ, nor did they explicate the mind of the empty Christ in their teaching. But they did circumscribe the way we may speak of Christ and of God,[74] precisely by excluding theologi-

---

73. Fee, *Paul's Letter to the Philippians*, 208.

74. See Joseph O'Leary, "Who Is Jesus Christ?" *Christology*, December 21, 2007, http://joseph-soleary.typepad.com/my_weblog/christology.

cal attempts to explain things in terms that would overcome the paradox—either by grounding themselves in a notion of what God is or in a contrasting notion of what being human means. The Hellenistic theologies negate that Christ is either a docetic appearance of a well-established and known God or a man with supernatural and divine qualities. What "remains" after those endeavors is the *arcana* of the faith, the paradox of the empty Christ, and the simplicity of the incarnation.

We have here in Paul an inchoate confession that remains inchoate. Such kerygmatic confessions as occur in scriptures the world over can become the seed confession for faith across all cultures—Greek and Jewish, oppressed and free, feminist and gay, eastern and western. When scriptures are given canonical status, this intentionally detaches those texts from their particular context and makes them available for common use throughout many communities of faith, leaving them theologically underdeveloped and, as witnessed by the conundrums of exegetes everywhere, allergic to developmental metaphysics and available to the authentic ruminations of thinkers who are open to those scriptures and traditions. But the harsh dogmatic insistence that often characterizes the minds of theologians on ecclesiastical Ritalin tends to keep our confessions frozen in time and affixed to their ontologies; one can always argue more persuasively from within an ontology that is agreed to be absolutely true and necessary. Better to ease up and let our creative imaginations wander about a bit within the compass of scripture and tradition.

Most negators of the faith traditions negate not the traditions themselves, but merely the small part of those traditions they know. People abandon prayer because they conclude that their urgent petitions to an all-governing God are not producing results. They do not realize that prayer is not the arm-twisting of a managerial God, but rather an avenue into the emptiness of an experience of adoration that negates all self-concern. We do not pray to get things; we pray to get away from getting things—even those things that are much to be desired for the common good. Others abandon our theological traditions because they reject metaphysics, not realizing that any *via affirmativa* of theology is but one manifestation of the richer—because more inchoate—teachings of scripture and of the *via negativa* that is twinned with all affirmation. The primacy of scripture means that we return there again and again to meditate anew on the meaning of faith, not to discard traditions but rather to restate them. How else do we have access to our own scripture? We go back to it to witness to scriptural meaning and to nurture the growth of its seeds into new realms of meaning and new cultural philosophies. As Luther (but not Harnack), knew so well, scripture does not merely bring us back to some earlier and more pristine layer of faith, it also germinates within us ever new appreciations of its teachings, expanding all our boundaries within the tradition and thereby enabling us to challenge later institutions, whether structural or theological.

Emptiness is the expeller of viewpoints. This point is emphasized by sixth-century Yogācāra commentator Sthiramati. Speaking of "unreal imagining" (Skt.

abhūta-parikalpa) in his *Commentary on the Differentiation of Middle and Extremes* (*Madhyābtavibhāgatīkā*), Sthiramati writes: "Unreal imagining is the imagining of the grasped and the grasper" (*grāhya-grāhaka-vikalpa*).[75] The everyday pattern of our apprehension of what's what does not "represent" the reality of what's what. Sthiramati teaches that "emptiness is apart from these mental states of grasped and grasper within unreal imagining." But this does not mean that we do not apprehend or that we can hang out in emptiness aloof from living and thinking. Rather, "unreal imagining exists [as subject and object] only in emptiness."[76] To function within the context of emptiness is to recognize that our subject-object pattern may indeed represent an evolutionary upsurge, but it is nevertheless dependently arisen over the varied biological and cultural histories of men and women. We derive cogency and truth when we attend to our actual experiences in our varied cultures and societies and seek to understand scripture and tradition and commit ourselves to faith practice. Scripture and creeds are not once-and-for-all formulas and were never intended to be; they were enunciated in particular terms as frameworks for the ongoing skillful enunciation of the mystery of our being here. They circle around our lives, offering varied openings for the careful reader into the *arcana* of faith.[77]

"Being equal to God," for Jesus, is neither that which is grasped (L. *raptus, res percara avide arripienda*) nor the act of grasping (*rapina*).[78] This is far from the later theological metaphysics of incarnation, which focused on precisely the objective content of understanding Christ—his two natures clearly understood. But here in the mind of Jesus, as declared in this Philippian hymn, there is no philosophy at all. Its understanding of the mind of Christ evinces no split between subjective consciousness and objective consciousness. Christ has emptied himself of that dichotomy. He is in the form of God, equal to God, without regarding that as anything to be apprehended. We do not grasp either what God is or how God is, nor are we given any clear notion of what "is" means in our theistic affirmation that God "is." Moreover, we are born with no assured identity as humans; we have to construct our sense of self over the first year-and-a-half of life.[79] Being empty of self, how could we possibly pretend to know what a divine identity might be? Conflicts about identity, wherever they occur,

---

75. On the Yogācāra critique of meaning, see Keenan, *Meaning of Christ*, 152–72.

76. YAMAGUCHI Susumu, *Sthiramati, Madhyāntavibhāgaṭīkā: Exposition Systématique du Yogācāravijñaptivāda* (Tokyo: Suzuki Research Foundation, 1965) Tome I, 13–20; Tome II, 17–26. See Keenan, *Study of the* Buddhabhūmyupadeśa, 118. On Mahāyāna philosophies of emptiness, see Nagao, *Foundational Standpoint*, and his essay "Emptiness" in Nagao, *Mādhyamika and Yogācāra*, 209–218.

77. See Johnson, *Quest for the Living God*. See also Roger Haight, *Jesus: Symbol of God* (Maryknoll: Orbis, 1999).

78. O'Brien, *Epistle to the Philippians*, 212; Max Zerwick, *Analysis philologica Novi Testamenti graeci* (Rome 1953) 449.

79. Julian Paul Keenan, *Face in the Mirror*, 67–68.

are shadowboxing matches in which we swing about wildly in the theological ether and never land a single knockout punch.

This reading of 2:6 is further bolstered by Werner Jaeger, who argues that the full textual phrase, both the verb and its object—"he did not regard it as *harpagmos*" (οὐκ ἁρπαγμὸν ἡγήσατο), means "to regard something as a stroke of luck, a windfall, a piece of good fortune."[80] Jaeger explains that this was a commonly used idiomatic expression for the spoils of war, as when the victor in a battle enjoys his booty or other good fortune. Despite the unlikeliness of this meaning in such a theological discourse as Philippians, that is exactly what the text does say: Jesus didn't take it as a particular stroke of good fortune that he was equal to God. Perhaps other Christ followers did insist on their good fortune in having Christ for their God, and perhaps that stance did not sit well with the Philippians who composed this hymn, preferring to exclude boastful theology and assertions of self-sufficiency.

In any case, we are left with no ascertainable metaphysical Jesus, or indeed any portrait of a historical Jesus. Just a life being of one mind with Christ, supplied by the Spirit. Just Jesus, whose path carves out the inner spaces in our minds and hearts to provide scope for a reformation of consciousness. Such a reading harmonizes with the notion that Jesus empties himself of all particular characteristics that might separate him from the full range of being human. He really is fully human and has about him no whiff of divine presence. This passage further emasculates any metaphysical pretensions (metaphysicians tend to be male), for the claim here—that it is nothing so very important that Christ exists in the form of God—is entirely foreign to the notion of self-enclosed essence in Greek philosophy.

Nor does Christ offer us a readily available image in which we may espy something special. No preciously distinctive mode of existence. Just the visible appearance (form) of a godly living that forgets altogether about being godly. As the hymn progresses, Christ's character becomes an emptying of the form of God on which we might have thought Jesus to focus. This entails the invitation to "meditatively and attentively focus" (φρονεῖτε) on this same mind that is in Christ Jesus: not on any divine self, but always on an emptying self. In this early christological hymn, the divine form or essence is permeable. It allows us to acknowledge that we ourselves construct all our notions of God, and it refuses to collapse the mind of Christ into theological viewpoints or to delimit or define its contours. To cultivate this mind of Christ is to focus our attention on Christ's emptying of all his being. We too are to empty all our being so that we might meet the risen life of Christ in the empty sky where we receive spiritual bodies, just as he wills.[81]

---

80. Werner Jaeger, "Eine stilgeschichtliche Studie zum Philipperbrief," *Hermes* 50 (1915) 553.

81. The images of risen bodies in Cor 15:35–41 are visionary images, not unlike the visions seen in dreams about the end-time. But they are grounded in the present experience of being in Christ and sharing his resurrection.

"... he emptied himself ..." (2:7)

2:7 Rather, he emptied himself, taking the form of a slave, being born as are all humans and being found as human in visage.

2:7 ἀλλὰ ἑαυτὸν ἐκένωσεν μορφὴν δούλου λαβών, ἐν ὁμοιώματι ἀνθρώπων γενόμενος: καὶ σχήματι εὑρεθεὶς ὡς ἄνθρωπος.

After declaring that Christ did not regard it as very special to be equal to God, the hymn goes on to announce that Christ "emptied himself" (ἑαυτὸν ἐκένωσεν). Many and varied are the commentators on this striking statement, from Christian theologians to Zen philosophers. Nowhere else in the New Testament do we find the like. Indeed, what could it possibly mean that Christ emptied himself?

Unlike the concept of "form," the notion of "emptying" has no history in Greco-Roman thought, nor does it feature prominently in any Mediterranean philosophy. And so exegetes, attached as they are to metaphysics, take it metaphorically.[82] Pre-Socratic Heraclitus had offered an analogous idea in his insistence that all things are radically transient; he pointed out that change, not permanence, is what is real.[83] But rather than follow Heraclitus in this, the Greeks opted for the philosophic path of his counterpart Parmenides, who sought to identify the real core of being, or that which is beyond transience and change. As ontological philosophy became dominant along with the rise of the sovereign church, any proponents of radical transience and change were relegated to the sidelines along with other variously unorthodox thinkers. And

---

82. On "emptied himself" in verse 2:7, Vincent writes: "Not used or intended here in a metaphysical sense to define the limitations of Christ's incarnate state, but as a strong and graphic expression of the completeness of his self-renunciation" (Vincent, *Critical and Exegetical Commentary*, 59). There have been western philosophies of nothingness: see Carlo Ossa's *La Attiche Memorie del Nulla*, in which Ossa presents a number of medieval discourses on "nothing," summarizing their thought clearly in an introduction (Carlo Ossa, *La Attiche Memorie del Nulla* [Rome: Edizioni di storia e letteratura, 2007] vii–xlvii). Often they echo the quietism of Miguel Molinos, but seldom are they able to account for this varied world in which we live and experience our being as not simply nothing. That is why they never gained purchase in western theology and were for the most part forgotten by the time of Nietzsche. Molinos and others in the apophatic tradition were unable to soften the onslaught of Christian ontology precisely because they never developed their own persuasive account of the varied patterns of human consciousness or offered a contrasting understanding of discriminative language as failing to grasp the really real. The Mahāyāna philosophies of Mādhyamika and Yogācāra, by contrast, do offer a rich and extensive body of philosophical materials that support the primacy of empty silence over verbalized doctrine, while upholding the enunciation of doctrine as something that is skillfully true and efficacious. The lack of philosophical discourse in the apophatic traditions is what allowed their marginalization in Christian thought, shunted off as they were into their silent corner as mere adjuncts to theology. That attitude toward the apophatic continues among scholars who refuse to delve into eastern traditions; they adduce the same arguments as those often employed against quietists and relativists, captiously applying them to entire traditions of which they know little.

83. Cited by Edward Conze, *Buddhism: Its Essence and Development* (New York: Harper Torchbooks, 1959) 140–41. For a considered essay, see Thomas McEvilley, "Greek Philosophy and Mādhyamika, *Philosophy East and West* 31 (1981) 141–64.

the rest, as they say, is Platonic history—the history of the classical ontologies and ontotheologies.[84]

However, beyond our western *mare nostrum* horizons, there does exist an ancient and profound philosophical tradition of emptiness. Indeed, emptiness is the central theme of Mahāyāna Buddhist thought. It questions all ontology, even the many ontologies that underlie the thinking of quite orthodox Buddhists. The Buddhist philosophy of emptiness arose in the early centuries of the Common Era and proliferated thereafter throughout India, China, Tibet, Korea, and Japan, more recently penetrating the west as well. It is this Mahāyāna philosophy of emptiness that serves as our aid here—a handmaiden like the Greek ontologies of the past—in our theological and exegetical reflection on the meaning of the empty Christ.

Despite its jarring import, Phil 2:7 clearly asserts that Christ emptied himself not of this or that attribute, but of being divine, which subjectively he did not regard as an object to be apprehended or grasped. Exegetes, however, are often induced by their own essentialist enthusiasm for "being" to reduce the term "emptied" here to a metaphor with little meaning. As Gordon Fee asserts, "This is metaphor, pure and simple."[85] Emptying, to these exegetes, becomes synonymous with the outpouring of love from within the essential being of God. But if Christ did not "apprehend," or grasp, his divine equality, then this hymn already marches to a different drummer. No apprehended, self-identified God stands in opposition to one who apprehends. Christ empties himself, and there is no self-identified God to be apprehended. It is not an uncommon theological notion that in basic meaning God is not an object, but rather that which draws people from their mediated realms of meaning to abide in the silence of unknowing.[86] And yet this notion has never had much influence on the doing of Christian theology. Like all mystical thinking and practice, it has been shunted to the periphery.[87]

In their desire to harmonize this Philippian hymn with traditional ontological assumptions, commentators often read it as a two-staged schema—the absolute being of God and the human Jesus—as though a cosmic drama unfolds from the depths of the divine nature.[88] Some commentators think that in emptying himself through

---

84. See Étienne Gilson, *Being and Some Philosophers* (Toronto: Pontifical Institute of Medieval Studies, 1971), in which the chapters move from being and the one, to being and substance, being and existence, existence versus being, and knowledge and being, sketching the four possible options of Plato, Plotinus, Avicenna, and Thomas Aquinas. Gilson argues against the philosophy of Avicenna as it wends its way through the Christian west, to consider existentialists like Søren Kierkegaard, and finally to champion Aquinas and his notion of being as "the act of existing (*esse*)" (ibid.).

85. Fee, *Paul's Letter to the Philippians*, 210.

86. Lonergan, *Method in Theology*, 29, 33, 106.

87. On the marginalization of the apophatic traditions within a doctrinal theology intent upon clarity of presentation, see Keenan, *Meaning of Christ*, 113–15.

88. Käsemann calls this a "sequence of occurrences in an event unified in and of itself" (Ernst Käsemann, "A Critical Analysis of Philippians 2:5–11," in *God and Christ: Existence and Province*, edited by Robert W. Funk, JTC 5 [New York: Harper & Row, 1968] 70, cited in Reumann, *Philippians*,

the humiliation of the incarnation and the cross, Christ accepted from the Father a divine "vocation," all the while remaining God.[89] He did not then truly empty himself, but only seemed to do so because of his vocation. This geography of the divine landscape—as though God were indeed the Father-up-there and Christ the Son-down-here who has descended from a preexistent state into his human existence, from the form of God to the form of a human slave—reduces Christ's incarnational emptying to a task he accepts as "vocation" from the Father. One is forced to assume either a duplicity of diverse consciousnesses within God or to adopt a docetic christology wherein the eternal Son only visits this world—however much we may insist on our Chalcedonian tradition that Christ is fully divine and fully human.[90] Such docetism, however, is not to be found in this hymn or anywhere in Paul's letters. He insists upon the reality of the incarnation, the central teaching of our tradition.

The creeds and traditions developed by the Greek Fathers of the church during the first five centuries do not address the truth and efficacy of the empty Christ of the Philippian hymn. They reflect instead then-current notions of what is really real about Christ. Our ancestors in the faith had available to them no philosophy of emptiness that they might employ in their struggle to understand incarnational faith without recourse to doctrinal ontology. They had no philosophy that picked up on the phenomenological confession of the Philippians. Ontology, or metaphysics, was in those times the queen of all science and knowledge. The church fathers were willingly constrained by their context to focus on what being real entails, and, albeit with firm and devout faith, they directed their thoughts not to Christ's emptiness, but to the real being of Christ as defined in terms of ontology. The cultural scope of their argumentation and of the teachings that became the orthodox center of faith and practice was—as perforce is always the case—a limited scope: the question of whether the real in Christ is precisely the real of God or a lesser real. If understood as a definition

---

348).

89. Morna Hooker, "Philippians, 2:6–11," in *Jesus und Paulus, Festschrift für Werner Georg Kümmel zum 70. Geburtstag*, edited by E. E. Ellis and E. Grässer (Göttingen, Germany: Vandenkoeck & Ruprecht, 1975) 152; and N. T. Wright, "ἁρπαγμός and the Meaning of Philippians 2:5–11," *JTS* 37 (1986) 345–46. Similarly, Fabricatore notes that Paul's "starting point is Christ as God. Paul does not begin with Christ as man who later was exalted as God which is assumed in a two-stage christology" (Fabricatore, *Form of God*, 145). That seems to read the hymn not in stages, but in the later ontological differentiation of divine and human. But the authors of the hymn had no insider information about the divine nature; this is more a confessional groping than the later ontotheologies. There is no mention in the hymn of a divine vocation.

90. Full-blown docetic theologies are never affirmed by our commentators, yet often such notions that Christ only *seemed* to be human do find their way into print. Vincent, in discussing verse 8 on "the likeness of men," states that this "expresses the fact that his mode of manifestation *resembled* what men are," but "the totality of his being could not appear to men, for that would involve the *morphe theou*" (Vincent, *Critical and Exegetical Commentary*, 59). Being found in fashion as a man is interpreted by Vincent as "confined to the outward *guise* as it appealed to human observation" (ibid., 60, italics added). But if Jesus did indeed retain his divine nature, then we mock the passion narratives of his sufferings by having to maintain that, even forsaken, in his divine nature he still enjoyed the bliss of the beatific vision.

of faith, the ontological confession of Christ as divinely and humanly real came to exclude any notion of Christ as empty of full equality with God. And this ontological confession leaned—at times toppled—into a common docetic understanding of the person of Jesus of Nazareth as not really very human at all.

More to the point of the present discussion, this insistent ontology disenables theologians from focusing upon the quite early faith confession that appears in this Philippian hymn—a confession that bluntly affirms that Christ emptied himself and did not regard himself to be God's equal. A more circumspect notion of the real as something that is beyond essence and without definable markers would surely cause us to pause before speaking of divine and human ontology. It would distrust human claims to know reality just as it is, whether those claims of knowledge are made in a "high" metaphysical mode or in a "reductionist" historicist mode. For Plato and Aristotle and for the medieval schoolmen, the really real is an essence—the very being of what is real—while for historicists, the real is the ascertainable portrait of Jesus of Nazareth as unearthed by theological archeology.

By contrast, in Mahāyāna's philosophy of emptiness, the real may be skillfully suggested in words and images, but it always slips away from clear definition, passes beyond languaged experience, resists being pinned down in essentialist categories. Notions of essence, the "whatness" of God or of humans, are always circumscribed by cultures and histories, while a theology of emptiness that is attuned to the negation of self is truly able to attend to the Philippian hymn's early confession that "Christ emptied himself"—a confession that predates both John's Gospel and the Letter to the Hebrews and comes centuries before the Patristic theologies based on those scriptures. Despite the many efforts that have been made to wrestle Philippians back onto the reservation,[91] the empty Christ of this hymn does offer an approach to the central and deepest mysteries—of who we are, who God is, and who Christ is—and that approach is at the same time distinct from and complementary to those later ontological commitments.

The medicine for our present ontological malaise is not, as some would maintain, its historicist rejection, but rather a ratcheting down of ontological discourse to a recognition of the human, dependently conditioned discourse it always has been. Scholars seeking the historical Jesus tend to work within a positivist and rationalist philosophy. Rejecting ontotheologies, they reduce everything to what can be ascertained from careful analysis of texts and cultural context to produce historical character sketches. The hymn of the empty Christ, however, also empties the historical character of Jesus and focuses the kerygma solely on his emptying of divine equality,

---

91. Silva, *Philippians*, 114: "In similar fashion, we may want to dispute that the passage speaks primarily to ontological issues regarding the nature of the Trinity, but it would appear futile to deny that Phil. 2:5–7 has some strong implications for these issues. These verses cannot serve as the total basis for a formula regarding the two natures of Christ, but the description of Christ in this passage reflects certain ontological commitments that lead rather naturally to the later orthodox formulations."

his suffering and dying on the cross, and the ineffable exaltation whereby he is raised above all imaginable categories.

This, to Paul and the Philippians, is the mind of Christ, the heart of the matter. And Paul never bothers much to draw the contours of the life of Christ from the Jesus traditions that circulated among the Christian communities in his time, before the gospel accounts were written down. The actual contour of risen life was then-and-there Philippian. Attention is focused upon the Christ who in dying emptied himself of both theological notions and historical details, leaving us simply with the invitation to share in his risen life within our own historical narratives.

True, our traditional creeds circumscribe, and by so doing protect, the paradox of the indivisibility of human and divine in Christ, and Christians are enjoined to respect and confess those creeds. But clinging single-mindedly to ontological categories can plunge us into voids that are too murky to engage our minds or engender practice. So we should not dismiss Christ's self-emptying as mere desultory metaphor in the Philippian hymn. Nor is it necessary to introduce the two-staged natural and supernatural schema of later theology into our interpretation of this ancient hymn, as if the early Pauline communities were working within that Hellenistic ontology. The hymn states simply that Christ emptied himself, not that he *manifested* the form of God in the form of a slave.[92] It is not that Christ acted as a mediator between divine nature and human nature, at least not here. It is not that he dramatically "exchanged" the form of God for the form of a slave, later to take up his divinity once more. This emptying is rather the very being of Christ—the being of nonbeing—and this is why he "took on the form of a slave," the greatest nonentity in the Greco-Roman world. This hymn is not depicting some pre-cosmic drama, nor is it speaking of a preexistent Logos, as does the prologue of John's Gospel. It simply says that Jesus, although in the form of God, emptied himself, and that that very emptying is the being of Christ.

It was sometime around the second century of the Common Era that Buddhist practitioners elaborated to our common benefit the Mahāyāna teaching of emptiness. Before the development of Mahāyāna thought, the notion of emptiness had long been used in Buddhism much as it was in Qoheleth: to describe the vanity and transience of all things to which humans might cling. But the famous chapter 24 of Nāgārjuna's *Stanzas on the Middle*, which treats the fundamental truths of the Buddha's teaching, asserts that emptiness describes not only the deluded objects of our greed and passion, but even the very core truths of the scriptures that contain the Buddha's teachings.

From that time on, the Mahāyāna traditions employed emptiness as a self-corrective hermeneutic designed to lead practitioners along the path of no-self and away from any form of faith empiricism, whether sacral or secular. The very truth of the earliest and most central of Buddhist doctrines—including the Four Noble Truths,[93] the Twelvefold Chain that results in this world of suffering, and indeed all that by

---

92. *Pace* Bruce, *Philippians*, 70; O'Brien, *Epistle to the Philippians*, 216.
93. The truth of suffering, of its origins, of its cessation, and of the path to that cessation.

which one might identify oneself as a disciple of Buddha—are themselves emptied of any stability. The path of doctrine and practice corresponds to no set world of meanings; all stable and fixed meanings have been dissolved in the waters of emptiness so that they might now flow through our river-minds and irrigate our parched hearts.

Just as many Christian commentators would limit the significance of Christ's self-emptying to a weak and pious metaphor, not all Buddhist thinkers wished to accept Nāgārjuna's rigorous emptiness critique as applicable to their own doctrine. There was an early and continuing divergence in views on this. Some thinkers in the Tathāgatagarbha lineage[94] maintain that the Buddha mind—the Buddha Nature—is original and quite real, that it is the always real and always present "seed/womb" (Skt. *garbha*) of an awakened Tathāgata. What is empty, they say, are all the "adventitious defilements" that cover over that mind and prevent its innate light from shining forth; the pure mind itself is the stable and very real core of our being. There is a realm that is really real, they maintain, apart from emptiness, variously identified as the "Reality Realm" or "the Original Mind of Enlightenment," and it is richly filled with good qualities and is the basis for all that is real. In these Tathāgatagarbha traditions, the pure Buddha mind is empty of defilements, which only obscure it like dirt over the pure surface of a lustrous mirror. But they insist that after emptying those defilements there remains something that is really real, and this is one's inner "Buddha Nature."[95]

Nineteenth and early twentieth-century Kenotic theologians Gottfried Thomasius and P. T. Forsyth resembled those Tathāgatagarbha thinkers in their conclusion that "what remained" after Christ's self-emptying could not be further emptied—and *that* was an essential core of divinity.[96] Nevertheless, arguing that Christ "must have 'emptied himself' *of something*,"[97] they launch into a quest for the "missing genitive" by asking, "Of *what* does Christ empty himself in order to move from stable divinity into human likeness?" A glass may be emptied, but still it is a glass emptied of *something*, they reasoned. And so, without any scriptural or traditional witness, they elaborate a theology that construes the Philippian hymn as protecting the core being

---

94. On the Tathāgatagarbha lineage, see Keenan, *Meaning of Christ*, 146–48.

95. There are Mahāyāna scriptures and commentaries in the Tathāgatagarbha lineage that move from self to self-negation in emptiness and then to the "great self" (Skt. *mahātma*) of the true self realized in awakening. These texts diverged from the classical Mahāyāna philosophies of Mādhyamika and Yogācāra, but they found much resonance in China and were affirmed by some schools, especially Chan (Zen), as the "self of no-self." I understand the "self of no-self" as a skillful means for affirming the conventional reality of an awakened person, not as the affirmation of an essential self. See Youru Wang, "De-Substantializing Buddha-Nature in the Tathāgatagarbha Tradition," *International Journal of Field-Being* 1 (1) 2:10 (2001).

96. Compare the classical essay by Nagao, "What Remains in Śūnyatā," in Nagao, *Mādhyamika and Yogācāra*, 51–60. What is emptied is the pattern of "unreal imagining" (Skt. *abhūta-parikalpa*) that clings to self-essences so as to reveal the unrestricted horizons of being as it is (*tathatā*) in all its breadth and depth. In a Mahāyāna theology, emptiness is not a privation in the ontological order, but rather an erasure of the suzerainty of that entire order, to reclaim the truth of our conventionally powerful scriptural discourses.

97. Fee, *Paul's Letter to the Philippians*, 210.

of Christ while emptying him of only those attributes deemed incompatible with his being human—attributes such as omniscience or omnipresence that clearly are not evidenced in the gospel narratives of Jesus.

The approach of these Kenotic theologians is almost that of a divestment theory that seeks to identify less essential elements of Christ's divine nature as the things of which he emptied himself. Convinced that Christ could not empty himself of his essential divinity, they conclude that he emptied himself only of the *relative* attributes of divine being—omniscience, omnipresence, and omnipotence—while retaining the *essential* attributes—holiness, love, and righteousness.[98] This reading finds little support among exegetical commentators,[99] however, for it flies away from the text as given and appears once again to interpret Christ's emptying as a modal move from stable divinity to human likeness. Moreover, Paul and the Philippian hymn make no such ontological differentiation between God's essence and God's attributes; such thinking could only have emerged within the horizons of the ontotheology that was a later development.

As indicated above, the classical Mahāyāna philosophy that we employ here is not the Tathāgatagarbha lineage that posits a core, nonempty Buddha Nature, but rather the early Indian and Chinese Mahāyāna schools Mādhyamika and Yogācāra, which insist that *all* is empty. For them, there is *nothing* that might constitute a firm inner support for a religious practitioner. All things and all views are emptied of their very essence (Skt. *svabhāva*), and there is no stable, fundamental core. It is not that their essence is emptied of something else. There simply *is* nothing solid and abiding that might be empty of something else—no inner Buddha Nature that might be purified.[100] Gordon Fee says that "Christ did not empty himself *of* anything; he simply 'emptied himself,' poured himself out."[101] So that which Christ emptied is stated in the text—he emptied *himself* (ἑαυτὸν). He did not empty himself of anything else, and there is no discussion here of the essential being of God. Rather, we are to empty our minds of any notion of Christ's superlative being, for risen life in Christ is not a grasping after

---

98. Collange, *Epistle of Saint Paul*, 102. On 2:7, see also O'Brien, *Epistle to the Philippians*, 218–23; and Bruce, *Philippians*, 70. J. B. Lightfoot renders: "'he divested himself,' not of his Divine nature, for this was impossible, but 'of the glories, the prerogatives of Deity'" (Lightfoot, cited in Bruce, *Philippians*, 70). Collange similarly affirms that Christ remains but that God renounces the exercise of the power of God: "He emptied himself of the fullness of this power" (Collange, *Epistle of Saint Paul*, 101).

99. Collange, *Epistle of Saint Paul*, 102: "K. Barth in particular has reacted violently to this view; in his opinion to tamper with anything relating to the divinity of Christ is to call in question the reality of salvation itself (*Church Dogmatics IV*)." Bruce adds, "The use of the Greek verb here [i.e., emptied] has given the name *kenosis* to a once popular christological theory (the 'kenotic' theory), which in fact has nothing to do with the meaning of the present passage" (Bruce, *Philippians*, 77).

100. Matsumoto Shiro, "Laṅkāvatāra ni iteratarashūnyatā," *Komazawa Daigaku Bukkyō Gakubu Ronshū* 21 (1982) 350–43. Matsumoto here shows that in the *Laṅkāvatāra-sūtra*, the scope of emptiness (*śūnyatā*) is limited, being "an absence of this in that (*iteratara*)," for the originally pure mind remains beyond the scope of emptiness. The *Laṅkāvatāra* combines Yogācāra philosophy with Tathāgatagarbha doctrine.

101. Fee, *Paul's Letter to the Philippians*, 210.

anything, however orthodox. To grasp after a self-enclosed truth invalidates that truth and is not a skillful teaching of true doctrine enunciated in apophatic awareness.

"A monk asked Nan-ch'üan, 'Is there a fundamental truth that has never been expounded for people?' Nan-ch'üan said, 'There is.' The monk said, 'What is the fundamental truth that has never been expounded for people?' Nan-ch'üan said, 'It is not mind; it is not Buddha; it is not beings.'"[102]

The awakened mind of Christ faith is not a grasping after an innately ontological Christ. It is something experienced in the visceral immediacy of prayer and meditation, supported by common liturgy, learned through scriptural attentiveness, and practiced in compassionate engagement. To those who fear the demise of ontology, all this undoubtedly sounds quite nihilistic. But this teaching of emptiness, far from leading people over the cliff of despair, enables them to reclaim their own experienced lives as dependently arisen "in Christ." They are then able to think doctrine validly in light of their experience within their culturally available philosophies, without any presumption that the knowing structure of our minds is capable of capturing the being of all that is real. By contrast to ontological theologians, who find it necessary to defend their epistemology and metaphysics against other philosophies and sciences, the risen life experienced by Christ followers frees them to learn and to employ many intriguing scientific and philosophic insights that were unavailable to our ancestors, critically appropriating them to deepen our gospel awareness.

Our conventional minds, structured as they are by genetics and the development of neural pathways, stretch out for deeper insight, even in awareness of our many limitations.[103] A true, and thus efficacious, path is to empty ourselves of all pretense to ultimate truth, precisely so that we may reclaim the dependently arisen truth and efficacy of that path and eventually abandon ourselves in the exalted upsurge of a risen life. I believe that this Philippian letter speaks of this notion of the emptiness of everything. Christ here has not, by force of his vocation, taken a vacation from being God. He has actually brought being God to nothing, so that God may be all in all. He has emptied the very concept of God until all God concepts may be recognized as human constructs about a strangely benign presence glimpsed beyond any human image or idea. Only then may one reaffirm God, the Father of Jesus, who emptied the very being of God, and who now can no longer be conceived as the sovereign controller of the universe, but rather as the presence that encompasses us often in its absence, transcending the polarity of subject–object discrimination.

---

102. Aitken, *Gateless Barrier*, 171. Wu-men comments, "At the question, Nan-ch'üan used up all his personal treasure immediately and became quite debilitated." The account is an abbreviated form of Case 28 in the *Blue Cliff Record*, in which Nan-ch'üan finishes his Dharma words by saying "I don't understand" and Pai-chang replies, "I already explained it fully to you." The phrase "beings" includes everything that might be apprehended to be the core meaning of the Dharma teaching (ibid., 172–73).

103. See Stuart Firestein, *Ignorance: How It Drives Science* (New York: Oxford University Press, 2012).

Such an interpretation, employing this central Mahāyāna notion of emptiness (Skt. *śūnyatā*), does not lead to the dark nihilism of the void or to the existential loneliness of those who have lost faith.[104] Its "flip side" is the complementary teaching that explains the "dependent arising" (Skt. *pratītya-samutpāda*) of our faith practice. Employing the Mādhyamika philosophy of the Middle Path, we can see that while Christ empties himself (ἑαυτὸν) of his own being (*ātman-svabhāva*)—of any essence, any substance, any permanent status whatsoever—that very emptiness can be seen as identical with the conditioned and dependently arisen being of all that he is and all that we experience or encounter in living the risen Christ-life.

The Philippians sought no ground either in ontologies of Christ or in historical portraiture of Jesus and looked instead to their own experienced risen life in Christ. What they heard of the past, they experienced both in their present and in the hymnic confession they wrote for our future. There are no nonempty somethings, either divine or human, that might be identified statically in any two-staged schema or dramatically in a three-act sequence—first and always God, then becoming somehow human, and finally exalted back to divine Lordship. Everything arises from causes and conditions, and all our lives are marked by transience and impermanence. Like the bubbles foaming on the ocean waves or the ever-moving ocean tides, all things change and never remain still even for a moment. Even the stillness of a midsummer afternoon is vibrant with growing and surging life all about.

The teaching of Mahāyāna emptiness eschews mile-high perspectives as pretense and places us right where we are, in the flux of living. The emptying of Christ, moreover, entails the abandoning of all absolute views, for the teaching of Christ's emptiness is the expeller of views.[105] An empty christology urges us to cherish the dependently arisen being of Christ among us and affirms grace in the simultaneously ugly and beautiful life "in Christ" that we live right here—a life that goes beyond both the metaphysicalized claims of the institutional church and the reductionist claims of scientific and historical researchers.

The verb "to empty" (ἐκένωσεν) in 2:7 means in the literal sense "to make empty," or "to render something ineffective." It does not mean "to pour out." In Buddhist thought, "emptiness" is a very precise term that denotes the absence of any self-enclosed being. That meaning is more germane to this passage, where the object of Christ's emptying is stated—it is himself (ἑαυτὸν). If Christ cherished himself, then we could only relate to him as to another self. But nothing exists entirely in and for itself—no self-enclosed human selves, no self-enclosed divine Self. Here in the Philippian hymn, the no-self of Christ means that he is emptied of the very form of God so that he is among us as one of us and we may share in his other-power and grace.[106]

---

104. See Julien Barnes, *Nothing to be Frightened of* (New York: Vintage, 2009). "I don't believe in God, but I miss him" (ibid., 3).

105. Nagao, *Foundational Standpoint*, 3–19.

106. Heil, *Let Us Rejoice*, 87: "The audience were directed to adopt the mind-set of 'considering

The Philippian hymn's play with notions of form—divine and human—undermines the stability of the distinction; the form of God, identified with Christ, is emptied of that very form, and so now the very form of God becomes unstable. This, it turns out, provokes a theological rush to shore up the foundations of the faith.[107]

But commentators and Christian pastors have no need to protect Jesus from emptying himself so that he may retain his proper divinity while we retain our proper identity. A modal transition from being in the form of God to being in the form of a slave cannot be recommended to anyone, for we never abide in the form of God. Such an interpretation could apply only to the inner relationships within the triune God, and in that case Paul could never have recommended that we also have this mind of Christ in us. That, in the terms of our tradition, really is docetism: the doctrine that Christ, in his essential divine nature, passed into and *seemed* to become human by taking on the appearance of a human being. But docetism amounts to nothing more

---

(ἡγούμενοι) one another more important than yourselves (ἑαυτῶν), each of you looking out not for the things of yourselves (ἑαυτῶν), but everyone also for the things of others' (2:3–4)." If, with Reumann, we see the Philippians as the authors of the hymn, then that is how in fact they understood resurrection faith as self-emptying, bringing out even more strongly the close connection of this verse about Christ's self-emptying with 2:4, which emphasizes a focus on the benefit of others.

107. This rush is almost universal. "Hardly a 'kenosis of the Father' before Christology, or retreat from the world by God; rather, in conferring Kyrios on Christ, God 'gains the name of Father'" (G. Bornkamm, "On Understanding the Christ Hymn [Philippians 2:6–11]," in *Early Christian Experience*, trans. P. L. Hammer [New York: Harper & Roe, 1969] 118, cited in Reumann, *Philippians*, 360). By contrast, Slavoj Žižek and Milbank argue in *The Monstrosity of Christ* that Jesus' emptying does not signify an emptying of the Father. In *Form of a Servant*, Dawe sketches that history from the Fathers through the Reformers to Kierkegaard, who reintroduced the notion to modern thinkers; the dialectical theology of Hegel, who in his *Phenomenology of Mind* takes mutual emptying as the central focus for all creative process; on to the Kenotic theologians Gottfried Thomasius and P. T. Forsyth, for whom Christ's self-fulfillment consists of a gradual awakening that passes through kenosis (Gottfried Thomasius and P. T. Forsyth, *The Person and Nature of Jesus Christ* [London: Independent, 1953] 336); and then back to Søren Kierkegaard, who, arguing vigorously against the Hegelians of his day, sees the absolutely qualitative and paradoxical contradiction between God and man; on further to Emil Brunner, who sees Paul's Corinthian folly of the cross as the wisdom of God and thus regards "the *exinanitio*, the extreme point of the *kenosis*" as "the supreme height of the self-manifestation of God (Emil Brunner, *The Christian Doctrine of Creation and Redemption, Dogmatics*, vol. 2, trans. Olive Wyon [Westminster, 1952] 361); and again Karl Barth, who sees the very being of God as moved freely by love, so that Christ's "humanity is a vehicle for divine revelation." Dawe concludes that Barth was "unwilling to go beyond the Trinitarian formulas to read the New Testament historically" (Dawe, *Form of a Servant*, 176). Still, the constant peril of nineteenth-century Kenotic thinking within that ontological framework is a bent toward an unacknowledged docetism. Dawe, heeding Kierkegaard, for whom "Kenosis is the absolute paradox that brings to naught all attempts at giving the faith rational coherence" (ibid., 180), goes beyond the two ontological patterns found in kenotic doctrine up to the present time—the Greek and the "Romantic-idealistic" after Hegel (ibid., 185)—to new definitions of God, who, in Barthian terms, has enough "ego-strength" strategically and personally to involve himself creatively in this world. Dawe, to my mind, avoids the oft-made criticism that Barth's treatment of scripture was positivistic, taking its words as if they were given units or facts of revelation, but he does not altogether avoid going beyond a broader spiritual empiricism that attempts to sketch the narrative events of scripture as a creative expression of love directed by a dynamic God toward humans.

than theologians or commentators clinging to the divine nature as something very precious and very much to be exploited for our own theological agendas, often in service of maintaining ecclesiastical privilege. Behind every metaphysical claim lies a claim of power in service to selfhood.

"Rather" (ἀλλὰ), Christ emptied himself, "taking on the form of a slave" (μορφὴν δούλου λαβών). This phrase would seem to be an explanation of what it means that Christ emptied himself. But what does it actually signify for Christ to take on the form of a slave? John Reumann, in interpreting the words "He experienced humiliation for himself" in verse 8, convincingly argues—against the widely accepted sense of a virtuously "humble" Christ—for a *humiliated* Christ, one who suffers recognizable bondage in his life.

A divine drama of virtuous bondage is found in the interpretation of Ernst Käsemann, who pictures a preexisting Christ who voluntarily empties himself of his heavenly existence, thus becoming subject to bondage by the elemental spirits of the universe, which enslave people because they themselves are daemonic. Being a slave certainly means being subject to bondage. Still, Käsemann seems to read the hymn *ex parte Christi*, as if from the theological vantage point of a preexistent Christ. This, however, is simply to imagine a cosmic unfolding of some divine drama that takes place in a special, sacred time. But there is no such cosmic drama. We and all our viewpoints and vantages are enmeshed in the dependently arisen web of language,[108] wherein personal dramas are lived theater—creative works of our own personal artistry, formed in and by our many languages, in and by our many cultures, even when crafted through inspiration. In contrast to Käsemann's preexistent Christ, Jesus takes on historical identity in the various conventional identities of his followers, for simply to live is Christ.

Being faithful Christians does not raise us above our culture, and it does not make our cultural artistry preferable to anyone else's. Rather, it urges us to construct a life drama creatively and compassionately to the benefit of others, demonstrating agapaic love for one another in this very here and now. In Käsemann's reading, it seems to me, Jesus never really empties himself. He only voluntarily walks out upon the stage of our history, moving in a human direction by changing his status from preexistent

---

108. Arguing against Chomsky's universal grammar, Everett writes: "Like most unusual things I observed or heard among the Pirahãs, I realized ultimately that Xahóápati was telling me more than I had realized: that to speak their language is to live their culture. A few linguists today, in the tradition of early twentieth-century pioneers Edward Sapir and Franz Boas, also believe that culture impinges on grammar and language in nontrivial ways. But my reasons are different from most of even this minority. My difficulty in successfully translating the Bible owed largely to the fact that the Pirahã society and language are interconnected in ways that make even the understanding of grammar, a subcomponent of language, impossible without studying the language and culture simultaneously. And I believe that this is true for all languages and societies. Language is the product of synergism between values of a society, communication theory, biology, physiology, physics (of the inherent limitations of our brains as well as our phonetics), and human thought. I believe this is also true of the engine of language, grammar" (Everett, *Don't Sleep*, 210–11).

to incarnate. But there is no two-staged movement. Christ's emptying is itself Christ's taking on the form of a slave. Emptiness is dependent arising. To abandon the form of God is to take on the form of a slave. And Christ's self-emptying is the same as his more-than-exaltation (2:9) to cosmic ineffability.

C. D. F. Moule suggests that this passage is best understood against the background of slavery in the Hellenistic society that produced this song.[109] In Greco-Roman society, a slave is stripped of all rights and securities that apply to other people, as indeed Paul himself experienced. But Paul welcomed his imprisonment, whereas slavery is an extreme example of degradation imposed by others. One can hardly doubt that to the Philippians slavery was much more than a notional reality; there were slaves everywhere in the ancient world, and they could be beaten, raped, and killed with impunity.

Slavery is not a theological notion, and scholars are at times too quick to spiritualize slavery, seeing therein a laudatory example of servanthood. L. W. Hurtado contends that although it is not expressly stated, being a slave meant for Jesus not just a degraded status in human society, but also being a slave to God.[110] Thereby, for us, Jesus becomes the "lordly" example of what it means to be the incarnate God in service to humankind. Peter O'Brien sums up the various interpretations of this passage by acknowledging that its background is indeed the social institution of slavery as it existed in that time, and O'Brien understands the hymn to embrace Christ's "divine vocation" as displaying the form of God in the form of a human slave. Christ then "did not exchange the nature or form of God for that of a slave; instead, he displayed the nature or form of God in the nature or form of a slave, thereby showing clearly not only what his character was like, but also what it meant to be God."[111]

Yet I believe that the significance of this hymn goes well beyond any shifting of forms or any vocational theology we might produce to spiritualize enslavement and forced humiliation. This emptying of Christ's "being equal to God" entails a sense of abandonment by God-as-Father, much as Christ experienced in the Markan narrative of the cross. Such emptying unto slavery entails a reworking of all our notions of what "being omnipotent and all-caring God" means. With visceral force, it demands that we rework all notions of what "being human" means as well, for if Christ was enslaved, then there is no refuge from common suffering. Christ's self-emptying is Christ's God-emptying and—as the nineteenth-century Kenotic theologians recognized—this does offend all previous biblical and theological notions of God as the all-controlling sovereign being beyond the world. Whoever composed this Philippian hymn had experienced a personal self-emptying. Otherwise, how could he (Clement or Epaphroditus?) or she (Syntyche, Euodia, or Lydia?) have used these words? In Christ, God empties everything into our human and transient being, and we are left

---

109. See O'Brien, *Epistle to the Philippians*, 222–23.
110. Ibid.
111. Ibid., 224.

with the beauty and the cruelty of life just as we live it in Christ. This is why Paul can declare that for him "to live is Christ and to die is gain" (1:21).

But Christ as slave does not reflect the gospel narrative of Jesus' life. In the Synoptics, he is a teacher and a messiah (albeit unrecognized), while in John he is the sometimes-ethereal Word made flesh. In his lifetime, Jesus was not a slave in any social sense. Only in the passion narratives does he experience bondage and suffer a humiliating death such as any slave would fear. This is the reason that some interpreters spiritualize the term "slave" in this passage. Joachim Jeremias and Eduard Schweizer, respectively, understand "the form of a slave" to refer to the Suffering Servant of the Lord as found in chapters 52 and 53 of Isaiah, or to slavery as found in the post-biblical Judaic notion of the righteous one's obedience to suffering. In these two interpretations, Jesus is the righteous servant *par excellence*, and he remains the preeminent example of the faithful servant.[112] But although he was not a lifelong slave, Jesus' sufferings were real, dependently arising from the circumstances of his life, and his sufferings were not in themselves greater than those of other mortals. He really was forcibly arrested, mocked, humiliated, beaten, and, feeling forsaken by all, murdered. To move quickly from Jesus' taking on the form of a slave to the celebration of his preeminent servant status among humans is to lessen his shared humanness and encourage images of the beggar king, who was truly noble but unrecognized.

But there is no "contrast between the divine majesty and power of the preexistent one (μορφὴ θεοῦ) and the abased humble servant (μορφὴ δούλου),"[113] because his emptying and his exaltation are indivisibly the one mind of Christ that we are told to embrace. A shift between the two states—of being humiliated and then being exalted—is not a true emptying at all, but rather the correcting of a mistake. The contrast is overcome in our shared risen life in Christ by refusing to collapse the creative tension between living here in Christ and being there with Christ, between suffering in this body and risen life in the body of Christ.

The text of 2:7 continues by stating that Jesus "was born like other humans" (ἐν ὁμοιώματι ἀνθρώπων γενόμενος).[114] It is not that "Christ *always existed*"(ὑπάρχων) "'in the form of God'" and then, despite the present tense of the first participle and the

---

112. Ibid. 220–222. Collange comments on emptying: "[I]n 1911 W. Warren was already detecting an allusion to Isa 53:12: 'he poured out his soul to death' ('*he'erāh lammāweth naphshô* = LXX: '*paredothē eis thanaton hē psuchē autou*'). This suggestion has been energetically championed by Jeremias, who argues from the frequent rendering of the Hebrew '*ārāh*' by the Greek '*ekkenoun*,' of '*nephesh*' by the reflexive pronoun '*heauton*,' and from the fact that in Ps 141:8 the phrase 'do not pour out my soul' ('*al-te'ar naphshi*) also expresses abandonment to death" (Collange, *Epistle of Saint Paul*, 100–101).

113. Pace O'Brien, *Epistle to the Philippians*, 221.

114. On verse 7, "in the likeness of men," Silva explains, "As the NBE puts it, 'Así, se presentándose como simple hombre,'" which translates as "Thus, he presented himself as simply human" (Silva, *Philippians*, 106). In a Chalcedonian register, Christ is simple human and simple divine, with no admixture of one into the other.

aorist of the second, *"came into existence"* (γενόμενος) *". . . by human birth . . ."*[115] The only life to which we have any access at all is the life of constant becoming—we have no notion of any always-present "isness" in an "always existence." It is only in our intellectual pretense that we think we have captured the static being of anything anywhere. So for Christ to be born as a human being, in the likeness of human beings, means simply that he was fully human. What else?

The passion narratives of Christ show just how human he is. In Rom 8:3, he came "in the likeness of sinful flesh"; in Gal 4:4, he was "born under the law"; and again, in Rom 6:9, he submitted to the control of death. In the karmic theory of Mahāyāna, all human actions are driven within the cyclical pattern of our evolutionary heritage by delusion, anger, and greed; simply being human, one is caught in and enslaved by all these karmic forces until one awakens. Entangled in and subjected to the humiliation of samsaric power, Christ was caught in "bondage to the powers which dominated man's dark world"[116]—powers that enslaved a large portion of the population to the benefit of the rest. He was tortured and murdered.

The one sure thing Paul knew, and the Philippians knew, was that this Jesus Christ they celebrated in song was indeed Jesus of Nazareth, who after his dying was encountered by Paul on the Damascus Road and by the Philippians in their daily lives. This Jesus was born just as all humans are born, fully and completely, with organs, viscera, and muscles, with all systems go, human in full. The phrase "being found in the likeness of humans" (ἐν ὁμοιώματι ἀνθρώπων) refers simply to Jesus in his worldly and conventional life, as well as to our Christ-identity when we are living selflessly in our human lives, freed from entanglement in our worldly and conventional selfhood.

A selfless identity is a no-identity that moves without self-concern, heedless of any need to erect ramparts around the metaphysical castle of an ecclesiastical ontology. The Philippian hymn does not employ any metaphysics of static being that might take over and occlude our celebratory song of Christ's emptiness, nor does it enunciate a dialectical dynamic of mutual interaction. It is difficult indeed to abandon the surety offered by notions of a core identity or a central dynamic. Yet any two-tiered metaphysics that claims that although Christ became human, "even as man He remained at the core of His being what He had been before"[117] sinks into fuzzy thinking; we have no avenue to understand what that "before" might mean. As O'Brien notes, this "appears to come close to saying that Christ's likeness to humans was not real but merely apparent. Interpretations that tend in this direction can hardly avoid the danger of some form of docetism, even when the contrary is asserted."[118]

The term "likeness" (ἐν ὁμοιώματι) affirms Christ's full sharing in human being, just as it is, in all the joy of community and the ugliness of suffering. The historical

---

115. O'Brien, *Epistle to the Philippians*, 224.
116. Caird, *Paul's Letters from Prison*, 118.
117. *TDNT*, 5:197.
118. O'Brien, *Epistle to the Philippians*, 225.

forms of Christ's human likeness and our own do have their conventional identities. All identity markers are human; God has no identity. Not being bound by time or space, before and after do not apply. Not being finite, there are no identifying characteristics. We do not even know how to pronounce "the name above every name" that will be bestowed upon Jesus in 2:9 of this hymn—the ineffable name of YHWH, which the text itself cannot enunciate. We cannot point at God and trust that we are indicating anything other than the direction in which our own finger is pointing.

"He was found to be human in visage" (καὶ σχήματι εὑρεθεὶς ὡς ἄνθρωπος). The term "visage" refers to the outward appearance, perceptible form, or shape of a thing, and I take it here as synonymous with "form"—meaning the way in which Jesus appeared to his contemporaries—his visage or face. Still, we know almost nothing of that visage at all. Was he good-looking? Was he skinny? Tall or short? Did he enjoy good health as he journeyed about Galilee and Judea? Did he ever fall in love? Or fall ill? For Paul, as for the entire early tradition, the historical visage of Jesus had little significance, and so he never gives us anything like a description. And, because of our tendency to supernaturalize Jesus, we seldom allow any musing aloud about whether he ever fell in love with the girl next door. Or with the boy next door. Or whether, like the rest of us, he might ever have suffered nausea or a headache. Although we confess that he was like us in all things except sin, our images of Christ discourage us from entertaining such questions. Still, Jesus was human like humans everywhere, and so he was "found as human in visage." But the point never was Jesus' appearance. What *is* to the point is what follows when the hymn moves on to summarize the life "career" (the bodhisattva *carita*) of Jesus.

"... he humiliated himself..." (2:8)

2:8 *he humiliated himself and became obedient to the point of death—even death on a cross.*

2:8 ἐταπείνωσεν ἑαυτὸν γενόμενος ὑπήκοος μέχρι θανάτου, θανάτου δὲ σταυροῦ.

Christ, in the passion narratives, experienced humiliation for himself. The phrase "he humiliated himself" (ἐταπείνωσεν ἑαυτὸν) means that "he suffered humiliation" in his social world, not that he humbled himself as a model for later Christians, as most English translations suggest.[119] Humiliation is shameful, as reflected in the Tanach, where Ps 25 contains an elegy against humiliation:

> [1]To you, O Lord (Κύριε), I lift up my soul, O my God (Ὁ Θεός μου).
> [2]In you I trust (πέποιθα); may I not be put to shame (μὴ καταισχυνθείην), nor
>   let my enemies (οἱ ἐχθροί μου) deride (μηδὲ καταγελασάτωσάν) me.

---

119. Reumann, *Philippians*, 351.

> ³Indeed, none of those who wait for you shall be put to shame (μὴ καταισχυνθῶσιν); let those who are wantonly lawless be shamed (αἰσχυνθήτωσαν).
>
> . . . .
>
> ¹⁸See my humiliation ("Ἴδε τὴν ταπείνωσίν μου) and my trouble, and forgive all my sins.
>
> ¹⁹See my enemies, that they multiplied, and with an unjust hatred they hated me.
>
> ²⁰O guard my soul, and rescue me; may I not be put to shame, because I hoped in you (ὅτι ἤλπισα).[120]

Paul himself prays that he not be humiliated before his Roman judges, hoping that he may present a spirited defense of the gospel. Neither the Philippians' concern about social status nor the Psalmist's desire to avoid disgrace demonstrates a readiness to embrace humiliation or even suggests humility as a virtue. Humiliation leaves scars; it engenders anger and resentment. Victims of schoolyard bullies, sexual predators, or abusive spouses often feel such ongoing shame that they remain silent about the violence done to them. For decades, even entire lifetimes, they may bury their feelings of humiliation. When they do finally speak, very often they are humiliated again, this time by lawyers hired by abusers or institutions (including churches who fear liability) to impugn their credibility in court. Such humiliation heaped upon humiliation discourages others from coming forward. Humiliation causes soul death, and when inflicted by religious leaders who follow a Christ who was himself a victim of power abuse, it discredits the gospel itself.

Here in the Philippian hymn, "he was humiliated" builds on the phrase "he emptied himself." Both expressions are meant to indicate that Jesus lived not in a make-believe world of messianic or divine man fantasies, but in the world just as it is—a world that is gripped by fear and that refuses to entertain the very notion of no-self. The Jesus celebrated here did not avoid shame and disgrace in his world. By following his kingdom path, he was brought to the lowest kind of degradation in his mock trial and ultimate crucifixion. Paul insists that we keep that historical fact in mind, for if we are to share life in Christ, any self-aggrandizement is wiped out in the blood of the cross. "He was humiliated" does not describe a Jesus who disparages the lives we live. The Jesus we see in the gospel narratives understands and accepts life just as it occurs—what the Mahayanists call "suchness" (Skt. *tathatā*). Living with that wisdom is the goal not only of Christians, but also of Buddhists. The entire life course (Skt. *carita*) of bodhisattva practice is to empty the self in order to engage compassionately in this world of deep and extensive suffering. For Christians, it is to be filled with the risen life of Christ who suffered. Unlike the Buddha Śākyamuni, who throughout his life was revered as the "World Honored One" (Bhagavān), Christ was honored

---

120. Pietersma and Wright, *New English Translation of the Septuagint*, 558.

neither by the authorities (Mark 6:1–6), nor even by his own village or family (Mark 3:19b–21; Matt 13:54–58).

Translating the phrase ἐταπείνωσεν ἑαυτὸν as "he humbled himself" suggests a divine act of laudatory virtue. But this does not capture the gospel concreteness of Jesus' humiliation. Even in the course of his teaching, Jesus frequently encountered rejection, and the passion narratives vividly recount the disgrace of his arrest, the jeering treatment by the guards and the crowds, and his death by crucifixion as the most humiliating form of execution. Self-emptying takes on concrete meaning in social and cultural context, and the Philippians knew very well that they were taking on the mind of a social outcast. "Philippians knew humiliation in daily life, 'put in their place' by betters in the social structures of the Roman world, its hierarchy of authority, and economic networks. All could identify with a figure who suffered humiliation."[121] This interpretation by John Reumann recommends itself precisely because it is so very concrete and socially congruent with ordinary human experience. Entire cultures are built on the avoidance of shame and humiliation.[122]

No one wishes to be humiliated by others. But Jesus was not only humiliated by others in his career and in his dying—the Philippians hymn teaches that he "humiliated himself," where ἐταπείνωσεν is an active indicative verb form. He willed this humiliation, and he became obedient to the point of death. That "he became obedient" (γενόμενος ὑπήκοος) hearkens back to the Suffering Servant in Isaiah and to the post-biblical Jewish witnesses of a devout and loyal servant, so it casts this early understanding of Jesus' passion and death in familiar categories. But it does not mean that to embrace humiliation is something good in itself. Paul prays that he will not be put to shame before his judges. In the gospel narratives, Christ accepts the brute fact that he is teaching goodness in a world that, with all its institutional violence, cannot bear to hear it. Yet an acceptance of humiliation is entailed in Christ's broader resolve not to abide in a realm of innocuous supernatural fantasy, but rather to live deeply and teach in opposition to the common greed and anger that pervade his world. The emptiness hymn of Philippians, for all its mystic meaning, is grounded in the secular life of Jesus of Nazareth.

Nor does this passage mean that Christ was acceding to the august will of his Father that he should die to appease that offended paternal figure, although some commentators think just that: "According to E. Lohmeyer, only a divine being can accept death as obedience; for ordinary human beings it is a necessity, to which they are

---

121. Reumann, *Philippians*, 370.

122. When I lived in a small town in Wisconsin some years back, an elderly gentleman of sterling character but failing memory walked out of a local store without paying for a small item he had inadvertently put in his pocket. He was arrested for shoplifting. The store had a "no exception" policy for shoplifters, and so even though everyone recognized that the man had no intention of stealing, they still pressed charges. Two nights later the man committed suicide rather than appear in court and be humiliated before his community.

appointed by their humanity (Heb 9:27)."[123] Yet no one, not even the best of commentators, can speak for what God might accept or not accept. What does a commentator know of how a "divine being" can or cannot act? Such a notion of father-God makes him simply an offended party in a cosmic drama, imagined to favor us humans over other beings if only his just anger might be appeased by Jesus' humiliation and death. But no such plaintive yet almighty god exists. The fatherly care of this silent God never saves the schooling fish that form those bait balls porpoises and tuna feed upon in the deep oceans. God is not the director of any cosmic drama, and God does not demand the death of Jesus. Jesus was snatched by timorous officials, abandoned by his disciples, tried by self-serving power-seekers, and executed without much thought, just as people today are treated in many parts of our modern world.

The trinitarian theology that developed not long after the scriptures were written insisted that the three persons of the Trinity had one and the very same will and intelligence. It was not as if one person, the Son, had a different will than the Father's and could thus, in his human mode, obey the Father's will. Any notion that makes too much of the Isaiah parallel of the Suffering Servant leans away from the indivisibility of Christ and the Father and toward tritheism—three gods, and that we have never entertained. Whenever in the scriptures it is said that it was necessary (δεῖ) for Jesus to die, this does not signal some theological necessity imposed by God or obedient acquiescence on the part of Jesus of Nazareth. It signifies, rather, that in our scriptures, we are dealing with interpretation of older scriptures and looking back to Hebrew texts that so often speak of the Suffering Servant. It means that, as Paul and his readers expect, those ancient scriptures are fulfilled in the actual events that occurred in the dependently arisen life of Jesus of Nazareth. It does not mean that we are dealing with theological drama. No metaphysical viewpoint is adequate to the dependently arisen diversity of Jesus' life or of our own. Jesus did not have to die for us. He just did.

To what, then, is Christ obedient? The text says he was obedient even "to the point of death" (μέχρι θανάτου). Above, in 1:21, Paul writes that for him to die is gain, for he longs to be dissolved to be with Christ. For Paul, the fact of death is more than a necessity that is hardwired into his genetic code, although it is indeed hardwired, for we all age and die. This is what the Pāli scriptures of early Buddhism identify as "old age/death" (Skt. *jarā-maraṇa*), a single stage in the twelvefold dependent arising of our samsaric lives. It is the final humiliation to age and lose control over our organic bodies, to become dependent upon the help of others, and to be deprived of our humanness. In the Christ wisdom here celebrated, obedience to the point of death means the acceptance of that humiliation and acknowledgment of our dying as the literal deconstruction of our organic being. To die is gain only in the light of thereby sharing in the body of Christ, enlarged to encompass all beings in a new configuration of risen living.

---

123. O'Brien, *Epistle to the Philippians*, 230, citing Ernst Lohmeyer, *Kyrios Jesus: Eine Untersuchung zu Phil. 2, 5–11. Zweite Auflage* (Carl Winter, 1961) 95–96.

What happens, then, when we die? We'll all die; no one can deny it. All who have seen someone else die recognize full well what happens: the organic functions cease, and the living person is replaced with an inert corpse. There are plenty of reasons why people die, but there are no theological answers to that question at all. There are books and films describing people who are cursed by the inability to die—they often depict such lives as dreary in the extreme, lives that no one in their right mind would ever choose.[124] Yet here in my "golden years," I find myself desiring to live on for many years more, just to see what it might be like. But I cannot. We die.

So it was that early Buddhist teaching began with the simple, stark acknowledgement that we humans suffer and die. Buddhists inherited from their Indian culture an acceptance of the cycle of transmigration (Skt. *saṃsāra*). They sketch the twelve causes and conditions that lead from primal ignorance all the way around to the final stage in life, which is described as "old age unto death" (*jāra-māraṇa*) as a single discrete stage in life. Then the cycle of birth, life with all its suffering, and death is repeated over and over again. This cycle was intended, in the scriptures and commentaries of the tradition, to emphasize the continuing suffering that is entailed in being alive. However, it also offered comfort to some to imagine a future life much like this one, only perhaps somewhat better because of good karmic deeds performed in the present. Unable to imagine undertaking the ascetic path-practices required to reach *nirvana*, such people were willing to postpone final cessation.

Here in the Philippian hymn, we too confront the culmination of all humiliations—the end of organic continuity. But the self-emptying of Christ also means that we have no self to lose by dying, for there exists no self in living. It is the emptying that enables the mind of wisdom to patiently embrace harsh life conditions, humiliations, and finally death itself. When first we are born, we have no ability to perceive or to process the buzzing world of sensations that surround us. No one remembers being slapped on the buttocks at birth. No one can recall that first primal cry that rushed oxygen into our infant lungs. It takes time for our brains to develop to the point of processing what our senses present to us: the sights and the sounds, the smells and the touches, the taste of milk from our mother's breast. In beginning to perceive what our senses sense, we also begin to distinguish ourselves from others. First we distinguish our bodies from our mothers, because mothers are not always and immediately present to our needs.[125] And as we begin to distinguish our bodies, very soon we begin to

---

124. See David Ewing Duncan, "How Long do You Want to Live?" *The New York Times Sunday Review*, August 25, 2012.

125. Julian Paul Keenan, *Face in the Mirror*, 70: "It appears that the sooner we 'detach,' or start to become independent from our parents, the sooner we become self-aware!" Keenan adds, "Preyer believed that exploration of the body was important to forming a sense of self, and he used keen examples such as a child trying to bite its own toes!" (ibid., 61). The Yogācāra texts describe the emergence of the sense of selfhood as beginning with the awareness of a separate body, which leads to the sense of a separate self that—while valid and necessary for everyday living—has no core reality that might be apprehended as that which must survive. Neuroscientists often devote their efforts to accounting for the sense of self, since there are no clear neural locations for the perception of self within our brains.

distinguish our selves—our inner selves. Our sense of who we are is arrived at by a precarious and sometimes fragile process of constructing a self-image by mirroring ourselves in the eyes of others.

It is that self-awareness that, as we come of age, becomes the director of all of our life activities and guides our life orientations. But it is a fragile construct, even when nurtured more or less healthily. Sometimes something goes organically wrong and infants do not develop a sense of their own being-here, for self-consciousness is not given by the mere fact of being born; it has no inherent status whatsoever. It is this construction of the self that Mahāyāna thinkers explain as dependently arisen, and thus empty of essence. There is no me to be me and no mine to be mine, for we live in "interbeing," growing within a web of relationships.[126] Life comes to us as a pure gift, and as we engage the amazing abilities of our brains and our bodies, so our minds begin to direct affairs, always within the context of our families, our friends, and our communities and with cherished hopes towards an ever-fuller engagement in life.

But, alas, if we've missed the Dharma boat somehow and have begun to suppose our self to be the center of our world, then we fall back into the murky waters of confusion, turning life back upon itself as we become fixated upon avoiding death. It is this pattern that the Yogācāra philosophers call imagined (Skt. *parikalpita*), whether found in amoral psychopaths, political movers and shakers, or identity theologians. Nevertheless, life for all of us is pure gift. If a gift when we are born, so likewise it is a gift when we die. Dying remains a fragile gift—in the shared risen life of awakened resurrection. Eternal life is not just the eternal life of some inner spiritual part of us. For Paul it is a shared risen life, and that is what it means to be "with Christ." We do not have an imperishable inner core. We have no souls, if by that we understand an eternal, imperishable core to our being. When Christ becomes obedient unto the point of death, he does not take refuge in the immortality of his human soul. The mind of Christ wisdom is coreless, for he has emptied his self. We construct our lives, whether in delusion toward endless suffering or through practices of wisdom that take us forward in life and lead us into the fields of wise and compassionate practice designed to gladden and benefit all sentient beings. One need not be worried about losing life. Our lives cannot be lost because they are not ours in the first place.

Yet our passage through this life is not just a meaningless blip in the natural evolution of the cosmos that devolves into a deluded struggle for survival. It does

---

Buddhists concur that self-awareness is a construct (*vijñapti*) but insist that we remain aware that, being so constructed, it has no final status.

126. Thich Nhat Hanh, *Interbeing: Commentaries on the Tiep Hien Precepts* (Berkeley: Parallax, 1987). The fourteen Tiep Hien precepts are those of the Tiep Hien Vietnamese Order founded by Master Nhat Hanh for the School of Youth for Social Service during the Vietnam War. They are the traditional Buddhist moral precepts formulated in 1964 for engaged and nonviolent practice on the many issues that face modern people. "Tiep" means "to be in touch with," and "hien" "to realize and make present." This Zen (Son) order was and still is engaged in working out the implications for practical living of the pure mind as empty and dependently arisen in everyday life.

matter that we live and, in whatever measure, it will matter to future generations that we have been here and done what we have done. In the Markan account, Jesus comes to preach a kingdom whose reality is as yet unfinished. It is an eschatological realm; it has no static essence or reality, but we entrust ourselves to the gospel in order to make it real. Our actions are always—to some extent and within the determinative context of our collective living together—free. The debate about free will versus a hardwired determinism never took place among Buddhists, both because they regard samsaric life as conditioned by our karmic heritage and because within that entanglement there is always at some point the spark of a fundamental desire for awakening (Skt. *bodhicitta*). That initial spark emerges everywhere. Why else do people over the globe strive to find a better life, even in face of the brute fact that our worlds have always constrained that freedom in fear of unbridled self-indulgence?

To counter the self-indulgence and disorder that flow from unbridled greed and hatred, we can consciously strive with compassion to increase the realm of freedom by creating communities of justice where truth may prosper. The task of compassion is not softhearted condescension toward the unfortunate, but rather engagement in a path that liberates beings from injustice and oppression, which frees even those most fortunate who enjoy a goodly share of the earth's wealth. The Buddha Śākyamuni was born to privilege, wealth, and pleasure. But the discovery that sickness and death bedevil us all caused him to abandon his palace confinement and embark on the quest for awakening. Our own quest for awakening can become embodied in our actions, flowing beyond the streambeds of our own bodies and our own skins, building up communal realms of freedom through practices of justice and peace. Not being static, the reality of the kingdom cannot be grasped within any single viewpoint, for it does not yet fully exist. Our reality becomes real only when individuals realize faith and their practice constructs the kingdom.

Christ himself, in his life and in his death and in his resurrection, lived a bodhisattva career of compassionate love. That is, he undertook acts of compassion and wisdom and was obedient to the path he himself preached—the good news of the kingdom—come what may. He was killed not because of the will of an arbitrary god. Rather, he was obedient to the path of authentic human living, in no way clinging to divine or human status of self. His obedience was not to a father figure, whatever Freud or Deleuze or Guattari may have thought, but to the very humanness we all share, even to the point of death. It was this human life that "led to his dying" (μέχρι θανάτου) not peacefully in bed surrounded by friends and family, but ignominiously and shamefully "hanging from a tree" (θανάτου δὲ σταυροῦ)—the very tree-death excoriated in Deut 21:22–23 as the most disgraceful of all deaths. He was killed because he obediently followed that commitment. Christ followers in Philippi and beyond are likewise called to further gospel freedom in the world, sometimes in a political sense, but always in that deep personal and communal sense whereby our world becomes the kingdom preached by the prophets, so that we humans may rise ever higher above our biological and evolutionary heritage of competitive struggle. Often this does require political engagement, for we shape the world to be as it is through our collective actions.

Evolution is held by many to be the upward thrust of our cosmic being. Teilhard de Chardin, in his book *The Phenomenon of Man*, presents a mystic vision of an ever-increasing evolution of consciousness from the earliest seed elements in the cosmos to the final Omega point that is the celebration of the Christ Mass upon the earth. Yet as I contemplate the evolutionary history inscribed in the earth itself, and as I witness the rapacious feeding of one creature upon another in vivid nature programs on my television screen, it seems to me that evolution is not such an altogether bright prospect—at least not in human terms. Our biological development over the centuries seems simply to engage us in struggles that become ever more vicious and ever more rapacious. Indeed, the tenacity of our self-attachment, as recognized by Mahāyāna Buddhism, is simply animal life become conscious of its own self-needs. Augustine describes this as original sin. We truly are born into a dog-eat-dog world.[127] Teilhard's Omega point does not come about through the natural force of evolution. Indeed, the record of our evolutionary karmic past is limned by greed and anger and fueled by delusion. Teilhard is breathtaking in the scope of his vision, but even though the pace of evolutionary development may be hastening,[128] I do not think we can count on a spontaneous evolutionary upthrust.

Without a path of wisdom and compassion to tame selfhood, we stumble from one bright dream to the next delusion. If indeed we live and have our being within the evolutionary struggle, then it is no surprise that political liberation movements seldom live up to their visions. The underlying evolutionary urges quite frequently appear in the form of replacement governments that are as inept as (and sometimes more rapacious than) their predecessors. This does not mean that political revolutions and liberation movements are not needed. Sometimes indeed they are, for one has to struggle to bring about justice and peace. But what it does mean is that the gospel

---

127. Gazzaniga, *Who's In Charge?*, 8: "Our brains are a vastly parallel and distributed system, each with a gazillion decision-making points and centers of integration. The 24/7 brain never stops managing our thoughts, desires, and bodies. The millions of networks are a sea of forces, not single soldiers waiting for the commander to speak. It is also a determined system, not a freewheeling cowboy acting outside the physical, chemical forces that fill up our universe. And yet, these modern-day facts do not in the least convince us that there is not a central 'you,' a 'self' calling the shots in each of us. Again, that is the puzzle, and our task is to try and understand how it all might work." The gospel task is more than to understand the genesis of self-consciousness as an adaptive evolutionary event—it is to understand how self-awareness is driven by delusion, greed, and anger, and then to turn those impulses toward selfless love.

128. Haidt, *Righteous Mind*, 215: "The actual speed of genetic evolution is a question that can be answered with data, and thanks to the Human Genome Project, we now have that data. Several teams have sequenced the genomes of thousands of people from every continent. Genes mutate and drift through populations, but it is possible to distinguish such random drift from cases in which genes are being 'pulled' by natural selection. The results are astonishing . . . : genetic evolution *greatly accelerated* during the last 50,000 years."

freedom we seek involves liberations that expand our boundaries beyond either/or alternatives, until there are no boundaries of self-interest and we open upon that constructive community Paul calls the "body of Christ." That path is always strategically nonviolent, in recognition of the oppressive demons that lurk in our inner heritage. We follow this quest obediently in acknowledgment of the dark days of our dying, even as Christ died on his tree. We are to learn the mind of Christ's self-emptying that we may fill the world with the sure hope of awakened and risen life.

There is an "upward call" in 3:14 of Letter C, in which Paul asserts the resurrection power of knowing Christ, but no identifiable upward force drives us, willy-nilly, toward justice and peace.[129] Thus, we are called to abandon self-love and turn toward the Christ mind of emptying. The reality of that which is empty is the eschatological reality that we strive to realize and construct. In a world of constant change, no static or fixed viewpoint can capture what is real. But the kingdom of the risen grows from within converted minds to emerge beyond present facts, and it emerges as an "upward call" to stretch forth toward an unfinished world of wisdom and love.

So if our lives are not our own possession and cannot be lost, then what happens when we die? When we die, we lose the biological life that surges through us and enlivens our bodies. Yet Paul's life "in Christ" and life after death "with Christ" do not signify a loss. Instead, they signify an ongoing risen life that, surging and striving toward expanding freedom, insight, and wisdom, does not disappear at his dying but flows instead into the organic body of Christ that constitutes the kingdom of God.[130] Shared life in Christ enables us to become free individuals—free from the confines of our ethnic identity, our religious denomination, our very skin—who are also free to form communities that, by stretching forth over the generations, can create for others yet unborn endless experiences of joy and gladness. That is the promise of the gospel. That is the reality of the kingdom of God: engaging in a very human fashion in a freedom quest that challenges death and makes end-time hope real. It guides our path efforts into that dark mystery that holds everything together. Nameless though it remains, we call it "the kingdom."

---

129. See Gazzaniga's *Who's In Charge?* on how "[t]he same genetic predisposition can result in divergent psychological outcomes, depending on an individual's cultural context," in relation to easterners and westerners (Gazzaniga, *Who's In Charge?*, 185).

130. See Haidt's *Righteous Mind* on major evolutionary transitions: "Major transitions are rare. The biologists John Maynard Smith and Eörs Szathmáry count just eight clear examples over the last 4 billion years (the last of which is human societies). But these transitions are among the most important events in biological history, and they are examples of multilevel selection at work. It's the same story over and over again: Whenever a way is found to suppress free riding so that individual units can cooperate, work as a team, and divide labor, selection at the lower level becomes less important, selection at the higher level becomes more powerful, and that higher-level selection favors the most cohesive superorganisms" (Haidt, *Righteous Mind*, 201). The body of Christ becomes here the "superorganism" of life lived individually beyond the boundaries of any recognizable organic life form, yet cohesively together with all who share that awakening—whether living or not living in the flesh.

Life horizons stretch forth beyond the professional careers of scientists and theologians (who seem persistently to resist learning from one another's insights), so that our life after death is neither that of a narrowly constricted self destined simply to disappear, nor the sweet continuance of that selfhood. Our culture, in various ways, encourages us to cherish such delusions: atheists grabbing for another moment of joy and the faithful for moonbeams. But there is no precious inner self to continue into imagined realms. Our after-dying life is a new creation, not the continuance of the old order. It is the flowing of the river of our personal life actions into the great sea of an awakened wisdom that is more personal than individual. It is impossible to imagine and thus cannot be defended, because before we have died none of us have experienced what lies beyond, and after we have died, no brain activity remains to support any images. How could we imagine bodiless life when the very body that enables experience has ceased to function?[131] Indeed, thoughtful people doubt that any describable thing does lie beyond for us, as if the self were just to continue on and on and on. It doesn't. There is no self-life after death. Rather, when self dies—when we lose ourselves—then we live beyond the boundaries that separate life from death and beyond the confines of our conventional selfhood.

Jesus not only was obedient throughout his life of preaching freedom and salvation to others; he was obedient "even to death, death on a cross" (μέχρι θανάτου, θανάτου δὲ σταυροῦ).[132] That death on the cross stands shockingly as the negation of all projects of the self to further its own career and success in life. Jesus did not succeed in life. He was an utter failure, in worldly fact, his brief career as a Galilean teacher cut brutally short. This Jesus made himself obedient even to the most ignominious of deaths—a form of death that to Jews was an abomination, for no honor was accorded to one who died by hanging upon a tree.

---

131. Gazzaniga, *Who's In Charge?*, 101: "Once again we see the integration of disparate behaviors into a coherent framework. Order has been made from chaos. In doing so, behaviors originating from the right hemisphere were being incorporated into the conscious stream of the left hemisphere and we could see, hear it happening right in front of our eyes." In the transmigratory context of Indian religions, there is a continuity of consciousness (Skt. *vijñāna-saṃtāna*) from death to life and life to death, repeated until one realizes cessation and discovers a nirvanic bliss beyond selfhood. Never having adopted the Aristotelian distinction between matter and form, they could not appeal to souls separated from bodies. Neither in fact did Paul, for the Christian adoption of the Aristotelian anthropology came after Paul. See Keenan, *I Am / No Self*, which attempts throughout to read the ironic discourse of the Gospel of John within the Heart Sūtra's anthropological understanding of the emptiness of self and the emptiness of the five constituent factors that we experience as selfhood.

132. Reumann sees verse 2:8c, "even to death on a cross," to have been added by Paul (Reumann, *Philippians*, 353, 374–76). That bolsters his later argument that 4:7–11 "corrects" the christology of the emptiness hymn by adding the missing emphasis on sharing the sufferings of Christ. But this seems a roundabout argument.

Emptiness Letter B, Part 2

"... God did more than exalt him ..." (2:9)

2:9 Therefore God did more than exalt him, for he gave him a name above all names.

2:9 διὸ καὶ ὁ θεὸς αὐτὸν ὑπερύψωσεν καὶ ἐχαρίσατο αὐτῷ τὸ ὄνομα τὸ ὑπὲρ πᾶν ὄνομα,

Scholars debate the interpretation of "therefore" (διὸ) in this verse. Some understand it to indicate that Christ's exaltation is in consequence of his humiliating death.[133] M. R. Vincent, interpreting "therefore" to mean "consequently," notes that those who refuse to accept that clear meaning do so because of their Reformation theology, wherein no one earns any salvific result. He criticizes Calvin, who "attempts to evade it by explaining διὸ [*dio*] as *quo facto*, which is utterly untenable."[134] But the image that results from Vincent's view is that Christ endures the cross to come out on the other side risen, as the best of all heroes who pass through trials and tribulations, even death, and emerge victorious. Karl Barth has argued that the "therefore" (διὸ) does not divide the hymn into two separate parts, but simply marks another aspect of what came before: "It does not say that he who was humbled and humiliated was afterwards exalted ..."[135] Meanwhile, O'Brien disagrees with Barth in asserting that a staged sequence is precisely what it means: "God has in fact vindicated Christ's self-chosen humiliation and conferred on him the name above all others."[136]

I am persuaded by Barth and Calvin, who maintain that this passage merely explicates the meaning of what it means to live in Christ—that humiliation and dying are indivisible from the eschatologically-realized risen life we now share. Certainly, in a Mahāyāna reading Calvin would be spot-on, for *quo facto* means "by that very fact." By the very fact of his cross, Christ's over-exaltation is indivisible from his abject humiliation, suffering, and death. In Christ, we are invited to erase the margins that delimit life here from dying and renewed life there. That is, it is a matter of one and the same indivisible life coursing through the cosmos.

This is not a dramatic story in which the outcome of Jesus' acceptance of suffering and his abandonment of divine equality is that he arises in victory mode. His lungs do not once again oxygenate his blood, and his heart does not pump blood through his wounded body. We confess Christ to have risen, not to have been resuscitated,

---

133. On verse 9, Martin writes, "*Therefore* (giving the result of his obedient submission to death) *God exalted him to the highest place* (giving the verb an elative or superlative sense, which is probably correct) is a phrase including the resurrection which is tacitly assumed, but it is aimed primarily at expressing the truth of the ascension as in Acts 2:33 (cf. Acts 5:31). The lxx uses the same verb, here translated *exalted*, Isaiah 52:13" (Martin, *Philippians*, 108).

134. Vincent, *Critical and Exegetical Commentary*, 61.

135. Barth, *Epistle to the Philippians*, 66.

136. O'Brien, *Epistle to the Philippians*, 234.

thereby affirming the indivisibility between his emptying of all identity and the fulfillment that is so much more than an empirical victory parade into heaven.¹³⁷ Telegenic resurrection events—although they resonate in the imagination—are not reported in any of the scriptures of our Christian traditions. There is in scripture no cosmic victory drama.¹³⁸ It is not as if Christ was at first in the form of God; then, second, emptied himself to take on the form of a slave and die; and finally, third, was exalted by the Father and given a superlative name. That is not how we read the passion and resurrection narratives. The resurrection is an eschatological event already operating in Christ and also in us when we live in Christ.

In the phrase "God more than exalted him" (ὁ θεὸς αὐτὸν ὑπερύψωσεν), we have a rare compound. Indeed, the verb "exalted" (ύψωσεν) with the prefix "more than" (ὑπερ, hyper) is a *hapax legomenon*, appearing only here in the New Testament. The meaning of the verb "to exalt" (ύψωσεν) is plain enough, but combined as it is with the prefix *hyper* (ὑπερ-), "over," it is open to interpretation.¹³⁹ The Philippian hymn employs a new term. Paul himself frequently invented new compound words; in fact, "Paul virtually holds the copyright on *hyper* compounds in the New Testament."¹⁴⁰ Scholars adduce various possible sources for this compound word. Bruce avers that "[t]he expression is drawn from Psalm 110:1, where the Davidic King is invited in an oracle to share the throne of Yahweh, sitting to the right side of him,"¹⁴¹ noting also that the "simple verb ['to exalt'] is used at the beginning of the fourth Isaianic Servant song (Isa 52:13): 'he will be exalted' (*hypsōthēsetai*)."¹⁴² In the Septuagint Greek, Isa 52:13 reads: Ἰδοὺ, συνήτε ὁ παῖς μου, καὶ ὑφωθήσεται, καὶ δοξασθήσεται σφόδρα,

---

137. See Reumann, *Philippians*, 372. Reumann refuses to see "therefore" as "because of" and explains, "If *dio* means 'because of this,' we are not told why, not even 'because of Christ's obedience'; only that God has swung into action" (ibid.). That renders God as previously inactive, for although Christ was not attached to his privileged status, God now "swings into action" to correct Jesus' mistaken disregard and affirm him as God's equal. The ontological insistence on selfhood is also found in Caird's comments on verses 10–11: "his self-forgetful love has been declared by God to be the only true greatness, to be indeed the very character of God himself" (Caird, *Paul's Letters from Prison*, 123). But in the hymn, the very character of God is emptied of self, so why reintroduce the strange notion of God's self?

138. Except for the noncanonical Cross Gospel, which pictures an immense Christ rising from the grave accompanied by a host of the just to proclaim the common vindication of Israel's faith. See Crossan, *Cross That Spoke*, 297–403, in which he proposes a textual interplay between the Gospel of Peter, discovered in 1886 in Egypt; the canonical Gospels; and an earlier Cross Gospel, the root source for all the passion and resurrection narratives still discernibly embedded in the Gospel of Peter. It is this Cross Gospel that presents the mythological and dramatic image of a superhuman Christ arisen at the head of the immense multitude. This text, embedded in the Gospel of Peter, did not figure in the ongoing tradition—not because it failed to support the missionary mandate to a closed group of apostles (ibid., 403), but precisely because it pictured the risen Christ in such overblown and ethereal images.

139. On 2:9, writes, "'Exalted' is a compound verb meaning, as Loh and Nida point out, 'God hyperexalted him' (*Translators' Handbook*, 61)" (Thurston, "Philippians," 84).

140. Fee, *Paul's Letter to the Philippians*, 221.

141. Bruce, *Philippians*, 72.

142. Ibid., 79.

translated as: "See, my servant shall understand, and he shall be exalted and glorified exceedingly."[143] The Isaiah passage does not, however, add the preclitic *hyper*. Possibly the Philippian composers of the emptiness hymn had been introduced to the Isaiah passage by Paul but added the prefix to the simple verb used there.

Most commentators, including Peter O'Brien, take the compound verb to signify a superlative degree, as in the verb "I was *overjoyed by* your coming," which expresses a high degree of joy. In this sense, the term would refer to Jesus' supreme degree of exaltation to a position over the whole creation. And yet, the prefix ὑπερ (*hyper*) can have not only the sense of intensifying to a superlative degree the verb it introduces, but also a sense of "going beyond" what that verb signifies. I would prefer to translate the compound here in this latter sense, as "more-than-exalted" or "over-exalted." Oscar Cullman, to the point, understands the term to mean "more than exalted" him.[144] This meaning is to be preferred, for it avoids an image of an empirical victory drama. Christ's humiliation is reversed, but it is not an empirical reversal. The exaltation to risen life is not conventional life restored and intensified. John Reumann looks to W. Thüsing on exaltation as resurrection to argue that risen life is a shared exaltation—the common life in Christ both of Paul and of the Philippians, as well as the invitation for human participation in the incarnate grace that flows from the indivisibility of Christ's dying and rising, engendering the fearlessness of discipleship.[145] So I believe that the meaning of the phrase here is not "exalted him exceedingly" or "exalted him to a superlative degree," but rather "more than exalted" him.

The prefix "hyper" does seem here to indicate going beyond or exceeding the action of the verb to which it is added.[146] Not only Paul, but also the apophatic theologians Gregory of Nyssa, Pseudo-Dionysius, and Maximus Confessor likewise generously use the prefix *hyper* (ὑπερ-). Imagine a dominant image of Christ Pantocrator as the center of the universe, present in luminous rays of grace and spirit creativity—a very highly exalted position, indeed. Imagine, by contrast, that at the center of this universe and all known universes there is a vast black hole that holds in tensive being

---

143. Pietersma and Wright, *New English Translation of the Septuagint*, 865.

144. Oscar Cullman, *The Earliest Christian Confessions* (London: SCM, 1949) 180, 217, 235.

145. Reumann, *Philippians*, 354. Reumann cites Thüsing, "Erhöhungvorttellung und Parousieerwartung in der ältesten nachösterlichen Christologie (SBS 42; Stutgard: KBW, 1979) 41–55.

146. *Oxford English Dictionary*, 2nd ed., s.v. "hyper-.". Verbs that mean "going beyond" what the unprefixed verb signifies abound in Patristic writings. Examples of such verbs where the prefix (ὑπερ-) itself signifies "going further or beyond what the verb signifies" are: "to go beyond, transcend" (ὑπερεκβαλινω) as used by Athanasius (*Contra Gentes* 33 in Migne 25.65d); "to extend or stretch out beyond" (ὑπερεκτείνω), as used by Gregory Nazianzenus in *Carminum libri duo* 1.2.9.57 in Migne 37.671. Adjectival uses are: "more than pure" (ὑπεράγνος) by Pseudo-Dionysius Areopagitus in his *De caelesti hierarchia* 10.3 in Migne 3.273c; "more than true" (ὑπεραληθής) by Maximus Confessor in *Mystagogia* 5 in Migne 91.680d; "the truth that is more than truth" (ὑπεραληθῶς) by Pseudo-Dionysius in his *De ecclesiastica hierarchia* 1 in Migne 3.1065A; "more than divine" or "supremely divine" (ὑπέρθεος), respectively by Pseudo-Dionysius' *De divinis nominibius* 2.3 in Migne 3.646, and by Athanasius "On the Trinity, in his *Homilia in annuntiationem deiparae* 1 in Migne 28.917A. Examples could be multiplied.

all stars and all worlds and into which, sooner or later, all return. That is not an exalted place at all; it centers nothing we much like to imagine. But God dwells, as the early apophatic mystics insisted, in darkness, not in light, and we are enlivened by the rays of divine darkness that encompass us and push us forward into life and into that dark bosom of the Father. Suns are the centers of their solar systems, but black holes lie at the center of galaxies composed of many solar systems.

Theistic concepts that were so persuasive in the small world of the ancients are hardly intelligible to us with our expanded knowledge of the vastness of the universe. It is not that these theistic concepts are not true, but that they cannot even be understood; indeed, the occasional arguments between atheists and theists seem to be taking place in echo chambers of archaic notions. Beyond the many suns in their solar systems and the many black holes in their galaxies lies the sheer mystery of not knowing. Mahayanists call that ultimate mystery the realm of the real (Skt. *dharmadhātu*), and they endow it with the compassionate visage of the Buddha body (*dharma-kāya*). Christians identify the same mystery as the father of Jesus, often then drawing on Greek ontology to fill out the image of an omnipotent and omniscient God and, as a result, getting stuck defending ideas of God taken wholesale from classical pagan philosophy. A Mahāyāna approach would favor abiding in the apophatic wonder of not knowing while avoiding the polarity of subject-object consciousness. That approach maintains the complete otherness of God from any conceptual understanding, even while reading the meaning of God in the self-emptying and the more-than-exaltation of Christ.

In Paul's letter, we hear of living in Christ—not of Christ's vindication in a cosmic drama that occurred some two thousand years ago. So God more than exalts, more than raises him up. God goes beyond any exaltation. God goes beyond any triumphant restoring of Christ—in order to give him a name beyond every named name. The implications of this are important: We do not claim that in the end Jesus is the exalted winner in a competition of religious heroes. (In contrast to Joseph Campbell's Vedantist reading of all world religious figures within a universal pattern of exaltation of heroes who undergo various trials and sufferings to attain a final victory.[147])

We have never called Jesus our hero. *Christus Victor* signifies that the victory of Christ's resurrection is the erasure of any final boundary between life and death for us all, not that his resurrection is the highest honor a conventional person might attain. Paul knows well that there is no male or female, no Jew or Greek, no slave or free, and thus no winner or loser, for God addresses all people everywhere with the same silent message of life and grace. It does not matter what name is affixed to a person, for any

---

147. See Campbell, *Hero with a Thousand Faces*, vii–viii: "It is the purpose of the present book to uncover some of the truths disguised for us under the figures of religion and mythology," which task is carried out by understanding "the grammar of mythology," under the aegis of "modern psychoanalysis." Campbell's analysis issues in "an amazingly constant statement of the basic truths by which man has lived throughout the millenniums of his residence on the planet," and concludes that, "as we are told in the Vedas, 'Truth is one, the sages speak of it by many names'" (ibid.).

such designation has only a worldly and conventional basis and thus falls away when we address the crucified Jesus we call "Lord." Nevertheless, here it is the named God who graces and gives to Jesus (καὶ ἐχαρίσατο αὐτῷ) a new name.

Do our names have real importance? The phrase "a name beyond every name" (τὸ ὄνομα τὸ ὑπὲρ πᾶν ὄνομα) offers a clue, for the hymn again uses that same overreaching preposition *hyper* (ὑπὲρ). Once again, this term does not indicate that the name God gives Jesus is a superlative name or even a really, really good name. It is a name that goes beyond naming; it is the name that cannot even be pronounced, for it lacks vowel sounds that might enable one to utter it—the name YHWH, which may be voiced only by recourse to different name, Adonai.[148] God is not nameable. So Jesus, then, is incomparable—not just the head of the class, but in a class without members. This Lord is not to be placed on any comparative listing of world teachers or world religious leaders not because he is better, but because in gospel matters there is no contest. God has given to him a name that is no name at all. Names are used to distinguish one person from another person. But this more-than-a-name is not a stable designation, for the unpronounceable name serves as a conventional marker for the erasure of all naming. In the final eschatological reckoning, we likewise retain no class divisions or ethnic designations, but are instead a new creation in an absence of conventional naming. The Chinese philosopher Chuang Tzu taught that the reason things have names is because we give them names: "What makes a thing so? Making it so makes it so!"[149] So the name that is bestowed upon Christ is not a stable identifier; it is the primal name of God, who has no name and who thus, when asked, revealed his no-name to Moses.[150]

This is the gracious gift that Christ receives: the name that is used in the Septuagint to represent the personal name of the nameless God. The point, I think, is that in the emptying whereby Christ does not claim his divine form, he takes upon himself all the dependently arisen stature of being fully human, and so in his life he was named Jesus. In Paul's preaching, he received Christ as his surname, and in his more-than-exaltation, he received the name YHWH, signaling his embrace within the vowelless presence of God, who is absent from all discriminative naming. We cannot speak the

---

148. Caird, *Paul's Letters from Prison*, 123: "There is an obvious difficulty, however, in identifying a name given at Christ's exaltation with that by which he was known to his contemporaries during his earthly life. For this reason the majority opinion is that the new name is 'Lord' (Acts: 2:36)," in which "Lord" is the Septuagint translation for Adonai, the stand-in name for the unpronounceable YHWH.

149. Chuang Tzu, *Complete Works*, 40: "What is acceptable, we call acceptable; what is unacceptable we call unacceptable. A road is made by people walking on it; things are so because they are called so. What makes them so? Making them so makes them so. What makes them not so? Making them not so makes them not so." In more modern parlance, we live within worlds constructed by language, which reflects commonplace, conventional insights and oversights.

150. Keenan, *Meaning of Christ*, 8: "When he (i.e., Moses) requests that Yahweh reveal himself by name, he is given the cryptic reply, 'I am what I am' (*ehyeh asher ehyeh*, Exodus 3:13), which implies, not that God's name is 'being' (ὁ Ὤν), but that Yahweh cannot be named or defined in any manner whatsoever."

name of God, but we can write down its consonants so as to emphasize that we cannot speak the name of God. Likewise, here Christ's over-exaltation crosses out the stability of his naming altogether, leaving us with the dependently arisen Jesus—the human name that points to what lies beyond names in his shared risen life. This entails the dynamism of constant tension between emptiness and dependent arising, between the nameless and our human names.

Christ lives and dies because he is empty and dependently arisen, and therefore he goes beyond being exalted as a victor in battle or as a resuscitated leader who might come back and claim his triumph. In the resurrection narratives, Christ arises only shortly to be removed from this earth, so that he may be enlarged in the lives of those who share in that resurrection. The movement of this hymn is not a temporal narrative, but rather a tensive circumscribing of emptiness within dependent arising, and then again within an emptiness wherein names have no purchase.[151]

Yet we're always talking about "Jesus Christ," and we confess him to be "Lord," the very name of the ineffable. Jesus, in the phrase of Ignatius of Antioch, is "the voice of the Father from silence," as the outflow from the ultimate truth that encompasses us all in our conventional world.[152] Our given names remain what they are so long as we live. The Chinese, in their practice of filial piety, extend their remembrance of ancestors by name to seven previous generations; thereafter all are subsumed under the common category of "ancestors." Only the sages continue to be remembered by name throughout the generations, for they have set the patterns of civilized order and moral living. For Christians, no other name is given but that of Jesus Christ, because his path splits the heavens to reveal that which is nameless—evoking possibilities for salvation and inviting us to overcome our entanglement in greed, anger, and delusion. We invoke the name of Jesus in our prayers; his more-than-exalted name means for us new life in Christ, and thus we name him to be Lord of our eschatological futures.

---

151. The sixth-century ce Buddhist T'ien-t'ai Master Chih-i contextualizes these mutual inherences as the threefold truth of emptiness 空, everyday living 假, and the middle path 中, wherein each is indivisible 即 from the other two, offering a pattern for trinitarian thinking that has yet to be taken up by Christian theologians. Chih-i's *Great Calming and Contemplation* consists of a series of Dharma lectures on meditative practices for monks and laypeople, systematizing the many Mahāyāna traditions then recently introduced into China. For a clear presentation of the history of this text and its impact, see Neil Donner and Daniel B. Stevenson, *The Great Calming and Contemplation: A Study and Annotated Translation of Chih-i's Mo-ho Chih-kuan* (Honolulu: University of Hawaii Press, 1993) 1–96. For more on how Chih-i drew his trinitarian schema from Nāgārjuna's Mādhyamika philosophy, see Paul L. Swanson, *The Foundations of T'ien-t'ai Philosophy: The Flowering of the Two Truths Theory in Chinese Buddhism* (Berkeley: Asian Humanities, 1989) 1–17.

152. In chapter 3, section 12 of the *Mahāyānasaṃgraha*, Asaṅga speaks of the seeds of contact (Skt. *sparśa-bīja*) that come from hearing doctrine and enable the practitioner to experience (*anubhāva*) the Dharma body of awakening. In chapter 10, section 4, that "contact" (*sparśa*) is realized by non-discriminative wisdom, apart from the pattern of subjects apprehending objects and expressing meanings in language. The claim that experience comes before and goes beyond the reach of language is widespread, because it is "just" experience, bereft of insight and judgment, whether that experience arises in the course of everyday living or is nurtured within meditative abiding.

Grounding ourselves as we do within this dependently arisen Christian tradition, with all of the ambiguity and historical sin that our personal names entail, we have a mixed heritage. Many Christians have worked courageously for peace and justice, remembering the hope for the coming kingdom and abiding in awareness of the benign transcendence of the non-achieving Father. Yet at times we have also veered from the path of the emptying Christ and sinned against many in his very name. We have persecuted Jews. We have colonized entire populations. We have turned away from the poor and the sick, celebrating our own status in service of a magical market that trickles down wealth upon the few and suffering upon the many. In so doing, we have besmirched the very name of Christ and made it into a marker of self-delusion. We are to repent of these sins done in the name of Christ. Drawn to this nameless living in Christ, we may then claim the name that for us, being more than a name, leads not only into the silence of the saints,[153] but also into compassionate solidarity with those who have suffered by our hands and by those of our ancestors.

"... every knee shall bend ..." (2:10–11)

2:10 *So that at the name of Jesus every knee shall bend, in heaven and on earth and under the earth,* [11]*and every tongue shall acknowledge that Jesus Christ is Lord, to the glory of God the Father.*

2:10 ἵνα ἐν τῷ ὀνόματι Ἰησοῦ πᾶν γόνυ κάμψῃ ἐπουρανίων καὶ ἐπιγείων καὶ καταχθονίων, [11]καὶ πᾶσα γλῶσσα ἐξομολογήσηται ὅτι κύριος Ἰησοῦς Χριστὸς εἰς δόξαν θεοῦ πατρός.

Because we live in a metagalactic cosmos of vast and expanding dimensions, each of our successive attempts to enunciate the ultimate meaning of our living takes on ever-broader cosmic dimensions. Perhaps, as some would argue, our future actually lies beyond the confines of this planet earth. That prospect has long fired our imaginations and inspired cinematic depictions illustrating the wonder and excitement of discovering entire new world realms. In the vistas of astrophysics, the Philippian hymn passage seems both overblown and underwhelming, for it moves within a much more restricted world vision: the surface of this earth, the sky above, and the underworld below. Aware as we are of our pluralistic world with its many cultures, the all-encompassing claims of this passage can cause some discomfort, for they do sound grandiose. And if proffered belligerently in an interfaith context, they are indeed embarrassing. However, when enunciated in the lived context of practitioners,

---

153. Nagao, *Foundational Standpoint*, 67: "Absolute denial, therefore, cannot consist in speech and reasoning. It must be a unique silence beyond all language. Vimalakīrti's silence in *The Scripture of Vimalakīrti* is said to resound like thunder. In his *Lucid Exposition*, Candrakīrti states that 'ultimate meaning is the silence (Skt. *tuṣṇīmbhāva*) of the saints.'" The citation from Candrakīrti is from the *Prasannapadā*, 57:7–8: "*paramārtho āryāṇaṃ tūṣṇīṃbhāvaḥ*."

with the intention of grounding their minds in the self-empty and over-exalted Christ, the import of these words is not to assert any manner of superiority. Just as the gospel does not constrain us to adopt either Paul's cultural stratagems or the social norms of the first-century Roman Empire, neither does it require us to narrow our cosmological vision to Paul's *mare nostrum* world.

Buddhists, with their culturally Indian image of countless world realms, can sound even more grandiose than these Philippians, whose cosmic vision centered upon the earth upon which we live sandwiched between the heavens above and regions below. But even within that rather limited perspective, this Philippian hymn magnifies the truth of our central teachings to cosmic hyperbole, proclaiming the exaltation of Christ to be "for the glory of God the Father" (εἰς δόξαν θεοῦ πατρός). In Paul's world, as is often noted, fathers enjoyed the role of paterfamilias with absolute authority over their households but limited power in the wider world. Imagining God as a benign paterfamilias with full authority over the household of the cosmos was a leap, but it was still an intelligible move.

However, our picture of the cosmos today far surpasses any earth-centered cosmos depicted in either Hebrew or Christian scriptures and beggars even the notion of the many replicated world realms found in classical Buddhist thinking.[154] This hymn's image of the exalted Christ envisages a world made one in the household of faith and practice. Each tradition strives in its fashion to touch the very heart of cosmic life, and thus the grand cosmic visions found in their scriptural texts. Scripture, however, does not offer any astrophysics of the universe to compete with the knowledge we have gleaned from our Hubble telescope. If we wish to speak of God in the context of that vast cosmos, we must develop newer images and concepts even to be intelligible. Certainly it does not serve to insist on God the Father as paterfamilias when the very structure of Greco-Roman households has long since disappeared from any of our social contexts. With no model of a paterfamilias among us, insisting on that image makes the faith a nostalgic remnant of an archaic past.

Even if Paul did envision the skies filled with "powers" inimical to Christ's gospel, the faith is not served by science fiction views of Jesus as an imagined Lord of lords with his angelic Jedi knights locked in battle with the dark forces of evil.[155] Biblical

---

154. See the clear and accurate presentation in Akira Sadakata, *Buddhist Cosmology: Philosophy and Origins* (Tokyo: Kōsei, 1997). That cosmology is as archaic as the Roman Empire's, but its imagination reached beyond this world to envisage what Edward Conze named the great trichiliocosm: "A universe which comprises 1,000 suns, 1,000 moons, 1,000 heavens and hells, etc" (Conze, *Perfection of Wisdom*, 323–24).

155. But see Clinton E. Arnold, *Power and Magic: The Concept of Power in Ephesians* (Eugene, OR: Wipf & Stock, 1989) 171. Arnold argues that the "powers" were experienced as threatening and diabolical by common people in Ephesus (and thus also in Philippi) and therefore concludes that post-Pauline letter is not engaging in cosmic speculation but rather addressing fears that have been endemic to humans from the beginning of our being. Walter Wink, in his trilogy *Naming the Powers: The Language of Power in the New Testament* (Philadelphia: Fortress, 1984), *Unmasking the Powers* (Philadelphia: Fortress, 1986), and *Engaging the Powers: Discernment and Resistance in a World of*

apocalyptic visions have been taken over by Hollywood and, with appropriate name changes, blended with cosmic visions from eastern religions; thus in *Star Wars* we see Yoda instructing us all in how to feel the Brahman force that pervades all being. These movies entertain with their artistic wizardry, discrediting the scriptural cosmologies as clearly archaic, impotent, and unworthy of much wonder or engagement. Perhaps exegetes should construct a new scriptural genre of science fiction that employs the cosmology of modern astrophysics, just as the ancients themselves used their own cosmic visions to engender meaning in their lives.

If the name that has been given to Jesus is above every name—and indeed is the ineffable, unpronounceable name that is voiced as "Adonai," or "Lord"—then not only has Jesus emptied himself of the form of God and refused to cling to equality with God, but his emptying also reformulates for us the very notion of God. In Ps 25:11–14 we read:

> ¹¹For the sake *of your name* (ἕνεκα τοῦ ὀνόματός του), O Lord—you will expiate (ἱλάσῃ) my sin, for it is great.
> ¹²Who is the person that fears (φοβούμενος) the Lord? He will set a law for him in the way he chose.
> ¹³His soul will abide in prosperity, his offspring shall inherit land.
> ¹⁴The Lord is empowerment (κραταίωμα) for those who fear (τῶν φοβουμένων) him, and his covenant is for making clear to them.[156]

The Philippian hymn focuses "on the name of Jesus" (ἐν τῷ ὀνόματι Ἰησοῦ 2:10), not as a replacement name for the Lord in the Psalm, but as himself sharing in "the name of the Lord" (ἕνεκα τοῦ ὀνόματός του). So Jesus takes on the same title, "Lord" (Κύριος, *Kyrios*), that is celebrated in the Psalm and throughout the Tanach as the present embodiment of the absent and unnamable God, promising an end-time fulfillment that flows continuously through the cosmos.

Clearly, the name Jesus Christ itself is not ineffable—we say it all the time—and yet he has been given a name "above all names" that cannot be enunciated. Thus, there is constant tension here between the conventional name of Jesus of Nazareth or Jesus the Christ and that ineffable name that is never uttered and can be written only without vowels.[157] We write his conventional names, both Jesus and Christ, to indicate that therein our faith comes to ground and abides among us. But never do any of us have a name that is absolute: Our history witnesses that absolutized names lead to

---

Domination (Minneapolis: Fortress, 1992), interprets those powers, however imagined by the ancients, as still actively embedded in corporate and institutional structures that embrace sacred violence, bedevil the many, and oppress people even yet.

156. Pietersma and Wright, *New English Translation of the Septuagint*, 558.

157. On the name YHWH and on reading (Qere) the written name (Kethibh) YHWH as "Adonai," see J. Weingreen, *A Practical Grammar for Classical Hebrew* (1939; Oxford: Clarendon, 1959) 23. The divine name *always* has to be read differently from its written expression in the scriptures, so it is called the "Qere Perpetuum," or the perpetual reading.

violent behaviors. We undertake crusades and jihads, persecution and oppression, for the sake of nothing more than our claimed identity. It is troubling to me that over the last few decades the churches seem to have placed more emphasis upon defining their own identities than upon teaching and living the wisdom of the risen Christ.

We are to focus our attention not upon our own constructs, but rather on the ineffability of what in our scriptures cannot be pronounced. On this particular point, every tradition says the same thing: that however we may envision or describe ultimate meaning, all names fall short. Which leaves us with the heightened, because emptied, understanding that all names are conventional. And so in 2:9–10, after God gives Jesus the "name above all names," thus identifying him as the end-time Lord, the passage reverts to his very conventional name, Jesus. The tensive and never-to-be-bridged otherness—between the everyday name of Jesus and the ineffable God who dwells in light inaccessible—is to be the focus of our attentive reading and meditation. For to interpret everything as captured by the conventional name of Jesus Christ is to refuse to acknowledge the empty Christ proclaimed in this hymn and to insist that our conventional Jesus is the best of all conventional religious figures. That is a secular, reductionist christology. It turns away from the expansiveness of Christ wisdom to build constricted ramparts behind which we might persuade ourselves that we are orthodox and safe.

"At the name of Jesus every knee shall bend" (ἵνα ἐν τῷ ὀνόματι Ἰησοῦ πᾶν γόνυ κάμψῃ 2:10) "and every tongue shall acknowledge" (καὶ πᾶσα γλῶσσα ἐχξομολογήσηται 2:11). This striking passage is often interpreted as signaling our human abasement and submission before the majesty of God. It is based on Isa 45:23, where the Lord God says, "By myself I swear, my righteousness goes forth from my mouth; my words will not be turned back, because to me every knee will bow and every tongue will acknowledge God" ("Ὅτι ἐμοὶ κάμψει πᾶν γόνυ, καὶ ὁμεῖται πᾶσα γλῶσσα τὸν Θεὸν).[158] But the key to understanding the Philippian passage lies in how it reconfigures and rewrites these words of God in Isaiah. Where the Septuagint Greek translation of Isa 45:23 has "by myself" (ἐμοί), the hymn substitutes the phrase "at the name of Jesus" (ἐν τῷ ὀνόματι Ἰησοῦ), shifting the perspective from that of the majestic Lord God to the minds of the Philippian composers of the hymn.

In echoing these words of Isaiah, the Philippian passage calls us to acknowledge that the source of the cosmos does not lie within our own purview; it is beyond any purview, in majesty incomparable. Christians are to bend the knee to Jesus as did our ancestors to the Master of the universe, for the vast emptiness of the deep cosmos is indivisible from the shared life of Christ. Nevertheless, the teaching of this empty Christ does not support any manner of religious one-upmanship. We do not replace God with Jesus. Rather, the Philippian hymn replaces Jesus' nameable name with God's ineffable name, suggesting a teaching that undermines any standalone name. The life we live in Christ is the same cosmic life that circulates throughout the entirety

---

158. Pietersma and Wright, *New English Translation of the Septuagint*, 860.

of creation—the life of what is and what yet is to be. Such cosmic life emerges from the physical elements of all life, bursting forth in the creation of galaxies and coming to abide within our bodies and expand within our consciousness.[159] To attentively live such a life is to live in Christ as the eschatological Lord of a risen life that reaches beyond its own enunciation.

Certainly the notion that all creatures will fall down and worship the Master of the universe is well attested in our scriptural texts.[160] The phrase that at the name of Jesus "every knee shall bend" (πᾶν γόνυ κάμψη 2:10) is somewhat more puzzling. It is not that, as some maintain, one is to assume a proper posture, for there is no proper posture across cultures. Kneeling was not then an ordinary position for prayer; many texts describe instead standing before the sheer mystery of the unknown, because unnamable, Lord of life beyond life and death. It is questionable whether it was even the Philippian Christians' practice to kneel when they gathered to acknowledge the ineffable lordship of the empty Christ. In its classical usage, this expression most often meant "to sit in order to rest," not to kneel.[161] One bent one's knees to sit and stop moving about, there to rest from all labors. In any event, this "bending of the knee" appears to signify abiding in attentive acknowledgment. These ancient Christians not only celebrated the Lordship of Christ, they also sat in quiet "acknowledgement" (ἐξομολογήσηται 2:11) of that Christ in their hearts, attending to his named absence in their minds.

To one nurtured by Buddhist texts, this phrase suggests bending the knees to sit in meditative quiet—taking full cognizance of the ineffable name of the empty Jesus, who is beyond any exaltation-as-reversal, and concentrating upon this more-than-exalted Christ mind in prayerful acknowledgment that the source of this life of ours lies outside the confines of self. Having received the ineffable name that is beyond all names, this Christ remains the transparently empty mirror of the Father, standing before us as an invitation to empty all our self-referential religious ideas.[162]

In 2:11, the hymn concludes with the declaration that all creatures in the known cosmos shall acknowledge the exalted lordship of that unnamable Lord Christ who has already forgotten he is equal to God: "every tongue shall acknowledge that Jesus Christ is Lord" (καὶ πᾶσα γλῶσσα ἐξομολογήσηται ὅτι κύριος Ἰησοῦς Χριστὸς). Yet it

---

159. See Gazzaniga's comments on emergent consciousness: "I think conscious thought is an emergent property. That doesn't explain it; it simply recognizes its reality or level of abstraction, like what happens when software and hardware interact, that mind is a somewhat independent property of brain while simultaneously being wholly dependent upon it" (Gazzaniga, *Who's In Charge?*, 130). Neuroscientists struggle to account for the emergence of conscious thought, which seems located at no single nodule in the human brain and beyond the explanatory reach of any deterministic philosophy.

160. O'Brien, *Epistle to the Philippians*, 242.

161. Sumney, *Philippians*, 49.

162. Keenan, *Meaning of Christ*, 226: "[Jesus'] total focus is to mirror the presence of God as Abba and to embody the rule of compassion. His being is found in that continuing transparency as the mirror of the Father." See Edward Schillebeeckx, *Jesus: An Experiment in Christology* (New York: Seabury, 1978) 304.

is obvious to us that even now, after almost two thousand years, most creatures have not in fact come to such an acknowledgment. Most do not name Jesus as the Lord or Master of the universe. There are Buddhists and Hindus aplenty. There are more than a billion Muslims and many millions of Jews. Many others are interested in religious matters but altogether neutral on matters of doctrine.

What, then, are we saying here? At the last day, will we Christians somehow see all people falling to their knees to acknowledge that our Jesus is their Lord? Will we Christians at the last wear the laurel wreath of victory? No, we will not. No way. That is the conceit of an imperialist missionary program that still seeks cultural sovereignty after all the old ecclesiastical social controls have failed—that somehow we will apocalyptically overcome the world and force it to acknowledge the lordship of our Christ. Such a concept of mission itself negates and turns away from the empty Christ proclaimed in Paul's gospel. If we instead would follow this Jesus, we would not be concerned to make him everyone's acknowledged Lord, for he did not regard being equal to God as important, realizing that no name ever comes to rest in what is real.

Knowing that Jesus is more than simply exalted to a superlative status, we can acknowledge that he has an ineffable "name"—one that is beyond our language and thus empty of any claim whatsoever—while we simultaneously proclaim the Jesus name as the empty path to an eschatological life of being in Christ and with Christ. Missionary endeavors are not about getting other people to accept our doctrinal propositions but about inviting people where they live to enter into that anticipatory fullness of life we call life "in Christ." What is important is to live that life, not to name it properly. The invitation is to become conformed to the mind of Christ, who did not think it so special to be equal to God and so becomes enfolded in the ineffable name of a God who still draws the cosmos forth toward fullness of life in Christ. Likewise, although fully confessing the truth of our tradition, we ought not to insist on its divine status as though that were the heart of the matter, for the real is not statically defined. The reality of Christ wisdom emerges from baptismal initiation, which means first and foremost entering into the dying and rising of Jesus, only then to learn the meaning of doctrine as defining the parameters of our practice.

To be one with each other in the Spirit-supplied Christ entails emptying our own self-interested thoughts—even our missionary self-interest, even our religious desires, even our personal faith—so as to witness to that faith transparently and to pay universal homage to the mystery we call God, embodied in acknowledgement of an end-time sharing in life beyond all constructed margins, for that is where the Spirit binds us together in Pentecost gatherings. That is the meaning of Jesus Christ as the Lord (ἐξομολογήσηται ὅτι κύριος Ἰησοῦς Χριστὸς) of the eschaton. But we are not to impose such submission upon others. We may bend only our own knees in acknowledgment of the Lordship of Christ and, by sitting at rest, preach his peace and life everywhere in the Spirit of the empty Christ.

The emptiness hymn celebrates this "over-exalted" status of no status at all as something that has taken place already. The ineffable name has already been granted, despite appearances to the contrary. So we are charged with the mission of living and preaching the gospel of Jesus, and we are driven by our own deeply felt need to reach beyond the margins of our own lives and cultures, as well as by a compassionate desire to announce and enunciate the unnamable name of Jesus throughout the world. But saying that "Jesus is Lord" creates a deep tension between preaching the conventional name of Jesus Christ on the one hand, and acknowledging the ineffable name of Jesus that encompasses all living beings in all cultures, in all places, in all stages of life—precisely because Jesus' name now becomes unpronounceable. Christ followers are to lose their cherished identities in order to witness to the empty Christ who is exalted beyond naming. This tension between naming and silence is found across traditions among those who are aware that we clothe our faith commitments in words whose meanings constantly escape their lexical definitions.

Following the empty Christ, we are not allowed, by the very force of the gospel, to pretend that our faith is expressed in any absolute or divine form (μορφή θεοῦ), for this too has been emptied. If Christ himself makes little of divine equality, then the faith of his latter-day followers is likewise not "equal to God" (τὸ εἶναι ἴσα θεῷ); it too is not something to be clung to or anything very special. If we are to follow the empty Christ, we too "more than exalt Christ" when we refuse to overcome his emptying, or when we resist hallowing him with our religious admiration as the pinnacle of all our faith delusions. Our path is rather to follow the empty Christ by hollowing out our own core identities and carving out the cancerous innards of prideful delusion so that we may be of use in preaching the gospel everywhere without claim to any special insight into divine intentions or special perspectives on absolute truth.

Our path is just the gospel path to awakened and risen life, preached to all people, to all sentient beings "in heaven, on earth, and in the world below" (ἐπουρανίων καὶ ἐπιγείων καὶ καταχθονίων), wherever sentient beings might be found to hear and heed this Christ-emptiness. This can occur only inasmuch as an ineffable Christ is our eschatological Lord, precisely because he emptied himself "to the glory of God the Father" (εἰς δόξαν θεοῦ πατρός), and only so long as it does not entail any cultural agenda of trumpeting our own languaged versions of Jesus Christ. Trumpets are called for only at the end time, and although its reality is at hand, still it has not come. The gospel analogue to the Mahāyāna doctrine of emptiness is this pervasive eschatological discourse that we find throughout the scriptures, for the end time—already here and not yet here—is to be the cleansing of all self-defined perspectives and interests. Eschatological reality stands over against and negates metaphysical reality as but a once-glimpsed view of the whole seen from a moving train. Missionaries are gospel servants, for like those appointed in Acts they serve the needs of people, and like Stephen they preach Christ, who empties everything because he is risen.

This is what sixteenth-century English theologian Richard Hooker calls the "interchange" whereby Christ becomes what we are and we are enabled to become what he is.[163] And this is the significance of emptying ourselves of all our imagined privileges and all our deluded resistance to giving up cherished and comforting ideas and ideals. Jesus of Nazareth did not come to impart new ideas but rather to share his living and dying in self-emptying and in more-than-exalted personhood. Becoming conformed to the empty Christ is not to imitate Christ as moral paradigm, for he is exalted here to the vanishing point into the glory of the Father. The Philippian hymn is an invitation to conform our minds to the empty Christ even at that vanishing point.

And so the hymn concludes here with the affirmation that the acknowledgement of Christ as eschatological Lord is directed "to the glory of God the Father" (εἰς δόξαν θεοῦ πατρός). As noted above, the perceptible and experienced glory of God's form has been emptied in the humiliation of a slave, and the hymn now ends in recognition that such glory is proper to God the Father apart from the purview of selfhood. Glory connotes power—a power that moves powerlessly to accomplish risen life even here in Christ, and also there when we die in passionate longing to live together with Christ. In the final phrases of this hymn, it is the glory of the Father that shines through the empty Christ into the minds of the disciples who learn Christ.

---

163. Weary of the unprofitable and "fierce contentions" on the theology of Eucharist, and setting aside the question of "whether with change or without alteration" of the Eucharistic elements, Anglican theologian Richard Hooker (1554–1600) in his *Ecclesiastical Polity* (ed. Keble, v, lvii, 12, p. 359) depicts Christ as addressing the communicant thus: "This hallowed food, through concurrence of divine power, is in verity and truth, unto faithful receivers, instrumentally a cause of that mystical participation, whereby as I make myself wholly theirs, so I give them in hand an actual possession of all such saving grace as my sacrificed body can yield, and as their souls do presently need, this is to them and in them my body" (Horton Davies, *From Cranmer to Hooker 1534–1603*, vol. 1 of *Worship and Theology in England* [Princeton: Princeton University Press, 1970] 122).

5

Emptiness Letter B, Part 3

The significance of the empty Christ for the Philippians (2:12-13)

2:12 Consequently, my beloved, just as you have always been obedient, not only in my presence, but much more now in my absence, work out your own salvation with fear and trembling; ¹³for it is God who works in you both the willing and the working beyond delight.

2:12 Ὥστε, ἀγαπητοί μου, καθὼς πάντοτε ὑπηκούσατε, μὴ ὡς ἐν τῇ παρουσίᾳ μου μόνον ἀλλὰ νῦν πολλῷ μᾶλλον ἐν τῇ ἀπουσίᾳ μου, μετὰ φόβου καὶ τρόμου τὴν ἑαυτῶν σωτηρίαν κατεργάζεσθε· ¹³θεὸς γάρ ἐστιν ὁ ἐνεργῶν ἐν ὑμῖν καὶ τὸ θέλειν καὶ τὸ ἐνεργεῖν ὑπὲρ τῆς εὐδοκίας.

The hymn has concluded, but Paul the apostle here goes on to speak of the consequences (Ὥστε) of embracing the mind and the practice of emptiness.[1] Having just sung the Philippians' hymn of the empty Christ who became obedient to being fully and totally human, spreading life, and enduring death, Paul turns his attention to his friends (ἀγαπητοί μου) the Philippians. He urges them not merely to imitate Christ as a model "out there," but actually to reconfigure their minds and abandon all self-referential images. They are personally to embrace the emptiness embodied in Christ—"as you have always been obedient" (καθὼς πάντοτε ὑπηκούσατε) in the practice, not merely "when I was among you" (μὴ ὡς ἐν τῇ παρουσίᾳ μου μόνον), "but even more so now that I am absent" (ἀλλὰ νῦν πολλῷ μᾶλλον ἐν τῇ ἀπουσίᾳ μου).[2]

---

1. Reumann, *Philippians*, 404: "Following the indicative mood account in 2:6–11, 2:12–18 continues the paraenesis, in 1:27–2:5. 1:17 *Exercise your citizenship in a manner worthy of the Gospel of Christ* stands over 2:12–18 as its imperatives treat how believers relate to one another and with the *politeia* of city and Empire."

2. Ibid., 409: "The Philippians seem generally to have supported Paul's Gospel through

No longer does the Paul we met in Letter A claim to be self-sufficient. From the Philippians' hymn of self-emptying he has learned not to cling to status, and he has been assured that his friendship with them does not entail heirarchical roles of client and patron. Now Paul can and does call the Philippians "my friends" (ἀγαπητοί μου), and he calls their attention to the fruits that flow from emptying one's self and living in the obedience of Christ. It is not that they are to be obedient to a stable and standalone Christ, or perhaps to the deacons and overseers who were mentioned in the first verse; they are to practice throughout their lives Christlike obedience to gospel freedom. Ecclesiastical cults of obedience seldom exhibit mutual self-emptying; generally, one party retains sovereign status while insisting that the other empty selfhood.

It has become clear in their hymnic confession that the Philippians have "always been obedient" (πάντοτε ὑπηκούσατε) to the empty and exalted Christ (as evidenced in their composition of the hymn)—not that they have always "obeyed me [Paul]," as one English translation has it. Nor, as *The Jerusalem Bible* has it, "Continue to do as I tell you." That is wrong: Paul is not asserting that the Philippians have always followed his advice or submitted themselves to authoritative figures in the church.[3] Here, "to be obedient" has a narrow focus and signifies just what it meant earlier in verse 9 when used of Jesus. Just as Christ, when emptied of all godly form and identity, became obedient (ὑπήκοος) by being fully human (γενόμενος ὑπήκοος μέχρι θανάτου, θανάτου δὲ σταυροῦ)—without pretensions, without privilege, without self—likewise, the constant obedience of the Philippians is to be found in their acknowledgment of the full humanity of life and death and in their emptying of all pretense and self-serving religious attitudes. Indeed, "No mention is made of the object of their obedience: ὑπηκούσατε is used absolutely."[4]

We should not conclude that because Paul speaks elsewhere about obedience to himself or obedience and submission to Christ that he is here instructing the Philippians to submit to the demands of either an imagined Christ seated far above in glory or to his apostle Paul sitting in his prison. Christ's more-than-exalted status remains empty of stable identity; as eschatological Lord, he has ascended beyond our purview. The present verse echoes the hymn passage, whose meaning is not that the Christ out there somewhere, or hovering in our imaginations, is to be obeyed. Nor are the teachings of Jesus a special object of our obedience. They do not in fact differ significantly from the teachings of such sensitive and intelligent Pharisees as Gamaliel. Paul, like Jesus, never urges people to abandon Torah, even though for Jesus some of "the traditions of the elders" are dismissed precisely because they do excuse people

---

evangelization and support for his mission work, though (4:10) contact had slackened for a time. 2:12b is genuine commendation of the Philippians, if with some hyperbole."

3. Collange rejects the notion that obedience means obedience to the apostle or to the authority figures of the community ("*hupēkoos*," v. 8) (Collange, *Epistle of Saint Paul*, 109).

4. O'Brien, *Epistle to the Philippians*, 275.

from Torah observance.[5] For Paul, circumcision, dietary regulations, and festival observances are erased because they create sharp, defining boundaries between Jewish and Greek Christians. This is the reason that some Jewish Christ followers regarded Paul as disobedient to Torah, the voice of God. In any case, in this passage Paul is urging his friends subjectively to embrace the obedient mind of Christ, even to death, however it may come.

We do not have a complete picture of Jesus, as the many "historical Jesus" studies have so amply demonstrated. We have only a few strokes toward a portrait but not enough to silhouette him clearly against his contextual background. This is why the historical questers come up with so many different portraits. We cannot know "what Jesus would do," for the scriptures do not place him within the compass of our often troubling questions. As usual, Paul is about other business: He wants the Philippians to radically reorient the entire way they perceive the world, themselves, and God, all to accord with the hymn to the empty Christ they delivered to him after their monetary gift caused him to be so hesitant. To be obedient to this Christ is to share in his suffering, in acknowledgment of being human, and moreover to share in his risen life, in even deeper acknowledgment of being human. That is the eschatological pattern of faith in the here-and-not-here Christ. That is the reality of the emptied real.

Paul follows a Christ whose very emptiness engages him in discerning what is best to do in concrete situations, as he elaborates in 4:8–9. No doubt when writing Letter A, Paul was disinclined to accept wholeheartedly the Philippians' friendship gift because of its patron-client implications, and thus he countered there with his claim of self-sufficiency. But in Letter B, he has accepted the Philippians' hymn about being empty in Christ, and so he drops any such claim of self-sufficiency to follow that empty Christ. Putting on the mind of the empty Christ is concretized in an obedience that acknowledges the upward call of the gospel that Paul mentions in 3:14 of Letter C on risen life—a call to empty oneself to live in the eschatological hope of a risen reality that is more than exalted, despite the humiliating circumstances that being in Christ often entails. It is not obedience owed to some person who stands over against us; it is an obedience inscribed into our very being, an obedience that transforms our cognitive understanding of life and death. This path does not establish a fixed identity that is assured by slavish obedience to an ecclesiastical authority. Rather, it entails ongoing practice learned by constantly renewed obedience to the elusive call of the gospel as we work out its meaning in the many concrete situations we encounter. It embraces the full spectrum of Christian churches, wherein the Spirit who supplies Christ breathes, and it sweeps beyond their margins toward engagement with all other traditions as well.

Still, there is little specific guidance for us in the New Testament on how to discern gospel obedience in times and cultures so vastly separated from those of Paul and the Philippians. It is immoral, many Christians (and Buddhists) agree, to use

---

5. See Keenan, *Gospel of Mark*, 172–83, on "Traditions."

contraceptives simply to escape responsibility in sexual encounters, for it is immoral to deny responsibility for our own actions. But most would also agree that it can be responsible, and moral, to use contraceptives to exercise responsibility within marriage; the issue is responsibility, not the use of contraceptives. However, when issues become complex, common agreement collapses. It is immoral to snuff out life just as it begins, for we agree that we are not to kill. But is it not also immoral to turn a blind eye to instances when good Christian sense and the cherishing of life indicate the abortion of an unviable fetus?[6] Pornography is wrong because it entices toward inordinate lust and it degrades those involved in its production, especially children. Yet even the moral theology manuals of my celibate seminary training stated that alluring pictures of naked women are acceptable in the context of the marriage bed for those who might find them useful, for if the central purpose of marriage is to conceive children, then anything that furthers that end is moral. Such issues become complex and seldom yield to the simplistic answers of moral theologies about intrinsic acts. We are tasked with discernment as to how our own actions best follow the gospel, and we cannot hand off that responsibility to distant and uninvolved authorities.

Theologies of intrinsic acts, whether good or bad, move within the ontotheological frame of essentialist thinking and bully the weak toward obedience and irresponsibility, all the while maintaining the authority of the ecclesiastical curators of the faith. Yet if faith is to be a sure refuge and a cure, it cannot be curated. The questions raised in the wake of Vatican II still await proper answers, including the question of how celibates, who have no experience and little insight into sexually engaged familial responsibility, have the authority to lay down normative codes on such matters. The only responsible sexual actions for them are abstinence, for everything else is sinful. Celibate clerics meditating on the empty exaltation of Christ ought to imitate Paul in attending to the hymnic confession of the Philippians and in abandoning all claims to ecclesial self-sufficiency.

We Christians have had many an argument over how one "puts on" the mind of Christ and what our obedience entails. The Reformers said we are saved by the faith of Christ and held that this clarifies what faith is not: it is not works. But this hardly clarifies the question of what faith means. I would suggest that it means we are to put on the empty mind of Christ and to allow our consciousness to be reconfigured in Christ-like obedience to the prompting of the gospel spirit, for only by that Spirit is Christ supplied. Luke Timothy Johnson contends that the genitive term "of Christ" ($\chi\rho\iota\sigma\tau o\tilde{u}$)

---

6. In 2010, Sister Mary McBride, administrator of Pheonix, Arizona's St. Joseph's Hospital, permitted an abortion to save the life of a mother rather than accept the inevitable death of both the mother and her unviable fetus. Her compassion incurred—in the words of Bishop Olmstead—an "automatic excommunication." The moral theology on abortion has hardened in the Roman Catholic Church since my seminary days over fifty years ago. See *Right and Reason: Ethics in Theory and Practice* (St. Louis: Mosby, 1959) 284. In recent decades, celibate men in the church have decided that without any doubt human personhood begins at the moment of conception, and they wage legal campaigns to enforce that new judgment upon all citizens, regardless of religious affiliation.

in Paul's phrase "the faith of Christ" (πίστις χριστοῦ) is a subjective genitive—Christ's faith—not an objective genitive meaning our faith *in* Christ, much less faith in Christ's church as a stand-in for Christ.[7] The church is the body of the risen Christ among all its members, not a substitute for Christ. An objective genitive reading of "the faith of Christ" would mean it is we who "have faith in Christ," which suggests it is our faith placed in Christ that saves, and thus that we are the agents of that faith, distinguished as more or less faithful by the intensity or conviction with which we confess it. But this is self-engendered salvation, moving always within the margins of conventional affirmations.

Rather, having "Christ faith" means that we are saved by "Christic faith," that is, the faith that the empty Christ expresses in his full obedience to the Father, who exalts him eschatologically—in which exaltation we are invited to share. For by transforming our minds and hearts, it is both we ourselves who work out our salvation and God who is working within us. In the empty Christ mind, all lines of demarcation between Paul and Christ, or between the Philippians and Paul, or between either of those and Christ, who has no bounded nature, are vacated of any final meaning. In Christ there are no differentiations between Jew and Greek, Buddhist and Christian, clergy and layperson.

Yet if one clings to the empty Christ while forgetting the dependently arisen everyday life of eschatological abiding, then the Christ who nullifies himself and does not cling to his divine nature may become an amorphous Christ who can morph into almost any embodiment. The self-emptying Christ is here identified with Jesus, who was obedient even to death on the cross and who is made concretely real when his followers take on the risen form of his life, now freed from our karmic heritage. And yet there are no universal liturgies or theologies, for we are human beings who always live within particular histories and particular cultures.

Our common Reformation history witnesses to deep and pervasive disagreements about just what salvation is and how it comes about.[8] Today, however, consensus seems to have been reached on many issues: We are indeed justified by faith through the grace of God and not by our own efforts to justify ourselves.[9] We do not

---

7. See Luke Timothy Johnson, "Rom 3:21–26 and the Faith of Jesus," *Catholic Biblical Quarterly* 44 (1982) 77–90.

8. The theme of D. A. Campbell's *Deliverance of God*, which argues powerfully for overcoming the traditional "Lutheran" Justification theory—rooted in the common reading of Romans that becomes a "fortress" theology, with its individualistic and contractual notions—in favor of a more apocalyptic understanding of Paul's christocentric mysticism. This is a forcefully staged argument, in stark disagreement with the conventional model of Justification theory and in critical dialogue with the "New Perspective" identified with E. P. Sanders and James D. G. Dunn's *The New Perspective on Paul*. Campbell's is an exegetically difficult volume with a strong tendency to logically unfold the implications of various theological positions, often to the point of unintended and unacceptable entailments.

9. Hans Küng's *Justification: The Doctrine of Karl Barth and a Catholic Reflection* (1964; Westminster, John Knox, 2004) was a pioneering endeavor to look beyond theological retrenchment toward a

and cannot "save" ourselves. But this common theological truth does not guarantee that we apprehend and live it faithfully. There are, I think, Christians who, in their own personal pilgrim's progress, embrace a wooden and other-excluding morality and then spare no effort in urging others to follow the same "correct" path. Some believe they have already been saved by grace and are therefore free to sit back and rejoice. Others see an imperative for the church to engage in social and political issues, as though the gospel calls for yet one more—quite progressive—nongovernmental organization. We all know full well that the salvific grace we have received is to be shared. Yet both the earnest Christian conservative and the enlightened liberal practitioner seem at times to miss the mark, for neither evinces the "fear and trembling" Paul speaks of when he writes to his beloved brothers and sisters in Philippi. Liberation theologian Camilo Torres' image of Christ as a revolutionary is not congruent with the obedient servant we see in the hymn of the empty Christ—however urgent the human need for revolution against oppressive exploitation may be.[10] Nor are the values promoted by a staunch conservative like William Donohue, who envisages a narrower but more faithful observance of Catholic virtues.[11] Both are spiritually obese, having filled their own minds and bodies with the junk food of religion.

Paul says that we are to "continue (κατα) to work out our own salvation" (τὴν ἑαυτῶν σωτηρίαν κατεργάζεσθε 2:12), and not regard it as a *fait accompli*. This entails a lot of individual and communal effort. The main verb here means "to carry out" a task, to bring it to completion.[12] If salvation is something already accomplished, then we would be free from fear and trembling altogether and excused from any need for the path of gospel salvation in our everyday lives. But Paul talks about effort, calling for frightening reconfigurations of our samsaric consciousness in the furtherance of the gospel. The gospel is not something that has already been achieved by us or for

---

deeper understanding of the commonality and differences in Justification theology.

10. See the sociological and political essays in Camilo Torres Restrepo, *Revolutionary Writings* (New York: Herder & Herder, 1969). Torres' analyses are cogent, and his conclusions led him to join the National Liberation Army (ELN) in the Columbian jungles. He once said in a Spanish-language article that "If Jesus were alive today, he would be a guerrillero" (*Si Jesús vivera, seria guerrillero*). A Roman Catholic priest and professor, he left both university position and clerical orders to join the guerilla forces, where he was shot in the head and killed in his first encounter with government forces in 1966. Some regard him as a predecessor of the Liberation theologians, which seems an ambiguous evaluation, for later Liberation theology—embodied in Archbishop Oscar Romero and many Latin theologians, although embracing Torres' witness against oppression of the poor—eschewed revolutionary violence. Still, it seems to me that Torres' shadow lies behind the subsequent Vatican fear of Liberation theology, even in its nonviolent embodiments. I applaud Torres' courage in joining the revolution, but I do not think that Jesus supported his platoon. The "fear and trembling" comes from having the courage to commit oneself against sin and oppression, without any supernatural warrant for being sinless or even being sure. Political liberators seldom usher in end-time peace and justice even after replacing dictators who must be replaced.

11. William Donohue, *Why Catholicism Matters: How Catholic Virtues Can Reshape Society in the Twenty-first Century* (New York: Image, 2012).

12. Fee, *Paul's Letter to the Philippians*, 234.

us by grace. The death of Christ on the cross brings about our salvation. It is only in the ontological theologies of the churches, however, that salvation is the direct result of the cross of Christ, for they see that event as having altered the ontological state of human nature by appeasing God and thereby opening the sluice gates of grace. There is none of this in Paul,[13] who teaches that we are to attend to the empty Christ who becomes human in negating divine nature. We are to reconfigure our minds through grace in the spiritual obedience of the empty Christ, which presages our own eschatological exaltation with Christ to the reality of risen life.

Medieval thinkers thought Christ transformed our human nature, opening it to the inrushing grace of a supernature. But here in Philippians, the empty Christ abandons his supernature, which means that we encounter him simply as human (καὶ σχήματι εὑρεθεὶς ὡς ἄνθρωπος 2:7). Obedience likewise is grounded in the practice of emptiness, engaged in the continual work through which we further the gospel in our daily lives within a communal awareness of the ineffable emptiness of Christ and of the need for full engagement in the world, with all of its sweat, blood, and tears. That is the Christ path: the tensive practice of both empty Christ awareness and full engagement in the dependently arisen world of human affairs. Neither an enlightened bettering of the sad and benighted world, nor a dramatic imaging of one who descends from above to experience suffering and death and then returns to be reestablished and reabsorbed into his former high status. Such status is the unliving stasis of the spiritually dead.

That theme of "descent/ascent" is the rhetorical structure of the Christ hymn we have just sung, from high to low and then again high. But the hymn uses that schema only as a rhetorical format, signaling this in its forceful words about Christ's disregard for grasping the divine nature and in its more than superlative language about his exaltation. There is no up-and-down frame actually to be lived or embraced in the meditative path of living, for we end where we begin, seated on the cushion or kneeling in the pews. The emptying of Christ is his fullness, and we ourselves as his followers should not correct his obedience to the cross by our own efforts to exalt him. God has already done much more than exalt him and has given him a name we do not know and cannot enunciate—although we can write it down in Hebrew and see that it is the word reserved for God alone. The crucified and executed Christ is more than exalted and restored to his prior position precisely because that position has itself been emptied. The reality of God becomes itself eschatological, abandoning all static

---

13. Reumann explains that the term *sōtēria* is "used here for the third time in the letter body. 1:19, in a phrase from Job, spoke of Paul's *deliverance* (from prison, with suggestion of his eternal salvation) through the Philippians' *entreaty and Jesus Christ, whom the Spirit supplies*. Human and divine elements are involved. 1:28 had a terse reference to the Philippians' *salvation* eschatologically. A firm stance on their part and God's own endtime action are involved. 'Salvation' is not used in 2:6–11, though many call the verses a 'hymn or song of salvation.' The encomium [that is, the hymn] presents high points of the kerygma. But the Philippians' composition [the hymn] did not assert the results of Jesus' death 'for us,' [as] *sōtēria* for those who believe and confess his lordship" (Reumann, *Philippians*, 408).

notions of benign and/or powerful deity. Being present in all things, God is that which draws them forth and unfolds the truth of risen life.

So, then, we are to work out our salvation. This salvation of ours is something to be learned, to be brought about, to be concerned about. The term "salvation" (σωτηρία, *sōteria*) is extensive in meaning; it can signify that we have been saved from sin, from imprisonment, from meaninglessness, from ennui, from hatred, from greed, from anger—from anything that imprisons us within our self-referential core of being. We are saved so that the primal energies already working within us will enable us to intend and to will, and then to carry out those intentions in gospel action. The Christ mind is not simply given, enabling us to appreciate our having been "made right" with God; indeed, Paul tells his Philippian friends to keep their attention on mind-of-Christ emptiness and engagement.

The empty mind of Christ means blood and tears as we abandon a protective God so that we may affirm a provident God in Christ. It means that we then abandon Christ himself so that we may, by emptying our minds of any "form of God," enter into the obedient mind of Christ. This is not an imagined intimacy with Christ that issues in better human relationships.[14] Christ can become an idol for those who cling to religion. And that is what so often has happened—in the adoption of Roman order by Christian hierarches, in the Crusades, and in all efforts to force the gospel upon others. By contrast, identity with Christ is the self-abandonment by which we live the same risen life and share the same mind,[15] which sets us free to seek the salvation of all our brothers and sisters. Nothing is accomplished by one's own self-power, and yet our efforts are energized by the other-power of God, day by day and year by year.

Still, for Paul and the Philippians, the task of working out salvation "with fear and trembling" (μετὰ φόβου καὶ τρόμου) was twinned with the task of furthering the gospel under the leadership of an empty Christ who, no matter how exalted, did not provide any assurance of success on either front. It is something of a shock, but surely fear and trembling does signify the abandonment of self-power. It is "not self-assurance, but defenselessness."[16] Absent of any self-defense, still Paul prepares to defend the gospel, well aware that the larger social world is too big for him to manage, for it surpasses the sphere of his influence. That background of small groups of Christ followers facing the institutional might of a huge empire throws into relief the fragility of Paul's stratagem of witnessing to the powers of Rome. This situation lies behind Lightfoot's[17] interpretation that Paul longed for the final witness of martyrdom, both for himself and for

---

14. *Pace* Collange, *Epistle of Saint Paul*, 108. Collange translates "For it is God who promotes among you the will and the action for good relationships" (ibid.). Good (and bad) relationships occur everywhere, both within the traditions and among those who confess no tradition.

15. See Paul de Jaegher, *La vie d'identification au Christ Jésus* (Juvisy, Seine-et-Oise: Editions de Cerf, 1927). On the transformative "indwelling" of the three persons of the Trinity, see Paul Galtier, *L'habitation en nous des trois personnes* (Roma: Pontifica Universita Gregoriana, 1950).

16. Fee, *Paul's Letter to the Philippians*, 236.

17. See J. B. Lightfoot, *St. Paul's Epistle to the Philippians* (London, 1881).

all the Philippians. When prospects for success are distant and improbable, people do at times stand witness with their lives. Here, however, Paul insists on continuing engagement, opting to remain within the eschatological consciousness that, while it longs to be with Christ, yet abides in living day to day in Christ. Either alternative embraces the same reality.

These early Christ followers did not put up barricades around themselves. They embraced the fearful absence of an already assured salvation while yet resisting the disillusionment that eschatological dreams are only pipe dreams. They did not become aggrieved victims in a dance of fools. The terms "fear and trembling," used nowhere else in the New Testament, have concrete points of reference in the lives of Paul and the Philippians. Indeed, "There is no precise Hebrew equivalent for *phobos kai tromos*" (fear and trembling).[18] Some interpret the phrase devoutly to suggest reverence and awe, while others take it to mean pure terror.[19] The former spiritualizes the meaning of the phrase and becomes ethereal—a recommendation for a virtuous consciousness, as if the salvation here envisaged were the subjective state of a standalone seeker looking for reassurance. But Paul does not use these words just to trouble the mind of Søren Kierkegaard, and salvation is not an individual endeavor.

What about interpreting it as "pure terror"? Paul draws upon, and yet distances himself from, the sentiments of Ps 111:10, which has it that "[t]he fear of God is the beginning of wisdom" (Ἀρχὴ οφίας φόβος Κυρίου), even as that fear is lessened and bolstered in the following Ps 112:8 with an assurance that a wise person, "firm in his heart, will never be afraid" (οὐ φοβηθῇ) but will witness the demise of his enemies. The two psalms combine the reverential fear that issues in wisdom with an absence of fear in seeing that others experience the wrath of the Lord. We have a German word for that—*schadenfreude*, meaning pleasure taken from the misfortunes of others. Scriptural *schadenfreude* can be justified by attributing it all to God, deleting Christ's emptiness and celebrating a God who, if feared, then empowers the fearful toward victory.

I opt for a different and less bellicose reading of this fear and trembling—not pure terror, but rather the natural reaction of Paul to the self-emptying of Christ in the Philippians' confession. If indeed there is no firm ground upon which to stand, how can one not tremble at that thought? If even Jesus is emptied of self and takes no refuge in his divine nature, we are shaken to the very core of our being. Because we also have no core being, Paul's trembling is more than just being afraid of the dark powers of the Empire. It signals a physiological shaking of our bodily frame, such as might well occur in taking on the form and visage of a slave (μορφὴν δούλου λαβών 2:7). Our minds are fearful because reality is indeed eschatological and not graspable.

Paul's advice comes at us tangentially—not to create factions, whether within the communities or between the emergent churches and the political powers, however dark those powers may be. He instead advises his listeners to practice "continuous,

18. *TDNT*, 9:199.
19. Reumann, *Philippians*, 386.

sustained, strenuous effort."[20] Even in the face of intractable sin and delusion encrusted in institutions of power and sovereignty, still we are to work out (κατεργάζεσθε 2:12) our common salvation, for this is a communal endeavor, not a personal quest for self-affirmation or self-fulfillment. Paul does not enter into disputes about divine and human causality; he speaks simply of human effort and endeavor.[21] Like all Jewish thinkers of his time, Paul is committed to Torah practice, and although he rejects what he regards as the overbearing view of those who would require the observance of dietary laws and circumcision by even non-Jewish members of the communities, he cannot conceive that a committed life of faith would not somehow entail strenuous practice.[22]

Although Paul does not engage in the kind of theological discussions about divine grace and human effort that came long after his time, he does write about the Christ energies that are at work within humans, propelling us to engender acts of willing (τὸ θέλειν) and to carry out those acts in deed (καὶ τὸ ἐνεργεῖν). So he sets the stage for later theologies on freedom and grace, for it is not we who engender those acts of the will or their translation into committed practice. It is God who works within (θεὸς γάρ ἐστιν ὁ ἐνεργῶν ἐν ὑμῖν). If we, following the model of the self-emptying Christ, have no core self upon which to ground conscious actions, then we have no innate self-sufficiency that might impel us toward selfless acts that are contrary to self-survival. Theologians who grapple with such questions often speak of a supernatural grace by which God "adds" to our natural abilities, but this presumes an entire realm of supernatural truth and reality over and above what we by nature are capable of doing.

I would take a different tack, for people the world over—even without recourse to the theological riches of our tradition—can and do learn to act morally, even against self-interest, by devoting themselves to the common good of peace and justice. The energies Paul speaks of are not the energies of any core self, but rather energies that flow within all of us to will and to put into effect that which we will, here to build character and community. Despite many obvious differences, both Christian and Buddhist traditions strive to redirect human energies from self-interest to shared and awakened life. Jews and Christians teach of a Creator God who, always present to all of his creation, gifts us with Torah law to direct our lives. Buddhists teach of an unknowable yet compassionate encompassing reality countering the pervasive karmic causality that creates the deluded world we experience. Both recognize that the primal and present source of human endeavor surpasses anything within the construct of selfhood. Both accounts insist that we are responsible for the way things are in our own lives and in the wider world, even though the center of our energy and power lies elsewhere.[23]

20. O'Brien, *Epistle to the Philippians*, 279.

21. According to Vincent, work means "to put forth power," and will "expresses a determination or definite resolution of the will" (Vincent, *Critical and Exegetical Commentary*, 66).

22. On Torah observance, see Keenan, *Wisdom of James*, 73–83.

23. See Perry Schmidt-Leukel, "The Unbridgeable Gulf? Towards a Buddhist-Christian Theology

Paul writes simply that "it is God who works in you" (θεὸς γάρ ἐστιν ὁ ἐνεργῶν ἐν ὑμῖν 2:13) as the primal fountain of all our experiences, thoughts, and judgments. In a traditional Buddhist context, all those experiences, thoughts, and judgments flow from clusters of causes and conditions that stretch far and wide in space and far back in time beyond anyone's ability to calculate. The human individual is not the source and ground of all that she thinks and is. Even the very thought of awakening comes, not from ourselves, but from hearing the teaching as it flows from the compassionate reality that transcends self-effort, a teaching that is an outflow from the original mind that encompasses the cosmos.[24]

Paul, too, teaches that "faith comes from hearing" (ἄρα ἡ πίστις ἐξ ἀκοῆς Rom 10:17), triggering larger visions of personal participation in a community without borders. At the same time, he is engaged in the ambiguous struggles that mark all human endeavor. Had Paul known more of neuroscience, he may have recognized the impact of gospel hearing and learning on the neural conditioning of our energies, or those electric messages that circulate in our bodies and brains.[25] He does recognize a primal source for the energies that lie within each person and urges all toward a reconfiguration of our survival energies to apply beyond the scope of personal well-being, extending toward the furtherance of gospel salvation to embrace the entire community, and indeed, the entire world. It does no good to save oneself if the world is lost.[26]

This primal God works in us "both the willing and the working" (καὶ τὸ θέλειν καὶ τὸ ἐνεργεῖν) in order to enable us to realize eschatological reality and rise with Christ. It is God who "works" (ἐνεργῶν), and it is our "willing" (τὸ θέλειν) and our "working" (τὸ ἐνεργεῖν). So, both humans and their source, God, "work" (ἐνεργεῖν, energein). One is drawn to conclude that there are no fixed margins to the energies that flow through our minds and bodies, for humans do not construct a sense of identity in isolation from others. I embody my ancestors, and I write footnotes to acknowledge the presence of the many absent scholars who have had a part in forming my mind, such as

---

of Creation," in Perry Schmidt-Leukel, ed., *Buddhism, Christianity, and the Question of Creation, Karmic or Divine* [Burlington, VT: Ashgate, 2006] 111–77. Schmidt-Leukel has written intelligently and perceptively here about the issues and assumptions underlying Buddhist rejection of a creator deity and affirmation of karmic causality vis-à-vis Jewish and Christian affirmations of a transcendent Creator who creates time-bound creatures to be free and responsible without the Creator himself becoming entangled in time and space. No matter how they differ in their conceptions of ultimate meaning, both traditions insist on an unnamable ultimate, and both insist on moral living.

24. See Hakamaya, "Realm of Enlightenment."

25. Vincent translates in 2:13 "and it is for this that God energises your will and stimulates you to work," and notes that "grace itself engenders moral faculties and stimulates moral exertions" (Vincent, *Critical and Exegetical Commentary*, 64–65). I read that in terms of neuroscience, to describe the "stimulation" of the pathways whereby we construct character and community.

26. See Reumann, *Philippians*, 409. Reumann notes "Your salvation" focuses "on the corporate whole of believers, those in the church community whose lack of consideration for others among them and concentration on their own (individual) interests have been criticized in 2:3–4" (ibid.).

it is. Beyond those ancestors and scholarly predecessors lies some primal energy that bursts forth from metagalactic events light-years beyond our seeing.

Buddhists see this as the *dharmadhātu*, or the all-encompassing real, which empties itself into lives driven by karmic defilement into blindness—or through awakening into bodhisattva lives that invite all toward the practice of selfless awakening and fulfillment. When Mahāyāna thinkers come to consider what causes awakening, they identify the influence of the Buddha and his teaching as a dominant causality (Skt. *adhipati-pratyaya*), meaning that the teaching can tame karmic patterns of greed and anger and thereby dispose the practitioner to engage in the path of awakened practice.[27] But the direct cause (*hetu-pratyaya*), which in western theology is called the efficient cause, remains the effort of sentient beings who are turned either toward awakening or toward lust after power and glory.[28] The point is not to affirm that we ourselves cause either our own salvation from delusion or our own awakening, for there are no selves. Unaware as Mahāyāna thinkers were, and are, of our Reformation disputes, they always insist that the "working" of the Dharma acts as counteragent to selfhood and its myriad deceits. This working is identified apophatically in the Pure Land Buddhist traditions simply as the "other-power" of limitless awakening in the figure of Amida Buddha, the personal face of compassionate reality.

Paul adds that all this willing and working is "beyond delight" (ὑπὲρ τῆς εὐδοκίας). In the empty Christ, Paul writes, both setting out to work and working take us "beyond delight" (ὑπὲρ τῆς εὐδοκίας). Here is yet another use of "beyond" or "more than" (ὑπὲρ, *hyper*). So the outcome is not simple joy or delight (εὐδοκία); rather, risen life in Christ stretches forth to an eschatological joy that goes beyond any transient or delightful emotive state we have ever experienced.

Again, I do not think this "beyond delight" signifies a superlative degree of delight, as if being under the God-influence offers the marvelous, shining assurance of

---

27. Haidt speaks of our innate neurostructures as "the first draft of the mind" (Haidt, *Righteous Mind*, 172). The end result is a process sometimes called "self-domestication." Just as animal breeders can create tamer, gentler creatures by selective breeding for those traits, our ancestors began to selectively breed themselves. In the sutras, Buddha is often described as the tamer of humans, and gospel learning is likewise meant to domesticate humans so that they may expand their biological horizons to encompass the totality of life.

28. Bandhuprabha offers a brief analysis: "Furthermore, because the Tathāgatas' mirror wisdom is the object (*ālambana*) [that structures their minds] in the continuity of other beings, all the images of senses, their objects, and [the resultant] consciousnesses of world-transcendent and good worldly *dharma*s (*lokattara laukikakuśaladharma*) appear, because if there were no mirror wisdom, then all these *dharma*s would not so appear. They arise and are realized because of the force of this [mirror wisdom]. This means that the Tathāgatas' mirror wisdom is their dominant, enabling cause (*adhipatipratyaya*), and because of this, all the senses, sense objects, and their consciousnesses of all world-transcendent and good worldly *dharma*s arise, just as a multitude of images appear in a bright mirror. Although each sentient being has his own causal force (i.e., *hetupratyaya*), yet only because mirror wisdom is their dominant enabling cause (*adhipatipratyaya*) do these [images] come to arise. It is just like seeds, which would not produce sprouts without the earth, etc., or the images of things, which would not be reflected without a mirror" (Bandhuprabha, *Interpretation of the Buddha Land*, 126).

a felt belonging. Commentators argue about whether this "good pleasure" (εὐδοκία, here translated as "delight") pertains to humans living in harmony with one another, or to God, whose "good pleasure" is the final goal of God's active working in our minds. That it is God's delight is theologically congruent, since God made the world "for himself," without any need or ulterior motive, but simply as the outflow of delight and generosity.[29] This notion hearkens back to Bonaventure, for whom God works our salvation for his own good pleasure, since it is God's nature to love and overflow in grace. But in Paul, the salvation that God works within our willing and our working leads to a salvation that has little to do with subjective states of heavenly pleasure for God; it is a salvation "among you" (ἐν ὑμῖν), in the plural.[30]

So the phrase "beyond delight" (ὑπὲρ τῆς εὐδοκίας) is rather vague.[31] Perhaps its meaning is not simply delight or pleasure, whether God's or ours. It may suggest, rather, "that which seems" (δοκίας) "to be good" (εὐ), for the verb meaning of εὐδοκέω includes "to consider good, or to resolve."[32] The point, then, would be that the willing and the working—or the intent and the translation of that intent into action—goes beyond (ὑπὲρ) any present consideration of what appears to be good. The end purpose of the primal and cosmic energies that come before us and flow through us is beyond our power to see or imagine. The maxim has it that man proposes but God disposes; often human projects conceived with the best of intention have unintended side effects. The complex webs of our interactions are so vast that it is impossible to foresee the future effects, not only in natural ecologies, but also in human actions. Perhaps the science of an expanding universe with borders that fade from any defined view suggests a primal God who is not above in any heaven that first-century Christians could envisage, but who is at the centerless center of a never-ending expansion of new galaxies in an unfinished cosmos. Physics beggars anyone's imagination, even a physicist's. Theology should learn from the wonder of physics and freshen the concept of the God conceived by Paul as "my God" (τῷ θεῷ μου 1:3; ὁ δὲ θεός μου 4:19) to go beyond what

---

29. See Liddell and Scott, *An Intermediate Greek-English Lexicon* (1889; Oxford: Clarendon, 1990) 833b, in which ὑπὲρ followed by the genitive can signify "beyond" or "above" something—here, τῆς εὐδοκίας.

30. On delight, Collange writes: "Once again, '*en humin*' must be taken with reference to the community ('among you') and not individualistically ('within you') . . . Further, '*eudokia*' should not here be given the meaning it usually has in the Bible of 'God's good pleasure' (against the majority of commentaries). This would involve giving the unacceptable meaning of 'in conformity with' to the preposition '*huper*' ('*eudokias*'), a meaning so alien to it that B-D (231.2) feel obliged to attach '*huper tēs eudokias*' to the following sentence, which only raises more problems than it solves. The only interpretation which really takes account both of the context and grammatical rigour is the one which gives '*eudokia*' its anthropological meaning of 'good understanding'" (Collange, *Epistle of Saint Paul*, 110–11).

31. Reumann renders the phrase "above and beyond goodwill" but elsewhere opts for taking "*eudokia*" as "goodwill by and among human beings" (Reumann, *Philippians*, 388–89, 410).

32. Bauer, *Greek-English Lexicon*, 319.

anyone with the cosmological understanding of his time could have conceived as the primal source and final end of all meaning.

In Gregory of Nyssa's understanding, there is no final limit to the "stretching forth" that the gospel inscribes on our minds and hearts, and no consideration or commitment can set its definite boundaries. Nevertheless, even those vast vistas must always come to ground in the everyday lives that we live in commitment to the gospel of freedom and justice. This is not about viewpoints, however expansive, but about practice enfleshed in the worldly actions of Christ followers.

Empty Murmuring (2:14–16)

> 2:14 *Do all things without murmuring and arguing,* ¹⁵*so that you may be blameless and innocent, children of God without blemish in the middle of a crooked and deformed generation, in which you appear like stars in the cosmos.* ¹⁶*It is by your holding on to the word of life that I can boast for the day of Christ, because my running and laboring have not been empty.*

> 2:14 πάντα ποιεῖτε χωρὶς γογγυσμῶν καὶ διαλογισμῶν, ¹⁵ἵνα γένησθε ἄμεμπτοι καὶ ἀκέραιοι, τέκνα θεοῦ ἄμωμα μέσον γενεᾶς σκολιᾶς καὶ διεστραμμένης, ἐν οἷς φαίνεσθε ὡς φωστῆρες ἐν κόσμῳ, ¹⁶λόγον ζωῆς ἐπέχοντες, εἰς καύχημα ἐμοὶ εἰς ἡμέραν Χριστοῦ, ὅτι οὐκ εἰς κενὸν ἔδραμον οὐδὲ εἰς κενὸν ἐκοπίασα.

Paul's stricture against murmuring and arguing (χωρὶς γογγυσμῶν καὶ διαλογισμῶν 2:14) is aimed at taming the natural disobedience that would refuse to acknowledge that we are neither masters of our own lives nor architects of our own salvation. We do not have to author our own salvation, but we are to endeavor to work at it, to "do all things" (πάντα ποιεῖτε) while refraining from "murmuring and arguing."

Nonetheless, Paul himself was a very argumentative apostle. As we saw in Philippians Letter A, he murmured about being self-sufficient and able to cope on his own in all circumstances—albeit with a nod to some help from the Lord. In Gal 2:9, Paul murmurs aloud about those who are acknowledged as "pillars" (οἱ δοκοῦντες στῦλοι εἶναι) in Jerusalem. And above, in this Letter B of Philippians (1:15–18), he grumbles about Christ preachers who have selfish motives. Later, at the very beginning of Resurrection Letter C (3:2), he goes beyond grumbling, castigating as "dogs" those Christian teachers who fail to understand the power of Christ's resurrection and insist upon circumcision. Apparently not *all* contention and argumentation are without merit to Paul, for he argues often and harshly against any closure of gospel freedom.

So here, when Paul objects to "squabbling" or "bickering,"[33] he must have something else in mind. First and foremost, the issue is that argument over views or ideas distracts and leads our focus away from the gospel disclosure of risen life, diverting

---

33. Pace Fee, *Paul's Letter to the Philippians*, 236, 245.

attention to partisan alliances. The working out of our salvation is to flow from our oneness with the self-emptying Christ. We are to abide in faith consciousness without being constricted by any expression of that faith that was freeze-dried at one particular moment of the ongoing tradition. That is Paul's issue in 1:15–18 with those ill-intentioned preachers. Within the languaged world of our dependently arisen hereness, words and images change over time. This situation can impel us to cling to orthodox opinion rather than to the gospel that would free us from clinging to our own images of divine truth. And so Paul argues for the gospel and not for any final viewpoint, however theologically astute.[34]

Paul did not invent the phrase "murmuring and arguing" (χωρὶς γογγυσμῶν καὶ διαλογισμῶν). It echoes the Hebrew scriptures' Exodus description of the children of Israel murmuring and grumbling against God in the wilderness (Exod 16:7; Num 11:1). The arguing and contention Paul has in mind recalls the questioning and complaints of those early ancestors as they wandered back and forth in the desert. Some exegetes see this section of Paul as an extended "appeal for unconditioned self surrender to God in Christ."[35] Yet these words have their referents in Paul's time as well—particular individuals who are identifiable to his readers at the time, if not to us. Some exegetes believe that litigation in civil courts was common in Philippi[36] and that Paul wishes such legal argumentation to stop. Paul himself, of course, is attempting to defend his citizenship claim in the courts. But perhaps his intent here is to temper some contention within the Philippian congregation, which he will allude to in 4:2.

The Greek *goggusmōs* (γογγυσμῶς), translated as "murmuring," is onomatopoeia, much as the English word "murmuring" imitates the sound of people mumbling and muttering. Such a grumblingly resentful attitude assumes that one possesses an unappreciated truth that others should, but do not, recognize. But it is the second term, "arguing" (διαλογισμῶν, *dialogismōn*), that holds the key here. In our Greek philosophical heritage, Plato's *Dialogues* are described with the same term: "Dialogues" or "Conversations"—that is, arguments—wherein Plato leads his readers, point by point, through clear reasoning to purify their minds. Plato lifted the minds of tyro philosophers from material things to the contemplation of pure and unadulterated insight by means of a rhetorically measured, back-and-forth question and answer conversation. For philosophers, such argumentation (διάλογος, *dialogos*) is not seen at all as a hindrance to a full, rich, and rewarding life; for Plato and his heirs, this kind of discussion

---

34. See Hans Conzelmann, *1 Corinthians: A Commentary on the First Epistle to the Corinthians* (Philadelphia: Fortress, 1975) 33–38, esp. 38: "Paul defines his position first of all in negative terms, as a nonstandpoint." Paul is not concerned with "the propagating of [any] *Weltanschauung*, but [with] the destruction of every attempt to regard a *Weltanschauung* as the way of salvation" (ibid., 47).

35. Joachim Gnilka, *Der Philipperbrief [Herders theologischer Kommentar zum Neuen Testament]* (Freiburg, 1976) 151.

36. See Martin, *Philippians*, 117–18: "It is conceivable that the plague of settling quarrels at pagan law-courts had broken out at Philippi as at Corinth (see 1 Cor 6:1–11)."

is one of the first steps away from entanglement in the barbarous mud of this world and toward the light of understanding.

An early Christian who had read or listened to Plato's *Dialogues* might think to reach such mystical insight from reading the gospel in the Platonic idiom. And many of the Greek Fathers of the church did just that.[37] The result was the clothing of gospel insight in terms of Greek philosophy.[38] Yet here in Paul's writings, such dialogue or arguing (διαλογισμῶν) is not seen as a first step on the mystic path upward from matter to spirit, but rather as an obstacle to following the always-enfleshed truth of the Jesus path. Paul is not trying to capture the reality of things in their intelligible forms. Rather, he is seeking to lead his readers into an always-unfinished eschatological reality in Christ. Paul is not Plato, and he appeals to a gospel that is much more fleshy and visceral than Plato's philosophy. In the historical event, until Aquinas reintroduced Aristotle to Christians in the thirteenth century, Christian Platonism held sway in theology, placing the focus not on our organic life in Christ, but on theological ontologies—definitions of the nature of God the Father, Jesus the Son, and the Holy Spirit. And these definitions repeatedly splintered the church as each ecclesial party drew red lines that no shared life might cross.

There is clear awareness in our scriptures, as indeed in the scriptures of most religious traditions, that human reasoning is not necessarily conducive to wisdom, however useful such reasoning may be in the development of doctrine. Again and again, the old familiar arguments fence our minds within their accustomed positions. But in a harmonious world where selfless argument reigns and contexts of meaning are mutually understood, we can and do build upon the previous insights of wise teachers in whom we have confidence. We then move forward at each stage of an argument until, by the cumulative weight of practiced thinking, we may reach a fresh but solid and existential conclusion.[39] However, self-interest is seldom absent, contexts seldom agreed upon, and assumptions often unrecognized—all serving to confuse rather than to clarify.

Perhaps especially in religious argument, we all too often fail to proceed within a fixed and agreed context of meaning to build insight upon insight derived from all sides and than to move toward a shared and celebrated conclusion. Even Plato wrote

---

37. See A. Festugiere, *Contemplation et vie contemplaire selon Platon* (Paris: Vrin, 1950) 5: "The movement that issued from Jesus has given a new life to a preexistent organism, the structure of which leads back to Plato. When the Fathers 'think' their mysticism, they Platonize." Jean Daniélou, in his *Platonisme et théologie mystique: Doctrine spirituelle de Saint Gregorie de Nysse* (Paris: Aubrier, 1944), agues that Gregory of Nyssa counters Platonic "light" mysticism by focusing on the unknowability of God in entering the cloud of darkness.

38. Keenan, *Meaning of Christ*, 48–50.

39. See Bernard Lonergan, *Insight: A Study of Human Understanding* (Toronto: University of Toronto, 1992). Lonergan's critical philosophy sketches at length the pure, unrestricted desire to know, both in its biased delusions and in its clear progress. I have been much influenced by Lonergan, but I cannot concur when he appeals to the "isomorphism" of subject and object to ground the enterprise of metaphysics.

his *Dialogues* as a work of fiction, not as a report on actual discussions. Indeed, apart from those scripted and liberating dialogues, our discussions most often do follow accustomed ruts from which we argue for a winner-take-all victory that rarely satisfies anyone. Debate contests are exercises to determine who best presents an argument, and it hardly matters which side of the issue one is assigned. If one can successfully ignore one's opponent's arguments and score points, one wins the contest. In a televised presidential debate not too long ago, when the moderator asked one candidate a very specific question, he proceeded to give a completely unrelated answer. Asked again to address the question, the candidate replied with "You have your questions. I have my answers." A famous passage from Mahāyāna's *Scripture on the Explication of Underlying Meaning* describes a scene of Buddhist scholars gathered in a forest glen to argue with biting tongues and fiery speech, each one denouncing the others. Each leaves the discussion without a single new insight but with an even more tenacious attachment than before to the view he had embraced from the beginning.[40]

It is this kind of "quarrelsome argument over opinions" that Paul envisages as an obstacle to life in Christ,[41] for it mistakes the ideas and viewpoints being discussed—however correct they might be—for the gospel path that is to be practiced viscerally, under the impetus of the Spirit. James, in his epistle, describes this type of argument as the opposite of wisdom. For him, wisdom does not discriminate between this viewpoint and that viewpoint; wisdom is about adopting no single viewpoint.[42] If truth and reality are empty and eschatological, they cannot be pinned down in terms of viewpoints.

The Mahāyāna doctrine of emptiness directly critiques all viewpoints as themselves empty (Skt. *sarva-dṛṣṭi-śūnyatā*). And it is not only incorrect viewpoints that are to be emptied; no viewpoint or opinion whatsoever can capture the truth. The overarching problem is not the validity of viewpoints, but rather the viewpoint-engendering mind that proliferates views from a putatively secure stance of self-interest. All views are themselves empty of essential characteristics; they take their validity only from polymorphous causes and conditions, which often are not common to the two sides of an issue and which lead each side to think their views into language and then cling to them as guides for thinking and for validating our own "knowing." Yet arguments that are assumed to be normative and beyond challenge merely

---

40. See *The Scripture on the Explication of Underlying Meaning* (Saṃdhinirmocanasūtra), trans. John P. Keenan (Berkeley: Numata, 2000) 14–15. The Bodhisattva Dharmodgata describes the scene: "I once saw seventy-seven thousand heretics gathered in one place with their teachers to consider the descriptive marks of the ultimate meaning of all things. But although they thought, pondered, investigated, and thoroughly examined these marks of the ultimate meaning of all things, in the end they were unable to reach any conclusion. They went no further than to exclude certain interpretations, delineating and modifying their own interpretations. They confronted one another and argued fiercely. Their mouths emitted barbed comments, pointed, captious, angry, vicious; and then each went his separate way" (ibid.). In Mahāyāna, there are no descriptive marks of ultimate meaning.

41. Reumann, *Philippians*, 389–90. Reumann adds "wrangling" and "bitching."

42. On non-discrimination and non-partiality, see Keenan, *Wisdom of James*, 64–59.

draw people toward illusion, leading them to substitute opinionated conviction for practice of the path. And it is the path that is important. It is the path that is occluded by contentious argumentation and complaints that one party's position has not been graciously accepted by the other.

Our Christian history since the Reformation has witnessed much divisive argumentation, with each church party murmuring against its competitors. Arguments over justification were accompanied by harsh disagreements over papal authority and marked by Luther sinking into Paul-like insult and mockery.[43] The entire history of denominational fracturing in England and America hovered around issues of church "polity" or "structure" as Anglicans rejected the burgeoning papacy, Methodists eschewed tedious liturgy, Presbyterians replaced bishops with councils of elders, Congregationalists located authority in the local parish, and Quakers brushed aside all clerical offices in their communal silence. Always the issue was power: How to understand and locate ecclesial authority? Postmodern thinkers have made us particularly sensitive to the fact that issues of power often underlie the theological arguments and ecclesial positions. Many who have learned Christ and been formed by the liturgies of the church have remained loyal to the institutions, continuing to practice despite repeated revelations of power hoarding and clerical cover-ups. Others are so dispirited and disillusioned by these revelations that they simply chuck the entire business.

In any case, Paul advises us to avoid murmuring so that we "may be blameless and innocent" (ἵνα γένησθε ἄμεμπτοι καὶ ἀκέραιοι 2:14). What does it mean to be "blameless"? In Letter C at 3:6, Paul says that he was blameless (ἄμεμπτος) in regard to righteousness mediated to him through Torah. In this passage, it is the entire Philippian community, including Paul himself, that is to be blameless and without reproach. So it seems that, for Paul here, being blameless and innocent is adapted to the concrete social and cultural situation. The Philippians are to be "irreproachable, living a life at which no finger of criticism may be pointed."[44] They are to be blameless in the context of their shared public life in Philippi, for the point is how this Christian community is to negotiate a space for itself within a Roman colony. Yet the text here does not prescribe some unchanging core of Christian behavior for the centuries.

It has appeared to many that Paul radically changes his conception of Torah and has made a shift from the letter to the spirit of the law. He alludes in this passage to the Hebrew scriptures, referencing Deut 32:5 about blame and shame, Gen 1:17 about that storied perverse and crooked generation's murmuring in the wilderness, and Dan 12:3 about stars in the sky and the day of the Lord—"the wise shall *shine as luminaries*" (φωστῆρες) "in the sky."[45] Although he is writing to a Gentile community, Paul himself is grounded in these Torah teachings. His understanding of Torah content has not

---

43. Erick H. Erickson, *Young Man Luther: A Study in Psychoanalysis and History* (1962; New York: Norton, 1993) 98–125, on "Allness or Nothingness," and 223–60, on "Faith and Wrath."

44. Martin, *Philippians*, 118.

45. See Fee, *Paul's Letter to the Philippians*, 242.

changed greatly since his youth, and the moral injunctions he frequently offers differ little, if at all, from those of his Jewish ancestors. But he refuses to mediate Christ grace through Jewish (or any other) cultic or ethnic identity markers.[46] His objective is to negotiate a cultural space for the new communities of the risen Christ, and with this in mind, he advises the Philippians in 1:27 to act as good citizens in full awareness of the faith depths of the gospel of Christ.

While Paul seems to have negotiated his Torah learning within the cultural norms of his day, he never identifies the gospel with any particular culture. He is sensitive to the people he is working among, realizing that they live "in the middle" (μέσον) of the crooked world, not in a sheltered community that holds itself apart.[47] And yet, being in the world does not mean that one is to measure truth by worldly values. Paul differentiates cultural expectancy from gospel faith. He sees circumcision as it must have been seen by Greeks in his day: as a defining mark of being Jewish, of being a member of the elect, the covenant people. Thus, he thinks it inappropriate that Greeks be required to submit to that ritual, which in their eyes mutilates the beauty of the body. He also thinks it unnecessary to change people's diets to conform to the requirements of Torah. But even while rejecting the imposition of Jewish identity markers, Paul sees no need to replace them with Christian identity markers. We share in the very risen life of being in Christ just as we are. Paul never argues for a Christian identity as opposed to another cultural or social identity: in Christ there is neither Jew nor Greek, male nor female, slave nor free.

So Paul urges here that these Philippians to whom he writes be not only blameless, but also "innocent" (ἀκέραιοι), meaning "unmixed" or "undiluted" by the crooked world, even the crooked world of religious argumentation.[48] But to be innocent here does not mean to be naïve or unaware of the world about us; it is simply to be able to recognize other people authentically and to respond to them without a mindset warped by pride, greed, or anger. It indicates not so much innocence before God as selfless relationships with others. In other words, Paul is instructing the Philippians, along with all accidental readers of this letter, to be blameless and innocent "in the midst of this crooked and deformed world" (μέσον γενεᾶς σκολιᾶς καὶ διεστραμμένης

---

46. Dunn, *Theology of Paul the Apostle*, 371: "The danger which he particularly confronted was that ethnic identity would in the event count for more than the gracious call of God or significantly determine and qualify that call."

47. Martin, *Philippians*, 120: "The vocation of believers is to be found and fulfilled *in* (lit. 'in the middle of,' *meson*) such a world. The small Greek word *meson*—Paul's insertion into the citation from the lxx—has great significance." The citation Martin refers to, Deut 32:5, describes the Israelites murmuring and arguing in the desert: "They have dealt corruptly with him (i.e., God), they are no longer his children (lxx, *tekna*) because of their blemish (lxx, *mōmēta*); they are a perverse and crooked generation (lxx, *genea skolia kai diestrammenē*)."

48. Vincent, *Critical and Exegetical Commentary*, 67.

2:15). The image is striking: we envision blameless and innocent children of God living in the midst of a perverted world ruled by Roman delusion.[49]

Not only are we to be "children of God" (τέκνα θεοῦ),[50] we are to be "without blemish" (ἄμωμα). "Unblemished" renders the Hebrew word *tāmin*, which describes the absence of defects in an animal to be offered as sacrifice. As specified in Exod 29:1, only a spotless and perfect sacrifice is fit to be offered to God. But the implications of this are disturbing. Are we, as spotless children, to be a sacrificial offering to God? The language, in any case, is sacrificial. Perhaps the image derives from the humiliation that Christ brought on his own head. While in 2:17 Paul speaks of himself as a libation poured over the sacrificial altar of the Philippians' faith, in the hymn of the empty Christ, it is Jesus himself who accepts humiliation even to the point of death on the cross. Sacrificial language permeates Paul's writings.

What, then, would it mean to be an innocent and perfect sacrifice to God? What God might that be? What is this world into which we have been born, if it calls for such a sacrifice? But Paul is not talking about the will of a sadistic God. When he writes that "this generation is crooked" (γενεᾶς σκολιᾶς), Paul uses yet another expression from the Hebrew scriptures, specifically from the Song of Moses in Deut 32:5, which laments human inability to walk in straightness and uprightness. The world is crooked, not straight, as everyone agrees—progressives in that they want to improve it, conservatives in that they want to restore lost virtue, moral philosophers in that they want to retrain our behavior.[51] No one thinks that the present age is quite all right as it is.

The first of Buddhism's Four Noble Truths is that life in this world necessarily entails suffering, for it lacks reliable constancy. In fear of the loss that change always brings, the world of men and women becomes bent and distorted; we blame others for all the problems. The world has scoliosis of the soul. Just as our spines may be bent, so too our souls can become crooked when we do not walk upright before God. So Paul describes his generation as "deformed" (διεστραμμένης), from a verb meaning to deform or pervert. The contrast could not be starker: Paul portrays unblemished children of God living a life without murmuring or argumentation in the midst of a crooked world that distorts everything in service of self. Paul's description of the world reveals no bright-eyed optimism about human progress or prospects. Indeed, it is difficult to read his words attentively and continue to think of him as either a social conservative promoting traditional values or a starry-eyed reformer.

49. This crooked world "carried implications in the Greco-Roman world, quite apart from Old Testament background" (Reumann, *Philippians*, 392).

50. Martin, *Philippians*, 121: "They are *children of God*; and also 'the children of light' (1 Thes 5:5), a title also claimed by the sectarians of the Qumran community."

51. Haidt, *Righteous Mind*, 190: "So far in this book I've painted a portrait of human nature that is somewhat cynical. I've argued that Glaucon was right and that we care more about *looking* good than about truly *being* good."

And yet Paul tells his readers that in this world we are "to appear as stars in the cosmos" (ἐν οἷς φαίνεσθε ὡς φωστῆρες ἐν κόσμῳ 2:15). The verb "appear" (φαίνεσθε), in its starry context here means "to shine." Some interpret this phrase as describing what we already are[52]—that we are already living in the light of Christ. Some strains of the Mahāyāna tradition emphasize that everyone possesses an original mind of primal enlightenment, explaining that although we are entangled in karmic defilements and distortions, we all are at base "originally" enlightened.[53] But to interpret Paul's words as affirming a starlight quality for "the saints," which distinguishes them from this crooked generation, is to imagine that we Christians do not live in this world. Affirmations of our already-present life in Christ are aspirational and conative; they encourage us to strive to realize our embryonic potential and become luminous witnesses to the already-present risen life shared in Christ.

Still, Paul—the least of the apostles—is talking about standing out in contrast to one's contemporaries, whose perverted and crooked world is characterized by sin and delusion. He envisages winning the race, but stardom there is not a supernatural aura illumining those who live in Christ. To be luminous means to light up risen life in a way that attracts others. But this is often a faint witness, flickering among the clouds in distant skies. In the Gen 1:14–19 creation narrative, the luminaries are placed in the firmament by the Creator, and they "do not shine for their own sake; they shine to provide light for all the world."[54] So here, the experience of risen life as the now-empty structure of an eschatological fulfillment is to live in the empty Christ whose light reaches throughout the cosmos.

Within the imagery that is available to Paul, everything centers on this earth, with the waters below and the stars above. In the cosmos as we perceive it in our day, neither sun nor moon nor stars—which we now know to be suns in other worlds—are cozily related to this home planet of ours. Still, Paul does not hesitate to hold that goal before us so that we may persevere in our striving: We are to be as stars in the night sky, beckoning with a faint luminescence. We are not to lord it over others as though the sun and the moon rise and set at our direction. We are not the center of anything cosmic. From Paul's—and our—earthly perspective, stars shine quietly in the night, not even causing tides to ebb and flow. They are indifferent to the magical uses humans may make of them, whether as astrological omens or as cosmic bodies attesting to the Lord above. They are just there, shining with no discernible purpose.[55]

---

52. Silva reminds his readers that "the most basic New Testament incentive to holy living is an emphasis on what we already are," noting a parallel in Matt 5:14–16, where "Jesus describes his disciples as ones who *already* are 'the light of the world'" (Silva, *Philippians*, 127).

53. See Sallie B. King, "Buddha Nature Thought and Mysticism," in *Buddha Nature: A Festschrift in Honor of Minoru Kiyota*, ed. Paul J. Griffiths and John P. Keenan (Reno: Buddhist Books International, 1991) 139–52.

54. Bruce, *Philippians*, 85.

55. The ten similes for the pure Dharma Realm in *Interpretation of the Buddha Land* describe the Dharma realm in its unconditional purity as spontaneously encompassing all sentient beings without

But they do lighten the darkness of the night sky, betokening worlds hardly imagined and reminding us that we are not the center of all life.

We become like stars in the cosmos when we "hold on to the word of life" (λόγον ζωῆς ἐπέχοντες 2:16).[56] This "word" (λόγον), including Paul's inventive words of gospel defense, is not the same thing as the endless words of argumentation (διαλογισμῶν) he rejected in 2:14. Paul does not shrink from an argument, but seldom does he accept the either/or dichotomy of most disputes. There is an unbridgeable difference between resurrection faith and all forms of philosophical debate on life. Thus, "the word of life" (λόγον ζωῆς, *logon zōēs*)—a phrase that appears only here in Paul—hearkens back to the constant tension between Paul's longing for the cessation that is death and completing his worldly task of enunciating the gospel of continued life in the risen Christ. As Paul prepares to plead his case before the Roman authorities, he wishes not to bring shame on the gospel, but rather to witness to its living power to transform lives away from self-absorption and toward living in Christ. Never shy in his rhetorical endeavors to preach to the Gentiles and refute his critics, Paul announces a word of life that—by erasing the final boundary between death and life—abides in equality wisdom (Skt. *samatā-jñāna*) between this world and our eschatological inclusion now *in* Christ and the not-yet experience of life *with* Christ beyond.

Paul's distaste for the kind of argumentation that contents itself with urging viewpoints is the reason he withdrew so silently from engaging with the philosophers of Athens (Acts 17:16–34), for their words do not capture any absolute right or wrong. The "word of life" enunciates the speaking of the Father from silence, the speaking that flows from identification with Christ—it does not contend. From the beginning, from the beginningless beginning, such life-words are enunciated not to argue people into compliance, but to open new horizons wherein they may experience life and—disregarding self-referential goals and possessions—practice the emptying of self for the sake of the Father and living authentically for the sake of others in freedom. This word gives life simply because it opens up marginless possibilities and visions to living beings, liberating their lives from the prison of delusions that define an upside down world as really real. We are to work out our salvation, for we have been given a word of life. This is the gospel that Paul preaches.

Paul says all this "so that I may boast" (εἰς καύχημα ἐμοι 2:16), and yet there follows no claim to self-sufficiency, no boasting on his own behalf. He takes pride instead

---

eliciting any activity (Bandhuprabha, *Interpretation of the Buddha Land*, 97–121).

56. Pace Vincent, *Critical and Exegetical Commentary*, 69. Vincent renders the phrase as "holding forth the word of life" (ibid.). For a summary of discussions around the verb *epechō* here, see Reumann, *Philippians*, 394. Suggested meanings have included "hold fast," "hold forth," or "direct attention to a matter." The latter would repeat the theme of attending to or focusing on the mind of Christ in 2:5, the introductory sentence to the hymn. It seems to me less likely to mean "to hold forth," as in proclaiming the gospel word, but rather to keep a focused mind on the empty Christ. Perhaps a dynamic rendering might be "to display" or "make present" the word of life, so that you may be irreproachable in the eyes of others.

in the gospel accomplishments of others as unblemished children of God (τέκνα θεοῦ 2:14) whose silent witness is enunciated in the emptiness hymn. The success of Paul's career is not found in his accomplishments, but in the Philippians' shared lives. Even so, he boasts not of them but "because of" their endeavors, taking the participle "holding on" (ἐπέχοντες 2:16) as causal. As I read the passage, Paul's celebratory boasting seems based upon something that goes beyond the cause-and-effect flow of time. His boasting "for the day of Christ" (εἰς ἡμέραν Χρίστοῦ) is based upon eschatological hope. The day of Christ is Paul's evocation of the reality of the day of the Lord, a notion found in the prophet Amos and throughout the Hebrew scriptures, as well as in the New Testament. It is the day of the coming of Christ, the *parousia*, the once-again presence of Christ that is now supplied by the Spirit among us. That "day" is that toward (εἰς) which all gospel efforts tend and by which they are structured[57]—an end-time awakening to a life that erases the world-boundaries between living and dying. It is an eschatological consciousness that envisages, however much in mirrored enigma, risen life in its more than exalted fulfillment, beyond any images of restored heroes or afterdeath imaginings.

We do await the coming of Christ, for the Christian path is an ongoing endeavor that does not come to a linear end. As structured within the mind of Christ wisdom, that end is overflowing and unending life, reaching toward ever fuller truth in eschatological hope beyond all our words, all our worlds. And that, I think, is what the coming of Christ means—not a particular point in linear time when an exalted Christ returns and declares us winners of the contest. Racing through life in a struggle for survival has meaning only in terms of an evolutionary competition for self-benefit. But attentiveness to the day of Christ is the very timeless structure of our time-segmented lives, compelling us forward today, tomorrow, and the same forever.

Paul uses the term "to boast" (καύκημα) elsewhere to mean prideful self-promotion, but here he boasts of the Philippians. The community in Philippi stands as his eschatological witness; he can boast on their account within the horizon of "the day of the Lord." Holding on to this life-word has opened their minds and awakened them to life in the empty Christ. Paul "can boast for the day of Christ" because his "running and laboring have not been empty" (ὅτι οὐδὲ εἰς κενὸν ἔδραμον οὐδὲ εἰς κενὸν ἐκοπίασα 2:16) and because the truth he pursues is the unfinished reality of eschatological faith in risen life. It is not a "labored running" or straining of muscles in the attempt to keep up the pace.[58] Paul's running the race to achieve the furtherance of the gospel has not been in vain. It has had an effect and is not empty, for it moves from glory to glory.

---

57. Reumann, *Philippians*, 395.

58. Ibid., 396. Reumann notes that Paul employs the same verb, *trechō*, "to run," as "exertion" (Rom 9:16; cf. 1 Cor 9:26). Reumann cites Gal 2:2, where Paul's mission to the Gentiles is agreed upon in Jerusalem, "lest somehow I should be running or had run in vain" (μὴ πως εἰς κενὸν τρέχω ἢ ἔδραμον). To bolster his point that the gospel calls forth exertion and effort, he translates ἐκοπίασα, not as "laboring," but as "struggling" (ibid.).

Paul's work here is "not empty" (οὐκ εἰς κενὸν 2:16) and "not without effect" (οὐδὲ εἰς κενὸν), for he follows the Christ who in emptying himself (ἑαυτὸν ἐκένωσεν 2:7) is by that very deed (*quo facto*) more than exalted (ὑπερύψωσεν 2:9). Risen life entails the indivisibility of powerless emptiness and the eschatological upward thrust toward a fulfillment that is beyond powerful. Similarly in 1 Corinthians, after celebrating the mystery of resurrection faith, Paul urges his friends to "be steadfast, immovable, always growing in the work of the Lord, for you know that your labor in the Lord is not empty of effect" (ὁ κόπος ὑμῶν οὐκ ἔστιν κενὸς ἐν κυρίῳ 15:58).

Pouring out Life (2:17–18)

2:17 *But even if I am being poured out as a libation over the sacrificial altar of your faith, I am glad and rejoice with all of you—*[18]*and in the same way you also must be glad and rejoice with me.*

2:17 ἀλλὰ εἰ καὶ σπένδομαι ἐπὶ τῇ θυσίᾳ καὶ λειτουργίᾳ τῆς πίστεως ὑμῶν, χαίρω καὶ συγχαίρω πᾶσιν ὑμῖν: [18]τὸ δὲ αὐτὸ καὶ ὑμεῖς χαίρετε καὶ συγχαίρετέ μοι.

As with every scripture in our tradition, Paul's letter to the Philippians has been carefully scrutinized again and again throughout the ages. In contrast to the Buddhist canon, with its many thousands of scriptures and commentaries, the Christian canon of the New Testament is relatively brief, consisting of only twenty-seven texts. And every single word of those texts has been squeezed and massaged for every possible meaning. Thus it is not surprising that even the adversative force of the first word in 2:17, "but" (ἀλλὰ), is read differently by different commentators. It appears perhaps to indicate some kind of break with, or contrast to, what has gone before. However, Paul is writing a letter, not a coherent essay containing theological statements that proceed in logical sequence and that might well be balanced by any number of "yes buts." In itself, a conjunction like "but" (ἀλλὰ) has little specific meaning, so it may simply serve to move the letter along. In this instance, however, it seems to signal a rather abrupt change of subject.

After describing his pride and joy in the faith of the Philippians who place their faith in the empty and exalted Christ, Paul now suddenly alludes to the imminent possibility of his death under imperial charges. He is looking to the end game: his own dying. In the old Latin translation of Phil 1:23, Paul now looks toward "being dissolved and being with Christ" after closing his own personal accounts and resting from his labors. The Mahayanists would call this *parinirvāṇa*, or the entrance into blissful peace and the cessation of all suffering following the end of all labor and all need for labor.

Paul writes of himself here as "a libation poured out" (εἰ καὶ σπένδομαι) "over the altar of sacrifice" (ἐπὶ τῇ θυσίᾳ καὶ λειτουργίᾳ). The term "pour out" (σπένδομαι) is often used of a sacrifice: a drink offering or libation of wine or olive oil poured over a propitiatory sacrifice. To Paul, it suggests the sense of spent energy in his race for the furtherance of the gospel. He must also have had in mind the shedding of his blood, perhaps as in the sacrifices of some pagan cults, but he uses the sacrificial term metaphorically.[59] More to the forefront of his consciousness, no doubt, is the blood that poured from the broken body of the crucified Christ—understood here in this early Christian scripture as the sacrifice through which Christ emptied himself. The point is Paul's willingness to spend his life for the sake of the gospel and, in that endeavor, to empty himself. He sees his life as a libation that will be poured out over the execution ground, as if that place of dying is the altar of sacrifice. He does not regard his life as something to cling to. It is nothing special. Rather he "rejoices" (χαίρω) in the pouring out of his apostolic service, for that will be credited to the account of the Philippians who have responded to his gospel.[60]

A parallel notion is expressed in 4:6 of the Deutero-Pauline epistle 2 Timothy, where the author—writing as Paul—says he is "on the point of being sacrificed, for the time of my departure has come" (Ἐγὼ γὰρ ἤδε σπένδομαι, καὶ ὁ καιρὸς τῆς ἀναλύσεώς μου ἐφέστηκεν). Second Timothy echoes Paul's words in Phil 2:17—where he writes that he is poured out (καὶ σπένδομαι)—in saying he is "about to be poured out" (ἤδε σπένδομαι). And the term translated "departure" (ἀναλύσεώς) in the 2 Timothy passage calls to mind Phil 1:23, where Paul writes that his desire is to depart (ἀναλῦσαι) and to be with Christ. The author of that Deutero-Pauline letter clearly has in mind Paul's references to departing and to the pouring out of his blood as expressed in Philippians. If we live in Christ, we also are to die in Christ.

The notion of Jesus' death as sacrificial appears frequently in the New Testament (Eph 5:2; Heb 9:26, 10:12). The idea does not, however, find great favor among many theologians and thinkers today, for it seems to imply that God requires the appeasement of a bloody sacrifice before saving human beings. It suggests a bloodthirsty God and the desirability of victimhood. The medieval theology that Christ had to make satisfaction for our sins by his death on the cross implies that God's majesty needed to be appeased by a sacrifice befitting his divine status, and it was for this that he sent his true and only Son. Although this notion may be consonant with feudal structures in the time of Anselm, who taught such a theology, it is simply repugnant in today's more democratic world. What kind of God would demand that anyone suffer and die for any reason at all? This suggests not a benign father who loves all his children, but rather a tyrannical father who nurses his wrath at being wronged by his children.

Our scriptures and tradition do, however, speak of sacrifice; it was a common and accepted practice in the ancient world. In fact, self-sacrifice is not an uncommon idea in our modern world. Martin Luther King Jr. famously preached that without sacrifice there is no living of the gospel. And indeed he lived that sacrifice to the very

---

59. O'Brien, *Epistle to the Philippians*, 306.
60. Ibid.

pouring out of his own blood. People all over this world of ours, in every religious tradition, spend themselves in the furtherance of wisdom and compassion. But we do not today offer bloody sacrifices on our altars. Zoroastrians offer grain, fruit, and flowers on their altars. Christians likewise bedeck their altars with flowers and sometimes incense, offering their sweet aromas to God's nostrils. And we know of people the world over who dedicate themselves and all their life energies, even to the point of transgressing the boundary between life and death, to further the gospel of wisdom and compassion. Moreover, we speak of the Eucharist as a "sacrifice of praise and thanksgiving," whereby we express gratitude for the emptying Christ who pioneered the path of our emptiness and liberation from the serfdom of sin and delusion.

It is in this sense that Paul speaks in 2:17 of pouring out his very lifeblood as a sacrifice for the sake of the Philippians so that they may participate in the anticipatory reality of eschatological resurrection. Paul's blood is poured out "upon the sacrificial altar of your faith" (ἐπὶ τῇ θυσίᾳ καὶ λειτουργίᾳ τῆς πίστεως ὑμῶν), for only faith entrustment opens up unrealized vistas of eschatological reality. The term "sacrifice" (θυσία, *thysia*), the usual word for sacrifice in the New Testament, is here twinned with the term "liturgy" (λειτουργία, *leitourgia*), the Greek word for a "public service." This term appears infrequently in the Christian scriptures, and most understand it here not to refer to a cultic rite, but rather to the service Paul renders to the Philippians. That is to say, the two terms "sacrifice" and "service" are here a hendiadys, or a figure of speech in which two words are used together to express a single notion. In this case, the combination (ἐπὶ τῇ θυσίᾳ καὶ λειτουργίᾳ) signifies a "sacrificial service" or, since they are introduced by the preposition "on" (ἐπὶ), perhaps more imaginatively, "on the altar of sacrifice,"[61] since altars are set up in public, open spaces. Accordingly, Paul is willing to pour out his lifeblood on a sacrificial altar, specified as the altar of the faith of the Philippians. This phrase "of your faith" (τῆς πίστεως ὑμῶν) thus explains what that publicly open sacrificial altar concretely is. The Philippians' faith in the empty Christ is the sacrificial altar for which and upon which Paul is willing to sacrifice his very life.

Of course, neither Paul nor Jesus died upon an actual altar of sacrifice. Especially since the European Age of Reason, critics have argued that things recounted in the Christian gospels never actually occurred. Embracing a philosophy of historical empiricism, they attribute reality only to what can be sensed directly. Accordingly, to their mind, much that is recounted in the gospels, including Paul's "altar of sacrifice," cannot possibly be anything more than airy metaphor. Some Christian believers respond by adopting the very same empirical approach while insisting that everything in the Bible is indeed empirically true, having been witnessed directly by trustworthy people who attest to that truth. But such a theology merely pits a supernatural empiricism against a naturalistic empiricism, although neither has much to do with truth. Both limit the real to what is directly perceived, all the while dismissing insight into

---

61. Sumney, *Philippians*, 57.

unfinished meaning and eschatological commitment to practice as mere afterthoughts. But insight and understanding lie at the heart of the gospel; we are to learn and take on the mind of Christ. Commitment is central, for we are saved by Christ faith, and that entails conscious decision and commitment. And here, since the sentence is conditional ("But even if," or ἀλλὰ εἰ καὶ), Paul's sacrificial decision does necessitate even his dying. His share in the risen life of Christ need not have—and is not recounted in any of our sources as actually having had—any empirical verification. There can be no empirical proof of resurrection or of awakening.

When Paul says, "But even if I am being poured out as a libation over the sacrificial altar of your faith" (ἀλλὰ εἰ καὶ σπένδομαι ἐπὶ τῇ θυσίᾳ καὶ λειτουργίᾳ τῆς πίστεως ὑμῶν), he is no longer claiming self-sufficiency as he did in Letter A. The Philippians' hymn countered that stance, and now he embraces the empty Christ, recontextualizing his own life in those terms. The "liturgy" (λειτουργία 2:17) concretely signals the public liturgy wherein the Philippians celebrate the empty and exalted Christ, and that liturgy speaks clearly of his sacrifice (θυσία) on the cross as an emptying of self. Paul's eschatological boasting in the Philippians is elicited specifically by their presentation to him of this hymn from their liturgies, which flows from their faith (τῆς πίστεως ὑμῶν), praising Christ's sacrifice. This sentence is not just metaphor; it speaks of the concrete practices of the Philippians when they gather together in faith confession to the empty Christ. Paul, then, in his prison, embraces Christ as so celebrated and seeks to conform his life to the mind of Christ.

Against common expectations, Paul tells his hearers that "I am gladdened" (χαίρω 2:17) and "you too are all to rejoice" (καὶ συγχαίρω πᾶσιν ὑμῖν) in his willingness to die within the empty faith of Christ, so that in their [now] "mutual joyous togetherness" (καὶ ὑμεῖς χαίρετε καὶ συγχαίρετέ μοι 2:18), they "join in the very same endeavor" (τὸ δὲ αὐτὸ) of pouring out their life energies for the sake of the gospel of life. Paul talks about their interbeing, their mutual relationships that go beyond separate individuals standing alone over against one another, now no longer hampered by considerations of who is patron and who is client. As it turns out, their gift to him did not mean that they wished to reduce him to a dependent client by which one party is beholden to the other. Paul now realizes, after reading and meditating upon the emptiness hymn, that his relationships with the Philippians are affirmed in mutual and healthy dependence upon one another. It is their faith that is expressed in their liturgy of the self-emptying sacrifice of Christ, and Paul now takes refuge in that empty Christ with hope in this newly enunciated exaltation of risen life beyond empirical categories.

The evolutionary struggle impels us to consume one another in competition for scarce resources as we contend for status. But the gospel counters that organic imperative by stressing wisdom and compassion, even to the point of sacrificing our own benefit—even our very lives—for others. Paul's recommendation of shared joy is elicited from his awareness that he shares life with the Philippians, and indeed, in the gospel path, with the entire world. There is but one life in which we all share, and it becomes life in Christ when we realize that we do not have to consume others or construct our security upon the impoverishment of others. There is but one life through which we approach the ineffable cosmic mystery of our many lives in as many tongues as we can enunciate.

One does wonder sometimes about Paul: Did he really face dying with such equanimity? Empty of any abiding core being as we are, how do we face death with equanimity and face living in peaceful awareness of our dying? People often do die bravely, but it helps to have a little support from one's friends. And so here Paul takes heart from the Philippian hymn as he anticipates pouring out his own lifeblood. Our scriptures present Paul as living in Christ: as being one with Christ and thereby being one with his brothers and sisters in Philippi, and Ephesus, and Corinth, and throughout the world of his day on into our worlds of this new Jerusalem and this new America. But he became so only through a constant stretching forth in sustained dialogue with all those people with whom he shared faith. The image of Paul as a standalone saint, inspired by his singular experiences to impart the truth to the less than faithful, discounts his humanity. There is nothing to be gained by pretending that Paul himself did not draw strength in the fields of the Lord from the many others who labored with him there. His many relationships involved far more than a one-way flow of insight and understanding from him to them, for they all were engaged in a common endeavor.

Paul frequently expresses his affection for, and friendship with, the Philippians in his struggle for the furtherance of the gospel. We know that he did have his problems with people, as they did with him. Indeed in 2 Corinthians, immediately after writing of his ineffable experiences—his visions and revelations in Christ (12:1–6)—Paul ceases "boasting" in the strength of his flesh and in his self-power to report on the "thorn in his flesh" that bothered and pained him and that never was healed. He is not an aloof man who focuses primarily on the peace that comes with dying. Indeed, in 2 Cor 11:23b–29, Paul lists an amazing series of sufferings that have attended his gospel endeavors:

> I have worked much harder, been in prison more frequently, been flogged more severely, and been exposed to death again and again. Five times I received from the Jews the forty lashes minus one. Three times I was beaten with rods; once I was stoned; three times I was shipwrecked. I spent a night and a day in the open sea. I have been constantly on the move. I have been in danger from rivers, in danger from bandits, in danger from my own countrymen, in danger from Gentiles; in danger in the city, in danger in the country, in danger at sea; and in danger from false brothers. I have labored and toiled and have often gone without sleep; I have known hunger and thirst and have often gone without food; I have been cold and naked. Besides everything else, I face daily the pressure of my concern for all the churches. Who is weak, and I do not feel weak? Who is led into sin, and I do not inwardly burn?

Paul did have his arguments with false brothers who would circumscribe the gospel, but he made his peace with true brothers and sisters in the empty, uncircumscribed Christ. And the Philippians taught him to live in the reality of that empty Christ.

As we marvel at Paul's many adventures and the sufferings he endured, perhaps we underestimate his weakness. He himself frequently says that he is weak, and he cites all the sufferings he endured as reasons why he is weak. The chronic disease he suffered, whatever it was, must have taken its toll. The beatings must have left their mark on his body. Surviving in the open sea for a day and a night after being shipwrecked must have had its own effect. So I think that when Paul says he is weak, he is not making a theological point so much as describing his mature, perhaps aging, body. He is worn out and weak, aware of the impermanence of his bodily form. He has experienced the transience of his own being-here. When he speaks of his body, he does not speak negatively, rejecting it, but he is aware of its frailty.

In the end, the body never does prevail for long. Paul writes from deep personal knowledge that all life is unsatisfactory, suggesting that all embodied life is characterized by suffering and pain. And so he configures his life in the empty Christ. We have no similar records of Jesus suffering before the time of his passion and crucifixion, for he died young and at the height of his adult vigor. By contrast, at the time Paul is writing this letter, he is imprisoned and awaiting trial and sentencing, all the while vividly aware that his energies are waning and his days are numbered. Still, to die is gain, and he would rather die to be with Christ.

Paul is aware in the sinews of his body of the incarnate presence of the risen Christ, of the Christ who was obedient even to death on the cross. So Paul speaks in 1:23 of longing to depart and be with Christ. He is not belittling the energy he demonstrated as a younger man. However, the energetic zeal he first felt for the Torah has since been redirected to the furtherance of the gospel—a Torah-less Torah. It is not that Paul has rejected Torah as if his zeal for it were somehow just a big mistake. Never does Paul say anything of the kind! But he rejects his previous attitude, which circumscribed the presence of the spirit of God to what he now perceives as an overbearing orthodoxy. He has worked long and hard for the gospel. He has visited and written letters to churches throughout the Hellenistic world—to communities in lands now known as Turkey, Macedonia, Greece, and Italy. The letters he received in return are now lost, but no one keeps sending letters when replies are not forthcoming.

Paul travels toward Rome in his chains, and yet he still has plans to go on to Spain. Imprisoned, anticipating his day in court, it is no wonder that he has a deep sense of the equality of life and death. The abiding joy for mystic Paul, in the living and the dying that is our very being, has become for him a felt presence; he has a vivid awareness that our lives here in these bodies are always, as the existentialists say, life unto death. Death is not simply an interruption in an otherwise energetic and successful life career. It is an unavoidable part of the natural structure of our mortal living and acting. It seems that Paul's mystic revelations in Christ have brought him to a point of meditative fearlessness. He does not boast bravely as he faces his own mortality, nor does he, like Dylan Thomas, advise us to "Rage, rage against the dying of the light."[62] In confronting the prospect of death, Paul is neither a courageous soldier facing an enemy, nor a defiant artist. Death is not an enemy to Paul. All his endeavors have been in and of the Christ who not only lived, but who also died to rise again in a life ineffably real beyond measuring friend and foe.

But here in his letter to the Philippians, as indeed in his other writings, Paul speaks as one much reduced by constant physical struggle and by the suffering he has endured. He is simply worn out. However, he embraces being sacrificed for Christ faith; he does not engage in murmuring and resentment against his varied oppressors or his Roman guards. He knows well that we should not engage in "murmurings" against anyone and that we should not "argue" ourselves to death, as church people are wont to do. He is willing, however, to launch attacks upon those he perceives to be enemies of the cross of Christ by their assertions of a victorious religious selfhood. In Letter C, the Resurrection Letter, he will even call such people "dogs" (3:2).

Paul knows how to defend the faith, and his polemics are energetic to the point of insult. Apparently, his efforts were sometimes successful. The unidentified judge or teacher Paul excoriates in Romans fades from Christian awareness, so that now we do not even know his name.[63] Yet Paul reserves such harsh language for those who would circumscribe gospel freedom. He launches no diatribe against the Athenian philosophers who held forth on the Areopagus, for they never came back to consider Paul's apologetics for the cross; they had no deleterious effect on the openness of the emergent communities. Of course, there really is no apologetic defense for crucifixion. The cross stands as its own sign that all divine apologetics fail in the darkness of the ongoing march of human history and cruelty. In any case, Paul clearly has grown tired. He is willing to be poured out as libation on the sacrificial altar that is the faith of the Philippians, enunciated in their hymn of the empty Christ. His life is now grounded upon the eschatological structure of the Philippians' faith in the emptied and exalted Christ. He is not a standalone guy. Paul's life is not his life alone.

Travel Plans (2:19–30)

> 2:19 *I hope in the Lord Jesus to send Timothy to you without delay, so that, knowing about you, I may take heart.* ²⁰*I have no one like him with such genuine heartfelt concern for you.* ²¹*In general people look out for their own interests, not those of Jesus Christ.* ²²*But Timothy's worth you know, how like a son with a father he has slaved with me for the Gospel.* ²³*I hope therefore to send him as*

---

62. Dylan Thomas, "Do Not Go Gentle into That Good Night," https://www.poets.org/poetsorg/poem/do-not-go-gentle-good-night.

63. See D. A. Campbell, *Deliverance of God*, 519–600, on "Rereading Romans 1:18—3:20 —Indictment reconsidered," which treats Paul's rejection of "The Teacher's system."

soon as I see how things go with me; ²⁴*and I trust in the Lord that I will also come soon.*

²⁵*Still, I think it incumbent on me [immediately] to send to you Epaphroditus—my brother, co-worker, and fellow soldier, your letter-carrier who ministered to my need;* ²⁶*for he has been longing for all of you, and has been distressed because you heard that he was ill.* ²⁷*He was indeed so ill that he nearly died. But God had mercy on him, and not only on him but on me also, so that I would not have yet another sorrow.* ²⁸*I am eager to send him with all haste, so that you may rejoice at seeing him again and that I may be less anxious.* ²⁹*Welcome him then in the Lord with all joy, and honor such people,* ³⁰*because he came close to death for the work of Christ, risking his life to make up for those services that you could not give me.*

2:19 Ἐλπίζω δὲ ἐν κυρίῳ Ἰησοῦ Τιμόθεον ταχέως πέμψαι ὑμῖν, ἵνα κἀγὼ εὐψυχῶ γνοὺς τὰ περὶ ὑμῶν. ²⁰οὐδένα γὰρ ἔχω ἰσόψυχον ὅστις γνησίως τὰ περὶ ὑμῶν μεριμνήσει, ²¹οἱ πάντες γὰρ τὰ ἑαυτῶν ζητοῦσιν, οὐ τὰ Ἰησοῦ Χριστοῦ. ²²τὴν δὲ δοκιμὴν αὐτοῦ γινώσκετε, ὅτι ὡς πατρὶ τέκνον σὺν ἐμοὶ ἐδούλευσεν εἰς τὸ εὐαγγέλιον. ²³τοῦτον μὲν οὖν ἐλπίζω πέμψαι ὡς ἂν ἀφίδω τὰ περὶ ἐμὲ ἐξαυτῆς· ²⁴πέποιθα δὲ ἐν κυρίῳ ὅτι καὶ αὐτὸς ταχέως ἐλεύσομαι. ²⁵Ἀναγκαῖον δὲ ἡγησάμην Ἐπαφρόδιτον τὸν ἀδελφὸν καὶ συνεργὸν καὶ συστρατιώτην μου, ὑμῶν δὲ ἀπόστολον καὶ λειτουργὸν τῆς χρείας μου, πέμψαι πρὸς ὑμᾶς, ²⁶ἐπειδὴ ἐπιποθῶν ἦν πάντας ὑμᾶς, καὶ ἀδημονῶν διότι ἠκούσατε ὅτι ἠσθένησεν. ²⁷καὶ γὰρ ἠσθένησεν παραπλήσιον θανάτῳ· ἀλλὰ ὁ θεὸς ἠλέησεν αὐτόν, οὐκ αὐτὸν δὲ μόνον ἀλλὰ καὶ ἐμέ, ἵνα μὴ λύπην ἐπὶ λύπην σχῶ. ²⁸σπουδαιοτέρως οὖν ἔπεμψα αὐτὸν ἵνα ἰδόντες αὐτὸν πάλιν χαρῆτε κἀγὼ ἀλυπότερος ὦ. ²⁹προσδέχεσθε οὖν αὐτὸν ἐν κυρίῳ μετὰ πάσης χαρᾶς, καὶ τοὺς τοιούτους ἐντίμους ἔχετε, ³⁰ὅτι διὰ τὸ ἔργον Χριστοῦ μέχρι θανάτου ἤγγισεν, παραβολευσάμενος τῇ ψυχῇ ἵνα ἀναπληρώσῃ τὸ ὑμῶν ὑστέρημα τῆς πρός με λειτουργίας.

Paul's now openhearted friendship and fellowship with the Philippian community shines through these verses. Timothy, Epaphroditus, Paul, and the Philippians are all on the same page, sharing the space that has been hollowed out in their lives by the empty Christ. In these twelve verses, Paul becomes rather chatty and introduces no major theological themes. He does not write of the empty Christ, nor does he discuss the sacrificial meaning of his own life and death as configured in terms of the Philippian liturgical celebration of Christ. At least this passage is not explicitly theological.

Paul turns here to news of, and plans for, his coworkers: Timothy, who often accompanied him, and Epaphroditus, the letter carrier from the Philippian community who was perhaps an overseer or agent deputed for that specific task. Peter O'Brien notes that these verses "appear at first glance to have little significance," noting that this section of Paul's letter accordingly has "often been treated as such."[64] This seems to me fair warning not to wrestle the text back into the theological arena in order to

---

64. O'Brien, *Epistle to the Philippians*, 313.

make it say something profound, for the passage introduces no explicit doctrinal or theological theme, its grammar is fairly straightforward, and it is free of interpretive conundrums. Its significance lies in its communicative friendliness and its lack of any of the status concerns evident in Self-Sufficiency Letter A. Paul is simply writing to his friends and addressing mutual concerns. He has read their correspondence, which expressed their liturgical understandings, and he no longer shows signs of queasiness about status issues that initially inclined him to claim self-sufficiency.

Paul offers Timothy as the model of a selfless worker for the furtherance of the gospel. Timothy has a genuine concern for the Philippians and their work in furthering the gospel—"how you are getting on" (τὰ περὶ ὑμῶν; literally, "those things [τὰ] about [περὶ] you [ὑμῶν]" 2:19). Paul himself hopes to be freed from his chains and to visit the Philippians at some point; meanwhile, he hopes to send Timothy "without delay" (ταχέως) so that he may remain in contact with his friends in Philippi. All of these travel plans are contingencies, however. Paul "hopes in the Lord Jesus" (ἐλπίζω δὲ ἐν κυρίῳ Ἰησοῦ) to send Timothy and also to visit the Philippians himself. But all the while he is not in control of his own affairs, for he is still in chains. A parallel thought, found in the letter of James, is expressed as "if the Lord wills" (ἐὰν ὁ κύριος θελήσῃ 4:15). In Christian commentarial circles, this expression of James (Jacobus), which acknowledges the limitations of our own human reach, is called the "Jacobean condition." It is the Muslim *Insha'Allah*, "if Allah wills." Paul expresses the same recognition in saying that his hope is in the Lord Jesus, beyond the troubled time and confined conditions in which he now lives his life in Christ, who is the wisdom of the Father.

Timothy is Paul's soul mate, for Paul has no one "equal in soul" sharing the same Christ-life (ἰσόψυχον 2:20) with him, so Paul "takes heart" (εὐψυχῶ 2:19) in sending him to Philippi. Paul and Timothy are in accord; the same vital life force that flows through Paul equally flows through Timothy, and the two are one in Christ. But Paul, Timothy, Epaphroditus, and all those who work together for the furtherance of the gospel are not simply submerged in being one in Christ—each and every one of them has a name. Paul chooses to send Timothy without delay, but only after his situation becomes clear; before that, he will send Epaphroditus immediately. One may speculate as to why Paul has decided on that sequence, but he does not bother to share much more information than that.

Paul contrasts Timothy's selfless work to the self-absorption of others, knowing that unlike the Christ who emptied himself (ἑαυτὸν ἐκένωσεν), people generally look after their own interests (οἱ πάντες γὰρ τὰ ἑαυτῶν ζητοῦσιν). He is speaking in general about humans, foreshadowing the Darwinian observation that evolution is driven by the self-interest of striving for survival in a competitive world. Perhaps Paul has in mind here those preachers mentioned in 1:15–17 who act out of their own partisan concerns. Perhaps also, as suggested by 4:2–3 of this Letter B, he is thinking of some in Philippi who hold different opinions on his citizenship strategy—among others who are named, Euodia and Syntyche. Possibly because Epaphroditus brought the

Philippians' letter to him, Paul judges that he will be the more able immediately to assuage their concerns, while Timothy and then Paul himself can address the issues when they arrive in Philippi.

Buddhists say that all people, because of their attachment to self, are caught in primal ignorance and the delusion of being able to protect that supposed self from impermanence. We seek those things we think will provide enduring support in a world we have created for ourselves, while we reject and push away in anger anything that might threaten our own survival or security. Even when we veil raw self-interest behind the many masks of selfhood—including masks of party or religion—we still, as Paul asserts in 2:21, look out for our own interests.[65] The obverse to seeking one's own interest is to "seek the interest of Jesus Christ" (ζητοῦσιν . . . τὰ Ἰησοῦ Χριστοῦ), literally to seek "the things" (τὰ) of Jesus. But Christ is beyond being benefited, not in victorious self-sufficiency, but in emptied exaltation. Still, the text contrasts seeking "whatever" redounds to self (τὰ ἑαυτῶν ζητοῦσιν) against "whatever" redounds to Christ (τὰ Ἰησοῦ Χριστοῦ).

What, then, does Paul mean by "seeking the things of Jesus Christ" (τὰ Ἰησοῦ Χριστοῦ 2:21)? It is not that Jesus actually needs anything from Paul—except that Paul stop persecuting him, and Paul has long since stopped persecuting Jesus' followers. Timothy never took part in such persecution, and it is he who is here offered as an example of seeking the things of Jesus Christ. He works together with Paul and others for the furtherance of the gospel. Paul is well aware that this Jesus Christ is the Jesus from Nazareth of Galilee who lived and preached, died, and rose from the dead. Yet when Paul says we are to seek the things of Jesus Christ, he has expanded the meaning of Jesus Christ. It is indeed the flesh-and-blood Jesus of Nazareth, but no longer restricted to his historical presence as still remembered by some in Paul's day or as sought by scholars in our day. For Paul, Jesus Christ is the one who died and, in rising, shares his risen life among the many.

This enlarged meaning of Christ, to which Paul witnesses before his judges, reaches beyond the dependently arisen, historical Jesus, who never in his lifetime traveled to Damascus in Syria or to Philippi in the Greek peninsula. In the emptiness hymn, Jesus Christ breaks boundaries of time and space and, within the gospel scope, invites all to a shared and authentic life. He makes us aware of the delusion of self by

---

65. A quick visit to the blogosphere reveals stunningly intense hateful speech deployed in church controversies as well as in political disputes. Before the advent of the Internet as a public forum, one heard and read about different platforms and positions but generally discussed the issues in person among friends and acquaintances. Because they were friends and acquaintances, the human hesitancy to offend others tended to preclude rank insults and meanspirited put-downs. This is dramatically different in the context of today's blogs, populated by anonymous people hiding behind internet monikers, spewing hatred and issuing anathemas with utter disregard for courtesy or even reasoned argument. I do not know how these online discussions will alter our common consideration of social, cultural, or gospel matters as time goes on, but as it is now, they witness to our common self-interested assumption that our own opinions capture the truth.

breaking the boundaries of death and thus dissolving the need for self-interest. That is the Jesus Christ of Paul the apostle, and to work for his interests means to serve others.

Timothy has "a proven worth" (δοκιμή 2:22), for his character has been tested. He does not seek his own benefit, but rather the benefit of the Philippians, and that concretizes the sense of the benefit of Jesus Christ. Timothy works together with Paul as a slave, a servant of God. At one with the empty Christ, he follows the Jesus who emptied himself of everything and took on the form of a slave. Timothy's ongoing commitment is for the sake of the gospel, concretized in the community of living people, not as a particular plan or ideology. Timothy lives within that pattern of consciousness that has turned from self-interest to the interest of others.

Paul has another friend, the Philippian Epaphroditus. He was not one of Paul's traveling companions, and he is mentioned only this once in the New Testament during the interchange between Paul and the Philippian churches. In writing to his friends in Philippi, Paul speaks more than once of shared friends, some of whom he names and many of whom he never bothers to identify. Apparently, he does not imagine his letters will have later readers who might be curious about these people. Although Christians have long regarded Paul's letters as scripture, this does not mean Paul himself was able to foresee their later canonical usage. So although we recognize valuable teachings in these missives, we must be content to realize that we are looking over the writer's shoulder at what are essentially long "postcards" whose context is often unknowable.[66]

Peter O'Brien surmises that "Epaphroditus was probably the bearer of the letter" from the Philippians that occasioned this Letter B from Paul. O'Brien notes that Paul expresses his loving regard for Epaphroditus by calling him "brother" (τὸ ἀδελφὸν 2:25) as well as a fellow worker and comrade in the struggle for the gospel.[67] Christians often speak in terms of being brothers and sisters to one another, for in our effort to overcome our rapacious evolutionary heritage we do share a family lineage. For Paul, and indeed throughout our tradition, belonging to the community surpasses biological genealogy. It is about the shared life we actually lead so as to overcome that heritage. This is what it means to live in Christ: We are one with Christ and therefore with all people, even enemies, even sectarian enemies, even those who would destroy the unity of the church, and even those who obstruct all of our efforts for the furtherance of the gospel—all of these share the very same life. This is what, in a gospel commitment, being brothers and sisters means.

So Epaphroditus, Paul's brother, is a "messenger who serves my needs" (ὑμῶν δὲ ἀπόστολον καὶ λειτουργὸν τῆς χρείας μου 2:25). Again, the word for "public service" (λειτουργὸν, leitourgon) appears, signifying here the "public" services provided concretely by the Philippians to Paul. His needs were probably monetary, for he is in

---

66. The image is from Stephen D. Moore, *Mark and Luke in Poststructuralist Perspectives: Jesus Begins to Write* (New Haven: Yale, 1991) 38–47, on "Jesus' Postcards."

67. O'Brien, *Epistle to the Philippians*, 330.

chains and not at present able to ply his tentmaking skills to earn his living. Nor does he have the ongoing support of a Christian community, for although his role is pastoral, he holds no paid position. Paul requires some money to meet his human needs, and perhaps that is exactly what the Philippians, living in a major trading center on the Via Egnatia trade route, were able to supply him through Epaphroditus. Perhaps he also needed money to expedite his legal case.

In addition to monetary support, Epaphroditus carried letters between Paul and the Philippians. The previous letter he delivered to Paul from Philippi about the empty Christ had allowed Paul to learn of the Philippians' public, "liturgical" celebration of Christ. And so Paul also calls this brother and coworker a "fellow soldier" (καὶ συνεργὸν καὶ συστρατιώτην μου 2:25), a military term consonant with Paul's understanding of the tasks of the gospel as struggle but more concretely referring to Epaphroditus' committed journeying back and forth along the routes that separated Paul from the Philippians. The same roads were built and used by the Roman legions that marched along them to maintain the harsh Roman peace throughout the Empire.

Communication did flow back and forth along the trade routes, and so the Philippians have heard that Epaphroditus has been sick. Indeed, says Paul, he almost died, but God took mercy on him. The text does not say that God restored him to glowing health, just that he had mercy on him, at least to the extent that he could now be sent back to the Philippians. They will be able to see that Epaphroditus is still alive, and Paul will be spared yet another sorrow to burden his bruised body and mind—in his words, "so that I might not have sorrow piled upon sorrow" (ἵνα μὴ λύπην ἐπὶ λύπην σχῶ 2:27). Paul will send Epaphroditus back "with all haste" (σπουδαιοτέρως 2:28), immediately, without waiting to see how events transpire, to allay their worry so that they "may rejoice at seeing him again and that I may be less anxious" (ἵνα ἰδόντες αὐτὸν πάλιν χαρῆτε κἀγὼ ἀλυπότερος ὦ 2:28). Everybody here had anxieties. Although neither Paul, nor Timothy, nor the Philippians—including, one would suppose, Epaphroditus—feared death for themselves, they were indeed concerned for one another.

Epaphroditus had come to the point of death because of "the work of Christ" (διὰ τὸ ἔργον χριστοῦ 2:30). He had been endeavoring in the gospel, the work of the Christ—who is our life among us—so that we might open the frontiers of our minds and break through the limitations we put upon our hearts to share the risen life of Christ that assuages our anxieties, even without removing them, and allows us to live for the benefit of others. Such a thing neither comes naturally nor flows from any cherished ideology. Here the phrase that Paul uses of Epaphroditus, that "he had been at the point of death, had been near to death" (μέχρι θανάτου ἤγγισεν 2:30), echoes the phrase in the hymn of the empty Christ who himself came to the point of death on the cross (μέχρι θανάτου, θανάτου δὲ σταυροῦ 2:8). Peter O'Brien recognizes a deliberate echo here, as though Paul "is presenting Epaphroditus as a model of unselfish service to the Philippians."⁶⁸

Finding Refuge (3:1)

3:1 For the rest, my brothers and sisters, rejoice in the Lord. To write to you these very things [about the empty Christ] does not trouble me, for it provides you with a refuge.

3:1 Τὸ λοιπόν, ἀδελφοί μου, χαίρετε ἐν κυρίῳ. τὰ αὐτὰ γράφειν ὑμῖν ἐμοὶ μὲν οὐκ ὀκνηρόν, ὑμῖν δὲ ἀσφαλές.

The opening phrase of this passage, translated often as "finally" (Τὸ λοιπὸν), means literally "as for the rest." It indicates that Paul is summing up and now "moves toward 'what remains.'"⁶⁹ There is a discourse in Mahāyāna philosophy about "what remains" after the critique of emptiness has negated everything that we might cling to as a support for the self.⁷⁰ Some—the Abhidharma philosophers—insist that what remains is the real reality of essences, to be understood by analysis and then focused upon in meditation. Others advance the view that the emptiness of all essences scarcely differs from pure nothingness; according to them, what remains after the critiques empty all viewpoints of supposed truth, as well as all meditative objects, is the experience of nothing at all. They assert that that very empty nothingness is itself awakening.⁷¹ However, the great schools of Mahāyāna thinking follow neither this nihilistic approach nor the Abhidharmists' realism. They teach that, once the critique of emptiness has been applied, "what remains" is the broad and varied world in all its multi-textured, variously beautiful, and dependently arisen richness. Indeed, this dependently arisen

---

68. Ibid., 343.

69. Fee, *Paul's Letter to the Philippians*, 291.

70. See Nagao, "What Remains in Śūnyatā: A Yogācāra Interpretation of Emptiness" in Nagao, *Mādhyamika and Yogācāra*, 51–60.

71. See Nagao's rejection of Jizang's (Chi-tsang's) identification of the "overcoming of falsehood with the manifestation of truth," for that leaves one solely with negation and the empty void (Nagao, *Foundational Standpoint*, 21–23). See also Nagao, "Fa-tsang no sanshō setsu ni taisuru jakkan no gimon" (Some Doubts about Fa-tsang's Explanation of the Three Natures), in Nagao, *Chūkan to Yuishiki*, 503–25. Here, Nagao critiques Fa-tsang's understanding of the three patterns of consciousness as recasting critical Yogācāra thought within Tathāgatagarbha categories, perhaps because of undue influence by the Taoist traditions of Lao Tzu and Chuang Tzu. Issues of being and nonbeing were treated in detail by Indian Mādhyamika and Yogācāra thinkers, but these Indian Mahāyāna philosophies encountered a very different cultural configuration when introduced into China, where "primal Nonbeing" is seen not as pure negation, but as the fecund, yet nameless source behind being itself. As in Section xl of the *Tao Te Ching*: "The myriad creatures in the world are born from Something, and Something from Nothing" (天下萬物生於有.有生於無), where that "Nothing" is understood, as in Section xxv, to be "a thing confusedly formed, Born before heaven and earth. Silent and void, it stands alone and does not change" (Lao Tzu, *Tao Te Ching*, trans. D. C. Lau [London: Penguin, 1963] 101, 82).

and interdependent world itself is the content of a Buddha's awakening, present all along from the very primal beginning and seen now as it is, in its suchness.

"What remains" now for Paul is the rejoicing. This attitude sums up his advice to his friends in Philippi, and indeed his entire theology. However, it does cause a problem for folks who insist on the centrality of self-survival, for rejoicing offers no surety against Epaphroditus' illness unto death, or against imprisonment and execution for Paul. The Philippians are getting their dear Epaphroditus back sound and safe, but they did have a scare, for they know that he might well have died. And Paul himself writes from his own distressed circumstance, under threat of execution as he is. Still, Paul concludes that this empty Christ—who by taking the form of a slave and being executed on a cross—limns our lives and is cause for rejoicing. In our sinews and bones we know that God has "more than" exalted him and given him the name that we cannot even pronounce. At the same time, all this rejoicing is a bit scary. Who wants to follow emptiness to a remainder that appears so very fleeting and transient?

Nevertheless, Paul says that although we may indeed be distressed and troubled by the empty Christ, "to write to you these very things does not trouble me" (τὰ αὐτὰ γράφειν ὑμῖν ἐμοὶ μὲν οὐκ ὀκνηρόν). The phrase "these very things" (τὰ αὐτὰ) refers to the faith confession that forms the heart of Letter B,[72] and which now constitutes the base of Paul's friendship with the Philippians: that Christ crucified is the empty Christ who invites us to abandon our very self-identity and to acknowledge that we are not self-sufficient, so that we may be enabled to work for the furtherance of the gospel. Those who dedicate themselves to that ideal do crave the friendly recognition that such dedication brings in its train; and in 2:16 Paul boasts in these Christ followers and basks in the recognition of the Philippians. Yet in the empty Christ, all standalone boundary markers are emptied and status claims abandoned, bringing liberation from things that are not real, delusions that engender and intensify strife, anger, and greed. "For the rest" or "finally" (τὸ λοιπόν) is thought perhaps to have been added here lest Paul be perceived as hesitating to repeat those themes.[73] He not only cites the emptiness hymn at 2:6–11 in Letter B, but he "writes the same things" in 3:7–11, to concur in the Philippians' confession of the empty Christ and to "help you be steadfast" (ὑμῖν δὲ ἀσφαλές 3:1).[74] Although Paul may have experienced some sense of uneasiness about the figure of the self-emptying Christ in the Philippians hymn, even in his Roman prison he welcomes the empty hollow that Christ carves out within the core of his own being and recognizes it as something in which to rejoice. He seems not to be overcome by existential anxiety at the prospect of dying, for he assures the

---

72. Reumann, *Philippians*, 453.

73. On ὀκνηρόν: "involvement in *oknos*, causing hesitation, reluctance, (such as) to shrink from . . ." (ibid., 454).

74. Ibid., 454–55: "Steadfastness, *asphalēs* (ἀσφαλές), *es* (only here in Paul) = *alpha* privative + *sphallō*, 'trip up'; 'not slipping or falling.'"

Philippians, and therefore me, that none of this is troublesome to him, that it causes him no anguish.

Paul further assures us that such discourse as he undertakes is for us "salutary and makes you safe" (ὑμῖν δὲ ἀσφαλές). The term translated as "safe"—above as "refuge"—occurs only here in Paul's writings. An adjectival form is used in Hebrews 6:19 for "a *sure* and steadfast anchor." The empty present becomes an eschatological moment in the unfurling of truths and realities beyond present-tense experience, and so we take refuge in a reality yet to unfold fully. It all has to do with security, even though that is precisely what the image of the empty Christ on the cross threatens. If we are unable to control and direct our lives, how can we be secure in the very possession of these lives? Paul offers, as a refuge for the anxieties that grow out of our self-clinging, the very teachings that he has just sung in the hymn of the empty Christ. The teachings themselves become a refuge, just as the teachings of the Buddha Śākyamuni are described in that tradition as a refuge. When one joins the Buddhist community, one "takes refuge" in the Three Jewels of Buddha (wisdom being), Dharma (teaching), and Saṅgha (community). It is not that the Buddha himself, or the teaching or the community, magically assuage the protean and polymorphous anxieties that spring from human living, but they counter our delusions, invite us to eradicate the habits that support them, and enable us to build upon the traditions of our elders to realize the reality of awakening to life abundant.[75]

Personal Affairs and Struggles (4:1-3)

> 4:1 *Therefore, my brothers and sisters, whom I love and long for, my joy and crown, stand firm in the Lord in this way, my beloved.* ²*I urge Euodia and I urge Syntyche to be of the same mind in the Lord.* ³*Yes, and I ask you, true yoke fellow, help these women, for they have struggled beside me in the work of the gospel, together with Clement and the rest of my coworkers, whose names are in the book of life.*

> 4:1 Ὥστε, ἀδελφοί μου ἀγαπητοὶ καὶ ἐπιπόθητοι, χαρὰ καὶ στέφανός μου, οὕτως στήκετε ἐν κυρίῳ, ἀγαπητοί. ²Εὐοδίαν παρακαλῶ καὶ Συντύχην παρακαλῶ τὸ αὐτὸ φρονεῖν ἐν κυρίῳ. ³ναὶ ἐρωτῶ καὶ σέ, γνήσιε σύζυγε, συλλαμβάνου αὐταῖς, αἵτινες ἐν τῷ εὐαγγελίῳ συνήθλησάν μοι μετὰ καὶ Κλήμεντος καὶ τῶν λοιπῶν συνεργῶν μου, ὧν τὰ ὀνόματα ἐν βίβλῳ ζωῆς.

---

75. In order to follow the continuing flow of this correspondence between Paul and the Philippians, I omit here 3:2–3:21, which passage constitutes Resurrection Letter C; it will be treated in sequence below. Letter B now flows directly into verses 4:1–9, and then—passing over 4:10–20, already treated as Letter A—into 4:21–23. The advantage of this gerrymandering of the text—although cumbersome when referring to the canonical version—is that it allows us to see the likely sequence of communications between Paul and the Philippians, and to get an impression of the developing relationship between them.

Letter B on the emptily exalted Christ now moves forward with reference to personal matters among Paul's Philippian coworkers in spreading the gospel during these early years. He begins a conclusion to this second letter with a forthright expression of "love and affection for my brothers and sisters" ("Ὥστε, ἀδελφοί μου ἀγαπητοὶ καὶ ἐπιπόθητοι 4:1), who are his "joy and crown" (χαρὰ καὶ στέφανός μου). This is a joy that he has frequently encouraged his readers to experience: Let us rejoice in the very being that we have, loving life and awaiting with ardor our hope of being transformed into "light bodies" of glory through the Christ power that pervades the universe, for he empties himself of all power so as to become our slave.

Elsewhere, Paul has written of running a race to win the victor's crown of laurel. But in this passage, his Philippian correspondents themselves are the sign of his victory, his "crown." And yet this curious victory is not accomplished through any effort of Paul's own; one could hardly list it on a curriculum vitae. And when Paul does list his lineage and accomplishments in Resurrection Letter C (3:4b–6), he treats them as less than nothing. The accomplishments here, moreover, are not his. This victory crown is won only in and through the interdependent practice of prayer and engagement whereby we all acknowledge our ignorance and live into the knowledge of Christ and of "heavenly politics" that negate any reality in the "realpolitik" of the world.

Paul tells the Philippians to "stand firm in the Lord in this way, my beloved" (οὕτως στήκετε ἐν κυρίῳ, ἀγαπητοί 4:1): in awareness of being one with the self-emptying Christ who—now no longer "standing" anywhere himself—gives us the strength to stand firm. In Christ-living, we are encompassed by empty love, with neither role expectations nor guarantees. Despite the fact that love is all too often interwoven with self-serving longing and inordinate desire, Christians talk a great deal about it. Buddhists, by contrast, generally eschew talk of love, aware as they are of the entanglements of passion and power.[76] They do speak of the friendship (Skt. *maitrī*) of the awakened buddhas and the loving kindness (*maitrī*) of bodhisattvas toward all sentient beings. And the Mahāyāna liturgical formula when taking refuge in Buddha, Dharma, and Saṅgha (the equivalent of Christian baptismal commitments), includes a compassionate vow to save all sentient beings.[77] For the most part, Buddhist discourse focuses on compassion (Skt. *karuṇā*) as it flows from the awakened wisdom (*prajñā*) that limns the Dharma reality of everything.

---

76. But see Makransky's *Awakening Through Love* on the Tibetan Buddhist tradition of Dzogchen. Although Buddhists most often shy away from talking about love—for its many distortions are apparent—Makransky, who has taught among the many Christian interfaith thinkers at Boston College, appreciates the centrality of disinterested love (*agapē*). Makransky celebrates the everyday love of such figures as Mahatma Gandhi, Mother Teresa, and the Dalai Lama, and he grafts his meditations on love onto Buddhist methods to unleash its power across religious boundaries.

77. See Habito's *Living Zen, Loving God* on the four bodhisattva vows, which are: "Sentient beings are numberless; I vow to free them. Delusions are inexhaustible; I vow to extinguish them. The Gates of Truth are countless; I vow to open them. The enlightened way is unsurpassable; I vow to embody it" (Habito, *Living Zen, Loving God*, 91).

The Christian use of love is rather more treacherous and open to misunderstanding, for in actual living it can easily slip toward the self-satisfying *agapē* of the overly concerned, or perhaps even self-gratifying *eros*. The very first instincts of human beings are to reach out—to father and mother and then beyond, often in seeking a mate with whom to share life, nurturing children, living in community. And all this longing and stretching toward fulfillment does push us to transcend the bounded self and its appetites and to be of service to one another. The same primal longing moves us to seek to overcome loneliness by living our life as the one body of Christ, in acknowledgment of the organic evolutionary pull of our heritage in the vast universe of visible and invisible matter, stretching beyond our individual lives and genealogical heritage.[78]

Who are the individuals named in this passage? Disappointingly, we know little more of them than their names. Paul "urges" two women, "Euodia and Syntyche" (Εὐοδίαν παρακαλῶ καὶ Συντύχην παρακαλῶ 4:2) to be of the same mind, to direct "their focused attention (φρονεῖν) singly (τὸ αὐτὸ) in the Lord" (ἐν κυρίῳ). Apparently, they are in disagreement about something, but we do not know the specifics.[79] He also asks someone he calls "true yoke fellow, comrade" (Syzygus: γνήσιε σύζυγε 4:3), "whom he calls upon" (ναὶ ἐρωτῶ καὶ σέ) to help "these women" (συλλαμβάνου αὐταῖς) in Philippi, for "they have all joined together with me in the work of the Gospel" (αἵτινες ἐν τῷ εὐαγγελίῳ συνήθλησάν μοι). There are others, including someone named Clement, "who have struggled and worked alongside me" (μετὰ καὶ Κλήμεντος καὶ τῶν λοιπῶν συνεργῶν μου). All these are Paul's fellow workers in the gospel endeavor; they are not the self-serving Christ preachers mentioned in 1:15–17. Whatever the differences among them, these people "have struggled with me in the Gospel work" (αἵτινες ἐν τῷ εὐαγγελίῳ συνήθλησάν μοι). They are named as members of this singular Philippian community, which again and again has supported Paul as he travels from place to place spreading the word, and which has shared with him its celebration of the emptily exalted Christ. Euodia, Syntyche, and Clement clearly are fellow practitioners in the gospel work.

The name Syzygus (σύζυγε), or "yoke-fellow," has elicited much commentarial discussion. "Yoke-fellow" suggests someone who is joined, or yoked, with others in a

---

78. We are not, however, to cling to a counterfeit transcendence, whether lustfully to the detriment and harm of others or rapaciously to assert an overweening sovereign power over them. Such have been the temptations and sins of the churches since they first had power and demanded a uniform turning away from organic love and sexual desire. See A. W. Richard Sipe, "Celibacy, Sex, and the Catholic Church," http://www.awrsipe.com.

79. Dahl argues that the disagreement between these "two outstanding and influential members of the church in Philippi was the chief problem faced by Paul" (N. A. Dahl, "Euodia and Syntyche and Paul's Letter to the Philippians," in *The Social World of the First Christians*, edited by L. M. White and O. L. Yarbrough [Minneapolis: Fortress, 1995] 3–15). And M. Tellbe describes the Philippians as "a community in disharmony" (M. Tellbe, *Paul Between Synagogue and State: Christians, Jews, and Civic Authorities in 1 Thessalonians* [Stockholm: Almqvist & Wiksell, 2001] 228–30). Both are cited by James D. G. Dunn, who considers Tellbe's description to be "overstated" (James D. G. Dunn, *Beginning from Jerusalem*, vol. 2 of *Christianity in the Making* [Grand Rapids: Eeerdmans, 2009] 1018 n. 264).

common endeavor. Some think it to be a personal name, or possibly even a term of endearment for Paul's wife. The latter interpretation would, of course, presuppose that Paul had a wife and that she lived in Philippi. Theologian and church father Clement of Alexandria (d. ca. 211) did understand Syzygus to refer to Paul's own wife, one upon whom he could call for help when needed (*Stromata* 3.6.53). But scholars tend to dismiss this possibility because the grammatical gender of Syzygus is masculine. Or Syzygus may refer to a "yoked" comrade in a theological sense, reflecting the words of Matthew: "Take my yoke (ζυγόν) upon you and learn from me for I am meek and humble of heart and you will find peace for your souls. For my yoke is easy and my burden light." (ἄρατε τὸν ζυγόν μου ἐφ'ὑμᾶς καὶ μάθετε ἀπ'ἐμοῦ, ὅτι πραΰς εἰμι καὶ ταπεινὸς τῇ καρδίᾳ, καὶ εὑρήσετε ἀνάπαυσιν ταῖς ψυχαῖς ὑμῶν. ὁ γὰρ ζυγός μου χρηστὸς καὶ τὸ φορτίον μου ἐλαφρόν ἐστιν Matt 11:29–30). Because of the rhythmic, balanced structure of this Matthean passage, some commentators believe that it may be part of a Christian liturgy, perhaps a hymn sung at eucharistic or baptismal services.[80] Of course, the present Gospel of Matthew dates to around the year 80 and is thus later than Paul's epistle, but if used in the liturgies of the early communities, those or similar words may well have been familiar to Paul and the Philippian congregation.

Or possibly in these early days in Philippi, as at other times and places, Christians adopted a special name at the time of their baptism, and "Syzygus" is simply a name that was commonly chosen as a baptismal name by a disciple of Christ (μάθετε ἀπ'ἐμοῦ) who takes "his yoke" (ζυγός *zygos*) upon his shoulders. It seems unlikely that Syzygus is an ordinary name for an individual, for it occurs nowhere else in Greek literature. All we know is that, like the others mentioned, this person was a coworker and that all "their names are in the book of life" (ὧν τὰ ὀνόματα ἐν βίβλῳ ζωῆς 4:3). We really know nothing more of these various people than that they are much beloved by Paul and, like him, their focus is on understanding and spreading the gospel word.

In 4:3 Paul is letting us know that our names—the names of all his coworkers in the gospel—even though they may pass into unrecorded and forgotten history, are nevertheless written in "the book of life." What book is that? Possibly there were civil registers of citizens in Philippi that serve as the immediate background for this image.[81] But Paul is not speaking of a registration or membership list but rather a list of those who live, a book never actually written, no source for genealogical research. Perhaps it is an empty, eschatological book that we will be able to read only when the last page is written. But surely it includes Paul and Clement, Epaphroditus and Timothy, Euodia and Syntyche, as well as Syzygus—whoever that may be—together with the risen Christ, who was more real to them than their own life stories.

Scholars sometimes speak of the "lost history" of Christianity. But this misses the point. Paul himself felt no pressing need to record that history for posterity. His focus

---

80. W. D. Davies and D. C. Allison, *Matthew: 8–18*, International Critical Commentary (1991; London: T. & T. Clark, 2004) 293.

81. On civic registers in Philippi, see Reumann, *Philippians*, 611.

is the gospel of grace and freedom, which is ever again experienced as liberative and transcendent, not something confined within historical boundaries. Even if we possessed detailed records about the Philippians, their witness would remain ancient and distant; we cannot relive their lives. But our histories and our names, even unrecorded, are not "lost." Past and present careers of compassionate engagement create faith traditions that liberate and expand ever more outward to realize justice and peace.

Buddhists negate self, and then immediately begin to sketch the bodhisattva career of the awakened, selfless person who lives on in the world for the sake of others.[82] No-self is not a denial of personal life; it does not erase the lineaments of saintly practitioners whose silent wisdom reverberates with the sound of thunder. Because of our philosophical heritage, Christians often conflate self and person; certainly we do not wish to sink into a nameless nihilism wherein no one is ever at home and nothing matters. But it is possible to speak of person as distinguished from self. Let us understand "self" to mean a center of consciousness that is experienced as subject and regarded as our core inner identity, separate from but related to objects that are deemed to stand alone in the outer world. The instinctual urge of such a self is to nourish, protect, and prosper itself, bringing itself into the most advantageous relationship with other selves. By contrast, we may understand "person" to mean a subjective center of dependently arisen consciousness, which is aware of being transient and empty *because* dependently arisen; and with this awareness, it is enabled to focus upon a life course of benefiting and gladdening others.

Descartes' I-consciousness (L. *cogito*) is the experience that all of us have of being here.[83] But the different awareness entailed in understanding that experience as either "self" or "person" leads to different insights and understandings, and thus to different paths of life practice. If we cling to self as something central and stable, all our efforts center upon the value of bolstering that core through our own karmic actions, whether good or bad. Bad actions (Skt. *karma*) tend to inscribe habitual greed and anger in the service of a me-first life, while good actions may create a sterling character that still clings pridefully to the illusion of an essence that does not exist. Even good karmic lives never open one to awakening, which will occur only apart from the calculus of selfhood.

However, when we understand ourselves as persons, as the result of ever dependently arising insights and understandings, we are enabled to abandon our narrow

---

82. See the concise article by Nagao on "Buddhist Subjectivity," in Nagao, *Mādhyamika and Yogācāra*, 7–12. On the doctrine of no-self, see Steven Collins, *Selfess Persons: Imagery and Thought in Theravāda Buddhism* (Cambridge: University of Cambridge, 1982).

83. Seeking to locate the neural basis for self-awareness, Haidt writes of Antonio Damasio's *Descartes' Error: Emotion, Reason, and the Human Brain* (New York: Putnam, 1994): "Damasio's interpretation was that gut feelings and bodily reactions were *necessary* to think rationally, and that one job of the vmPFC [ventromedial prefrontal cortex] was to integrate those gut feelings into a person's conscious deliberations" (Haidt, *Righteous Mind*, 33). The neurobiology gets complex precisely because there is no neural center for self-awareness, as there is for other human activities.

preoccupation with self-profit and self-views and thus to hear about and experience oneness with that eschatological mystery we Christians identify not as self but as Christ, who being both empty and exalted received a nameless name. To be a person and live in Christ means first and foremost to live not in self-concern but in awareness of a risen life that enables us, weak and sinful though we are, to turn our focus to others, day by day, from beginning to end. Personhood thrives within the web of interbeing in Christ, within a web of beings who each exist empty of any fixed being.

We do not have to know about Euodia's history, for she has contributed to who we are—she is a part of the dependently arisen tradition that has shaped us all along. We do not need to know much about Clement or Syntyche, for we have in our lives many such models of Christian living. Nor do we need to unearth all the historical details about Jesus, for it simply does not matter much what was said in his conversations with family, friends, or lovers. The tradition of Christian practice is not a mere link to a pristine Jesus of history, but rather an ongoing experience of risen life—beyond the boundaries of life and death—scripted by our scriptures in the person of Jesus and modeled again and again over the ages in lived lives.

Eschatological Joy (4:4–7)

4:4 Rejoice in the Lord always; again I will say, Rejoice. ⁵Let your gentleness be known to everyone. The Lord is near. ⁶Do not worry about anything, but in everything by prayer and supplication with thanksgiving let your requests be made known before God. ⁷And the peace of God, which surpasses all understanding, will guard your hearts and your minds in Christ Jesus.

4:4 Χαίρετε ἐν κυρίῳ πάντοτε· πάλιν ἐρῶ, χαίρετε. ⁵τὸ ἐπιεικὲς ὑμῶν γνωσθήτω πᾶσιν ἀνθρώποις. ὁ κύριος ἐγγύς. ⁶μηδὲν μεριμνᾶτε, ἀλλ' ἐν παντὶ τῇ προσευχῇ καὶ τῇ δεήσει μετὰ εὐχαριστίας τὰ αἰτήματα ὑμῶν γνωριζέσθω πρὸς τὸν θεόν. ⁷καὶ ἡ εἰρήνη τοῦ θεοῦ ἡ ὑπερέχουσα πάντα νοῦν φρουρήσει τὰς καρδίας ὑμῶν καὶ τὰ νοήματα ὑμῶν ἐν Χριστῷ Ἰησοῦ.

In 4:2, Paul has encouraged the Philippians to be of one mind. In 1:27, he recommends the duties of citizenship (πολιτεύεσθε) to all, and in his final letter, Resurrection Letter C, he will again speak of the Philippians' "civic engagement from the heavens" (ὑμῶν γὰρ τὸ πολίτευμα ἐν οὐρανοῖς ὑπάρχει 3:20). He stresses public engagement (πολίτευμα) and transcendent (ἐν οὐρανοῖς) emptying of ideology. It is in that sense that he urges people here, not once but twice, to "rejoice" (χαίρετε ἐν κυρίῳ πάντοτε. πάλιν ἐρῶ, χαίρετε 4:4), whatever the surrounding social and political situation. Eschatological joy hovers between here-and-now practice and the vision of transcendent fulfillment.

Paul consistently rejects "party spirit" in their community life, for it is this that can divide people who are one in the body of Christ. Possibly his particular concern at this juncture is a difference of opinion about public strategy among the Philippians, or between some of them and Paul. So he urges the Philippian community to be gentle, not contentious. And to "let that gentleness be known to all people" (τὸ ἐπιεικὲς ὑμῶν γνωσθήτω πᾶσιν ἀνθρώποις 4:5). "All people" here (πᾶσιν ἀνθρώποις) includes all those with whom the Philippian believers interact in their public life. The gentleness of this community will be made known to the people of Philippi.

Philippi was a Roman colony, but its people managed many of their own local affairs. Like people everywhere, they no doubt had among them various political factions and also guilds that protected the various trades. Meanwhile, they needed to maintain workable relations with the Roman authorities. Paul takes no particular stance on local political and social matters, but his stance as a Roman citizen before the authorities must have caused some worry in this Roman colony.[84] Paul did not take part directly in political controversies in any of the cities of the Hellenistic world, although he did once come into conflict with the silver workers in Ephesus when his preaching against idols made of silver had political and economic repercussions. But in general he recommends that believers in this gospel eschew ideological stances, demonstrating their "gentleness" (ἐπιεικὲς) to all people. Because he himself is not a political partisan, he is confident of his acquittal in the Roman courts. He stands firm only in the gospel. And, in the event, it does appear that his strategy was effective, for Letter C contains no mention of his continued imprisonment.

However, Paul's joy is equally because "the Lord is near" (ὁ κύριος ἐγγύς 4:5). Some commentators understand this phrase as referring to the "presence" of the Lord to those who pray.[85] This would be supported by Ps 145:

> [18]Near is the Lord to all who call on him (Ἐγγὺς Κύριος πᾶσι τοῖς ἐπικαλουμένοις αὐτὸν), to all who call on him in truth.
> [19]The will of all who fear him (θέλημα τῶν φοβουμένωμν αὐτὸν) he will do (ποιήσει), and to their petition he will hearken (καὶ τῆς δεήσεως αὐτῶν ἐπακούσεται) and will save them (καὶ σώσει αὐτούς).
> [20]The Lord watches over all who love him (Φυλάσσει Κύριος πάντες τοὺς ἀγαπῶντας αὐτὸν), and all the sinners he will destroy (καὶ πάντες τοὺς ἁμαρτωλοὺς ἐξολοθρεύσει).
> [21]Praise of the Lord my mouth will speak, and let all flesh bless his holy name (καὶ εὐλογείτω πᾶσα σὰρξ τὸ ὄνομα τὸ ἅγιον αὐτοῦ), forever and forever and ever.[86]

This psalm describes the nearness of the Lord as his presence to those who call upon him in truth, who work out their salvation in fear and trembling. The Lord not only will hear their prayer, but will also respond to save them while destroying their enemies,

---

84. Reumann, *Philippians*, 635: "Dual citizenship in church and civic community (1:27) continues to play out in Paul's letter."
85. Ibid.
86. Pietersma and Wright, *New English Translation of the Septuagint*, 618.

the sinners. Commentators who refer to this psalm as Paul's inspiration here tend not to note that the Christ of the Philippians, although he prayed in Gethsemane, was not saved from the cross; he died in anguish feeling abandoned by God. *His* enemies were not destroyed, but he emptied himself so as transparently to mirror the harsh love of the Father.

Many commentators believe that when Paul writes that "the Lord is near," he expresses his expectation of the imminent coming of Christ in linear time, breaking through the clouds of heaven and arriving as lord and savior of Paul's *mare nostrum* world. Some argue that this is the reason Paul remained aloof from the dirty politics of this world: he expected his heavenly politics actually to arrive from the clouds. But I believe that this is a mistaken interpretation. When Paul says that the Lord is near, he is not working within the structure of linear human expectations but rather of human hope. He is not thinking in linear time. For him, the Lord is already near in eschatological dreamtime. Indeed, if the gospel is a programmed set of scheduled expectancies, then we are fated to bleak disappointment, over and over again. In liturgical and ritual acts, however, the anticipated fulfillment of all that is real becomes present—sacramentally and effectively in the minds and hearts of the community.

Ideological programs always invite counterprograms,[87] whereas the gospel invites conversion and transformation and lays upon our shoulders the task of skillfully entering into public debate on behalf of the poor and marginalized. The nearness of the Lord is not a linear measure of when one might expect this Lord to arrive with political placards announcing correct positions. It is rather the very structure of our lives as Christians, lived in the tensive practice of eagerly awaiting the coming of the Lord, who is always near, while stretching our horizons to learn anew the import of our eschatological dreams.[88] For Paul, the Lord is Jesus Christ, for he has seen in "the face of Christ" (ἐν προσώπῳ Ἰησοῦ χριστοῦ 2 Cor 4:6) the very light of divine wisdom. And the hymn in 2:6–11 has attributed the name "Lord" (κύριος, *Kyrios*) to Jesus, who emptied himself of everything and was more than exalted. It is the very unpronounceable name of YHWH as the mystery beyond enunciation. In the Greek Septuagint translation of the Hebrew scriptures that Paul read, *Kyrios* (κύριος)—"Lord"—is used throughout.

The point is important: When we speak of Jesus Christ, we are not naming the Lord as the soon-to-arrive agent of our salvation. Not only has the physical return

---

87. See Emmaniel Lévinas, *Difficult Freedom: Essays on Judaism*, trans. Sean Hand (Baltimore: John Hopkins, 1990). Lévinas' work has been critiqued by Oone Eisenstadt, "Anti-Utopianism Revisited," *Shofar: An Interdisciplinary Journal of Jewish Studies* 24 (2008) 120–38. I concur with Kalmanson's recasting of the issue of messianic hope and expectancy in terms of Dōgen's Zen teaching of the indivisibility of practice and realization; see Leah Kalmanson, "The Messiah and the Bodhisattva: Anti-Utopianism Re-Revisited," *Shofar* 30 (2012) 113–25.

88. "Dream" here is not meant to suggest illusion, but the vision of Caedmon or Cynewulf in "The Dream of the Rood," a seventh-century English poetic vision of Christ mounting the cross to defeat death.

of Jesus Christ to this world not occurred for these past two thousand years, but the expectancy that it will occur soon—or within any measurable span of time—is delusion, a basic error. The eschatological structure of faith has nothing to do with expectancies in linear time, not in the future nor at any particular time at all. Nor is the coming-again of Christ something that has already happened while we weren't paying attention. The coming of Christ is the transcendent structure of this very present, ever-so-secular life, grounded in the past experiences we have had of God in the face of Christ and in his very person (ἐν προσώπῳ Ἰησοῦ Χριστοῦ), as we stretch always back and always forward to realize and prepare for that ever-coming Lord.

Engaged in this always-expanding quest for insight into life, "we are not to worry about anything" (μηδὲν μεριμνᾶτε 4:6), Paul says, even though we know full well that bad things not infrequently do happen to good people.[89] We live in a world of suffering and dying, and there are many things of which we must be aware, including some that we do well to fear. The frightening import of Charles Darwin's *Origin of the Species* was not that he was the first to speak of evolution, for many before him had accepted the idea. The disconcerting feelings he triggered in the piously religious sprang from his demonstration of the radical change that had occurred within space-time, thereby undermining the classical and cherished philosophical theology that had developed in the preceding millennium—a theology that arranged the world into an elegant hierarchical order of beings.[90] The beauty of that well-ordered vision was that each set of beings was analogically—in proper measure—placed and cared for within its station. This applied not only to turtles (among which could be great variation just so long as all were turtles), but also to human beings, who were set at the pinnacle over the animals (as affirmed in Gen 1:26) and especially cared for by God's providence. Those who relied upon this underlying philosophy of hierarchical being, wherein all share in being analogically in their proper station and in their proper degree, saw Darwin's work as undermining our secure place as a loved and redeemed species. What human person would want to be demoted from being the apple of God's eye to being one of many interconnected species in a nonhierarchical ecology?[91]

---

89. To borrow from Harold S. Kushner, *When Bad Things Happen to Good People* (New York: Anchor, 1981). Kushner's book is more than a theological apologetic for the goodness of God despite human suffering; it is a modern embodiment of Job, who even in his suffering remained embraced within the mystery of life and death.

90. See Arthur O. Lovejoy, *The Great Chain of Being: A Study in the History of an Idea* (Boston: Harvard University Press, 1976). Lovejoy examines the notion that all things have their graded being within a fully complete hierarchy of being, from God down through the material world, tracing the idea from Plato to the modern world, for it has long served as the accepted plan and structure of the world. It is still alive in ontological theologians' notion that all beings share in being by analogy (*analogia entis*), thus grounding our being and our knowledge within a continuous ladder of being and knowing. This was the operative theology behind Christian critiques of Darwin, whose ideas about evolution blurred set boundaries and dispensed with the upper levels of angels and God.

91. Edward O. Wilson, *Sociobiology: The New Synthesis* (1975; Cambridge: Harvard University Press, 2000). Wilson presents an update on natural selection to account for the communal and altruistic behavior of insects, animals, and humans within their shared social and ecological worlds. Critics

Nonetheless, we are indeed part of a much larger divine ecosystem, and we are not to become enemies of the cross by claiming special privilege, or to expect that the Lord will come and save us from being so frighteningly human. No matter how preoccupied we may become with the health of our bodies, the fact of nature's ferocious and unrelenting struggle is true. We are as tossed about by the waves of disease and disaster as are all other creatures and, as old age comes upon us, our fears are only compounded by the "wonders" of medicalized survival far beyond any possibility for quality of life. The Indian classic *Bhagavad Gita* famously depicts the ravages of time itself as consuming all beings.[92] Time does have sharp teeth, and we all without exception pass through its jaws. If not at the mercy of William Blake's tiger burning bright in the night, then of cancer or some other disease chewing away at our innards. Our Christian heritage—expressed here in Paul's advice not to worry about anything—is not meant to blind us either to the organic surge of life's beauty or to our own distressing diminution and ending. The cross is not the cross of Christ alone. Awaiting with its grim threat, it is the cross of each and every one of Christ's disciples. Better to join the Lord in his suffering and dying that we, too, may move beyond all worry, taking on the mind of the Christ who emptied the divide between living and dying. Death is not unique to Christians or to Buddhists. But both traditions refuse to acknowledge the divide between life and death as final—Christianity in its teaching of resurrection faith, Buddhism in its emphasis upon awakening (Skt. *bodhicitta*).

Although Paul tells us that we should not worry, he knows full well that there is much to be worried about. He worried about Epaphroditus, and about how worried the Philippians were about their friend. It may be that people in the colonial market

---

objected to Wilson's inclusion of humans, as if people were determined by their biological impulses to act for the common good in society. A Mahāyāna perspective, however, is less concerned with the specialness of humans, for the scope of the Buddha's compassion embraces all sentient beings as they cycle through lives. In the Mahāyāna reading of sin and delusion, the evolutionary history that Wilson explains is our karmic heritage, our primal and "original sin," not because we are so Eden-like special, but because we are not. Pierre Smulers notes that Teilhard de Chardin's evolutionary vision was never able to successfully formulate a notion of original sin, while the Genesis account depicts a primal purity and bliss before Adam and Eve sinned. See Pierre Smulers, "Evolution and Original Sin," *Theology Digest* 13 (1965) 172–76 (Smulers' article is a digest of his "Evolution et péché originel," Appendix III of *La vision de Teilhard de Chardin* [Paris: Desclée de Brouwer, 1964]). Indeed, for many theologians the fall from primal bliss is the reason for the incarnation, for if humans had not fallen, there would have been no need for their redemption. In a more sensitive exegetical mood, however, one might see Genesis not as providing a primal history so much as a mythic truth that sketches our eschatological dreams, for there never was any garden, and "adam" means simply "earthling." So Adam stands in for us all.

92. *The Bhagavad-Gita: Krishna's Counsel in Time of War* describes Krishna counseling the hesitant Ārjuna, who faces his beloved relatives in battle, to perform his allotted duty without attachment to its actual results: "I am time grown old, creating world destruction, set in motion to annihilate the worlds; even without you, all these warriors arrayed in hostile ranks will cease to exist. Therefore, arise and win glory! Conquer your foes and fulfill your kingship! They are already killed by me. Be just my instrument, the archer at my side!" (Barbara Stoler Miller, trans., *The Bhagavad-Gita: Krishna's Counsel in Time of War* [Toronto: Bantam, 1986] 103).

The Emptied Christ of Philippians

center of Philippi did not experience the Roman Empire as particularly oppressive, for they lived in a thriving center of economic activity. Yet the very nature of empire is to oppress masses of people. And in Philippi during the Roman Empire many slaves were forced to work without hope in the nearby mines; they could not have gathered for worship with Paul and Epaphroditus, Euodia, and Syntyche. As widely traveled as Paul was, he was well aware of how poor people then lived. Still, he tells the Philippians they are not to focus on earthly things alone, but to abide in awareness of a harshly benign transcendence that ratchets down the surety of having answers to all problems.

The stance Paul recommends to the Philippians is one of human gentleness rather than confrontation. In 4:6 he advises: "in all things present your requests before God by prayers and petitions" (ἀλλ' ἐν παντὶ τῇ προσευχῇ καὶ τῇ δεήσει ... τὰ αἰτήματα ὑμῶν γνωριζέσθω πρὸς τὸν θεόν) and "with an abiding sense of thankfulness" (μετὰ εὐχαριστίας), they are to know that already they have been gifted in living life and living life in Christ. He tells them simply to make their prayers known "before God" (πρὸς τὸν θεόν) and not get caught up in the contention and party spirit that would demean the gentle gospel, distorting it and casting it as just one of many social and political options.

It is enough simply to "let them [our requests] be known," enunciating our prayers and requests into the vast spaces that cover God's presence, for then when we abandon our anxiety, "a sense of transcendent peace is allowed to filter into our minds and hearts" (καὶ ἡ εἰρήνη τοῦ θεοῦ ἡ ὑπερέχουσα πάντα νοῦν φρουρήσει τὰς καρδίας ὑμῶν καὶ τὰ νοήματα ὑμῶν ἐν Χριστῷ Ἰησοῦ 4:7). This peace is greater than the weary cessation of hostilities between parties, and so Paul calls it "the peace of God" (ἡ εἰρήνη τοῦ θεοῦ), a peace "that goes beyond the mind" (ἡ ὑπερέχουσα πάντα νοῦν), and thereby can guard our hearts and our thoughts in Christ Jesus (φρουρήσει τὰς καρδίας ὑμῶν καὶ τὰ νοήματα ὑμῶν ἐν Χριστῷ Ἰησοῦ). We are not to worry about sickness, suffering, and death, and we are to show gentleness to everyone.

Given the by-then distant history of Greek thought, the ideas of Plato must have precipitated into the broader Hellenistic culture of Paul's time—including the notion that, in addition to the perceptive ability to sense earthly things, we also possess a mystical organ, the *nous* (νοῦς), which enables us to see into the really real truth of things.[93] But the godly peace of which Paul speaks here goes beyond (ἡ ὑπερέχουσα) any such ethereal insight. It surpasses the mystic mind entirely (πάντα νοῦν, *panta noūn*), settling into the marrow of our bones and the interstices of our neural synapses despite the controller mind that worries about its purchase on the life of self.

The phrase "surpasses all understanding" (ἡ ὑπερέχουσα πάντα νοῦν) contains yet another *hyper* (ὑπερ) preclitic. As in Paul's earlier usages of this prefix, it does not here signify a superlative peace that comes from a superlative God. Rather, "surpassing" (ὑπερέχουσα) means more than (ὑπερ) having (ἔχουσα); it "goes beyond" (ὑπερ) having altogether. The verb ὑπερ-ἔχω, "beyond having," signfies the reversal of self-interest

---

93. Keenan, *Meaning of Christ*, 66–70, on "The Platonic Form of the Mystic Tradition."

and grasping, as in the emptiness hymn Christ does not consider divinity as "something to be grasped." The self-emptying person in an ungraspable and eschatological exaltation abandons worry (μηδὲν μεριμνᾶτε); there is no need for anxiety once the boundaries between success and failure, life and death, have been obliterated by Christ wisdom.

Discernment (4:8–9)

4:8 *As for the rest, brothers and sisters, whatever is true, whatever is honorable, whatever is just, whatever is pure, whatever is pleasing, whatever is commendable, if there is any excellence and if there is anything worthy of praise, take account of these things.* ⁹*Keep on doing the things that you have learned and received and heard and seen in me, and the God of peace will be with you.*

4:8 Τὸ λοιπόν, ἀδελφοί, ὅσα ἐστὶν ἀληθῆ, ὅσα σεμνά, ὅσα δίκαια, ὅσα ἁγνά, ὅσα προσφιλῆ, ὅσα εὔφημα, εἴ τις ἀρετὴ καὶ εἴ τις ἔπαινος, ταῦτα λογίζεσθε: ⁹ἃ καὶ ἐμάθετε καὶ παρελάβετε καὶ ἠκούσατε καὶ εἴδετε ἐν ἐμοί, ταῦτα πράσσετε: καὶ ὁ θεὸς τῆς εἰρήνης ἔσται μεθ᾽ ὑμῶν.

Here is Paul's public social stance, what he would do concretely in particular situations, and it is not any kind of definitive stance at all. He does not recommend that the Philippians stay aloof from all political engagement. Even as a people in Christ, they are not set apart, above the hurly-burly of down-and-dirty human politics. They have engagements as citizens. They are to stretch forth and engage in attentive insight and judicious commitment. This is Paul's social gospel to the Philippians, and it is no set program at all.

Writing "as for the rest, brothers and sisters" (Τὸ λοιπόν, ἀδελφοί 4:8), Paul signals that he is bringing this discourse, Letter B, to a conclusion.[94] He had already used this phrase at 3:1, but that passage clearly was not the conclusion; he had more to say. But here, "the rest" of what? In the present context, it must refer to the rest of our human affairs—that about which we are not to worry, the social and political engagements and disputed stratagems of the Christ gatherings vis-à-vis their world. It is not that Christians are to stay aloof. Believers in Christ, who have appreciated the oneness of their community, are nevertheless not to absent themselves from the councils of the city. They are not to avoid social commitment or political involvement. Still, gentle participation in such affairs, Paul insists, is to exemplify the best of the public virtues admired in that world.

He still promotes no particular political stance. Politics are complex, and the needs of the moment shift according to time and place. If indeed the good news that we have experienced in Christ reaches beyond the boundaries of self—outward toward

---

94. Sumney, *Philippians*, 69.

other people, back in time to before the patriarchs, and forward in our eschatological hopes for a just and peaceful future—it cannot be captured in any simple slogan or partisan claim. Through the Philippian liturgies celebrating the empty Christ and in prayers made known before God, we are to emerge beyond personal and group boundaries, all of which are erased. Nevertheless, human affairs in the light of the gospel remain human affairs. They are to be carried on in a spirit of gentleness made known to all, for never do any strategic decisions usurp the place of the word of the gospel. And so Paul provides only a general formula: Whatever commends itself to our considered understanding, be engaged in that and do that. For anyone who places faith in this gospel, "whatever is true" (ὅσα ἐστὶν ἀληθῆ), "whatever is honorable and just" (ὅσα σεμνά ὅσα δίκαια), "whatever pure" (ὅσα ἁγνά), "pleasing" (ὅσα προσφιλῆ), or "commendable" (ὅσα εὔφημα)—those things ought to be done. We are indeed to heed the prophetic call to justice that long we have heard in the scriptures. This, however, will become concrete in the practice of civic virtue. "If anything is found to be excellent" (εἴ τις ἀρετὴ) "or praiseworthy" (καὶ εἴ τις ἔπαινος), we are to "take into account these things" (ταῦτα λογίζεσθε). Paul's advice is pragmatic but strikingly nondirective.

Paul's list of "whatevers" does not mean, however, that the options we choose do not matter: We are to do what is honorable and just. Probably Paul himself did not make up the list he presents; many scholars believe that in cataloging these virtues, Paul relies on a textbook list of ethical qualities that were broadly accepted within the broader culture. He uses the material "in much the same way as pagan moral philosophers of his day when instructing their adherents."[95] Just as his advice above on not worrying reflects Epicurus' advice on tranquility, so his advice here reflects Stoic moral values.[96] And although the Christian gospel in its social implications and theological depth counters the Roman politics of that ancient time, it is not simply a countermovement to Roman power. Indeed, the gospel counters political structures of that and every time, for we have not yet realized the kingdom that Jesus in the Gospel of Mark says has drawn near (ἤγγικεν ἡ βασιλεία τοῦ θεοῦ 1:15a). That kingdom is still just over the hill, for we humans do not yet all share the experience of conversion (μετανοεῖτε καὶ πιστεύετε ἐν τῷ εὐαγγελίῳ 1:15b) that would mark that realization.

Paul's list of virtues here are not specifically or uniquely Christian. Philosophers and thinkers across cultures and through time commonly have recognized the first six items as virtues: truth, honor, justice, pure motivations, and pleasing and commendable behavior. These not only are generally recognized human values, they are also values that every follower of this gospel would affirm. Who is not to be concerned about truth, honor, and justice? What Jew could have read the prophetic books of the Tanach and not be committed to justice? Which Stoic thinker would not wish to act in a way that is pure and apart from selfish motives? What conscientious government counselor would not want to act in a way that would please others and would

---

95. O'Brien, *Epistle to the Philippians*, 501.
96. Ibid., 502.

be commended by them? But Paul is not recommending these virtues alone to his readers; he advises that whatever else they find to be virtuous, with that they are also to identify. Pressing the point, he adds that "whatever [his readers] might find to be excellent and praiseworthy" (εἴ τις ἀρετὴ καὶ εἴ τις ἔπαινος), that too "they are to take into consideration" (ταῦτα λογίζεσθε). A less programmatic or ideological commitment could hardly be imagined. In other words, no follower of the gospel is to consider himself or herself aloof from social intercourse and engagement, and there is no specific set of Christian directions, for there is no Christian identity apart from the Christ who emptied his self-identity.

Still, our practice—"that which actually we do" (ταῦτα πράσσετε 4:9)—is to reflect the nurture and training we have received from the gospel teaching. Paul tells his hearers that their engagements should be consonant with "the things that you have learned and received and heard and seen in me" (ἃ καὶ ἐμάθετε καὶ παρελάβετε καὶ ἠκούσατε καὶ εἴδετε ἐν ἐμοί). This does not free us from "thinking rationally" (λογίζεσθε 4:8), but it does provide the context in which we are to do so. Any political or social course of action that negates the gospel teachings is to be rejected, no matter how pleasing it may seem, no matter how excellently conceived, no matter how expediently necessary. Violations of justice, whether by government or by those who oppose government, do not harmonize with this gospel. Crusades to spread the faith by the sword negate the very gospel they pretend to follow. Cheating and stealing are wrong for high-profile financiers and bankers as well as for petty cheats and common thieves. The gospel is indeed a critique of all actions that support a false sense of self. And any supposed "virtues" of a standalone self that would shrug off the needs of the poor are merely variations on greed and anger, masked as affirmations of confident and socially respectable self-identity.[97]

In all their worldly engagements, the Philippians are to reflect upon and consider their actions, just as Paul considers himself to have done. But they are to prosecute such actions without anxiety and without party spirit. This is something of a difficult task. Party spirit abounds even in church politics, and drives the repetitive fracturing of church communities. It is difficult to avoid. Arguments can be pursued not only in the press and during meetings and conferences, but also—perhaps even more intensely—in the penumbra before sleep and in our everyday musings about being heard and appreciated. They go "viral" in the blogosphere, with more anonymous anathemas than any church official ever issued. Competing narratives become fortresses behind which people can hide, cling to righteous anger, and launch vituperative assaults.

---

97. Including Ayn Rand's "objectivism," which celebrates rational egoism and the rejection of ethical concern for others in favor of laissez-faire capitalism as the protector of individual rights. See Rand's *Atlas Shrugged* (New York: Random House, 1957), which pictures a dysfunctional United States that controls its creative industrialists, who go on strike, thereby "stopping the motor of the world" by their withdrawal. Her philosophy of self-interest still exerts influence on right-wing politics, particularly on such libertarian thinkers as the Cato Institute's. In any gospel terms and in Mahāyāna doctrine, the entire approach of "objectivism" is regarded as sin and delusion.

"Idealists" who think that nothing is so real as their own ideas clutch their opinions to themselves and engender both anger and fear. Nevertheless, Paul tells us, we are to eschew contentiousness and party spirit. We are simply to make our needs known "and the God of peace will be with you" (καὶ ὁ θεὸς τῆς εἰρήνης ἔσται μεθ'ὑμῶν 4:9). Note that the passage does not say that God will hear and fulfill our needs—at least not in linear time.

Good Wishes and Grace (4:21–23)

> 4:21 *Greet each and every saint in Christ Jesus. The brothers and sisters with me greet you.* ²²*All the saints greet you, especially those from the household of Caesar.* ²³*The grace of the Lord Jesus Christ be with your spirit.*

> 4:21 Ἀσπάσασθε πάντα ἅγιον ἐν Χριστῷ Ἰησοῦ. ἀσπάζονται ὑμᾶς οἱ σὺν ἐμοὶ ἀδελφοί. ²²ἀσπάζονται ὑμᾶς πάντες οἱ ἅγιοι, μάλιστα δὲ οἱ ἐκ τῆς Καίσαρος οἰκίας. ²³ἡ χάρις τοῦ κυρίου Ἰησοῦ Χριστοῦ μετὰ τοῦ πνεύματος ὑμῶν.

It is with the hope for an end-time consciousness that Paul concludes this letter. He instructs all his readers "to greet" (Ἀσπάσασθε) everyone without regard to any clear agreement on political strategy, but simply and elegantly "in Christ Jesus" (ἐν Χριστῷ Ἰησοῦ). To be in Christ Jesus marks a reorientation of the consciousness, from self-delusion to grace-full living. It is a reorientation that is triggered by abandonment of self-markers and conformation to the empty mind of Christ. The result is a social engagement of no ideology, a philosophy of pragmatic approaches to the complexity of the dependently arisen world. It is not a philosophy that upholds traditional values unerringly, for traditions change, as do cultures.

There is in Christ neither slave nor free, even though the Greco-Roman world flourished on slave labor. Even the book of the Apocalypse, whose Revelation was decidedly anti-Empire, never called for the abolishment of slavery. Paul's gospel did little in his time to benefit the enslaved mineworkers bound by servitude and constant humiliation.[98] Roman economic might could no more do without slavery than we so far have been able to do without oil to power our civilization, despite the suffering thereby inflicted on others. Paul here is not writing to slaves who cannot read, but to Philippians who can. For Paul, and perhaps even more for the Philippians, the focus lies simply and starkly on the elegant mind of the empty Christ, into which we may be enlightened, and from which we are encouraged to develop our own social and cultural commitments as best we can.

Throughout this Emptiness Letter B, and indeed throughout Paul's writings, to be one in Christ Jesus is the gospel consciousness that enables people to empty

---

98. Ruden, *Paul Among the People*, 133: "Pacifism seems never to have gone further then the question 'Why aren't we fighting barbarians rather than our neighbors, who are fellow Greeks?'"

themselves and focus their attention upon one another. Furthermore, it is this transformed and enlightened consciousness that enables Paul to speak of the early gospel practitioners as "each and every one a saint" (πάντα ἅγιον), here meaning that they are culturally pure in their crooked world,[99] adopting in their practice the virtues that Paul lists as cultural values. It means that all who listen to the words of Paul and attend deeply may experience the seed potential that will germinate and enable people both to engage in their world intelligently and to be content in the face of suffering and dying, for it empties all self markers and pushes people to abandon their enclosed worldly lives.

Using a formula of politeness, Paul assures his Philippian readers that all "the brothers and sisters who are with me" (οἱ σὺν ἐμοὶ ἀδελφοί) also "greet you" (ἀσπάζονται ὑμᾶς), and "all the saints" (πάντες οἱ ἅγιοι),[100] "especially those of the Emperor's household" (μάλιστα δὲ οἱ ἐκ τῆς Καίσαρος οἰκίας), "greet you" (ἀσπάζονται ὑμᾶς). In this, the next to last line of Paul's Letter B, he mentions almost offhandedly that some of those who are with him—some of the saints whose minds are being transformed by the empty Christ, some of those people—are themselves members of Caesar's household. This is a surprise. How is it that Paul has dealings with the imperial house at all? We just do not know.[101]

Perhaps some of the Roman Christians were indeed members of, or servants in, the bureaucracy of the Empire. Perhaps Paul is imprisoned somewhere under a Roman administration with "imperial" guards who have become his friends, since they recognize that he is in chains for Christ. We simply do not know, and so the commentators offer nothing more than guesses. It is interesting that Paul feels no hesitation to identify some of the "saints" as members of the imperial household. He seems not at all allergic to people because of their political or social employment, even if they are part of the oppressive empire. The gospel is to have vast social impact, for the kingdom of God is the eschatological hope for a world of justice and peace. Paul nowhere denies this, and yet he tends to speak less of the nearness of God's kingdom as found in the Synoptic Gospels, and more of the eschatological nearness of Jesus who structures our minds.

Even though for Paul there is neither male nor female, Jew nor Greek, slave nor free, and even though the Empire takes in many different peoples and enforces its culture upon them with cruel power, still, for Paul, Rome is not the whore of Babylon. Apparently, for him, there is neither Roman nor Christian. His strategy is for citizen acceptance of the gospel; and indeed less than three hundred years after Paul's time

---

99. Paul, on the children of believers (1 Cor 7:14): "Otherwise, your children would be unclean, but as it is, they are holy."

100. See Reumann, *Philippians*, 728: The saints have become the identity marker of those who, emptying themselves, live "in Christ," as members of the community of the spirit.

101. Ibid., 739: "Possibly a house church [in Ephesus] made up from the *familia Caesaris*, slaves and, or those who have gained freedom in the Emperor Nero's lower-level civil-service bureaucracy."

the gospel and the Empire will be amalgamated, forming a Christian Roman Empire that continues Roman state sovereignty and power. In the later Deutero-Pauline letters, Christian accommodation to the values of power has so increased that by the time of the Pastoral Epistles the emerging churches are modeling themselves upon hierarchical patterns to enforce ecclesiastical conformity and order. And Paul could hardly have envisaged that within just a few generations, the emperor of the Roman Empire would find in Christian practice and institutions a ready ally for his imperial desires.[102]

But the gospel that Paul expresses in Philippians challenges us first and foremost to empty our hearts of all identity markers, to eschew power for weakness, and to reason among ourselves as to the best course forward. To bypass union with the empty Christ by pretending that we have achieved some kind of a new Christian identity or new Christian order is to render the gospel sterile. With minds focused upon the empty Christ, we are to expand our social, cultural, and political horizons to create a just and peace-abiding world without accommodating to the power fixations of some selves over other selves. The identityless expansion of our horizons will never come to a conclusion, nor will it compete with Buddhists, Hindus, Muslims, or atheists, but it will witness always with gentleness to the transformative life in Christ that such competition would occlude.[103]

Paul thus ends his Emptiness Letter B on the empty Christ with the wish that "the grace of the Lord Jesus Christ" (ἡ χάρις τοῦ κυρίου Ἰησοῦ Χριστοῦ 4:23) will "permeate your minds" (μετὰ τοῦ πνεύματος ὑμῶν), for it is to "your spirits" (πνεύματος ὑμῶν) that his efforts have been directed,[104] just as it is the Spirit who supplies Christ to their consideration.

---

102. See Mitchell, *Church, Gospel, and Empire*; and John Howard Yoder, *The Politics of Jesus* (Grand Rapids: Eerdmans, 1994).

103. On Paul's use of military imagery and on putting self-identity and competition aside, see Ruden, *Paul Among the People*, 130.

104. Heil equates spirit with "the human 'spirit' that animates and is synonymous with their persons" (Heil, *Philippians: Let Us Rejoice*, 178).

6

Resurrection Letter C

This last of the three letters in Paul's Philippian correspondence is comprised of verses 3:2–21 of the canonical epistle. No doubt this missive originally included both a proper introductory passage and a conclusion like those we see at the beginning (1:1–2) and end (4:21–23) of the unified letter. We have used 4:21–23 as the conclusion to Letter B above. As it stands without its opening, Resurrection Letter C begins with a harsh polemic against those who demand the identity marker of circumcision as a prerequisite to Christ-identity as a righteous person—a demand that is in direct contradiction to the self-emptying Christ. Paul then addresses the issue of his own identity, which he regards as so much offal that is to be discarded, just as Christ of the Philippian hymn regarded his divine status as nothing to cling to in self-definition. Paul describes his self-emptying not as a matter of acquiring a new identity as a righteous Christian, however, but rather as knowing Christ, participating in his resurrection power, and sharing in his sufferings.[1]

The emptiness hymn of 2:6–11 has long been seen as central to the Philippian epistle, and rereading Philippians in this three-letter schema allows us to glimpse the process whereby Paul himself has come to appreciate and adopt the Philippian community's teaching of the emptying mind of Christ. In this last of the three letters that comprise the canonical letter to the Philippians, Paul expresses again that recently acquired insight, this time in terms of resurrection faith.

Canine Confidence (3:2–4a)

3:2 Just look at the dogs, at those who do harm, at those who mutilate the flesh!
³We are the circumcision, who serve by the spirit of God and boast in Christ

---

1. Silva, *Philippians*, 150: "Here in Philippians the listing of credentials has a more direct theological purpose—to serve as a foil for his exposition of the Christian message in verses 7–11."

Jesus and take no confidence in the flesh—⁴even though I, too, have reason for confidence in the flesh.

3:2 Βλέπετε τοὺς κύνας, βλέπετε τοὺς κακοὺς ἐργάτας, βλέπετε τὴν κατατομήν. ³ἡμεῖς γάρ ἐσμεν ἡ περιτομή, οἱ πνεύματι θεοῦ λατρεύοντες καὶ καυχώμενοι ἐν Χριστῷ Ἰησοῦ καὶ οὐκ ἐν σαρκὶ πεποιθότες, ⁴καίπερ ἐγὼ ἔχων πεποίθησιν καὶ ἐν σαρκί.

Although there is no recorded presence of a synagogue in Philippi, we know that Paul contended elsewhere with "Judaizers" who insisted that to be Christ followers meant being fully Jewish. So it may well be that itinerate preachers with such views had arrived in Philippi and were demanding that even the Gentile Philippians in this gospel community conform to Jewish customs. In any case, Paul here is responding to attitudes that would draw members of the community back into fear and conflict, into denial of the empty Christ in favor of clinging to a false sense of security and a deluded identity. So Paul tells them to "Look out" (βλέπετε) for "the dogs"—people who take stances that would denigrate the empty life we live in Christ.

As elsewhere, the Greeks of the Philippian house churches did read the scriptures—that is, Torah—and no doubt were attracted to the beauty of the Hebrew faith but not to some of its cultural practices. They sought the God who, as Abraham Joshua Heschel teaches, was seeking them;[2] but they were not at all keen on being circumcised. In their Greek culture, where open nakedness was accepted as normal at least in some contexts, the notion of changing the appearance of the sexual organs was much to be abhorred. Why on earth would God want to mutilate the beauty of his human creation? These new followers of Christ would have found it difficult culturally to accept and follow the practice of circumcision.[3] Paul is addressing these culturally Greek members of the community in this message.[4] They would have felt pressured by the charges of Judaizers, from whatever quarter they came, that they could not be Christ followers without becoming full-fledged Jews. At the same time, Judaizers would have been upset at Paul's interference; given their hope that someday God-fearers would accept not only faith in the Lord but also Jewish cultural patterns and religious customs, they would have considered Paul a thorn in the side.

---

2. Abraham Joshua Heschel, *God in Search of Man: A Philosophy of Judaism* (New York: Farrar, Straus & Giroux, 1955).

3. Reumann discusses the widespread practice of circumcision among many ancient peoples: "Circumcision came into even greater prominence for Jews when Antiochus IV Epiphanes (176–71 CE) banned it (1 Macc 1:48, 60–61). The practice became something to die for, also when Hadrian (117–38 CE) placed circumcision on a par with castration . . . as a barbaric custom, akin to murder . . . For Greeks, to circumcise was to mutilate the body, something barbaric . . . In Greco-Roman culture there were social implications for circumcised man. The Greek gymnasium (even in Jerusalem) and Roman baths assumed nudity. The Jewish badge of membership in the covenant people brought stigma" (Reumann, *Philippians*, 472–73 n. 12).

4. See Crossan and Reed, *In Search of Paul*, 38–45.

Even if the Philippian community was thoroughly Gentile, that they would feel pressure from Christ followers elsewhere to uphold all the norms of Torah is not unreasonable, for none of the early communities of Christ followers regarded themselves as a replacement for the Israel of God.[5] "Paul, it needs to be emphasized, knows nothing of a 'new' Israel; for him there is only one people of God, who are now newly constituted—quite in keeping with Old Testament promises—on the basis of Christ and the Spirit; and it is by the Spirit in particular that Gentiles have entered into their inheritance of the blessings promised to Abraham (Gal 3:14)."[6] Indeed, the term "new Israel" appears nowhere in the New Testament.[7]

Philippian house gatherings, formed around the experience of the empty and risen Christ, were in a culturally ambiguous situation. Their new Christ faith did not mean a rejection of older, more Jewish communities that went back to Jesus' Palestine and the early apostles, and they had not as yet drawn a divide with Israel and the rabbis as reported in Acts 15:6. They did not reject Hillel (d. ca. 15 CE) and his grandson Gamaliel (d. ca. 54 CE), or the patriarchs Moses and Abraham, or prophets like Isaiah and Elijah—all of whom figured in their own narrative history. On the other hand, many gatherings of Christ followers, especially in Philippi with its absence of synagogue and Jewish cultic life, barely identified with the social and cultural practices that identified Israel as the chosen people. In Paul's mind, life in Christ indeed reshaped and reconfigured his own past, but if we listen to what he actually says, this did not invalidate the covenant or create something new called Christianity. The solution for the Philippians was their negation of the ongoing value of any chosen identity, and this is what they celebrate in the hymn to the empty Christ—that they are neither Jew nor Greek. And Paul embraces that emptying of identity, as becomes clear in 3:4–11.

The later separation of church from synagogue is prefigured in this reaction of Paul to the demands of those Jewish Christ followers who insist upon retaining the ancient identity markers of the chosen people, whom Paul himself often calls "the saints." But as Paul meditates on the empty Christ of the Philippian hymn, everything becomes new in Christ and those old identities fall away. Emptied, Christ threatens no one; he represents no divisive position that might harden ideologically or institutionally. And yet that empty Christ, in the concrete situations where Paul lived and preached, did eventually mean a break with the cherished cultural identities and traditions maintained by some Jewish Christians, and perhaps also by Greek Christians who in some communities had already fully joined the synagogue and accepted circumcision.

---

5. Some think that here in Phil 3 we find the beginning of the transposition from the Israel of the Old Testament to the Christian Church as the new Israel. But as Reumann argues, "*peritomē*-ecclesiology,' even when interpreted in terms of the Spirit, would have little or no place in an increasingly Gentile church after 70 CE, a church of uncircumcised believers" (Reumann, *Philippians*, 475).

6. Fee, *Paul's Letter to the Philippians*, 299. See also Sanders' pivotal *Paul and Palestinian Judaism*.

7. Arnold G. Fruchtenbaum, "The Use of Israel in the New Testament," *Middletown Bible Church*, http://www.middletownbiblechurch.org/reformed/israelaf.htm.

The question for Paul is: Are these clearly biblical norms binding forever, and on all those who have been freed in Christ? Does their scriptural witness mean that Greeks, too, must follow customs that seem alien to them? Why mutilate the good body God has given? What overriding religious reason is there for not partaking of shellfish? These issues may seem almost trivial to Christians today, but we have seen their counterpart in our culture wars over the past several decades: Despite what Jesus says about the indissolubility of marriage, may not divorced people be remarried in the church? It is true that passages in both Old and New Testaments link homosexuality to the idolatry of those times, but may not faithful gay Christians today receive communion at our common table? Or marry in the church? If baptism is the entrance into the community of the church, may we not share the Eucharist with those who, although unbaptized, approach our common table to share our common life? The same intensity that marks these modern clashes between tradition and our changing culture characterized the emotional issue of circumcision for Paul and the Judaizers against whom he rants here.

Paul, born and raised in a Hellenistic culture, deeply immersed in the Jewish tradition, and reconfigured in Christ faith, teaches that the important thing is the transformation of mind and heart, not the cultural norms through which that is expressed. The distinction is old but difficult to work out in practice. It was Jeremiah who first spoke of the new covenant, inscribed not on tablets of stone but on the very flesh of the human heart. Yet Jeremiah never faced an influx of non-Jews into his community. What parts of a tradition are to be regarded as merely cultural and thus dispensable when cultures change? For Paul, nothing is indispensable, for there is nothing in our daily lives that does not change. All fixed and essential identities are deconstructed by the empty Christ. It is not that Paul will lose his old Jewish identity and take on a Christian one. Paul will lose his identity altogether.

The empty Christ provides the people in Philippi with a safe harbor from the fears and delusions that spring from self-clinging. But they must look out for those who insist that cultural identity is more important than the reorientation of heart and mind that comes from focusing upon the empty Christ. Paul growls: "Look out for the dogs, the injurers, and [their] mutilation" (Βλέπετε τοὺς κύνας, βλέπετε τοὺς κακοὺς ἐργάτας, βλέπετε τὴν κατατομήν).[8] The Greek word for circumcision is *peri-*

---

8. Reumann considers the possibility that the reference to dogs suggests itinerant Cynic philosophers, whose "crude *adiaphoria* or shameless indifference to conventional behavior—'constant barking, scavenging, urinating, and mating in public' (*Anchor Bible Dictionary* 1:1233)—made them unwelcome" (Reumann, *Philippians*, 471-72). But Reumann thinks not, for "what follows in 3:2 is specifically Jewish—one would not call wandering Cynic freeloaders 'workers,' and 'incision, circumcision'" (ibid.). Bruce notes: "Dogs were regarded as unclean animals (cf. Rev 22:15) because they were not particular about what they ate," suggesting that kosher norms were also in play (Bruce, *Philippians*, 105). Caird takes the "dogs" of verse 2 as "an admonitory example and not a group of menacing enemies against whom the Philippians must be on their guard. For they are allowed to drop into the background, and the contrast from now on is between Paul the Jew and Paul the Christian" (Caird, *Paul's Letters from Prison*, 134-35). Better stated, the contrast lies between a well-defined, religious

tome (περιτομή), but here Paul uses instead the term *katatome* (κατατομή) denoting a "mutilation," a cutting or chopping as perhaps by the downward motion (*kata*) of a knife. He is saying this cutting *around* the foreskin, which has heretofore been the sacred mark of participation in the people of God, is really nothing more than *chopping off* of the flesh.[9] All that it accomplishes is injury to the most sensitive of male organs. We are to beware of such culturally required mutilation, and those who "would do harm" (τοὺς κακοὺς ἐργάτας) to our bodies. We are warned to watch out for "dogs" (τοὺς κακοὺς), a term that in its very harshness expresses the emotional intensity surrounding this issue.

Commentators often attempt to determine precisely who it is that Paul is disparaging as the "dogs" in this passage. J. M. G. Berkeley and Gordon Fee call it "mirror reading" when commentators attempt to determine the identity of Paul's opponents from what he says about them.[10] In letters A and B, which are not especially polemical, we do not discern any definable groups of opponents. But here in letter C, it seems that there are some particular people who in their zeal for the traditions threaten the Philippians' endeavor to take on the empty mind of Christ. Possibly Paul is using the image of dogs in a generalized way, to refer to anyone who would attack and tear apart the human body. Dogs in Paul's world are not seen as loyal pets but as ritually impure scavengers that feed on carrion and excrement. Thus it is particularly indelicate of him to use this unsavory image to describe those who preach a different gospel,[11] demanding of all Christ followers cultural conformity to practices of circumcision, dietary restrictions, abstinence from food used in pagan sacrifices, and the observance of the religious festivals.

Passing quickly from images of ravening canines, Paul avers that "we already are" (ἡμεῖς γάρ ἐσμεν 3:3) "the circumcision," using here *peritome* (ἡ περιτομή), the proper Greek term for Jewish circumcision. But for him, as with Jeremiah, that sign of faith has shifted so that it no longer means a visible bodily mark at all.[12] Now, "we" are described as "those who serve by the Spirit of God" (ὁι πνεύματι θεοῦ λατρεύοντες),

---

Paul and the empty person he—and the Philippians—emulated in Christ.

9. Thurston, "Philippians," 113: "Jews circumcise; pagans mutilate. The prophets of Baal slashed themselves (1 Kgs 18:28) and the followers of Cybele cut themselves in religious ecstasy."

10. Fee, *Paul's Letter to the Philippians*, 7.

11. Still, Paul's rejection is brutal. See Reumann, *Philippians*, 473: "Hence his outburst, in Galatians 5:12, 'I wish they'd go castrate themselves' (wordplay on *peritomē* and *apokoptō*) . . . Paul's rhetoric is boisterous, rude, and even crude. But not here aimed at Judaism itself or what Jews do in their community, but against missionaries who in Galatia (probably in Corinth, perhaps in Ephesus), wanted to make Paul's converts really saved and blessed by adding this rite for Gentile believers. Paul turns a proud identity marker for Jews back in the face of the enemies by an insult term." On identity markers, see Dunn, *New Perspective on Paul*, 474–75.

12. Reumann, *Philippians*, 478, on "We are the Circumcision": "At issue in Paul's day was Christian identity in a Roman *colonia*, not via Jewish circumcision, but through Christ in a community with a heritage and the Spirit." Still, that identity is a cultural and social construct, not a physical mark of Christian status.

by the Spirit who supplies Christ, the emptying Christ who carves out space in our minds for faith commitment. Still, such public service in the world (λατρεύοντες) arises within the context of liturgical service (λατρεύοντες), whence the celebration of the empty Christ has emerged. This "service" encompasses the entire orientation of our daily lives,[13] including liturgical worship—liturgy. It is the very same service that Paul has just described in his own life, poured out as a libation on the altar of service (λειτουργίᾳ) for the faith of the Philippians. Throughout, it is our commonality with Christ in living and dying that is at issue.

"In saying that 'we,' both Jews and Gentiles together who have put our trust in Christ, 'are *the* circumcision,' Paul indicates that the primary issue is not the Philippians' salvation, but rather [the working out of] the identification of the people of God under the new covenant."[14] As it turns out, that identification does not mean a reconfigured, stable identity for the "Christian," a prospect that was never envisioned by Paul. Rather, it will be an identity-less sharing in the organic life of Christ through knowing the power of his resurrection and participating in his sufferings. It is because of this that we also rejoice in Christ Jesus. We find ourselves one with the Lord of emptiness who clings to no identity whatsoever, for he has emptied himself of all identifiable forms except that of slave and criminal. It is thus that we "boast in Christ Jesus and have no confidence in the flesh" (καὶ καυχώμενοι ἐν Χριστῷ Ἰησοῦ καὶ οὐκ σαρκὶ πεποιθότες 3:3). There is no refuge in selfhood.

What does it mean to boast in Christ Jesus? Paul has written that our boasting may abound in Christ Jesus (1:26), and that he can boast in the steadfastness of the Philippians who "hold on to the word of life" (2:16). In speaking here again of boasting, he draws his meaning largely from Jeremiah 9:23–24, where the wise person boasts not in wisdom, might, or wealth, but rather in the Lord.[15] In lieu of boasting of our individual status or accomplishments, the ultimate expression of a self-centered life,[16] we are to boast in our emptying. In our new identity with Christ, we are not to cling to old identity markers like circumcision in the community of Torah. "The future, therefore, is not to be found in taking on Jewish identity; in other words, the future does not lie in his [Paul's] religious past."[17] Nor, I would add, does it lie in the assertion of a new future of static and self-assured Christian identity.

Most of the commentators I have read contrast Paul's boasting in Christ Jesus to the self-affirmation that was intrinsic to his previous Hellenistic Jewish identity. According to O'Brien, "The apostle's references to boasting need to be understood

13. Reumann notes that the phrase "who serve by the spirit of God" tempted later scribes to interpret it as a "spiritual worship" (ibid., 476). But, he argues, worship is not the topic here and the verb means "serve." The usual sense of *pneuma theou* holds, viz., "by the Spirit of God" as instrumental dative. Reumann's take is that it means being "in daily life" (ibid.).

14. Fee, *Paul's Letter to the Philippians*, 298.

15. Ibid., 154, 301.

16. Ibid., 303.

17. Ibid., 306.

against the contemporary backgrounds of the professional practices of the sophists, among others, and of the Jew whose basic attitude was one of self-confidence before God, convinced that his keeping of the law would bring honour to himself. As Paul attacked the doctrine of justification by works, so he opposed all boasting based on self-trust."[18] But this is, I think, too narrow a reading: Paul is contending not just against Greek philosophy or rabbinic teaching, but against the universal human practice of boasting in oneself, whatever the contours of that self.[19] Nor are we to boast in our new identity; Christ washes away all personal and social markers that afford us a false sense of security.

Paul having declared the outward marks of Torah covenant to be unnecessary for Hellenistic Christian communities, one might assume that he will advocate something new, something that goes beyond old Jewish identity markers, perhaps a new Christian identity rejecting circumcision and kosher laws for all. He does not do this, however; he asserts only that Jewish cultural norms *need not* apply to Greeks, while Jewish Christians are to continue following Torah practices. In our reading, it is not a question for Paul of which cultural identity a Christian is to assume, for being in Christ is no cultural identity at all (however much both church and state enlisted the gospel to serve as guarantor of western cultural superiority in later centuries). Paul urges the Philippians to recall his prior warnings "against those who would entice them to submit to Jewish 'boundary markers' and thus be identified with Israel's former covenant while they also identify with Christ . . ." Rather, they are "to find their joy in the Lord . . . [and] hold fast to . . . their sure hope of Christ's coming . . ."[20] I hesitate before this interpretation, however; I see Paul as simply reaffirming Jeremiah's "new covenant" written surgically upon our hearts.

Paul's gospel is much more radical than any mere shift in identities. He does not recommend that Jewish Christians abandon their traditional practices. At the same time, he goes much farther than that, inviting *all* to abandon any identity markers whatsoever. Paul does not know, nor does he say, that he has become a Christian. There is nothing about "being a Christian" anywhere in Paul's writings. Simply because the experience of the living Christ has taken hold of him, he now would break through all cultural boundaries that would bar participation in that graced awakening—ethnic boundaries for Jewish people and cultural boundaries for the Gentiles. Paul is not drawn to recast his faith in terms of Hellenistic culture with all its philosophic riches; he makes no move to employ Greek philosophy to filter the gospel (although our later ancestors in the faith did precisely that). Paul in fact critiques the identification

---

18. O'Brien, *Epistle to the Philippians*, 362.

19. See Sanders, *Paul and Palestinian Judaism*. He was among the first Christian scholars to question and demonstrate the inaccuracy of caricatured images of the Jewish faith as legalistic and phony. Others followed him in this evaluation, among them James D. G. Dunn, who coined the term "the New Perspective," focusing attention on a more careful historical image of Jews in Jesus' time.

20. Fee, *Paul's Letter to the Philippians*, 286–87.

of faith and culture that runs throughout the ancient Hebrew narrative. Offering no newly constructed Christian identity, he speaks of living "in Christ" in terms so mystical and indefinable that they could never serve as visible markers for any stable thing.

We are not to find comfort in our biological heredity—our "flesh." The question is: What is this flesh (σαρκὶ, *sarx*) in which we are to take no refuge, to have no confidence?[21] "Flesh" here means the embodied self that we take to be so central to our living that we circumscribe by using clear and visible marks of our belonging: flags and emblems, necklaces with crosses for Christians, head scarves for Muslim women, beards and turbans for Sikhs, and for all, ideas and viewpoints that hedge us into monolingual worlds.[22] It is not that Paul himself has no personal history. He presents his identity here, constructed out of who he was and who he has come to be. So when he says we should "take no confidence in the flesh" (καὶ οὐκ σαρκὶ πεποιθότες 3:3),[23] still he confesses, "even though (καίπερ 3:4) I, too, have (ἐγὼ ἔχων) good reasons to do so." And then immediately below he discards that identity as so much offal.

Paul's Identity (3:4b–6)

3:4b *If anyone supposes to take refuge in the flesh, even more so can I.* [5]*I was circumcised on the eighth day, a member of the people of Israel, of the tribe of Benjamin, a Hebrew born of Hebrews; as to Torah, a Pharisee;* [6]*as to zeal, a persecutor of the church; as to righteousness under Torah, blameless.*

3:4b εἴ τις δοκεῖ ἄλλος πεποιθέναι ἐν σαρκί, ἐγὼ μᾶλλον: [5]περιτομῇ ὀκταήμερος, ἐκ γένους Ἰσραήλ, φυλῆς Βενιαμίν, Ἑβραῖος ἐξ Ἑβραίων, κατὰ νόμον Φαρισαῖος, [6]κατὰ ζῆλος διώκων τὴν ἐκκλησίαν, κατὰ δικαιοσύνην τὴν ἐν νόμῳ γενόμενος ἄμεμπτος.

There is no escaping our lineage or history; we are who we are as the result of our dependently arisen past. But neither is there any refuge to be had in that lineage or history. No form of self-identity is any kind of refuge, although it is a persistent temptation and, as Paul says, there are those who "suppose to take refuge in the flesh" (εἴ τις δοκεῖ ἄλλος πεποιθέναι ἐν σαρκί 3:4b). To take refuge means to rely or depend upon (πεποιθέναι). But this is only an "apparent" (δοκεῖ) refuge; there is nothing finally, firmly set about its dependently arisen course. Nevertheless, people everywhere,

---

21. Reumann, *Philippians*, 477. Note that the definition above for *sarx* parallels the Buddhist notion of *saṃsāra*, entanglement within the enfleshed selfhood of our bodies.

22. Flesh (*sarx*) "covers justification by the Law and even by man's own religiosity or spirituality" (Collange, *Epistle of Saint Paul*, 125). Caird adds, "What Paul means by *confidence in the flesh* becomes clear in the following verses: It is any claim to superiority, whether it is based on inherited privilege or on personal success" (Caird, *Paul's Letters from Prison*, 134).

23. The grounds for confidence are "not self, but God or, here, Christ," in contrast to which, "*sarx* denotes the whole person, human life destined for demise and destruction before God, not something which real life and future hopes can be built" (Reumann, *Philippians*, 477).

including Paul's opponents, do depend upon the assumed reality of their self-identity. We do not want to regard our very selves and the histories of our lives as empty.

Jesus may not have regarded being in the form of God, or being equal to God, as something precious to cling to, but it is difficult for us to translate such an attitude to our own lives, where identity markers play such an important role in our ability to live in and cope with the world. It is all just too unsettling to think that in the deepest part of our here-and-now being we are empty of any core whatsoever, that we have no assured and delineated self or identity markers. For if we accept the truth of that, we would have to acknowledge that we have nothing within ourselves to depend upon. And if we cannot depend upon our own selves down here, how can we depend upon a God up there who mirrors our human concepts?

This is the issue that Paul struggles against, for he is preaching a gospel that is both personally and culturally disruptive. This gospel threatens all self-affirming life scripts that rest upon assumed personal narratives and accepted cultural patterns. But those narratives and patterns, if promoted beyond their dependently arisen grounding, are illusion—what the Mahayanists call the primal delusion (Skt. *avidyā*), the mind functioning in the pattern that imagines the self to be real. Paul sees this attachment to an imagined self as boasting "in the flesh" (ἐν σαρκί), that is, according to "human standards."[24] And that delusion—whether religious or not, whether Christian or Jewish, whether Torah fundamentalist as in Romans[25] or Hellenistic secularist as on Athens' Areopagus hill—forms the context in which he has to negotiate and contend. Whatever the unique makeup of the Philippian community, in all probability most of the communities of Christ followers in the Hellenistic world with whom Paul dealt contained both observant Torah Jews and Gentile God-fearers who were attracted to Torah faith in the Lord of the universe.

Paul himself, however, is not an outsider to that Torah tradition, and so he can boast in his lineage "better than" (ἐγὼ μᾶλλον 3:4b) anyone else. He was born into, and all his identity markers were nurtured by, that tradition. And although he rejects others' demand that all Gentiles be circumcised, he himself was properly "circumcised on the eighth day" (περιτομῇ ὀκταήμερος 3:5).[26] Ethnically, he is indeed "from the people of Israel" (ἐκ γένους Ἰσραήλ), more specifically "from the tribe of Benjamin" (φυλῆς Βενιαμίν); so he can claim full and complete membership within "the Hebrew people" and tradition (Ἑβραῖος ἐξ Ἑβραίων).[27] Not only was he raised within the tradition and

---

24. O'Brien, *Epistle to the Philippians*, 363.

25. See the argument of D. A. Campbell, *Deliverance of God*, 313–468, on "The Conventional Reading and Its Problems."

26. Reumann comments on circumcision: "Jubilees 15:11–14, a male child not circumcised on the eighth day 'has broken my covenant' (J. H. Charlesworth, *Old Testament Pseudepigrapha* [Garden City: Doubleday, 1983] 1:86)" (Reumann, *Phillipians*, 482).

27. On identity markers, Reumann writes, "The first four items can each be paralleled by a phrase Roman citizens might use for their heritage. As counterpart of circumcision, the *toga* (*virilis*) can be claimed, chief garment of a free-born Roman male . . . The counterpart for a Roman citizen was *civis*

nurtured in its teachings, he adhered intently not only to the demands of Torah but also to the Traditions of the Elders as learned from his teachers. To wit, "in his Torah observance he was a Pharisee" (κατὰ νόμον Φαρισαῖος), those "separated ones" who insisted that all life be permeated by an awareness of the Lord of the universe and the guidance of Torah.[28]

It was Paul's felt "zeal"[29] for Torah observance that led him "to persecute the church" (κατὰ ζῆλος διώκων τὴν ἐκκλησίαν 3:6), those early Christian communities who themselves felt "called out from" and separated from the world of delusion and sin, just as the Pharisees in their authentic practice felt themselves "separated" by their dedication from nonobservant people. We have little historical information about how effective Paul's persecution of the nascent church was. Perhaps he only wanted to silence them; Acts reports that he stood silently at Stephen's demise and did not himself take part in the stone throwing. But by his own account, as a law-observant Pharisee dedicated to reform,[30] he did indeed zealously attempt to persecute the Christian movement, which was regarded as an unorthodox option for any Hebrew who believed the "Shema Israel"—that God is one, without another. In this regard, Paul confesses, he was "as to righteousness under Torah, blameless" (κατὰ δικαιοσύνην τὴν ἐν νόμῳ γενόμενος ἄμεμπτος).[31] In 2:15, Paul tells the Philippians to be "blameless

---

Romanus; for Paul, 'born a citizen'" (ibid., 512–13). The terms "Hebrew" and "Tribe of Benjamin" help "imply Saul of Tarsus once studied in Jerusalem (Acts 22:3; 23:16, his sister presumably lived there now), that he spoke Aramaic, but not necessarily that he was of Palestinian parentage ... The counterpart Roman term for family identity (Pilhofer 1:126–27) was *(Cai)filius*, 'son (of Caius)' (or whoever)" (ibid.). Silva adds, "Pilhofer (*Philippi*, vol. 1, Die erste christliche Gemeinde Europas. Wissenschaftliche Untersuchungen zum Neuen Testament 87 [Tübingen: Mohr Siebeck, 1995] 122–26) sheds interesting light on Paul's self-description. Pointing out that the residents of Philippi were part of the *tribus Voltinia* and had thus both Philippian and Roman citizenship, Pilhofer states that a Philippian citizen whose family name, for example, was Caius would be identified with this pattern: *civis Romanus, tribu Voltinia, Cai filius*. With a deliberate threefold contrast, Paul replaces Rome with Israel, Voltinia with Benjamin, and his family name with Hebrew (of the Hebrews). Pilhofer then goes on to expand on the issue of citizenship, concluding that the Christians would have been regarded as being outside—and thus as enemies of—the Roman order" (Silva, *Philippians*, 150 n. 5).

28. According to Bruce, "The term Pharisees means 'separated ones'" (Bruce, *Philippians*, 109). Bruce notes further that in "a later rabbinical commentary, *Leviticus Rabba*, the injunction, 'Be holy because I, the Lord your God, am holy' (Lev 19:2) is amplified: 'As I am holy, so you must also be holy; as I am separate, so you also must be separate *perûshîm*'" (ibid. 111).

29. Reumann, *Philippians*, 514: "Heroes exhibited zeal from Phineas on, leading to 'zeal for the Law' in Maccabean times and Paul's day, but not yet identified with avowedly political Zealots." Reumann adds, "In the Greek world, *zēlos* = commitment to a person, cause, or goal" (ibid., n. 32).

30. On Pharisees, Reumann writes: "the fundamental and most influential religious movement within Palestinian Judaism between 150 B.C. and A.D. 70," with "a particular relationship to the Law." The term appears "almost 100 times in the New Testament; Philippians 3:5, the only example outside the Gospels and Acts (there only in Jerusalem; of Paul at 23:6 and 26:5). Most treatments of the Pharisees stress their origins (probably 2nd century B.C.); 'separation' from the unholy; written *and* oral law, applied in daily life; openness to newer ideas like resurrection; communal life. More recent analysis stresses political origins (conflict with later Hasmonean rulers; not necessarily opposed to Herod or Roman rule), a movement to change society" (ibid., 484).

31. Ibid., 515–16: "This self-description has stung many commentators, and not only Protestants,

and innocent" (ἄμεμπτοι καὶ ἀκέραιοι) in this crooked world; here he asserts that in his Torah observance he was "blameless" (ἄμεμπτος) but not that he was "innocent" (ἀκέραιος).

It is a common assumption that Paul, as the apostle of Christ, abandoned his old Jewish identity to take on his Christian identity. After all, he stopped persecuting the church! But, he does not write that he is no longer a Pharisee. Indeed, Acts 15:5 makes clear that in the early communities there were Pharisees "who believed in the Gospel" (τινες τῶν ἀπὸ αἱρέσις τῶν Φαρισαίων πεπιστευκότες) while insisting that all Gentiles be circumcised. In the account of Paul before the Sanhedrin in Acts 23:6, Paul identifies himself as a Pharisee in the present tense: "I am a Pharisee, a son of Pharisees" (ἐγὼ Φαρισαῖός εἰμι, υἱὸς Φαρισαίων),[32] on trial because of his resurrection faith, a faith that was common to all Pharisees. He may in fact have been a follower of Rabbi Hillel.[33] Yet, clearly Paul has moved away from the Pharisees' traditional understanding of Torah observances, at least as regards the necessity of circumcision and kosher laws for non-Jews. His old identity remains as his historical grounding, albeit reconfigured in light of the enlightening Christ. Furthermore, as is clear throughout his writings, especially in his letter to the Romans, he no longer regards his own blamelessness before the law as efficacious.

The entire Reformation theology that Martin Luther developed from reading the scriptures is grounded in Paul. And like Paul before him, Luther experienced justification and became blameless only as a gift that comes from the Father through the Lord Jesus.[34] Nothing Paul of Tarsus could do, nothing Luther could do, and nothing we can do, will bring about our justification. No zeal avails. There is no righteousness or justification that comes from exact and zealous observance of anybody's Torah.[35] Likewise, there is no righteousness or justification that comes from exact and zealous observance of the gospel. Paul confesses that although he followed that path of zeal

---

as outrageous," but "Being blameless was no impossibility among Greeks, 'unblamed by friends,' 'faultless justice' (as in Plato, *Legibus*)."

32. For a discussion of the Pharisaic schools of Hillel and Shammai, see Allen Ross, "Christian Pharisees in the Bible" http://bible.org/seriespage/pharisees.

33. On Paul's being a Pharisee, see Reumann, *Philippians*, 513 n. 30. Also see J. Jeremias "Paulus als Hillelit," in *Neotestamentica et Semitica, FS M. Black*, edited by E. E. Ellis and M. Wilcox (Edinburgh: T. & T. Clark, 1996) 85–94. Saul was a follower of Hillel: "That Luke and Paul studied at the feet of Gamaliel (grandson of Hillel) in Jerusalem (Acts 22:3, cf. *New Jerome Biblical Commentary*, edited by Raymond E. Brown [Englewood Cliffs, NJ: Prentice-Hall, 1990] 79:18) supports the Hillelite proposal, as do many of Paul's exegetical methods. Paul and Hillel agreed on resurrection and Gentile mission (Pes. 8:8), as in H. Danby, *The Mishnah* (Oxford: Oxford University Press, 1932) 148." Caird adds, "It was more than three centuries since Hebrew had given place to Aramaic as the vernacular language, but it was still studied in the rabbinic schools and had never quite ceased to be a spoken language" (Caird, *Paul's Letters from Prison*, 135).

34. A point stressed in Krister Stendhal, *Paul Among Jews and Gentiles* (Minneapolis: Fortress, 1976).

35. As rabbinic literature fully recognizes. See Sanders, *Paul and Palestinian Judaism*.

assiduously he "found it empty and meaningless; hence he insists for the Philippians' benefit that there is 'no future in it.'"[36]

Paul is doing more than presenting his curriculum vitae in 3:5–6. He is not simply listing what he has done, but telling us who he thinks himself to be. His ethnicity has not changed; he is still Hebrew of the Hebrews. And his argument here is not against representatives of mainstream contemporary Jewish faith or practice; it is addressing Torah-observant members of the early church communities. The controversies reflected in his writings are not part of high-level dialogues with Jewish teachers like Hillel or Shammai, but rather intra-church disputes with other leaders among contemporary communities of Christ followers. It is because Paul is immersed in Torah and trained in exegetical commentary that he can argue strongly that his opponents are not more Jewish than he. Nor are they more zealous for the law than is Paul, who was trained as a Pharisee. He has read the scriptures, the Hebrew scriptures, even if most often in their Greek translation.[37] As we can see from his letters, the words of those scriptures echo through his thoughts, enwrap his mind, and flood into his rhetoric.

Do we not then discern a shift in cultural identity here? Surely that is so, for Paul is engaged in Hellenistic cultural realms. However, he seems never to have rejected his Jewish identity in order to take on a Christian identity. He has certainly changed, from zealous persecutor to apostle to the persecuted, now charged to work for the furtherance of the gospel. But I think it a shallow interpretation to see Paul's radical reorientation as a simple shifting of identity markers. He is much too subtle and theologically perceptive to think that life in Christ is merely one individual's exchange of social or cultural identity markers.[38] It is the radical reorientation of the whole framework in which identity markers function.

This may become clearer if we briefly examine a parallel passage. When Paul in 2 Corinthians says that "many boast in worldly things" (ἐπεὶ πολλοὶ καυχῶνται κατὰ σάρκα, 11:18), he insists that they are fools, sunk in their own delusion. The issue in that passage is similar to this Philippian passage in that Paul presents his *bona fides* as equal to anybody's. "If anyone presumes to play the fool, so can I likewise presume" (Ἐν ᾧ δ᾽ ἄν τις τολμᾷ, ἐν ἀφροσύνῃ λέγω, τολμῶ κἀγώ, 2 Cor 11:21b). He then lists the same markers of his former identity: Hebrew, Israelite, descendent of Abraham (Ἑβραῖοί εἰσιν; κἀγώ. Ἰσραηλῖταί εἰσιν; κἀγώ. σπέρμα Ἀβραάμ εἰσιν, κἀγώ, 2 Cor 11:22). These cultural and ethnic identity markers have not disappeared, and so Paul

---

36. Fee, *Paul's Letter to the Philippians*, 310.

37. Reumann, *Philippians*, 483: "*Hebraios* = an Aramaic-speaking Jew." Paul was "likely bilingual, Greek his first language; Acts 6:1, *Hebraioi*, 'Jews who, while able to speak Greek, knew a Semitic language' also; *Hellēnistoi*, (Jews) 'who spoke only Greek' (AB 31:347; C. F. D. Moule, 'Once More, Who Were the Hellenists?' *Expository Times* 70 [1958–59] 100–2)."

38. Even Segal—who emphasizes conversion as ideological shift in "The Consequences of Paul's Conversion"—stresses the onging nature of Paul's understanding of the implications of his conversion (Segal, *Paul the Convert*, 117–49).

can use them to support his claim for the gospel. But Paul then expands his argument, for apparently in this letter to the Corinthians some of his opponents who identify themselves as Christians wish to substitute that identity for another. And so Paul says that if "they are servants of Christ, I am more so" (διάκονοι Χριστοῦ εἰσιν; παραφρονῶν λαλῶ, ὑπὲρ ἐγώ, 2 Cor 11:23). But he interjects a phrase in the middle of the verse to say that in speaking like this, *"I am speaking as a fool"* (παραφρονῶν λαλῶ). The issue is not then what one identifies oneself to be, Jewish or Christian, but rather the very tenacity of one's identity-seeking, which in all its sundry variations encloses persons and their groups within narrow, scripted narratives about their own precious lives and self-careers. That is to speak as a deluded fool. In another translation of the same verse from 2 Corinthians, we read that to talk like this about identity markers is to be "out of one's mind (παραφρονῶν λαλῶ)," beyond (παρα-) any mental centering (φρονῶν). It is simply a presumption (τολμᾷ . . . τολμῶ) to claim any such identity markers as central, whether they are Jewish or whether they are Christian.

Christian identity certainly is no stronger or more to be desired, for Christians—who lack power even over their own selves or their status—must take on the form of slaves in service of the gospel. In his 2 Corinthians letter, after belittling these identity claims as the ravings of a fool, Paul goes on to speak of his life as he remembers experiencing it. He lists his sufferings and trials in service of the gospel, his beatings and appearances before judges, his imprisonments. He is a man well acquainted with suffering. But he also recounts the mystic experiences he has had—visions and revelations of the Lord that go beyond his ability to enunciate. These too, however, are peripheral. "We shall not boast of them," he says, for identity-boasting is the enunciation of error and delusion.

When, however, Paul does attempt to enunciate his oneness with Christ, he speaks the truth and does not speak as a fool, even if in Christ he might boast (Ἐὰν γὰρ θελήσω καυχήσασθαι, οὐκ ἔσομαι ἄφρων, ἀλήωειαν γὰρ ἐρῶ, 2 Cor 12:6). Oneness with Christ is the erasure of identity markers, not for him a new identity marker. The identities we construct from the variously conditioned histories of our lives do function in the world and maintain a validity if only in our awareness of their day-to-day erasure. We are not enclosed within a supposed reality of who and what we are, but must constantly stretch forth and break free. This is so, not only that we might become one with Christ in God, but also that we may reach across our constructed boundaries of ethnicity, religion, and everything else—in order truly to be brothers and sisters to others in furthering this gospel.

This identityless emptying is the life that Paul leads. It is the sum of all his endeavors—the life pushed forward by those deep experiences that first occurred on the Damascus Road and that continued to draw him to stretch forth beyond Damascus, never to reach a final term. Cultural observances, even revealed Torah, enjoy only a worldly and conventional role as encouragement to us to follow the path. Even the churches, as is all too apparent today, enjoy but a worldly and conventional role in encouraging us to follow the path. Inspired and guided by the shared Spirit who supplies Christ, they do not as institutions occupy a sacred space carved out from an otherwise secular and godless world. An empty christology entails an empty ecclesiology. Paul's gospel does not allow us to carve out a set-apart sacred space, for we do not know and cannot attempt to say clearly where it all leads. For, in leading to oneness with Christ, it surpasses every worldly boundary.

Self-reckoning (3:7–11)

3:7 *Yet whatever was [accrued as] gain for me, all that I regard as loss because of the Christ.* ⁸*Furthermore, I continue to regard everything as loss because of the value beyond evaluation of knowing Christ Jesus my Lord, because of whom I have lost all things, and I regard them as shit, so that I may gain Christ* ⁹*and be found in him, not having my own righteousness from Torah, but that which comes through faith in Christ, a righteousness from God grounded on faith,* ¹⁰*[all] in order to know him, and the power of his resurrection, and participate in his sufferings by being conformed to his death,* ¹¹*if in some way I may reach to what goes beyond the resurrection from the dead.*

3:7 [ἀλλὰ] ἅτινα ἦν μοι κέρδη, ταῦτα ἥγημαι διὰ τὸν Χριστὸν ζημίαν. ⁸ἀλλὰ μενοῦνγε καὶ ἡγοῦμαι πάντα ζημίαν εἶναι διὰ τὸ ὑπερέχον τῆς γνώσεως Χριστοῦ Ἰησοῦ τοῦ κυρίου μου, δι' ὃν τὰ πάντα ἐζημιώθην, καὶ ἡγοῦμαι σκύβαλα ἵνα Χριστὸν κερδήσω ⁹καὶ εὑρεθῶ ἐν αὐτῷ, μὴ ἔχων ἐμὴν δικαιοσύνην τὴν ἐκ νόμου ἀλλὰ τὴν διὰ πίστεως Χριστοῦ, τὴν ἐκ θεοῦ δικαιοσύνην ἐπὶ τῇ πίστει, ¹⁰τοῦ γνῶναι αὐτὸν καὶ τὴν δύναμιν τῆς ἀναστάσεως αὐτοῦ καὶ [τὴν] κοινωνίαν [τῶν] παθημάτων αὐτοῦ, συμμορφιζόμενος τῷ θανάτῳ αὐτοῦ, ¹¹εἴ πως καταντήσω εἰς τὴν ἐξανάστασιν τὴν ἐκ νεκρῶν.

Paul is speaking of the radical reorientation of his life, sketching what the mind of Christ means to him personally.[39] Although the basic human structure of his experience, understanding, judgment, and commitment remains as it was in his old life, the patterns in which all those activities emerge have now been turned around, from sin and delusion to grace and truth. He has undergone an inner conversion, not simply an emotion-laden experience but a complete reorientation of experience, insight, and judgment. Paul's insights fill his letters. His judgments are sometimes brutally concise as when he denounces the "dogs," and sometimes carefully deliberative as when he argues his citizenship strategy. It is not just that he is no longer moved by zeal for Torah. It is the experience of oneness with Christ that encourages him to empty all the patterns of his thinking, but then to reclaim those same ways of thinking as the

---

39. On the agenda in 3:4–11, see Reumann, *Philippians*, 505. Regarding the 'I'-form: "Begun at 3:4a, it continues through verse 14." Used in "giving personal testimony to religious experiences" (ibid.).

conditioned understandings that they are while still affirming his commitment to the unconditioned gospel, which escapes the margins of all human insight. This is what is entailed in Paul's awakening to oneness with the empty Christ. It is a restoration of his Hebrew heritage, not a substitution for his dependently arisen past.

And so Paul reckons up his accounts. He was a merchant, a tentmaker who likely traveled about with the trade caravans, where tents would be most needed. Even during his missionary travels he continued his trade, which probably provided his daily bread. Engaged as he was in business, he no doubt was familiar with the language of accounting; and so in writing the Philippians here, he looks at his balance sheet. Terms such as "gain" (κέρδη 3:7) and "loss" (ζημίαν)—borrowed from trade and finance[40]—are found throughout the New Testament. Occasionally they refer specifically to financial matters, as when Paul endeavors to raise funds for the support of the poor in Jerusalem. But most often the accounting envisaged is not financial. Here, clearly he is not speaking of money but rather of his career, his curriculum vitae: "all the things that before were gains" ([ἀλλὰ] ἅτινα ἦν μοι κέρδη), these now he regards as loss (ταῦτα ἥγημαι . . . ζημίαν). It is not that he has had a reversal of fortune; he still possesses those things, but they have lost their value "because of the Christ" (διὰ τὸν Χριστὸν).[41]

Paul's radical reappraisal of his personal account is more than simply a change of attitude or the adoption of new ideas. The Yogācāra philosophers of ancient India write extensively about such radical conversion, which they call "the conversion of support." In their thinking, "support" (Skt. āśraya) signifies the basic consciousness that supports all our other mental activities. This consciousness, they contend, arises as the result of a host of causes and conditions. We experience our world through our five senses and perceive what we encounter through our sense organs, but our karmically defiled thinking distorts these valid experiences, engendering deluded ideas. So the many ideas that rule our lives and direct our actions are not, as they seem to us, neutral and objective appraisals. They are not accurate pictures of anything real out there in the objective world.[42] Instead, our ideas are driven toward delusion and focused on self by force of our karmic heritage. This defiled thinking (kliṣṭa-manas),

---

40. On gain and loss, see ibid., 488: "Some see Mark 8:36 parallel (Luke 9:25), 'What will it profit people if they gain (kerdēsē[i]) the whole world and forfeit (zēmiōthē[i]) their life?" On 3:7, Thurston adds: "The verse's drama comes from the opposites 'profit, loss.' The connotation is that of deliberate judgment" (Thurston, "Philippians," 123).

41. Reumann, Philippians, 528, relates that Garland, in "Composition and Unity of Philippians," 171 n. 103, "cites commentators who parallel 'Christ's self-emptying and Paul's account of his own self-emptying'; but Paul does not set Law and circumcision aside in order to resume them later, as Jesus apparently does with whatever he gave up in becoming human [as some interpret the emptiness hymn." Paul continues to accept Torah and "allows" Titus to be circumcised, although he demotes the practice from any definitive status. Christ's self-emptying is not reversed by once again taking up his ungrasped divine status, for he is more-than-exalted.

42. For the many critiques of the real understood as the "already-out-there-now," see Lonergan, Insight: A Study of Human Understanding, "Patterns of Experience," 204–31.

under the ageless influence of our primal ignorance, is evidenced in our evolutionary survival struggles against others and expressed in our personal and social histories as greed and anger. Paul experienced such a radical conversion, from delusion and sin to truth and grace.

Underlying all sensation, perception, and thinking is what the Yogācāra thinkers call "the storehouse consciousness" (Skt. *ālaya-vijñāna*), wherein the seeds from past actions of many lives lie dormant, ready to germinate into the false ideas about "me and mine" (*ātma-ātmīya*) that control our lives and engender all manner of delusion displayed over and over again in deeds of greed and anger. This is the classical Mahāyāna teaching about an originating state of sin and delusion that cycles through the ages. All this does not negate human endeavor or personal creativity, nor does it preclude the scope of free will. But it does shift the register in which all life values are understood, and it calls for faith-commitment (Skt. *adhimukti*; Chi. 信解) to tame the unruly mind and to seek the path toward awakened wisdom.

The conventional self-awareness whereby we manage our lives in the world—acquiring food and keeping warm, making a living, raising a family, pursuing a career like teaching school, working for the poor, or marketing shoes—structures our life and our identity. But upon conversion—once we are freed (解) from our body-centered and deluded karmic entrapment in the primacy of selfhood—these same activities can emerge from awakened compassion, enabling us to commit (信) to a selfless personal life in authentic bodhisattva fashion. The goal, however, is not simply release from delusion. Bodhisattva life leads not only away from delusion but into engaged wisdom, which is never ablated into some cloudy escapism. The Yogācāra philosophers teach that we are to abandon attachment to self and seek wisdom as a selfless person. Although there is no inner self, no stable and preciously wrapped entity at the center of our universe, we can reclaim our human lives as selfless persons working toward the common good.

The self-interested consciousness that Yogācāra, and Paul, would seek to convert is precisely the mark of our modern secular culture. This is the unquestioned motive force behind the laissez-faire policies that drive our economies. And yet the Yogācāra thinkers insist that, in point of philosophic reality, our embodied living does not support any view of a stable self, and that the competition between selves moves to the rhythm of greed and anger. Their critical philosophy of mind affirms instead the healthy presence of the selfless and transient person who functions for a lifetime among others in dependence on the images we perceive and the insights they trigger in our other-dependent minds, but aware both of the transcendent otherness that goes beyond any thought and of the need for compassionate engagement in the world as we find it. We are called to consider carefully the meaning of our experience of the world until insights are triggered, then to judge the truth that emerges from those considered insights, and to commit ourselves accordingly to wise and compassionate living.

Otherwise, with an unawakened, multi-dependent consciousness, we fall—as Augustine taught—into the original sin of projecting a world that we can imagine only in terms of either profit or loss to our selfhood. We live then within, and according to, the fixed and frozen maps of that imagined world, finding ourselves imprisoned, separated from others and from Christ awakening. All this is living "in the flesh"—according to fleshly standards and measures. It is this cherished delusion that is turned around and con-verted (Skt. *parivṛtti*) in awakened wisdom (*bodhi*). This Yogācāra understanding of conversion, I would suggest, offers insight into what happens in moments of radical reorientation, and indeed what happened to Paul. Having turned away from his old life, which was focused on his variously stellar identities, he finds himself bereft of any self support whatsoever—and all "because of Christ" (διὰ τὸν Χριστὸν 3:7), upon whose cross all dreams of self-victory were extinguished when he was crucified.

When Paul, in describing what has changed, writes that what he formerly regarded as gain he now "regards" as loss, he uses the verb "I regard" (ἥγημαι) repeating the same word twice in the next verse. This is a pivotal verb in the mystic hymn of the empty Christ, wherein Christ does not "regard equality with God as something to be clung to, as something precious" (οὐκ ἁρπαγμὸν ἡγήσατο τὸ εἶναι ἴσα θεῷ 2:6); and now Paul uses it in describing his own life.[43] Indeed, "to regard" is a key term in this correspondence, for both in the hymn and in this passage it refers to the mind of wisdom whereby one turns away from delusion and toward wisdom and engagement—germinating for Paul in seeking uplifting experience through prayer and meditation, gaining insight into the world of faith, and making decisions to live for others, all by taking on the mind of Christ. For him, as for the Philippians who composed the panegyric, being of one mind with Christ is a radical repatterning of consciousness that enables one to say, "No longer do I live, but Christ lives within me."[44]

Interpreters are often tempted to gloss over this radical conversion of Paul—our earliest example of what it means to follow the Christ path. Some read it as a kind of superlative personal encounter in an unusual vision; more commonly, it is seen as Paul abandoning his former self only to substitute a new Christian identity. Both interpretations are shallow, and neither reflects the text here. If Paul's experience is confined to a personal vision, it would have little meaning for anyone else. And if it were merely a shift in his affirmed identity, there would be no room for Christ to live in him, nor he in Christ. But Paul here regards his personal identity markers as worthless so that he may "gain Christ," who did not regard his own self as something to be concerned about. It is not that Paul has simply changed his mind; he has reoriented the patterns

---

43. Silva, *Philippians*, 155: An "indication of the character of this passage is the way it appears to echo 2:5–11 . . . It contains "explicit verbal parallels: *hēgeomai* (2:6, 3:7–8), *morphē* (2:7; cf. *symmorphizō* 3:10), *heuriskō* (2:7; 3:9), *kyrios* (2:11; 3:8)."

44. Reumann, *Philippians*, 506: "Some see Philippians 2:6–11 behind what Paul says in 3:8–11, with *pistis Christou* in 9c as link, 'Christ's faith(fulness).'" I would include myself among these "some."

in which his mind functions, recognizing the base level of his unconscious drives and reconfiguring everything in wisdom.[45] He does not just abandon old identity markers for new ones; in his present life as gospel advocate, he regards all identity markers as loss. They remain his identity markers, but now they are ratcheted down to their conventional status. He is still Jewish and still a Pharisee trained and zealous, but the flow of his energies has been reversed, its polarity shifted.

Verse 3:8 presents a strange concatenation of linking particles that move the sense along rather rapidly. Paul begins with a conjunction "but" (ἀλλά),[46] then follows by joining together three particles, "however," (μεν), "then" (οὖν), and caps the sentence off with "indeed" (γε), followed in 3:9 by another conjunction "and" (καί). The writer seems to be hemming and hawing. However, the discourse is moving at a deeper level, attempting to stress and reinforce the re-patterning of all Paul's experiencing, thinking, and judging as these flow from his abandonment of identity markers. Not only does he abandon his old identity markers, he abandons his new ones too. He has not found a new religion to define himself.[47] With the model of the Christ who emptied himself and regarded being equal to God as nothing precious, Paul here does not regard his new Christian endeavors as providing him with yet another self-identity, for that new identity also is nothing so very special or precious. In fact he rejects it, for it would constitute yet another example of self-boasting—Paul's term for the self-righteousness that bedevils preachers everywhere. Instead, he continues to "regard everything to be loss" (ἡγοῦμαι πάντα ζημίαν εἶναι 3:8). The emptying of Christ flows over into the emptying of Paul.[48]

Why does Paul empty himself? Is it just that he has found faith? We often have regarded faith, not as radical reorientation and conversion of mind, but as a shift in viewpoint, something that may be acquired through thoughtful reading. But that could hardly account for what sent the blinded Paul to follow Ananias into Damascus and drove him to write these letters to Philippi. It is not that Paul has found a new relationship with the risen Christ in glory. He never discourses on his relationship with Christ, remaining content with being "in Christ" here and eschatologically "with Christ" hereafter. Although he speaks repeatedly of being in Christ, he never speaks as though he has a relationship that he might develop. Relationships not only draw people together, but also distance them, for they rely on a sense of "me" in here and

---

45. Caird, *Paul's Letters from Prison*, 136: "[H]e is not so much attacking real contemporary enemies as the ghosts of his own past."

46. On the "great But" at the beginning of verse 7: "we omit it" (Reumann, *Philippians*, 517).

47. Stengel rejects the notion that Paul experienced conversion as a "change of religion." See K. Stengel, "The Apostle Paul and the Introspective Conscience of the West," in *Paul Among Jews and Gentiles* (Philadelphia: Fortress, 1976) 78–96.

48. Collange, *Epistle of Saint Paul*, 128: "The apostle's movement away from the assets and values mentioned above is reminiscent of that of the hero of the Christological hymn in 2:6."

"you" over there, distinguishing one from the other. Paul speaks only of being "in Christ," never of having a relationship "with" him.[49]

Paul has emptied himself "because of something that surpasses value" (διὰ τὸ ὑπερέχον), using yet another finance term—here to describe "knowing Christ Jesus my Lord" (τῆς γνώσεως Χριστοῦ Ἰησοῦ τοῦ κυρίου μου)—with yet another example of the preclitic *hyper* (ὑπερ). Prefixed to the verb "to have" (ἔχον, *echon*), it forms the important term (ὑπερέχον, *hyperechon*) to mean "beyond or surpassing" anything that can "be had." As above in the hymn of the empty Christ, the resulting compounded word signifies not simply a superlative degree of having a great and surpassing possession; it is something that goes beyond having altogether.[50] It is that which is realized in the emptying of anything one could possibly possess. It is a personal version of the notion that God "more than exalts" the empty Christ (ὑπερύψωσεν 2:9), not that God "exalts him exceedingly." Paul, I think, combines words in unusual ways because it is almost impossible to express in any language what he understands by being one with Christ.

Languages function always in terms of subjective knowers and the objectively known, and yet the wisdom traditions of the world insist that there are some experiences that cannot be filtered through such dichotomous acts of bringing disparate things (or persons) into manageable relationship. Whatever Paul experienced as being in Christ, and whatever he felt as he penned these lines to the Philippians, their significance is not captured in conventional subject-object speech. And so Paul plays with language, stringing together conjunctions, bending speech to new meanings, adding untoward prefixes and suffixes, playing with semantics to suggest extra-ordinary meanings. It is not that Paul has emptied himself of his identity markers because of the surpassing value that he now has found *out there*, perhaps on the road to Damascus, and thus subjectively has a Christ experience *in here*. It is something beyond the range of having and not having, something that undermines the patterns of understanding of any such appropriating mind—whether the Hebrew mind of Paul's youth or the Christ mind of his later years.[51]

---

49. *Pace* Silva, *Philippians*, 168, on τῆς γνώσεως Χριστοῦ Ἰησοῦ: "The gloss on BDAG 203, (s.v. γνῶσις, meaning 2), 'personal acquaintance with,' is generally accepted by scholars, regardless of their position on that debate [on the meaning of knowledge]."

50. Reumann thinks the translation of "*to hyperechon*" as "surpassingness catches the abstract noun form" (Reumann, *Philippians*, 489). The Mahāyāna analogue is a similar abstract noun, *prajñāpāramitā*, the wisdom (*prajñā*) that has gone beyond (*pāramitā*).

51. A synonym for the storehouse (or warehouse) consciousness of Yogācāra, with its latent karmic seeds and habits, is "the appropriating consciousness (Skt. *ādāna-vijñāna*)." It reaches out from the preconscious mind of karmic evolution, with its deluded sense of being a permanent self, to grasp at objects that—in its delusion—it regards as that which is real in the world. See David F. Germano and William S. Waldron, "A Comparison of Ālaya-Vijñāna in Yogācāra and Dzogchen," *Buddhist Thought and Applied Psychological Research* (New York: Routledge, 2006) 36–68.

On Paul's final balance sheet, then, he has subtracted his zeal for Torah. But the law for which he was so zealous is not the rabbinic Torah of later history.[52] Paul never read most of what we now know as Mishnah or Talmud, for the simple reason that neither had yet been written. When we talk about the Jews in the New Testament, we would do well to keep in mind Abraham Joshua Heschel and his classical Jewish theology.[53] Heschel evinces a sensitive and encompassing understanding that resembles not at all the Christian commentators' frequent portrayal of Paul's Jewish opponents as stubborn sticklers for laws and regulations. It is a grave error for Christians to lump Paul's opponents under the banner of Jewish legalism. In any case, Paul's opponents cannot be identified as over against Christians, for they themselves are members of the emergent Christ churches—Christ followers who insist that, even while believing in Christ, they must cling to Torah as a religious identity marker. They are rather like Christian fundamentalists today who conflate faith and culture. But such people, who are to be found everywhere, do not define a tradition, however diligent their efforts to act as its curators. Paul has emptied his ledger of the avaricious drive that pretends to serve God while in actual fact sowing division and harming human practice.

The ancient paths of Jainism and Buddhism stress *ahimsa*, explaining that we are not to harm beings of any kind. And in accord with Guru Nanak's admonition—"Realization of Truth is higher than all else. Higher still is truthful living"[54]—Sikhism rejects all discrimination between religions as harmful. No religious doctrine and no religious commitment should work to the harm (Skt. *hiṃsā*) of any living being. One of the central questions of our own day is how to develop robust and committed faith living within a tradition that neither apologizes for its own faith commitments nor undertakes proselytizing campaigns that would harm others by defining their supposed needs and then rushing our gospel in as the appropriate answer to those needs.[55]

When Paul says that he has lost all things "because of Christ" (διὰ τὸν Χριστὸν 3:7), it is is not for him a matter of balancing between, on the one hand, his previously

---

52. Sanders spends the first 420 pages of his work *Paul and Palestinian Judaism* describing Tannaitic Literature, the Dead Sea Scrolls, Apocrypha, and Pseudepigrapha, to sum up Palestinian Judaism as "covenantal nomism" from 200 BCE to 200 CE, all but forcing recognition of the falsity of Christian depictions of Judaism as obsessively legalistic and hypocritical. Neither was Paul to be taken as a member of the sect called Zealots. See Reumann's critique: [I]t is 'anachronistic' to see before 68 CE 'members of the sect called Zealots,' political revolutionists against Rome (D. Rhoades, ABD 6:1045; cf. 1043–54; O. Betz 1977:59; Hengel 1988:159, 168–71)" (Reumann, *Philippians*, 485).

53. Heschel, *Man Is Not Alone: A Philosophy of Religion* (New York: Farrar, Straus, & Giroux, 1951).

54. Geoff Teece, *Sikhism*, Religion in Focus (London: Watts, 2008) 4.

55. On "The Intrinsic Difficulties" and "The Systematic Difficulties" of scripting peoples' actual need so as to fit the answers provided by Reformation grace and justification, see Campbell, *Deliverance of God*, 38–95. Campbell takes aim at Reformation thought, but his argument could be made with equal force against any of the many professions that filter human need through the sieves they provide. See the work of postcolonial thinker Homi Baba, especially his essay "Signs Taken as Wonder: Questions of Ambivalence and Authority under a Tree Oustide Delhi, May 1817," in *The Location of Culture* (New York: Routledge, 1994) 102–22.

cherished and now lost gains and, on the other, this newly discovered Christ. There is no balancing going on, for the Christ is not on one side to which Paul has committed; Christ is rather our middle path, in that he collapses opposition and brings peace. Thus Paul can "know him" (τῆς γνώσεως 3:8) not simply by name as Christ Jesus but he also "experiences" (τῆς γνώσεως) Christ as "my Lord" (Χριστοῦ Ἰησοῦ τοῦ κυρίου μου), the director of his life. Indeed, in the emptiness hymn, God has more than exalted Jesus, and he has also given him the name that is above any name. And that which surpasses value is not simply to do things because motivated by this august Lord, Jesus Christ; it is rather to act within that radical transformation of consciousness whereby one's experiences break the boundaries of selfhood and enable one to live ever more in the wisdom and knowledge of Jesus Christ.[56] This is not a matter of an anxious subject apprehending Jesus as a pain-assuaging agent; it is a knowing that empties the dichotomy that is defined by boundaries between subject and object and, having so emptied them, can then reengage precisely in the world where gospel tasks are to be undertaken. Christ is not "the person of supreme worth,"[57] for he has emptied himself of any worth whatsoever.

The expression Paul uses here—about the beyond-value, and thus valueless, value of "knowing Christ Jesus"—is literally "the gnosis of Christ Jesus" (τῆς γνώσεως Χριστοῦ Ἰῆσοῦ), an expression found nowhere else in Paul, and in fact nowhere else in the New Testament. This, so the commentators explain, is a bridge term suggestive of Hellenistic ideas, perhaps even Gnostic ideas, of a wisdom that goes beyond ordinary knowing.[58] And it is a difficult term to interpret. What does it mean to know Christ? What is Christ "gnosis"? Commentators often interpret this "knowing" in terms of personal relationship with Christ. O'Brien, for example, asserts: "Here at Philippians 3:8 Paul is speaking about 'his own personal relationship with Christ,' something that is absolutely basic and fundamental to his being a Christian."[59]

---

56. Collange, *Epistle of Saint Paul*, 130: "Experience of his Lordship is therefore essentially a dynamic experience which sets one on the road. That road, from self to Christ, is a long one."

57. Pace O'Brien, *Epistle to the Philippians*, 385.

58. Reumann, *Philippians*, 490: "Nowhere else does Paul use 'knowledge of Christ Jesus' . . . . English commentaries favor the Old Testament as source and often seek to exclude Gnosticism (Fee, *Paul's Letter to the Philippians*, 318 n. 21). German commentaries are often open to more than Old Testament-Jewish background (e.g., Gnilka 192–93; U. B. Müller, 152, "Der Brief aus Ephesus. Zeitliche Plazierung und theologische einordung des Philipperbriefes im Rahmen des Paulusbrief," in *Das Urchristentum in seiner literarischen Geschichte, Festschrift Jürgen Becker*, eds., U. Mell, U. B. Müller [Berlin: de Grutyer, 1999],155–72)."

59. O'Brien, *Epistle to the Philippians*, 388. Similarly, for Reumann it is about "'getting in' and 'staying in' a right relationship with God" (Reumann, *Philippians*, 521). But on the phrase "in him" (*en Chrisōt[i]*), Reumann wavers between a "personal relationship" and a "realm, including the church, where Christ is Lord" (ibid., 493). Relational categories are so pervasive because they are taken to be the things most real to us, but for Paul what is real is the transformation whereby we become conformed to Christ, not related to him as subjects relate to objects. Reumann is aware of the issue; interpreting 3:8 on gaining Christ, he writes: "The overall eschatology—future in 8e, present status in 9a—is best taken as 'already but not yet' (Fee, 320–21). Paul is 'in Christ' now, a personal relationship

I began to think in such personalist terms many years ago after reading Remy G. Kwant's *Encounter*, his phenomenology of what it means to be a person in relationship with other people.[60] Certainly, personalist discourse about encountering the face of another is a valuable discourse that echoes themes long practiced in Christian devotion and commitment. Nevertheless, I think personalist interpretations of Paul's relationship with Christ run the risk of encouraging inner images that do little to embody the presence of Christ in our lives. There is a danger in devoting prayer time to imaginative mind games. If one has "encountered" Christ and cherishes a "personal relationship" with him, one's theology tends to become resistant to scripture that emphasizes "being *in* Christ," and any critique of a cozy relationship with Jesus images is heard as an insult to a friend, the best of all friends, Jesus himself. But Paul calls Christ Jesus his Lord and endeavors to take on the mind of Christ by emptying his being to be *one* with Christ. This is not a simple relationship between individual persons. In Christ, Paul has lost everything and therefore he has found everything, precisely because there is nothing to be found at all.[61] Everything once precious has been lost. In that Christ, and "because of that" (δι' ὅν 3:8) Christ, Paul has "forfeited everything" (τὰ πάντα ἐζημιώθην), and now he "regards everything once precious as nothing more than shit" (καὶ ἡγοῦμαι σκύβαλα).

Paul, I think, was never a person of delicate sensibilities. And here he does indeed speak of shit, perhaps apropos of the "dogs" he mentioned earlier.[62] Unsurprisingly, this is the only place in the New Testament where the term shit (σκύβαλα) occurs. Hesitant to offend, translators and commentators generally do a little euphemistic sidestep and opt for "refuse, rubbish, or dung." A Zen practitioner once went to his master to find out how best to realize the ideal of awakening. He said, "Master, what is Buddha?" The master, so the kōan reports, answered, "A dried shit-stick!" (an implement then used as toilet paper in the privy). This kōan is meant to disabuse practitioners of thinking that Buddha, the enlightened one, is something so very precious or special.[63] The

---

under Christ's lordship, but realized only in part; to be perfected at the final Day, when Paul (and others) will be 'with Christ'" (ibid., 520). But—*pace* Reumann—being in Christ, as eschatological, seems ill-fitted to any "partial relationship" with him and one wonders how that "partial" might be understood.

60. Remy G. Kwant, *Encounter* (Pittsburg: Duquesne University Press, 1960) 15–24, treats "The Primordial and Irreducible Nature of Intersubjective Contact," then to be carried into the realms of science, philosophy, and theology.

61. Collange translates 3:8: "be despoiled of all things" (Collange, *Epistle of Saint Paul*, 127). Thurston renders it in contemporary slang as "'On account of Christ I became a loser.' Paul has chosen to empty himself of familial, theological, and religious status for the sake of knowing the Christ" (Thurston, "Philippians," 124).

62. Fee, *Paul's Letter to the Philippians*, 319. Collange explains, "In Jewish eyes the dog is unclean and feeds on excreta" (Collange, *Epistle of Saint Paul*, 124). Silva adds, "Moreover, there is some evidence that the ancients understood *skybalon* as deriving from *to tois kysi ballomenon*, 'that which is thrown to the dogs'" (Silva, *Philippians*, 158).

63. See Aitken, *Gateless Barrier*, 137–41, on "Case 21: Yün-men's Dried Shitstick."

point the Zen master is driving home is that the practitioner is to abandon all supports for selfhood, whether they be matters of greed, pride, anger, or envy, or conversely, things that are cherished or idealized as sacred. Making Buddha special removes Buddha from our ordinary, day-to-day lives, in all their commonplace places. Anything that serves to support us in our delusions, no matter how awesome its pedigree, is shit.

Paul, too, knows that such "specialness" is not only useless but toxic, and this is to be avoided if we are to gain Christ and live resurrection faith. His own identity markers, past and present, are so much worthless shit, "so that I may gain Christ" (ἵνα Χριστὸν κερδήσω 3:8). Christ for Paul is the prize towards which he strains and for which he neighbors the Philippians. But that does not mean that Christ can be grasped and held high as a prize hard won; this is a prize that one in fact never attains. Perhaps this is why Christians prefer to talk about having a relationship with Jesus, something that can be worked on continually until his coming and the cessation of all work. But no one possesses a relationship with Christ—that is yet another false and deluded boast. Christ is always other to the calculus of selfhood.[64] To gain Christ means to stretch forth, as Paul will emphasize in 3:13, not to rest contentedly in possession of an intimate friend one might relate to as "Christ."

It is not even that Paul looks forward to the consummation of his relationship with Christ on the last day, for that final day is already here, in the present age. Paul's "gain" that is Christ becomes the conative drive of his human life "in Christ," the motive force for his engagements and labors. His is not to be the peaceful awakening described in some Buddhist sūtras. Paul does not for a moment attempt to remove himself from the fray with all its pain and suffering; he runs through his sufferings as though they are mere obstacles. Thus, perhaps, his fondness for athletic imagery—his many mentions of runners in a race, his allusions to striving and endeavor and gymnastics. He tells us that he does not beat the air uselessly; he lands his punches. He trains himself for the contests and endeavors of furthering the gospel.

In writing to the Corinthians, Paul describes those endeavors by saying that he attempts to be all things to all people, Jew to the Jews and Gentile to the Gentiles (1 Cor 9:20–22). And this was indeed his strategy. To him, the struggle is not a matter of contention between cultures; faith is a sign of the failure of any final cultural option, an acknowledgement of that which goes before and perdures beyond any human culture, however ecclesiastically treasured. Apparently, however, even though Paul is no longer in chains when he writes this final Resurrection Letter to the Philippians, his overall strategy did not work out. The Jews never did accept his version of "deepening" a renewed, shared tradition. However we may interpret it, there was a parting of the ways, and the gospel communities became increasingly—and then all

---

64. Collange, *Epistle of Saint Paul*, 126: "It is not from any weakness or cowardice or lack of personal assets that Paul recommends reliance upon Another." The teachings of Shin Pure Land Buddhism stress reliance on Other Power (Js. *tariki*).

but entirely—non-Jewish. Paul's all-inclusive strategy failed. No other conclusion is, I think, possible.

As a deeply engaged human being, all of Paul's passions and all of his commitments were directed toward the furtherance of this gospel. But, like many another human being, he was so engaged that in his strategic approach perhaps he sometimes failed to see beyond his own horizon. We may expand our horizons by attending to the many cultures and religions of our world, but no one sees beyond what he can see at the time. Indeed, if we believe in the doctrine of the incarnation—that Jesus was found in human visage, born into his time and place—his vision, too, was bound by his own horizons. There are no divine vantage points in this world, even for Jesus.[65] Yet Paul has abandoned self—not for a Jesus "out there" in the bright light, as described in the dramatic account in Acts 9 of his Damascus Road conversion—but for the Jesus who inwardly drives us toward outward endeavors in this weary and painful world. Paul's Christ offers no cessation of pain and suffering. Rather, he lays upon us the command (κεῖμαι 1:16) to engage in labors for the nurturance of the gospel seed that it may germinate in purified minds, enabling us to work together in unity for justice and peace.

It is not only a matter of Paul striving "to gain Christ," for immediately he describes the very same experience in other words, as being "found in him" (καὶ εὑρεθῶ ἐν αὐτῷ 3:9). Commentators explain that the two phrases are essentially the same.[66] But I think there is something more involved, for if Paul had said only that he practices in order to gain Christ, it might well seem that it is all about his own effort. The active verb "to gain" is therefore clarified (explained "epexegetically") by the passive verb "to be found." Clearly, then, Paul does not claim to have done something by his own self-power, to credit his own decisions and endeavors for the course his life has taken. But some commentators focus so much on this passive language that they neglect Paul's actively chosen self-abandonment: Paul is "under command"; Paul is "found in Christ"; Paul is "obligated" (κεῖμαι). He is seen not as moving his own life, but rather the "Christ who lives in him" moves him, "becoming the focal attention of his mind."[67] This does not mean, however, that Paul did not actively strive to further the gospel. As we see in the descriptions of his many adventures and trials, he never shrinks from engaging in robust promotion of the gospel. For Paul, being in Christ collapses the difference between passive and active voices.

But Paul does not boast of being righteous; he attributes everything to the one who empowers him. He says that, "from Torah I have no righteousness of my own" (μὴ ἔχων ἐμὴν δικαιοσύνην τὴν ἐκ νόμου 3:9). He does not reject Torah, but rather his

---

65. No mixing of divine and human *idiomatum*, as taught in the Chalcedonian confession.

66. O'Brien, *Epistle to the Philippians*, 392.

67. *Pace* Reumann, *Philippians*, 492. Reumann interprets "to be found in him," as "to project a possible realm" of life in Christ (ibid.). Rather, that possibility is being here and now "in Christ," within an eschatological resurrection faith; there is no separate "realm" to be attained.

own "righteousness from Torah," for that is the base error.[68] What he describes as his *own* righteousness from Torah is a righteousness accomplished by the human effort to be faithful in actualizing Torah in one's life; and so he is critiquing his own self-validating practice of Torah and perhaps also that of some of the people with whom he argued during his career. The rabbis, however, never taught that the righteousness that flows from Torah is a matter of self-actualization, nor that one ever attained "self-righteousness" from Torah. Ancient and modern Jewish theologians agree: Torah is a gift from God, enabling us to live deeply and faithfully. Nevertheless, from Paul's words we can perhaps mirror-read his opponents to have insisted on strict Torah observance as the identifying characteristic of faithfulness and thus of righteousness. Paul was not, I think, involved in dialectical conflict with the broad Jewish tradition, but specifically with opponents within the early Christian congregations.[69]

Righteousness is one of the central themes of the Tanach. It is the "doing of the commandments" in the endeavor to create a world of justice, gathering the people together around a common worship of the master of the universe. It is this very righteousness that Paul says he has received through faith in Christ—"that righteousness that comes from God and is grounded upon Christlike faith" (ἀλλὰ τὴν διὰ πίστεως Χριστοῦ, τὴν ἐκ θεοῦ δικαιοσύνην ἐπὶ τῇ πίστει 3:9).[70] In so claiming, Paul is echoing the Torah theme that righteousness comes from God and is grounded upon faith in God, but must be embodied in practice, in "doing the commandments." There is no new content here, except in that this righteousness is further described as received through faith in Christ. Christ here brings to ground that realm of spiritual practice characteristic both of the Hebrew scriptures and of the gospel narratives, so that Christ followers are to deepen and make concrete the ancient traditions we all have received. If Paul had been engaged with Hillel as his interlocutor—the famed rabbi who lived shortly before Jesus—perhaps these early arguments about faith and Torah would never have occurred with the intensity that caused the split. Hillel, however, lived a generation

---

68. Reumann, *Philippians*, 510: "Rather, a Christ, Torah antithesis that has to do with 'community identification,' righteousness as a 'membership term,' two kinds of righteousness expressing 'mutually exclusive boundary markers, rival ways of determining the community of salvation,' by Torah or by Christ." Again, I see the contrast to lie between bounded identity and the unbounded identity of the empty Christ, no matter how often Christians have constructed their own identity boundaries.

69. Vincent comments that Patristic writers hesitate to so disparage the Law. But still, he says, "The law was a light, but unnecessary after the sun had arisen. It was a ladder, useful to mount by, but useless after one had mounted" (Vincent, *Critical and Exegetical Commentary*, 101). Compare the common Mahāyāna critique leveled, not at unacceptable teachings, but at the Mahāyāna Dharma itself, which in the Prajñāpāramitā scriptures is likened to a raft that—having taken one to the far shore of wisdom—may be left behind, lest one's compassionate teaching career (Skt. *bodhisattva-carita*) be burdened by unnecessary portage.

70. Reumann, *Philippians*, 527 n. 54: "It is worthwhile beginning [to consider] Paul's views on justification with this astutely theological, experiential self-description, rather than the exegetical passages in Romans or polemical narrative in Galatians; cf. [John] Reumann, ["Justification by Faith in Pauline Thought: A Lutheran View," in *Rereading Paul Together: Protestant and Catholic Perspectives on Justification*, ed. D. E. Aune, 108–30 (Grand Rapids: Baker Academics, 2006)].

before Paul and sadly was not available for these foundational Christian discussions. Of course those conversations took place within the inner circle of gospel practitioners. Moreover, Paul had little opportunity, and no need, to engage in "interfaith" dialogue.

So it is far too facile an interpretation to contrast self-righteousness as Jewish and the righteousness that comes from God as Christian. That is not the dichotomy at work here. It is not that Paul has received from God "a different kind of righteousness."[71] That is just one more Christian boast—that we have a special way of being righteous. Paul has abandoned all self-justification because there *is* no righteousness that comes from self-achievement. And there never was. Any Christian reading that would interpret Paul as announcing a momentous shift in the salvation history of the world is unhelpful; that is simply a Christianized version of history, while in fact there is only our one, ever complex and multifaceted, history. E. P. Sanders has cogently demonstrated that righteousness in the ancient Hebrew tradition is not something that denies grace or that takes confidence in self-achievement.[72]

What Paul is stressing here is the abandonment of self, creating the scope for growth into Christ without the necessity of observing cultural practices—here those Torah practices that define Israel's specialness—that might be an obstacle to that abandonment. We are to hollow out a space in which Christ may take up residence. So Christlike faith is groundless living; it takes the ground from under our feet. The new "realm" of Christ faith is the consciousness of Christ followers who have embraced an empty wisdom. To rely on God as a support for religious selfhood is to rely on nothing much at all, for across traditions faith is the recognition of our very radical transience, not a removal of it. We are to have faith in Christ and, on the basis of faith-righteousness, to be delivered from sin and delusion to fully engage in the world, as was he who emptied himself to take the suffering form of a slave.[73] So Christ is not "the one" because there is no one.[74] There is no authentic faith in a Christ who hovers out there as some object of our imagination. Rather when Paul speaks of the faith of Christ, he means it both as the faith lived by Christ and our Christlike faith, for πίστις Χριστοῦ (faith of Christ) is a subjective genitive, indicating a faith-filled Christ

---

71. Pace O'Brien, *Epistle to the Philippians*, 395.

72. E. P. Sanders, *Paul, the Law, and the Jewish People* (Philadelphia: Fortress, 1983) 154–59, on "Paul's Critique of Judiasm and of Legalism in General."

73. D. A. Campbell sees Christ's "obedience" and "submission" and indeed, all the ὑπακου- words as overlapping with πιστ- words in Paul. Christ' faithfulness (πίστις χριστοῦ) is his disclosure of God's deliverance and not an act whereby the individual exerts faith in Christ as object. Such Christ faith is coterminous with his "obedience" and with his "self-emptying" (Campbell, *Deliverance of God*, 612–13).

74. Pace Reumann, *Philippians*, 517: "Not 'loss *for (the sake of)* Christ,' as if Saul sacrificed his past glories for Jesus, but the One *because of* whom Saul changed his view on what mattered to him."

mind that overcomes the split between subject-object patterns of imagined religion and blurs the fixed and stable patterns of our self definitions.[75]

Paul has then "lost everything" (πάντα ζημίαν 3:8) "so that I may know him" (τοῦ γνῶναι αὐτὸν 3:10). If to know Christ entails losing everything, then we do not just replace one set of gains with a different set of gains. To insist that in gaining Christ, Paul has gained the great prize is not to understand this "everything" (πάντα). Literally, it is to see only Paul's "escalating" language.[76] It is best to understand this passage as moving beyond the accounting of profit and loss to undermine the entire pattern of conscious grasping after any profit imagined to be found in any object. This Christ-knowing, or gnosis, surpasses anything one might have or grasp, even in prayer and meditation. It signifies an awakening, an empowerment through emptying the self, not any superior value. It is non-analogical.

So it does not go far enough to say, as O'Brien does, that "from the moment of his conversion on the Damascus road Paul had come to know the risen and exalted Lord. He had been brought by grace into an intimate personal relationship with the Son of God, and from that time on he had made it his ambition to know him."[77] For Paul, to know Christ signifies something quite different from a subjective knower apprehending and establishing a relationship with the objectively present person of Jesus. To know Christ is not to continue in this subject-object pattern at all, but rather to experience and participate in the same risen life. It is more than one friend knowing another. Friendship relates one person to another, and the notion of such a relationship can indeed serve as a skillful means to aid us in understanding what it is to know Christ. And yet when Paul in the following clauses proceeds to spell out what it means to know Christ, he makes no mention at all of relationship. To know Christ is to know and experience "the power of his resurrection"(καὶ τὴν δύναμιν τῆς ἀναστάσεως αὐτοῦ 3:10), to "participate in his sufferings" (καὶ (τὴν) κοινωνίαν (τῶν) παθημάτων αὐτοῦ), and to be awakened to a risen life beyond imagination.

The sequence in 3:10 suggests that in coming to know Christ, one first experiences the power of his resurrection, and only then participates in his sufferings. But

---

75. Scholars argue whether "faith of Christ" (πίστις Χριστοῦ) in verse 9 is a subjective genitive, signifying Christ as subject of faith in God, or an objective genitive, signifying our faith placed in Christ. There are arguments for both options. Reumann entertains the idea that it is perhaps a subjective genitive, "knowledge which Christ has of us" (Reumann, *Philippians*, 491). But "We find a good case for the objective genitive at 3:9, 'faith in Christ'" (ibid., 496). Similarly, Collange opts for the objective genitive. But, he notes, "Certainly the genitive could be taken as subjective, i.e., the knowledge which Christ has of us" (Collange, *Epistle of Saint Paul*, 129). See Dunn, *Theology of Paul the Apostle*, 380. I take it here to mean a Christlike faith, embodied in dying and rising to new life, shared organically with Paul and the Philippians; this avoids the choice forced by the subject-object polarity of conventional knowing.

76. Reumann, *Philippians*, 517.

77. O'Brien, *Epistle to the Philippians*, 401–402. Likewise, one wonders why Reumann says that faith "is the means for believers to appropriate righteousness from God, through faith in Christ" (Reumann, *Philippians*, 509). Why "appropriate"?

this order of things seems to reverse the theology that the path to resurrected life is through suffering accepted bravely in following Christ on his *via dolorosa*. So, does one first experience the resurrected élan of being one with Christ and *then* share in the suffering and anguish that are common to all humans, albeit now enabled to taste the power of life even in sickness and in dying? The answer apparently is to avoid mapping things on a linear time line so that one either first experiences resurrection power and then participates in suffering, or first suffers and then is rewarded with resurrection. Neither sequence is affirmed in the received text. Suffering and resurrection are not only joined by the conjunction "and" as: τὴν δύναμιν τῆς ἀναστάσεως αὐτοῦ καὶ τὴν κοινωνίαν [τῶν] παθημάτων αὐτοῦ, but in the text that scholars take as most likely to be original, the definite article (τὴν) is omitted before both "participation" and "sufferings," with the result that the expression "participation in sufferings" is conjoined with the "power of his resurrection" under one definite article before "the" power (τὴν δύναμιν).[78] Thus the two phrases "power of his resurrection" and "participation in his sufferings"—are to be taken as indicating the single content of "knowing Christ"; there is no linear progression from one to the other. Resurrection power and shared sufferings are not two distinct items, one following upon the other in sequence, but they are twinned with one another in synergy. Just as the sufferings of Christ do not cause his resurrection, for us also the former do not bring about the latter.[79]

Without question, people do suffer and people everywhere look forward to an end to suffering. Yet, even as humans who suffer, we experience of the power of resurrection in these our very bodies. It is not a surcease of suffering that Paul intends to communicate here: rather, the power of the resurrection is experienced in sharing human suffering. The one does not cancel the other. Suffering does not mean that one has not and cannot experience the power of the resurrection. And that resurrection experience does not preclude the presence of sufferings, however intense they may be. The power (δύναμις, *dynamis*) of this resurrection enables people to abide in their bodies of suffering; it is not a separate operative force (ενέργια, *energeia*) rushing in from somewhere else to ease their condition medically.[80] Rather, resurrection faith empowers human experience to abide in being human, which is described by Paul in Rom 5:18 simply as "justification of life" (εἰς δικαίωσιν ζωῆς).[81] It neither removes people from their lives nor liberates them from death, but it plunges them ever more deeply into being human: "The Christian life . . . takes its origin from a death, the death of Christ, which translates itself for every believer into a death to sin and to

---

78. Ibid., 403.
79. Pace Fee, *Paul's Letter to the Philippians*, 228, 332.
80. Reumann, *Philippians*, 499, on 3:10.
81. Vincent, *Critical and Exegetical Commentary*, 104.

self."⁸² "[T]o know Christ" is "to experience the power of his resurrection"⁸³ within the eschatological contours of the mind of empty wisdom.

Paul appends another explanatory phrase, "being conformed to his death" (συμμορφιζόμενος τῷ θανάτῳ αὐτοῦ 3:10). This stands in apposition to "knowing Christ,"⁸⁴ describing "the manner by which Paul will come to know Christ's power and fellowship, 'by becoming like him in his death' (NRSV; JB, 'by reproducing the pattern of his death')."⁸⁵ External resemblance is not at issue, for few of us are likely to replicate Jesus' death. But "suffering is an entry into the life of Christ himself, albeit imperfect, a way of sharing his experience."⁸⁶ And O'Brien emphasizes the "continuity" of the process of the Christian disciple's being conformed to Christ's death.⁸⁷ Just as "Christ emptied himself, taking the form of a slave" (ἀλλὰ ἑαυτὸν ἐκένωσεν μορφὴν δούλου λαβών 2:7), so the Christian is to live moment to moment as a disciple, furthering the gospel call to emptied and engaged self-abandonment. "We are to be one form" (συμ-μορφιζόμενος 3:10), not simply with the exalted and absent Christ, but at the same moment "with his death" (τῷ θανάτῳ αὐτοῦ), viscerally in our living and dying.

It would be far more pleasant to be one only with the living Christ, but that is not what the text actually says. We are to be conformed to his death. After all, whether we like it or not, inevitably we all do die. The question is whether in our suffering and dying we can be conformed to the death of Christ, and how we may approach it. How are we to live fully so as to die intentionally? The Gospel of John depicts Jesus' dying on the cross in terms that seem strangely aloof, reflecting little of the pain and agony one might expect; Jesus utters no cry of dereliction in John. John's language instead evokes images of equipoise and calmness. Paul suggests the same here, in his blunter, theological (rather than narrative) account. We are to be conformed to the death of Christ in that we are to empty our lives, taking on the form of a slave and transcending selfhood, even to the last moment of our dying.

What then might afford continuity between this fragile life and being risen with Christ after we die? Paul has no notion of humans as composed of body and soul. He teaches nothing about the immortality of the soul, for the immortal soul was too Platonic a Greek notion to find purchase in his gospel understanding.⁸⁸ Paul speaks, rather, of an "inner person" (ἔσω ἄνθρωπος) and of the heavenly continuance of his

---

82. Collange, *Epistle of Saint Paul*, 132.
83. Bruce, *Philippians*, 115.
84. Vincent, *Critical and Exegetical Commentary*, 105.
85. Reumann, *Philippians*, 502. Braumann writes, "The death of Christ acquires a morphē in the death of the apostle" (G. Braumann, *NIDNTT* 1:705, 707). Fee comments, "Very likely . . . the participle is 'modal'" (Fee, *Paul's Letter to the Philippians*, 333 n. 65).
86. Thurston, "Philippians," 128.
87. O'Brien, *Epistle to the Philippians*, 408.
88. Although it is found in 1:3–15 and 2:23–24 of the Wisdom of Solomon, which was written in Greek at just about the same time as these Philippian letters.

selfless I (ἐγώ)[89]—expressed in Ephesians as a "new humanity" (καινὸς ἄνθρωπος 4:24)—which is realized in being grounded in the one body of Christ. In the empty Christ, Paul has no clear idea about the mechanism of risen life. It all comes down to "being conformed to his death" (συμμορφιζόμενος τῷ θανάτῳ αὐτοῦ 3:10), knowing that the emptied form of Christ energizes inert bodies by resurrection power to something more than a continued self-exaltation.

All of this, then, is meant by knowing Christ: the power of his resurrection and participating in his suffering, and being conformed by that knowledge and wisdom to his dying, "so that we may somehow attain to the resurrection from the dead (εἴ πως καταντήσω εἰς τὴν ἐξανάστασιν τὴν ἐκ νεκρῶν 3:11). The expression "if somehow" (εἴ πως) signifies that Paul does not know how. Resurrection faith does not come with a user's guide. When Paul speaks of Jesus, he does not have in mind the historical accounts of Jesus; we are not engaged here in a masochistic quest to repeat the sufferings of a criminal executed in the days of the Roman Empire. Tradition has it that Paul himself was beheaded, and he recommends no particular form of death to his Christian hearers. It really does not much matter. There are many ways to suffer, many ways to die. Beyond these lies resurrection.

The term Paul uses here for resurrection is not the usual *anastasis* (ανάστασις). He appends the prefix *ek* (ἐκ, here ἐξ) to give us the uncommon *exanastasin* (ἐξανάστασιν), signifying "resurrection from," here from death (εἰς τὴν ἐξανάστασιν τὴν ἐκ νεκρῶν 3:11). But the prefix is superfluous, and most English translations ignore it. There is a verb *exanistēmi* (ἐξανίστημι), which means to wake up or rise up. So I would take Paul's unusual term for resurrection here to mean awakening from the sleep of death, with perhaps a stress on the "upward" sense of risen and awakened life, as when in 3:14 Paul writes of "the upward call of God in Christ Jesus" (διώκω εἰς τὸ βραβεῖον τῆς ἄνω κλήσεως τοῦ θεοῦ ἐν Χριστῷ Ἰησοῦ). This "upward" pattern, this impulse to reach beyond bodily survival, has been deeply inscribed in our genes over the course of our entire biological and human history. It is not a magic act like Harry Potter's return from his afterdeath conversation with Dumbledore. Such images of magical restoration elicited in the Philippians, as they do in ourselves, a deep skepticism.[90] As well they should. But resurrection faith here is to be understood as taking refuge in "simply" being human, with all the promises written deep within our minds and with the enabling power of sharing in risen life. However difficult it may be to acknowledge our primal source in the unknown—now more than ever benign in that our ongoing lives are encompassed in the Christ awakening from the dead self—the resurrection promise occupies the center of our faith.

89. See Thrall, "Paul's Understanding of Continuity."

90. Reumann, *Philippians*, 523: "A clash over resurrection is apparent . . . . Problems with Jesus' bodily resurrection and implications for believers were endemic to Paul's congregations in Macedonia and Greece. . . . From the Jesus story, verses 10-11 pick out his *death* (10b) and *resurrection* (10a), not how he believed or any detail in his life, like circumcision or being under the Law, points to which Paul could have alluded (Galatians 4:4-5)."

We frequently speak in this way. At funerals we talk about the deceased being at rest or asleep, and pray that they too will rise with Christ. At Buddhist funerals, the recently deceased is entrusted to the same reality of awakened life, even receiving a new name as an awakened buddha; and this is yet another form of the same human yearning. Paul is playing with words that mean both to awaken from sleep and to arise, but he does not know the contours of such a resurrection any more than does Chuang Tzu when he talks of waking from his butterfly dream.[91] Theologians often, in their desire to clarify the scriptures, will nail down meanings in bright images, leaving little in the shadows. But those sharp images leave me wondering how they know these things so clearly. Paul's words are much less definite, as we see in his subjunctive introductory phrase "if in some way" (εἴ πως) I may attain to this resurrection." My grammar school catechism was clearer: We die and, if we have lived the gospel, our souls will go to heaven, where, disembodied, we/they await the bodily resurrection at the end of time. N. T. Wright's *Surprised by Hope* similarly fills in the picture. Yet that is such a wooden depiction that it arouses doubt and skepticism by its very clarity about things that we do not and cannot know.[92]

Despite his verbosity, Paul does understand the limits of words. He is aware that we make them up in an attempt to express meaning that we have consciously experienced but have no ability to understand or articulate. When we speak of the meaning of life, or the underlying meaning of the multiverse, we name our yearning, which gives us no avenue for further insight. Paul's effort here to express the power of his experiences is in the main inadequate, although at times he is rather quite skillful and wise. Still, insights do not spring fully formed and luminous from the depths of the unknown darkness, and so Paul not infrequently resorts to making up words in the attempt to express what he wants to say—here "waking up," or perhaps "resurrection up from." Scholars often interpret the purpose of his adding the preposition *ex-* as merely to "*reinforce* the significance of" the subsequent phrase "from the dead."[93] Thus, "so that I might experience resurrection up from the dead." The very redundancy of this phrase seems to emphasize that Paul is forcing words to bear the weight of what surely lies beyond any horizon available to us.[94]

---

91. See Chuang Tzu, *Complete Works*, 49: "Once Chuang Chou dreamt he was a butterfly, a butterfly flitting and fluttering around, happy with himself and doing as he pleased. He didn't know he was Chuang Chou. Suddenly he woke up and there he was, solid and unmistakable Chuang Chou. But he didn't know if he was Chuang Chou who had dreamt he was a butterfly, or a butterfly dreaming he was Chuang Chou. Between Chuang Chou and a butterfly there must be *some* distinction! This is called the Transformation of Things."

92. In his book *Surprised by Hope: Rethinking Heaven, the Resurrection, and the Mission of the Church* (New York: HarperCollins, 2008), Wright engages in a kind of supernatural empiricism.

93. O'Brien, *Epistle to the Philippians*, 415.

94. Vincent, *Critical and Exegetical Commentary*, 106: "ἐξανάστασις occurs only here in the Bible . . . Why the compound word was selected instead of the simple ανάστασις, we cannot explain."

This term *exanastasin* (3:11) is modeled perhaps on the "more than exalted" term in 2:9 of the emptiness hymn. There it was argued that the term *hyper-upsōsen* (ὑπερύψωσεν) signifies a state that is more than, or beyond, "highly exalted." *Exanastasin* is similar in that Paul is doubling up here on the meaning of resurrection to suggest—perhaps in the manner of later mystic theologians like Dionysius the Areopagite and Maximus Confessor—that the truth of our resurrection faith surpasses its own content in such a way that it cannot be humanly imagined. Paul certainly wants us to reach beyond notions of mere restoration or resuscitation from the dead.[95] He is not simply speaking in the superlative; he is crafting his words so as to communicate the inadequacy of *any* account that might suggest the form of this risen life. And just as we are not to cling to the empty Christ, neither are we to cling to risen life.

Paul makes it clear that the resurrection from the dead of which he speaks is not something reserved as an afterlife experience. Its power is experienced in his and our own living, corporeal life. We do not know the shape of our own human future, much less the shape of what lies beyond this life. Nevertheless, our path is limned by hope in something that goes beyond the living body, beyond mere bodily restoration from the dead. Paul does not mean that we are to survive as ethereal spirits. He makes that clear in 1 Cor 15:37–41, where he teaches that our present bodies are seeds or kernels that germinate into bodies differently given as provided by God, each in accord with its seed potential: "And what you sow is not the body which is to be, but is a bare kernel, perhaps of wheat or of some other grain. But God gives it a body as he has chosen, and to each kind of seed its own body" (ὁ δὲ θεὸς δίδωσιν αὐτῷ σῶμα καθὼς ἠθέλησεν, καὶ ἑκάστῳ τῶν σπερμάτων ἴδιον σῶμα 1 Cor 15:37–38). He tells us that these different bodies include animals, birds, fish, the stars, the sun, and the moon, all distinctive, for even "star differs from star in glory."

In short, we simply cannot imagine the body of the resurrection. Paul's Corinthian vision is cosmic, embracing everything, not just the bodies of flesh that we now inhabit. Paul never identifies the risen body in terms of any body that we actually have experienced. Unclear though the form of his hope is, we are nevertheless to strive to reach beyond death and beyond mere bodily restoration.[96] In the shared power of risen life and sufferings, the margins of life and death have been erased by the Christ

---

95. Reumann cites A. Oepke in explaining that "in the Greek world 'resurrection' was impossible; at best, an isolated event in stories about the physician Aesculapius or Apollonius of Tyana. Upon dying, one faces a shadowy existence in the abode of Hades; at times notions of the 'immortality of the soul' or 'transmigration of souls' (Plato *Resp.* 10, the myth of Er) . . . Resurrection of the body is not found in most of the Old Testament, only in late texts like Isaiah 26:19 and Daniel 12:2 . . . . 'Resurrection-restorations of the people of God' (Hosea 6:3; Ezekiel 37; Isaiah 53:10–12 . . .) came to be applied to Jesus (1 Corinthians 15:4 'according to the scriptures') . . . Possibly [the phrase here is a] genitive of apposition, 'the power that his resurrection is' (. . . Vincent, 104)" (A. Oepke, *TDNT*, 1:368–72, cited in Reumann, *Philippians*, 500).

96. Jews and early Christians "could not conceive of any worthwhile life after death except in bodily terms. Thus the body, together with the physical universe with which it is inseparably linked, must be included in the redemptive purposes of God" (Caird, *Paul's Letters from Prison*, 140).

who empties the divide between God-dwelling-in-final-rest from his creative labors and humans still struggling on the surface of one of many billions of worlds. The take-away from this is overflowing joy in the celebration of a life abundant that both surpasses imagination and confounds theological exposition.

Some commentators are concerned that Paul speaks tentatively in the phrase "if in some way I may reach (εἴ πως καταντήσω) to what goes beyond the resurrection from the dead" (εἰς τὴν ἐξανάστασιν τὴν ἐκ νεκρῶν 3:11). He has already experienced the power of resurrection faith, and yet his language when he expresses his hope to attain to the reality beyond resurrection "seems to introduce a note of doubt or uncertainty."[97] Many wish that Paul had a more unambiguous confidence,[98] but "total elimination of uncertainty for *ei pōs* [if somehow] is hard to pull off."[99] Having found his sure refuge in Christ, does Paul yet doubt that he himself will rise? Is he not completely confident in his beliefs? But Paul's ambiguity here elegantly expresses the difficulty that humans in every tradition encounter when attempting to cloth in words their deepest experiences—whether of life in Christ, of Buddha awakening, of true Jewish discipleship, of Islamic servanthood, of Hindu oneness with Brahman, or of Taoist harmony with the breath/energy of the cosmos.

The experienced power of the resurrection is not lessened by the ambiguity of words that can never capture its contours in sharp relief. The awakened life of Christ comes before and goes beyond words. The ambiguity and doubt relate to "how" (πως, *pos*) one shares in risen life to be with Christ, for this is an eschatological hope, not a firmly held tenet. At their best, all traditions demonstrate a deep awareness of the inadequacy of human language. Only positivists think that words fully express meaning. These are experiences that cannot be reduced to indicative or hortatory sentences. Subjunctive discourse, with its note of probability and doubt, is much truer to the authentic path experience of Christians who are engaged in the teachings of Paul and in following the path of the empty Christ. A faith confession that ignores our humanness, and claims with certainty to have captured the fundamental truth of the cosmos, negates by its very certitude life as it is actually lived in all of its ambiguity and all of its hope.

Like the emptiness hymn in 2:6–11, the present passage about resurrection power and shared suffering has been somewhat overlooked in discussions of the christology of Philippians. V. Koperski, however, contends that the passage in 3:7–11 is "one of the strongest christological statements in Christian scripture," stronger even than

---

97. O'Brien, *Epistle to the Philippians*, 412.

98. On "if," Reumann writes, "Many see *pōs* suggesting doubt or uncertainty in the apostle's mind" (Reumann, *Philippians*, 502). Thurston comments, "Does *ei pōs* imply conditionality about resurrection itself? Almost everyone concludes, 'no'" (Thurston, "Philippians," 128–29). Then what about fear and trembling?

99. Reumann, *Philippians*, 525.

2:6–11.¹⁰⁰ John Reumann agrees, noting that "the striking new note in 3:8–11, compared with 2:6–11, is *resurrection*, Christ's (3:10a) and ours or at least Paul's (11)."¹⁰¹ Reumann suggests that Paul added this passage to correct the theology of the emptiness hymn, which does not emphasize the sufferings of Christ or his bodily resurrection.¹⁰² And yet the emptiness hymn does describe Christ as becoming "obedient to the point of death," even if—as Reumann contends—it was Paul who added the phrase "even death on a cross." I think it better to understand this passage not as correcting the hymn's theology so much as restating it in terms of the Jesus tradition's more familiar, more pervasive, emphasis on the death and resurrection of Christ as we share and participate in their ongoing reality. Indeed, 3:7–11 speaks of bodily resurrection within the same eschatological hope, the contours of which in 2:6–11 remain hidden to humans and are less likely to be imagined as bodily restoration or resuscitation. In both passages, Christ appears in wisdom categories, whether in the self-emptying and more-than-exaltation of the hymn of 2:6–11, or here, as the gnosis of knowing Christ indivisibly in his sufferings and resurrection power.¹⁰³

Despite the comparatively little attention given to Phil 3:7–11 by commentators on Paul's christology, its emphasis on Christ's death and resurrection is congruent with the overwhelming focus of the tradition's theological discourse over the centuries, while the emptiness theme of the Philippian hymn has remained comparatively unexamined. So it seems right and proper that "3:7–11 does not occupy a place anywhere near the towering influence of 2:6–11,"¹⁰⁴ whose focus on the empty Christ expresses a very early christological confession. Yet 2:6–11 has rarely been recognized to be as centrally important to our christology as the Prologue of John's Gospel.

Stretching Forth (3:12–14)

> 3:12 *Not that I have attained already or already been perfected. Rather, I press on if I also may take hold, for I have been taken hold of by Christ (Jesus).* ¹³*Brothers and sisters, I do not calculate that I myself have apprehended. Just this single thing: forgetting what lies behind and stretching for what lies ahead,* ¹⁴*bearing*

---

100. V. Koperski, *The Knowledge of Christ Jesus my Lord : The High Christology of Philippians 3:7–11* (Leuven, Belgium: Peters, 1996) 1, 287–321.

101. Reumann, *Philippians*, 507.

102. Ibid.: "Is this a place where the theology of the Philippian 'hymn' was vulnerable? It ignored Old Testament-Jewish bodily resurrection and implications for believers. Greeks had problems with the resurrection and its meaning . . . ." Bolstering his interpretation, Reumann takes the phrase "even death on a cross" in 2:8, not as part of the Philippain composition, but as a corrective added by Paul himself (ibid., 506).

103. See C. Marvin Pate, *The Reverse of the Curse: Paul, Wisdom, and the Law*, Wissenshaftliche Untersuchungen Zum Neuen Testament Reihe 114 (Tubingen: Mohr Siebeck, 2000). Pate argues that Paul used the wisdom theme to separate Christ as God's wisdom from the Law.

104. Reumann, *Philippians*, 526.

down attentively I press on toward the prize of the upward call of God in Christ Jesus.

3:12 Οὐχ ὅτι ἤδη ἔλαβον ἢ ἤδη τετελείωμαι, διώκω δὲ εἰ καὶ καταλάβω, ἐφ᾿ ᾧ καὶ κατελήμφθην ὑπὸ Χριστοῦ [Ἰησοῦ]. ¹³ἀδελφοί, ἐγὼ ἐμαυτὸν οὐ λογίζομαι κατειληφέναι· ἓν δέ, τὰ μὲν ὀπίσω ἐπιλανθανόμενος τοῖς δὲ ἔμπροσθεν ἐπεκτεινόμενος, ¹⁴κατὰ σκοπὸν διώκω εἰς τὸ βραβεῖον τῆς ἄνω κλήσεως τοῦ θεοῦ ἐν Χριστῷ Ἰησοῦ.

Paul has not captured, or apprehended, Jesus. And he has had no defining experience that brings him to a full realization of the power of resurrection faith. In 3:8–10 he writes that he has abandoned all things for the sake of knowing Christ and experiencing the power of his resurrection in being conformed to the sufferings of his death. Now, having emptied all previous supports for his subjective selfhood, he proceeds to negate even the very actions of attaining, taking hold of, or apprehending. "Verse 12 has five verbs, never a direct object, no nouns except at the end, *by Christ Jesus*."[105] Paul's point in 3:12 is not to assert that his own progress on the path of knowing Christ is only partially complete, but rather to negate the verbal force of attaining (ἔλαβον), apprehending (κατειληφέναι), or becoming perfect (τετελείωμαι).[106] The wisdom of Christ does not function within the framework of subject apprehending object, and Paul overcomes that kind of dichotomy through continued engagement in the path of awakened life in Christ.

In Mahāyāna theology, awakened resurrection is not a path that leads from this world of samsaric and sorry suffering to a realm of pure nirvanic peace.[107] For the Mahayanist, awakening is overcoming the dichotomy between these two poles, whereby an awakened person empties not only *this* world of endeavor, disappointment, and suffering, but also *that* world of cessation and calmness, of beyond-it-all peace. I think Paul is saying something very similar here. He emphasizes that knowing Christ is not a once-and-for-all apprehension of Christ as object, that knowing comes only from seeing the faces of Philippians who live in the Christ supplied by the Spirit, and who through their hymnic confession have taught Paul to live in the empty Christ as well.

The Christ mind that Paul shares with the Philippians abandons the naïve realism of subject living in opposition to putative objects, whether those objects are worldly possessions or imagined religious personages. Churches that exalt Christ as the heavenly object of devout practice surround Christ with luminous imagery and ontological surety because they themselves have been caught up in secularizing Christ

---

105. Ibid., 552.

106. Ibid., 55: "The verbs are what Paul negates."

107. *Pace* Reumann, *Philippians*, 551: "Perfection is *not* his, even now in Christ, the way it *will be* one day, with Christ. This holds for every Christian—existence means tension between what has already been received and what still lies ahead." Rather, Paul collapses time frames into eschatological emptiness, fulfillment consciousness, present in being in Christ and presently structured to being with Christ, at death.

in a framework of worldly self-assertion.[108] By contrast, Paul's non-attainment is not a special spiritual cult for the assiduous practitioner, but rather a reclamation of our dependently arisen human knowing of Christ through experiencing the visceral power of his resurrection and being embraced in his sufferings. By refusing the hegemony of the dualistic and imagined pattern of consciousness that would restrict us to distant images of an otherworldly savior, we may engage the world as it actually is, in a Christ wisdom that acknowledges all our transience and all our suffering.

We do not know Christ in finite stages, but in Paul's eschatological wisdom, we embrace an always-tensive hope and ongoing compassionate engagement; it is not a journey that follows a roadmap to a particular destination. He does not know where he is going, but he does know where he stands, here in Christ. Still, to know Christ is not to have gotten him, not to have attained anything; rather, it is to be constantly engaged in the activities of discipleship and endeavor for the sake of the gospel. That is Paul's eschatological hope and the present structure of his elastic mind, which stretches forth to meet his brothers and sisters in shared fellowship. Paul speaks not of something that has been attained, apprehended, or grasped, but rather of his *effort* to attain. He "has not yet attained" (Οὐκ ὅτι ἤδη ἔλαβον 3:12) anything; and he never will in any imagined eschaton, for there is no attaining and nothing to be attained. Here and elsewhere throughout this letter, Paul is recommending a radical shift in our consciousness, and his focus is upon a constant and unending deepening of knowing the mind of Christ. He says that he has not already received anything, that he has not already been made perfect or come to the final term or end point (ἢ ἤδη τετελείωμαι). When we speak of salvation and justification, we often forget that these, likewise, are not objects to be attained.

Still, just what is it that Paul has not yet obtained? In 3:11, he hopes that "I somehow may take hold" (εἴ πως καταντήσω) of the resurrection from the dead that leads beyond categories.[109] Then in 3:12 he shifts from active to passive voice to say "for I have been taken hold of by Christ (Jesus)" (ἐφ' ᾧ καὶ κατελήμφθην ὑπὸ Χριστοῦ [Ἰησοῦ]). The grammar again is about to collapse. Will he now somehow take hold of it? Some commentators answer that what he has not yet attained is the full power of the resurrection, but he has received knowledge of Christ and enriched his personal relationship with the risen Lord. Although Paul supplies no object for the first transitive verb in 3:12 (ἔλαβον, "have attained"), some scholars feel free to supply what they think Paul intended to say.[110] But in fact he says only "I have not yet attained." We

---

108. See John A. T. Robinson, *Honest to God* (Philadelphia: Westminster, 1963).

109. On εἰ καὶ καταλάβω, Reumann writes, ""Thus it expresses 'an uncertain expectation associated with an effort to attain something' (ZBG 403, suppy "to try [if I can ...])" (Reumann, *Philippians*, 537).

110. On "bewildering" variety of objects suggested, Vincent writes, "Meyer says that βραβεῖον is the bliss of Messiah's kingdom; and that ἔλαβον is to be explained of his having attained in ideal anticipation(!)" (Vincent, *Critical and Exegetical Commentary*, 107). Rather, I take the meaning to express that no arhat bliss lies in the future. On "not attained," Reumann writes, "Again no direct

should hesitate to fill in objects that we envision Paul as attaining, for the category-less resurrection is not an attainable object at all. To fill in Paul's missing objects is to rewrite the text, not to interpret it. A better understanding is that Paul deliberately omits any object for his transitive verb precisely because he is not focusing here on the object apprehended or received.

Other, more perceptive, commentators point out that the focus should be not upon what is received but upon the very act of attaining or receiving.[111] One might suggest the translation, "I have not got it," where the object "it" is not a definite any-thing, leading to the possible conclusion that Paul, in humbly disclaiming that he has achieved fulfillment of the aspirations he has just listed, simply was not so very far along the laddered path. One commentator argues just this: " . . . that which Paul disclaims having already obtained is the ultimate and complete 'gaining' of Christ."[112] But this leaves intact the notion that Christ wisdom is an attainable goal, even if Paul himself has not yet attained it. More insightfully, G.B. Caird writes: "He is denying that achievement itself has any place in the life of faith."[113] Another scholar rightly points out that Paul rejects "the fundamental attitude of being satisfied, gained from knowing 'I have arrived.'"[114] I conclude that the focus here is entirely upon the con-figuration of consciousness with which one follows the gospel. It is not about having or getting anything at all, for there is nothing at all to be gotten. Already, all is gift, this empty and beautifully transient life of ours.

It seems clear to me, with my Mahāyāna philosophy, that if Paul does not define the goal and does not say what it is that he has or has not obtained, then we have no call to name his objective. It may help us to envisage a City on the Hill, but such visions are merely a skillful means to encourage our practice, for once we arrive there, it turns out to be yet another way station.[115] We do not travel along a path toward a someday attainment of the final Christ objective. In our day-to-day practice, we may make advances in uprooting and taming the evolutionary urge to assure our own survival and selfhood, progressing in the formation (Greek, *paideia*) of a virtuous mind,[116] but we

---

object in Greek," so "some add 'it,' or supply 'the finish line'" (Reumann, *Philippians*, 538). Silva thinks that "all three [of the verbs obtain, be perfected, and grasp] have the same referent in view, namely, the attainment of Paul's ultimate goal" (Silva, *Philippians*, 173).

111. O'Brien, *Epistle to the Philippians*, 421. "The abrupt verbs and their uncertain objects did not arise out of thin air" (Reumann, *Philippians*, 553).

112. Ibid., 420 n. 4.

113. Caird, *Paul's Letters from Prison*, 142.

114. G. T. Montague, *Growth in Christ: A Study of Saint Paul's Theology of Progress* (Fribourg: Regina Mundi, 1961) 125.

115. As in the parable of the Conjured City in the Lotus Sūtra. See Gene Reeves, *The Stories of the Lotus Sutra* (Boston: Wisdom, 2010) 94–99, on "A Fantastic Castle City."

116. Werner Jaeger, *Paideia: The Ideals of Greek Culture*, trans. Gilbert Highet (Oxford: Oxford University Press, 1956) traces the growth of Hellenistic cultural training through the development of cultural learning toward character formation. Jaeger treats the Hellenistic cultural context within which the early Christian communities developed in Werner Jaeger, *Early Christianity and Greek*

have no way to measure progress toward a final goal. Never are we even halfway there, for this gospel is an ongoing path at each moment fulfilled in experiencing the unrestricted power of Christ resurrection and participating in Christ sufferings.[117] Even as Paul awaits the eschatological coming of Christ, still he strives on, for that striving is the eschatological structure of his Christ mind.[118] The "yet" (ἤδη) in the passage does not mean that at some future date he will have attained, merely that as yet he has not. Nevertheless, he offers himself as model and paradigm to his readers then and now. This further explains why Paul confesses in 3:11 that he strives "in some way" (εἴ πως) to realize risen life "with outstretched, empty hands."[119]

Paul has "not yet come to my endpoint perfection," (τετελείωμαι 3:12) and he never will. This term is reminiscent of the mystery religions of his Hellenistic world. Perhaps some of his correspondents have heard talk of initiates who "had been already perfected," who had "attained the end point." That seems to have been a feature of Gnostic movements in Paul's day, with their focus on a special "gnosis," or knowledge that rises above this sorry world to the perfection of a stable wisdom. Whether or not we can discern behind this term a whiff of these mystery religions—about which we know very little because of scant textual evidence[120]—Paul himself has not arrived at any perfected endpoint. He has not been initiated into any mysterious secret. There is no perfected state that might mystically terminate his striving to be conformed to Christ. Rather than projecting some blissful end state, the culmination of a life of practice, Paul celebrates the power of Christ resurrection identified in his life as sufferings, all conformed to the empty mind of Christ.

Paul did die, likely executed during the persecutions of Nero. We cannot ask him what he meant by this or that in his writings, and yet I think that Paul's letters do serve for the furtherance of this emptying gospel. In his dying, he no longer suffers beatings or imprisonments, but is one with the risen Christ, organically and personally part of the groaning cosmos that in us spontaneously births a new world of justice and peace, of wisdom and compassion. That is why he can say that one is to overcome life and death, or, more exactly, to experience the power of the resurrection and share in the sufferings of Christ. What ends with death is effort, not the ongoing life that circulates throughout all our worlds.

Thus, Paul must still "press on so that he will attain" (διώκω δὲ εἰ καὶ καταλάβω 3:12). When he writes in 3:6 of "persecuting" the church, he uses the very same verb

---

Paideia (Boston: Harvard College, 1961).

117. Keenan, *Meaning of Christ*, 86–119, on "A Mysticism of Darkness."

118. Fee, *Paul's Letter to the Philippians*, 348: "the eschatological consummation of what is 'already' his in Christ."

119. Barth, *Epistle to the Philippians*, 107.

120. On *teleios* and *epiteleō*, common terms in Greek philosophy, Reumann writes: "'the perfect man' attains *phronēsis* or 'firm, true views'" (Reumann, *Philippians*, 536). Perhaps with Gnostic overtones, but "Whatever one decides on 'Gnosticism,' mystery cults existed in Paul's day, at Eleusis (near Athens); Dionysus cult (pertinent to Philippi)" (ibid.).

diōkō (διώκων), the basic sense of which is zealously to pursue an objective.[121] Yet, he is unable to identify clearly what that objective is; or perhaps better said, he has identified it as a wisdom consciousness that entails an ever deeper knowing of Christ without any graspable objective. He strives and presses on, so as to apprehend, so as to obtain . . . what? I don't think he really knows, which is precisely why he says that he must press on so as to attain and "get a hold [of it]." The subjunctive tenor of 3:11—*ei pos* (εἴ πως), literally, I strive "if (εἰ) I may possibly lay hold [of it]" (δὲ εἰ καὶ καταλάβω)—is repeated in 3:12, where the same hesitancy is expressed in the words "If I also may take hold" (δὲ εἰ καὶ καταλάβω). Faith is marked by hesitancy, not by the tenacity of firmly held views or beliefs.

Theologian Jean Daniélou focused on Gregory of Nyssa's commentary on this passage, particularly on the notion of "stretching forth" (ἐπεκτεινόμενος) in Paul.[122] Gregory developed a theology, not of getting and having, but of stretching forth constantly from any point, here in this life and even after this life has come to its end. It is not that Christ will come at a certain point, and we will all be happy ever after in some Christian Elysian field.[123] It is not that, once arrived in heaven, people sit around being beatifically happy. Rather, the entire cosmos groans and stretches forth ever more to enter into the depths that we Christians identify as knowing the power of Christ's risen life. In Rom 8:22-24, Paul talks of this stretching forth as a cosmic groaning for bodily redemption: "We know that the whole creation has been groaning in labor pains until now, and not only the creation, but we ourselves, who have the first fruits of the Spirit, groan inwardly as we wait for adoption, the redemption of our bodies."

To know Christ does not mean the once-and-for-all enrichment of a stable religious self that now can stand confidently in relation to a Jesus out there, but rather a constant striving, in abandonment of any stability, toward becoming conformed to

---

121. Collange explains: "The stress lies on the effort required because '*diōkō*' properly speaking does not mean 'to run' but 'to chase,' 'to pursue after,' 'to hunt down' (cf. 3:6)" (Collange, *Epistle of Saint Paul*, 133). Also see Thurston: "'Pursuing' implies hunting down a quarry, hunting down animals" (Thurston, "Philippians," 122). Collange adds: "*Diōkō* appears as a *terminus technicus* for Paul's attitude before his conversion—Acts 9:4; 22:4, 1, 1; 1 Cor 15:9; Gal 1:12, 13)" (Collange, *Epistle of Saint Paul*, 127).

122. Jean Daniélou, *Platonisme et théologie mystique: Doctrine spirituelle de Saint Gregorie de Nysse* (Paris: Aubier, Éditions Montaigne, 1944) 257. In his *Fourth Homily on the Beatitudes*, Gregory writes: "Thus the great apostle Paul, who has tasted the fruits reserved for Paradise, seems to me to have been satisfied with what he has tasted, and yet to have always thirsted: 'Christ lives in me'; and yet he always 'stretches forth (*epekteinetai*) toward that which is ahead,' until he states, 'It is not that I already know that for which I reach nor that I am already perfect'" (cited in Herbert Musurillo, *From Glory to Glory: Texts from Gregory of Nyssa's Mystical Writings* [Crestwood, NY: St. Vladimir's, 1979] 167).

123. Reumann, interpreting the "heavenly call," sees Paul's Damascus Road call "not completed till the goal is reached, at the parousia or the individual's death" (Reumann, *Philippians*, 550-51). He notes other visions that were available to the Philippian readers: an interim kingdom on earth, Utopian communities: "Alexarchus is said to have founded a town about 316 B.C. on Mt. Athos, some fifty miles south of Philippi, named Uranopolis, 'City of Heaven' . . . Portefaix [*Sisters Rejoice*] assumes that 'this was known in Philippi,' including anecdotes on egalitarian status for women in Uranopolis" (ibid., 153-54).

Jesus; for he has emptied himself of everything so that, having abandoned everything, we too may be more than exalted. This is something more than an individual striving or experience; the entire cosmos shares in stretching forth to an ever more organic and bodily risen life, the birds and the fishes, the sun and the moon, and all the varied stars in the sky. Our evolution, when reconfigured by path-practice, is not limited to an afterlife of self-survival but is liberated from that evolutionary imperative that we may reach beyond any known limit. If Teilhard de Chardin had been a more assiduous student of scripture, he might have grounded his mystic geology upon these Pauline scriptures. Then again, perhaps they were inscribed in his evolutionary consciousness. Our life in Christ is to expand beyond known horizons, just as the cosmos itself is expanding without margins. Indeed, we now know that the multiverse is at every moment becoming larger and larger, with no identifiable boundary to contain it. Risen life is not an escape to a blissful and godly narcotic absorption, but a bodily resurrection wherein as God wills it we remain bodily awakened and ever participate in the eschatological fulfillment of the reality of the cosmos.

The fact that Paul is unable to know or to say does not mean that he has not experienced the power of the resurrection. Often we are conscious of things that cannot be expressed in mediating words or concepts.[124] The enabling power that structures Paul's life is knowing the Christ he has consciously experienced in the fullness of his living and dying, in the richness of his rising and being exalted, and to somehow communicate that in his teaching and committed practice. This is how Paul understands the ultimate point of living and dying. But it is not a known goal like any other aspirational target, and although Paul is fond of athletic metaphors that speak of racing to the finish line, that finish line has already begun and will never end. Thus, he immediately qualifies his attempts to attain and take hold, using another of his mystical clarifications: "for I have been taken hold of by Christ (Jesus)" (ἐφ'ᾧ καὶ κατελήμφθην ὑπὸ Χριστοῦ ['Ιησοῦ] 3:12).

The experience of attaining Christ is an experience of being attained *by* Christ. This grasping is a being grasped and encompassed in the benign embrace of the risen Christ by being conformed to suffering, by being human. Paul did not set about to survey and analyze his world, reaching the judgment that enfoldment in Christ is the proper objective of his endeavors. Rather, in the midst of striving to attain (διώκω δὲ εἰ καὶ καταλάβω) the eradication of what he saw as a threat to Truth, he was apprehended, knocked down, and pinned down in blindness by Christ. What he was doing on that Damascus Road was "pressing on," to reach and to extirpate the Damascus community of disciples of the Jesus path. But as he pressed on, his goal disappeared in an experience of blindness and confusion. Likewise here, the objective of his endeavors

124. According to Lonergan, being in love with God without limits is a dynamic state of consciousness. But "to say that a dynamic state is conscious is not to say that it is known. For consciousness is just experience, but knowledge is a compound of experience, understanding, and judging. Because this dynamic state is conscious without being known, it is an experience of mystery" (Lonergan, *Method in Theology*, 1–6).

is not self-constructed. He presses on because he has been pressed by Christ to slave away at the oars to further propel the gospel ship. Not a self-motivated reaching out for anything, but being emptied by the emptying Christ.

In Mahāyāna philosophy, the truth of ultimate meaning is literally the truth of the final (Skt. *parama*) end target (*artha*), that which draws one forth, and towards which one aims, without ever reaching any final point, for the simple reason that our conventional capacities—dependent as they are on the pattern of subject apprehending object (*grāhya-grāhaka*)—are not designed for attaining such a goal. Structured as they are for coping and surviving in a world of competition, they must be tamed by gospel practice. Which is why, again and again, the Mahāyāna scriptures insist that the truth of ultimate meaning (*paramārtha-satya*) is a goal of no-goal. We do not have arrows in our mental quivers to reach that target. Still, the mind that is reconfigured with the intention of embodying the ultimate meaning may follow the path that reaches its final point by emptying all points of any final status and engaging in compassionate action toward emptying the world of any final suffering.

Similarly here, Paul has a goal that constitutes no final point, no finish line. The final point and ultimate goal, beyond all human endeavor, lies in Paul's "stretch practice" whereby, yoga-like, he empties himself into the vacuum that is the empty Christ, who was in the form of God yet did not cling to his equality with God, becoming fully and completely human and thus, in his faith, Christlike. That is the final objective: to be one with Christ whose final resting point on the cross was emptied precisely by being more-than-exalted. In the Gospel of Mark, as Jesus dies, the curtain in the Holy of Holies in the Temple is torn apart, revealing the absence of any identifiable location wherein God might dwell.[125] Here Paul talks about the goal, but he does not know the final contours of life in Christ. He is silent on most of these matters. In fact, he found it necessary to curb the eschatological zeal of the Thessalonians, who thought the end point imminent. For a time he shared their linear expectation of, and perhaps their enthusiasm for, an imminent parousia, but eventually turned that expectation into a hope that was inscribed in the very fibers of his questing mind.

Paul stresses, "I do not reckon that I myself have apprehended" (ἀδελφοί, ἐγὼ ἐμαυτὸν οὐ λογίζομαι κατειληφέναι 3:13). Even after he has been apprehended by Christ and has experienced things that he says that he cannot enunciate, still he avers that he has not attained anything and does not consider himself to have laid hold of and grasped Christ within his own personal compass. Indeed, there is no Christ to be so grasped—he, Christ, has emptied himself of anything we might wish to apprehend. To learn Christ is then to learn to be empty as Christ was empty. So Paul does not reckon that he has apprehended anything. He does not "calculate" (λογίζομαι 3:13) his own spiritual profit.

Shinran Shōnin (1173–1263)—the architect of Japanese Shin Pure Land Buddhism and master of Buddhist theology—describes the everyday foolish self as

---

125. Keenan, *Gospel of Mark*, 385–87.

bootlessly trying to control the universe by means of *calculation* (Js. *hakarai*), that constant human endeavor whereby we bob and weave, advance and retreat, all in the quest to figure out and ensure the security of a self which, construction that it is, has no enduring reality.[126] Paul refuses to engage in such "calculation," for he knows that he has not apprehended anything. This is why he speaks in such enigmatic terms and why his rhetoric and theology are so paratactic, lacking clarified objects, prone to adding preclitics to words and to tying things together with ambiguous conjunctions. He is not being clever; he just does not know, for the eschatologically experienced content of conversion lies beyond the pattern of mediated knowing. We are not reading here a clear presentation by a scholar in control of his field, but a paratactic theological "stretching forth" by a man deeply and obediently engaged in the upward call of Christ to further the gospel in his own world.

If then Paul does not identify an object that he might attain, why does he talk about attaining at all? Because, grasped and taken hold of by Christ, he is driven to stretch his energies in the everyday service of this Christ. This is a passive experience, as indicated by the many "divine passives" that fill Paul's letters as well as the rest of our scriptures. But it is a passive enfolding that drives one to act. These "passive voice" descriptions do not function within the ordinary polarity of active and passive grammatical voices. They signal conscious experiences that are distinctive in that they disrupt the subject's ability to reach toward an object, or to translate experience into insight and knowledge. And yet, across the traditions, such conscious experiences impel people to commit themselves to practices whose validity lie beyond any polarity of apprehender and apprehended, effective practices of wisdom and compassion. By their fruits, you will know the authenticity of such practices.

Churches and sanghas (Buddhist communities) attempt to pin down such conversions of consciousness in their doctrines, for empty experiences do have a tendency to dismay, precisely because they lie beyond and beneath all the controls of exact speech. In their varied theologies, religious traditions attempt to present doctrine as welcoming and reassuring, assuaging fear and offering refuge. Unfortunately, in the process of bringing such experienced truth into the accustomed parameters of secular life, with its patterns of stable acquisition, they sometimes tend to trivialize the experienced truth of life in Christ, or of Buddha awakening. The church is old. The sangha is older. The Torah is older yet. Each of these religious traditions contains a mystery ever ancient and ever new, to borrow the words of Augustine. They and their institutions are archaic. One can spend a lifetime studying their many twists and turns

---

126. In Pure Land Shinshū theology, true abandonment of self-power and "entrustment" well up from the encompassing Other Power of Amida Buddha, and flow into the chanting of the Buddha's name, the *nembutsu* (念佛). See Unno's comments: "The saying of nembutsu is neither a religious practice nor a good act. Since it is practiced without any calculation (*hakarai*), it is 'non-practice.' Since it is not a good created by my calculation, it is 'non-good.' Since it is nothing but Other Power, completely separated from self-power, it is neither a religious practice nor a good act on the part of the practicer" (Unno, *Tannisho*, 13).

through history. The archaic nature of religious institutions becomes most obvious, however, when their adherents cling to every detail of traditional doctrine and practice, substituting those details for the very experience of conversion and renewal that their practices are meant to enunciate and encourage. In such instances, practitioners become, not disciples of the empty Christ or disciples of the awakened Buddha, but rather deluded persons seeking a false security in ideological and theological rigidity. The gospel is all about *metanoia*, that conversion—*change*—of mind that enables one to engage in stretching forth to make real the kingdom that is always at hand. It is not about having "The Truth."

Here Paul is stretched and pulled out of himself, and he strives to attain an objective beyond any identifiable object.[127] How then is he to explain this? He does so in terms of the singleness of his practice—"Just this single thing" (ἕν δέ 3:13). He sums up by stating that this "one point" (ἕν) is displayed in his continual efforts for the gospel and in his experiences of mystical union with Christ. It is his single-minded mental focus, his one-pointed meditative practice. But he does not leave it at that; he fills out what such a single-minded focus on knowing Christ entails—following the example of the empty Christ without a thought for what came before, "forgetting all that lies behind and stretching for what lies ahead" (τὰ μὲν ὀπίσω ἐπιλανθανόμενος τοῖς δὲ ἔμπροσθεν ἐπεκτεινόμενος 3:13).

It is this "stretching forth" (ἐπεκτεινόμενος) that Gregory of Nyssa identified as the characteristic mark of the Christian life. It is an ever deepening experience of oneness and non-duality with Christ, both here in our endeavors and beyond in painless peace, passing from glory to glory, from one attainment to the emptying of that attainment, for all attainments are themselves empty and lead to launching again, over and over, into daily deepening experiences beyond the compass of our bounded selves.[128] For Paul, the characteristic feature of knowing Christ is this constant stretching forth beyond the margins of his self-consciousness, striving to bring about a world of Christlike harmony and peace wherein the calculus of power itself is canceled. That calculus was canceled for Paul by his experience on the Damascus Road, when the boundaries that he had seen as fixed and immovable, between his native Hebrew

---

127. Caird notes that Paul is concerned that his readers might "expect his Christian experience of union with Christ to give him an even greater sense of superiority than he had as a Pharisee. So he pauses for a moment in his argument to point out that he makes no claim to possess any assets that he can call his own or to have reached his goal" (Caird, *Paul's Letters from Prison*, 141). Caird goes on to explain that "Paul has not only written off the assets he once enjoyed . . . [W]hen he speaks of regarding his Jewish advantages as loss, this is no mere figure of speech. He has actually *suffered the loss* of them" (ibid., 137). But he still has his pursuit, transformed in the service of the empty Christ, and he is still a Pharisee trained in the scriptures and skilled in rabbinic argumentation.

128. Reumann notes that some who overemphasize faith as a struggle (*agōn*; boxing, footrace) "against others toward a heavenly prize" find themselves in "a position (the need for moral effort to attain salvation) for which they criticized Judaism" (Reumann, *Philippians*, 545–46). On "stretching," Vincent writes: "The word has passed into sporting language—'the home stretch'" (Vincent, *Critical and Exegetical Commentary*, 110). But this homestretch keeps stretching forth without a finish line.

culture and the emerging Christian communities, were erased. That is why, in all of his endeavors in the various churches in the Greco-Roman world, Paul fights almost intemperately against any reimposition of boundaries. He is not a Christian fighting Jews, but a gospel preacher fighting against members of his own various communities who would reinstate such boundaries.

Although clearly Paul fights his intramural opponents' tenacious clinging to the signs of the ancient Hebrew covenant, there is no indication that he ever entered into discussion with learned rabbis or even other Pharisees. What he seeks is boundless peace, a peace so that one may practice knowing Christ in the furtherance of this gospel for the wellbeing of the world, the whole multicultural and bifurcated world of ethnic belonging (Jew or Greek); gender difference (male or female); and social stratification (slave or free). This is the reason he stretches forth. This is why he does not rest on his laurels, content with the depths of his own experience of mystic union with Christ. One does not actually forget the past but, as Paul recommends here, one can cease to attend to it. In 3:4b–6 above, he recalls his past in the list of his own distinguishing characteristics as a Jew. However, he does not offer a new set of distinguishing markers for a would-be Christian, for the empty Christ has no markers that would distinguish him from other enlightened teachers, and hardly even a proper biography. Thus, we are to leave behind the distinguishing features of our own life stories and stretch toward the future.

Paul is grounded in time. And even while he eagerly longs for the eschatological coming of Christ, he stretches forward for the future wellbeing of his world. Eschatology is not a time chart upon which to record God's or Christ's actions, but rather the constant structure of the empty mind, both attentive to what lies transcendentally beyond and intent upon the tasks of the present moment. It always entails our stretching beyond our personal and social margins. So here we see Paul using an athletic image. It is "drawn from the games, and it pictures a runner with his eyes fixed on the goal, his hand stretching out towards it, and his body bent forward as he enters the last and decisive stage of the race."[129] Paul extends that image, saying "I press on single-mindedly toward the prize of the upward call of God in Christ Jesus" (κατὰ σκοπὸν διώκω εἰς τὸ βραβεῖον 3:14). Pressing on with zeal, he employs the same term, "to pursue" (διώκω), that he used in describing his former quest to persecute Jesus' followers. And he presses "toward the goal" (εἰς τὸ βραβεῖον), which term is "taken directly from the athletic imagery of the games."[130] One imagines that in his younger days, Paul himself may have been something of an athlete, running in races and entering wrestling competitions, for he knows all the vocabulary. He races toward the goal "single-mindedly" (κατὰ σκοπὸν), with the one-pointed focus of a racer eying the finish line. Indeed, the phrase "single-mindedly" (κατὰ σκοπὸν) contains the term

---

129. O'Brien, *Epistle to the Philippians*, 429.
130. Ibid.

skopos (σκόπος), which lies behind our English word "scope" and indicates specifically an endeavor that engrosses one's total attention, thus defining one's scope of activity.[131]

This verse, 3:14, (κατὰ σκοπὸν διώκω εἰς τὸ βραβεῖον τῆς ἄνω κλήσεως τοῦ θεοῦ ἐν Χριστῷ Ἰησοῦ) poses problems for the interpreter. The RSV unpacks the grammar to translate: "I press on toward the goal (κατὰ σκοπὸν) for the prize (εἰς τὸ βραβεῖον) of the upward call of God in Christ Jesus." Reumann, taking *skopos* (σόπος) to mean "a goal or target at which one aims," translates: "I run in pursuit (διώκω) toward the goal at the finish (κατὰ σκοπὸν), for the prize (εἰς τὸ βραβεῖον), to be called upward by God (τῆς ἄνω κλήσεως τοῦ θεοῦ), in Christ Jesus (ἐν Χριστῷ Ἰησοῦ)."[132] This is the only use of the noun *skopos* in the New Testament, but the verbal form appears in 2:4, meaning to "look out for" the interests of others, and in 3:17, meaning to "look into" or "examine," and so imitate, what one finds in Paul.[133] It is used for "one who watches out for (in a good sense, cf. 3:17, *skopeite*) or watches over a city, and then a goal or target at which one aims."[134] The verb form *skopeō* (σκοπέω) means "to look out for, notice, keep one's eye on."[135] Thus, in 3:17 (σκοπεῖτε) it means to examine or notice Paul's character. But *skopos* in 3:14 is introduced by *kata*, a preposition that means "bearing down,"[136] in contrast to the "upward" call that identifies the "prize" for which Paul strives.

I interpret the phrase to mean that Paul strives with a downward (κατὰ) look (σκοπὸν) for the prize of being called upwardly. Paul is running for the goal, all the while looking down to mark where he runs. The meaning of *skopos* here is the same as in 2:4 and in 3:17: to look out for, to examine and notice. I would then translate: "bearing down attentively I press on toward the prize of the upward call of God in Christ Jesus." Runners on ancient tracks did not have the advantage of well-groomed, level surfaces, but had to watch their step, lest they trip over a rough spot and fall flat on their faces. So while keeping the finish line in view, they also constantly had to be aware of the earth on which they ran. The takeaway point for Paul, then, is that while pressing on for the eschatological prize, he remains focused on this bumpy earth where people have different ideas and do not necessarily agree on strategies for furthering the gospel.

Paul goes on to describe the prize as "the upward call of God in Christ Jesus" (τῆς ἄνω κλήσεως τοῦ θεοῦ ἐν Χριστῷ Ἰησοῦ 3:14). That is an unusual prize, hardly a final goal in any sense, for the prize in this race is not something one receives but is yet another call, an upward call to the eschatological structuring of the wisdom-mind of Christ. That is the prize that beckons Paul and draws him upward, away from earthly contests, to hear and witness to Christ above in this life here below. This "upward"

---

131. Ibid., 430.
132. Reumann, *Philippians*, 533, 556.
133. Ibid., 539.
134. Ibid., 556.
135. Bauer, *Greek-English Lexicon*, 756.
136. Vincent, *Critical and Exegetical Commentary*, 110.

or heavenly (ἄνω) call provides a contrast to those whom Paul goes on to describe in 3:19—people who have their minds on earthly affairs alone,[137] assuming that they have here a permanent abode for self, for its programs and designs. But Paul tells of an "upward (ἄνω) call," one that beckons us to pay attention to what cannot be seen (σκοπὸν) below (κατὰ)—"the inner man" (ἔσω ἄνθρωπος) of 2 Cor 4:16–17, our authentically tensive personal life.[138]

Here, "upward" or "heavenly" does not refer to the blissful state of an arhat who is rapt in unworldly awakening, but rather a cosmic beckoning to our deepest Christ consciousness, the inner person standing in wonder at the star-filled night sky.[139] We have no permanent home. The call from God to transcend is embodied in the Christ who came and died and rose again, and comes ever again, enfleshed in the body of the community. This is not a vertical transcendence or transport to a supernatural location; but neither is this call merely a horizontal influence from the example of Christ to Paul, as if Christ were a teacher teaching pupils and spreading his influence far and wide. Nor is it some kind of "divine" vocation granted to an elite few and not to others. The upward call of Christ power and participation—resurrection and suffering—does not function within the bounded horizons of our human constructs. It is an upward call to an awakening, an invitation to reform our organic minds so as to transcend all our pretenses and become aware of the risen life of Christ that is available to all, assuaging the pain of all, and drawing us back into the world for the sake of others.

The Mind of Abiding without Clear Answers (3:15–16)

3:15 So then, as many as are perfect, let us have the same mind. If any of you form your mind differently, for you God will bring light to the issue. ¹⁶In any event, let us march forward along the very [path] along which we have come.

3:15 Ὅσοι οὖν τέλειοι, τοῦτο φρονῶμεν· καὶ εἴ τι ἑτέρως φρονεῖτε, καὶ τοῦτο ὁ θεὸς ὑμῖν ἀποκαλύψει· ¹⁶πλὴν εἰς ὃ ἐφθάσαμεν, τῷ αὐτῷ στοιχεῖν.

The suggestion in 3:15 that some are perfected leads scholars to see irony in this passage, for in 3:12 Paul clearly states that he has not yet been perfected.[140] But it is this

---

137. Fee, *Paul's Letter to the Philippians*, 350.

138. Thrall, "Paul's Understanding of Continuity," 291.

139. Reumann, Philippians, 540, notes parallels to this upward call within the larger society: Philo of Alexandria writes that "those craving wisdom and knowledge (*epistēmēs*) . . . have been called upwards (*anakeklēsthai*) . . . those who have received [God's] down-breathing (*katapneusthentas*) should be called up to Him (*anō kaleisthai*). Hermetica 70, 'the mind (*dianoias*) . . . stirred . . . by heavenward yearning, drawn . . . upward (*anō*).'"

140. Ibid., 546: "Irony is likely with *teleioi* (15a)." Reumann notes: "an oxymoron, 'in the Christian vocabulary, *perfect* can only mean 'conscious that we are not perfect' (cf. Aquinas, *Phil.* 105)" (Haupt, 142, cited in ibid., 559 n. 21).

irony that clarifies what "perfection" does *not* mean here. In a gospel of radical self-emptying, "perfection" can hardly indicate individual, personal achievement.[141] In the same sentence as the phrase "As many of us as are perfected" (Ὅσοι οὖν τέλειοι), Paul counters any idea of personal achievement by saying: "let us have the same mind" (τοῦτο φρονῶμεν), the same focus. We speak of perfection, but there is no perfection, and that is why we speak of perfection. The introductory verse to the hymn of the empty Christ (τοῦτο φρονεῖτε ἐν ὑμῖν 2:5), employs the same verb (φρονέω, used also in 3:19 and 4:2), "to focus one's mind upon, to attend to, to ponder, to think." This kind of attentive focusing remains the point throughout: that our subjective consciousness is to be reoriented—away from imagined patterns of apprehending and controlling the objective world of anybody's theology, and toward a mind of Christlike wisdom that can abide in the suchness of our fragile and transient lives. "To have the same mind" is neither to have a static mindset nor to apprehend any set content, but rather to actively "attend" to the same (τοῦτο) mind that was in Christ Jesus, embodied in the knowledge and wisdom of Christ, manifested in the power of his resurrection, and witnessed by sharing in his sufferings.

Many commentators have understood this sentence in 3:15 to mean that Paul is recommending his own outlook,[142] his correct thinking,[143] or his point of view.[144] But that interpretation creates some difficulty with the following sentence, in which Paul acknowledges that at least some others do not in fact accept his viewpoint at all,[145] but "think differently" (ἑτέρως).[146] I would disagree with the initial assumption that Paul is here recommending a set of correct theological ideas. Rather, he is urging a new pattern of consciousness that will enable us to abide in the unmediated wisdom of eschatological openness, and thus to bring that experience of being in Christ to bear on life commitments through the enunciation of the teaching of Christ. The viewpoint-grasping mind is an immature mind, whatever its claims to have reached maturity and perfection (τετελείωμαι 3:12). By contrast, the "same" as in Christ moves

---

141. Caird, *Paul's Letters from Prison*, 144: "[T]he notion that Christians are to be spiritual virtuosos, each pursuing his own inward development in keeping with his individual attainments is quite out of keeping with Paul's concept of the church as a living organism."

142. O'Brien, *Epistle to the Philippians*, 420.

143. Fee, *Paul's Letter to the Philippians*, 354.

144. Caird, *Paul's Letter from Prison*, 143–44, as reworked by Fee, *Paul's Letter to the Philippians*, 354.

145. Silva explains, "It is the second sentence . . . that has proved especially baffling. As Martin (*Philippians*, New Century Bible, 1976, 141) puts it, Paul gives the impression of 'saying that agreement with his teaching is a matter of indifference and that those who dispute his statements are entitled to their views'" (Silva, *Philippians*, 178). Fee writes of the tenor of the sentence, which is "almost nonchalant—a kind of 'throw away' sentence—which makes one think that no great issue can be in view" (Fee, *Paul's Letter to the Philippians*, 358).

146. Vincent, *Critical and Exegetical Commentary*, 113: "Ἑτέρως, only here in N.T. 'Otherwise' than what?" Vincent offers his solution: "[T]he apostle is not dealing specially, if at all, with differences of opinion, but rather with dispositions which underlie the spiritual life" (ibid., 114).

us away from our constant need to attain self-engendered perfection through proliferating viewpoints, and toward knowing Christ experientially—living simply as human, enabled both to embrace the power of the resurrection and to accept, and thus be conformed to, suffering and dying.

The passage on knowing Christ in 3:7–11 links phrase after phrase in a meditation upon the import of Christ resurrection as indivisible with Christ suffering. This is not a theological systematics that offers a clear position to which Paul's readers are expected to assent. Rather, we are to engender by faith one and the same emptying and ever over-exalted Christ mind. Paul often tacks together such extended passages without providing any assistance to help his readers understand. His rhetoric is paratactic, even disjointed; it does not move on a level where clear and concise viewpoints are systematically interconnected to comprise a well-articulated theology. Nor can the perfection that Paul mentions be taken as any kind of mapped schema for a lived life. We are left with just that resurrection power and that shared suffering, their contradictions encompassed in the living Christ. The connecting links between life and death, like those pesky Pauline particles, do not allow for an unambiguous reconstruction of Paul's thought. Thus it is that the many commentators who have attempted to elucidate Paul's theology differ so much among themselves.[147] Paul even undermines any kind of distinct, subjective self who might have the capacity to grasp objective ideas.

Overcoming the dichotomy between subject and object—a move that is basic to the Yogācāra interpretation of emptiness[148]—is the hallmark of mystical thinkers everywhere. These thinkers move in inchoate teachings. And as one who is encom-

---

147. See Dunn, *Theology of Paul the Apostle*, 1–26, "Prolegomena to a Theology of Paul." Here, Dunn negotiates his approach to Pauline theology, questioning whether such an endeavor is even possible to accomplish with such an allusive and "multilayered" thinker (ibid., 17). Taking Romans as the template for Paul's theology, Dunn does, however, write an 800-page theology of Paul, weaving together the intersecting themes we find in his writings. But it is the work of a skilled weaver rather than a bricklayer.

148. See Nagao, *Foundational Standpoint*, 91–93, on "The Middle Path in Vijñaptimātratā: The Being of Non-Being." Nagao treats the other-dependent pattern of subject-object understanding as "unreal imagining" (Skt. *abhūta-parikalpa*), in wisdom seen to abide in the emptiness of any final or essential ground to either subject or object, yet to be conventionally valid because dependently arisen. For a more detailed treatment with stress on the recognition of liberation from karmic obstructions that enables one to acknowledge the margins and the validity of conventional knowing, see Dan Lusthaus, *Buddhist Phenomenology: A Philosophical Investigation of Yogācāra Buddhism and the* Ch'eng Wei-shih lun (London: Routledge Curzon, 2002) 219–28, on "Madhyamaka and the Two Satyas," and 228–42, on "Closure and Referentiality." Leen offers a contrasting, but congruent, meditation on the indwelling of the Spirit within the souls of those who are freed by grace (Leen, *Holy Ghost*, 193–97). He teaches that by grace, we see God, darkly—not by apprehending any idea, but immediately—for we apprehend and grasp ideas in acts of cognition but do not thereby hold the concrete reality thereby represented. By contrast, in the indwelling of the Spirit, God becomes present *in* the soul, not *to* the soul. "The Divine essence itself must fulfill with regard to the creature's intellect the role of idea" (ibid., 197), reconfiguring subject-object patterns by transforming the operative activity of knowing by the direct presence of God within and of loving in an immediate act of encompassing love.

passed in Christ and finds mere words wholly inadequate to contain Christ wisdom, Paul is indeed a mystic.[149] His words here recommend, not a shift in mindset or a change of ideas, but a reorientation of the very pattern in which our minds function. This reorientation is grounded in a cognitive reordering of the experience of attending. It requires turning away from the self-interested apprehension of ideas to the phenomenally experienced presence of the absent Christ in our lives—whereby we gain apophatic insight into the Christ who emptied himself even of being God so that he might die in the most excruciating and shameful human fashion, that we might kataphatically judge his gospel to be a path to life—to be risen and more than exalted so that, one with him in the taste of this ever-benign and ever-silent God, we too may share compassionate commitment in the chosen course of our lives.[150]

"As many as are perfect, let us have this one mind," Paul writes. This ironic "perfection" (τέλειοι 3:15) of no-perfection contrasts with the attitude of those in Paul's wider world who thought of themselves as being already mature, beyond the common thinking of the *hoi polloi*. It is such deludedly "mature" people that commentators on

149. It seems to me that Crossan and Reed treat Paul's mysticism of his "being in Christ" as peripheral to his anti-Roman kingdom program (Crossan and Reed, *In Search of Paul*, 276). After speaking of Paul's blurred identity with Christ, they write: "Does Paul think, therefore, that only mystics can be Christians or that all Christians must be mystics? In a word, yes" (ibid., 280). Because, they observe, they live the resurrection faith. Yet, it seems to me that these themes are so central to Paul that his vision of God's kingdom against the Roman Empire is not his central message, for any factional program occludes the self-emptying Christ. Certainly, here in Philippians, Paul offers no counter-Roman advice to anyone, and he hardly mentions the Synoptic theme of the coming kingdom. Contrast Leen, who speaks of those who "stand back, as it were, from the picture portrayed in the Gospel, to study it in a good light and from a favorable angle. They admire the beauty of the different virtues that go to complete that perfect work of the divine Artist painted in human colours, namely, the moral character of Christ" (Leen, *Holy Ghost*, 87). Leen goes on to complain of those whose attitude is one of mere admiration, and probably has in mind scholars such as Albert Schweitzer and his *Quest of the Historical Jesus*. Leen's theological perspective is Thomistic theology, considering its substitution of the sanctifying union with God for the apocalyptic vision of both Jesus and Paul, yet his discourse on Jesus as the path of transformative grace is persuasive. Crossan, by contrast, focuses in many of his works on what is available from historical reconstructions, often giving short shrift to the path-practices that are entailed in taking on the mind of the empty Christ. My preferred approach is to meditate on the empty Christ, as scripted in the sacred texts and developed in the traditions, as the dependently arisen course of the gospel faith. The empty Christ is not recovered as a pristine Jesus long forgotten, nor are our scriptures and traditions themselves more than dependently arisen, i.e., fully historical.

150. Gazzaniga insists on the organic ground of mental activity: "When thinking about these big questions, one must always remember, *remember*, remember that all these modules are mental systems selected for over the course of evolution" (Gazzaniga, *Who's In Charge?*, 103). That organic base, however, can be tamed and move from self-survival to action for the common good. Even beyond beehive-like activities for the common good, some neuroscientists insist that mental activity can be driven by collective emotions to open upon a selfless realm of sacred silence. See Haidt's comments: "Durkheim believed that these collective emotions pull humans fully but temporarily into the higher of our two realms, the realm of the *sacred*, where the self disappears and collective interests predominate" (Haidt, *Righteous Mind*, 226). Haidt quotes Ralph Waldo Emerson's trancendalist vision: "Standing on the bare ground,—my head bathed by the blithe air and uplifted into infinite space,—*all mean egotism vanishes*. I become a transparent eye-ball; I am nothing; I see all; the currents of the Universal Being circulate through me; I am part or particle of God" (Emerson, cited in ibid., 227).

Paul's letters often identify as his opponents in the various Hellenistic communities. And to be sure, then as now, there are indeed some who believe that they have moved beyond the generality of their fellows to occupy an especially "enlightened" position. Clerical status, for instance, is often accompanied by the unreal expectation that by preparing for that elevated role in the church one has come to a full understanding of the gospel and can thus with confidence edify a receptive, but immature and poorly informed, laity. In practice, a perfection that is assumed by virtue of sacramentalized status most often smothers gospel liberation, pressing it into the narrow confines of whatever conventional ideas are favored by the favored.

Paul in his letters often does critique just such people, as some commentators conclude, but it appears that here he is making a different point. By speaking ironically of the so-called "perfect people," Paul is actually saying that there is a true maturity, a true perfection, that consists precisely in emptying oneself of perfection, accepting authentic human living in the power of ongoing discipleship and common participation in suffering and resurrection faith, manifested in being conformed to Christ's death. That perfection in turn entails detaching ourselves from the surety of our theological position or our ecclesial status, and attending with gospel wisdom and skill to the dependently arising course of human events.

Paul is redefining maturity and reimagining perfection. For him, "to be perfect" means to be authentically and humanly one with Christ in the endeavors of the gospel. In light of the immediately preceding passages, this means that those of us who would be perfect, hearing the heavenly call to transcend this world and its values, "stretch forth" toward our future endeavors, forgetting everything that lies behind in our lives, forgetting and regarding as nothing special the entire karmic history of our checkered past, none of which determines who we are to be. Being found in Christ entails no fixed hold on what one has received, but rather a future-oriented traditional faith that is open to whatever the tasks of the gospel will come to be.

So Paul says that, "If any of you form your mind differently, for you God will bring light to the issue" (καὶ εἴ τι ἑτέρως φρονεῖτε, καὶ τοῦτο ὁ θεὸς ὑμῖν ἀποκαλύψει 3:15). I do not believe that Paul is insisting here on his own viewpoint. If he were, the sentence should perhaps be translated as: "If any of you think differently, God will reveal this [correct viewpoint] to you."[151] This is indeed a possible translation of the words, but it makes Paul out to be narrow-minded, assured that only *his* thoughts are correct thoughts, while others must somehow toe his line. If that is indeed Paul's intent, he has done a very poor job of articulating the ideas that we are to accept, with rhetoric that is replete with dangling phrases resisting comprehension in the context of any semantic whole, and even full stops that arrest the flow of all images and ideas. Again and again, Paul's circulating themes withhold clarity from the calculating minds of theologians and slip through the fingers of the exegetes. Paul's focus is not

---

151. F. W. Beare, *A Commentary on the Epistle to the Philippians* (London: A & C Black, 1950) 131: "[Paul] is ready to wait until God opens the minds of the others to the truth as he has expounded it."

upon the clear articulation of ideas. His concern is a different approach to life. If one takes an erroneous path, then "God" (θεὸς) "will bring light" (ἀποκαλύψει) to "this" issue (τοῦτο) "for you" (ὑμῖν). It is God who will disclose,[152] not Paul. Paul preaches Christ, empty and exalted, not ideas or viewpoints *about* Christ.

Within the Christian tradition are many different spiritual approaches and prayer strategies. The practice of Mother Teresa—who dedicated her life to assuaging the sufferings of the poor and enabling them to die with dignity—differs markedly from the practice of Dorothy Day, who while serving the poor in New York neighborhoods also advocated forcefully for social justice and peace. When the two met, Mother Teresa honored and recognized Day as a fellow worker. And yet Teresa never protested anything, while Day was arrested time and again for her refusal to accept the cultural values that lead to war and social injustice. The eloquent devotions of Lancelot Andrewes, late-sixteenth and early-seventeenth-century Anglican scholar and bishop, embody a deep sacramental practice that differs entirely from the vigorous spirit of someone like Ignatius of Loyola, sixteenth-century Spanish founder of the Jesuits. When the plague came to Andrewes' London parish, he prudently retired to his country estate to wait out the pestilence in prayer. Had Liberation theologians been around in those days, they might well have challenged his decision. Nonetheless, Lancelot Andrewes continues to be acknowledged as a writer of deep and penetrating works of authentic devotion. There is no one-size-fits-all pattern of Christian maturity.

Indeed, the Christian churches that look especially to Paul for theological insight differ among themselves historically and theologically in some important areas. And yet all draw from the same Paul. He himself acknowledges that there are different spiritual gifts, but the same spirit of Christ. He does not have the final or the only idea; he offers no universally applicable instructions on how Christ followers are to live and to practice. He leaves it to God to lead people into the light. Paul is saying that if you have reconstituted your mind in Christ in a different fashion, then let us leave the matter to God, who he trusts will bring to light all of these issues. In a word, this gospel is not an ideology that is to be implemented without regard to social and cultural context. Yet Paul is no relativist, recommending just any approach at all. While not dismissing the faith and endeavors of others (with the one exception of the culturally exclusive withdrawal of Peter, and then for good reason),[153] he does say: "In any case, let us march forward along the very [path] along which we have come" (πλὴν εἰς ὃ ἐφθάσαμεν, τῷ αὐτῷ στοιχεῖν 3:16). "In any case," he says, let us take on the mind of Christ. The phrase "in any case" (πλὴν) means under any circumstances, whether you see things my way

---

152. Vincent, *Critical and Exegetical Commentary*, 114: "Ἀποκαλύπτειν is to *unveil* something that is hidden, thus giving light and knowledge." What is both hidden and to be revealed is that nirvanic resurrection is indivisible with saṃsāra and suffering.

153. Gal 2:11–14.

or not.[154] The gospel path is always the Christ path and none other can be efficaciously followed, but within that common context there are many viewpoints.

The phrase "let us march in line" (τῷ αὐτῷ στοιχεῖν 3:16) is an imperative infinitive. "[T]he earliest and shortest reading of this clause . . . is elliptical (literally, 'let us march by the same'"[155] (τῷ αὐτῷ)—to which we supply the word "path," knowing that Paul, with his fondness for vigorous images, is envisaging the road ahead. As noted, Paul is fond of manly metaphors, references to masculine games and military actions. For this reason, images of Saint Paul clad in ornate ecclesial vestments and illumined by a Persian halo always appeared incongruous to me, and intended to bring him into the sheepfold of church leaders. Paul himself tells us that all his endeavors are because he is "under orders," like a lieutenant in the military. He is an officer commissioned to preach the gospel, instructing us here to march in step with our fellows, as soldiers do. But we are not to march just anywhere; the point is that we are to continue to march ahead along "the path we have already come" (εἰς ὅ ἐφθάσαμεν), "from the point we have reached."[156]

This final phrase in 3:16 means literally "toward that which we have already come," but this requires a bit more interpretation. It could mean to "behave in conformity to [the rule of faith] to which we have already come." Some have interpreted it just that way, deriving the sense of 'rule' (*kanoni*) from Galatians 6:16, a passage that uses the same verb in wishing peace and mercy upon all who march by this rule (ὅσοι τῷ κανόνι τούτῳ στοιχήσουσιν).[157] However, as Gordon Fee notes, it is likely that "it does not here refer to some external 'rule' that he and they [Paul and the Philippians] have in common."[158] Caird points out that "when we consider the phrase as a whole, τῷ αὐτῷ στοιχεῖν, which is so reminiscent of τὸ αὐτὸ φρονεῖν ('have a common mind') in 2:2 that it is most naturally taken to mean 'have a common rule of behaviour.'"[159] That norm is not, however, a set of clear instructions but has already been given: We are to stretch forward from any point of attainment to live the eschatological faith in ever-new incarnate endeavors.

No matter how we may approach the mystery of Christ, or how we may attend to and understand the needs of the gospel task, we are all to hold fast to the clear and central rule of the Christ who, although in the form of God, has emptied himself that we might do the same. Marching in an army that prizes peace and submits to its enemies is surely counterintuitive, but this is the order given through Paul to Christ followers. In short, this epistle to the Philippians—which is accepted as one of the authentic letters of Paul and is possibly the very earliest New Testament scripture—teaches that

---

154. Fee, *Paul's Letter to the Philippians*, 360.
155. O'Brien, *Epistle to the Philippians*, 441.
156. Ibid.
157. Reumann, *Philippians*, 563.
158. Fee, *Paul's Letter to the Philippians*, 361, esp. n. 39–40.
159. Caird, *Paul's Letters from Prison*, 145.

Patterned Imitation (3:17)

3:17 Brothers and sisters, become imitators of me and with me, and examine those who walk according to the pattern you have in us.

3:17 Συμμιμηταί μου γίνεσθε, ἀδελφοί, καὶ σκοπεῖτε τοὺς οὕτω περιπατοῦντας καθὼς ἔχετε τύπον ἡμᾶς.

Paul appears yet again to have coined a new Greek word: "conjoined imitators" (Συμμιμηταί). This word occurs nowhere else in the New Testament or in the rest of Greek literature. But then, Paul has made up words before. There is a perfectly good, and simpler, Greek word for "imitators" (μιμηταί), and Paul could have used that term had he simply meant to write "imitate me." In 1 Cor 4:14–16, he does use that term to say that he, as their "father through the gospel," can call upon them "to be imitators of me" (μιμηταί μου γίνεσθε). In 1 Cor 11:1, after advising his readers not to give offense in their daily activities but to seek the benefit of others, he uses the word again to admonish them to "imitate me, as I Christ" (μιμηταί μου γίνεσθε καθὼς κἀγὼ Χριστοῦ).[160] In 3:17 of our text, however, he is saying something different. Having learned to imitate the empty Christ (3:4–11), he reflects the Philippians' practice in this and writes "the same" back to them. So he adds the prefix "with" to the word "imitators" (μιμηταί) to form a compound. And this move creates difficulties for translators. Some render the compound as "join together in imitating me," while others say "unite in imitating me." Another possibility is "be fellow imitators of me." It is indeed a troublesome term. Most of the lexical difficulty disappears, however, if we see Paul's relationship with the Philippians as a mutual sharing in Christ, rather than as a patron educating his Philippian clients. In any case, Paul clearly is recommending that his readers join him in shared "imitation." The only question remaining is what they are to imitate and how.

People commonly imitate one another.[161] Some ask, "What would Jesus do?" More troubling perhaps—especially to those who believe that the Deutero-Pauline letters with all their household codes were written by Paul himself—is the question "What would Paul do?" Are we to enforce those cultural norms even though they have

---

160. Bruce, *Philippians*, 127: "These last words [from 1 Cor 11:1: κἀγὼ Χριστοῦ] are crucial: it was not that Paul wished to set his own life up as an ethical standard; he presented Christ as the absolute standard...."

161. Gazzaniga notes, "Babies first enter the social world through imitation" (Gazzaniga, *Who's In Charge?*, 143). Gazzaniga adds, "Mimicry is what makes babies copy their mothers' expressions, sticking out their tongues when they do and smiling when they do. The consequence of this tendency" is "known as emotional contagion" (ibid., 163).

long been regarded as archaic, "even outmoded in their own time?"[162] Shall we recommend that slaves serve their masters with cheerful faces?[163] We all have our models for living and doing—from parents and older siblings, to professional basketball stars whose moves we attempt to copy, to sages and saints who model life itself.[164] Art and film build on this desire of people to find role models and live for a brief time in another person's shoes. Seymour Chatman, in his *Story and Discourse: Narrative Structure In Fiction and Film*, sketches how discourse and rhetoric work their desired effect, providing signs and clues that lead the reader or viewer to identify with the story and imitate some of its characters. He also demonstrates how such narratives may divert and befuddle the reader, setting the stage for reverse insights that bring about the desired effect, and always doing more than simply imparting information.[165]

This is true of scriptures as well, for they set out to preach a path of life and in so doing provide models for imitation.[166] The gospels do this by offering clear, if selective, narratives of the life, death, and resurrection of Jesus of Nazareth. The significance of those narratives for us is not their imparting the facts of Jesus' life, but rather in leading us to embrace resurrection faith. Jesus is the scripted model, leading us all straight through his teaching to dying and rising again, in a shared communal awaiting of the day of the Lord. And if these narratives do not provide any description of Jesus' "hidden years" of growing up in Nazareth, it is because those years were not hidden at all but merely ordinary. Luke-Acts is the grandest of our ancestral stories, filling in some remarkable details, as did my grandmother, mother, and aunts when they told

---

162. Sarah J. Tanzer, "Ephesians," in *Searching the Scriptures: A Feminist Commentary*, edited by Elisabeth Schüssler Fiorenza (New York: Crossroad, 1994) 2:330.

163. Castelli, in *Imitating Paul*, sees Paul as enforcing sameness over diversity and otherness, interpreting his call for imitation as a call for a servile obedience that excuses mature differences. Reumann comments that Castelli's "attention to 'textual effect rather than the textual meaning' is a corrective" not only to social innocence, but to all commentarial endeavors that are content to read Paul only within his Sitz im Leben, ignoring the great impact of these texts on our traditions and practices (Reumann, *Philippians*, 587).

164. Gazzaniga, *Who's In Charge?*, 164: "People do not mimic the faces of those with whom they are in competition nor with politicians with whom they do not agree. More recently it has been shown that the relationship between the observer and the observed is relevant for mimicry reactions and not all emotional expressions are equally mimicked. Happiness is always mimicked, negative expressions are not, depending on who is being mimicked . . . Voluntary imitation, however, . . . is a potent mechanism in learning and acculturation."

165. See Chatman, *Story and Discourse: Narrative Structure in Fiction and Film* (Ithaca: Cornell University Press, 1978) for the interplay between the presented story of what happened and the structuring discourse whereby that story is told. Chatman's understanding of discourse has inspired some to develop deeper understandings of our scriptures, such as Robert M. Fowler, *Let the Reader Understand: Reader-Response Criticism and the Gospel of Mark* (Minneapolis: Fortress, 1991). Our scriptures are not treasure troves of solid and factual information about Jesus or about Paul, but are instead accounts received in the churches, structured to encourage following the path that draws us in and transforms our minds. Absent that transformative path, what does it matter whether these accounts provide accurate information?

166. Reumann notes, "No significant OT background" (Reumann, *Philippians*, 567). The theme of imitation and example "is Greek, not from the Old Testament" (ibid., 584).

our family story—what was done and what happened, and how people felt about what happened. Paul, however, provides no such biographical narrative about Jesus. He adds little color to the story of Christ dying and rising. Nevertheless, he argues the same brief—about our own death and resurrection as here we await the day of Christ Jesus.

So what does it mean when in 3:17 Paul offers himself as a model to imitate? Paul has written that he regards as loss anything in which he might glory, including all identity markers of his ethnic and religious self—not only his upbringing in Torah, but also anything from his experience of oneness with Christ. He has emptied himself, like Christ, who although in the form of God emptied himself. What then are the Philippian "brothers and sisters" (ἀδελφοί) to imitate? It seems clear from the rhetorical onrush of Paul's writing that they are to imitate his practice of abandoning all self-markers and—forgetting what lies behind their various stories—to hear, like Paul, the upward call that launches them on their here-and-now endeavors, marching forward toward that which comes ahead in the context of their conventional lives and beyond.

Paul's admonition to imitate means that we, going beyond any fixed pattern of doctrine or ideas, are to take on the character that we see embodied in his endeavors and Timothy's,[167] as well as in the arduous travels of the messenger Epaphroditus. "Together" (συμ-) Paul's hearers are to "model" (μιμηταί) their path on the empty Christ, about whom they have confessed their faith. He goes beyond generalities, clarifying how that imitation is to be accomplished—by examining "those who walk according to the pattern you have in us" (καὶ σκοπεῖτε τοὺς οὕτω περιπατοῦντας καθὼς ἔχετε τύπον ἡμᾶς).

In 2:4, Paul writes of people "looking out" (σκοποῦντες) for their own interests or the interests of others. In 3:14, he says that he runs while scoping out the path ahead (κατὰ σκοπόν). Here the same meaning obtains: we are to attend to and critically "look into" (σκοπεῖτε) the pattern of those whose life-walk follows Christ wisdom, emptying self to experience fulfillment beyond any measure. It is not the general character of persons we are to investigate, but specifically how they live (περιπατοῦντας) that "pattern" (τύπον) of life. Many live virtuously apart from resurrection faith, but their lives do not model this pattern; the gospel is not simply about virtuous living. It is neither Paul's nor the Philippians' life that is to be imitated, but the "pattern" (τύπος, *typos*) or configuration of their minds, and this is not a model that can be slavishly copied in cookie-cutter fashion. It is a life lived in an energetic and practiced "stretching forth" to that which lies ahead, toward ever-expanding horizons, a becoming one with Christ in the overcoming of the final horizon between living and dying.

---

167. Collange, *Epistle of Saint Paul*, 136: "[T]he apostle often presents himself to his readers as a pattern in order to emphasize the importance of 'sufferings' (1 Thess. 1:6; 2:14; cf. 2 Thess. 3:7–9) and of self-giving (1 Cor. 11:1) in the life of one who 'imitates Christ' (1 Cor. 11:1; 1 Thess. 1:6; cf. Eph. 5:1; 2:6–11)."

Horizons are never stable or enduring, for the farther we can see the more there is to see. So the attempt to model ourselves upon a pattern calls for attentiveness and critical examination (σκοπεῖτε) of how it is embodied in actual living (οὕτω περιπατοῦντας). This requires us to focus on the mind of Christ (τοῦτο φρονεῖτε ἐν ὑμῖν 2:5), which burrows into our mental and cognitive structures to reorder our impulses and then, through prayer and meditation, to form gospel habits of wisdom and compassion. When Paul relates the facts of his life history, he speaks of his sufferings and his accomplishments—how many times he was shipwrecked and how many times beaten; how often dragged into court and threatened with punishment and death; his excellent ethnic and religious pedigree; and how he pursued and persecuted the church for the sake of his religious beliefs. But the events of Paul's life, even his gospel adventures, are not models for our imitation. The models of risen life for us are those individual Christ followers in every generation—included in the word "us" (ἡμᾶς) in Paul's phrase "imitate us" (3:17)—who have demonstrated that same stretching forth toward oneness with the empty Christ.

In his day, Paul did not model himself on the "pillars" of the church in Jerusalem; in fact he kept his distance from them,[168] for they seemed only begrudgingly to affirm his apostolic mission to Gentiles who lived beyond their own Palestinian horizons. When Peter came to Ephesus and refused to eat with the Gentiles in accord with Jewish dietary laws, Paul admonished him in no uncertain terms (Gal 2:11–14). Likewise, Paul's own restricted horizons preclude the possibility of our taking him today as a cultural model. Even he and his Gentiles never traversed the trade routes across inner Asia and beyond to encounter the ancient cultures of China or India, both of which possessed rich religious and philosophical wisdom traditions entirely unknown to them. But Paul's life "in Christ" does stretch beyond any particular cultural world, to be embodied again and again throughout the ages.

Much like "historical Jesus" scholars—who attempt to fill in what the gospels omit and then urge that their reconstructed image of the historical Jesus is more real than the Jesus of the New Testament texts—specialists on Paul strive to fill in details about him from his historical milieu. But there is little warrant for most of these reconstructions. This "historical" view might perhaps be the most rational approach if the lack of historical detail in the New Testament were merely a matter of inadvertent omission. But I consider it to be otherwise—that the skeletal New Testament portrait of Christ intentionally reveals only what was of central import to the early church—its witness to the benign Father's silent love. And for similar reasons, when Paul tells his readers to "become" (γίνεσθε) "imitators" (μιμηταί) "of me" (μου)[169] in 3:17, he adds the prefix *sum* (συμ, "together") because it is not his personal characteristics that he

---

168. On Paul's relationships with Peter and the Jerusalem community, see Chilton, *Rabbi Paul*, 75–170.

169. Reumann, *Philippians*, 591: "Phil 3:17a agrees in wording with two uses of *mimētai mou ginesthe* at 1 Cor, where Paul calls converts to his stance and orientation."

wants his readers to copy, but rather the life orientation that he shares with others and according to which he lives his life. The pattern to be imitated is found "in us" (καθὼς ἔχετε τύπον ἡμᾶς), not just in Paul; he himself is not the perfect model and there is nothing to boast of in his attainments. Indeed, Paul was a work in progress, and he died a work in progress, as do we all. Thus, in order to give full weight to the term "co-imitators," I translate "become imitators of me and with me"—that is, imitators of the life to be discovered in the empty Christ. Paul is recommending intensive living that strives always for a goal that is attained ever more deeply in its non-attainment. He has not yet reached it himself, and he does not want to encourage others to imagine that there is any particular point that they may one day claim to have reached.

Paul contrasts knowing the risen Christ with choosing *not* to know Christ—choosing not to experience the power of his resurrection and rejecting the emptying that is embodied in the cross. One pattern of living is to remain tied to images that we ourselves have created, dedicating ourselves to attaining imagined goods or resisting imagined evils (Skt. *parikalpita-svabhāva*). This is the pattern of delusion that Paul sees embodied in those who are hostile to the cross of Christ. He recommends instead that we live in the perfected pattern (*pariniṣpanna-svabhāva*) of Christ wisdom, which refuses to rest in any delusion of stable perfection but instead always strives to move forward so as to attain, but without any defined expectations. That kind of attainment is never a once and for all event; it is grounded in the very structure of our dependently arisen hearts and minds with their synergistic insight into our experience (*paratantra-svabhāva*).

So Paul tends not to envisage the goal toward which we strive as located on some road map where we move from starting point through set stages—a quarter mile, half mile, three-quarters of a mile—toward a destination. The final goal towards which we strive always recedes beyond attaining, all the while exercising its gracious effect upon our lives by structuring our minds and hearts to reach ever forward beyond today, beyond tomorrow, beyond the cross, beyond even the final resurrection, yet to be grounded right here—that, conformed to the death of Christ, we may experience oneness with him beyond any imagined Christ reality. In Paul's eschatological faith, it is not only the universe that expands beyond its former boundaries, so also does the Christ wisdom that unleashes human minds.

It is not that at the end of a long, continuous path of progress, we will encounter Christ sitting there on some golden throne dispensing awards. It is not that at the end of a certain period of time Christ will appear, coming again to walk familiarly among us. Paul did expect the coming of Christ at some point, and yet he writes of this coming as beyond linear time constraints. In any linear expectations that Paul may have had, he was mistaken; but in his eschatological hope for being with Christ always, he provides a model of being in Christ now. And so Paul urges his fellow imitators to strive and to press attentively toward the prize.[170]

---

170. O'Brien, *Epistle to the Philippians*, 447.

The point is to have the mind of Christ Jesus so that we may live according to the authentically human pattern of his life, freed from fixation on images. That is the prize: continually to empty deluded images in the search for further insight. Never are Christ followers to be satisfied with the world as it is, but always to strive to make it better. Now and later, these injunctions mean that all of us Philippians are to remain dissatisfied with spiritual attainments, whatever those might be—for in any case they are not "our" attainments—and always to work for the furtherance of the gospel. To adopt such a pattern of life and follow this model of the empty Christ as presented in the Philippians' hymn is indeed an imitation of Christ. Becoming one with Christ, we ground our faith and practice on a tradition that has been passed down to us by its model practitioners—those saints throughout the ages, who still come stumbling in.

It is not as though today we Christians need somehow to leap back over the millennia to verify our scriptures and their teachings: Did we really receive Torah as gift through Moses from God? Did Jesus really say all those things? And rise from the dead? If, before engagement, we had first to come to some conclusion about all these matters, no one would ever begin practicing the path. But we live nested within a communion of practitioner saints, in their thousands and millions, and may entrust ourselves and our lives to that enlightened path as a sure refuge. It will not do for me to practice a bare scriptural spirituality (*sola scriptura*), for I need Ignatius of Antioch with his second-century letters, and I need Gregory of Nyssa with his trinitarian theology and mystic insight. I need Francis and Clare of Assisi. I need the popes in their varieties and the heretics in theirs. And all the rest, who in their idiosyncratic lives, lived this empty Christ in service of others and for the furtherance of the gospel.

Hostility to the Cross (3:18–19)

> 3:18 *For, as I have often told you of them and now I repeat with tears, many walk their life path, hostile to the cross of Christ.* [19]*Their end is destruction; their god is the belly; and their glory is found in their shame. Their minds are fixed on earthly things.*

> 3:18 πολλοὶ γὰρ περιπατοῦσιν οὓς πολλάκις ἔλεγον ὑμῖν, νῦν δὲ καὶ κλαίων λέγω, τοὺς ἐχθροὺς τοῦ σταυροῦ τοῦ Χριστοῦ, [19]ὧν τὸ τέλος ἀπώλεια, ὧν ὁ θεὸς ἡ κοιλία καὶ ἡ δόξα ἐν τῇ αἰσχύνῃ αὐτῶν, οἱ τὰ ἐπίγεια φρονοῦντες.

Paul "has already told" the Philippians (πολλάκις ἔλεγον ὑμῖν) about these people (οὕς) who live in delusion. In 3:2 he wrote of dogs who do harm (Βλέπετε τοὺς κύνας, βλέπετε τοὺς κακοὺς ἐργάτας), attempting to impose the visible signs of bodily "mutilation" (βλέπετε τὴν κατατομήν 3:2) on Christ followers. Here Paul is speaking of fellow Christ followers who want the exaltation without the suffering that marks our lives. "[T]hey would not be called *enemies of the cross of Christ* unless they at least claimed to be Christian."[171] He "talks about them here with tears" (νῦν δὲ καὶ κλαίων λέγω 3:18),[172] his emotions breaking through his words in his regret for these people. He cries for them, these Christ followers—"the many who walk their path" (πολλοὶ γὰρ περιπατοῦσιν) and adopt an attitude "in hatred of the cross of Christ" (τοὺς ἐχθροὺς τοῦ σταυροῦ τοῦ Χριστοῦ), living lives as enemies of the cross. Paul does not specify clearly who these people are;[173] but most likely they are Christ followers who reject not the resurrection, but the cross. Like most of us, they want to be winners, and the cross is an embarrassing sign of humiliation and loss.

In 3:2, Paul is referring to those who would denigrate gospel freedom in Philippi, threatening to undo the path of Christ-emptiness by laying identity demands on the congregations, no doubt with the intent of assuring them of a permanently enduring spiritual selfhood. These "Judaizers" demand the public observance of the ancient identity markers.[174] But perhaps something different is at play in this passage: Those who are "hostile to the cross" would abandon the empty Christ and thus occlude the power of his resurrection. They want the status of risen persons but without the suffering of the cross. They do not simply have a different social strategy like the self-interested Christ preachers, or demand identity markers like the "Judaizers." More significantly, they would eviscerate the empty Christ who is celebrated in Philippi. And thus Paul marshals all his rhetorical resources here to attack them as negators of the gospel faith that regards resurrection and suffering as indivisible. As Reumann writes, "*The cross of Christ* is the polemical heart of Paul's gospel (1 Cor 1:18; Gal 6:12)."[175] In the Deutero-Pauline letters to the Colossians and to the Ephesians, Paul's successors do teach that already we are risen, and the cross falls from view. Perhaps, even as Paul writes these words to the Philippians, he has already become aware of such teachings.

Paul is not making the case for doctrinal understanding of the significance of Christ's dying, but rather for the simple acknowledgment of the cross that we share in

---

171. Caird, *Paul's Letters from Prison*, 146. Reumann notes, "Not 'enemies of the lordship of an exalted Christ' but hostile to *the cross*" (Reumann, *Philippians*, 593).

172. On tears, Reumann writes, "*klaiōn* is not of 'theological significance'" (Reumann, *Philippians*, 569). Here, these enemies of the cross reject suffering and expect escape through perfection.

173. Caird sagely notes regarding the vagueness of the enemies in 18–19: "If we find this passage tantalizing . . . that is the penalty for reading private correspondence" (Caird, *Paul's Letters from Prison*, 146). Collange adds: "The violent denunciation commencing in verse 18 now continues but in such general terms that they do not allow the personalities of those who are under attack to be discerned with any clarity" (Collange, *Epistle of Saint Paul*, 137). Silva, on doing heresy hunt, writes: "It would appear that the descriptive clauses in Phil. 3:19 do not by themselves specify the nature of the heresy in view" (Silva, *Philippians*, 182).

174. On enemies, Reumann notes: "Some phrases and themes in 3:12–16 stem from 'the enemies' (18–19), introduced in 3:2–4a. . . . Fee tends to dismiss 'mirror readings' but here Paul's 'disclaimers' ('not perfect yet') may reflect 'Judaizers' and 'the idea that Torah observance makes one more complete in Christ'" (Reumann, *Philippians*, 545).

175. Ibid., 570.

our dying. He calls those he is criticizing "enemies" of the cross because they live in forgetfulness of what it means to be human—to be here only for the brief, biologically allotted span of our lives. They live their lives in rejection of any images of death, and focus solely on risen life. For Paul, an ongoing sharing in Jesus' crucifixion, practiced in meditative synergy with the experienced power of resurrection, is the source of hope in things unseen. That is not a natural move, and these "enemies of the cross" do not make it. Paul contends that, rather than experience risen life, they focus only on their present organic life. "Their god is their belly" (ὧν ὁ θεὸς ἡ κοιλία), and they cannot lift their attention from the things of this earth (3:19). They are fixed on their own life story lived on their terms.

To fight against the cross, to be an enemy of the cross (τοὺς ἐχθροὺς τοῦ σταυροῦ τοῦ Χριστοῦ 3:2) means to follow Christ *without the cross*, to share in the exaltation without the self-emptying. Centuries later, in Christian legend, Emperor Constantine had a vision of the cross as a victory symbol (L. *in hoc signo vinces*, "in this sign you will conquer"), a harbinger of his imperial victory and signifier of his sovereign power. But that came long after Paul. In his day, the cross had as yet acquired no victorious connotations, even for those walking the Christ path. For Paul and for the Philippians, the cross was the sign of a humiliating death abhorred by all, and this is precisely the reason that it figures so prominently in Paul's gospel.

"Enemies of the cross" would block out the images of death and suffering that the cross evokes and so make "their god to be their own *inner being*" (ὧν ὁ θεὸς ἡ κοιλία 3:19). This last term (κοιλία, *koilia*) is often and properly translated as "belly" or "stomach," a powerful image because the primary means we have for supporting our life is to consume adequate food to fend off illness and the ravages of aging. But the term also refers to any empty space, hollow, or cavity; and as such, it is used metaphorically for "the inner person," a synonym for one's inner heart.[176] The Gospel of John uses this term when it says that, out of Jesus' "innards" will flow streams of living water (John 7:38). The word may also connote "the womb and the genitals, the male sex organ." It may then refer to the penis, of which, "if uncovered, one should be ashamed,"[177] and this is consistent with the charge that they "glory in their shame" (καὶ ἡ δόξα ἐν τῇ αἰσχύνῃ αὐτῶν). Despite all our delusions and bootless attempts to make our bodies into precious temples, they do remain weak and fragile, unable to provide anything that we may reliably depend upon or long glory in.

For those who "focus on earthly things" (οἱ τὰ ἐπίγεια φρονοῦντες 3:19), those things constitute their only horizon of meaning. They dismiss the proffer of the gospel of the empty Christ as irrelevant, as pie in the sky. This rejection does not rouse Paul's polemic temper when he hears it from the Athenian philosophers, but his innards churn with anger when he hears it within a community that professes faith in the emptied yet exalted Christ. "Their end will be their destruction" (ὧν τὸ τέλος ἀπώλεια

---

176. O'Brien, *Epistle to the Philippians*, 455.
177. Reumann, *Philippians*, 572–73.

3:19),¹⁷⁸ not as punishment, but simply because, willy-nilly, they too will die. Everyone is instinctively hostile to a cross that symbolizes a humiliating death. But if we reject the cross, perhaps we will be able to maintain the pretense that we are not mortal and that our selves will perdure forever and ever, or at least for a very long time. So Paul critiques these people, saying, "they focus on the things of this earth" (οἱ τὰ ἐπίγεια φρονοῦντες),¹⁷⁹ but "they too will end up dead" (ὧν τὸ τέλος ἀπώλεια). In introducing the hymn of the empty Christ (2:5), Paul has told us that we are to focus (φρονεῖτε) on the emptying of our Lord Christ, for we follow where our mind leads. People who focus on the things of this earth are thus confined to this earth. For them, there is no upward call; they have to content themselves with being content—practicing tranquility, reducing stress, and perhaps taking a yoga class or two.¹⁸⁰

Paul contends that such people occlude the power of the resurrection because they are afraid of, indeed hostile to, sharing in the sufferings of Christ. And they are left simply with dissolution and destruction as their final end. In 1:28 of the Emptiness Letter, Paul uses the term "dissolution" (ἀπώλεια) to refer to those who oppose the gospel. But the connotations of this term are not altogether negative, for in 1:23 he employs a synonym in asserting that he longs to be dissolved (to depart ἀναλῦσει) and be with Christ. So when Paul writes of "destruction" here in 3:19, he means simply the dissolution of our embodied selves, the falling apart of our bodies and their going down to the grave—downward, in willful ignorance of the upward call that might enable us to receive the power of resurrection beyond life and beyond death. It is as if this upward call exercised a magnetic pull upon ionized bodies, drawing them into a new risen life—but only if the currents of living in Christ here still circulate.

"Enemies of the cross of Christ" refuse to acknowledge the fact that all life entails suffering—the very first of the Four Noble Truths enunciated by the Buddha. Life entails suffering because life is impermanent. It is impermanent precisely because we cannot control our own organic metabolism. The self that we cherish so dearly cannot be preserved. But as John Hick points out in *Death and Eternal Life*, we humans are

---

178. On "destruction in 3:19, signifying "annihilation, ruin" (ibid., 571). *Koilia* means literally "hollow," or the abdominal cavity where food is digested. Perhaps it can be rendered: "their end is annihilation; their god is their empty hollowness," for they ineptly dismiss the emptiness of their own inner being.

179. Vincent, *Critical and Exegetical Commentary*, 117: "οἱ τὰ ἐπίγεια φρονοῦντες: 'who mind earthly things.'" Better: "Whose mind is affixed on earthly things."

180. Classical Yoga, by contrast, is an intense spiritual practice meant to reconfigure consciousness through physically concentrated meditations. See Jean Varenne, *Yoga and the Hindu Tradition* (Chicago: University of Chicago, 1973). In its Hindu form, it entails the cosmic "eternal norm" (Skt. *sanātana dharma*) of the Vedas and the Upanishads. However, yogic practice pervades Indian traditions, as witnessed in the name of the Yogācāra school of Mahāyāna, which means "Practitioners of Yoga," and its practices in almost parallel form are found in the Tantric Buddhist schools of Tibet. Our contemporary western practice of "yoga for health" is generally a pale imitation of an ancient spiritual practice and tradition.

the only species who know that we are mortal, and yet we fail to believe it.[181] These enemies of the cross of Christ push away the undeniable truth of the suffering and death we experience in this life, a truth that I encountered as a child taken to one Irish wake after another. It is not so much that people "deny all that the cross of Christ stands for,"[182] but that they simply hate the cross as an image of our inevitable dying, our being abandoned and beyond all possible support. This is what we dread. But to ignore death as if it were not real is to occlude the risen life of being with Christ.

Perhaps it is because we find it so difficult to face the stark reality of dying that we manufacture claims to self-sufficiency, as even Paul does in his first, begrudging letter of thanks to the Philippians (4:11). Paul, however, did come to relinquish that insistence upon self-sufficiency and to embrace the empty Christ of the Philippians' hymn. By choosing to live within the tensive both/and of living and dying while celebrating the empty and exalted Christ, our dread of dying can be reconfigured so that rather than fleeing from our mortality we may share the suffering of Christ in resurrection faith and hope. But it never becomes an easy dying or a cozy suffering, for suffering is fully as real as risen life.

The rejection of eschatological hope flows from willful ignorance of organic life-unto-death, and it consigns us to live as animals. The better alternative, which Paul articulates in 3:13–14, is "stretching for what lies ahead, bearing down attentively . . . toward the prize of the upward call of God in Christ Jesus (3:13–14)"—so long as we are able—and then abandonment to the awakening that overcomes death. Attentive to that upward orientation, we move forward in conventional living because of a transcendent awareness of risen life in Christ, which is completely other from our earthy life.

This "upward" movement is the here-and-now, reconfigured structure of eschatological consciousness, flowing from a transcending silence that thunders the emptiness of all things. This upward call frees us from the self-imposed confines of our own ideas and viewpoints. Now that technology has enabled us to see into the cosmos far beyond this earth, we no longer have to limit our view to the ancient cosmologies of a natural earth and a supernatural heaven. We are aware that we are surrounded by the sheer mystery of an ever more fully known universe, even as all its parts rush away from our grasp. In any case, resurrection faith does not depend upon a particular "view" of the universe; it takes refuge instead in experiences and insights that lift us up, assuage our pain, and drive us ever more to stretch our being and our energies to benefit and gladden all sentient beings on this earth. But we need to attend to the empty Christ in order to turn off the ambient noise and let the sounds of transcendent

---

181. John Hick, *Death and Eternal Life* (Louisville: Westminster, John Knox, 1994) 55. See his tantalizing section on "The Idea of a Global Theology of Death," for it is a notion common to all civilizations that in some sense we live beyond dying (ibid., 29–34).

182. *Pace* Bruce, *Philippians*, 129.

silence reverberate within our minds and bodies. Thus the next, and final, section of Paul's Resurrection Letter turns to imagining the contours of risen life.

Governing Councils and Cosmic Reconfigurations (3:20-21)

3:20 *But our governing council from the beginning is in the heavens, whence we ardently await the Lord Jesus Christ as savior.* [21]*He will reconfigure our lowly body that it may be conformed to his glorious body, in accord with the energy that enables him also to have dominion over all things.*

3:20 ἡμῶν γὰρ τὸ πολίτευμα ἐν οὐρανοῖς ὑπάρχει, ἐξ οὗ καὶ σωτῆρα ἀπεκδεχόμεθα κύριον Ἰησοῦν Χριστόν, [21]ὃς μετασχηματίσει τὸ σῶμα τῆς ταπεινώσεως ἡμῶν σύμμορφον τῷ σώματι τῆς δόξης αὐτοῦ κατὰ τὴν ἐνέργειαν τοῦ δύνασθαι αὐτὸν καὶ ὑποτάξαι αὐτῷ τὰ πάντα.

After recommending in 3:15 a single-minded focus on the mind of Christ, and stressing in 3:17 a communal imitation of the tensive pattern of being both here living "in Christ" and there, after dying, "with Christ," Paul now reminds the Philippians that "our governing council" (ἡμῶν γὰρ τὸ πολίτευμα) is from the heavens, not confined to this world. The term he uses, *politeuma*, translated here as "governing council," is of particular interest as it appears nowhere else in the Bible.[183] Some render *politeuma* as "commonwealth," or "colony," suggesting thereby that the true home of the Philippians is not here in the Roman colony of Philippi but rather in the heavens.[184] Emperor Octavian established Philippi as a colony in 42 BCE, and extended Roman citizenship to its aristocratic males.[185] It was "governed as if it was on Italian soil and its administration reflected that of Rome in almost every respect."[186] Its people would have been well accustomed to the back-and-forth of political discussion, although participation would have been restricted to those properly qualified males recognized as citizens. Those men may well have gathered to discuss the life of the city, their "polis" (πόλις),

---

183. Reumann, *Philippians*, 596–97.

184. Vincent, *Critical and Exegetical Commentary*, 118: "Due emphasis must be laid on the use of the present tense [ὑπάρχει]. The believer *now is*, in this present world, a citizen of the heavenly commonwealth." Note also Benoit's assertion that "pour nous, notre cité se trouve dans les cieux, d'où nous attendons ardemment, comme sauveur, le Seigneur Jésus Christ." (For us, our city is found in the heavens, whence we ardently await, as savior, the Lord Jesus Christ.) (Benoit, *Les épîtres de saint Paul aux Philippiens*, 34).

185. On "citizens of heaven" in contrast to Roman citizenship, Caird comments, "Rome had given the full franchise of the imperial city to towns and individuals in the provinces in order that they might represent and spread in their neighbourhood the Roman way of life, its laws, customs, and culture, until the whole heterogeneous mass of the empire should be united in sentiment, outlook, and loyalty as well as in political and military fact" (Caird, *Paul's Letters from Prison*, 147).

186. Andrew T. Lincoln, *Paradise Now and Not Yet: Studies in the Role of the Heavenly Dimension in Paul's Thought with Special Reference to His Eschatology*, Society for New Testament Studies Monograph Series 43 (Cambridge: Cambridge University Press, 1981) 100.

and that would have been their "politics" (*politeuma*). I doubt, however, that Paul was concerned with the city politics of Philippi. Clearly, all Christian writers carried forward the ancient Hebrew call for justice, but nowhere does Paul present the gospel as any manner of political program.

John Reumann, who has delved most deeply into the history of the term *politeuma*, states that it signifies "a civic association." For the Philippian Christ followers, it would have been "an association within the society of a Greco-Roman city, where their version of 'heaven on earth' took form—governed by beliefs and praxis of the missionaries, probably not incorporated legally but a *politeuma* in parlance of the day."[187] *Politeuma* then "referred to a smaller ruling council, not the whole *politeia*, all the people, or even all the citizens; and to voluntary associations for cultic, social purposes and mutual support among ethnic aliens."[188] Not a grandiose kingdom in the heavens, then, but more like "a *thiasos* or *collegium*," perhaps a club or a guild, and thus Reumann translates "civic association."[189] We might see it here as a kind of church council, formed from the local churches and charged with general oversight and particular duties, such as Epaphroditus' mission to carry funds to Paul. Someone had to make the decision to do that.

The issue here for Paul and the Philippians seems to have been not how to escape this life for a heavenly abode, but how the nascent Christ gatherings might carve out the social space in which to function in the context of conventional everyday life in a Roman colony, while at the same time maintaining an awakened awareness of their upward call to a completely other, risen life in Christ. Paul is speaking of an association of Christ gatherers, perhaps constituted by a number of house churches led by people he has named—Epaphroditus, Euodia, Syntyche—guided by the overseer, and served by the deacons. He urges these Christ people to curb the interests of any one party among them as they seek to make commonly supported decisions, reminding them that at best such negotiations will tame the calculus of self-benefit and power grabbing.

Civic associations in Philippi, as throughout the Roman Empire, were surely quite restricted and without political power; perhaps most were focused on issues of trade and taxation in Philippi, for that city's important status derived from its position on the trade route to and from Rome. Yet Paul is addressing, not trade or taxation, but rather the same issue that landed him in prison—how to heed the upward call to risen life while living within the brutally dominant Roman political order. As an alternative to "party spirit" (κατ'ἐριθείαν) or "selfish ambition," (which in 2:3 he condemns in no uncertain terms), Paul offers here "a civic engagement that flows from the heavens" (τὸ πολίτευμα ἐν οὐρανοῖς ὑπάρχει 3:20). "Our governing council" "from the beginning is in the heavens," because it has "its origin in, comes into existence, derives from,

---

187. Reumann, *Philippians*, 597.
188. Ibid., 576.
189. Ibid.

and thus is" from the primal beginning (ὑπάρχει; ὑπ+ἀρχή). This term occurs also at the beginning of the hymn of the empty Christ, where it is said that Christ, "although being" (ὑπάρχων 2:6) in the form of God, yet emptied himself. In that passage, the gerund "being" (ὑπάρχων), likewise means "being from the beginning." In 3:19, Paul has said of those who divinize their own self-interests (whose "god is the belly") that "their minds are fixed on earthly things." Now he urges the Philippians to abandon a mundane fixation on the calculus of self and instead to stretch forth to benefit others in their awakened awareness of being in Christ.

Paul, however, provides no specific description of what the political program of such a heavenly governing council might be. Any ultimate stance soon tumbles from its pretense and is revealed to be just as worldly and contextual as any other stance. So the phrase "in the heavens" (ἐν οὐρανοῖς) is not a locator for some heavenly brand of politics;[190] it is simply a rejection of self-fixated values. Such values are dethroned by appeal to an unrestricted horizon that reaches beyond. Even Paul's own effort to press his citizenship rights was a subject of some dispute, and so he recommends it merely as a conventional strategy that harmonizes with this gospel of the empty Christ and as an approach that is possibly useful for the Philippians, some of whom likely enjoy the rights of citizenship themselves.

Politics may indeed always be local, but the gospel is unlocatable. In any debate over ideas and programs intended to translate partisan ideas into power over others, the gospel serves to reverse our constant calculation of self-interest. Paul preaches no set program. He insists instead on radical reorientation of our minds toward an awareness of the empty Christ—a position of no position. He stretches forth, seeking a conventional stance that will benefit and gladden all others; this is the reason he desires to present a defense of the gospel before those Roman powers that hover over the affairs of the emergent gatherings of Christ followers. Paul was not a liberation theologian; within the horizons of the Greco-Roman cities he served, no such possibility could be envisaged. Liberation theologians thus look to the Synoptic Gospels, with their demand for a kingdom of justice and peace. There was social and political unrest in Palestine, and New Testament texts written there map a path of liberation in Christ by nonviolent witness against oppression.

Still, the "heavens" of which Paul speaks in 3:20 are not a special place or special state of mind apart from this sad and weary earth. In 3:20–21, he is imagining the eschatological pattern of being with Christ as a transformation of our bodily being here. That transformation does not come from our being here, however; it is completely other, in the unimaginable silence of ultimate meaning. And the heavens are the "there" from "whence we ardently await the Lord Jesus Christ as savior" (ἐξ οὗ καὶ σωτῆρα ἀπεκδεχόμεθα κύριον Ἰησοῦν Χριστόν 3:20). What, however, does it mean to await Jesus' coming? Paul is not, like Thomas Aquinas more than a millennium

---

190. On the heavens as "transcendent abode," see ibid., 575. But "it is associated more with final eschatology than creation" (ibid.). The place of emptiness, it too is empty.

later, speaking of a beatific state of the soul's union with God.[191] Nor is he describing a mystic experience. In his conventional cosmological framework, "the heavens" simply mean the sky space above us and beyond our reach. The verb "to eagerly await" (ἀπεκδεχόμεθα 3:20) describes an eschatological waiting, a waiting in hope. It catches the sense of the unrestricted "stretching forth (ἐπεκτεινόμενος) for what lies ahead" in 3:13—a looking forward without knowing when the Lord will come, because his coming has no "when" measure. We await "the Lord Jesus Christ" (κύριον Ἰησοῦν Χριστόν), who has passed beyond life and death, because he emptied death and rose to life.

Paul refers to Christ here as "savior" (σωτῆρα, sotēra). In the gospels, the title *Christ* (Χριστόν) means Messiah, the "savior" or deliverer from sin and delusion. To the Greeks in Paul's day, however, a savior was the patron deity of a particular club, guild, or association. Perhaps for that reason, Paul's authentic letters use the word "savior" to refer to Jesus only in this one instance, in the context of "our governing councils."[192] The absence of any mention of Jesus as savior elsewhere in the writings of Paul—our earliest Christian witness—parallels the absence of "kingdom" themes in his writings as well. Paul and his Philippian friends were no doubt cognizant of the dangers of presenting Jesus as any kind of Messiah who would liberate them from Caesar. Well aware from the received tradition that Jesus was executed when perceived by some to be a king, they would have known that to use terms like "kingdom" or "savior" would hardly benefit their effort to carve out a space for Christ followers living under the purview of Roman power. But "to ardently await" (ἀπεκδεχόμεθα 3:20) Jesus Christ is not a matter of linear expectancy; and in any case a Jesus arriving from the sky would be so unthreatening as to elicit little concern from Rome. (If Paul was in fact killed in the course of Nero's persecution of Christians in 46 CE, it was not because Christ was a threat to Nero but rather because Nero needed a scapegoat to blame for burning Rome.)

As it happened, Jesus did not soon return from the eschatological skies, so Paul and the early "watchers" readjusted their timetable to think of time in different terms.

---

191. For Aquinas, although heaven was not a locatable place, it was a state characterized by the beatific vision—a direct and immediate union with God wherein nothing is seen because the vision is not discriminative. Paul is not, however, speaking of any disembodied state of the beatific soul, for he knows nothing of such a notion.

192. On savior: "of Christ, in Paul's acknowledged letters, here only," while *sōtēr* is "... patron deity in voluntary associations. In the Greek world, a common title for a god who delivers, frees, protects, preserves, or heals a *polis* and its citizens" (Reumann, *Philippians*, 577). Collange notes: "The modern reader is at first surprised to learn what little use the New Testament makes of the title 'Saviour,' accustomed as he is to seeing it given an important place in the devotion and the theology of the churches. Paul only has it here (cf. however Eph 5:23) and only the *Pastorals* and *2 Peter* give it a special place" (Collange, *Epistle of Saint Paul*, 140). In the gospels, however, the term "Christ" translates to "messiah," the anointed deliverer or savior. Paul, by contrast, enunciates a Christian faith without a savior! Martin notes: "V. Taylor explains this neglect of the term [saviour] in early Christian literature as due to the popular use of the designation in Greek religion where the gods were hailed as 'saviours,' and in Caesar worship which gave this honorific title to the emperor" (Martin, *Philippians*, 163–64). See V. Taylor, *The Names of Jesus* (New York: Macmillian, 1962) 109.

Rather than saying that he is "expecting" our savior Jesus Christ to arrive from the sky at a particular time, Paul speaks rather of "ardently awaiting" (ἀπεκδεχόμεθα) the coming of Christ, which is not a scheduled structure of expectancy to be fulfilled so much as a tensive stretching forth, moment to moment, for the always imminent coming of Christ, who in his risen exaltation transcends every conventional expectation and every worldly category.

Paul's accustomed world order has been torn apart, and his self fragmented, shorn of all identity markers. Somehow or other, something has broken through his mapped identity to set him free to ardently await resurrection. Attuned to the unforeseen events and uncontrollable circumstances that upset all human plans, he now simply "awaits" the moment of risen awakening, stretching his here-and-now ardor onward and upward toward the coming of Christ. There is no linear measure and no metaphysical language that can possibly represent what he is talking about.[193] To await the coming of Christ is to live in Christ wisdom, experiencing the power of his resurrection and participating in sufferings in conformity with his empty dying, that we may rise with him and live as one body. Without expectancy, and yet constantly awaiting Jesus the savior. The *Tractate Sanhedrin* (88b) says: "Ulla said: Let him [the Messiah] come, but let me not see him. Rabbah said likewise: Let him come, but let me not see him. R. Joseph said: Let him come and may I be worthy of sitting in the shadow of his ass's saddle."[194]

This "savior" (σωτῆρα) for Paul here is the patron of our gatherings, quite different from the Jesus of the Gospel of Mark, who saves by his passion and death.[195] Jesus in Philippians 3:20–21 is savior in that "he will reconfigure our lowly body that it may be conformed to his glorious body, in accord with the energy that enables him also to have dominion over all things." For Paul here, to be saved is to be reconfigured, viscerally and bodily. Reconfigured from "our lowly body" (τὸ σῶμα τῆς ταπεινώσεως ὑμῶν 3:21). Both "reconfiguration" (μετασχηματίσει) and "being conformed" (σύμμορφον) refer to a trans-formation, a re-formation, that con-forms our very being to its roots, because those roots are not "our" roots to begin with. Again we hearken back to

---

193. See Emmanuel Levinas, *Difficult Freedom: Essays on Judaism* (Baltimore: Johns Hopkins, 1990), translated from the 1963 French edition by Seán Hand. "One has failed to say anything about the Messiah if one represents him as a person who comes to put a miraculous end to the violence in the world, the injustice and contradictions which destroy humanity but have their source in the nature of humanity, and simply in Nature" (ibid., 59).

194. Ibid., 59–96. On "Messianic Texts," commenting on four passages from the final chapter of Tractate Sanhedrin. The constant refrain about the messianic age is "the eye hath not seen, O God, beside thee, what he hath prepared for him that waiteth for him." One can picture an expectation, but not a hope.

195. See Keenan, *Gospel of Mark*, 356. When Jesus arouses his disciples from sleep in the garden, saying, "It is all over. The hour has come" (Mark 14:41), the phrase "it is all over" (ἀπέχει) literally denotes the closing of an account or the payment of a bill. Eta Linnemann translates it there "the account is closed," as signifying the entire event of the passion (*Studien zur Passionsgeschichte*, 24–28 [1970], cited in Adela Yarboro Collins, *The Beginning of the Gospel: Probings of Mark in Context* [Minneapolis: Fortress, 1992] 96).

that hymn of the empty Christ, which in 2:6–7 says that although Christ was in the form (ἐν μορφῇ) of God, he emptied himself and took on the form of a slave (μορφὴν δούλου λαβών). He was found in "visage" or "figure" to be human (σχήματι εὑρεθεὶς ὡς ἄνθρωπος), which means the visible structure of one's very being. That means that both we and Christ are rooted in our social and cultural worlds and, further back, in the entire evolutionary tree of life on earth, for that is what it means to be human. And that is what is to be reconfigured by Christ wisdom.

Here in this final passage of the Resurrection Letter, that same empty-exaltation is expressed as a sharing in the resurrection power that is indivisible from participation in the sufferings of Christ. Our bodies, then, from being weak and always vulnerable to humiliation, will be reconfigured and appear in a different aspect. The notion of conforming here has nothing to do with conforming to a known pattern or template, since there is no pattern or rule for the risen body of Christ that Paul ever described. This conforming is a transforming into that presence of risen life *in* Christ, which Paul experienced, and life *with* Christ, which Paul anticipates as he writes.

In Matt 11:29, Jesus tells his disciples to take his yoke upon them and learn from him because he is meek "and humble of heart" (καὶ ταπεινὸς τῇ καρδίᾳ). Paul uses the same term here (ταπεινώσεως) to describe our bodies, so it seems that he is characterizing the physical body as humble. Some translators thus render the phrase as "lowly bodies," perhaps mirroring the "weakness" of those who fearfully move away from the cross toward a pretend glory (καὶ ἡ δόξα ἐν τῇ αἰσχύνῃ αὐτῶν 3:19). It is true that we have "weak mortal bodies,"[196] or "bodies of humiliation,"[197] in the same sense as 2:8 of the hymn of the empty Christ, where it says that Christ humiliated himself (ἐταπείνωσεν ἑαυτόν), meaning that Christ took upon himself a weak body that was subject to sickness and death, with its inevitable end at the grave.[198] Indeed, the present passage weaves its meaning by constant allusion to, and echoes of, the emptiness hymn in 2:6–11. That hymn remains at the heart of this correspondence.[199]

---

196. O'Brien, *Epistle to the Philippians*, 464.

197. Sumney, *Philippians*, 91.

198. According to Reumann, our body of our humiliation "means here our human state in contrast to promised future glory . . . We live in *tapeinōsis* now, Christ in glory. *Body* refers to Christ as an individual and to each individual believer, *sōma* (singular, but corporate) for those in Christ as a collectivity" (Reumann, *Philippians*, 599).

199. Thurston notes that Reumann makes the strongest case that 3:20–21 is a hymn fragment (see John Reumann, "Philippians 3:20–21—A Hymnic Fragment?" *NTS* 30 [1984] 593–609). Even if it is not, Thurston continues, "Paul is consciously using the same vocabulary that appeared in the Christ hymn. Paul wants those hearing the letter read aloud to be put in mind of the hymn, and this for at least two reasons" (Thurston, "Philippians," 137). First, that Christ is pattern (of wisdom); and second, that "the theological point of 2:6–11, that Jesus emptied himself of status and thus was raised up by God, is precisely the matter at hand in 3:1–4:1" (ibid.). Reumann agrees that in the redacted letter there is "a greater tendency to associate 3:20–21 with 2:6–11 . . . as linked by vocabulary and ideas" (Reumann, *Philippians*, 601). Bruce also notes that "J.-F. Collange (ad. loc.), R. P. Martin (ad. loc.), and others point to a striking series of parallels between this passage and 2:6–11" (Bruce, *Philippians*, 135).

The point is not to reconfigure some stable inner core of one's identity,[200] but rather "a complete metamorphosis of thinking, willing, and conduct,"[201] brought about by a "transfigured self-abasement,"[202] in the likeness of the transfigured Christ who emptied himself.[203] But this is a self-abasement that frees our conscious thinking, willing, and conduct to become selfless persons entangled with Christ's emptiness when we accept being here just as we are, while still stretching forth in eager awaiting for the "body of his glory, to which we will be conformed" (σύμμορφον τῷ σώματι τῆς δόξης αὐτοῦ 3:21). Such a glory body shows no "continuity between the present and the future,"[204] as if risen life maintained any clear linkage with the identity that we construct and experience over the course of our conventional, earthly lives. But here these ideas are so closely linked with the emptiness hymn[205] that their import is that we also share in Christ's more-than-exaltation. One of the unintended side effects of the Christian adoption of the Platonic notion of soul was to blur this discontinuity and to allow persons to imagine risen life in continuity with life in the flesh—only now the glorified flesh.

The transformation imagery—being "reconfigured" and being conformed "to glory"—is perhaps an extravagant attempt to limn the contours of the conscious stretching forth that might enlarge our bodies as in 1:20 Christ is enlarged in Paul's own body. The organic margins dividing one body from another are washed away. In the enlarged Christ of 1:20, there is no male or female, Greek or Jew, slave or free, for all are one in the body of Christ. The term "body" (σῶμα, soma) is singular here, both in referring to our body of humiliation and to the glorious body of Christ. But in contrast to this fragile, earthly body of ours, Paul presents as our final life, not the dead and dusty body of our decay, but "the body of his glory" (τῷ σώματι τῆς δόξης αὐτοῦ 3:21), the body of shining light (δόξα) that is Christ, the glory body of Christ. Such restructuring and conforming denotes radical change and restructuring of our bodily being. Yet, being here, we await that restructuring of the abundant life we share in our

---

200. Reumann writes of form "which constitutes one's identity" (Reumann, *Philippians*, 580). Vincent interprets that a change of σχῆμα is "not a destruction of personal identity" (Vincent, *Critical and Exegetical Commentary*, 120). Mahāyāna, with its teaching that form is emptiness and that very emptiness is form, envisages not a destruction of formal identity, but a recognition that all identity is conventionally constructed.

201. Reumann, *Philippians*, 598 n. 40.

202. T. Engberg-Petersen, *Paul and the Stoics* (Louisville: Westminster John Knox, 2000) 125.

203. Thurston, "Philippians," 134: "'Change' ([μετασχηματίσει, from] *metaschēmatizō*) has as its root the term 'likeness' (*schēma*), which was of such importance in 2:7. It means to change the outward form or the appearance of something."

204. Pace Fee, *Paul's Letter to the Philippians*, 383.

205. Reumann commments, "Being conformed" (σύμμορφον) here is correctly "often linked to 2:6 and 7," meaning that this bodily conformation to Christ "will occur (*metaschēmatisei*) under the working power of Christ (21b), either 'in the heavens' (20a) or in 'mid-air' when Christ comes (cf. 1 Thess 4:17)—regardless of where one supposes the future completed kingdom will be (1 Cor 15:24-28), 'above' or a 'renovated earth,' or new Jerusalem (a question Paul does not answer, so pictures from the Book of Revelation or elsewhere have often been imported)" (Reumann, *Philippians*, 599).

common experience, for the transcendent source from which we spring—no matter how conceived—sets the primal horizons of who we are at the ever-present moment.

All this brings to mind the Taoist notion of the "transformation of things" (Chi. 變物 *p'ien-wu*), whereby the constant, ever-alternating yin-yang flow of the cosmic Tao rearranges the vital energy (気 *ch'i*) of things in ever new and surprising ways. This Taoist notion turns attention to the ongoing cyclic flow of life, recommending a conscious harmony with the primal Tao in recognition that we are indeed a part of the energy that pervades the cosmos.[206] Paul does not say anything of this kind, but neither does he mention later Greek Christian teaching on life after death that speaks of the "immortality of the soul." That terminology is found neither in Paul nor anywhere else in the New Testament. It first appears in the Wisdom of Solomon, a Jewish text of about the year 50 CE, written in Greek in Alexandria, from whence it makes its way into Patristic theology.

Perhaps Paul's description of the heavenly reconfiguration of our risen life is more congruent with the Mahāyāna notion that this body life of mine is not really mine—that the inner hegemonic "I" who creates the image of a self in control, and insists on its truth, is merely a construct that is necessary for everyday living but has no lasting value. In Yogācāra theology, awakening entails realization of the universal body (Skt. *kāya*) of the real, in contrast to this deluded self. We awaken to the Dharma body (*dharmakāya*) of all the awakened buddhas.[207] Christian teaching, by contrast, insists on the value of personally living into the organic body of Christ, for without our bodies we are not persons at all. And yet to be a risen person is not a final point in the life of a standalone individual but rather the final reconfiguration of an organic unity within the risen body of Christ who energizes all. Our organic lives here and now are not, however, to be brushed aside in ethereal afterlife images. We do live here in the ardent awaiting of the Lord, who when he appears as savior will transform us to the full mature measure of being selfless persons.

We are about the building up of the body of Christ, not about escaping from this world; and our lives and efforts take on a meaning beyond what we can imagine in the building up of the body of the faithful, in the broadest possible sense of that word. Although all our canonical scriptures witness to the resurrection of Jesus, Paul does not give us descriptive details about the transformation of risen life. Even the gospels offer no actual description of the rising of Christ. We cannot imagine what it means to live a risen life, for we are risen only in germ, by sharing already in the Christ-life that is given. We do not know what shape or figure that germ will take. We have no experience of a "glorious body," a body of light, and can only imagine it in terms of some

---

206. See Derk Bodde, "Harmony and Conflict in Chinese Philosophy," *Essays on Chinese Civilization*, edited by Charles LeBlanc and Dorothy Borei (Princeton: Princeton University Press, 1981) 237–98; Kuang-ming Wu, *Chuang Tzu: World Philosopher at Play* (New York: Crossroad, 1982) 61–88; and Max Kaltenmark, *Lao Tzu and Taoism* (Stanford: Stanford University Press, 1969) 19–46.

207. See Asaṅga, *Realm of Awakening*, 241–44, on "One Dharma Body and Many Buddhas."

luminous image, perhaps a radiant Jesus merging into the golden light breaking from the sunlit heavens. But we need not simply discard such images as if they have nothing to do with our hopes for living beyond the boundaries of self and thus beyond; they do, and they derive from our religious traditions. The Pure Land traditions in China and Japan often depict Amida Buddha as approaching a deathbed and encompassing the dying person in Amida's Other Power (Js. *tariki*), receiving him or her into that Buddha's infinite light (Skt. *amitābha*). Indeed, in Pure Land theology Buddha is identified as both "Infinite Light" (Amitābha) and "Infinite Life" (Amitāyus). These images are not to be taken literally, but that does not mean they are easily translated into some more comprehensible expression.

It has always been difficult to imagine what a risen body would be like,[208] which is why many deny it altogether. In an attempt to counter nineteenth-century rationalists and deists who rejected the reality of the resurrection, Christian theologians began to insist that indeed it is our very empirical, physical bodies that rise in heaven. But rather than embracing such supernatural empiricism, we do better to maintain the apophatic silence of poorly understood images, admitting that our imaginations are not up to the task of envisioning the risen body. Such a not-knowing of what that new configuration of life might entail then frees our attention to focus on the life force that we all do experience now, that energy presently coursing through our minds and our bodies. And we do experience that vital energy. Paul knew from his youth that life was a gift given by creation. It is this life energy, breathing through even the frailest of bodies, that is reformulated and transformed in the ongoing energy of each and every person within the body of Christ, across all boundaries.

In the transfiguration account of Mark 9:2–8 (which bears some resemblance to gospel accounts of appearances by the resurrected Jesus), the overpowering and blinding light that engulfs Christ's terrified disciples is, in the final analysis, found to be nothing other than "just Jesus."[209] The more one meditates on these bodies of ours, the more one is forced to face their mortality. And the more one meditates on the light of Christ, the deeper one enters into an awareness of the pure light of emptiness.[210] This is not some supernatural magic trick, but the very light that surrounds us and enables us to live. Indeed, all light is supernatural in that it originates beyond this natural world in which we live.[211]

---

208. As N. T. Wright attempts to do in *Surprised by Hope: Rethinking Heaven, the Resurrection, and the Mission of the Church* (New York: HarperCollins, 2008). Wright writes to disabuse Christians from imagining a bodiless heaven to which our souls go, stressing the corporate and bodily resurrection preached by the church. Yet I think Wright overstates his point by presenting clear images of a bodily resurrection that cannot be imagined.

209. See Keenan, *Gospel of Mark*, 208–34, on "The Epiphany of Just Jesus."

210. See Makransky, *Awakening Through Love*, on the Zen-like Tibetan tradition of Dzogchen and its stress on "pure light."

211. *Pace* Thurston, "Philippians," 135: "The term for 'power' (*energeia*) is used in the NT only of supernatural power." Better, such power is not self-power (Js. *jiriki*), but the outflowing compassion of

All this reconfiguration and transformation is "in accord with the energy²¹² that enables him also to have dominion over all things" (κατὰ τὴν ἐνέργειαν τοῦ δύνασθαι αὐτὸν καὶ ὑποτάξαι αὐτῷ τὰ πάντα 3:21). Paul here is echoing the concluding verses (2:10–11) of the emptiness hymn, which describe the more-than-exalted Christ as exalted over all other cosmic forces. Lest one misunderstand, Paul is not saying that Jesus is more powerful than all other powerful persons. He *is* saying that in Jesus flows the energy of the universe, upholding us all in these lives we live. And Christ offers us a share in the creative energy that courses though life everywhere; it courses through his body then and now, beyond all ownership and all self-appropriation. All comes as grace and gift, beyond any of our our tenacious attempts to control life and assure its continuation.

When Paul speaks in 3:20 of that "energy," he alludes to Psalm 8:4–6, taking the Psalm's mention of "the son of man" (ἤ υἱὸς ἀνθρώπου) to refer to Jesus as the eschatological son of man, thus exalted beyond measure. This Lord who, the Psalm says, "is crowned with glory and splendor" (δόξῃ καὶ τιμῇ ἐστεφάνωσας αὐτὸν) and "set over all the works" of the creative hands of God, "to whom all things have been subjected (πάντα ὑπέταξας)," is echoed in the words of Philippians 3:20, where Paul writes of the creative energy "that enables him (Jesus) also to have dominion over all things" (καὶ ὑποτάξαι αὐτῷ τὰ πάντα).²¹³ Echoing Psalm 8, Paul attributes the creativity of God to the Lord Jesus, the son of man. And the intertextual echoing does not stop here, for the Psalm itself alludes to Genesis 1:26, where God "creates man and woman in his image and likeness (ποιήσωμεν ἄνθρωπον κατ'εἰκόνα ἡμετέραν καὶ καθ'ὁμοίωσιν), thereby giving them dominion (καὶ ἀρχέτωσαν) over all and setting them in charge of the fish in the sea, the birds in the sky, all cattle and over all the earth (καὶ πάσης τῆς γῆς), as well as over snakes who slither on the earth."

The Hebrew psalm, as written, celebrates the creative energy present in human beings, who are loved by God and graced with dominion over the animals. Paul attributes the same creative power and energy to Jesus, for that energy enables him to have dominion over dying. The theological point is that Jesus, not standing alone and apart, but as the presence of the empty and risen Lord among us, shares with God the same creative energy of the cosmos. This is the very same creative energy present at

---

being encompassed in the other-power (Js. *tariki*) of infinite light. See Martin's assertion that "power, *energia*, represents energy in effective action" (Martin, *Philippians*, 166).

212. On *energeia*, Reumann writes, "In the final five Greek words of 21b, Paul quotes from both Psalm 8:6 and himself at 1 Cor 15:27, in a treatment about the End. Two words are brought over from 15:27 into 3:21 (*put into subjection* and *all things*, article added), but with a significant change. In 1 Cor 15:23–28 God subjects 'the powers' and Death ('all things') to Christ; in 3:21b Christ subjects the universe to himself. Phil 3:21b is Christocentric, while 1 Cor 15:27, in using Ps 8:7, remained within the OT sense of God subjecting all things; in the Psalm under the feet of humans, in 15:27 to the Son" (Reumann, *Philippians*, 600).

213. Reumann notes that "to have dominion, to subject" (ὑποτάξαι) "[A]ackgrounds in military use, the citizen and the state (Rom 13:1, 1), and in codes about superior and subordinate in a household (Col 3:18; Eph 5:21)" (ibid., 581).

creation, not an added power gained somehow through church or scepter, an energy that flows through Christ into the risen lives of all. Paul sees Jesus Christ's reconfiguring and transforming of death to be his shared risen and awakened embodiment of the creative energy that the Psalmist attributes to the "son of man," the same energy that was present in the very primal creative act of Genesis. Paul understands the resurrection energy of this Jesus as savior, not as some added power previously unknown and now given to Jesus, but as the outflow of the all-encompassing creative élan we read of in the mythic account at the very beginning of Genesis.

7

Postscript
On the Interfaith Reading of Paul

In this reading of Paul, I am influenced by all I have read from the first moment I began to read the meaning of my life. In particular, convinced as I am of the elegance and truth of Mādhyamika's philosophy of emptiness and of Yogācāra's critical philosophy of mind, I approach Paul from an angle that diverges from accustomed patterns of western interpretive theology. By now in this my western culture, Mahāyāna Buddhist thought is somewhat well-known and not so very alien. And yet, because it originates from such a culturally distant religious tradition, its potential remains unrecognized in Christian theologizing.

In my youth, I read Paul and indeed all of the scriptures within the context of Greek ontology and classical metaphysics. I liked that philosophy then; I like it now. But it is only one pattern of thought among a great panoply of cultural options. Any philosophical framework channels one's reading and understanding in a particular direction; there are no frameless or directionless readings. So I would urge that we will only enrich our understanding of our own scriptures when we open ourselves to the deep world traditions of the human endeavor—Confucian notions of humanness, the Hindu conception of the characterless Brahman embracing all, Taoist sensitivity to the organic flow of life that interrelates everything. For me, Mahāyāna thinking on the emptiness of all philosophy offers new avenues into understanding Christian scripture. But new avenues are all too often blocked by doctrinal insistence on the suzerainty of our medieval ontologies.

There are many potential pitfalls in interfaith theology.[1] One may be tempted to conclude that no particular traditional discourse actually means what it says but that all are simply expressions of a universal truth accessible to all. This is indeed a pitfall, for it assumes the existence of a universal experience, or of a single truth

---

1. See Keenan, *Grounding Our Faith*.

that all traditions express in their varied, halting, and culturally conditioned ways.² In point of actual fact, the various traditions describe different constellations of human consciousness, each in its own milieu regarded as authentically revealed and confessed as scripture. An equal pitfall, I think, is to rank the great religions of the world, placing one's own tradition alone at the top above all others, which are regarded as lesser versions of the truth most fully expressed in *my* tradition. This practice reduces religious traditions to linear examples of the same order, regardless of the fact that each confesses itself to be beyond any linear ordering at all. That practice, however, is not uncommon: Eusebius did define Christian identity as against the "lesser" Jewish tradition.³ ABE Masao did re-inscribe Christian ideas into his Zen perspective.⁴

I have no desire to subject all Christian discourse to the categories of Buddhist philosophy. I do not believe that Mahāyāna emptiness constitutes a metalanguage that we can employ in thinking Christian doctrine and scripture, for emptiness is a contextual discourse that feeds off other contextual discourses and indeed insists upon the contextuality of *all* discourse. At the same time, I do not wish to privilege western ontologies as though somehow Christian revelation confers upon them an assured and special status.⁵

Indeed, because emptiness in Mahāyāna philosophy functions as a critique of *all* views, Mādhyamika and Yogācāra thinkers regard even Buddhist views as misleading when they are held tenaciously as though having captured the ultimate truth. Those same thinkers turn their criticism upon the very notion of emptiness itself—when emptiness is held as though it is yet another viewpoint, the viewpoint of emptiness. But the salutary "effect" of such emptying is to unleash awakening from the confines of ideas and viewpoints, whether the foolish ideas of this crooked world or the doctrinal viewpoints of ecclesiastical curators. There can be no overarching perspective or ultimate philosophy. Emptiness that is understood as some kind of ultimate viewpoint itself, the Mahayanists insist, is "emptiness ineptly apprehended"; they compare this to

---

2. The final stance of Abe and his "Dynamic Emptiness," but hardly confined to him. It is the position of many pluralist theologians. See, for example, John Hick, *God and the Universe of Faith* (New York: St. Martin's, 1973) and Paul F. Knitter, *No Other Name? A Critical Survey of Christian Attitudes Toward World Religions* (Maryknoll: Orbis, 1986).

3. On Eusebius of Caesarea, the first chronicler of church history who, in aligning the eschatological peace of the gospel with Roman sovereign order, could then define Roman Christian identity against all others, see Mitchell, *Church, God, and Empire*, 28–59. He argues that the twinned sovereignties of church and empire constitute a "godly polity," perhaps taking that term from Letter C to the Philippians in 3:20, where τὸ πολίτευμα ἐν οὐρανοῖς means a civic association on a local level, not the empire itself.

4. Abe's approach subsumes Christian doctrine within a Zen metaphysics of emptiness that regards the central Christian teachings—of Christ, his incarnation, and thus all trinitarian theology—as but an example of a more universal and cosmic self-emptying that stands at the beginning of all things. See Keenan, "Mahāyāna Emptiness or 'Absolute Nothingness'?" for a discussion of Abe's dialogue with Christianity.

5. Étienne Gilson, *A Gilson Reader: Selections from the Writings of Étienne Gilson*, edited by Anton Pegis (New York: Doubleday, 1957).

a medicine that remains in the stomach without circulating throughout the body, thus poisoning the entire organism.[6]

Everything is truly empty, the Mahayanists tell us, even emptiness itself. When it is not recognized as itself empty, the very notion of emptiness is vain and deluded. Similarly, here in Philippians, the empty Christ is not to be clung to as a vague and mystic force, but immediately to be identified as the eschatologically absent Lord who proleptically structures our everyday existence in his Spirit presence. When so recognized, the self-emptying Christ leads us into the silence of the Father, enunciated in the Spirit-speaking of this Jesus word. And insight into the emptiness of Christ can trigger an upsurge of the inchoate power of a wisdom that plunges down, below the reach of ideas and viewpoints, and wells up and bubbles forth from a consciousness no longer ensnared by the power games of language fabrication.[7] As the emptiness hymn tells us, Christ has nothing to gain or to cling to. His disciples, likewise, are to empty their most cherished notions of who they are, that they may awaken to the word of life that augurs risen life beyond stable categories altogether.

Paul does not teach the empty Christ as the symbol of an ultimate place of no place called emptiness.[8] Paul experiences Christ as very real, as a man who died and rose from the dead and was disclosed to Paul in a vision as he traveled about pursuing his "blameless" zealotry. It is precisely because Christ was such an empty man—who emptied even death of final meaning—that Paul now sings the Philippians' hymn to the empty Christ. He himself has experienced Christ beyond death and thus beyond his own life, and beyond the reach of any language that we employ in our world. However brief and fleeting, an encounter with the living Christ who has once died shatters the zealotry of self-righteousness. However, that Christ-emptiness is present only in the conventional discourse that we call gospel and not in any biographical account. Thus, Paul is reticent to describe his moment of conversion. He is neither an ontotheologian who speaks about the essence of Christ, nor a theological relativist who clutches emptiness ineptly, as a final view that would encompass all other views.

In Buddhist lands, to be empty marks the dawn of an awakening that renders the practitioner free to be skillfully effective in benefiting and gladdening all sentient beings through the preaching of Dharma. Some in the west, however, choose to cling to a kind of emptiness that is thoroughly negative; when they perceive the fragility of the gospel narrative from that negative stance, they reject all religious faith as beyond

---

6. Nāgārjuna, *Mūlamadhyamakakārikā* [Stanzas on the Middle] 24:11. See Garfield, *Fundamental Wisdom of the Middle Way*, 299: "By a misperception of emptiness a person of little intelligence is destroyed, like a snake incorrectly seized or like a spell incorrectly grasped."

7. On John 16:16–33, see Keenan, *I Am / No Self*, 243–46, on "The End of the Questioning Mind."

8. In the context of Buddhist-Christian dialogue, and true to his Kyoto School roots, ABE Masao chooses to interpret Christ's emptying as the "locus" of absolute nothingness, overcoming every affirmation and every negation. See Abe, "Kenotic God and Dynamic Sunyata," 9–17.

belief and do not allow themselves to be grasped by the ever-awakening faith of that fragile gospel.

I am convinced that Mahāyāna notions of emptiness, no-self, and the dependently arisen status of doctrine can be adopted and applied validly as but one philosophical option that may serve in interpreting Christian scripture and in broadening Christian thinking. I believe that these notions have the potential to enhance the hearing of the gospel—whether by cultural Christians who have become "hard of hearing" through over-familiarity with narrow interpretations of the Christian gospel, or by people of different cultures and languages whose ability to hear is impaired from the start when the gospel is presented in a philosophical tongue that is quite alien to them.

Selected Bibliography

ABE Masao. "Kenotic God and Dynamic Sunyata." In *The Emptying God: A Buddhist-Christian-Jewish Conversation*, edited by John B. Cobb Jr. and Christopher Ives, 3–65. Maryknoll: Orbis, 1990.

Aitken, Robert. *The Gateless Barrier: The Wu-men Kuan (Mumonkan)*. San Francisco: North Point, 1990.

Asaṅga. *The Realm of Awakening: A Translation and Study of the Tenth Chapter of Asaṅga's Mahāyānasaṃgraha*. Translated and annotated by Paul J. Griffiths, Noriaki Hakamaya, John P. Keenan, and Paul L. Swanson. Oxford: Oxford University Press, 1989.

———. *The Summary of the Great Vehicle* (Mahāyānasaṃgraha). Translated by John P. Keenan. Berkeley: Numata Center for Buddhist Translation and Research, 2003.

Bandhuprabha. *The Interpretation of the Buddha Land* (Buddhabhūmyupadeśa). Translated by John P. Keenan. Berkeley: Numata Center for Buddhist Translation and Research, 2002.

Barth, Karl. *The Epistle to the Philippians*. Translated by J. W. Leitch. Richmond, VA: John Knox, 1962.

Bauer, Walter. *A Greek-English Lexicon of the New Testament and Other Early Christian Literature*. Translated and adapted by W. F. Arndt and F. W. Gingrich. 2nd ed. Chicago: University of Chicago Press, 1979.

Benoit, Pierre. *Les épîtres de saint Paul aux Philippiens, à Philémon, aux Colossiens, aux Ephésiens*. Paris: Éditions du Cerf, 1953.

Bruce, F. F. *Philippians*. New International Bible Commentary. Peabody: Hendrickson, 1989.

Caird, G. B. *Paul's Letters from Prison in the Revised Standard Version*. New Clarendon Bible. Oxford: Oxford University Press, 1976.

Campbell, Douglas A. *The Deliverance of God: An Apocalyptic Rereading of Justification in Paul*. Grand Rapids: Eerdmans, 2009.

Campbell, Joseph. *The Hero with a Thousand Faces*. Princeton: Princeton University Press, 1958.

Campbell, William S. *Paul and the Creation of Christian Identity*. London: T. & T. Clark, 2008.

Castelli, Elizabeth A. *Imitating Paul: A Discourse of Power*. Louisville: Westminster John Knox, 1991.

Chilton, Bruce. *Rabbi Paul: An Intellectual Biography*. New York: Image, 2005.

Chuang Tzu. *The Complete Works of Chuang Tzu*. Translated by Burton Watson. New York: Columbia University Press, 1968.

Collange, Jean-François. *The Epistle of Saint Paul to the Philippians*. Translated from the French by A. W. Heathcote. Epworth, 1979. Reprint, Eugene, OR: Wipf & Stock, 2009.

Selected Bibliography

Conze, Edward. *Buddhist Wisdom Books: The Diamond Sutra and the Heart Sutra.* 1958. Reprint, New York: Harper Torchbooks, 1972.

———, trans. *The Perfection of Wisdom in Eight Thousand Lines and Its Verse Summary.* San Francisco: Four Seasons Foundation, 1973.

Crossan, John Dominic. *The Cross That Spoke: The Origins of the Passion Narrative.* San Francisco: Harper & Row, 1988.

Crossan, John Dominic, and Jonathan L. Reed. *In Search of Paul: How Jesus's Apostle Opposed Rome's Empire with God's Kingdom.* New York: Harper, 2004.

Dawe, Donald G. *The Form of a Servant: A Historical Analysis of the Kenotic Motif.* Philadelphia: Westminster, 1963. Reprint, Eugene, OR: Wipf & Stock, 2011.

Dunn, James D. G. *The New Perspective on Paul.* Rev. ed. Grand Rapids: Eerdmans, 2008.

———. *The Theology of Paul the Apostle.* Grand Rapids: Eerdmans, 1998.

Everett, Daniel L. *Don't Sleep, There Are Snakes: Life and Language in the Amazonian Jungle.* New York: Pantheon, 2008.

Fabricatore, Daniel J. *Form of God, Form of a Servant: An Examination of the Greek Noun μορφή in Philippians 2:6-7.* Lanham, MD: University Press of America, 2010.

Fee, Gordon D. *Paul's Letter to the Philippians.* The New International Commentary on the New Testament. Grand Rapids: Eerdmans, 1995.

Garfield, Jay L. *The Fundamental Wisdom of the Middle Way: Nāgārjuna's Mūlamadhyamakakārikā.* Oxford: Oxford University Press, 1995.

Garland, D. E. "Composition and Unity of Philippians: Some Neglected Literary Factors." *Novum Testamentum* 27 (1985) 141–73.

Gazzaniga, Michael S. *Who's In Charge? Free Will and the Science of the Brain.* New York: HarperCollins, 2011.

Habito, Ruben L. F. *Living Zen, Loving God.* Somerville, MA: Wisdom, 1995.

Haidt, Jonathan. *The Righteous Mind: Why Good People Are Divided by Politics and Religion.* New York: Pantheon, 2012.

Hakamaya Noriaki. "The Realm of Enlightenment in *Vijñaptimātratā*: The Formulation of the Four Kinds of Pure Dharmas." Translated by John P. Keenan. *Journal of the International Association of Buddhist Studies* 3 (1980) 21–42.

Heil, John Paul. *Philippians: Let Us Rejoice in Being Conformed to Christ.* Atlanta: Society of Biblical Literature, 2010.

Illich, Ivan. *Celebration of Awareness: A Call for Institutional Revolution.* New York: Doubleday, 1969.

———. *In the Mirror of the Past: Lectures and Addresses 1978–1990.* New York: Boyars, 1992.

Johnson, Elizabeth A. *Quest for the Living God: Mapping Frontiers in the Theology of God.* New York: Continuum, 2007.

Johnson, Luke Timothy. *The Apostle Paul.* Audiobook with course guidebook; 6 compact discs, 360 min. Great Courses 1. Chantilly, VA: Teaching Company, 2001.

———. *The Writings of the New Testament: An Interpretation.* Philadelphia: Fortress, 1986.

Keenan, John P. *The Gospel of Mark: A Mahāyāna Reading.* Maryknoll: Orbis, 1995. Reprint, Eugene, OR: Wipf & Stock, 2005.

———. *Grounding Our Faith in a Pluralist World—with a Little Help from Nāgārjuna.* Eugene, OR: Wipf & Stock, 2009.

———. "The Intent and Structure of Yogācāra Philosophy: Its Relevance for Modern Religious Thought." *Annual Memoirs of the Ōtani University Shin Buddhist Comprehensive Research Institute* 4 (1986) 41–60.

Selected Bibliography

———. "Mahāyāna Emptiness or 'Absolute Nothingness'? The Ambiguity of Abe Masao's Role in Buddhist-Christian Understanding," *Revue Théologiques* (Université de Montréal) 20 (2012) 341–63.

———. *The Meaning of Christ: A Mahāyāna Theology.* Maryknoll: Orbis, 1989.

———. *A Study of the* Buddhabhūmyupadeśa: *The Doctrinal Development of the Notion of Wisdom in Yogācāra Thought.* Berkeley: Institute for Buddhist Studies and Bukkyō Dendō Kyōkai America, 2014.

———. *The Wisdom of James: Parallels with Mahāyāna Buddhism.* Mahwah, NJ: Newman, 2005.

Keenan, John P., and Linda K. Keenan. *I Am / No Self: A Christian Reading of the Heart Sūtra.* Christian Commentaries on Non-Christian Sacred Texts. Leuven, Belgium: Peeters; Grand Rapids: Eerdmans, 2011.

Keenan, Julian Paul. *The Face in the Mirror: How We Know Who We Are.* New York: HarperCollins, 2003.

Leen, Edward. *The Holy Ghost.* New York: Sheed & Ward, 1953.

Lonergan, Bernard. *Method in Theology.* New York: Herder & Herder, 1972.

Makransky, John. *Awakening Through Love: Unveiling Your Deepest Goodness.* Somerville, MA: Wisdom, 2007.

Marchal, Joseph A. *Hierarchy, Unity, and Imitation: A Feminist Rhetorical Analysis of Power Dynamics in Paul's Letter to the Philippians.* SBL Academia Biblica 24. Atlanta: Society for Biblical Literature, 2006.

Martin, Ralph P. *A Hymn of Christ: Philippians 2:5–11 in Recent Interpretation and in the Setting of Early Christian Worship.* Downers Grove: InterVarsity, 1997.

———. *Philippians: An Introduction and Commentary.* Downers Grove: InterVarsity, 1987.

Mitchell, Roger Haydon. *Church, Gospel, and Empire: How the Politics of Sovereignty Impregnated the West.* Eugene, OR: Wipf & Stock, 2011.

Mu Soeng. *The Diamond Sutra: Transforming the Way We Perceive the World.* Somerville, MA: Wisdom, 2000.

Nagao Gadjin. *The Foundational Standpoint of Mādhyamika Philosophy* (中觀哲學の根本的立場, *Chūkan tetsugaku no konponteki tachiba*). Translated by John P. Keenan. [Original Japanese published in Nagao, 中觀と唯識 *Chūkan to Yuishiki* (*Mādhyamika and Yogācāra*), 3–144. Tokyo: Iwanami, 1978]. Albany: State University of New York Press, 1989.

———. *Mādhyamika and Yogācāra: A Study of Mahāyāna Philosophies.* Collected papers of G. M. Nagao. Edited, collated, and translated by Leslie S. Kawamura. Albany: State University of New York Press, 1991.

O'Brien, Peter T. *The Epistle to the Philippians.* The New International Greek Testament Commentary. Grand Rapids: Eerdmans. Reprint, Bletchley, UK: Paternoster, 1991.

Pelikan, Jaroslav. *The Christian Tradition: A History of the Development of Doctrine.* 5 vols. Chicago: University of Chicago Press, 1975–1991.

———. *Credo: Historical and Theological Guide to Creeds and Confessions of Faith in the Christian Tradition.* New Haven: Yale University Press, 2003.

Pietersma, Albert, and Benjamin G. Wright, eds. *A New English Translation of the Septuagint.* Oxford: Oxford University Press, 2007.

Portefaix, Lilian. *Sisters Rejoice: Paul's Letter to the Philippians and Luke-Acts as Received by First-century Philippian Women.* Coniectanea Biblica, New Testament Series 20. Stockholm: Almqvist & Wiksell, 1988.

Reumann, John. "Oikonomia-Terms in Paul in Comparison with Lucan Heilsgeschichte." *New Testament Studies* 13 (1966–1967) 147–67.

———. *Philippians: A New Translation with Introduction and Commentary.* Anchor Yale Bible. New Haven: Yale University Press, 2008.

———. "Resurrection in Philippi and Paul's Letter(s) to the Philippians." In *Resurrection in the New Testament*, edited by R. Bieringer et al., 407–422. Leuven, Belgium: Leuven University Press, 2002.

Ruden, Sarah. *Paul Among the People: The Apostle Reinterpreted and Reimagined in His Own Time.* New York: Image, 2010.

Sanders, E. P. *Paul and Palestinian Judaism: A Comparison of Patterns of Religion.* Philadelphia: Fortress, 1977.

Schweitzer, Albert. *The Mysticism of Paul the Apostle.* Adam & Charles Black, 1931. Reprint, Baltimore: John Hopkins University, 1998.

Segal, Alan F. *Paul the Convert: The Apostolate and Apostasy of Saul the Pharisee.* New Haven: Yale University Press, 1990.

Silva, Moisés. *Philippians.* 2nd ed. Baker Exegetical Commentary on the New Testament. Grand Rapids: Baker, 2005.

Stowers, Stanley K. *A Rereading of Romans: Justice, Jews, and Gentiles.* New Haven: Yale University Press, 1994.

Sumney, Jerry L. *Philippians: A Greek Student's Intermediate Reader.* Peabody: Hendrickson, 2007.

Thrall, Margaret E. "Paul's Understanding of Continuity between the Present Life and the Life of the Resurrection." In *Resurrection in the New Testament*, edited by R. Bieringer et al., 283–300. Leuven, Belgium: Leuven University Press, 2002.

Thurston, Bonnie B. "Philippians." In *Philippians and Philemon*, edited by Daniel J. Harrington, 3–163. Collegeville, MN: Liturgical, 2009.

Unno, Taitetsu. *Tannisho: A Shin Buddhist Classic.* Honolulu: Buddhist Study Center Press, 1984.

Vincent, Marvin R. *A Critical and Exegetical Commentary on the Epistles to the Philippians and to Philemon.* International Critical Commentary. Edinburgh: T. & T. Clark, 1897.

Žižek, Slavoj, and John Milbank. *The Monstrosity of Christ: Paradox or Dialectic?* Cambridge: MIT Press, 2009.

www.ingramcontent.com/pod-product-compliance
Lightning Source LLC
Chambersburg PA
CBHW080726300426
44114CB00019B/2499